Wesleyan Theology Today

A Bicentennial Theological Consultation

Edited by Theodore Runyon

104994

Kingswood Books

An Imprint of The United Methodist Publishing House

NASHVILLE

WESLEYAN THEOLOGY TODAY

Copyright © 1985, The United Methodist Publishing House

ISBN   0-687-44452-7

PRINTED IN THE UNITED STATES OF AMERICA

Contents

FOREWORD

The Bicentennial of United Methodism was observed by the Division of Ordained Ministry of the General Board of Higher Education and Ministry through a celebration of contemporary United Methodist scholarship. Four significant volumes were either published or encouraged by the division in a series entitled *An Informed Ministry: 200 Years of United Methodism.* They were: *Ministerial Education in the Methodist Movement* by Gerald O. McCulloh (1981); *A Source Book of American Methodism* by Frederick A. Norwood (1982); *Practical Divinity* by Thomas A. Langford (1983); *An Educated Ministry Among Us: United Methodist's Investment in Theological Education* by G. Melton Mobley (1984).

In addition to these publications, the celebration of scholarship continued with two outstanding consultations initiated and managed by the division. In April 1983, Drew University was the site for historians to gather under the theme of *Methodism and Ministry: Historical Explorations.* Emory University was the location in August of that year for the second consultation, *Wesleyan Theology in the Next Century*, at which theologians from across the church met to review our denomination's theological task for the next century.

These consultations constituted the largest and most representative scholarly events in the history of our denomination—an appropriate recognition of two centuries of commitment to scholarship in the Wesleyan tradition. Those privileged to attend the consultations were inspired and stimulated by the high quality of major addresses and workshop papers. The Division of Ordained Ministry applauds The United Methodist Publishing House in making many of the documents from both occasions available to a wide audience throughout the church. Superbly edited by Dr. Russell Richey of Drew University, assisted by Dr. Kenneth Rowe, and Dr. Theodore Runyon of Candler School of Theology, these volumes will be valuable resources in the continuing historical and theological exploration of our Wesleyan tradition.

May readers discover some of the excitement and inquiring spirit these papers reflected in their original presentation.

Donald H. Treese
Associate General Secretary
Division of Ordained Ministry
General Board of Higher
  Education and Ministry
The United Methodist Church

PREFACE

It is with a sense of accomplishment that the Division of Ordained Ministry of the General Board of Higher Education and Ministry and The United Methodist Publishing House are able to make available this record of the Bicentennial Consultation, "Wesleyan Theology in the Next Century: United Methodism Reviews Its Theological Task." Held on the campus of Emory University in August of 1983, the event was sponsored, or funded in part, by the Council of Bishops, the Division of Ordained Ministry, and the General Board of Global Ministries of The United Methodist Church; Candler School of Theology, Emory University; and the Vivian G. Crummey Benevolent Trust.

The Steering Committee for this event was chaired by Theodore Runyon of Candler School of Theology, who also serves as editor of this volume. Other committee members included Richard W. Cain, representing the Association of United Methodist Theological Schools; Charles F. Kirkley, representing the Division of Ordained Ministry; Bishop Calvin D. McConnell, Seattle Area, representing the Council of Bishops' Committee on Theological Education; Jim L. Waits, also representing Candler; and Donald H. Treese, *ex officio*, Associate General Secretary, General Board of Higher Education and Ministry. The vision held by this Committee was threefold: (a) to examine critically those elements within the Wesleyan Tradition which may lend identity and direction to the Methodist movement today; (b) to explore the affinities between our heritage and the most creative trends in contemporary theology and ethics; and (c) to stimulate research, teaching, and publication in the area of United Methodist Studies. The papers contained in this volume are but one expression of the many ways in which these goals were realized.

The Division is pleased to have this opportunity for partnership with The United Methodist Publishing House, as together we identify those resources necessary for our theological task.

John L. Topolewski
Project Manager,
   Bicentennial Observances
Division of Ordained Ministry
General Board of Higher
   Education and Ministry

INTRODUCTION

Theodore Runyon

More than two hundred theologians, ethicists, and others interested in Wesleyan theology assembled in Atlanta at Emory University in August of 1983, to examine and discuss the resources to be found in the Methodist heritage for theologizing today.

This Consultation was the second of two sponsored by United Methodist agencies in connection with the bicentennial observance of the founding of American Methodism, whose independence from British Methodism was confirmed by the Christmas Conference of 1784, held in the port city of Baltimore in the newly independent United States. Although under United Methodist sponsorship, the Consultation consciously sought to think beyond the limitations of one branch of the Methodist family and included participants from most of the churches which trace their origins to the Wesleyan revival or Methodist developments in the United States.

The first Bicentennial Consultation, at Drew University, focused on historical themes. The Emory Consultation had as its mandate "to examine critically those elements within the Wesleyan tradition which may, if recovered and reinterpreted, lend identity and direction to the Methodist movement today." In the chapters that follow, therefore, despite frequent references to the past, the predominant interest is not so much historical as teleological—the search for a viable way into the future.

This task was undertaken by eleven working groups, most of which reflected contemporary directions in theology and ethics that exhibit some affinity with the Wesleyan mode of theologizing. The organizing themes of these working groups supply the chapter titles of the book. Liberation theologies are represented—black, feminist, and Latin American—along with process theology, neo-evangelicalism, faith-development theory, ethics of character, and the new interest in the religious affections. The perennial issues of mission and evangelism, ecumenism, and constructive theology also claim the attention of the contributors. The result is a volume that is by no means a finished product but gives access instead to the creative ferment that is found in contemporary Methodism.

The group on *Wesleyan Constructive Theology*, chaired by Thomas Langford of Duke University, sought to identify the theological strengths of the heritage, analyze the weaknesses that have become evident in its two-hundred year history, and chart a theological course for the future that would build upon the first and correct the second. The main resource for Methodist theology is of course the thought of John Wesley. The fact that Wesley never wrote a systematic theology, a seeming disadvantage to Methodist academic theology in the past, may prove to be a blessing. Every attempt to reduce Wesley to a system (Fletcher, Watson, Miley, Wiley, etc.) has failed to do justice to one aspect or another of his thought. And now developments in theology, especially in Latin America and the third world, are raising questions about system-building as the most viable mode of doing theology. Wesley's praxis-oriented sermons and essays are closer to what is proposed as an appropriate way for thinking and reflection to occur within the life of the church in today's world. If so, the theology of Wesley may be peculiarly suited to speak to the new situation.

The affinity between Wesleyan modes of thought and Process Theology has often been remarked, but not until this Consultation has there been a concerted effort to clarify this relationship. The working group on *Process Theology and Wesleyan Thought*, under the leadership of John B. Cobb of the School of Theology at Claremont, analyzes various approaches to Process Theology—systematic, feminist, liberationist, and evangelical—and notes in each case the affinities between the concerns, presuppositions, and methods, of a Process approach and those of Wesley. His appropriation of empirical modes of thinking, his regard for the created world, and his speculations about the continuity of matter through constant change, mark Wesley's thinking as not uncongenial to the abstractions as well as the concrete implications of Process thought.

Every analysis of Wesleyan theology must take into consideration the place given to Scriptures as both the primary source and the norm of theologizing. The contributors to the section on *Methodism and Biblical Authority*, headed by Donald Dayton of Northern Baptist Theological Seminary, seek to identify the distinctive hermeneutic with which Wesley approached the Scriptures, comparing him with biblical scholarship of more recent generations. Wesley's principle—always to interpret more obscure passages in the light of those in which the meaning is clear, and to interpret individual passages in terms of "the whole tenor of Scripture"—may offer a way through the thicket of competing claims to inerrancy and infallibility which have been raised again in our time.

Liberationist perspectives are advanced by the working groups in feminist and black theology and by those seeking to interpret mission and evangelism in a global context. Rosemary Keller, of Garrett-Evangelical Theological Seminary, served as convenor of a group that brings a variety of biblical, historical, and systematic perspectives to *Constructing a Feminist Theology in the Wesleyan Tradition*. After a thorough review of the biblical texts which speak for and against women's leadership in the church, the historical sources are recounted which demonstrate the significant contributions which women have made to the Methodist movement from its inception. Wesley's own high regard for the capabilities of women, and the training afforded them, first as class and band leaders and then as local and even itinerating preachers, meant that Methodism opened the way for many to exercise leadership roles denied them in the larger society. This is not to say that the record has been universally bright, for these chapters also recount the discrimination against women in Methodism. But in the Wesleyan emphases upon freedom, responsibility, service, and transformation, the theological foundations were laid for a creative feminist approach.

Early Methodism's stand against slavery, plus the relative freedom which black people experienced in the Methodist forms of preaching and worship, combined to give Methodism a special appeal to black Americans, according to the group on *Black and Ethnic Religion and the Theological Renewal of Methodism*, chaired by C. Eric Lincoln of Duke University. Indigenous leadership developed quickly among black people, and black Methodist denominations emerged. The eloquence of these preachers, from Harry Hosier to the present, is legend, though historians have not always recognized the importance of their role in shaping black identity and survival. The preachers provided the basic biblical picture of reality and the imagery within which a life of suffering could be interpreted and endured in the hope of a coming freedom. But how does this heritage speak to the dilemmas of racial minorities today? Laurels from the past are not sufficient. Can the black experience now feed into Methodist theology in such a way as to revitalize it? This is the question with which the reader is left.

According to the working group on *Wesleyan Mission and Evangelism in Global Context*, led by Roy Sano, previously of Pacific School of Religion and now Bishop of the Denver Area of The United Methodist Church, a theology of evangelism and mission cannot be formulated today without taking into account the worldwide context of the Christian church and especially the needs of the third world. The gospel is global in its intent, and gives hope to human history as well as to individuals. A specifically Wesleyan contribution is seen in the positive valuation Wesley placed on the orders of this world, which he saw as positive agencies of God's grace and not simply in their negative function of restraining sin. Thus there is a word of good news to structures and systems. To be sure, they are imperfect and sinful, but like individuals they are reformable and subject to being perfected. They too must be called to repentance and, in the hope of the transformative power of the Spirit of justice and truth, they can be enlisted to serve human needs more adequately.

An example of how this not only has worked in the past but can work in the present is given in the comparison of eighteenth-century class meetings and their role in empowering the poor and the "base communities" now emerging in Latin America. Here is method of evangelism which, both in Wesley's time and today, puts the common people directly in touch with the Scripture, organizes them into groups for nurture and mutual support, makes them responsible for each other, and recognizes the role of structures in bringing about change both in individuals and in society.

In all approaches to evangelism, individual experience is not to be neglected but remains a key element. In the Wesleyan understanding, faith experiences are not static but grow and mature, and are enlisted in the service of love. It is this love, experienced personally but inevitably social in its implications, which according to Wesley prevents Christianity from understanding itself as a private religion.

The contemporary theme of religious experience was taken up by the working group on *Religious Affections and the Knowledge of God*, convened by Don E. Saliers of Emory University. The concern with the religious affections, though the subject of much recent interest in both American and European theological circles, is hardly new, and its classic expression goes back to Wesley's contemporary, Jonathan Edwards, whose *Treatise on the Religious Affections* Wesley abridged and included in his *Christian Library* series, thus making it available to a wide readership. For both Wesley and Edwards the knowledge of God and of religious reality is dependent upon a spiritual empiricism, a "spiritual sense," awakened by the divine Spirit, which gives access to the transcendent realm. According to the Lockean epistemology which they employed, transcendent reality makes its imprint on the spiritual senses analogously to the way the external world makes its impressions on the mind. These experiences then shape the Christian life in terms of the two archetypal affections, love and joy; and true religion consists in large part in the living out of these affections.

This explains why from Wesley's standpoint religious experience is both necessary and cannot be understood solely in subjective terms. For empiricist epistemology, experience is the avenue of access to reality. But experience is induced by that which is experienced. To live out the implications of one's experiences is to live from the other, in response to that which has been introduced into one's life from beyond. Nineteenth-century Methodism and later revivalism tended to forget these important distinctions, identifying the subjective feeling as the reality itself and the guarantor of salvation. The twentieth-century reaction to this subjectivism has tended to err in the opposite direction and discount religious experience altogether, insisting that only the objectively given is to be trusted. Apart from the immense problems created by such an oversimplification, the fact remains that experience brings with it a kind of self-evident authority and conviction, a participation in that which is trusted. And when it is absent religious commitment is difficult to initiate or maintain. According to Wesley, such religious experience is not anti-rational. It is not simply a matter of the heart but is appropriated by the mind working in concord with the heart and affections to enable the whole person to participate in divine reality.

One of the roles of worship therefore is to kindle the affections, to form life in response and service to the God known in the worshiping community. Thus Wesley gave no little attention to the forms of worship and the means of grace as the channels through which divine reality is experienced and allowed to mold and transform human life. This is evident in the care he gave to the Sunday Service, the prayerbook and hymnal he edited and sent with Thomas Coke in 1784 to the fledgling Methodist movement in America.

In an age that puts a premium upon personal experience but is locked into subjectivism, do Wesley's fundamental insights into religious experience have something to teach us that can inform our worship and evangelism, and our understanding of faith and commitment?

Closely related to the recovery of the affections as an important theological category is the "ethics of character," here represented by two essays from the working group, *The Ethics of Character and the People Called Methodist*, led by Robin Lovin of the University of Chicago. In contrast with most ethical approaches, which concentrate on commands and resulting actions, the ethics of character focuses on the doer—the disposition and "constancy" out of which the agent acts. What makes an act ethical is not just a deed that can be labeled good or bad but the being and motives of the doer which help to determine the moral texture of the event. The sanctification of the agent thus becomes a prime consideration for determining whether or not a given action is Christian. Actions which flow out of the experience of the love of God extend that love into the life of the world. Thus an ethics of character draws together the personal and social dimensions of Christian discipleship in a unified approach which overcomes the dichotomies between "individual" and "societal" that have so plagued recent moral thought as well as the church's self-understanding.

The interest in religious experience and sanctification in Wesley has parallels with yet another contemporary movement, "faith development" theory. James Fowler of Emory University headed the working group on *Spirituality, Perfection, and the Human Vocation: Wesley and Human Development*, which brings religion into dialogue with recent theories of psychological and moral development. Strictly speaking, the approach of the developmentalists is descriptive and not normative, and the stages they describe are in the cognitive appropriation of a religious tradition rather than the *ordo salutis* as such. Nevertheless, Wesley's understanding of salvation as a continuing process rather than a one-time event comports well with the developmentalist's empirical observations. Wesley's doctrine of prevenient grace understands the divine to be at work in the human situation on a pre-conscious level, which then moves into consciousness with "the first faint stirrings of the heart." The relationship with God thus evolves from unconscious but real participation in grace, to conscious appropriation of a religious symbol system, to a life which is permeated in every aspect by the consciousness of divine presence and meaning. Accompanying this maturation is a universalizing expansion of one's love, rooted in a participation in the divine will to reconcile all of creation, along with an awareness of the relativity of all concrete symbol systems to capture the divine—though without any lessening of the intensity of commitment to the liberating proclamation expressed in one's own symbol system. Each of these stages can be traced in Wesley's own development. And in his pastoral efforts he constantly urged his followers to "go on" toward the ever greater appropriation of the promises of the gospel.

The working group on *Wesleyan Thought and Christian Social Ethics*, led by Philip Wogaman of Wesley Theological Seminary, entered into its discussion well aware that Methodists have traditionally been accused of being long on practical activity and short on theory. This may be traceable to Wesley's own impatience with doctrinal disputes that kept Christians from uniting to undertake together what they could not hope to accomplish separately. Wesley was inclined to bracket disputes over the finer points of the law in order to cooperate toward what all could agree God requires. Sorting out the principles of this kind of practical ethic was the task of the working group. Convinced that it is not sufficient merely to catalogue Wesley's positions on slavery, economics, the state, war, poverty, etc., the group sought to identify the theological roots which nourish the stands he took. The wider horizon that becomes evident, when one asks the context in which all of these efforts toward reform are couched, is *creation* and *consummation*. The original intention of the Creator is read from the destiny in the Kingdom prepared for God's creatures, a kingdom which is not just reserved for the future but comes to earth to work its transforming effects. As a result, Methodists have generally assumed the reformability of this world's institutions and have worked in cooperation with other agencies, both religious and secular, toward that end. Wesley's doctrines of creation and kingdom also help to overcome the tendency toward an individualistic approach to morality that has so plagued Methodist perfectionism on the American scene.

A body of social doctrine has, as a matter of fact, evolved in Methodism—exemplified in the Disciplinary statement of Social Principles—which now needs to be reviewed critically and built upon in an ecumenical context, as the churches seek to speak clearly to the moral issues of the present and the future.

Since the time of Wesley's own efforts to overcome rancor and build cooperation between Calvinists and Arminians, Anglicans and Non-Conformists, Catholics and Protestants, Methodists have been committed to ecumenical endeavors. The working group on *Ecumenism and Methodism: Issues in Ministry, Sacraments, and Order*, chaired by Gerald F. Moede, General Secretary of the Consultation on Church Union, was not content to repeat the obligatory affirmations of ecumenical good intentions, but tackled the concrete issues arising from the Roman Catholic-Methodist bilateral dialogue and from *Baptism, Eucharist and Ministry*, the milestone Lima accord of the World Council of Churches.

Dialogue with other traditions is sending Methodists back to their sources and enabling them to discover there points of contact with other Christians. The result is not only a basis for more substantive dialogue and cooperative efforts that have greater integrity but an increased appreciation of the resources the Wesleyan heritage has to offer the larger church.

Some readers may wish to test the waters here and there in areas of their special interest. Others less daunted by the sheer bulk of these proceedings will want to wade through the entire document. Either way, one can hope that these pages will communicate something of the sense of discovery and excitement experienced by the participants in the Bicentennial Consultation as the full range of the potential of the theological heritage began to emerge into view. And the contributors would want to assure the reader that what is found here is not the final word on the Wesleyan tradition but only a beginning word, an inviting word, and perhaps even an enticing word.

I. PLENARY PAPERS

1. WHAT IS METHODISM'S THEOLOGICAL CONTRIBUTION TODAY?

Theodore Runyon

As a keynote address this lecture is supposed to answer the obvious but not always easily resolved question: "Now that we are here, why have we come?" One could say that we have been summoned together by the Methodist family of churches in order to supply theological legitimacy to the future of the movement. The only thing wrong with that answer is that it is not true. To be sure, the Consultation is co-sponsored by the United Methodist Council of Bishops. But I do not have the impression that the Council is holding its collective breath waiting upon what transpires here to see whether the Methodist movement should continue. If Methodism has survived two hundred years in this country without an official ideology and without legitimation by its theologians, I suspect it can continue to do so in the future. So much for the vital and indispensable task of theologians as purveyors of ideology!

Some of you who have just come from the World Council of Churches Assembly in Vancouver may wonder how what we are doing here affects our ecumenical commitments. As we focus on Wesleyanism, will the inevitable result be to raise denominational consciousness and to promote a kind of Methodist chauvinism? Given the persistence and vociferousness of attacks on the ecumenical movement, is not our first responsibility to downplay denominational consciousness, ignore denominational heritages, circle the wagons, and join to defend ecumenism? There is much in me that wants to do just that. Yet the ecumenical movement does not operate in a vacuum, and its theological reflections are not produced out of whole cloth. They emerge from the creative confrontation of various historic traditions in interaction with the challenges that emerge from the needs of the world. And the ecumenical movement as such can only respond to these challenges by drawing on the theological resources available to it from the various traditions. To be ecumenical means to believe that the riches developed within the branches of Christ's church belong to all of us, and ought to be made available to all. All should be able to benefit when the theology of one or another of our traditions proves especially effective in meeting certain kinds of challenges.

For example, when Nazism threatened to extend its sovereignty over all of life and sought to co-opt the church in its totalitarian schemes, the absolute sovereignty of the God of Calvin, mediated by Barthianism, was required to provide the backbone to the churches to stand against the pressures and enticements of that absolutist regime. That same Barthianism lent American Protestantism the critical tools to question cultural Christianity in our own setting. Little wonder, then, that neo-Reformation theology dominated Protestant thought after the Second World War, which was the formative period of the WCC and Protestant ecumenism. Moreover, many Methodists can testify to the benefits of a dose of Barthian realism as an antidote to the dominant subjectivism of much of popular Methodism. Something of a cloud hung over Wesleyan theology during the Barthian era, however. "Religious experience" was a highly suspect category, both for being "religious" and for being "experience." Major works on Wesley during this period, written by Cell, Cannon, Hildebrandt, Deschner, and Williams, went to some pains to show how Wesley was really more in tune with the concerns of Reformation theology than he previously had been represented as being.

Now, however, the theological scene has changed. Vatican II brought a new openness on the part of Catholicism to ecumenism in general and to Protestant theology in particular, making the strident Protestant confessionalism of an earlier era no longer necessary. In an equally significant development, churches that were only recently classified as mission churches have now become full-fledged partners in the theological endeavor, with the effect that the focus of theological attention has shifted away from the European–North American axis to the concerns of third-world Christians, who by the year 2000 will constitute the majority of all Christians, and are rapidly coming into their own. Their burning issues are not those of the Reformation or even those of neo-Reformation thought. This is no less true for the daughter churches of the Reformation than for others. Namibian Lutherans are at the forefront of the fight for freedom and self-determination in their land. But when they seek inspiration in Luther they find admonitions to abide by the status God has assigned to them, take comfort in their spiritual freedom, and look forward to release after this life. Across the border in South Africa black theologians in the Reformed tradition are trying to wrest Calvin out of the grip of the whites for whom a distorted Calvinism has provided an ideology of election and a predetermined order in which black people have an inferior status in this world. Blacks are supposed to take comfort in the fact that the subordinate status ordained for them on earth may not reach to heaven, where they too may be among the elect.

While these may be extreme examples they only serve to illustrate the fact that in the new situation of today's world Reformation models are no longer perceived as answering the most pressing questions. Are their other historical resources that could prove more useful to an ecumenical theology?

Enter John Wesley. He is not a perfect fit by any means. He was no revolutionary. His sympathies for the monarchy and his opposition to the revolution of the American colonies are well known. He was no friend of anarchy, and for good reason. On more than one occasion he came close to losing his life at the hands of an unruly mob, and only the opportune intervention of constabular authorities saved him. Yet, in a time of far-reaching changes in the social and economic order caused by the Industrial Revolution and early capitalism, changes paralleling those to which the third world is being subjected in our own time, he identified with the victims caught between the millstones of history. He pled the cause of the small farmers and peasants driven off the land by the enclosure laws which eliminated common grazing lands and absolutized the property rights of landlords. He sought out these dispossessed masses who huddled unemployed and hungry in the burgeoning cities, the only place they could go—a familiar pattern in the third world today where industrialized agriculture, often introduced by multinational corporations promising to maximize profits of local landlords, is replacing a peasant economy. The poverty in the urban sprawl of Latin American parallels exactly the poverty in Wesley's time. It affects the same people in the same ways. In eighteenth-century England the unorganized factory workers, the unorganized agricultural workers, the unorganized miners, were all at the mercy of their employers and the vagaries of the economy. With unemployment running at 20 to 40 percent, long lines waited to take the jobs of any who were not content with subsistence-level wages.

What did Wesley do for these proletarian masses who responded to his movement? He organized them and trained them in organizational skills. (Today's community organizers ought to make him a patron saint. He was the first of their breed.) He organized his followers into societies and the societies into classes and bands. Those with natural abilities and the call became lay preachers and exhorters. In the class meetings every tenth or twelfth person was a leader by definition, with specific pastoral duties and records to keep. Leadership required literacy, and Sabbath schools emerged in Methodism well before the time of Robert Raikes to teach people to read the Scriptures. To be able to read the Holy Writ was to be put directly in touch with liberating power without the necessity of a mediating authority, the clergy or the scholar. The reverence for, and sometimes reactionary defense of, the Scriptures cannot be understood apart from this fact, and ought to explain also why the Scriptures are reverenced even if seldom read. They are a symbol of immediate access to divine authority. To question them is to threaten to interpose the expertise of scholar between the people and the Word of God.

Others in the growing Methodist societies filled the role of stewards in charge of resources and funds. The system proved a remarkable seedbed for the cultivation of leadership, stewardship, and mutual assistance. And all were charged with the responsibility to care for one another. Their penny a week grew into credit unions that gave interest-free loans to those who had fallen on hard times. Methodists need no longer go to debtors prison. Wesley's concern for the unemployed eventuated in the establishment of cottage industries and the exchange of products among Methodists. Health services were virtually unavailable to the poor. They could afford neither the doctors nor the apothecaries. It was probably just as well. A popular couplet of the time summarized the general confidence in the medical profession:

The cannon shot and doctor's pill
With equal aim are sure to kill.[1]

Wesley published his *Primitive Physic: An Easy and Natural Method of Curing Most Diseases*, a self-help book of diagnoses and remedies from the best authorities of the time. (Most of the cures have since been proved to be, if not beneficial, at least harmless.) Where Wesley did get the cooperation of doctors and apothecaries, dispensaries and clinics were set up.

Can you grasp what this growing network among Methodists of social relationships, interdependence, and mutual care meant to the peasants and farmers in the countryside and the proletariat in the mines and the cities? It meant that they were no longer simply the victims of the society of which they were a part. They were enabled to become active agents with some degree of control over their own destiny. The French historian, Halévy, and his latter-day America disciple, Bernard Semmel, are absolutely correct when they see this development as turning proletarians into middle-class citizens, into members of the rising bourgeoisie. The first stage of liberation from the medieval peasant mentality is to recognize oneself as a agent, as capable and worthy of having some say in one's own destiny. This is what the slave and the peasant lacked. They lived in a world in which, according to the reigning ideology, God had fixed everyone's place. To revolt against this preordained order was to offend the Almighty. This is why the rising middle class which challenged that ideology was, as Marx himself observed, the most revolutionary class to date. And this is why consciousness raising, whether it takes place in a base community of Christian peasants in Latin America or a feminist group in Iowa, begins with questioning the traditional, taken-for-granted, divinely ordained order of things which previously has determined persons' identities and destinies.

The picture I have drawn of Wesley thus far may make him appear to be a rather robust Christian activist who accomplished an amazing amount of good. But is that a complete or even accurate picture? Already I can hear questions coming from two sides of the Methodist aisle, from the left and from the right.

From the left comes the objection, Haven't you been too easy on Mr. Wesley? Have you not assumed that the organizations he created and the institutions he brought into being were genuine solutions to the overwhelming problems of the time, whereas they may have only ameliorated the misery of those few he was able to reach and may have done little to challenge the fundamental injustices written into the social order. The British social historian, E. P. Thompson, argues that the "energies and emotions which were dangerous to social order . . . were released [in Methodism] in the harmless form of sporadic love-feast, watchnights, band-meetings or revivalist campaigns."[2] By diverting the energies of the working class into a round of religious activities, Methodism may have actually slowed the process of meaningful reform in Britain.

Moreover, for all of Wesley's talk about social holiness, did not his approach remain fundamentally individualistic, concentrating on the preparation of the individual soul for the life hereafter? And did not the preoccupation with personal salvation, which characterized Methodism on both sides of the Atlantic, lead to a rampant individualism that reduced religion to the private sphere and ethics to private virtues and vices, blinding us both to systemic evil and to the necessity of social solutions for it?

From the right come objections that are the mirror image of those from the left. Have I not emphasized too much the social effects of Methodism and left the impression that this was Wesley's primary concern? Is it not the case that any social changes his movement may have helped to effect over the course of time were very secondary to his commitment to the salvation of souls? Moreover, is not this loss of the passion for souls precisely what is crippling the mission of Methodism today, and can renewal come until we return to our first task, that of spiritual reform?

One could quibble with the details of these criticisms. E. P. Thompson has to take some account of Methodism's influence in the battle against the systemic evil of slavery, where Wesley clearly recognized and decried the coalition of economic and political forces that undergirded the system. And the importance of Methodism in the British labor movement, from the Tolpuddle Martyrs onward, is undeniable. Nor can one fail to be impressed by the fact that the last three speakers of the House of Commons have been Methodists, when Methodists constitute less than 5 percent of the population. Wesleyanism must do something to prepare its sons and daughters for political responsibility. Of course the claim which Methodists like to quote, made by a British labor secretary to a world congress of socialist parties, can be read two ways. He claimed that British socialism, "has learned more from John Wesley than from Karl Marx." Others are of the opinion that British socialism would be healthier had it paid more attention to Marx.

One might respond to the criticism from the right with the observation that evangelicals themselves are far less inclined today to write off this world in favor of the next. They also are looking for a spirituality that makes a difference here and now.

Is there a theological foundation in Wesley for combining the concerns of these two camps organically, a way which is not merely the coexistence of disparate and divergent values in a marriage of convenience called Methodist pluralism but a genuine unity in mission based on a common theological grounding? If such a foundation is there, and if it can be elucidated and made more readily available, it will be of interest far beyond the boundaries of Methodism. For we are talking of a conflict which runs right down the middle, not only of much of American Protestantism, but of Christianity worldwide, including the third world.

I want to explore the theological foundation that I believe is there in Wesley by looking first at a term and a phenomenon which is so much a cliché in Methodism that to view it afresh will not be easy. I am referring to "conversion." Only to mention the word is to conjure up associations of sawdust trails, mourners' benches, praying through, and warm hearts. But I want you, if you can, to put these associations aside for the moment and look at the theological substance. In examining conversion more closely I predict that we will discover that it cannot really be understood apart from being placed in a much larger context than Methodism traditionally has given it. These two factors: the indispensability of conversion and the indispensability of the larger context for understanding the meaning and purpose of conversion, will begin to help us to put some things together.

What is conversion for Wesley? Let us attempt first to look at it whole, without breaking it down into justification and regeneration or new birth. What happens in a Wesleyan conversion? Conversion takes place as the love of God which has shown forth in the face of Jesus Christ penetrates through the defenses of the human heart and begins its transforming action there. This love is experienced as the person discovers him or herself to be the *object* of God's caring action in Christ. In one sense, therefore, it is a passive event in which the subject, though unworthy, receives the inestimable gift of God's own self. In another sense, it is an active event in which the core of personal identity and action, known by Wesley as the "heart," has kindled within it a radical trust toward the source of the love. The passive side of this event is known as "justification," the active side as "new birth" and the beginning of "sanctification." But as Wesley saw clearly these are really not separable except for logical purposes. Sanctification continues only as the love which makes things right, i.e., the justifying grace, continues to be received and have its transforming effects. And the love which is extended in God's gracious self-giving achieves its purposes only as through the receptive creature God is enabled to intervene in a fallen creation to create anew.

In this last statement I have already begun to indicate the larger context of conversion which seems to me to be essential if we are to understand Wesley's own view.

It is interesting that Wesley's very first sermon after his ordination by Bishop Potter in 1725 was on the text, "Seek ye first the kingdom of God and his righteousness."[3] The emphasis in that sermon, however, as well as in one preached in 1747 on "The Way to the Kingdom," is on the demand for radical commitment. God requires nothing less than the whole person, and the human being responding to the sovereignty of God can give nothing less. Radical commitment which will be rewarded in another world, rather than the good news of the kingdom bringing renewal to this world, is the theme of the young Wesley.

By the time of his sermon on "Scriptural Christianity," preached in 1744 at St. Mary's, Oxford, before the university, we hear from Wesley a quite different note. Expositing the text from Acts 4:31-36, which begins with a Pentecost-like scene in which the apostles are gathered together for prayer and the place is shaken, and "they were all filled with the Holy Spirit and spoke the word of God with boldness," Wesley points out that in the verses which follow there is no mention of the extraordinary signs of glossolalia which had accompanied the first Pentecost, but instead the signs that accompany this filling of the Spirit are a new, more just society practiced by the disciples. Wesley traces the progression from the change in the heart of Peter to the hearts of others who are likewise changed. Peter was grasped by "a divine evidence or conviction of the love of God the Father, through the Son of his love, to him a sinner, now accepted in the Beloved."

Says Wesley, "He that thus loved God, could not but love his brother also; and 'not in word only, but in deed and in truth.' " The Jerusalem community reached out therefore and "fed the hungry, clothed the naked, helped the fatherless or stranger, visited and assisted them that were sick or in prison, (and) gave (their) goods to feed the poor."[4] Moreover, "neither said any of them that ought of the things which he possessed was his own; but they had all things in common. And with great power gave the apostles witness of the resurrection of the Lord Jesus; and great grace was upon them all. Neither was there any among them that lacked: for as many as were possessors of lands or houses sold them, and brought the prices of the things that were sold, and laid them down at the apostles' feet: and distribution was made unto every man according as he had need" (Acts 4:32-35). In this sermon the Spirit is the sign of the Kingdom, and introduces a new order among human beings. Wesley then inquires of the Oxford dons in the congregation, "Ye venerable men, who are more especially called to form the tender minds of youth. . . . Is your heart whole with God? full of love and zeal to set up his kingdom on earth? Do you continually remind those under your care, that the one rational end of all our studies is to know, love, and serve 'the only true God, and Jesus Christ whom he hath sent' . . . and that without love all learning is but splendid ignorance, pompous folly, vexation of the spirit?"[5] Not only piety but learning must serve to advance the reign of divine love and the changes in structures which that love initiates. (Incidentally, this was the last sermon Wesley was invited to preach before the university!)

Wesley's own desire to lead the Methodists in a communitarian direction was well known, and it was only the persistent opposition of some of his advisors which kept him from implementing the New Testament model in this way. We Methodists came within a hairsbreadth of being communistic!

That Oxford sermon had a note of eschatological fulfillment which gets picked up again and expanded in a remarkable series of sermons that were included in Wesley's Second Sermon Series, which he did not publish until 1788, and only then because someone threatened to collect them from the pages of the *Arminian Magazine* and bring them out. If they must be published "before I go hence," complains the eighty-five-year-old Wesley, "methinks I am the properest person to do it."[6] The collection is especially important because, though the sermons were not originally written for the purpose, Wesley put them together in such a way as to "throw light on some important Christian doctrines."[7] What we have here, therefore, is an acknowledged systematic approach, one which begins with sermons on eternity and the Trinity and proceeds through creation, the fall, predestination and human freedom, the purpose of Christ's coming, to the general spread of the gospel throughout the earth, and the new creation. This series spells out in much more detail, therefore, the setting within which Wesley wants conversion to be understood. Unfortunately, it is this larger context which is missing from most Methodist preaching and theologizing. Even Albert Outler and Colin Williams have not been very helpful at this point. Although the term they have popularized for understanding Wesley's comprehensive doctrine of salvation, the *ordo salutis*, has the virtue of preventing conversion from being

understood as an isolated event and treats it instead as a part of an ongoing process, the *ordo salutis* remains heavily individualistic, focusing on the stages of individual development. The term originated in Lutheran orthodoxy and was taken over by German pietism. It is significant that Wesley himself never used it. And these later sermons, written when Wesley was in his seventies and eighties, may give us a clue to why this was the case. For they reveal that the decisive event of conversion and the process of sanctification cannot be properly understood in a purely individualistic context. They must be seen in their organic relation to creation and kingdom. To interpret them in a more narrow way is to deprive them of their intended significance. Let us look more closely at that significance.

Conversion is decisive for Wesley because it is a participation in a new ontological reality, God's own renewing of the cosmos. Its fundamental significance is therefore as a sign of eschatological renewal. This is why Wesley must insist over against Luther and the quietists that the most fundamental nature of salvation is *actual* change and not just change in one's status before God. To exhaust the meaning of salvation in a change in God's disposition toward the sinner is to deny that the purpose of Christ's coming is the renewal of the world. The essence and purpose of "real religion," says Wesley, is "a restoration of man by Him that bruises the serpent's head to all that the old serpent deprived him of; a restoration not only to the favour but likewise to the image of God . . . . Nothing short of this is Christian religion."[8] For the Creator has given birth to Christianity in order to pursue his purposes of the renewing of the creation. He is the God who declares, "Behold, I make all things new."[9] And wherever his reconciling Spirit is at work Wesley is convinced that God "is already renewing the face of the earth."[10]

Wesley does not doubt that God could accomplish this renewal in an instant, in the twinkling of an eye, simply by divine fiat, as easily "as when God said, 'Let there be light; and there was light.' "[11] But such is not the way that he has chosen to work. "As God is One, so the work of God is uniform in all ages. May we not then conceive how he *will* work on the souls of men in times to come, by considering how he *does* work now, and how he *has* wrought in times past?"[12] Wesley concludes that God's preferred method of operation is one which does not negate human freedom but which maximizes "the understanding, the affections, and the liberty which are essential to a moral agent."[13] "The kingdom of God will not 'come with observation;' but will silently increase, wherever it is set up, and spread from heart to heart, from house to house, from town to town, from one kingdom to another,"[14] until "the will of God may be 'done in earth as it is in heaven,' . . . that all the inhabitants of earth, even the whole race of mankind, may do . . . the whole will of God in all things,"[15] (V, 337.). God has chosen to bring about his revolution in this way because he seeks not the destruction of his creation but its transformation. This even extends to the physical world. Not one atom will be destroyed, but all will be *transformed* (VI, 191f.). The biblical images of destruction refer fundamentally to this transformation, though all that which does not participate in transformation will indeed be finally lost.

Our access to this cosmic transformation is our own transformation. Thus the experience of conversion is important not so much in a subjective as in an objective sense. It takes it validity from the new order of which it is a proleptic sign. Part of our problem in understanding Wesley at this point lies in the change the term "experience" has undergone. Because of the intervening nineteenth-century, we habitually think of experience as subjective. Do not be confused by this. When Wesley insists that this change in the heart is the *sine qua non* of genuine religion, he is not concerned about an emotion. He is not insisting that persons should feel a certain way. In the eighteenth-century experience was the medium for receiving reality, for participating in the real world. Whether material or spiritual, it was the "sensible" evidence of the real world and the means of participating in that world. Unless one participates in the reality of God's redeeming history one cannot be empowered to become an agent of divine transformation. And this is what sanctification is all about—becoming an agent of the age to come, joining in the struggle against the forces of sin and corruption, claiming the promise of the new age and living in the hope that the victory over sin is indeed possible. Moreover, this hope is not blind wishing; it is grounded in the core experience of the power of a love that prevails, a love received at the center of one's existence. This hope *knows* whom it believes. Assurance is not feeling but evidence.

Does such a theology have something to offer the emerging world? I believe that it has. It operates out of a comprehensive vision of renewal that insists that we do not have to be content with the world as it is. God intends better things for his people. "He will not despise the work of his hand." Yet "he that made us without ourselves, will not save us without ourselves,"

says Wesley quoting Augustine[16], and God calls upon us to participate in our own renewal and that of our world. At the same time the Wesleyan epistemology of experience recognizes that persons are only deeply motivated when they are put in touch with a power which they sense in their bones is objectively real and which eventually will prevail over the powers of the present evil age.

Any struggle for liberation and change will encounter times of frustration and defeat. Opposition and hostility will wear down fair-weather recruits. Only those who in the depths of their being participate in the renewing power will be given the strength to persist. For oppressed peoples the love of God may even be mediated paradoxically through their rage against injustice and their awareness of a power that joins them in the struggle. But a core experience must be present among the oppressed of a power that is greater than all that opposes them if they are to be sustained and keep faith with each other and with the God of justice and love. Theological reflection on the nature of Christian experience is therefore an appropriate agenda item for third-world theologians. Their justifiable preoccupation with empirical analyses of the socio-economic situation in their lands as a basis out of which to do theology must not be allowed to obscure the theological and pastoral task of cultivating the religious affections which can sustain a prolonged effort against powerful, well-heeled, and entrenched forces. Analysis is effective only if it can also give rise to and clarify religious experience.

Thus there is no necessary antipathy between religious experience and social renewal. Indeed the opposite is the case. Experience sustains social commitment by putting it in touch with the Reality which cannot be defeated; and social renewal places experience in the larger context of God's re-creative activity in history. And the two wings of Methodism can discover a common ground and working theology in their Wesleyan heritage. *Conversion is our business* (Lonergan)— in every sense of the term.

The remarkable parallels between the base communities springing up in Latin America and Wesleyan class meetings are well worth investigating more fully. Other liberation communities have been empowered as well by the same structures of common shared experience, common tasks, common convictions, and a common vision of a new future. At least two of our working groups will be reflecting on this phenomenon and its implications.

We need to remind ourselves also that the

future of Wesleyan theology will not necessarily be carried by Wesleyans nor will it necessarily go by the name of Wesley. Others may discover the structures involved in the Wesleyan approach quite independently of us and carry them out more faithfully than do we. When the heritage was passed on to us it did not come with exclusive patent rights. We can only rejoice if others have discovered Wesley without knowing his name.

If the tradition is to have self-conscious advocates, however, we are they. No one else can be expected to feel the responsibility to do what is so obviously our task. If Methodism does indeed have much to contribute to an ecumenical theology at this point in history, and if we are the ones entrusted with the responsibility to teach and to reflect, then "a charge to keep we have." And this is no time to hide our light under a bushel.

NOTES

1. Oscar Sherwin, *John Wesley, Friend of the People* (New York: Twayne Publishers, 1961; p. 136).
2. E. P. Thompson, *The Making of the English Working Class* (London: Victor Gollancz, 1964), p. 36.
3. "John Wesley's First Sermon." (London: Chas. H. Kelly, 1903).
4. Wesley, *Works*, vol. 5, pp. 40, 41.
5. Ibid., p. 49.
6. Ibid., vol. 6, p. 185.
7. Ibid.
8. Ibid., p. 276.
9. Ibid., p. 289.
10. Ibid., p. 288.
11. Ibid., p. 280.
12. Ibid.
13. Ibid.
14. Ibid., p. 283.
15. Ibid., vol. 5, pp. 337-38.
16. Ibid., p. 281.

2. HOW THEOLOGY EMERGES FROM POLITY

James S. Thomas

When, in 1748, John Wesley wrote "A Plain Account of the People Called Methodist,"[1] He presented to the Rev. Mr. Perronet both a statement of polity and an outline of pastoral theology. Mr. Wesley's statement, that "everything arose just as the occasion offered," must be read in context. He was not one given to actions based on impulse, though he did show much more ability to accept innovations than is commonly thought.

I.

A careful reading of Mr. Wesley's letter reveals the theological and practical bases for his societies, the bands, the classes, and the persons needed to make them function properly. The societies grew out of a deep human need for the gospel. Person after person came to Mr. Wesley seeking help. They had searched the Scriptures, they wanted to lead new lives; but how? Mr. Wesley told them: "If you will all of you come together every Thursday, in the evening, I will gladly spend some time with you in prayer, and give you the best advice I can."[2]

Giving the practical and theological reasons for the societies, Mr. Wesley stated that these would-be-Christians were "fleeing from the wrath to come." In another place, one of his biographers paraphrases Wesley to say: "I am still convinced that the only lasting arena for perfection is the Society."[3] This joining of simple polity with the theology of perfection is a point of major significance. For Wesley, there was no point in polity without a faith to be expressed and there was no effective way to express that faith except through polity.

The other parts of the polity with which the early Methodists began were also attempts to live out a meaningful theology. When many people expressed the desire, Mr. Wesley divided the societies into bands. The rules for the bands and the theology out of which they emerged were clearly stated. It is true that Mr. Wesley regarded this elementary organization as "prudential helps, grounded on reason and experience," but it is no less true that he expected the general rules given in scripture to be observed and for each member of a band to be strengthened in faith by

a very close association with others of like mind. Robert G. Tuttle, Jr., gives a clear outline of Mr. Wesley's polity arrangements and functions both in graphic and narrative outline.[4]

Just as important as this structure by which these early Methodists grew are the leaders and servants that made the structure so effective. From the united society there came, on the one hand, the class meeting, the prayer meeting, and the strangers' society. On the other hand, there were the bands, the select societies, and the penitents. For all of these there were very clearly outlined instructions. As the needs developed, such leaders emerged as ministers, assistants, preachers, stewards, leaders, visitors of the sick, and schoolmasters. And the reasons for all of these were the people of God and the faith by which they desired to be saved.

That such a polity was effective is amply demonstrated by the growth of the early Methodists, both in faith and in numbers. Near the end of his "Plain Account," Mr. Wesley indicates something of how this organization served those in deepest need. The children were taught to read and write; a way was found to relieve the distress of the poor; a dignified type of relief was provided for widows. It was clear at this point that polity was emerging from theology both by a careful design of Mr. Wesley's and by the prudential helps that were suggested by obvious need.

This is the first point upon which some reflection is required. For many people, theology is a matter of doctrines, systems, and carefully stated beliefs which, when expressed properly, are the reasons for their membership in one type of church or another. According to them, there are systematic theologians and preachers, on the one hand, and there are the organization persons on the other. And their work is so different, both substantively and qualitatively, that there are few meeting places between them.

To the extent that this was true in the past, it obscured a very important area of theology. Pastoral theology, as Thomas Oden has recently observed, is "theoretical insofar as it seeks to develop a consistent theory of ministry, accountable to scripture and tradition experientially

14

sound and internally self consistent. . . . It is also a practical discipline, for it is concerned with implementing concrete pastoral tasks rather than merely defining them."[5] This bridge between the systematic and the practical is crucial at this time. It was the basis of John Wesley's theology and ministry.

When seen in this way, polity is more than a series of structures, interrelated according to the preferences of those who must make them work. Polity is both structure and a way of living out the theology which the church professes. It is both clear outline and discipline, on the one hand, and action within the context of widely accepted theology, on the other.

The first way in which theology emerges from polity is found in the process of teaching and nurturing the people of God. In a word, theology has always had to find some way to be practical. And when it does, it both produces and emerges from polity.

John Wesley understood this very well. In the introduction to *John Wesley's Fifty-Three Sermons*, Edward H. Sugden puts the matter pointedly. "John Wesley was a pragmatist before Professor James had popularized that term. 'His theology, if I may again quote Dr. Fitchett, is one which links doctrine to conduct. It has the salt of reality. Here are doctrines realized in human experience and tested by that experience.' "[6] Wesley not only linked doctrine with conduct; he found a most natural alliance between doctrine and polity.

II.

It is now appropriate to ask how this relates—if at all—to the extensive studies of Wesley's theology and the elaborate polity of the present United Methodist Church. Wesley was, after all, an Anglican clergyman who remained so throughout his life. He lived to see the Christmas Conference of 1784 and a rapid development of the societies in America. By 1784 there were as many as 83 itinerant Methodist preachers in America and 14,998 members. Coke, Whatcoat, and Vasey arrived in New York on November 3, 1784. It became clear that the Methodists were moving beyond a connection of societies and would, very soon, become a church.

Just how much of Wesley's polity was carried over in the American church, we cannot precisely determine. What we do know is that there were sharp divergences from some things that Mr. Wesley had in mind for polity, that the American preachers would soon make their voices heard on organization and procedure, and that Francis Asbury would soon become the architect of the polity which continued to emerge as the church grew in numbers and influence.

Given these facts, it will require another look at the total situation. Could it still be said that theology emerged out of polity when so much of that polity seemed to be formed by the insistence upon the American church to find its own identity? When polity faced the severe tests of controversy, were the major reasons given for it theological, cultural, sociological, or political? Was not the greatest task before this new church the clear statement of a self-definition, both theological and structural? Questions like these must lead us to a different kind of approach to our subject.

III.

When we turn from Wesley's basic ideas of governance for the societies to the American scene, we encounter a polity which is, in some ways, quite different from what Mr. Wesley had in mind. For Wesley, it was quite proper to appoint the superintendents for America. But Asbury not only refused to be appointed, he wanted the preachers to elect him and also he allowed himself to be called a bishop. This caused Mr. Wesley great concern. He expressed that concern to Asbury, but it was clear that the newly emerging church would have to be governed by a person with authority on these shores rather than by a beloved father who still belonged to the Church of England. Ferguson describes the break with Wesley's ideas of polity even more sharply. "The truth is that the Christmas Conference set in motion forces that in hardly more than two years' time left the Methodist Episcopal Church with hardly a veriform connection with the founder."[7]

This radical change in polity was at least as much a response to the new social situation in America as it was a reluctance to follow an honored leader. After all, the history of the Methodist Episcopal Church corresponds closely with the history of the new nation. It could hardly be expected that a church polity developed for a connection of societies would survive, unchanged, in a land where independence and freedom of thought were so highly treasured. In one way or another, the preachers would make their voices heard. And this has been an increasingly important note in Methodist polity ever since.

Such changes in polity, however, should not be overrated. In many ways, they were changes in degree more than in kind. At the same time, there were changes in theological emphases but no radical departure from the main themes of

Wesleyan theology. Gerald McCulloh begins his essay on "The Changing Theological Emphases" by saying: "In 1876 American Methodism, in spite of being divided in its organizational structure, was predominantly of one voice in its theology."[8] He goes on to outline four continuing emphases in Wesleyan theology: the universality of sin, salvation for all, the witness of the Spirit, and the call to Christian perfection.

The point to be made here is that there was a remarkable continuity in polity and theology and an interplay between them that provided the vitality of the rapidly growing church in America. Theology did indeed flow from polity, this time by deliberate reflection upon what the church should be and do amidst the changes of the times.

While Mr. Wesley believed that there was no final guidance in the scripture on matters of order, he also believed that the societies in America should develop in certain specific ways. Colin Williams points out how much Wesleyan theology found expression in the societies.

> The life of the kingdom that is ours now is an eschatological gift which is but a foretaste of the final kingdom and is subject to the vagaries of our unceasing conflict with the evil of this present world.
>
>   Nevertheless, Wesley believed that the Christian is called to work for social renewal and he rejoiced to see the transformations which (however incomplete and temporary) flowed from the life of the Societies.[9]

Just as Wesley was convinced that the people needed to be awakened and trained, he felt that the leader would be the key to the success of the movement. Snyder saw a direct connection between the development of the societies and the itinerant system.

> The society-class-band system would not have held together had it not been for the "itineracy"—Wesley's system of traveling lay preachers. These preachers were under Wesley's direct supervision. If Methodism in general looked like a quasi-monastic order, the itineracy was in fact an order—a preaching order which, if not celibate, certainly knew about poverty and obedience.[10]

This is why Colin Williams could write that "Wesley saw the organization of his Societies as an expression of one of the essential means of grace."[11]

Returning to the American scene, it may be profitable to define polity more carefully and examine ways in which theology emerges from it. This will be done by examining three continuing—and in some ways unique—themes of Wesleyan polity.

IV.

The serious student of Methodist polity soon discovers that connectionalism means more than legal relatedness by way of the *Book of Discipline*. In a much more profound way, connectionalism means a polity by which an entire fellowship of local churches and annual conferences all over the world agree to live out their life together. This is the overarching idea in the polity of The United Methodist Church.

In a statement read at the Conference of 1769, Mr. Wesley saw himself as a "centre of union." He wrote:

> You are at present one body. You act in concert with each other, and by united counsels. And now is the time to consider what can be done, in order to continue this union. Indeed, as long as I live, there will be no great difficulty. I am, under God, a centre of union to all our traveling preachers. They all know me and my communication. They all love me for my work's sake, and, therefore, were it only out of regard to me, they will continue connected with each other. But by what means may this connection be preserved, when God moves me from you?[12]

The answer to Mr. Wesley's question eventually came in a polity of local churches, Annual Conferences, a General Conference, and eventually Jurisdictional Conferences and a great deal in the life of the churches in between. These would preserve the connection. Within this connection of structure, action, and discipline three major themes are evident. It is the thesis of this paper that Wesleyan theology and its spirit both contributed to the making of this polity and emerged from it.

This first theme might be called Ministry/Itineracy/Episcopacy. These three are so interrelated in Methodist polity that any profile of one calls for a statement on the others. All three are parts of a doctrine of ministry. Within his theology of ministry, John Wesley made it clear that he believed episcopacy "to be scriptural and apostolical." However, it is also true as Howard Snyder points out that Wesley believed even more that, "at heart the church was the community of God's people."[13] Episcopacy therefore was for the service of the people of God. Bishops, or as he chose to call them, superintendents, were meant to enhance and extend the life of God's people. Now R.S. Bilheimer reminds us that the episcopacy in Methodism has never been a third order, but rather the investiture of an elder with certain definite executive functions and powers.[14] The importance of mentioning the bishop at this point is not to emphasize the importance of the office so much as to point out that as the polity developed, this office, at its best, became one of Mr. Wesley's "prudential helps." Indeed, it did so in ways he hardly could have imagined. Bishop Nolan Harmon has pointed out that the development of the Methodist episcopacy has been, and continues to be, the fundamental and constitutional part of the church's life. He went on to say that Mr. Wesley,

. . . fixed the itinerant Methodist system firmly in the Large Minutes of the English connection, and in time saw it established in the United States.[15]

The uniqueness of this episcopacy is found in the fact that no other Protestant church has ever tried what Bishop Harmon calls such an "iron clad episcopacy." This episcopacy is considerably less iron clad now than it was in Asbury's day, but it is still unique enough to be considered in the total context of an itinerant ministry.

One must always be aware of the danger of reading back into the polity, now hallowed by many years, a theology that was never really there. Nevertheless, it is clear that Mr. Wesley's view of the three orders of ministry were important to the polity that emerged later. One of the questions in the minutes of 1747 was:

Q. Are the three orders of Bishops, Priests, and Deacons plainly prescribed in the New Testament?

A. We think they are, and believe they generally obtained in the Churches of the Apostolic Age.

These orders of ministry, therefore, were not only matters of polity but of scripture and theology as well. Ministry was fundamental. Itinerancy was a way of doing ministry. And episcopacy was, among other things, a way by which order in the deployment of ministry could be maintained.

There is an even more fruitful area for theological research in the polity of ministry. If episcopacy can be seen both as a ministry that enables ministry, and with sufficient authority to do so, it can also be seen as an office in which theology is constantly being interpreted to the people of the local churches and the annual conferences. All of Mr. Wesley's major theological foundations emerge from the actual living out of the polity that has come out of two hundred years of testing, revising, reshaping, and renewing.

How, for example, does one explain to a pastor or a local church, where both are mutually agreed to live together for many years, that itinerancy still makes good sense? There are simply not enough reasons of sociology or preference or convenience to make a good case one way or another. But if ministry is fundamental to the life of the church, and if all ministers are bound together by covenant and ordination, and if the needs of the people of God in a given congregation are paramount, then the theological reasons for being where the people need such a person are far more powerful than the prudential ones.

The reverse, of course, is just as true. If the congregation or pastor agrees that it is time to itinerate, and if this case is put only on prudential grounds, either or both will miss the opportunity to see certain fundamental theological points. Ministry is for the people. And, in Methodist polity, ministers come out of a connection. If they are called rather than appointed, they can be sent in the same way. This neat way of putting it is, of course, inadequate to state the actual human situation. But the point is that the issues related to ministry-itinerancy-episcopacy have been under severe test since the days of James O'Kelley. And the further point is that these issues, while often settled in some heat and controversy, and usually on quite understandable grounds of human preference, must finally be discussed in the theological context to which they belong.

One additional word is necessary. The best stories in the area of polity cannot be told. They are too close to where people live, too delicate in their nature to be detailed, and often too inconclusive to allow a final judgment. Even so, every superintendent sooner or later faces situations in the lives of congregations and pastors that are too complex for human reason, too freighted with emotion for clear description, and too filled with pathos for ready alternatives. As one struggles to work through such complex problems of ministry and congregational life, there often emerge theological issues that the entire church would do well to reflect upon.

Theodore Runyon reminds us that, for Wesley, "Justification by faith is renewal and recreation in anticipation of and participation in, the future that is determinative. Sanctification has to do with growth in grace and the restoration of the person to wholeness."[16] While there is much more to Wesleyan theology than these two points, the generalization is no less true: all of these issues are faced and worked out in the actual struggle of bishops, pastors, and congregations to be the church and to move toward the perfection which Wesley emphasized so strongly.

In this case, theology emerges from polity in the testing places of congregational life, in the struggle to be the people of God in concrete social situations, and in the raising of fundamental questions of theology and worship. That the Holy Spirit enters and enables such struggle is a point that must be emphasized with great and grateful urgency.

The second theme in present United Methodist polity is the social outreach of the church. This area, controversial from the beginning, is fundamental in Wesleyan theology and his understanding of polity for the societies.

If one sees in the present structure of boards and agencies something of Mr. Wesley's works described in his "Plain Account," one will also see a continuing and—I think—indispensable part of Methodist theology and polity.

When Wesley is quoted as saying, "The world is my parish," it is a true reading of the way he viewed his ministry. But he said more than that on the subject. In one letter, he wrote, "I look upon all the world as my parish; thus far I mean, that in whatever part of it I am I judge it meet and right, and my bounden duty to declare, unto all that are willing to hear, the glad tidings of salvation."[17] The truth is that Wesley's "world" included not only the geographical areas to which he went but all the social issues of his time. His famous letter to Wilberforce, written in his last year, is just one case in point. Moreover, his point was theological: to declare the glad tidings. And he did this tirelessly not only to those who were willing to hear but to many others, including mobs, who, at first, were not willing to hear at all.

We now know this area of polity as a network of boards, agencies, and commissions, all of them responding to the inescapable challenge of Mr. Wesley's and all of them finding their rationale, finally, in lived-out theology. That this is an area that has caused much controversy in the church, no one would doubt. Nevertheless, it is clear that here polity both grows out of theology and produces a theology of praxis that is potentially rich in quality.

As Howard Snyder puts it, "For Wesley, holiness and good works were all of one piece. He saw faith, holiness, and good works as the root, the tree, and the fruit, which God has joined and man ought not to put asunder."[18] One could hardly be more theological than that. From the beginning, Wesleyan polity moved boldly away from a protected pietism that feared encounter with the world. As we know now from liberation theologians, this old word of the church is ever new. A theology that cannot speak to the hurting places of a sinful society hardly merits the name. And a polity that does not produce more theology of this kind is hardly worth keeping in place.

What remains to be said about congregational life and nurture has already been said in other parts of this paper. The people of God were the reason for polity in the first place. They needed to be organized, taught, nurtured, ministered unto, and inspired. If this took lay ministers, so it would be. If the numbers increased until there was a need for more careful supervision, that would be provided also. If order became important—as it certainly did—there would be those who would be specifically charged with ordering the life of the congregation.

In all of this, Wesley never ceased, as he never wanted his followers to cease, to offer Christ to the people. By whatever polity that was consistent with this desire and through whatever persons he could find with gifts and graces, Wesley felt that it was urgent to present Christ to the people.

As Albert Outler puts it:

> The burden of his evangelical message was always the same; the references are almost monotonous. He speaks of 'preaching Christ,' of 'offering Christ,' 'proclaiming Christ,' 'declaring Christ,' and so forth. And always it was the gospel of salvation by grace through faith, justification and deliverance through God's grace in Christ.[19]

By this statement, and many others, we know that Wesley saw no neat categories of polity on the one hand and theology on the other (indeed, he would do this, church or no church). What he did see and feel was a great passion to provide for the salvation of people through the means that became available.

Frank Baker makes a major point when he says:

> In all of this Wesley deliberately avoided any kind of rigidity either in teaching or organization. All was to be responsive to the needs of the moment and the workings of the Holy Spirit. . . . For John Wesley any theology which dealt only with a transcendent God, like any Church which remained merely an institution, was little more than empty speculation, fruitless organization.[20]

With such a spirit as this, theology would indeed emerge out of polity. It would do so by the original intent of Mr. Wesley's. Then, as the church in America grew, it would do so by reflecting upon its life and witness, both in conference sessions and at other times and places. More than that, theology would emerge from polity in those testing places of congregational and corporate life where the truth of pastoral theology becomes the life by which the church affirms both its Lord and itself.

NOTES

1. John Wesley, "A Plain Account of the People Called Methodist," *Works*, vol. 8, p. 248.
2. *Ibid.*, p. 250.
3. Robert G. Tuttle, Jr., *John Wesley, His Life and Theology* (Grand Rapids: Zondervan, 1978), p. 276.
4. *Ibid.*, p. 280.
5. Thomas C. Oden, "What is Pastoral Theology?" *Newsletter of the Theological School* (Drew University, Madison, N.J., vol. 3, no. 3.
6. Edward H. Sugden, ed., *John Wesley's Fifty-Three Sermons* (Nashville: Abingdon Press, 1983), p. 7.
7. Charles W. Ferguson, *Organizing to Beat the Devil* (Garden City, N.Y.: Doubleday & Company, 1971), p. 41.
8. Gerald O. McCulloh, "The Theology and Practices of Methodism," *The History of American Methodism*, ed. by Emory Stevens Bucke (Nashville: The United Methodist Publishing House, 1964), vol. II, p. 593.
9. Colin W. Williams, *John Wesley's Theology Today* (Nashville: Abingdon Press, 1960), pp. 196-97.
10. Howard A. Snyder, *The Radical Wesley*, Downers Grove, Ill.: Inter-Varsity Press, 1980), p. 63.
11. Williams, *Wesley's Theology Today*.
12. See 1763 Letter to the Clergy, *Letters*, vol. 4, pp. 235-39.
13. Snyder, *Radical Wesley*, p. 75.
14. R.S. Bilheimer, ed., *The Quest for Christian Unity* (New York: Association Press, 1952), p. 161.
15. Nolan B. Harmon, "The Growth of the Episcopacy," in *History of American Methodism*, vol. III, p. 17.
16. Theodore Runyon, "System and Method in Wesley's Theology," unpublished paper, Emory University.
17. Wesley, *Works*, vol. 1, pp. 201-2.
18. Snyder, *Radical Wesley*.
19. Albert C. Outler, *Theology in the Wesleyan Spirit* (Nashville: Tidings, 1975), p. 46.
20. Frank Baker, *John Wesley and the Church of England* (Nashville: Abingdon Press, 1970), pp. 117-18.

3. METHODISM AND NEW ISSUES
IN ECUMENISM

J. Robert Nelson

The two liturgical cries with which I feel compelled to begin this talk are these: *Alleluia!* and *Kyrie Eleison!* Those of us here who, only a week ago, were in Vancouver, attending the Sixth Assembly of the World Council of Churches, will probably agree with my sense of compulsion. One can hardly think about Methodism and ecumenism on this day without beginning with that assembly. And just as British Methodism's gift to Duke Divinity School, Geoffrey Wainwright, could subsume all systematic theology under the name of *Doxology*, so the many hundreds of us at Vancouver have come away with the deepest impression and lasting memory of daily doxological worship in the great tent.

It used to be the case at ecumenical conferences that we often felt most divided at worship, however sincere and warm our intentions and attitudes. This was because we tended to parade our various traditional and conventional styles of service. As one denominational group after another took charge of worship, there was always something to offend someone. Or else, there were artificial, synthetic liturgies which, because of their eclectic elements, were supposed to satisfy everyone; but most often they pleased very few.

Worship at Vancouver had an entirely different effect. It was an inexplicable phenomenon—unless we are prepared in faith to explain it by the effectual presence of the Holy Spirit. The services somehow proved to be both synthetic and authentic, rather than eclectic and hectic. Morning, noon, and evening in the huge tent the throngs of people manifested an almost palpable oneness. There was full participation in leadership, as some nine hundred laity and clergy spoke, read, sang, or danced. Strange musical instruments and drums blended with the Western piano and organ. New hymns, chants, and responses were contributed by Christians of the Pacific islands, Asia, Africa, and the Caribbean. The singing was of a lustiness and harmony which would rival the best Welsh Methodists. Each service had its special quality. The Orthodox Liturgy for the Day of Our Lord's Transfiguration was a two-hour experience of exaltation.

But even that, most agreed, could not equal the doxological ecstasy which caught up the three thousand or more who celebrated the Holy Communion according to the new Lima Liturgy, over which the Archbishop of Canterbury presided.

In almost all of these services we were learning the beauty and power of antiphonal praying: each brief spoken prayer was echoed by the sung response of the entire congregation. And the two ancient responses, Hebrew and Greek, predominated. *Alleluia* to the allegro rhythm of African and Jamaican music; and *Kyrie Eleison* from the Russian Orthodox Liturgy and from Taizé Community. So we continued with mixed moods. The *Alleluia* expressing joy, celebration, praise, and fulfilment; the *Kyrie* praying in contrition and penitence, a supplication out of our acknowledged sin. Both were present simultaneously. "Praise the Lord! Lord, have mercy!"

I suggest that this duality characterizes our earthly situation as Christians. It applies equally to the whole church, to the ecumenical movement, to the WCC and other councils of churches, and certainly to the attitudes of us Methodists to the *oikoumene* of God. Like the Vancouver assembly, we should be "sensors." Not "censors" with a *c* but hyper-sensitive "sensors" with an *s*. The joys and the pains of all the churches, and of all humanity, need to keep us constantly sensitive to the goodness and the tragedy of human lives, *la grandeur et la misère*, the agony and the ecstasy. *Alleluia* is response to all evidences of God's faithfulness and love for us; *Kyrie Eleison* is our confession of infidelity and despair about our own resources for life.

The main theme of the assembly gave us further symbols of ecumenical sensitivity. "Jesus Christ—the Life of the World" spoke to both the promise of "life in all its fulness" and the struggle with the "powers of death" in the world.

Was this theme sufficiently and successfully treated? I, for one, think it was not. That may just mean that it was not interpreted in *my* way. But, more objectively, delegates were often content to use the theme as a slogan, a cliché, a label taking the simple form, "life is a gift of God." Others duly and emphatically expressed understanding of problems of *how* this life is lived, rather than exploring *what* life is—especially as God creates, sustains, and redeems human life in and through Jesus Christ. Do we Christians believe—do we realize—that every human life and all of life owe existence to the divine creativity at work in and through the incarnate Life, Jesus Christ?

This theme really poses the ultimate ecumenical question. All of our programmatic concerns for church unity, mission, renewal, justice, and peace are subordinate to it. So we are not concerned only with the church, the churches, and Christians; but with the inherent value of each person in every place and time. God's *oikoumene* is defined by God's offer to each one who lives—the offer of a fully human existence; and it is obstructed by the numerous kinds of personal and social corruption which prevent the realization of God's promise. In other words, the sphere of ecumenical concern is delimited only by the extremities of human life itself.

This is not a brand new idea, minted at Vancouver. The understanding of ecumenism as embracing the whole of life of all humanity is a species of Christian universalism which has been growing steadily for two decades. In 1963 the Second Vatican Council opened at the word of Pope John XXIII, whose view of God's will was truly for *Pacem in terris*. At the same time, we in the WCC began speaking of church unity in relation to the unity of all humanity (without knowing exactly what we meant by this). But we have been learning how to think globally. The Vancouver assembly brought to it highest level so far this way of construing ecumenism as shared concern for the entire human race: that is, our shared creation by God, our shared responsibility for sin, and our shared hope for the realization of all persons' worth and enjoyment of life. The favored words in Vancouver texts and addresses included precisely "sharing," "participating," and knowing the many implications of *koinonia*. The constantly heard challenge to make ecumenism local, to bring its spirit and practice to the grass roots where people live, is perfectly justified. In fact, we were stressing the same mandate in 1961 at the New Delhi assembly by defining Christian unity primarily for "all in each place." However, to separate locality and universality as alternative choices of interest and commitment is now shown to be indefensible. Like the *Alleluia* and the *Kyrie*, they belong together.

A realistic question has to be posed, however. Can the diverse aspects of the whole human comedy and human tragedy be effectively comprehended in the kind of Christian concern we call ecumenical? If ecumenism applies to all life, can there be focus on particular issues? If not, we are doomed to disarray and dismay. If so, which are the priorities?

Revolting as the bureaucratic term "prioritizing" may be to certain literate sensitivities, much of the debate at Vancouver was over the question, What comes first? "Peace" and "justice" were key words in the rhetorical litany. People of the Northern Hemisphere are mainly concerned about securing peace in the time of nuclear weapons. Delegates of the Southern Hemisphere insist that social and economic justice are the primary need; and they fear that the powerful northerners will be so occupied with peace that justice will suffer below the Equator.

Another set of alternatives was constantly being set before us. Rather than acknowledging the relation between the unity and renewal of the church, on one hand, and the community and renewal of all humanity, on the other, some people separated these into disparate options. Moreover, within the scope of "churchly issues" the arguments for priority of either mission or renewal or unity presupposed the disparity of these three. All these categories, as well as others, can be claimed vigorously for preferential treatment. Each has its programmatic possibility. As in our own Methodist structures, there are program units for each major concern in the WCC; and with varying names they are present in the secretariats and congregations of the Church of Rome. But is it not evident that the alleged dichotomies and alternatives are false distinctions of priority? As human beings we do not live by either water or food or air or human relationships. So it is for the church and the ecumenical movement. The closing prayers at Vancouver were intended to resolve the separation of peace and justice in delegates' minds. "The root of the tree of peace is justice." To follow that metaphor, the root cannot live without the branches of peace as well as the green leaves of reconciliation and unity.

The idea may now seem obvious. But I stress the point that the ecumenical view must be synoptic and universal because I want to confute the unreflective idea which pervades our denomination and others, that ecumenical participation is only for those who make it a vocation or a hobby, and especially for those who have ecclesiastical expense accounts. There was a time when we could laugh at the designation "ecumaniac." And today there are indeed enthusiasts who wear WCC buttons and *Oikoumene* t-shirts; and no one need deride them. But the serious ecumenical business has now become every

Christian's business. An illustration of this development is found in our United Methodist organization. In 1972, here in Atlanta at the General Conference, some of us debated strongly in favor of having a General Commission for Ecumenical Affairs, rather than simply a division within the new Board of Global Ministries. Unfortunately, the majority voted in their belief that ecumenism belonged "somewhere out there" in the wide world of mission and international church relations, rather than "right here" wherever the church is found. Experience proved the minority to have been wiser; and now we have that General Commission. Yet, even with this functioning structure, the wrong impression can be drawn, that ecumenism remains a departmentalized, specialized function of the denomination, with its own particular column in *The Interpreter* magazine.

One of our favorite words in the churchly lexicon today is "commitment." That can mean a number of things. It has meant, for example, in past years the sending of mentally retarded persons to the "insane asylum." It also has a meaning for people active in the commercial market and in politics. But *we* use it to mean our serious, unqualified devotion to what we believe to be God's will. As Methodists, what is our ecumenical commitment? The first articles of the United Methodist Constitution of 1968 do, in fact, commit the church to the quest for unity with other churches. Do these also commit the church to the total, synoptic task of ecumenism? I am not sure whether any formal policy statements of Methodist churches has gone so far as the 1982 commitment of Lutherans; their official position is defined:

The Lutheran Church in America declares that the ecumenical commitment to the unity of the church is among the highest priorities under the proclamation of the Gospel. Therefore, this church recognizes that ecumenism must pervade its faith and life in its international, national, synodical and local dimensions.

The Decree on Ecumenism of the Second Vatican Council (1964), backed by the authority of that council, tacitly makes a similar commitment:

The concern for restoring unity involves the whole Church, faithful and clergy alike. It extends to everyone, according to the talents of each, whether it be exercised in daily Christian living or in theological and historical studies.

Do we have any policy statements for Methodists bearing comparable weight?

Yet, it is not the statements of councils, synods, and general conferences alone which convert the minds and sentiments of their members from parochialism, sectarianism, and denominationalism to an authentic commitment to ecumenism. The approving of conference resolutions and even constitutional articles is relatively easy as compared to the persistent, unrelenting task of communicating and educating for the formation of a Christian ecumenical outlook.

As for communication, we all know that this is the era of instant news— veritable cascades of news drenching us daily. In this country there is no good reason why church people should be mentally confined to the parochial ghetto. This inexcusability is valid even despite the alarming deficiency of our church journalism and electronic communication. Especially without excuse are two kinds of persons who by vocation share the Holy Spirit's *charismata*, the pastor-preacher and the teacher. To be sure, the pulpit and the lectern need not be turned into a news desk. But, to put the matter rhetorically in questions: How often do *you* preachers convey to congregations a well-informed sense of what God is doing in and through the church of the world just now? And how deliberately and consistently do *you* teachers—in local church, college, or seminary—relate your subject matter to the actualities of some phase of the church's ecumenical witness? If your answer is positive, blessed art thou! If negative—well, be your own judge.

My assignment is not to give an overall description of every issue within the scope of the ecumenical movement, but rather to deal with some new issues in ecumenism. This means having to make some arbitrary choices as to what is truly new and what merits our consideration just now. With your indulgence (and since this is a plenary meeting, that means *plenary* indulgence), I wish to speak briefly about the following issues. All of them, inevitably, were on the Vancouver agenda, and they will remain on the agenda of most churches for a good while.

(1) *Evangelical mission*, (2) *church unity*, (3) *human community*, (4) *the participation of all sorts and conditions of people*, (5) *scientific technology* and (6) *general justice and peace for all*. Note that none of these can be handled responsibly without some deep-plowing by theological analysis as well as varieties of sciences.

(1) When we speak of *"evangelical mission"* we are rightly avoiding the dichotomy of two vocations of the church, evangelism and mission. Go tell it in Nashville, go tell it in New York, that these two have become one flesh and one spirit. The artificial split between them is both concep-

tual and organizational, according to much United Methodist usage.

Fifty years ago the International Missionary Council was engaged in the project they called "rethinking mission(s)." Today we are still doing it. And while the social and cultural conditions of humanity keep changing so fast, we Christians will keep rethinking what is essential and immutable in our faith and what is properly subject to modification, as it pertains to the *Missio Dei* to humanity.

Except for the most dogmatic and inflexible of Christian mentalities, the mission of the church for the sake of the gospel of Jesus Christ has always borne problems of ambiguity. It poses fundamental questions of God's purpose for each person (i.e., salvation), and the radical question of the discontinuity of Jesus Christ from other religious leaders, saviors, teachers, and the soteriological beliefs which their lives have engendered. Thus we experience or witness two kinds of polarization today. First, there is for many people a polarization between Christians and the adherents of all other religions or ideologies; and this can be overcome, in their view, only by conversion of the latter. This causes, secondly, a polarization within the church's membership between Christians of rigorous orthodoxy (defined as you will) and those of (shall we say?) flexible faith and theology.

This tension resides also in the minds of particular men and women. While we may hold sincere belief in Jesus Christ as God's only Mediator with humanity, we also have an unpresumptuous understanding of other people's religious beliefs and hold an attitude of friendliness toward them in an atmosphere of religious freedom.

Ambiguity and polarization are being intensified today as the pluralism of religions and ideologies becomes much better known, and as, by means of easy travel, we come to know personally the kinds of Muslims, Hindus, and Buddhists which in former years one could only read about. At Vancouver, one of the most animated and earnest floor debates took place over the first draft of the report on "Witness in a Divided World." Judging by the estimated proportion of delegates who applauded interventions which criticized the report for seemingly subsuming evangelical mission under inter-religious dialogue, for not even mentioning the theme of "Jesus Christ—the Life of the World," and for providing only a diluted theological rationale for mission, it seemed that two-thirds to three-fourths of the people de-

manded a stronger, more kerygmatic and Trinitarian interpretation of mission. The rejection of that draft was unique in the assembly, although a second, much altered draft was accepted at the last hour. In my view, this action did not amount to a repudiation of dialogue with people of other faiths; indeed, the presence and the public speeches of prominent representatives of Judaism, Islam, Sikhism, Hinduism, and Buddhism were generally welcomed with appreciation. But a defensive posture was maintained against the idea that mission and dialogue are equivalent rather than complementary, or the more radical notion that dialogue is preeminent over evangelical mission.

About the diaconal aspects of mission, however, there has been little dispute within the ecumenical movement. The old colonializing concept of the so-called Great Century of Protestant missions has surely passed; and the commitments to the new churches' indigenization, self-determination, and equal participation are as well honored as the concerns for the liberation of peoples from forms of exploitation and the development of their societies.

Disagreements within the whole ecumenical community of the world over the theological understanding of mission, attitudes toward people of other faiths, and strategies for world and local mission will inevitably continue. They continue within Methodism and other world communions as well. However, at Vancouver there was a mood of reconciliation among the categories of Christians who have been rather suspicious of the authenticity of one another's faith and doctrine. Eastern Orthodox Christians no longer inveigh against Protestants, whom they formerly called "proselytizers." Roman Catholic missiologists work harmoniously with Protestants of various kinds. And at Vancouver, a group of leading conservative Evangelicals issued a letter in which they stated:

> Hence, we feel pressed to declare publicly our determination to be more actively involved in all efforts seeking the unity and renewal of the church. Because we have seen evidence of God at work here, we cannot but share our growing conviction that evangelicals should question biblically the easy acceptance of withdrawal, fragmentation and parochial isolation that tends to characterize many of us.

This verbal olive branch may or may not be welcomed by those who are content to be known as theological liberals. Those who would reject it are, it seems, betraying the very virtue of pluralism which is often extolled in relation to those who come from the opposite direction.

(2) *Church unity* as a realizable condition, in succession to the present state of denominational, racial, and class division, is regarded by many Christians as an obsolescent concept and evanescent goal. Rather than vitiating or abandoning the belief in God's will for unity, however, the delegates to the Nairobi assembly only seven years ago revised the constitution of the WCC to make its first function more prominent than ever. The council's first stated function is this:

> To call the churches to the goal of visible unity in one faith and in one eucharistic fellowship expressed in worship and common life in Christ, and to advance towards that unity in order that the world may believe.

Now, church unity is an old, much debated problem in the ecumenical movement and in every kind of Christian community. But today it has become a new issue, because a new solution has suddenly come before the public. This is the highly important document called *Baptism, Eucharist, and Ministry*, with the acronym *BEM*. It is, of course, the text of the converging towards consensus which was brought to final form by the Commission on Faith and Order in Lima, Peru.

To be honest, some of us *aficionados* of faith and order studies were pretty pessimistic about the program prepared for Vancouver. It seemed that very little space was being made for discussion of *BEM*, since the text was not subject to further revision. And this seemed to reveal a bias against church unity issues on the part of the assembly planners.

Nobody really supposes that Baptism, Holy Communion, and the ministry are the *only* matters over which churches are divided; for there are many doctrinal, liturgical, customary, and institutional barriers. But neither can anyone doubt that for more than sixty years in faith and order conferences and studies, long before the formation of the WCC, the sacraments and the ministry have been central problems, crying for some kind of resolution. For those who are still unpersuaded to support valid efforts toward achieving visible unity of two or more denominations it is easy to aim a cheap shot at *BEM*; it is saying sardonically that it has meaning for the settlement of domestic, intra-ecclesial differences which actually make no difference to the way the churches serve and witness in the world. The drafters of the text can hardly be accused of such isolationist mentality, however; and the text clearly refutes it. The same faith and order people who gave you BEM have for more than a decade been stressing the implications of Christian unity for renewal of human community, the community of women and men, the unacceptability of any form of racism, and the inclusion in all dimensions of the church's life of disabled and handicapped persons. As the British theologian, Mary Tanner, said: the recent study on the Community of Women and Men "challenged any belief that the unity of the Church can be limited to the coming together of ecclesial bodies on the basis of doctrinal agreement alone, or with the adoption of common structures of decision making."

But why this unexpected, amazing success of *BEM*? Why has the commendability of the text itself stimulated such positive ecumenical publicity, rather than the calculated publicity's having had to make people read the text? Briefly, I can see several reasons, as follows:

1. There was careful, critical preparation over a very long time. It is no exaggeration to say that *BEM* began in the preparations for the First World Conference on Faith and Order at Lausanne, 1927. In this ecumenical cuisine we used a low burner and stirred the pot slowly.

2. During the recent fourteen of these years there was full participation by Roman Catholic theologians along with the Eastern Orthodox and Protestants. At the Lima meeting, finally, there were no abstentions among the one hundred votes on the text.

3. The basis on scriptural texts, critical exegesis, and biblical theology was considered normative.

4. The general theology of the three parts of *BEM* is of clearly Trinitarian character.

5. The christological focus is well defined.

6. The power of the Holy Spirit is acknowledged throughout in *BEM*'s epikletic emphasis.

7. The text is positive, indicative, but not pontifical. The modesty of the drafters is illustrated by the use of commentary on difficult questions for which no final resolutions have been found.

8. *BEM* displays a comprehensiveness on matters of traditional dispute (such as infant and believer's Baptism), so categorical choices of one or another practice are transcended.

In addition to these intrinsic virtues of *BEM*, there can be no doubt that the celebration of the Lima Liturgy in the tent on July 31 propelled the document into the appreciative thinking of all present. Its authenticity was immediately grasped. I can readily confess that I had never known an occasion when the extravagant statements sometimes made about the Eucharist's being heaven on earth were so credible. In fact, I realized that an eternity of praising the Almighty God in heaven might not be so boring after all, but rather exhilarating. As for its inclusiveness, consider this: a Russian Orthodox Archbishop led prayers; a Roman Catholic bishop read the Scripture; a Church of South India bishop preached; and Dr. Runcie, Archbishop of Canterbury, con-celebrated with a Danish Lutheran, an Indonesian Reformed minister, an African Methodist, a Hungarian Baptist, a Moravian from Jamaica, and a pastor of the United Church of Canada. As the Faith and Order Director, William Lazareth, gloated: "That Lima Liturgy, presided over by Canterbury, was equal in value to fifty study conferences."

If this Methodist enthusiasm about *BEM* can be tolerated and now tempered, I must point out that everyone is not pleased with every detail of it. Certainly there are Christians of the so-called nonliturgical churches who cannot subscribe to various theses on Baptism, the Lord's Supper, and the ordained, three-fold pattern of ministry. Perhaps they would just as soon make an apostolic secession right now.

What is the intended disposition of *BEM*? Unlike dozens of other WCC reports and recommended study papers of the numerous bilateral conversations, *BEM* is not commended to the churches of the world for their casual consideration and possible action, if they feel like taking any. That is clearly the fate of a majority of such reports. No, *BEM* is intended to be *received*. What does that mean? As our man, John Deschner, asserted: " 'Reception' is a key word for what looks like a new ecumenical era in the WCC's quest for visible church unity;" it "refers not simply to deciding what to do with a document, but to a 'spiritual process' of appropriating new *life* in our churches." Or, to sharpen that meaning, Father Jean-Marie Tillard said, "This is the first time in the history of the Roman Catholic Church that Catholic bishops have been asked to accept a doctrinal document that did not originate with Rome." What boldness! To ask the many churches of the world to adopt into their own canons, orders, disciplines, and constitutional practices the recommended definitions and interpretations of this unique ecumenical document!

This is by no means a fanciful dream. As I have vainly boasted about the United Methodists recently, we actually began several years ago to accommodate our orders of worship to the sacramental theology upon which so many theologians of the *oikoumene* have agreed. And in the official response which we United Methodists sent to Geneva on the first full draft of *BEM*, 1977, carrying the *nihil obstat* of the Council of Bishops, we entered into a constructive give-and-take dialogue, which has borne fruit in the final draft. Moreover, the bilateral discussions which we have had with Roman Catholics on the Eucharist and with Lutherans on Baptism have already facilitated our way toward an agreement to the first two parts of *BEM*. What we have not yet done, and what we will certainly have to do, is grapple with the statement on ministry in a manner more consistent and thoroughgoing than has thus far been attempted.

In still another dimension of ecumenical engagement some of us Methodists, appointed by the church, have been appropriating and assimilating the ecumenical wisdom on sacraments, ministry, and ecclesiology. This is in our participation in the Consultation on Church Union. This consultation's influence has now far exceeded the boundaries of the study commissions and plenary sessions. The ten denominations "in quest of a Church of Christ Uniting" have this summer become nine, due to the union of the two Presbyterian bodies. All these have formally agreed at the highest level of their governments on the mutual recognition of members of all the churches. Presbyterians and Disciples have gone farther, by inviting persons from other denominations to become members of some of their standing commissions as full voting members—a significant ecumenical gesture. Now we are seeking the next stage: the mutual recognition of ministries. It has been proposed and accepted that this recognition be achieved by a process of covenanting to have in the future none but common ordinations. Perhaps that "right time," that *kairos*, is drawing near. We can only be sure that whatever happens in the coming few years will be strongly determined by the interplay of our nine denominations' handling of *BEM* and our progress toward agreement in COCU. To adapt Jim Kirby's story of the fisherman, we Methodists have been handed a stick of dynamite with a burning fuse. The time of decision is not far off. In Canada we worshiped with our ex-Methodist friends in the United Church, which was formed by union with Presbyterians and Congregationalists just fifty-eight years ago. Other ex-Methodist friends came also from twenty-six years of the experience of union in India. And our friend, Norman Young, is here from the Uniting Church of Australia, at one since 1977.

Historically considered, we have already passed the point of no return with respect to church unity. Perpetuating denominationalism indefinitely is an illusion at least, and an antitheological delusion, or deception, at most.

In this ecumenical century of the church, the

mandate and inevitability of church unity have been demonstrated by seventy-five years of church unions, fifty years of faith and order convergence, twenty-eight years of the WCC, and eighteen years of bilateral conversations—all of these within eighty-three years of intensified need of the earth's population—need for the justifying and reconciling power of God in Jesus Christ which can work effectually through the undivided People of God and Body of Christ.

Very briefly, now, I can mention four other *new* issues in ecumenism. Each is of great importance. None can at this time be given the emphasis it deserves.

(3) *Human community* as a Christian ecumenical aspiration is hardly a novelty; but there is clearly a new motivation, a new sense of urgency, and a new hope of some measure of success in achieving it. This is a "hope against hope" right in the face of the present fragmentation of human societies. We suffered no lack of reminders at Vancouver of the unjust and belligerent side of humanity's condition: the gross violations of basic human rights; the economic inequities which, at worst, mean destitution and starvation for millions; the persistence of oppressive racism, either by cruel laws in South Africa or by implicit, uncodified discrimination in many lands; and, permeating and poisoning the whole earth, the virulent nationalism and militarism which cause nations to waste their substance and keep building ever increasing threats to our order and survival.

Except for those Christians who seem eager to behold the universal carnage of an apocalyptic Armageddon, how can any of us not hope for what the World Council naively calls "the renewal of human community?" Yes, it is a naïve hope. It reflects the childlike trust in God's good purposes and in God's provision of strength to the poor in spirit, to the peacemakers, to the powerless people who nevertheless find "strength to love." It is the simple ecumenical faith, above all political sophistication and knowledge of human depravity, that God wills to us the church as the sign and instrument of justice and peace in the whole human community.

(4) *Participation*, then is the fourth issue to note. We perceive that this is not distinct from, but in operative line with, the previous issues of mission, church unity, and human community. The Vancouver assembly itself was a major manifestation of the principle of comprehensive participation. Some have judged it to have been so participatory as to exclude persons of high competence in special fields. And this is surely

the danger of thoroughgoing populism, whether in The United Methodist Church or the WCC. Categories are made more important than capability; quotas than qualifications. Yet, skill, experience, competence do not *have* to be the price paid for genuine participation in church councils or civil structures.

Who are designated as the ones now deserving overdue consideration for full participation? Women, to be sure, youth, elderly men and women, handicapped persons, the poor.

With the exception of one category, these were present and prominent at Vancouver as examples to all the churches. The missing category, of course, were the poor—the truly poor. Who would pay their expenses?

(5) *Scientific technology* has emerged as an ecumenical concern only since the Nairobi assembly where the Australian biologist, Charles Birch, proclaimed convincingly its wonders and terrors for humanity. Some aspects of it had previously been considered, such as nuclear weapons, other dazzling devices for mass killing, and also the adverse effects of the sudden imposition of technological industry and commerce upon poor, developing nations. The WCC conference on Faith, Science, and the Future, held four summers ago at M.I.T. in Cambridge, began a new venture in ecumenical effort. There, we could see what it means, for Christian theology and the churches' responsibility for human well-being, that our civilization in the Northern Hemisphere, especially, is moving from the *industrial* era to the *atomic* era, to the *cybernetic* era, and to the *biotechnological* era. While the military uses of scientific research and development frighten us immediately upon recognizing them, we are coming to see their application to human beings as such and to the human race as cause for both hope and alarm.

To be sure, in the ecumenical context, these are hardly church-dividing barriers in the usual faith-and-order sense. Baptism, Eucharist, and ministry may prove to be much simpler to resolve among churches than the problems we all will have to face in common:

(a) The growing power of scientific technology over economics, politics, and cultures.

(b) Scientific materialism as a world view, taught and accepted in schools and universities.

(c) Uses and abuses of genetic engineering, means of energy release, automation in production, and all the techniques of communication.

As worldwide disciples of the nontechnologi-

26

cal Jesus, we ask ourselves Who is sufficient for these things?

(6) *General justice and peace for all* is assuming ever-growing prominence on our ecumenical mandate. It is conventional to talk anxiously about threats to peace today. But as the prophet warned Israel, "There is no peace" to threaten, when we consider that since 1945 there have been more than one hundred conflicts large enough to be called wars! As was reiterated at Vancouver, the world is not at peace when each day of the year more than a billion dollars are spent on military preparations, equipment, and actual fighting. Nor is the world at peace when terrorism and torture are common-place; when the practice as well as the mentality of apartheid exist in every nation; when 85 percent of the world's population enjoys virtually no health services of preventive or therapeutic value; when civil criminality is on the grand scale.

So ecumenical peacemaking in the smallest and largest dimensions of society is our order of each day, even while war prevention and disarmament remain the special focus of much effort.

And as never before, I believe, we Christians, divided and confused as we are, are coming to see how all the above-mentioned ecumenical issues —evangelical mission, church unity, renewing the community of humanity, participation, uses of scientific technology, and struggles for human rights, justice, order, and peace— how all these are, as we say in theology, "perichoretic"—interpenetrating, mutually supportive—in the whole church's difficult but faithful discipleship.

So I can end as I began, *Kyrie eleison* and *Alleluia*!

II. Wesleyan Constructive Theology for the Future

1. WESLEYAN THEOLOGY: HERITAGE AND TASK

Durwood Foster

If to the theological challenges of our time the Wesleyan heritage brings significant assets of hermeneutic and substantive holism, of catholic openness and practical evangelical zeal, it also harbors liabilities of moralism, individualism, and shallow pragmatism that invite the corrective of today's wider Christian and world community. Within the dialogical horizons expanding in current theology the Wesleyan tradition thus both reflects the crises of Christendom and offers much to the setting free and making whole of the world that form the thrust of God's reign. In what follows I propose briefly to inventory the Wesleyan theological tradition and commend some directions it seems particularly fitted and obligated to pursue in the decades ahead.

I. Assets

1. Among the assets of theological Wesleyanism none is more conspicuous than its *hermeneutic holism*, meaning broadly here by "hermeneutic" what pertains in general to the right reading of the Christian "text": namely, the familiar quadrilateral of Scripture, tradition, reason, and experience. Whereas the history of Christian interpretation shows these elements chronically impugning or ignoring one another, from Wesley onward the movement bearing his name has been committed in principle to their careful interplay. Thus, for example, in spite of the categorical authority accorded the Bible, the motto *solo scriptura* was never adequate to Wesleyanism. And while biblicism as well as one-sided traditionalism, rationalism, and experientialism have all colored the stream from time to time, there was from the beginning a built-in Wesleyan resistance to each of these approaches pursued in isolation. Nor has sane balance in this respect been merely a matter of bland eclecticism. The respective corners of the quadrilateral have all been espoused by various Wesleyans with creative intensity—more so indeed than their ideal congruency has been achieved. Yet the individuating vigor with which the different elements have been exercized—unless they fall asunder—greatly potentiates, of course, the eventual force of their integration.

2. In the content of its witness even more definitive of Wesleyanism than its comprehensive hermeneutic has been a remarkable *double emphasis upon grace and freedom*. In no other particular stream of Christian sensibility has there been such a notable intonation of divine initiative in tandem with creaturely responsibility; it was first paramount in Wesley himself. The concerns of Augustine and Calvin have here married those of Pelagius and Arminius. If it belongs to the essential genius of biblical faith to envisage the creation, healing, and fruition of the world as indefeasibly a God-and-human enterprise—without weakening either end of the polarity—Wesleyan tradition has advocated that vision with unique insistence. In Ritschl's image, Christian life and thought comprise an ellipse whereof every point is determined by two focuses. Moral freedom is categorically valued in its own right, not simply as a concession to modernity, but as actualizing divine purpose. Beyond the antithesis, therefore, of other worldly mysticism and humanistic autonomy, authentic Wesleyanism exerts a potent impulse toward God-centered secularity.

3. Related but distinct is the further Wesleyan *dual stress upon justification and sanctification*. Christian experience generally has featured sometimes the one, sometimes the other of these pivotal moments, whereas Wesleyanism has passionately wanted to hold them together in tight embrace. The indicative, *Christus pro nobis, Gerechtsprechung* are inseparable from the imperative, *Christus in nobis, Gerechtmachung*. The subjectivity of faith is integrally bonded with God's prevenience. Faith is a gift, yes, but never arbitrarily imposed; and active righteousness is an expectation, but always with gracious empowerment. The necessity of divine mercy is underscored by accent upon the gravity of universal sin, even as its reality is sung with such evangelical fervor. Christian consciousness is joyfully comforted despair. This is the gospel's living water for the broken and hopeless, including those who may indeed have no future in this world. Yet *sola fide* cannot say it all, for blessed assurance of forgiveness continually issues into constraint toward perfection. Salvation as *Seligkeit* and as *Umwandlung*, so often disjoined, are here one. Together they form the *articulus stantis et cadentis ecclesiae*.

4. In principle there emerges from this kind

31

of religious consciousness a salient *synthesis of ecumenical openness and evangelical apostolicity.* All humanity are in dire need of the gospel, all are embraced by it, all are summoned by it. The atonement is not limited. God wills the salvation of all, and in virtue of the Christ event preveniently restores the responsible capacity of all. The service of such a catholic vision justifies, and also transcends, whatever institutional pragmatics may provisionally implement it. God is at work everywhere; and whenever hearts sense concord, in the parish that is the world, hands should join. At the same time, the perfection that always impinges as possibility and goal never cancels our dire need for mercy or precludes, short of death, the prospect and challenge of further growth. As Wesley and very many of his followers have been keenly aware, society—and very conspicuously so-called Christian society—is far from the Kingdom. Innumerable persons languish in misery, deprived of the good news and amendment of life intended for them. Taken seriously, this conviction would leave one never complacently content with the status quo of either one's individual or social facticity but would propel one zestfully outward in self-transcending stewardship and witness. One would gladly anticipate the precedence of divine grace and hurry forward to cooperate with it.

5. Already implied in the foregoing as another mark of Wesleyanism is a signal *conjunction of personal and social salvation.* While individual experience is accented, the Wesleyan style has always featured common worship, hymnody, fellowship, and social service. *Pace* William James, religion is never simply what one does with her or his solitude. As rather extremely exemplified in the original Methodist bands, soteriology is intensively a communal enterprise—yet one which, so far from submerging the individual in the group, would focus group energies upon the individual. Resonant with this is Wesley's concern for the dissemination of the spiritual classics and for the personal pursuit of perfection, the latter, however, abjuring mystical withdrawal and always embracing active love of neighbor with insistence upon personal rectitude and discipleship. If he did not attain to the purview of what we call the social gospel or liberation theology, the founder of Methodism nevertheless espoused some of their crucial principles so that when these developments appeared they could be readily drawn into alliance with the Wesleyan tradition, as long as they did not forfeit a concern for individual salvation for the sake of the social dimension alone.

6. The marked Wesleyan composition of

individuation and participation (as Tillich would call it) engenders finally a notable *junction of piety and praxis.* In part this has derived from the cooperation of different temperaments, so that some Wesleyans have been mainly pious and others mainly practical. Yet the paradigm established by Wesley himself has always called for a more unitive blend within each person. While holding a deep respect for knowledge, reason, and education, Wesleyan theology has consequently leaned toward praxis and has been strongly colored by the religious affections. If the split between technical reason and emotion is one of the basic problems of modern culture, the spirit of John Wesley has been and can still be a significant counterforce.

II. Liabilities

1. Having briefly noted some salient resources of the Wesleyan heritage in theology, it is in order next to assess similarly its difficulties and shortcomings. To a considerable degree these correspond to the assets already stated, in the sense, for example, that one major problem of the Wesleyan tradition is palpably a tendency toward hermeneutical disintegration or a splintering into biblicism, traditionalism, rationalism, and experientialism. The weakness here, however, is surely not simply the obverse of the virtue but rather the *lack of a unifying envisagement of the Christ norm.* In Wesley's unique personality the guiding power of this norm is implicitly effective in spite of inadequate systematic articulation. But as his definitive influence recedes in time or is one-sidedly appropriated, the various corners of the hermeneutic triangle begin to come unglued and collide. Not endowed with a systematic proclivity, Wesley never thematized intentionally enough even for his own time that the *rex et dominus scripturae,* as well as the *rex et dominus* of tradition, reason, and experience, is Christ. In any event his intellectual horizon could not, of course, encompass the crisis of biblical historiography beginning to erupt only at the end of the eighteenth century. Though he addressed discerning sermons to the Spirit's authority, to ponder systematically the relations of the historical, biblical, and living Christ lay beyond his time. Nor would it appear that even into our own period the Wesleyan tradition on the whole has succeeded in making good what the founder perforce left unprovided, though in this respect it has hardly been worse off than other streams of modern Christianity.

2. The lack of a cohesive vision of the Christ norm is also exposed in the Wesleyan *tendency, as freedom pulls loose from grace, to become a scheme of*

self-salvation. Although the counter movement of holiness supernaturalism was also evoked, a humanistic tilt was the main outcome of disjoining divine initiative and human responsibility. As in the wider Arminian tradition, where the compelling "Christic" union of divine and human fades from normative centrality there occurs an egregious shift toward creaturely autonomy—Pelagianism crowds out Augustinianism—which then creates a secular vacuum into which fundamentalism and the new religious movements eventually pour.

3. Closely correlated with the foregoing there has developed, from a growing cleavage of justification and sanctification, the *oppressive legalism* that haunts the Methodist ethos. Even if lately many have found relief from personal puritanism by heavily imbibing the "new morality," still for most social or political compunctions have taken up the slack. They are, of course, truer to their tradition than those who take the opposite tack and simply acquiesce in the cultural establishment. Wesley himself was deeply imbued with the pathos of the law; both before and after his conversion an acute moral sensibility—indeed a leaning toward moralism—pervades his cognizance of radical mercy and is always needing to be sublated by his unfailing grasp of love. Anchored in the Christic union of gracious indicative and transforming imperative, the themes of justification and sanctification could be both emphasized and balanced in the model Wesleyan personality. But since the ground and truth of this balance in Christ was never adequately thematized by Wesley, the widespread erosion in modern theology of a meaningful grasp of justification has tended to exacerbate Wesleyan moralism where it has not in fact been abandoned for mere convention or psychological group dynamics.

4. In the absence of a unifying norm tethering it to spiritual vision, the Wesleyan leaning toward praxis tends to deteriorate into a *theologically trivial pragmatism* that exercizes itself in various kinds of institutional self-satisfaction. Ordination to the ministry and success in it are monitored merely in terms of social leadership. Biblical and doctrinal criteria yield to having any viewpoint one can engagingly relate to current events. Pastoral care becomes semiprofessional psychotherapy; and worship and evangelism are measured by what works in membership, attendance, and budget.

5. As a corollary of this pragmatic utilitarianism, there is also from the beginning in Wesleyanism a certain *lack of sensibility for the divine mystery*, coupled with a danger of self-assurance. Abjuring mysticism and the *deus absconditus,*

Wesley's attention is absorbed by the revealed personal God who is Judge and Savior. One question here is whether and to what degree a confident hold on the gospel must exclude the abyss of transcendence, the primordial inscrutability of God, and if so, whether types of Christian piety and religious awe will not always dialectically need each other. In Wesley himself it is entirely clear that God-as-related can never become God-controlled-by-us; this is precluded by a profound intuition of holy righteousness and amazing grace. But especially the rational-empirical wing of later Wesleyan theology, when it does not share the biblical-traditional theocentrism of the founder, runs a much greater risk of putting God at human disposal, but also, for that reason, of portraying a God much less adequate to human need.

6. The last Wesleyan traditional deficiency I shall propose is the *lack of an eschatological envisagement of God's realm as an embracing frame of reference* for the salvific process. In spite of accent on transformation and the notable Wesleyan social impulse, justification and sanctification tend to be conceived merely as attributes of the individual. The blessed community of humankind and Christic dominion over all the world, including nature, hang therefore loosely unrelated to the Wesleyan *ordo salutis* in its primary focus and thrust. Directly implicated in this, of course, is the sticky discussion of whether John Wesley has a social ethic or whether one might at least be derived from his teachings. Certainly there are vital connecting links in Wesley for a vision of social salvation. At the same time, Wesleyanism stands seriously in need, as does most of traditional Christianity, of a more effective integration of the healing of the individual with the setting free and making whole of the world.

III. Tasks

1. While theology is a circle on which one can begin anywhere, the problems of the Wesleyan tradition—and indeed of modern Christianity across the board—would seem to ask initially for clarification of the authoritative foundation of Christian faith: that is, for a *rethinking of the Christ-norm as the galvanizing center of a comprehensive hermeneutic.* The Christ-norm embraces the converging normative functions of the historical, the biblical, and the living Christ. While it has been agreed that no objective biography of Jesus is possible, historiographical inquiry has issued—and will continually be issuing—in results which require assimilation into faith's image of the Christ. The present chasm between critical study of Jesus and the theological Christ sorely

needs bridging. Intimately involved in this, of course, is the ongoing study of the biblical witness to Christ, both of the Old and the New Testaments, in its variety and unity. But also integral to the interaction of the historical and biblical Christ(s), as a theological process, is the constant impingement of the living or risen and coming Christ, who is not to be differentiated from the Holy Spirit or the *testimonium spiritus sancti internum*—that is, the communally indwelling presence which will "bring to remembrance" all Christ has said and "guide into all the truth" (John 14:26; 16:13). The coalescence of these three Christs, or modes of Christ, may be expressed in the formula that the historical Jesus is normatively revealing so far as he becomes the biblically witnessed Christ, and the biblically witnessed Christ is normatively revealing so far as he becomes the risen and coming Christ who is always experienced as inseparable from the contemporaneous truth. The historical and biblical modes are as essentially self-transcending or preceptive as the living mode is essentially grounded in witnessed event. Each mode is a lens confirming and stereoscopically enhancing the other two. Historical facticity alone does not generate the normative image of Christ, nor does the biblical witness, unless its *fundamentum in re* be historically credible and corroborated by personal encounter with the community's living Lord. Whatever is shown to be nonhistorical, nonbiblical, or nonliving (i.e., noncontemporaneously transformative) does not in principle belong to the Christ-norm; in fact, of course, the content of each of the three factors is subject to the contextual relativity the church undergoes. The irremovable "space," so to speak, between them is a wellspring of open-ended self-transcendence for Christian faith. But in their mutual potentiation at a given time and place the three modes comprise the freeing and whole-making reality of Christ in its most intensive form. It would seem to be apodictically inherent in Christian faith—*a priori* so far as faith is decisional commitment, *a posteriori* so far as it is gracious experience—that, praise God, *there is* this integral saving reality: our Lord Jesus Christ. Without it, as Barth so well saw, trying to piece together Scripture, tradition, reason, and experience is a hopeless effort to reglue Humpty-Dumpty. At the same time, the Christ-norm is not given apart from the theological task, and with respect to all the terms we have been using here and their mutual applications there is a very weighty theological agenda confronting Wesleyanism and the whole church in our time.

2. Given the reality of the normative Christ (the only "article" that can plausibly be construed to decide the "standing or falling of the church"), Wesleyan tradition would seem to have a special vocation in the *attainment of a cohesive Christian hermeneutic integrating Scripture, tradition, reason, and experience*. Has any other particular stream of interpretation within Christendom (or for that matter—*mutatis mutandis*—world religion) so emphasized the interplay of the four elements, or been as much invested in them severally? Catholicism has been very strong in tradition, but not (till recently) in Scripture; whereas the Reformers came forward with the other foot. The Enlightenment and Protestant Liberalism have promoted reason in unison with general experience. The left wing of the Reformation and modern charismatic movements have stressed experience in its religious-ecstatic signification. Wesley, and to some considerable extent his theological heirs, have boldly insisted upon the mutual viability and ideal integrity of all four corners of the quadrilateral. Devolving from this now is an agenda that, using the touchstone of Christ, would test Scripture by tradition, reason, and experience just as much as in each particular relation *vice versa*. Tradition would be seen as the continuing trajectory (embracing numerous sub-trajectories) of faithful witness founded upon, but at the same time critically parsing and illuminating, the canon. Reason would be espoused as in its essential structure the God-given power of continuously demythologizing (i.e., existentially elucidating) both Scripture and tradition and mediating these to contemporary life; at the same time the sinful obscuration of actual reason would prompt constant recourse to biblical and traditional witness as well as prayerful openness to the risen and coming Christ. Experience, along with reason, would be the medium, in its more universal sense, of relating Bible, tradition, and ostensible rationality to the pragmatics of real human need (the "human question," as Tillich calls it). In its more specific religious sense, it would be the personal ecstatic encounter with the mystery of transforming grace—transcending, but by no means destroying reason, tradition, and the letter of Scripture.

For purposes of "Wesleyan constructive theology," a particular word is in order regarding personalism and process theology, under which rubrics have appeared the most illustrious examples of Wesleyan achievement within the field of reason. Both movements have shown concern and capacity to assimilate biblical and traditional as well as experiential elements and have commendably led the way toward a greater theological holism both hermeneutically and substantively, especially as they have become implicitly and explicitly more clearly Christ-centered in some of their representatives and more committed to the outreaching and liberating praxis of the Christian mission. But as valid and enriching as it is to employ all conceptualities, so far as they will serve the purpose (1 Cor. 3:21-23), in the fuller rendition of the theo-christic vision, and as needful as it is to establish metaphysically a base for thematizing the personal and processive dimensions of biblical faith, in both personalism and process theology there has lurked considerable ambiguity as to whether a particular philosophical system was supplanting Christ as foundational norm. In the degree this ambiguity has prevailed, both movements have taken on more of schoolish character and have resonated less with the biblical and traditional witness to sovereign holy mystery, to human deviance, and to transformative eschatological hope—or with universal need and Christian experience conformable with the same.

3. A further theme that Christ-centered Wesleyanism is naturally equipped to advocate forcefully in the future of theology is the *distinctive emphasis that the setting-free and making-whole of the world is thoroughly a divine and human process.* This indissoluble chord must be rescued from the exhausted debates of doctrinal history and grounded anew in the definitive model of God-humanhood beheld in Jesus as the Christ and experienced in the indwelling of the Spirit. It may then penetrate and illuminate the whole range of Christian thematization, into many loci of which it has never yet fully found its way. For this task contemporary biology, physics, and metaphysics offer fresh conceptual help, even as modernity languishes in deep pathos for authentic synthesis of creative autonomy and transcendent grace. Thought must break through the antithesis of absolute and relative, currently so pervasive, to affirm the irreducible reality of finite causality—material, formal, efficient, and final—in, with, and through a primordial and sustaining divine concurrence. Human responsibility must be anchored in and guaranteed by the sovereign God's inmost loving intentionality that becomes luminously real in Christ, as Wesley's motif of prevenient grace posits. Faith must be seen—as is not always clear in Wesley—to be both gift and decision, as works for their part are obedience and grace. Ontology must incorporate, as Whitehead for example beautifully does, the dependent primordiality of open contingency, allowing for the adventure of James's "half-wild" universe along with the ultimate constraint of righteous love. Much exacting reflective work beckons in this area in the decades ahead both in Christian doctrine itself and in the relational undertakings of philoso-

phical theology. The humanities, as well as other religions, will be eager participants in this dialogical enterprise.

4. A closely related task is that of *refurbishing the axial Wesleyan recital of justification and sanctification so that it is saliently clear that every human being is loved, forgiven, and called by God.* The paradoxical *Ineinander* of gracious indicative and summoning imperative is at the heart of the overall Christian message, and there is no locus in theology where the grounding of the Christ-norm is more needed or helpful. For the two foci of Ritschl's ellipse coalesce uniquely in Jesus' person. Both words, "justification" and "sanctification," have become today largely meaningless, or, worse than that, perniciously misleading. Even historically they were never adequately clear, for both functioned as complex ideas that partly overlapped and yet together did not either subsume or logically exhaust other notions such as reconciliation and perfection. But while much conceptual renovation is pending in this area, Christian theology—or rather the world—stands ever in dire need of the gospel of the God who loves *and* calls us to love as Jesus loved. Based on Christ, there is involved here an unimpeachable moment of self-esteem, *in spite of* (as Paul and Luther so profoundly knew) the horrific gravity of sin, combined with a distinct moment of expectation, constraint, and enablement to collaboration with God and neighbor in creation's fulfillment. Ritschl was right to insist we have to do here with a single doctrine in which the two moments are always in dynamic reciprocity. Justification is needed because of the constantly impinging law—that is, the vocation to sanctity—anticipated everywhere but consummated in Christ. Sanctification, on the other hand, becomes feasible only because the moral efficacy—the sense of self-worth—of the person is restored by faithfully apprehended justification. Faith as the noetic mode in which justification is recognized is actually a phase of sanctification and, in spite of much confusion in doctrinal history, must not be construed as a condition of the sinner's acceptance by God, which is unconditionally guaranteed by God's saving will in Christ. What is at stake in justification is that *nothing* be posited as required in the sinner, the absence of which could and would therefore become a torment, blocking the assurance of God's unmerited love. There is thus not merely a "justification of the doubter," as Tillich commendably proposed, but a justification of the exister by virtue of God in Christ. The totally hapless and helpless person can therefore truly take comfort in the thought of Milton that "they also serve who only stand and wait." On the other

hand, to believe that a person's repentant faith in her or his status, in spite of sin, as God's beloved child will engender growth in grace—gratitude, creativity, and rectitude—is intrinsically part of Christian faith, namely, Christian humanology. There is much to be done in these areas of reflection, for example, in explicating the work of Christ as well as the indwelling of the Spirit. But it is clear in any case that to divide sanctification from justification encourages the cheapening of grace and the oppressive moralism that is alas so notoriously a part of the Methodist image as well as Methodist experience.

5. To the extent that theological trivialization and self-perpetuating institutionalism are a problem in Wesleyanism, and widely in Christianity today, it is above all the fresh impact of the Christ-norm that could *revive powerfully the Wesleyan commitment to unrestricted ecumenical openness.* Original Wesleyanism strongly eschewed any self-reifying denominational intentionality. Its avowed purpose was simply the propagation of "scriptural holiness," as Wesley liked to put it. Surely this will to instrumentality, to complete transparence, is the authentic heritage Wesleyan theology needs now to assert: transparency to the gospel concretized in Christ, to the liberating and fructifying love of God for all the world, to the message of this entrusted to us, breaking down walls of hostility so that everywhere the blessed community may joyfully emerge. "Scriptural holiness" should be heard in the key of the Christ-norm, lest it sound biblicistic or emotionalistic and so not convey radically enough the universality of divine and human love beheld in Jesus. Wesley spoke of joining hands if there be a concord of hearts. This was not shallow sentimentality, as we know from his unremitting concern for essential Christianity, for example, in the dispute with Whitefield. But what was at issue for Wesley in "essential Christianity" was the necessity and availability of God's free grace for all. Even this kind of inclusiveness must exclude its opposite, which is exclusion, or more concretely, un-love. Commitment to Christ is commitment to openness, as we see openness in its most earnest reality in his life mission and his cross, which is the gateway to the world's renewal. Such commitment would mobilize ecumenical Christianity for transparent obedience to the way, the truth, and the life concretely imaged in the Christ. And in the emerging "larger ecumenism" of our time, there would be an eager readiness to extend hands wherever union of heart was sensed, in spite of all divisive labels. This would mean not only the welcoming but the promoting of

dialogue whenever it can occur, as well as glad collaboration in whatever purposes are compatible with Christlike love. "For all things are yours" if "you are Christ's" (I Cor. 3:21, 23). John Wesley was an eager learner; and from the separated sisters and brothers, not only of Christendom, but also of Judaism, Buddhism, Hinduism, and Islam, and in principle all traditions, Wesleyanism stands to deepen its sense of divine mystery and its tolerance for the variety of God's ways with human beings. Yet, if true to the Wesleyan heritage, Christian openness will be a discerning one, exercising critical rationality in its ardor of experience, as well as positively rooted in Scripture and tradition. What is claimed to be the Christic process under anonymous or alternative auspices may very well not be, as the fiftieth anniversary of the Barmen Declaration should well remind us. The process must continuously be tested by the image of Christ, even as the image opens us to the ongoing transformation of the process. In any event, as we move forward into uncharted experiences of interreligious exchange and mutual reconception, no particular tradition seems better fitted than the Wesleyan to steer between rigidness and dissolution, to boost morale and sustain trust in the Christlike God at work for good in everything with those who love (Rom. 8:28).

6. This brings us finally to a task poignantly incumbent upon Wesleyanism if it is to do justice to its own inmost original impulses as well as what might seem to be its emerging entelechy in the concourse of world Christianity and world religions, namely, *to develop a more integral linkage of individual salvation with the all-encompassing realm of God.* For Wesleyanism, along with its individualism, has also manifested a notable social concern—but without grounding this adequately in its basic theological perspective. A marriage of Wesley's personal evangelism with the covenant theology of Johannes Cocceius and the Puritan tradition would have been a healthy intermediate step. For justification and sanctification need to be seen as predicates of the emerging new community in Christ—or "anonymously," as Rahner says, wherever Christlike love is emerging, wherever the Christic process is identifiable. The justified community that is called to go on to perfection, and is promised the wherewithal thereto, is the nonexclusive community with whom Christ identifies—first of all the poor and the oppressed, but all who do not oppose and deviate from God's sway in their lives. So far as the Christian makes and can make no special claims for her or himself, that one is already embraced by Christ in this community, even though, as Luther incisively stresses, this

justified person is also simultaneously a sinner. It is then incumbent upon the Christian to seek the perfection or fulfillment of this community, to make straight the way for all, for the excluded minorities, for women, for the economically and politically violated, also for the psychologically injured and deprived (like Scrooge, e.g.). For God's reign is frustrated whenever created potentialities for love and joy are impeded. Beyond the relief of grievances, there is needed positive envisagement of the creative role in the divine reign (the realm of ends) of interpersonal relationships—not just in marriage and family but also in friendship. Moreover, the fructifying of all the potencies of life must be included in the vision of God's realm: the tilling of the earth, the increase of the talents, the release into liberty of the whole travailing creation. The scientific enterprise and the venture of human imagination in art and play need also to be seen as eligible to serve and exemplify the setting-free and making-whole of the world. Whenever the creative loving purpose of any part of the world is frustrated, our individual sanctification is vicariously frustrated; whenever this purpose is fulfilled, we are vicariously fulfilled. The blessing of our justification in Christ we share with all, as a love from which nothing can separate. The active hope for our mutual transformation in Christ we also share with all, pressing forward together with all who will, as mutual heirs of a glorious promise.

It goes without saying that for the Wesleyan theological tradition to grasp and parse, elucidate and implement, its formidable tasks over the coming years is both intimidating and exciting. Let us be grateful for so splendid a heritage, for such a company as we have of intrepid co-workers, and for a future that, given the God we believe in, is so fascinating and challenging.

2. JOHN WESLEY'S HERITAGE AND THE FUTURE OF SYSTEMATIC THEOLOGY

M. Douglas Meeks

Can John Wesley's theology be a vital and vitalizing resource for the future of systematic theology? This is a difficult question. It is often claimed that there is no system in Wesley's theology.[1] Was Wesley really more than a great evangelist and religious organizer? If he was only a "folk theologian" why even bother with our question? Wesley does not seem to fit well into recent Euro-American theology, which has been overwhelmingly concerned with theological method. Wesley, like Luther, was much more what Karl Barth called an "irregular" than a "regular" theologian.[2] Why then expect Wesley to contribute anything to the future of systematic theology?

The second, even more serious problematic within our leading question can be expressed this way: "Does systematic theology itself have any future?" For some time theologians influenced by historicism, positivism, and secularism, and now by third-world themes, have been questioning whether systematic theology as we have known it since Thomas Aquinas has not come to an end. It deserves at best, many contend, a decent burial. For some decades now a proper circumlocution has been sought not only for the term "dogmatic" but also "systematic." Candidates such as "constructive theology," "confessional theology," "sound teaching," and the like, have found currency. But what is meant by and done under these headings is as much in jeopardy as the classically construed "systematic theology."

In view of these seemingly indomitable objections—Wesley is not a systematic theologian, and systematic theology has no future—I will, with proper tentativeness, attempt to make a few small contributions to the claim that Wesley and his heritage *are* important resources for the future of systematic theology. If in the end we should somehow or other be able to say that Wesley *is* a systematic theologian, this would mean, it seems reasonable to assume, that we would at least have to rethink radically our conception of what systematic theology should be and do. In other words, I propose that *by rethinking Wesley, we rethink systematic theology.*[3]

I would begin with a preliminary, quite simple definition of the word "systematic," partly as an initial rationale of why I would stick with this term. Our word "system" stems from the Greek word *sunesthai* which is found in Colossians 1:17: Jesus Christ "is before all things, and in him all things *hold together.*" Systematic theology is the church's task of showing that all things "hold together" or "subsist" in Jesus Christ and of showing the implications of this for the church's mission in the world. Wesley's note on Colossians 1:17 summarizes quite well what is at stake in systematic theology. "The original expression not only implies, that he sustains all things in being, but more directly, all things were and are compacted in him into one system. He is the cement, as well as the support, of the universe. And is he less than the supreme God?"[4]

But what does it require to show that all things "hold together," "cohere," are "supported by," are systematized in Jesus Christ and to make the implications of this clear for the life and mission of the church in the world? Does Wesley's theology suffice for this task? Does Wesleyan theology represent an adequate model for engaging in this task today? What does Wesleyan theology actually contribute to the future of this task?

We could follow the lead of Albert Outler and many others in saying that Wesley's theology is principally a fruitful source for ecumenical theologizing.[5] The ecumenical character of Wesleyan theology itself is clear. (1) Wesley never intended his theology to be self-sufficient or closed; it was a theology for a movement of revival and reform within the national church of England. (2) It clearly intended to express "simple Biblical religion," but it appropriated many strands of the tradition. (3) It was a theology forged out of the pluralistic, public "ecumenical" debates of mid-eighteenth-century England. It would have been inconceivable without openness to and admixture of Anglican Evangelicalism, Eastern and Roman Catholic ascetical theology, Lutheran theology of justification by faith, Puritanism, Arminian Calvinism, Moravian and Spenerian pietism, revivalist "strategic" theology, only to mention a few of the church traditions whose appropriation in his situation formed Wesley's theology. (4) One principal characterizing strength of Methodist theology has been its influence for all of the above reasons, in occasioning ecumenical theology in the nineteenth and twentieth centuries. The ecumenical character of Wesleyan theology closely parallels its relatively positive relationship to modern theological and cultural pluralism. Thomas Langford has given full and insightful evidence of this in his book *Practical Divinity*.[6] But as Langford's analysis shows, it is much easier to demonstrate the irenic ecumenism, fructifying tolerance, and generativity of a healthy pluralism in Wesleyan theology than it is to track down its distinctive characteristics which promise actually to provide a concrete shaping power for the future of theology, church, and world.

The contribution of Wesleyan theology to the future of systematic theology will not have too much to do with Wesley's having created original loci or doctrines, but perhaps more to do with which doctrines he selected out of the Christian classics and how he put them together. Even more likely the real contribution will come from the form of Wesley's theology, the way his theology was done, and the locus and loyalties of his theology. Perhaps the most telling question of Wesley's theology will be *cui bono*, for whose good was his theology done?

The "Paradigm Shift" in Contemporary Theology

Most theologians in the North Atlantic community are well aware that the answer to the question, What does it require to show that all things hold together in Jesus Christ? is very much up for grabs. And thus there is almost everywhere among those who designate themselves with the term "systematic," or some correlative, an urgent search for a new key in which to do theology. It is widely announced that we are undergoing a paradigm shift. Some people have the impression that systematic theology is on hold while this question of a paradigm shift is being adjudicated.

What are the causes and signs of the deep "epochal shifts" we are living through now? Whereas Kuhn's thesis of paradigm shifts presupposed cultural continuity, Landon Gilkey argues that the transformation of the cultural form itself points to a phenomenon deeper than a paradigm shift: the crisis of the whole culture in which theology has been done in modernity.[7] Two examples of a cultural or epochal shift would be the rise of the modern scientific community itself and the emergence of the

Enlightenment culture that centered around the scientific community. These epochal shifts have largely determined theology's question field for the last two hundred years. The sea change of the Enlightenment made the crisis of cognitive claims a major focus of systematic theology, and the university more and more the setting in which theology had to be done. Theology sought at its core focus either to find a dimension of reality unaffected and untouchable by the Enlightenment scientific/technological methods or (and this has been the case increasingly in recent years) to show the similarity of theology to scientific method. Thus we had, on the one hand, theologies focussing on the self, the absolute subject, the internal human life, and, on the other hand, theologies focusing on a revised cosmology, scientific method and verification.

On both counts Wesleyan theology has not been a welcome partner in the efforts to make theology conform to the modern paradigm or epochal shift. Wesleyan theology often seemed to be self-consciously beyond the pale of the academy. Wesley seemed decidedly pre-Kantian, pre-Hegelian, and pre-Marxist. His amazing interest in science and technology seemed only antiquarian. He was not faced with the awesome successes or the horrendous destructive power of technology as the instrument of the industrial revolution and modern warfare. On the other hand, when it came to the development of a consciousness theology from Schleiermacher to Troeltsch or an existential theology from Kierkegaard to Bultmann, Wesley's theology stood out (or stood back) like a sore thumb because of his constant criticism of the subjectivization of faith. Though Wesley's theology may have provided much fuel for the fires of individualistic and privatistic tendencies in conservative theologies, it remains unmistakably opposed to the theological moves which are necessary to lodge faith and knowledge of God in the consciousness.

In the meantime, Wesleyan theology has been absorbed in what Outler refers to as three distinct phases: Phase One is "the scholarly aspect of a denominationalism preoccupied with itself and its founder."[8] From the days of Jabez Bunting down to our time it demonstrates a cultic fascination with Wesley as cult-hero and founder of a triumphalistic church. Phase Two, partly in response to new interpretations of the eighteenth and nineteenth centuries and partly as the result of the decline of Methodist "triumphs," breaks up the Wesley-Methodist symbiosis and connects Wesley with theories of social transformation, various philosophical and theological schools, the Lutheran and Calvinist renaissance in the twentieth century, and so on. This phase tends to emphasize only a limited aspect of Wesley's thought and to use Wesley as "authority" for judgments derived elsewhere. Phase Three, still nascent, would be, argues Outler, more concerned with "ecumenical theology and praxis." "Its first goal is that of basic reorientation—the 'repositioning' of Wesley in his own time and place, against his large background and in as wide an historical context as possible. But all of this is still in order to an 'application' of Wesley's relevance to issues in *our* times and *our* futures."[9]

If we are living though another "continental shift," what relationship, what relevance would a "repositioned" Wesley have for it? Gilkey argues that the new epochal shift is the result of the fundamental questioning of Enlightenment and post-Enlightenment culture. We have entered a time when the Enlightment's basic institutions tend to destroy rather than to strengthen its life. There is a growing crisis sense about the ambiguity of its basic institutions and powers: science, technology, and industry. Its promise and power have produced weapons which can destroy the entire world, even life itself; industrial production threatens environmental destruction; the technocratic progress of industry dehumanizes life. Most crucially it does not seem capable of producing institutions which will resolve the deepening crisis of worldwide economic injustice, depletion of life-resources, and international and intercultural conflict. The failure of the secular religions of progress, history, and science is occurring just at a time when the three monotheistic religions are giving rise to a faith in God that struggles for the liberation, dignity, and rights of human beings. On the world scale, as the result of the extreme ambiguity of Western culture, the other major world religions no longer appear clearly false, inferior, or less well-advanced.

The self and world-destructiveness of the Enlightenment powers and institutions has brought about the loss of confidence in the symbolic structure of Western life, both capitalist and socialist, that is, "the confidence in history's progress" by means of this culture's forms. This requires theology's radical rethinking of its connections to this culture in relation to which it has developed since the seventeenth century.

This period of paradigm shift is marked by extreme pluralism: a pluralism of paradigm shifts of the first century (primitive apocalyptic), the second (Hellenistic), eleventh (Gregorian/ Scholastic), sixteenth (Reformation), seventeenth and eighteenth (Enlightenment), and twentieth centuries (post-Enlightenment), which are all alive and represented as current options of Orthodox traditionalism, Roman Catholic traditionalism, Protestant, Fundamentalist, and Evangelical orthodoxy, and various forms of liberal and post-liberal theologies. Even within the Wesleyan tradition itself this pluralism rages. Major efforts have been made to connect Wesley principally and in principle to each of these paradigms, which in part explains the rich diversity and disturbing confusion in world Methodism/Wesleyanism. For theologians, like David Tracy, this uneasy pluralism threatens the whole project of theology.[10] Even though the ideal of pluralism can be applauded and even though it would be impossible to do away with the existing pluralism, the "conflict of interpretations" and the "conflict of plausibility structures" threaten to make theology no longer relevant to the publics of university, church, and society.

Tracy's desire to transform the destructive theological conflict into a *conversation* is similar to Wesley's great desire for calm, considered, reasoned, unprejudicial discourse among theologians and religious leaders of his own situation of intense theological conflict. Tracy has developed a typology for contemporary theology which is unequaled in its comprehensiveness and which proposes an analogical way for mediating (not just obviating, but putting in conversation) the conflicting paradigms. I believe it is useful to set Wesley's theology over against Tracy's typology in order to discern how Wesley might make a contribution to future theological conversation. Tracy's approach, from my perspective, falls far short of his intended goal. Some analysis of the reason for this might also shed some light on Wesley's own peculiar method and contributions to the future of systematic theology.

Tracy's well-known typology depends on a division of labor between three complementary theological disciplines which are each primarily related to three different publics. Each discipline has its special transcendental orientation and focal meaning. The typology can be roughly diagrammed as follows:[11]

1. Foundational Theology	Academic Public	Truth	Explication Verification
(Theologies of *Manifestation* through philosophical reflection, experience of the ordinary, mysticism, etc.)		(Metaphysics, dialectics)	
Catholic tendency			Disclosive
2. Systematic Theology	Church Public	Beauty	
(Theologies of *Proclamation*: Word, hermeneutics, etc.)		(Poetics, rhetoric)	Interpretive
Protestant tendency			
3. Practical Theology	Societal Public	Good	
(Theologies of *History and Praxis*: political and liberation theologies)		(Ethics, politics)	Transformative
Post-Enlightenment tendency			

Whereas Tracy shows great sensitivity to and learning from the so-called practical theologies (political and liberation theologies), the effect of his typology turns out to be exclusive instead of comprehensive. It prevents praxis theologies from doing the foundational and systematic tasks. This leaves open the suspicion that "Tracy's distinctions are unintentional ways of theoretically immunizing the disciplines of foundations and systematics against the claims of liberation and political theologies.[12] I will argue that the contours of Wesley's theological method are much closer to what Tracy calls "practical theologies" than to what he calls systematic and foundational theology. I am not maintaining that Wesley's theology exactly parallels in content contemporary liberation and political theologies. But on the questions of (1) praxis and (2) relation of theological substance to the poor, I believe there are crucial parallels. My primary intention here is not to "authorize" liberation and political theologies by appeal to Wesley but rather to propose a way of reading Wesley out of the contemporary situation of theology in dialogue with Wesley's own situation and the traditions out of which he lived. A first step in this direction would be to note the similarity of the response of the church, university, and societal publics of Wesley's day to his theology and the responses of these publics to liberation and political theologies today.

Whereas Tracy draws the basic ground rules for theological conversation from foundational theology, Wesley drew them from the practice of evangelization and mission aimed at the conversion of persons and conditions. Wesley certainly did not eschew the explicative, disclosive, and interpretive tasks of systematic and foundational theology (as defined by Tracy), but he understood these tasks to be united in and at the service of the transformative grace of God in concrete acts, relationships, and conditions.

The overall tenor of Wesley's theology suggests that the methodological search for an abstract paradigm may not be the way theology should function at all. Stephen Toulmin has raised some interesting questions along these lines. According to Toulmin, "Drastic paradigm changes are found only on abstract, theoretical levels; on concrete, practical levels, much continuity of experience and belief exists, despite all conceptual changes on the theoretical level."[13] Thus the first question about paradigms for theology should be, How far are theological issues abstract and theoretical, for example, those dividing Newtonian mechanics and quantum physics?

Whenever Christianity has sought to embody a rationally based cosmology, that is, whenever its truth has been made to depend upon the general intelligibility and convicting power of a world view, it has left itself open to near disasters. For example, from 1500 on the "new philosophy" discredited the traditional religious-metaphysical cosmology, and from 1750 on the developing natural, historical, and social sciences undermined the Newtonian cosmology on which Protestant orthodoxy had so heavily depended. Does theology in the 1980s need to borrow from the natural sciences or some other source yet another entire cosmological system?

Foundational/Catholic

According to Tracy the defining characteristic of foundational theologies is "a reasoned insistence on employing the approach and methods of some established academic discipline to explicate and adjudicate the truth-claims of the interpreted religious tradition and the truth-claims of the contemporary situation."[16] Wesley did not make a generally accepted world view the ground of the Christian truth or the necessary medium through which the gospel had to be interpreted or communicated. Nor did he fix an academic discipline as the canon for verification of Christian truth. In fact, Wesley's theology would cause us to ask fundamentally whether the Christian faith can be verified theoretically at all? To be sure, Wesley was able to depend on a kind of cultural monocentrism, and, furthermore, there were surely inherited philosophical world views reflected in his apologetic theology. But in his method and at the heart of his evangelical theology, he did not depend on them. Wesley's theological method was much closer to the traditional prudence of Jewish theologians. Wesley could say with Toulmin, it is "better to ground theological claims closer to the familiar facts of everyday life and experience—i.e., to remain near the concrete levels where certitude and continuity are available—and to base our critique of these ideas on that human experience, rather than on abstract systems of concepts or 'paradigms'." Perhaps the fecundity of Wesley's theology for the future is due partly to his lack of abstract paradigms. Wesley's choice was to have no other paradigm than the grace of God's love in the history of Jesus Christ. This left his theology open to read this history within the time and place in which the gospel was to be proclaimed.

Regaining our nerve to do theology in a Wesleyan mode may mean no longer being chagrined at the charge that Wesley was a "peoples' theologian" working for the communication of "plain truth to plain people." In Wesley's theology one can see what Johannes Metz calls a "non-regressive reduction of over-complexity" or a "non-trivial reduction of doctrine to life," of doxography to biography. Theology is different from the sciences, and its paradigm shifts will be different from those of the natural and social sciences. This is the case because theology is engaged in conversation with the believing and converting community. Theology, even as a science, is able to learn from the unlearned. It has often been observed that Wesley's own personal assurance and his certitude about his theology came from the response of those to whom he preached (not from his Aldersgate Street experience or from the confirmation of his university-trained peers).[15] A Wesleyan theology will thus maintain that church praxis concerns the stuff of method. Theological method cannot be created in abstracto from the life of the church. Wesley understood that the logos of theology always aims at a form of knowledge as a form of life. Wesley's is a theology less interested in the order of Christian truth (as in 'school theologies' generally) than in the Christian life.

This does not mean that many of the functions which Tracy ascribes to foundational theology cannot be found in Wesley's theology. Tracy argues that one of the most debilitating results of the conflict of interpretive paradigms is that theology, failing the ability to stay in conversation, becomes more and more private. Wesley, however, can be an important model for the explication and defense of the church's theology in a recognizably public way, where "public" refers to the "articulation of fundamental questions and answers which any attentive, intelligent, reasonable person can understand and judge in keeping with fully public criteria for argument."[16] "An Earnest Appeal to Men of Reason and Religion" remains a paradigm of such public theology. Despite the fact that Wesley sometimes claimed to be a man of "one book" (not unlike Calvin), the cruciality of his university training in the humanities and sciences for the formation of the Revival can be easily demonstrated. If systematic theology were again to be related to the church's evangelization and mission in our North Atlantic society, this would not mean less stress on the sciences of the human person, society, history, and nature, but indeed a much greater stress. Those who would be authentic evangelists and missionaries to our society require much deeper grounding in the university's critical disciplines than those who would view themselves as taking over already defined clerical positions of managing the internal psyches of persons or the structures of the church's organization. Many of the tasks of so-called foundational/philosophical theology are needed for missionary theology. But these tasks, too, should be praxis-grounded. This does not mean, however, that praxis must always precede theory, as some liberation theologies claim. Systematic theology must make sure that the tasks of theory and reason are grounded in the subsisting of the church's evangelization and mission to the world in Jesus Christ.

If Wesley did not engage in the mediation of religious reality via philosophical reflection or of transcendence through the experience of the ordinary or of the self, his theology nevertheless does demonstrate some Catholic/manifestation emphases. The emphasis on God's creative, operative, preventing grace as being always-already present is certainly a Catholic element. But this is not grounded in a theory of reality itself but in trust in the faithfulness of God. In the earlier stages of his theology Wesley's most distinctive contributions to the tradition—the doctrines of perfection and assurance—certainly had their ground in the Catholic tradition. Wesley took up Arminius' correction of Calvin's doctrines of election, predestination, and reprobation by emphasizing the possibility of the maturation of righteousness and holiness in this life. This emphasis on works, out of the Catholic ascetical and mystical traditions of holy living, was to remain throughout his life the decisive means of Wesley's arguments against the antinomian tendencies of Puritanism and Evangelical Calvinism. But Wesley's doctrine of sanctification cannot be properly understood if it is viewed simply as an outgrowth of the Catholic/manifestation traditions. It is rather a doctrine which goes beyond both the Catholic/manifestation and the Protestant/proclamation traditions and is indeed the mediating power between them.

Proclamation/Protestant

If we move now to what Tracy calls the focal paradigm of proclamation, in which is found, Tracy argues, the primary task of systematic theology, that is, interpretation of tradition and situation, we shall find a framework in which Wesley can easily be called a systematic theologian. Wesley certainly succeeded in what Tracy views as the major task of systematic theologians: interpreting the tradition for the present situation.[17] The systematic theologian as confessional theologian risks "faith in a particular religious tradition" and has the right to be formed by that tradition.[18] The proclamation/Protestant orientation shifts "away from all experiences of manifestation into the empowering experience of God's decisive word of address in Jesus Christ. No depth experience, no quest for the ultimate, no mysticism . . . can save us . . . only if God comes as eschatological event, as unexpected and decisive Word addressing each and all; only if God comes to disclose our true godforsakenness and our possible liberation can we be healed."[19] By June 18, 1738 in his sermon on "Salvation by Faith" Wesley reached the heart of his faith and theology through the appropriation of the Reformation doctrine of "justification by faith alone." Wesley declared, "All the blessing which God hath bestowed upon man, are of His mere grace, bounty, or favour; His free, undeserved favour; favour altogether undeserved; man having no claim to the heart of His mercies."[20] This seems to be a radical departure from Wesley's earlier emphasis on holiness through works. Atonement for sins can never happen through works. "For all our works, all our righteousness, which were before our believing,

merited nothing of God but condemnation."[21] Thus Wesley arrived at what remained the starting point of his theology for the rest of his life: "Grace is the source, faith the condition of salvation."

Wesley's starting point in justification by faith seemed to come close to a sectarian support of rampant antinomianism and to the doctrine of salvation by the imputation of Christ's righteousness, both of which Wesley was to spend a lifetime fighting. What prevented Wesley's theology from being simply a constant paradox between the Catholic and Evangelical elements at the heart of his theology? The key to a critical appropriation of Wesley's theology today is the question how Wesley mediated these two aspects of his theology: Catholic and Protestant, manifestational and proclamational, foundational and systematic (to use Tracy's terminology). The third element of mediation occurs in Wesley's new ordering of works and faith in his pneumatological doctrine of perfection. Wesley will be most fruitful for the future of theology when his is viewed as a praxis theology.

Transformational/Praxis

In important senses Wesley's whole theology is glued together and grounded in its third dimension: sanctifying grace. The emphasis on prevenient and justifying grace might be called the *disclosive* aspects, the emphasis on sanctifying or cooperative grace the *transformative* aspect of Wesley's theology. It is this aspect of Wesley's theology which impels us to rethink systematic theology so that, over against Tracy, it would include the several functions he assigns to foundational, systematic, and practical theology. Furthermore, systematic theology should locate and define its publics according to the church's mission in and to society, not by an abstract theory of conversation.

Wesley's theology, I believe, can be seen as adumbrating some important emphases of praxis theologies today. Wesley's doctrine of sanctification is a doctrine of the actual, concrete doing of faith in love. Holiness is not a condition or a consequence of justification but the concrete action of justification within historical conditions and relationships. In the debates with Calvinist antinomianism Wesley was pushed so far in the direction of Arminius as to say that without sanctification there would be no salvation, without inherent holiness, without works, faith would not avail. These were shocking theological judgments in Wesley's time—just as they are for many Christians today. We can be certain that in these statements Wesley is not going back to his earlier attempt to find salvation through holy works. Something much more radical and decisive is involved. What is at stake here for the method of systematic theology can best be seen in the methodological considerations of praxis theology.

Praxis theologies seek a radically different correlation of theory and praxis from those correlations found predominantly in the tradition. In the theory-praxis relationship required by Christian mission "the critical correlation is placed in praxis rather than theory." This means that "praxis itself as action or performance grounds the activity of theorizing. *Praxis is not only the goal but also the foundation of theory . . .* theory is critical to the extent that it explicates its own foundations in transformative praxis. No theory *qua* theory can be critically self-grounding. No theory *qua* theory can sublate praxis, although praxis can sublate theory."[22] Thus, norms are not grounded in the axioms or principles of further theories but in the concrete action of believing persons in specific historical and societal situations. Action here must be understood to include the life of spiritual discipline, prayer, meditation, and thinking. Praxis includes the whole active life of conversion. Furthermore, the conversion of praxis is constitutively a communal reality. Truth does not have a metaphysical or disclosive but a transformative character. Claims to truth and meaning in theology depend upon means of discerning the conversions of persons who make such claims. "Only radical and enduring personal transformation can ensure the presence of truth."[23]

In agreement with much of ancient tradition, Wesley understood the transformative reality of faith to be initially and primarily a matter of trust and of converted orientation. *Fides qua* always grounds *fides quae.* Wesley found his doctrine transformed and shaped in his praxis. For sometime Wesley had believed with Spener, Francke, Law, and Thomas a Kempis that the good Christian life was constituted not by correct doctrine but by new birth and the leading of a holy life. But it was not until his first exposure to open air preaching among the colliers in Kingswood that the "system" of Wesley's theology came into view. And that "system," that way of showing that all things hold together in Jesus Christ, was the life of preventing, justifying, and sanctifying grace to, for, and with the poor. This was the Wesleyan praxis which was the foundation and goal of the Wesleyan theory. It was the means by which the Protestant and Catholic, the Calvinist and Arminian elements of Wesley's theology were mediated. As regards the distinctive doctrine of perfection, the heart of Wesley's theology, the first field preaching and the response to it were considerably more important than the Aldersgate experience.

It is too early to say or prove historically how crucial the poor are to the formation of Wesley's theology. The work of scholars like John Walsh, however, is beginning to build up a case that Wesley's praxis theology has as its focal meaning God's relationship to the poor in Jesus Christ.[24] By "poor" we mean those whose humanity is threatened in the economic, political, cultural, and personal dimensions of life. Many persons qualify as being "poor" in one or two of these dimensions. It is clear, however, that the early Wesleyan praxis/theology was focused on those persons and communities who were poor in all of these dimensions, that is, persons who were like the am-aretz or those the Synoptic Gospels call the "crowd" (*ochlos*), or the "poor" (*ptōchoi*). For Wesley, it is clear theologically that these people represent the part of God's creation most threatened by death and sin. They, therefore, represent the point at which the power of God's grace must show itself if salvation for the nation and for the creation is to take on concrete significance. The logic of I Corinthians 1 is the logic by which Wesley's theology is grounded in the praxis with the poor.

Bernard Semmel and others have made much of the way the development of Wesley's understanding of perfection/holiness was related to his consuming struggle against all forms of enthusiasm and antinomianism which would fan the flames of revolution and civil war in England. Whereas evangelical enthusiasm (or perhaps better put, the energy of hope based on the eschatological promise of the gospel) was and is constitutive of Wesleyanism, enthusiasm could (as it had in the civil war) break out into armed political strife.[25] Thus, in tandem with the sanctified discipline of the religious life, Wesley argued for the divine right of kings, passive obedience, nonresistance, and the like. These are the factors most remembered of Wesley in the socio-political realm. Did Wesley have to argue these political convictions and stances (which he came by honestly from his Jacobite/Tory/nonjuror background) in order, as Semmel claims, to offset the radical energy, liberty, hope, and motivation for life which his proclamation of grace released so that this enthusiasm would not be lodged in the "epidemic madness" of "King Mob"?[26] Did he have to argue these points of view in order to prevent the repression of the Methodist movement by the establishment? Perhaps so.

But these conservative political positions in no

way prove that Wesley's praxis relationship to the poor was not actually constitutive of his doctrine of perfection. The brunt of his argument against Calvinist views of election, predestination, and "irrespective reprobation" was that they prevented solidarity with those who already seemed damned by their poverty and stultified the self-motivation of those who would be liberated from their poverty and indignity. It is Wesley's praxis identification with the poor, the forgotten, the ignorant, the exploited, which gave focal meaning, shape, constant self-criticism, and transformation to this theology.[27]

This praxis focus is nowhere more apparent in Wesley's theology than in his doctrine of God.[28] Wesley's theology of the divine compassion in relation to the poor redefines the nature of God's freedom and of human freedom.[29] God's freedom has traditionally been interpreted as absolute free choice, based on God's perfect, beatific self-sufficiency within the closed life of the immanent Trinity and on God's *apatheia*—inability to suffer. According to the Calvinist conception God's sovereign freedom meant God's groundless decision or decree, on which everything else, including God's love, was based. The Calvinist God thus took on the character of an arbitrary despot, the master of every event, the emperor who has the absolute power of the disposal of property. The theories of election and predestination were devices for the protection of God's omnipotence and absolute sovereignty.

Wesley's praxis solidarity with the poor makes a radical departure from this concept of God's freedom. For Wesley God's freedom is grounded in God's love. The notion of God's lordly freedom as "free choice," as domination, denies God's nature as love and goodness. This is the reason that "predestination" is "subversive of the very foundation of Christian experience."[30] For Wesley, because God cannot deny Godself, God does not have the choice between mutually exclusive possibilities: being love or not being love. Thus, a concept of freedom which would be appropriate to God's identification with the poor through the sheer grace of God's love cannot be derived from the language of domination. If God's eternal freedom is God's love, God's suffering, patience, and self-giving, then this determines the quality of the synergistic relationship between God and believers. Preventing, justifying, and sanctifying grace create a new human being with freedom to enter into God's history of redeeming righteousness with the world. The freedom of the will is not yet the freedom of the gospel. Justifying grace turns freedom lived under good and evil into conver-

sion of the believer's being, into liberation from guilt, liberation from fear of death, from self-possession, from idols, from personality cults, from our compulsion to dominate our environment, and from our dependence on necrophiliac security systems. Wesley's creative theological wrestling with God's power and freedom and with human freedom was the result of the focus of his theology as sanctifying praxis with the poor.

We have argued that Wesley is a systematic theologian, but on the basis of that claim have proposed that systematic theology will need to rethink its nature and task. We have argued that systematic theology should be coherent, comprehensive thinking about the life and mission of the church focused on God's identification with the poor in Jesus Christ. Praxis grounds the more theoretical work of interpretation and verification. These tasks too cannot be separated from the concrete life of the church's mission in the world. The truth of theology is precariously based on the conversion of those who do theology. This has vast implications for the questions of the locus of theology (especially theological education) and for the formation of theologians in what Wesley calls "practical divinity." We can conclude with the wager that on these matters we have only begun to scratch the surface of Wesley's significance for the future of systematic theology.

NOTES

1. Albert Outler has put the problem in this way: Wesley "seems never to have felt the impulse to produce anything resembling a comprehensive exposition of his theological ideas—and this may have been just as well. Short doctrinal summaries are scattered throughout his writings, and these give ample evidence that his thought was consciously organized around a stable core of basic coordinated motifs. But there is no extended development of his system, and for the simple reason that there never seemed to be a *practical* need for such a thing. His single, sufficient motive in theologizing was to reinforce the spiritual and ethical concerns of his societies in particular and the Church in general. Theology, in this context, was a dialectical affair: faith seeking self-awareness and self-expression. This neglect of a developed systematic statement, however, has encouraged all too many of his followers to misperceive the organic unity of Wesley's thought, or to ignore the pivotal place of rational understanding in his mind and method. Wesley himself cannot be invoked on behalf of an anti-intellectual attitude toward the Christian truth." *John Wesley,* ed. Albert C. Outler (New York: Oxford University Press, 1964), p. 27.

2. But for Barth "irregular" theological work was not only a part of "systematic" or "dogmatic" but was its foundation. By "irregular dogmatics" Barth meant "the enquiry into dogma in which there is no primary thought of the task of the school. . . .Dogmatics as free discussion of the problems that arise for Church proclamation from the standpoint of the question of dogma can and must be pursued in the Church outside the theological school and apart from its special task. Such free dogmatics existed

45

before there was the regular dogmatics of the school, and it will always have its own necessity and possibility alongside this. It will differ from it by the fact that it does not cover the whole ground with the same consistency, whether in respect of Church proclamation itself, the decisive biblical witness, the history of dogma, detailed systematics, or strictness and clarity of method. Perhaps for specific historical reasons it will take up a specific theme and focus on it. Perhaps it will be relatively free in relation to the biblical basis or its choice of partners in discussion. Perhaps it will be more of an exposition of results, and will take the form of theses or aphorisms, and will observe only partially or not at all the distinction between dogmatics and proclamation. Perhaps it will leave much to be desired as regards the explicit or implicit distinctness of its path of knowledge. In one respect or another, or even in many or all respects, it will be, and will mean to be, a fragment, and it will have to be evaluated as such. . . . It should also be noted that regular dogmatics has always had its origin in irregular dogmatics, and could never have existed without its stimulus and cooperation." *Church Dogmatics*, I/1 trans. G. W. Bromiley (Edinburgh: T & T. Clark, 1975), pp. 277, 278. According to Barth's reading, Wesley as "systematician" would be in the company of theologians such as Athanasius, Luther, J. C. Blumhardt.
3. In his paper, "A New Future for Wesley Studies: 'Phase III'," given at the Seventh Oxford Institute for Methodist Theological Studies, (*The Future of the Methodist Theological Tradition*, M. Douglas Meeks, ed. [Nashville: Abingdon Press, 1985], p. 48), Albert Outler grappled again with the question of Wesley and systematics: "The problem of a credible hermeneutics for Wesley is, as I know, a vexed one. Its nub, or so it seems to me, is whether the fact that Wesley never produced a systematic exposition of his theology (and never intended to) is to be reckoned as a weakness to be remedied or as a strength, to be exploited. Here, much depends on whether one sets the notion of 'systematics' over against its simple antithesis, 'unsystematic'. . . . There is, however, another possibility: viz. to think of theology as coherent reflection upon Christian living with all of its natural divagations. Wesley knew the history of 'systematic theology', from Peter Lombard's *Sentences* to Philip Melancthon's *Loci* and in the heroic labors of the Protestant 'dogmaticians'. He himself relied heavily on John Pearson's *Exposition of the Creed* (which comes as near to a 'systematics' as seventeenth century Anglicanism can show). But he also knew that the bulk of significant Christian literature, from the Scriptures, to the Fathers, to the classics of devotion, to the liturgies had focused on the Christian *life* and the intimations of Christian truth that could be drawn from them. . . . In whatever patterns Methodist theologies may continue to develop, it will be crucial for them to strike for new balances between 'faith' and 'life'."
4. John Wesley, *Notes* (London: Epworth Press, 1976), p. 743.
5. See, e.g., Albert Outler, "Towards a Reappraisal of John Wesley as a Theologian," *Perkins Journal*, 1961 (Winter): 14.
6. Thomas A. Langford, *Practical Divinity: Theology in the Wesleyan Tradition* (Nashville: Abingdon Press, 1983).
7. See *Reaping the Whirlwind: A Christian Interpretation of History* (New York: The Seabury Press, 1976), "Theology for a Time of Troubles," *The Christian Century*, April 29, 1981, 474-80.
8. See Outler, "A New Future for Wesley Studies: 'Phase III'."
9. Ibid.

10. David Tracy, *The Analogical Imagination: Christian Theology and the Culture of Pluralism* (New York: Crossroads, 1981).
11. This is an expansion of Matthew Lamb's typology. See his *Solidarity with Victims* (New York: Crossroads, 1982), p. 80. See Tracy *The Analogical Imagination*, esp. pp. 54-82, 97, 376-98.
12. Ibid., p. 81.
13. Stephen Toulmin, paper given at an international conference on the "present situation of theology" at Tübingen University, May 1983.
14. Tracy, *Analogical Imagination*: p. 62.
15. See Outler, ed., *John Wesley*, pp. 14-18; Bernard Semmel. *The Methodist Revolution* (New York: Basic Books, 1973), pp. 28-40.
16. Tracy, *Analogical Imagination*, p. 63.
17. Ibid., p. 64.
18. Ibid., p. 67.
19. Ibid., p. 386.
20. John Wesley, *Forty-Four Sermons* (London: Epworth Press, 1944), p. 1.
21. Ibid., p. 7.
22. Lamb, *Solidarity with Victims*, pp. 81, 83.
23. Tracy, *The Analogical Imagination*.
24. John Walsh, "Elie Halevy and the Rise of Methodism," Proceedings of the Royal Historical Society, February, 1974; "Methodism and the Mob in the 18th Century" in *Popular Belief and Practice*, Studies in Church History, vol. 8, C. J. Cuming and D. Baker, eds. (Cambridge: Cambridge University Press, 1972); C.D. Field, "The Social Structure of English Methodism, 18th to 20th Centuries," *British Journal of Sociology* 20 (June 1977): 199-255; R. Porter, *English Society in the 18th Century* (London: Pelican, 1982). Robert F. Wearmouth, *Methodism and the Common People of the Eighteenth Century* (London: Epworth Press, 1945).
25. This is the focal point of Semmel's argument in *The Methodist Revolution*.
26. Leon O. Hynson has recently argued that Wesley's support of the monarchy from 1770 on was actually a subtheme of his primary concern for religious and civil liberty. "A careful reading of Wesley suggests that he moved from an early emphasis on the 'divine, indefensible, hereditary right' of the monarchy to an emphasis on the divine right of human rights. His dedication to the monarchy was a real one but became in his later years the political instrument of his profound effort to preserve liberty for the people and the nation." "Human Liberty a Divine Right: A Study in the Political Maturation of John Wesley" *Journal of Church and State*, 25 (Winter 1983): 85.
27. I believe this is true not only for Wesley's theology and for his maturing political views but also for his changing economic views. Wesley's basic economic orientation was in the Aquinian ethic. As Wesley moved haltingly in his later years toward the "individualistic, entrepreneurial mood of a commercial England" and seemingly against the traditional ethic opposed to engrossing, forestalling "market" price and usury, he did this with the "cause of the poor" as his primary criterion. See Semmel, *The Methodist Revolution*, pp. 71-79; Kathleen W. MacArthur, *The Economic Ethics of John Wesley* (New York: Abingdon Press, 1936).
28. For the following, cf. my paper "The Future of the Methodist Theological Traditions," given at the Seventh Oxford Institute of Methodist Theological Studies.
29. This is one crucial sense in which Wesley's theological theory shapes praxis just as reciprocally his praxis with the poor shapes his theory.
30. *Journal*, vol. 5 (May 14, 1761), 116-17. Quoted by Semmel.

3. WESLEYAN CONSTRUCTIVE THEOLOGY?

Charles Wood

The variety of adjectives which may be found preceding the noun "theology" can be confusing. There is Jewish theology, biblical, liberal, feminist, and evangelical theology—the list could be extended into the dozens. These adjectives do not all perform the same service: some indicate an approach, some delimit the subject matter, others declare a particular commitment or concern. It is not always easy to tell just what is being indicated, or how the adjective qualifies the noun and the enterprise.

Few of these terms have escaped censure of one kind or another. Those who view revelation as the ground of theology may declare natural theology impossible. Systematic theology may appear overweening to those struck by the mystery and freedom of God. So-called liberal and evangelical theologies alike may seem to be question-begging efforts, in which the theologian's allegiance to a particular point of view compromises the inquiry from the start. Dogmatic theology may connote a narrow preoccupation with right beliefs and their formulation. Nearly every sort of theology which an adjective may suggest has been called into question, with more or less justice. The bare noun "theology" is, of course, intolerably uninformative, and anyone who intends to forswear adjectives and to study, teach, or practice just plain theology should be prepared for a reaction of skepticism or impatience from those to whom that intention is announced. But although the adjectives may be practically unavoidable, the problematic character of most of the resulting terms indicates the importance of giving careful consideration to their choice and use.

"Wesleyan constructive theology," the focus of our attention in this work-group, is, naturally enough, doubly suspect. It would be well for us to clarify the sense in which a theological endeavor might properly be "constructive" and "Wesleyan." This paper proposes such a clarification. Of course, one may fairly ask whether it is worthwhile to use the phrase or to pursue the enterprise thus designated at all. The paper will not answer this question, though it may contribute in some way to an answer.

I

Whether Christian theology ought to be constructive at all is a debated issue. To some, the task of theology is essentially analytical and descriptive: it is to identify and unfold the truths already received in the sources of the church's tradition. On this view, theological construction amounts to infidelity. To do "constructive theology" would be to prefer the product of one's own imagination to "the faith once delivered to the saints." To the extent that it is faithful to its task, theology avoids construction. To others, however, theology is essentially constructive; it is, to use a phrase prominent in the recent work of Gordon Kaufman, "imaginative construction," and the more fully this is acknowledged, the more adequate the construction is likely to be. To ignore or deny the constructive character of theology is to delude oneself. There can be no simply descriptive theology.

The force of this latter claim, against any naive and ahistorical attempt simply to recover and transmit the primitive, uninterpreted gospel, can readily be felt. We know that perception is already interpretation, that any theologian's description of the faith is influenced in countless ways by his or her circumstances, and that therefore theology will always in some sense be a constructive endeavor, whether intentionally so or not. And it makes sense, granting all this, to be candid and self-aware about this necessity. Theology, like all works of the human mind, is inevitably constructive.

But if all theology is constructive, what might be meant by the phrase, "constructive theology"? If it is not simply pleonasm, this phrase must designate a particular type or aspect of theology, distinguishing it from other types or aspects (however "constructive," in the first sense, they may also be). How might this be understood? At what point must Christian theology be particularly constructive, and what is the nature of this construction? To gain some clarity about this, it may be helpful to envision the task of Christian theology as a whole.

Christian theology may be defined as a critical

Reprinted by permission of the *Perkins Journal*.

inquiry into the validity of Christian witness.[1] That inquiry has three basic dimensions, each corresponding to an essential formal feature of the concept of "Christian witness." First, because Christian witness always conveys an explicit or explicit claim to be Christian, there is the fundamental question of its Christianness: Is this act of witness—past, present, or envisioned—truly Christian? Secondly because Christian witness also conveys a claim to truth, there is the fundamental question of its truth: Is this really true? Thirdly because Christian witness is an act of communication and not a performance in a vacuum, there is the fundamental question of its aptness as communication: Is this act of witness fitting to its context and to its purpose in that context? Is the Christian witness validly enacted here?

To each of these three fundamental questions there corresponds a principal theological discipline. We may, for convenience, call these disciplines by the familiar titles of historical theology, philosophical theology, and practical theology, respectively, though the titles are negotiable and relatively unimportant. Historical theology, on this usage, is not simply the historical study of the Christian tradition. It is a theological discipline which uses historical inquiry to pursue the critical question of the Christianness of Christian witness. It reflects upon the way the church has always appealed to elements of its own tradition to vindicate the Christian authenticity of its life and message, and it asks two main questions about this process: First, what is it in the past which may most adequately serve as the criterion or criteria for testing the representativeness of Christian witness, that is, its faithfulness to Jesus Christ about whom it claims to be? (What, in other words, is the "canon" by which the church's representation of Jesus Christ may be measured?) And secondly when may an instance of witness rightly be said to be "in accord" with the criteria thus identified? What does it mean to be faithful? Historical theology investigates the Christian tradition so as to inform and enhance contemporary reflection upon the problems of the identity, continuity, unity, and representativeness of Christian witness in its manifold and ever-increasing variety.

Philosophical theology—understood here as a discipline of Christian theology, not as a synonym for "natural theology" or "philosophy of religion"—uses the resources of philosophical reflection to pursue the question of the truth of Christian witness. It aims to discover and display the logic of Christian witness, that is, the principles governing its meaning, so as to clarify the sorts of claims it makes, and then to see what may be said about the truth of those claims.

Practical theology studies the practice of Christian witness, with particular attention, not to its origin (historical theology) nor to its nature (philosophical theology), but to its goal, its intention. It asks by what standards the practice of Christian witness ought to be judged in the light of its goal, and it proceeds to make the relevant judgments concerning a given instance of witness, past, present, or prospective. Because Christian witness is itself a matter of human conduct, and because it always takes place within a particular human situation, practical theology draws upon the various disciplines concerned with human behavior (e.g., sociology, anthropology, and psychology) as resources for its inquiry. It studies the ways in which society and culture shape Christian witness and influence its reception; but it goes beyond a description of this process, to make critical judgments regarding the adequacy of Christian practice, and to ask the normative question of how witness may be most fittingly enacted within a given set of circumstances.

Three principal theological disciplines thus take shape around the three fundamental critical questions which are to be raised about the validity of Christian witness as such. Put in positive form, the questions are: What is truly Christian witness? What is the truth of Christian witness? How is Christian witness fittingly enacted? Although these are distinct questions, none of them may be pursued in isolation from the others. It is, for example, impossible fully to determine the meaning and truth of an utterance apart from a consideration of its origin and its intention in a particular context. It is impossible to assess the fitness of a given act of witness, or even to identify the pertinent criteria for such an assessment, without attending to the nature of Christian witness as such, as well as to the variety of its historical expressions. And it is impossible to locate the criteria of Christian authenticity in the Christian tradition if one is unprepared to read the tradition as the history of Christian practice, that is, bring the resources of practical theological reflection to bear upon historical theology. These three inquiries are interdependent in many ways. That interdependence is also a feature of the cognate secular disciplines which correspond to these three dimensions of theology: neither "history" nor "philosophy" nor "the human sciences" names a single discipline with a single identifiable method; all are vast, unruly, and to some extent, undisciplinable fields of inquiry, interconnecting and overlapping with each other in various interesting ways.

Those familiar with the so-called "Wesleyan quadrilateral" of Scripture, tradition, experience, and reason as theological guidelines may recognize a parallel between those guidelines and their interaction, on the one hand, and the foregoing sketch of the three basic lines of theological inquiry and their interaction, on the other. At the considerable risk of oversimplification, let us see whether the parallel may be correlated fairly clearly with the inquiries here labelled (respectively) historical, philosophical, and practical theology. To test whether a given utterance or action is "scriptural" is to test its Christian authenticity, that is, its capacity to represent the Christ to whom Scripture bears definitive witness—assuming, of course, as Wesley certainly did, that it is "Scripture" and not something else which performs that function, and assuming that one has an appropriate way of understanding and applying Scripture so as to be able to determine when something is in accord with it. (For Wesley, "tradition" had something substantial to do with this question of how one reads and uses Scripture; but then, so did "experience" and "reason." Given the primacy of Scripture for him, it seems best to associate this dimension of theological inquiry with "Scripture" simply, and not with "Scripture and tradition"—though a case could also be made for the latter alternative.) The discipline of historical theology does not, of course, simply assume that "Scripture" has this role, since that is one of the things about which it has to inquire; but the underlying question as to the Christian authenticity of what the church says and does is the same.

"Reason," in the language of the quadrilateral, represents the question of the meaning and truth of Christian witness—the question of what is here called "philosophical theology." In Wesley's own understanding, the gospel is not only to be commended as true and believed to be true, it is to be apprehended as true. It is not only reasonable in the sense that it accords with the eternal *logos*, it is also reasonable in the sense that human reason—once in possession of the evidence of faith—can understand and affirm it through ordinary processes of inference and judgment.[2] "Scripture and reason" are both to be consulted. Or, to put it another way, we are entitled to satisfy ourselves as to the truth as well as the "scripturality" of what is presented as Christian witness before we affirm it for ourselves or proffer it to others. Indeed, apart from some exercise of reason along these lines, it is doubtful that we can be said even to understand it.

The category of "experience" may be correlated with the concern of practical theology: How may Christian witness be so represented as to achieve its own goal? Valid witness is known by its fruit, for example, by its capacity to transform personal and social existence in appropriate ways. A particular representation of the gospel will attest itself—or fail to—in the way it influences the lives of the persons and the society to which it is addressed. A form of witness which is suited to one situation may be ineffective, or negative in its effects, in another, and so practical theology must always be contextually specific as it works out the relationship between witness and experience.

"Scripture," "reason," and "experience" thus represent, in Wesleyan language, the three major tests to which Christian witness—"tradition," to use the fourth term of the quadrilateral—is subjected in theological reflection. "Tradition" and "witness" are functionally equivalent terms in this connection. Both can refer to the process as well as to the content, to the activity of "bearing" or "handing on" as well as to that which is borne or handed on. Tradition or witness is also that which, in a sense, bears us: comprehensively understood, it is the ongoing Christian movement through which we have our own Christian existence. Tradition, so understood, is less a "guideline" which we consult than it is the environment in which we find ourselves, and those with whose care we are entrusted.

Christian theology is critical reflection upon Christian tradition, both upon the tradition which has been inherited and upon the "traditioning" yet to be done. It subjects that tradition to a threefold test. We have seen that each of the three principal lines of theological inquiry is dependent upon the other two. We have also seen that the critical question central to each is also capable of positive or constructive formulation. Since critical inquiry presupposes criteria, some attempt to answer these positive questions (What is authentically Christian witness? What is its truth? How is it fittingly enacted?) is requisite to the critical task as such.

The pursuit of these positive questions as to the authenticity, truth, and fitting enactment of Christian witness drives these three inquiries into close interaction, indeed, into a unified pattern of reflection.[3] A fourth principal theological discipline thus emerges at the point of intersection of the first three. "Systematic theology," to use the conventional term, is constituted by the effort to bring the three basic theological inquiries together in a comprehensive and constructive fashion. It is "systematic" in three senses: First, it integrates the three basic inquiries, bringing the resources and insights of each to bear upon each of the others, and striving for coherence. Second, it is comprehensive in its scope: it attempts to deal with the whole of the Christian witness, giving attention to its consistency and integrity. And third, it is indeed constructive theology: it attempts to offer a positive answer to the question of what constitutes valid (authentic, true, and fitting) Christian witness, for a given situation or range of situations. The answer thus reached may find written expression in what is frequently called "a systematic theology," that is, a comprehensive statement of the Christian faith according to some explicit principles of interpretation and organization. But it need not. Occasional essays addressed to particular issues in the primary disciplines of historical, philosophical, and practical theology, focused treatments of specific doctrines or aspects of witness, and many other sorts of writing (and speech) may manifest the results of systematic theological reflection, as may—and should—the "enacted theology"[4] of actual Christian practice: church polity, worship, social witness, and the rest. "Systematic theology" in the strict sense properly designates a mode of theological reflection, and is applied only derivatively to its results. And we might well be wary of associating the term exclusively with one sort of literature, especially when what may be called for in a given situation is a quite different way of sharing the results of systematic reflection.

"Constructive theology," then, may be taken to designate this positive aspect of systematic theology, and, by extension, its working out into the various sorts of theological proposals which the exigencies and opportunities of Christian witness may seem to call for.

II

But what might *Wesleyan* constructive theology be?

It would appear that the term "Wesleyan theology" might be taken in at least two distinct senses—leaving aside its casual use to designate either Wesley's own theology or the theology produced by persons in the Wesleyan tradition, however defined. In one sense, "Wesleyan" refers to the theological criterion; in the other, it refers to the object of criticism. That is, Wesleyan theology could refer to the effort to identify that which is authentically Wesleyan, and to criticize church doctrine and practice in the light of that standard. Alternatively, it could refer to the

effort to subject the Wesleyan tradition itself to critical scrutiny—to test its adequacy as Christian witness.

Both sorts of Wesleyan theology have been pursued with more or less vigor in the past two hundred years, and both have their uses. At first glance, the former sort would appear useful to the church's concern—such as it is—for doctrinal discipline, by helping the church to identify, understand, and apply the standards of doctrine to which it is committed. It is, however, instructive that the "normative Wesleyanism" of, for example, the United Methodist doctrinal standards understands itself to be somewhat less than normative: it appeals constantly to the criterion of Scripture (cf. Article V of the Articles of Religion, and the prefaces—and contents!—of Wesley's *Standard Sermons* and *Notes on the New Testament*), takes responsibility for its own place within the broader Christian tradition, and holds itself open to the tests of reason and experience. A Wesleyan theology in this first sense which takes this fact seriously, rather than elevating Wesley's utterances as a material norm, is on the way to becoming a Wesleyan theology in the second sense: that is, a critical examination of the validity of the Wesleyan movement and message as Christian witness.

It is to this sort of Wesleyan theology that John Wesley himself exhorted his readers.[5] And if "constructive theology" refers to that aspect of the whole theological task which generates new possibilities for the understanding and furtherance of Christian witness, perhaps Wesleyan constructive theology is best understood simply as the sort of constructive theology which emerges out of such critical engagement with the Wesleyan heritage.

NOTES

1. For a fuller treatment of the following scheme, see Charles M. Wood, "An Orientation in Christian Theology," *Encounter*, Vol. 45, No. 3 (Summer 1984), pp. 243-57.
2. John Wesley, *An Earnest Appeal to Men of Reason and Religion*, in *Works* (Oxford), vol. 11, pp. 55-57.
3. There are, of course, a number of contrary forces to be reckoned with, as Edward Farley and Joseph Hough, among others, have recently pointed out.
4. John Deschner refers to Wesley's "articulated theology," "presuppositional theology," and "enacted theology" as three distinct resources to be taken into account in any attempt to take his theological measure. It is a distinction with wider possibilities.
5. The order and content of three of the questions traditionally asked of those seeking admission into full connection in an annual conference enforce this exhortation: "Have you studied the doctrines of The United Methodist Church? After full examination do you believe that our doctrines are in harmony with the Holy Scriptures? Will you preach and maintain them?" (*The Book of Discipline of The United Methodist Church*, 1980, para. 425.)

4. PERSPECTIVE
FOR A WESLEYAN
SYSTEMATIC THEOLOGY

H. Ray Dunning

Anyone who proposes to construct a systematic theology in these times of information explosion is bold beyond classification. Few minds have the breadth to encompass the field adequately and certainly I am not among them. However, the demands of the times seem to call for an effort to provide a reasonably consistent Wesleyan theological perspective. And, of course, one could probably ask which Wesleyanism? So let me say that I am working in that tradition which has latched on to Wesley's perfectionist emphasis and thus has not shown too much interest in what Mildred Bangs Wynkoop has called the whole Wesley. However, it seems to me that each partial Wesleyanism could be tremendously enhanced if it would make the whole Wesley its lodestar as perspective.

The problem, of course, is to identify the perspective. Yet that is the most crucial matter. As Paul Tillich says: "Systematic theology does not seek to be completely comprehensive so much as to address relevant problems from a particular perspective."[1] Gordon Kaufmann makes the same point:

> It is important to distinguish between the perspective that informs a systematic theology and the detailed analysis of theological doctrines. A theologian's perspective affects the way he frames questions as well as the answers he gives to them; it shapes his fundamental judgments regarding what is theologically important as well as his way of resolving issues; it works at every level of his thinking. . . . His perspective is, in short, the most important determinant of his thinking, though often it remains concealed and unknown, even to the theologian himself.[2]

This approach does not mean that one is seeking to reproduce John Wesley's theology, that is, it is not *per se* a historical discipline. Rather it seeks to identify the point of view which informed Wesley's theologizing and seeks to develop that in contemporary terms. This is to say that it is not of ultimate significance what Mr. Wesley said on this or that particular doctrine. In fact, I think it can be demonstrated that Wesley articulated some doctrines, for example, the atonement, in a way that radically conflicted with his fundamental theological stance. Thus the task of a Wesleyan theology today is to extrapolate the "point of view" in as fully consistent a way as can be done, in dialogue with the best of contemporary theological scholarship.

What I am speaking about is what Professor Tillich has called the "norm" of systematic theology of which he says: "Sources and medium can produce a theological system only if their use is guided by a norm."[3] I think he is furthermore correct when he suggests that such a norm must be existential in nature. As he puts it, it must arise out of the spiritual life of the church as it encounters the Christian message. One cannot produce a viable Wesleyan theology as a mere tradition. It would only be a museum piece. In Helmut Thielicke's felicitous phrase, it would be "tending the ashes rather than guarding the flame."

What I am proposing as a norm for constructing a Wesleyan systematic theology can be conceptualized as a series of concentric circles, each encompassing one informing the inner circle or circles.

The inner core I would identify as soteriological. Wesley's own expressed commitment supports the centrality of this concern. His actual theologizing was designed to explicate saving truth. L. M. Starkey, Jr., in his book on Wesley's understanding of the Holy Spirit says: Wesley's "concern with the doctrines of the Trinity and the Holy Spirit is decidedly non-metaphysical; he relates these doctrines immediately to man's redemption. Salvation is his primary doctrinal and practical concern. . . . Every doctrine of Wesley is centered in the context of vital religious experience."[4] Theology, then, from the Wesleyan point of view is not ivory-tower speculation. Every doctrine should finally be evaluated in terms of its saving significance. It appears to me to mean, for example, that an authentic Wesleyan theology would have—at best—peripheral interest in speculative eschatology, but clearly much in realized eschatology.

The soteriological focus of Wesleyan thought,

I take to be two-pronged. And here, I would modify the conceptualization. Instead of a circle, it seems to be more like an ellipse with two foci held in polar tension. These balancing foci are (1) justification by grace through faith and (2) sanctification by grace through faith. If either one is thought of as the center of a circle, the result is an imbalance that is not distinctively Wesleyan. When justification is placed at the center, the tendency is toward antinomianism; when sanctification is placed at the center, the tendency is toward legalism or moralism. The latter is a trap into which my own tradition has too often and too readily fallen.

Some have objected to this conceptualization by arguing that in practice, Wesley laid his stress upon sanctification and allowed justification to slip into a secondary role. But if this is true—and I have questions about that—it is a historical judgment. I am suggesting this as a normative judgment. However Wesley himself, in his sermon "On God's Vineyard," reflects this balanced relationship.

> It is, then, a great blessing given to this people, that as they do not think or speak of justification so as to supersede sanctification, so neither do they think or speak of sanctification so as to supersede justification. They take care to keep each in its own place, laying equal stress on one and the other. They know God has joined these together, and it is not for man to put them asunder: Therefore they maintain, with equal zeal and diligence, the doctrine of free, full, present justification, on the one hand, and of entire sanctification both of heart and life, on the other; being as tenacious of inward holiness as any mystic, and of outward, as any Pharisee.[5]

This synthesizing tendency in Wesley creates a model for his theological successors in walking a narrow path between partial perspectives.

Now to the second concentric circle, which we wish to identify with *prevenient grace*. The whole soteriological dimension of Wesleyan theology is spelled out in terms of this distinguishing teaching. In my own tradition, it has been given central attention but has usually developed in a truncated form. The implications of it are quite far-reaching. It has, or can have, both ontological and epistemological overtones and probably has the most pervasive character of any Wesleyan doctrine. I want to point out some striking ramifications of this idea, but so as not to get too far afield, let me quickly suggest that the third concentric circle is christological. Wesley explicitly grounded prevenient grace in Christology. Not only did he teach that grace is freely bestowed upon all men for the sake of Christ,

removing the "guilt" of original sin, but knowledge of God is also interpreted as the consequence of the grace of Christ. A Wesleyan theology will thus be uniquely christological in focus: justification, sanctification, and prevenient grace in all its numerous manifestations must be interpreted from this standpoint. Since the work of the Holy Spirit and preventing grace are virtually synonymous at one level, the work of the Spirit is seen by Wesley to be christological in nature (See the Pentecost hymns compiled by Timothy Smith.) In fact, the christological grounding of every doctrine should be the all encompassing character of the norm in a Wesleyan systematic theology.[6] Deschner argues that Christology is the presupposition of Wesley's theology, and comments: "The author's conviction is that an explicit examination of Wesley's great presupposition can lead to clarification and even correcting of preaching in the present-day Wesleyan tradition."

In my own tradition, this aspect of Wesleyan theology was abandoned, by and large, from the mid-nineteenth century on with less than happy consequences. In recent times, the interpretation of Christian experience in all but exclusively pneumatological terms has encountered a movement stemming from Wesley scholarship which has recaptured his christological emphasis with some interesting results. It was found that certain perversions followed as a partial consequence of this emphasis with no way of theologically guarding against them.

Let me now turn to some illustrations of how this "norm" would be implemented in particular doctrines. The central position of soteriological concerns may be seen in Wesley's own approach to the doctrine of the Trinity. In his sermon "On the Trinity," Mr. Wesley makes several suggestions that bear on the question. One of these involves a distinction between the *substance* of the doctrine and the philosophical explication of it; or in different terms, the *fact* and the *manner*. He is very flexible with regard to any and all explications of the teaching but feels that the Christian must be committed to the substance, or the fact. The substance he sees to be soteriological rather than ontological. Since the word "fundamental" is too ambiguous, he is reticent to declare which are fundamental truths, but he does hold that the doctrine of the Father, Son, and Spirit is one that we must know because it has "a close connexion with vital religion." He says further that there is no wisdom in rejecting what God has revealed (the fact), "especially when we consider that what God has been pleased to reveal upon this head, far from being a point of indifference, is a truth of the last importance, it enters into the very heart of Christianity: *It lies at the root of all vital religion*" (italics mine). He spells this out by suggesting that it is the basis of our acceptance with God (by which he means the work of the Son) and the basis of the witness of the Spirit. In sum, this would mean acceptance by the Father, through the Son, and witnessed to by the Spirit. He concludes: "Therefore, I do not see how it is possible for any to have vital religion who denies that the Three are One."

Let us look now at the *prevenient grace* motif. Here we have some help from one, if not the first, of Wesleyan "systematic theologian," John Fletcher. Mr. Fletcher worked out a rather full-scale interpretation of the ramifications of prevenient grace in terms of a doctrine of dispensations, which is first of all an epistemological category and only secondarily a historical one. A dispensation reflects a certain level of knowledge of God from the lowest (the dispensation of the Father) to the highest (that of the Spirit). It is the first which I want to look at here. Fletcher refers to this dispensation variously as "the natural law," "the remains of the Creator's image in the human heart," "the secret grace of the Redeemer, which is more or less operative in every man," "Gentilism," or "Judaism."

He supports and describes the dispensation of the Father scripturally by reference to those passages of scripture with speak of the universal knowledge of all men (Acts 17:26,27; Titus 2:11; I Tim. 4:10; Acts 10:34; Heb. 11:6; Micah 6:8). Although inadequate and falling far short of the full revelation of the soteriological provisions available in the "dispensation of the Spirit," this "revelation" is sufficient unto salvation if God is just. Otherwise "impartial justice" would have required that God had seen to it that there had been only one dispensation of grace and all men given full knowledge of it. Although all men do not have access to the same degree of truth,

> nevertheless, it is equally certain that every man, in what period of time and in what peculiar circumstances soever he found himself placed, has received sufficient light to discover, as well as sufficient power to perform what God has been pleased to require at his hands.[7]

This construction of Wesley's doctrine of prevenient grace is the developed implication of the teaching and is not contrary to Wesley's own mature understanding. John Allen Knight, in his dissertation (Vanderbilt) on Fletcher, argues that there is an implicit "theology of history" which came to expression in the later writings of Wesley so that his perspective broadened to include non-Christian believers, for example, Cornelius, who had never heard the gospel. He saw that God would accept them on the basis of their degree of faith and obedience to what light they had.

Fletcher becomes quite explicit in his statement about the extent and efficacy of prevenient grace in its "epistemological/soteriological" aspect:

> Such is the faith by which those Jews, Mohammedans and Pagans, whose hearts are principled with humility, candor, and the fear of God, have been, and still continue to be, saved in every part of the world. For the Father of mercies, who knoweth whereof we are made, will no more absolutely condemn such worshippers, on account of the extraordinary respect they have discovered for Moses, Mohammed, and Confucius, than he will finally reject some pious Christians, for the sake of that excessive veneration which they manifest for particular saints and reformers.[8]

Thus the Wesleyan doctrine of prevenient grace is the basis for a view of general revelation (not natural revelation, which is really a contradiction in terms) which provides a ground of rapprochement between Christianity and non-Christian religions. This puts Wesleyan theology in the tradition that Paul Tillich characterizes as Augustinian because "knowledge" of God is immediate and direct rather than inferential. Let me pursue this further by relating prevenient grace to the doctrine of the *imago* as I believe it should be constructed.

Wesley used the term "natural man" to describe the human condition apart from grace. He paints a dark picture of such a creature. Pertinent to our question in this discussion, he denies that such a man has any knowledge of God or that he could ever attain to any such knowledge. In his sermon on "Original Sin" he hypothesizes that if two infants were brought up from the womb without being instructed in any religion, they would have no religion at all and no more knowledge of God than wild beasts. In this description, however, he makes two stipulations: (1) parenthetically he notes the exception, "unless the grace of God interposed," and (2) that this result would occur apart "from the influences of God's Spirit."

In his sermon on "Working Out Our Own Salvation" he cashes in on these stipulations.

> For allowing that all the souls of men are dead in sin by *nature*, this excuses none seeing there is no man that is in a state of mere nature; there is no man, unless he has quenched the Spirit, that is wholly void of the grace of God. No man living is entirely destitute of what is vulgarly called *natural conscience*.

But this is not natural: it is more properly termed preventing grace. (Italics mine)

This grace which goes before is universal in its extent and is the source of all good in man, and of feelings of right and wrong which are the result of the activity of conscience. Furthermore, in reference to John 1:9 he says: "Everyone has some measure of that light, some faint glimmering ray, which sooner or later, more or less, enlightens every man that cometh into the world." The end result of universal prevenient grace is that "no man sins because he has not grace, but because he does not use the grace which he hath."

What we are suggesting here is that *prevenient grace* is simply another way of talking about that aspect of the *imago dei* as a relationship within which man perpetually stands while at the same time recognizing that this grace is not, in and of itself, saving grace, even though it may become so if responded to properly. Rather, what it is saying is that of all earthly creatures, only human beings are, in Mr. Wesley's words, "capable of God," and this is not a natural but a gracious capacity.

The long-standing question of nature and grace takes on unique contours from the Wesleyan perspective. Unlike the Thomistic solution, it does not hold to a "good" human nature which needs but to be supplemented by grace to complete man's full, two-fold telos. Nature is not "good" but radically fallen, perverted, corrupt, devoid of any redeeming qualities before God. Furthermore grace is not restricted to a segment of man's life, that part which has to do with the supernatural virtues. The distinctiveness of the Wesleyan view is that nature is graced so that the "natural man" is but a logical abstraction. This grace extends to the whole of human existence.

The implications of this for the theological definition of man are significant. Instead of identifying some quality such as reason, which distinguishes him from the brute creation, or attempting to find some Divine spark within that blurs the distinction between man and God, it defines the essence of man as man-in-relation-to-God. In other words, when prevenient grace is interpreted as an ontological principle, it is grace which constitutes the humanity of man. The very being of man *qua* man is his standing in grace. This clearly retains the Creator-creature relationship with all that entails.

In traditional theological terminology, this interpretation holds that God is first in the *ordo cognoscendi* as well as the *ordo essendi*. This is the consequence of holding, in accord with the Augustinian tradition, that God is the ground of all knowledge as well as the ground of all being. Knowledge of God, like the being of God, is not derived from knowledge of other things. This is the reverse of the traditional cosomological theistic proofs which begin with empirical knowledge of the world, or some aspect of it, and infer God's existence from this prior knowledge. The doctrine of prevenient grace as a principle of knowledge affirms that one's experience of the world raises the question of God because one is already aware of an impinging Presence. Knowledge of God is not secondary and inferential, but primary and direct.

Here is another place where Mr. Wesley's theological principles, when consistently applied, lead to a different conclusion than he himself affirmed. As we know, he did give some credence to arguments for the existence of God that began from an empirical base.

Prevenient grace may also provide a clue to a Wesleyan view of biblical authority. There is another working group concerned with this question, but systematic theology needs to address it as well. Mr. Wesley himself presents us with an ambiguous picture. He can be quoted in such a way as to support a fundamentalistic version of inerrancy. However, the basic thrust is much more classic Reformation, according to doctoral dissertation conclusions by Larry Shelton. I would suggest that prevenient grace applied to the issue would give the Wesleyan view a precise focus.

Most discussions of authority, with which I am familiar, fail to reflect an awareness that the fundamental aspect of authority is existential or personal in nature. Except in the case of physical coercion, which really does not have any relevance to the matter, any claimant to authority must be acknowledged as such in a personal decision of commitment. It is impossible to identify all the possible motives which precipitate such decisions. It may be fear or reverence or love or some other motive, or a combination of several. Regardless of what the particular motive or motives of the decision to submit may be, it is ultimately personal in nature. What determines such a decision? It cannot be exclusively in the objective character of the authority, or else everyone would respond in the same way. It must finally be acknowledged as a mystery which finds its locus in the hidden depths of human personality.

At this point we can draw a parallel to the traditional Reformation doctrine of the "internal witness of the Holy Spirit" and the Wesleyan doctrine of prevenient grace. Just as this grace is extended to all men, but not all accept, so the

Spirit works in the consciousness of all who are exposed to the message of the Bible. The reason some acknowledge its authority is this act of personal decision which, like the response to the offer of salvation, is a mystery hidden, not in the secret counsels of God , but in the equally impenetrable mysteries of human personality.

If this suggested norm for a Wesleyan theology is adequate or valid, I believe it can provide a constructive theology which will be distinctive in many ways. It will be able to do justice to the overall emphasis on Scripture without creating serious imbalances. I am interested to see just what shape the various doctrines will eventually take when seen from this perspective.

NOTES

1. Paul Tillich, *Systematic Theology*, 3 vols. (Chicago: University of Chicago Press, 1967), vol. 1, p. 59.
2. Ibid., p. ix.
3. Ibid., p. 47.
4. L. M. Starkey, *The Work of the Holy Spirit* (Nashville: Abingdon Press, 1965), pp. 37-38.
5. Wesley, *Works*, vol. 7, pp. 204-5.
6. Cf. Wesley, *Notes*, on Rom. 1:19 and John 1:9; John Deschner; *Wesley's Christology* (Dallas: Southern Methodist University, 1960), p. 92; Starkey, *Work of the Holy Spirit*, p. 41; Charles Allen Rogers, "The Concept of Prevenient Grace in the Theology of John Wesley," Ph. D. dissertation, Duke University, Durham, N.C., 1967. See Wesley, *Works*, vol. 6, p. 223; vol. 7, pp. 187ff., 373-74; vol. 8, pp. 277-78; *Sermons*, vol. 1, p. 118; vol. 2, pp. 43, 445.
7. John Fletcher, *Works* (Philadelphia: Joseph Crukshank, 1791), vol. 3, pp. 170-79.
8. Ibid., pp. 176-77.

5. CONSTRUCTIVE THEOLOGY IN THE WESLEYAN TRADITION

Thomas A. Langford

To explore the possibilities of constructive theology in the Wesleyan tradition requires, first of all, that we reflect on that tradition. To attempt to decipher the conveyance of a tradition need not be restrictive or an attempt to hide in the past. Rather, it can be a significant act of self-understanding and can create an opportunity to utilize the past for the present.

This is especially the case in the area of constructive theology. We have lived far too long with the myth that the Wesleyan tradition has not been concerned with theology. It is one of the best kept secrets in the history of doctrine that Methodism is also a theological tradition. To discover that tradition and to explicate its meaning can have significance for our present task; consequently, I want to discuss characteristics of the Wesleyan tradition which are informative for constructive theology.

Biblical Base

I want to begin where John Wesley began and claim that Wesleyan theology has, for the most part, been consciously rooted in the Bible. Theology underwrites the proclamation of the gospel, and what the gospel is must be ascertained from Scripture. For Wesley this was certainly true. Yet to refer to Wesley must be done with care, for Wesley is not important as a final authority or as the decisive shaper of doctrine. On the contrary, Wesley is important because he continuously pointed beyond himself to the more ultimate base of theology in biblical witness. For the most part, the Wesleyan tradition has agreed with the primacy of the biblical witness, and I say this recognizing that for half a century (the last decade of the nineteenth century and for at least four decades in the twentieth century) North American Methodist theology moved to a primary base in experience and some Methodist theologians continue to follow this route.

Even where there is agreement on the biblical base for theology, however, there have been changes in understanding that base. For Wesley to root theology in Scripture carried three presuppositions: (1) There is a unitary witness in the Bible; (2) there is a general consensus of interpretation which yielded classical Christian doctrines; and (3) the biblical message is made a living witness as it is interpreted through the internal witness of the Holy Spirit.

Today, the first two of these presuppositions are not secure. Biblical study has made it impossible to assume a neat unity in biblical thought or a general consensus about interpretation or resulting doctrine. Because of these changed conditions, Wesleyan theology, as biblically based, follows—closely or at a distance—the winding paths freshly marked by biblical studies. Rather than offering a firm anchor for received beliefs, a biblical base means a recognition of the primacy of Scripture as fallow soil for new growth. The biblical witness remains, but its message must continually be heard afresh through the witness of the Holy Spirit in every situation.

To say, therefore, that theology in the Wesleyan tradition is biblically based is not a conclusion, it is a challenge. A principal question today, and for us certainly, is How can the biblical witness be related to or be utilized by constructive theology? A scant outline of events in this century indicates the path of struggle over the issue. From the beginning of this century there was a growing distance between biblical study and constructive theology; the two disciplines have, for the most part, been understood to be disjoined. In the 1940s and 1950s, however, the era of biblical theology seemed to make the relationship more promising, and new interaction seemed possible and was explored. But that moment has passed, and once again the question of interrelationship presses upon us. To work out this relationship is the ongoing task of a tradition which explicitly acknowledges responsibility to both biblical authority and a specific culture.

How shall we attempt to relate the two today? I make my own comments as suggestive of the task we, as a tradition, must undertake.

1) There remains a non-objectifiability about God's action in Jesus Christ. The Jewish desire

for signs, the Greek desire for wisdom, and our desire for scientific certitude are unrequited. Neither historical statement nor theological construction can completely capture God's self-presentation in Jesus Christ. What we do have in Scripture are a variety of perspectives upon this central historical event, common witness to the lordship of Jesus, and the internal witness of the Holy Spirit. The believer—including the theologian—must attempt to see the meaning of Jesus synoptically by responsive sensitivity to the biblical message and the Holy Spirit.

To speak of biblical authorization of theology is to acknowledge that Christian life—including thought—is shaped by the life, death, and resurrection of Jesus Christ. Initially this must be affirmed as the formative power of God through the biblical witness. Scripture is authoritative as it authors a new self-identity. The biblical words are life-forming precisely as they lead to an indwelling of the meaning of Jesus Christ. This assumes that there is a consistent and adequate, if not a unitary and complete, kerygma which centers around (1) the historical Jesus, (2) who is confessed by the New Testament community by word and life both in terms of his person and sovereign status, (3) who is proclaimed as risen and exalted Lord, and (4) who continues to be present, as Holy Spirit, nurturing the Christian community's commitment and growth.

Authority is that which shapes life, it is legitimated—that is, acknowledged—power which integrates life around a commanding center and projects life toward accepted and final goals. Scripture is authoritative not as the conveyer of static truths but as the dynamic witness which organizes human life, both individual and corporate, and sets a way of being in the world.

2) Biblical authority is always mediatorial, it always points beyond itself to the authority of God in Jesus Christ. God remains free and sovereign over Scripture and in the utilization of Scripture. In the language of David Kelsey, the Scripture is a "normed norm." That is, it is God who inspires and guides the process from production to preservation to interpretation through the agency of the Holy Spirit. Biblically based theology is confessional; it witnesses to covenant life which is initiated, shaped, and projected by God.

3) The presence of God in Jesus Christ is community-structuring. To be a community is to be claimed by a shared center so that lives are held together by that center. The communal activity—the traditioning process—is informative to every subsequent interpretation of faith.

So the biblical witness informs a community which strives for corporate interpretation, and correction. The community stands with and over against individual interpretation of Scripture, not as controlling all legitimate interpretation, but as instructing through participation in faithful life-formation.

4) Christians are to live in the world in ways appropriate to God's sovereign and gracious rule. Here Scripture is the most immediate and necessary guide to Christian reflection, for God's way of being in the world is definitively expressed in the incarnation of Jesus Christ. It is crucial to emphasize that Christian theology is not predicated upon proof texts or explicit ethical codes but is a part of the formation which occurs as worship becomes a style of life in reflection on the incarnate reality of Jesus Christ. Christian responsibility is not so much an *imitatio Christi* but, as Fred Herzog has said, an *innovatio Christi*. Under the guidance of the Holy Spirit, the Bible is important for Christian faith, life, and interpretation as the medium for the creation and nurture of relationships.

5) Theology is a part of faithful living, seeking to understand and therefore critically assess the validity of faithful existence. That is, theology constantly questions the appropriateness of Christian life-form against the norm of the form of God's presence in Jesus Christ as this is addressed by the variety and varying New Testament witnesses. Christian life is not reducible to theological statement. Rather, theological language is expressive of and helps nurture a full-orbed thanking and obeying life.

The interrelatedness of biblical study to theology is crucial. The Scripture is the primary witness to God's presence in Jesus Christ, yet this must be continually interpreted under the guidance and the sovereignty of the Holy Spirit. In this regard, theology possesses both a freedom and a restriction. The freedom of theology is found in its renewing sensitivity to the fresh guidance of the Holy Spirit. Under the aegis of God's releasing grace, theology is called to question itself, its methods, its accepted results, and its most confident formulas. Theology is free because the truth of God is never in human grasp and can never be controlled by human beings, even by the most ingenuous and committed persons.

But theology is also restricted, it is centered in the reality of the singular historical event of Jesus Christ. This event constitutes the anchor of Christian existence and theological reflection. Yet this event, central and indispensable as it is, remains beyond our firm grasp even as it informs worship and life and reflection. Theology is Christian activity precisely as it enables and reflects on this event and attempts to understand how the Scripture has witnessed to its meaning, what consequences it has for our society, for the natural world, and for personal life-formation.

Enlightenment Context

The second characteristic of this tradition, which stands in dialectical relation to the first, is that Wesley inaugurated the first major religious movement after the inception of the Enlightenment. Not enough has been made of this fact, yet it is crucial and has several basic consequences.

First, a brief description of the intellectual situation. The Enlightenment, as described by Isaiah Berlin, was built upon the influences of Isaac Newton, who brought order and clarity into the realm of the physical sciences.

Yet the ancient disciplines of metaphysics, logic, ethics and all that related to the social life of man, still lay in chaos, governed by the confusions of thought and language of an earlier and unregenerate age. It is natural, and indeed almost inevitable, that those who had been liberated by the new sciences should seek to apply their methods and principles to a subject which was clearly in even more desperate need of order than the facts of the external world.[1]

"A science of nature had been created; a science of mind had yet to be made."[2] "To all of them the model was that of contemporary physics and mechanics."[3] Underlying this model was the cardinal belief that truth was one, single, harmonious body of knowledge. "But the central dream that all evils could be cured by appropriate technological steps, that there could exist engineers both of human souls and of human bodies, proved delusive."[4]

We must speak of Wesley's relation to the Enlightenment, but we must do so with caution. It is not possible to demonstrate direct reliance of Wesley upon Enlightenment thinkers—although he is clearly aware of and mentions Deists, Bacon, Locke, Newton, Hume, Hartley, Toland, Voltaire, Rousseau, Abbé Raynal, Frances Hutcheson, Lord Kames, and Montesquieu.[5] It is possible, however, to identify themes which are common, emphases which are related, sensitivities which are evident, and issues or problems which are addressed. Wesley's relation to the Enlightenment is more a matter of a shared cultural ethos, and it is important to indicate some of the ways in which Wesley responded to a cultural-intellectual situation which was becoming permeated by Enlightenment sensibilities.

Perhaps the most relevant paragraph is found in his sermon, "The Unity of the Divine Being."

How great is the number of those who, allowing religion to consist of two branches—our duty to God, and our duty to our neighbour —entirely forget the first part, and put the second part for the whole,—for the entire duty of man? Thus almost all men of letters, both in England, France, Germany, yes, and all the civilized countries of Europe, extol *humanity* to the skies, as the very essence of religion. To this the great triumvirate, Rousseau, Voltaire, and David Hume, have contributed all their labours, sparing no pains to establish a religion which should stand on its foundation, independent of any revelation whatever; yes, not supposing even the being of a God. So leaving Him, if he has any being, to himself, they have found out both a religion and a happiness which have no relation at all to God, nor any dependence upon him.[6]

Wesley takes the challenge seriously. Yet this is often overlooked in discussing his theology. An illustration of the failure to take adequate notice of Wesley's relation to the Enlightenment ethos is found in Gerald R. Cragg's introduction to *The Appeals to Men of Reason and Religion and Certain Related Open Letters*. In this introduction Cragg mentions Wesley's unacceptability to "a generation nurtured on John Locke, John Tillotson, and Samuel Clarke."[7] But rather than developing this insight he interprets the *Appeals* exclusively as a response to Wesley's critics from within the church, especially Warburton and Horne. Yet within the broad-gauged sweep of the *Appeals* Wesley is clearly also speaking to non-Christians, to Deists, and to people whose reasoning comports with Enlightenment themes (paras. 12, 28). He develops an epistemology which responds to John Locke's lead (para. 7) as Cragg acknowledges in a footnote on page 57. Wesley's stress on the sinful human condition strikes at foes both within and outside the church (para. 2). He explicitly mentions his opposition to Henry Dodwell, a deist (para. 36). Further he emphasizes the difference which Christian faith makes in the present world, not only in heaven (para. 42). All of this is enough to open the necessity of also seeing Wesley in relation to the Enlightenment, not simply to church opponents. Further, this emphasis of Cragg's runs counter to the evidence in Wesley's Journal where three and perhaps four of the six references to the *Appeals* refer to nonchurchmen—Deists, rational infidels, disavowers of religion—who respond to the *Appeal*.[8] The point is, Cragg continues a tradition of interpreting Wesleyanism as an intrachurch struggle. Much more clearly the interaction needs to be seen as one with a changed cultural-intellectual context. Several aspects of this situation are significant.

1) Because the Wesleyan movement began in the Enlightenment era it was different from the Protestant Reformation of the sixteenth century. The Reformation took place among people who shared basic assumptions; it was a struggle among Christians who were seeking the most adequate statement of Christian understanding and the most faithful mode of Christian living. The Enlightenment, on the contrary, set aside received assumptions, including the reality of God. On the throne of sovereignty it placed the autonomous, rational human being. Consequently, the confrontation for Wesley was not one among Christians but between Christians and an unbelieving world. This fact had several significant consequences.

2) To encounter an unbelieving world, Wesley did not provide a creed, rather he presented a kerygma. It is singularly important that the Wesleyan movement was not built upon a creedal base (this fact has made it difficult for historians of doctrine to know how to deal with this tradition, and especially when these historians come from Reformation traditions there is a tendency to say that Methodism is nondoctrinal—so much for parochial vision). The sermons and *Notes on the New Testament* constitute Wesley's deposit for the future, and these point to a kerygmatic core: Wesley attempted a restoration of apostolic Christianity in the spirit of a new age.

3) The Enlightenment context also affected Wesley's ecumenical attitude. To put the matter directly, when one's opponents are an unbelieving world, one catches the hands of all and any who stand on one's side. The threatening challenge from outside draws together those who share common if not identical commitments. Consequently, Wesley—and especially as he grew older—was catholic, open, and affirmative of other Christians.

4) In anthropology Wesley responded both in opposition to and in agreement with Enlightenment themes. In contrast to the Enlightenment's conviction that human nature is good and that there is a natural religion which is native to all people, Wesley forthrightly emphasized original sin and the destitute character of ordinary human life. On the other side, Wesley's emphasis on Christian perfection may be seen as a variation on a theme which the Enlightenment was reviving. Although Wesley predicated his hope for full salvation on God's grace and not

human attainment, his vision for human life shared a common telos of perfection with Enlightenment hopes.[9]

5) Again, the role which Wesley assigned to human response in the divine-human relationship was affected by the Enlightenment mentality. The Enlightenment emphasis on autonomous, rational humanity required that this be taken into account as neither Luther nor Calvin nor their successors had done. The fact of human freedom and responsibility could not be simply set aside, it must be dealt with. And this Wesley attempted to do as he struggled, often alone, to state his understanding of human ability to participate in redemption.

6) Finally, the effort of the Enlightenment to interpret human life on the model of natural science, especially those of physics and mechanics, was challenged by Wesley. To attempt to construct a science of the human mind on the model of the science of nature, Wesley believed, was wrong. It is important that in his discussion of predestination Wesley attacks the positions of Newton and Hartley. His opposition was to a mechanistic interpretation of distinctly human qualities, and this concern guided his discussion of the relation of human nature to God's grace.

All of these are important consequences of Wesley's being influenced by the Enlightenment. He was confronted by and faced the contemporary world with challenge, appropriation, and proclamation. And these attitudes have come to characterize the movement he fostered. One of the difficulties with deciphering the distinctive qualities of Methodist theology is that it has, and especially in the United State, lived so closely with the environing culture that it always is in danger of absorption, or at least confusion. North American Wesleyan theology, from the time of Asa Shinn and Nathan Bangs, has been engaging in the intellectual challenge of modernity. (The comment has been made that Methodism in the United States has produced more philosophical theology than any other tradition. One reason for this is its determination to engage the modern world.) Because of its sensitivity to its context, Methodism has changed as the context has changed and, again, its tradition is one of continual alteration not repetition (and this has puzzled historians of doctrine).

This leads to a major emphasis: constructive theology in the Wesleyan tradition should be a combination of confessional and apologetic theology. Its history precludes a bifurcation of theological responsibility. Wesleyan theology has found its vitality as it has lived with the tension of holding these two modes of theology together.

Theology and Praxis

Another decisively important characteristic of Wesleyan theology is its practical character. Theology, for John Wesley and much of the Wesleyan tradition, has been reflection for the enhancement of practice. Praxis is integral to theology as practical divinity. This is a critical issue, for in this tradition theology has not been, initially, an elitist or specialized task (early Methodist education was not ministerial education, and in this it represented a new movement in North American church education). Rather it grew immediately out of concrete life and functioned in services of mission. Theology was the thought of the living Christian community—it is difficult to overestimate the potential importance of the idea of "Christian conference" which Wesley included in the means of grace and which functioned in groups as small as bands and as large as annual conferences. The principle was that theology was undertaken as a Christian body and underwrote the service of that body. Wesleyan theology today is challenged to recover this largely lost character (lost to scholarly specialization and separate existential setting), namely, once again to become practical, to find its life in the life of the concrete Christian community, to acknowledge its social, economic, and cultural situation, and to accept its place among the community of believers, hearing diverse voices, responding to diverse needs.

Concrete life awareness calls forth ethical responsibility. The integral role which ethics plays in theological construction is distinctive of the Wesleyan tradition. In Wesley himself it is possible to argue that his social ethics derives from his theology (V. Schneeberger) or that his theology issues from his social engagement (M. Marquardt). This illustrates the close interweaving of the two in his thought and life. Social ethics has also been prominent in continuing Methodist doctrine and activity, and this helps to account for the fact that Methodist theology has been amenable to the social gospel and now to liberation theology.

It is also obvious that personal ethics has been prominent in this tradition. One of the remarkable facts is the number of theologians who have also written on ethics issues and were engaged as well in ethical activity. The pietistic and holiness streams have had a clear effect on the style of Wesleyan thought and spiritual life. And this should be remembered and honored as an important characteristic.

This theme leads into the Wesleyan tradition's understanding of the church in mission. It is remarkable how often Asbury claimed that Methodist preachers were "apostolic men." This implies not only a legitimacy to their ministry but a responsibility for carrying the gospel.

We have already stated that John Wesley gave his followers the mandate for proclaiming the kerygma, to be preachers of the the saving Word. So intense was this concern that Martin Schmidt has claimed that Wesley more thoroughly than anyone else in church history has stressed the fact that the church is mission. Whether or not this claim is wholly accurate, it does reinforce the theological praxis which is characteristic of the Wesleyan tradition.

Implications

There are several implications which flow directly from these comments.

1), The Wesleyan tradition has provided bases not conclusions, for constructive theology. There is a distinctiveness about the Wesleyan tradition, as we have mentioned, but there has never been—in its origination or continuation—a singular concentration upon its own unique emphases. Wesleyanism is, in fact and intention, Christian faith which acknowledges indebtedness to the widest Christian tradition. Nevertheless, there is validity in emphasizing the distinctiveness of the Wesleyan tradition in order to provide focus for some important continuing themes of Christian witness. At our best we attempt to express the integrity while also acknowledging and honoring the sincerity of other Christian traditions and while living in hope of inclusive Christian witness through life and word.

2), There is an order of importance held by this tradition to which God in Christ is primary as this is witnessed to by the Scriptures. From this there follows, not in sequential order but in multiple relationships, awareness of the world, of ethics, and mission. Methodist theology may be described as reflection upon the formation of life authored by Jesus Christ and continuing under the aegis of the Holy Spirit in the actual conditions of human living.

There has been no direct discussion in this paper of the quadilateral which has become symbolic of United Methodist theology. The quadilateral does point to the inclusive potential within this tradition, but the formula is so comprehensive in character and so general in scope that it is only as there is clearly structured priority and nuanced interrelation that it can contribute to theological construction. The quadilateral formula, as such, does not provide distinctive content or particular character to developed theological statement.

3), The Wesleyan theological tradition continues to be vital and ongoing; it is open and challenging. The resources which it has bequeathed are promising for theologians who accept the persistent task of interpreting the Christian faith. Because of its character, this tradition is best served, not by antiquarians, but by those who transpose inheritance into fresh creativity.

NOTES

1. Isaiah Berlin, ed., *The Age of Enlightenment: The 18th Century Philosophers* (New York: Mentor Books, 1956), p. 15.
2. Ibid., p. 16.
3. Ibid., p. 18.
4. Ibid., p. 29.
5. Some illustrations of Wesley's comments about these persons all add color to his thought. Voltaire, "Never was a more consummate coxcomb!" (*Works*, vol. 4, p. 287). "Did Mr. David Hume . . . know the heart of man? No more than a worm or a beetle does" (*Works*, vol. 7, p. 342). Rousseau, "a shallow, but supercilious Infidel, two degrees below Voltaire." (*Works*, vol. 4, p. 16).
6. *Works*, VII, 270-71.
7. Wesley, *Works* (Oxford), vol. 11, p. 10.
8. See esp. references in Wesley's *Journal* to Nov. 20, 1745, Jan. 6, 1748, and Sept. 20, 1748. It should be noted that *A Further Appeal* is more directly an answer to critics within the church, while the first *Appeal* carries one into the wider and critically important Enlightenment intellectual context.
9. Cf. Frank E. Manuel, ed., *The Enlightenment* (Englewood Cliffs, N. J.: Prentice-Hall, 1965), pp. 4-5. It should be commented that Wesley's retention of the emphasis on individual will as the source of sin, in contradistinction to social or contextual causes, constituted both a gain and a loss for his interpretation of Christian faith.

III. Process Theology and Wesleyan Thought

1. PROCESS THEOLOGY
AND THE
WESLEYAN WITNESS

Schubert M. Ogden

Among the stated purposes of the Bicentennial Theological Consultation is "to explore the affinities between the Methodist heritage and some of the most creative trends in contemporary theology and ethics." The assumption of this paper is that at least one of the things that could be reasonably called process theology sufficiently qualifies as just such a creative trend to justify exploring the affinities between it and the distinctively Wesleyan tradition of Christian witness.

Before we proceed with this exploration, however, it is important to be clear about some basic presuppositions. In assuming, as I do, that the process theology of which I speak is among the creative trends in contemporary theology and ethics, I naturally presuppose a certain understanding of Christian theology. According to the familiar analysis of "theology" as *logos* about *theos*, or thought and speech about God, Christian theology might be supposed to include all such thought and speech about God as is appropriate to the Christian witness of faith. But while there is certainly precedent for this very broad understanding of "Christian theology," it has long since come to be used more strictly to refer, not to all Christian thought and speech about God, but only to such as are involved in critically reflecting on Christian thinking and speaking more generally. Recognizing this, I myself use the term "Christian witness" to designate all Christian thought and speech about God (as well as the rest of Christian praxis) simply as such, thereby reserving "Christian theology" to be used in this stricter sense. Accordingly, I define the proper meaning of the second term as either the process or the product of critical reflection on the validity claims expressed or implied by Christian witness.

Any act of Christian witness, just like any other act of human praxis, necessarily implies, even if it may not express, certain claims to validity—for example, to the meaningfulness of what is said, to the sincerity of the speaker in saying it, to the truth of his or her assertions, or to the rightness of the norms regulative of his or her actions (Habermas: 174-79). Moreover, every act of

Christian witness expresses or implies a distinctive claim to validity—namely, the two-fold claim to be at once appropriate to what is normatively Christian and credible in terms of common human experience and reason. But this claim is obviously problematic in its one aspect as well as in the other, sharp differences between Christians themselves, rendering the appropriateness of their respective witnesses clearly questionable, and the even sharper differences between Christians and other interpreters of human existence, serving only to cast doubt on the credibility of any of their conflicting interpretations. Thus, by its very nature, the primary level of praxis of which Christian witness is a part creates the need for the secondary level of reflection that is Christian theology. For it is only by the process of critically reflecting on witness in the way theology has the task of doing that the problematic claim to validity such witness expresses or implies can ever be confirmed.

Given this understanding of Christian theology, the assumption that process theology is one of the creative trends in contemporary theology and ethics implies at least this: Process theology is one way of critically reflecting on Christian witness so as to validate its claim to be both appropriate and credible. I stress that the only process theology I myself have ever had any interest in doing is simply a certain way of doing Christian theology in this full sense of the word. While I should not question that some so-called process theologies are quite properly taken to be only or primarily philosophical—either because they are not Christian theologies at all—being instead a new form of natural theology—or else because their main contributions are to the philosophical rather than the historical or exegetical tasks of Christian theology—still process theology, in the only sense that I am willing to accept as proper, refers to a certain kind of Christian theology, and hence to critical reflection on the appropriateness as well as the credibility of Christian witness.

As for the other term, "the Wesleyan witness," its meaning, too, should be clearer now that some of my presuppositions have been clarified. I

Reprinted by permission of the *Perkins Journal.*

speak of "Wesleyan witness" instead of simply "Wesleyan thought," because I take "witness" to be appropriately the more inclusive term, covering not only speech and thought but everything else in Christian praxis. As such, it designates one important strand within the larger tradition of Christian witness that furnishes the privileged data for Christian theological reflection. Of course, there neither are nor can be any privileged data when it comes to assessing claims to credibility. By its very nature, any such claim is a universal claim, and any datum that is at all logically relevant to assessing its validity must be equally relevant with every other. But in assessing claims to appropriateness, a religious tradition is self-differentiating in assigning to some of its elements a normative authority over some or all of the others, some of the data it furnishes has a more or less privileged status in assessing any claim to be appropriate to its witness. Even so, for the Christian theologian, and hence also for the process theologian, the data furnished by any one strand of witness, such as the Wesleyan, do not and cannot have a primary normative authority. Whatever their authority for Christians who stand within this strand of tradition, they are but one of any number of such strands on whose appropriateness Christian theology has the task of critically reflecting by reference to the sole primary norm of the apostolic witness.

The other thing to note about the distinction I presuppose between witness and theology is that it is a relative, not an absolute, distinction. Just as in general the products of reflection may be integrated into contexts of praxis, thereby becoming part of the data for later reflection, so the products of theological reflection may be integrated into the contexts of Christian praxis, and thus become part of the witness on whose claim to validity subsequent theology has the task of critically reflecting (Habermas and Luhmann: 115, n. 20).

If what has been said to this point is important for understanding the argument of the paper, it is nevertheless extremely formal and at best preliminary to the exploration we have proposed to conduct. I have said that process theology is a certain kind of Christian theology, or a certain way of doing Christian theology, understood as critical reflection on the claim that is expressed or implied by Christian witness to be both appropriate and credible. But just what kind of Christian theology is process theology, and how exactly does it reflect on this distinctively Christian claim to validity? The answer to these questions may be given in two steps: first, by formally identifying process theology, and then, second, by materially describing it.

We may say formally that process theology is the kind of Christian theology that employs the insights, concepts, and methods of process philosophy and that it is in this way that it reflects on both the appropriateness and the credibility of Christian witness. By "philosophy" in general, I should explain, I mean a more or less reflective self-understanding that is comprehensive in scope and generally secular rather than specifically religious in constitution. As such, it properly includes, although it is not exhausted by, both a metaphysics and an ethics, by which I understand both a theory of ultimate reality in its structure in itself and a theory of how we ought to act and what we ought to do, given the structure of ultimate reality and its meaning for us. Thus, in speaking of process philosophy, I mean just such a reflective, comprehensive, and secular understanding of existence together with the metaphysical and ethical theories that explicate its necessary implications. And in formally identifying process theology as employing the insights, concepts, and methods of process philosophy, I intend to say that it is in terms of this self-understanding and these theories that it critically reflects on the meaning and truth of Christian witness.

Yet since even this is only a formal identification of process theology, we must take the second step of materially describing it. This we may do, obviously, by means of a material description of the distinctive self-understanding of process philosophy as well as of the metaphysics and ethics that it necessarily implies. But it is equally obvious that there are certain difficulties with any such description. Aside from the fact that limitations of space increase the risk of oversimplification, what is to be rightly taken as the sources of a normative concept of process philosophy and how these sources are to be correctly interpreted are both controversial questions among those who may fairly claim the expertise prerequisite to answering them. Notwithstanding these difficulties, however, the exploration we are now conducting requires that we attempt at least a summary description of the process philosophy in whose terms the process theology expressed by this paper seeks to carry out its task as Christian theology.

For this kind of philosophy, to be a self is not merely to be continually becoming, but also to exist, in the emphatic sense in which "existence" means that one is consciously aware of one's becoming and, within the limits of one's situation, responsible for it. Thus one is aware, above all, of one's real, internal relatedness—not only to one's own ever-changing past and future, but also to a many-leveled community of others similarly caught up in time and change and, together with them, to the all-inclusive whole of reality itself. But one is also aware, relative to this same whole of reality, of one's own essential fragmentariness and of the equally essential fragmentariness of all others. With respect to both time and space, the whole alone is essentially integral and nonfragmentary, having neither beginning nor end and lacking any external environment. This is not to say, however, that the whole of reality is experienced as mere unchanging being, in every respect infinite and absolute. On the contrary, insofar as the whole is neither merely abstract nor a sheer aggregate, it must be like the self and anything else comparably concrete and singular in being an instance of becoming, or an ordered sequence of such instances, which as such is always finite in contrast to the infinite realm of possibility and relative and not absolute in its real, internal relations to others.

On the self-understanding distinctive of this philosophy, then, to be human is to live as a fragment, albeit a self-conscious and, therefore, responsible fragment, of the integral whole of reality as such. In other words, for this philosophy, the meaning of ultimate reality for us demands that we accept both our own becoming and the becomings of all others as parts of this ultimate whole and then, by serving as best we can the transient goods of all the parts, to make the greatest possible contribution to the enduring good of the whole.

As for the metaphysics that this self-understanding implies, it is in every sense antidualistic, being in one sense monistic, in another sense a qualified pluralism. It is monistic in the sense that it recognizes but one transcendental concept, or one set of such concepts, in which anything that is fully concrete and singular can and must be described. Thus for process metaphysics there are not many but only one kind of ultimate subjects of predication; and no difference between one such ultimate subject and another amounts to an absolute difference in kind, whether it be a merely finite difference between one and another part of reality or even the infinite difference between the inclusive whole of reality and any of its included parts. Even the integral whole of reality as something concrete and singular is either an instance of becoming or an individual sequence of such instances in the same sense in which this may be said of any other thing that is more than a mere abstraction or aggregate. This explains, of course, why *the* transcendental concept for such a metaphysics is precisely "process," in the sense

that to be anything concretely and singularly real in the full sense of the words is to be an instance of becoming: an emergent unity of real, internal relatedness to all the things that have already become in the past, which then gives itself along with them to all the other such emergent unities that are yet to become in the future.

But if process metaphysics is in this way attributively monistic, it is nonetheless substantively pluralistic, even if in a qualified sense. This is the case insofar as it recognizes not one but many ultimate subjects of predication. Although anything fully concrete and singular is an instance of becoming of ultimately the same kind as any other, there are any number of such instances, each an emergent unity of real, internal relatedness ontologically distinct from all the others. Above all, there is the unique ontological distinction between the self and others as all mere parts of reality, on the one hand, and the one all-inclusive whole of reality, on the other. Even as each fragmentary becoming is ontologically distinct from every other, so each of them severally and all of them together are ontologically distinct from the integral becoming of the whole. And yet, as I have said, the distinction between part and whole is unique; and this means that the pluralism of process metaphysics, real as it certainly is, is also qualified. Although "part" and "whole" are indeed correlative concepts in that each necessarily implies the other, the symmetry between their two referents presupposes an even more fundamental asymmetry between them. For while there could not be an integral becoming of the whole without the fragmentary becomings of the parts, what the whole as such necessarily implies is not *this part or that* (since all of its parts, unlike itself, are merely contingent rather than necessary), but only *some part or other*—or, if you wish to put it so, that the intensional class of parts have at least some members and thus not be a null class. On the other hand, what each and every fragmentary becoming necessarily implies is not merely *some whole or other* (since the idea of more than one whole of reality is patently incoherent), but rather the *one and only necessarily existing whole*— the one integral becoming of which all fragmentary becomings are contingent parts and but for which none of them would be so much as even possible (Hartshorne, 1967: 64-65).

This brings us to the ethics of process philosophy, which, like its metaphysics, is thoroughly antidualistic. By this I mean that it recognizes at most a relative, not an absolute, difference between self-interest and interest in others and between how we are to act and what we are to do toward the others who, being consciously aware of their becomings, are insofar on the same level as ourselves, and how we are to act and what we are to do toward all those whose becomings take place at some lower, unconscious level (Hartshorne, 1970: 198 ff.). Because even self-interest is in its way an interest in others—namely, in one's own past or future instances of becoming—and because all instances of becoming that can be affected by how we act and what we do are attributively one even if substantively many, there is only one ethical principle, or one set of such principles, governing the whole of our moral life, whether this be spoken of, as I am speaking of it here, in terms of "judgments of obligation," or, alternatively, in terms of either "judgments of virtue" or "judgments of value" (Carney: 429). Of course, our moral acts themselves, if not also the modes of our action, must be differently specified in the different situations in which we are required to act and in relation to the different others and levels of others for whom we are responsible. But for a process ethics of obligation the one thing we are obliged to do in every situation and in relation to every other is to realize as fully as we can the intrinsic good that lies in each and every instance of becoming (Hartshorne, 1976).

This means, among other things, that there is always a specifically political aspect to our moral responsibility. This is so, at any rate, if "politics" is taken in a broad sense as having to do, not only with the formation of specific structures of government and the state, but with the formation and transformation of structures of order generally. Because all becoming, and hence the realization of all intrinsic good, necessarily presupposes an order more or less permissive of emergent unities of real, internal relatedness to others, one can promote the optimal realization of intrinsic good at all levels of becoming only by forming appropriate structures of social and cultural order (320 ff.).

So much, then, by way of a summary description of what I take to be properly meant by "process philosophy." Inadequate as it certainly is, it should be sufficient to mediate a material description of the process theology whose affinities with the Wesleyan witness we are concerned to explore. In other words, it should now be clear that such of the distinctive characteristics of process theology as warrant so speaking of it at all derive from the fact that it is in terms of the self-understanding and of the metaphysics and ethics that have just been described that it critically reflects on the meaning and the truth of Christian witness.

Proceeding with our exploration, we must now make a parallel effort to get beyond the merely preliminary clarification of the other term, "the Wesleyan witness." All that has been said so far to clarify this term is that it designates an important strand within the larger tradition of Christian witness on which any Christian theology, including process theology, has the task of critically reflecting. But, once again, we need to ask just what strand of tradition the Wesleyan witness is and exactly how it expresses the common witness of the Christian community. And here, too, we may answer our questions in two steps: first, by identifying the Wesleyan witness formally and then, second, by essaying a material description of it.

The first step is easy enough, and we may formally identify the Wesleyan witness by saying simply that it is the testimony borne by the community of faith and witness that originates with John Wesley and that the way in which it expresses the common witness of the Christian church is in accordance with the norms that are authoritative for this particular community. But here again there are obvious difficulties in taking the second step of materially describing the Wesleyan witness. Not only do the same limits of space compel one so to simplify as to risk distortion, but there are also analogous and equally controversial questions about what is rightly understood to be normative in Wesleyan Christianity and about the correct interpretation of its norms. Moreover, whether I may fairly claim to have the expertise necessary to answer these questions is even more uncertain than in the case of the earlier questions about process philosophy. Even so, there is no way to continue our exploration without attempting a material description, however summary and inadequate, of the distinctively Wesleyan form of Christian witness.

We may begin this description by directly addressing the question of what is rightly taken to be normative for the Christian community that traces its origin to Wesley. According to Thomas Langford, who has recently discussed this question in a thoughtful way, the Methodist tradition "cannot be understood by exclusive appeal to Wesley. Although Methodism cannot be understood apart from John Wesley, it also cannot be understood except as it has moved beyond Wesley. . . . Today the Wesleyan tradition is the result of its inclusive history. . . . Beginning with Wesley, it did not stop with Wesley—this is one important mark of this tradition" (260 f.). Having said this, however, Langford goes on to accept an analogy that C. K.

Barrett cites from the work of Helmut Flender: "Just as Paul, in faithfulness, not unfaithfulness, to Jesus, had in a new generation to say things that Jesus had not said, so Luke, in a third generation, had, in faithfulness to Paul, to say things Paul had not said" (261). If Langford's own statements might seem to imply that what is normative in the Wesleyan witness includes considerably more than Wesley himself, this is hardly the implication of his acceptance of Flender's analogy. On the contrary, if one applies this analogy as he presumably intends it, it is precisely faithfulness, not unfaithfulness, to Wesley that must alone finally decide whether or not any of the things that have been said by those who have followed him are normatively a part of the Wesleyan tradition.

My position is that it is just so that one ought to apply the analogy and that one rightly takes Wesley's own witness of faith to be the sole primary norm for all specifically Wesleyan witness. This is in no way to question, however, that there is indeed more to the Wesleyan tradition than simply Wesley. It lies in the very nature of a normative witness that it cannot possibly function as such except by being continually reinterpreted in each new situation. This means that there may be all sorts of things that must be said beyond anything said in the primary norm, depending on the extent of the change from the old situation to the new. Assuming, then, that there has indeed been change—in some respects, vast change—between Wesley's situation and those of his followers in the Methodist tradition, one would naturally expect that they have had to say things that he not only did not say but could not have said and that at least some of these things, also, have been and perhaps still are normative for the Wesleyan witness. To this extent, one can only agree with Langford that the Methodist tradition, even in the normative sense of the words, "cannot be understood by exclusive appeal to Wesley." This in no way alters the fact, however, that it is Wesley's witness alone that constitutes the Methodist tradition as a normative tradition and that it is always only by proving its faithfulness to this primary norm that any claim to stand in this tradition can finally be validated.

For this reason, we need only to look to Wesley's own testimony to complete a material description of the Wesleyan witness. Even then, of course, there remains the risk of oversimplification, and few points of interpretation are beyond controversy. But without minimizing such difficulties, I believe one may describe the Wesleyan witness sufficiently for our purposes by singling out three of the defining characteristics of Wesley's witness of faith.

First of all, his witness is characterized by a faithful restatement of catholic Christianity as recovered and reinterpreted by the Protestant Reformers. With good reason, I believe, Albert Outler has ventured to describe Wesley's distinctive doctrinal perspective as "evangelical catholicism" (Outler [ed.]: viii). For not only was the immediate source of his witness the tradition of Anglican divinity deriving from the English Reformation, but its "deeper wellspring," as Outler puts it, was the interpretation of the biblical witness by the Fathers of the ancient church, in whose thought and piety Wesley discovered what he came to regard as "the normative pattern of catholic Christianity" (viii, 122, 9). At the same time, if I were to point to a single bias in many of the more recent interpretations of Wesley's witness, it would be the tendency to differentiate it far too sharply from that of the continental Reformers. Such a tendency is apparent to the point of caricature, in my opinion, in Theodore Runyon's comparison of Wesley and Luther in his introduction to *Sanctification and Liberation* (9-48, 225-28). But even from as generally fair and balanced an interpretation as Langford's, one would never guess that the *particula exclusiva* of the Reformers has anything like the prominence in Wesley's own formulations that it actually has.

My point, of course, is not to suggest that Wesley's witness would be even more adequately described simply as "evangelicalism." But if I have no doubt that his Christianity is substantively catholic, I am equally certain of this in the case of Luther and Calvin (Pelikan). In him, even as in them, what is recovered and reinterpreted by the rediscovery of the gospel, and hence by *sola scriptura* and *solus Christus*, *sola gratia*, and *sola fide*, is the faith and witness of the early catholic church. This explains, among other things, why, like them, he everywhere assumes the authority of the Nicene dogma of the triunity of God and the Chalcedonian dogma of the two natures of the one person Jesus Christ.

On the other hand, it is equally characteristic of Wesley's witness that these dogmas, along with other conserving articles of faith, are not so much made thematic in it as presupposed by it. Thus, while he does indeed restate classical Christology and soteriology—albeit in terms that, in important respects, are his own (Deschner)—the center of his witness is the constituting article of salvation by grace through faith alone, which he knows Luther to have spoken of as the *articulus stantis vel cadentis ecclesiae* and the English Reformers to have called "the strong rock and foundation of the Christian religion" (Sugden [ed]: 1:50). Centering on this one theme of "salvation by faith," his preaching and teaching are typically concerned with such other evangelical themes as original sin, the use of the law, the necessity of repentance and good works, and, most distinctively of all, Christian perfection.

No doubt one reason for this "existential concentration," if I may so speak of it, is that Wesley is, above all, an evangelist whose divinity is a "practical divinity" immediately directed toward the decision of Christian faith and the formation of Christian life. But if he is therefore rightly classified as a "folk-theologian," rather than as one of "the great speculative theologians" of the front rank, one need not suppose that this is the only reason for so classifying him (Outler [ed.]: 119). It is arguable, I believe, that the deeper reason for the distinctive style of his theology, very much as for that of Luther's, is his firm theoretical grasp of the existential character of Christian faith and witness, which always have to do, not with the being of God in itself, but with the meaning of God for us, and hence also with our own self-understanding and praxis. But whatever the reason for it, a second characteristic of Wesleyan witness equally defining with the first is that his evangelical restatement of catholic Christianity is ever so much more practical and existential than speculative and metaphysical.

The third characteristic defining his witness is closely related to the second—namely, its distinctive stress within its overall existential concentration on the power of God's love in Christ to overcome the power of sin over the future as well as the guilt of sin from the past. It is just this stress, of course, that comes to expression in Christian perfection's being, as we noted, the most distinctive theme of Wesley's witness. But taking the full measure of this is not to be lightly assumed. If Langford is certainly correct that "the centering theme of Wesley's thought was grace, expressed in Jesus Christ and conveyed to individuals by the Holy Spirit," it is nevertheless important to bring out (more clearly, in my opinion, than Langford does) the distinctive nature of grace as Wesley conceives it—as always sanctifying as well as justifying, the ground of "real" as well as of "relative" change in human existence (Langford: 260). To be sure, one will not want to highlight the distinctiveness of Wesley's view by suppressing his own insistence that "faith is the condition, and the only condition, of sanctification, exactly as it is of justification" and by then contrasting it with a mere caricature of the views of the Reformers—

for example, by claiming that "for Luther . . . justification provides the substructure for heaven and our relationship with God—but not for our life in this world, which is left to be dealt with on grounds other than faith" (Sugden [ed.]: 2:453; Runyon [ed.]: 36). But as surely as one must acknowledge that Wesley's understanding of grace and salvation is—and is intended to be—entirely in accord with the real views of the Reformers, one will as little want to miss its distinctive emphasis on the transforming effect of God's love received through faith. As Wesley consistently understands the matter, to trust in the gift of God's love, and so to accept God's prevenient acceptance of us, is always to enjoy not only freedom from the *guilt* of sin and forgiveness of the past but also—and as he insists, "at the same time . . . , yea, in that very moment"—freedom from the *power* of sin and openness for the future (Sugden [ed]: 2:446).

These, then, are what seem to me to be the chief defining characteristics of Wesley's witness and, therefore, what may be properly taken as defining the entire tradition of witness of which his is the source. At best, of course, what emerges from such a summary is only the primary norm of this tradition, as distinct from all the secondary attempts, more or less successful, to reinterpret this norm in succeeding situations. But if I am right that it is Wesley's witness alone that is primarily normative for this tradition, what finally measures the success of any of these attempts, alone making it part of the Wesleyan witness, is that it, too, in its own time and place restates the catholic witness to God as recovered and reinterpreted by the Reformation and, within its existential concentration on the meaning of God for us, so expresses this witness as to point, above all, to the life-transforming power of God's love.

It is time now to complete our exploration by identifying certain affinities between the Wesleyan witness thus understood and process theology as it was previously described. I shall briefly consider six such affinities, some of which are more or less clearly implied by what has been said, others of which will require us, in effect, to extend our description of one or both of our two subjects. It is well to recall at the outset some of the more formal points with which we began, so as to keep in mind throughout the discussion that, although the distinction between theology and witness is relative and not absolute, all the affinities are such as are possible between a certain kind of Christian theology and a certain strand of Christian witness, on whose meaning and truth this theology, like any other, is supposed to be the critical reflection.

1. Not the least reason for characterizing the Wesleyan witness as, in its way, "catholic" is its explicit claim for the essential reasonableness of Christianity. To be sure, Langford is entirely justified in holding that Wesley's interpreters and successors, until recently, at least, have by and large followed his lead in acknowledging Scripture as the sole primary authority for Christian witness and theology (25 f., 264 f.). But if this acknowledgment has always sharply distinguished the Wesleyan witness from mere rationalism, it has certainly never warranted the adoption of sheer fideism. On the contrary, from Wesley on it has generally been interpreted as certainly compatible with, if not also demanding, the insistence that Christian witness is thoroughly reasonable (Cragg [ed.]: 43-90). In this, one may venture to believe, the Wesleyan tradition, like the catholic tradition more generally, rightly lays claim to the authority of Scripture. For the striking thing about Scripture is that it nowhere appeals to itself as the sufficient ground for the credibility of its claims, but points rather to God's decisive revelation and to prophetic or apostolic experience of this revelation as its explicit primal source. Furthermore, it does not point even to this revelation or to such immediate experience of revelation as alone supporting the credibility of its claims, but assumes instead that its claims are credible because they represent explicitly and decisively the same existential truth that is implicitly present in all human experience and reflection (Ogden, 1976: 413).

But be this as it may, insofar as the Wesleyan witness is explicit in claiming that what it says is in principle credible in rational terms, there is a close affinity between it and process theology— as well as, naturally, any other Christian theology that likewise accepts the responsibility of establishing the credibility of Christian witness in terms of common human experience and reason.

2. To say only this, however, is to assert an affinity between the Wesleyan witness and a general type of Christian theology, not process theology in particular. And there is another affinity that is very similar, in that it does indeed obtain between this witness and process theology, but hardly process theology alone. Perhaps the simplest way to formulate this affinity is to say that, while there is an important sense in which both the Wesleyan witness and process theology have their primal source in human experience, the experience in question is in both cases other and more than our external sense perception of ourselves and the world.

To put it this way, however, is not to affirm but to deny that in either case the only sense in which one can meaningfully talk about the primal source of one's witness or theology is to speak of human experience. If both cases are agreed that experience is indeed the *noetic* source of all our thought and speech about God, whether more spontaneous or more reflected, they also agree that the *ontic* source of our witness and theology is revelation: both the original revelation implied by Wesley's fundamental doctrine of "prevenient grace" and the decisive revelation through Jesus Christ that constitutes Christian existence (Ogden, 1975). In other words, process theology and the Wesleyan witness alike are objectivist not subjectivist in their understandings of experience, in that they both take it to be a primal source of our thought and speech only insofar as it is also a dependent source.

But where they are also alike is in clearly distinguishing the experience of revelation from what we ordinarily call "experience." Thus process theology contrasts the *existential* experience involved in understanding ourselves, the world, and God from the *empirical* experience involved in perceiving others and ourselves by means of our senses. Wesley, on the other hand, draws a similar contrast by way of qualifying the general empiricist dictum that "our ideas are not innate, but must all originally come from our senses." There is a difference in kind, he holds, between "external sensation" through your "natural senses," which are "altogether incapable of discerning objects of a spiritual kind," and "internal sensation" through your "spiritual senses," which are "exercised to discern spiritual good and evil." Consequently, "till you have these internal senses, till the eyes of your understanding are opened, you can have no apprehension of divine things, no idea of them at all" (Cragg [ed.]: 56 f.).

At this point also, then, the Wesleyan witness has a definite affinity with process theology. And yet, as I have said, process theology is hardly the only theology for which this could be claimed. A more than merely empirical understanding of experience is widely represented in recent philosophy, and a number of theologies employing the insights, concepts, and methods of different contemporary philosophies—from process philosophy and radical empiricism to existentialism and phenomenology—are all more or less similar (Ogden, 1969; 76-88). But if process theology is not unique in its understanding of experience, the affinity between it and the Wesleyan witness still seems to be close. In fact, except for "transcendental" theologies like Karl Rahner's and Bernard Lonergan's, it may be the only contemporary theology in which experience at its deepest level is conceived to have the same unrestricted scope that it presumably has for Wesley.

3. There is a further point, however, where the uniqueness of process theology is generally allowed even when it is compared with such other revisionary theologies as Lonergan's and Rahner's, with which it otherwise has much in common. I refer to the understanding of God or, more exactly, of God, self, and the world that process theology has elaborated in terms of the metaphysical theory of process philosophy.

A distinctive feature of this understanding is its interpretation of "God" as properly referring to the strictly universal individual, and hence to the integral whole of reality, whose many parts are properly designated respectively as "self" and "the world." If such an interpretation is monistic enough to bear a certain resemblance to pantheism, it is nevertheless distinctively different from positions that have been traditionally so identified. By distinguishing with process philosophy between the abstract identity of the whole as the one individual sequence of integral becomings and the concrete reality of these becomings, each in itself and as an ordered sequence, process theology is able to assert the sole necessary existence of God in contrast to the radical contingency of everything else, thereby maintaining the unique ontological distinction between God, on the one hand, and self and the world, on the other. To this extent, it is undoubtedly more like traditional theism than any form of traditional pantheism, although the pluralism it asserts in thus distinguishing God from self and the world is like that of the Metaphysical theory whose terms it employs in being a qualified pluralism. God is indeed asserted to be ontologically distinct from everything else, but everything other than God, whether self or the world, is held to be absolutely dependent on God, while God is only relatively dependent on it, being dependent for neither existence nor essential identity but solely for the becoming of God's own enduring good insofar as it is internally as well as externally related to the becoming of all transient goods.

My contention is that it is just such a qualified pluralism as process theology explicitly asserts that is necessarily implied by the Wesleyan witness, and specifically by its distinctive stress on both divine and human agency. If there can be no question that this witness is in entire agreement with the Protestant Reformers in affirming that we are saved by grace alone through faith alone, it nevertheless sharply breaks with a monergistic understanding of grace according to which faith is so created in us by God's act that we are saved without any free and responsible action of our own. The question, however, is whether Wesley's clear rejection of such monergism warrants the familiar interpretations of his position as synergism (Outler [ed.]: 14, 16, 30, 119; Runyon [ed.]: 28). My answer is that if a Wesleyan understanding of grace and freedom is properly described as "synergistic," it is so only in the sense in which process theology's understanding of God and the self may be said to be "pluralistic," which is to say, it is at most a qualified synergism that asserts a certain symmetry between grace and freedom only by presupposing an even more fundamental asymmetry between them. Thus it asserts that there is indeed a difference between God's gracious acceptance of all things and our faithful acceptance of God's acceptance, which is our own free and responsible act and not any act of God's. But it also presupposes that, whereas God would be God and would be a gracious God even if we had never existed, we could not so much as possibly exist, much less exist in faith, except for the radical prevenience of God's grace.

In sum: if the Wesleyan understanding of grace and freedom is synergistic, it nevertheless bears enough of a resemblance to monergism to imply a metaphysical understanding of God and the self that, like process theology's, is only a qualified pluralism.

4. Another feature of process theology's understanding of God, self, and the world is closely related—namely, its interpretation of the meaning of God for us as the gift and the demand of boundless love and of our authentic self-understanding, accordingly, as essentially involving an active moment of loyalty to the demand of God's love as well as a passive moment of trust in its gift. Whether talk about God's love is construed as a proper metaphysical analogy or is frankly accepted as only a symbol, it is not meaningful talk at all unless the structure of God in itself involves real, internal relatedness to others. This is so, at any rate, if "love" is understood in its ordinary sense as referring, first of all, to the acceptance of others and then, secondly, to action toward others on the basis of such acceptance. Clearly, to accept others as love does is to be really, internally related to them; and not to be so related to them is not to love them at all, even in an analogical or merely symbolic sense of the word. Conversely, to conceive God, as process theology does, as the integral whole of reality that in its very structure is eminently relative as well as eminently absolute, is to do all that a

theology has to do metaphysically in order to provide the basis for at least symbolic talk of God's love.

The primary meaning of such talk, however, is existential, rather than metaphysical, in that it expresses the meaning of God for us, thereby authorizing the authentic understanding of ourselves and others in relation to the whole. Thus, in speaking of the gift of God's boundless love, process theology represents the integral whole of reality as authorizing an existence in unconditional trust. Because the whole of reality is eminently absolute as well as eminently relative, it can be trusted without condition, not only to establish structures of cosmic order permissive of the optimal becoming of self and the world, but also to redeem their fragmentary becomings from the futility of sheer transience by accepting them unconditionally into its own everlasting becoming. With this in mind, process theology affirms with the Protestant Reformers that we are saved by grace alone through faith alone, in the sense that it is solely by trusting in God's love alone in all its absoluteness that we can realize our authentic existence as selves in the world.

But process theology also speaks of the demand of God's boundless love, thereby representing the same integral whole of reality as authorizing an existence in unconditional loyalty. Because the whole of reality is eminently relative as well as eminently absolute, it should be loyally served without condition, all the transient goods of self and the world being included in its own enduring good. Recognizing this, process theology also affirms—and, again, the Reformers—that the faith through which we alone are saved is an active faith that works by love, in the sense that it is only by loyally serving God's love in all its relativity that we can continue in the authentic existence that has its basis in trust.

In all of this, however, there is undoubtedly the closest affinity between process theology and the Wesleyan witness. This is clear not only from the existential concentration of this witness on the meaning of God for us, and thus on our own authentic existence, but also, and, above all, from Wesley's double insistence that faith is the only condition of justification and sanctification alike and that good works are necessary to salvation (Sugden [ed.]: 2:444-60). If interpreters of Wesley continue to regard this insistence as paradoxical, and, therefore, commonly tend to compose the paradox by tacitly introducing qualifications, there is not the slightest evidence, so far as I am aware, that he himself ever so regarded it. On the contrary, he constantly proceeds as though the two parts of the insistence naturally belong together, the only unnatural thing to his mind being the suppression of either of them by missing the point of the other.

The reason for this, I submit, is that Wesley is exactly like the process theologian in interpreting our authentic existence as essentially involving an active as well as a passive moment. If he himself characteristically speaks of these moments as "love" and "faith," thereby taking "faith" narrowly as referring to trust but not loyalty, he nevertheless everywhere assumes the teaching of the Edwardian Homilies that "that faith which bringeth [not forth repentance but] either evil works or no good works is not a right, pure and living faith, but a dead and devilish one, as St. Paul and St. James call it" (Outler [ed.]: 128). Verbal differences aside, then, the Wesleyan witness and process theology express essentially the same understanding of human authenticity: as passive acceptance of the gift of God's love as the sole ultimate ground of all reality and meaning and, on the basis of this acceptance, active obedience to the demand of God's love as the only final cause to which both self and the world exist to contribute.

5. I have appealed to Wesley's insistence that good works are necessary to salvation as confirming that he is exactly like the process theologian in understanding authentic existence to involve an active as well as a passive moment. But this is not the only thing that his insistence on the necessity of good works confirms. It also confirms the definite bias toward praxis that is one of the abiding characteristics of the Wesleyan witness.

This becomes clear as soon as one recognizes that in Wesley's view good works properly so-called are but one of two main ways in which faith working through love comes to external expression. If they are rightly regarded as its "practical" expression, it also finds "speculative" expression in "thinking" or "opinions," which Wesley systematically distinguishes from the "walking" or "practice" proper to works. Moreover, in explaining what is and is not "a catholic spirit," he is as concerned to distinguish it from "*speculative* latitudinarianism," in the sense of "an indifference to all opinions," as to distinguish it from "any kind of *practical* latitudinarianism," such as "indifference as to public worship, or as to the outward manner of performing it" (Sugden [ed.]: 2:129-46). In other words, for all of his insistence that a catholic spirit is an inward matter of faith and love distinct from all outward matters of either works or opinions, Wesley is as steadfastly opposed to any antinomianism of thought and belief as he is to any antinomianism of action and practice.

Even so, the striking thing about the Wesleyan witness is its preoccupation with the second kind of antinomianism and its insistence, accordingly, that good works are necessary to salvation, not right opinions. Although our active participation in God's love is outwardly expressed by how we think and what we believe as well as by how we act and what we do, the "outward salvation" with which Wesley is above all concerned is not orthodoxy but orthopraxis, or, as he himself puts it, "holiness of life and conversation" (Cragg [ed.]: 68).

Very much the same bias toward praxis is also evident in process theology, especially as it has developed more recently. Contrary to popular stereotypes, even the "process theologies" that are only or primarily philosophical have typically demonstrated practical as well as speculative interests. But in the case of process theology in the proper sense of the word, its most influential expressions have increasingly evinced a concern with praxis that is quite pronounced. Most of them, to be sure, have a broadly political character that goes beyond anything that can be explicitly found in Wesley's witness. But if this is due in some degree to process philosophy, whose ethical theory assigns special importance to structures of social and cultural order, it is due in even greater degree to the formative influence of modern historical consciousness, in which Wesley scarcely shared. For this reason, the pertinent question is how Wesley's own bias toward praxis could be expressed today by anyone fully sharing in this consciousness if not in terms validated by a specifically "political" or "liberation" type of theology (Runyon [ed.]; Ogden, 1981). But, then, if the answer to this question is the one I am suggesting, there must clearly be a close affinity between any adequate contemporary expression of the Wesleyan witness and the same bias toward praxis in process theology.

6. If a broadly political concern with forming and transforming structures is distinctive of modern theologies, process theology among them, the same is true of the concern to overcome homocentrism in Christian witness and theology. In this case, however, process theology has taken the lead, not only in being among the first to draw attention to homocentrism as a theological problem, but most especially in the relative adequacy of its proposals for a possible solution.

There is no mystery about the reason for such relative adequacy. Because the process philoso-

phy in whose terms it critically reflects on the Christian witness is in every way antidualistic, in its ethics as well as in its metaphysics, process theology is able to offer an understanding of self and the world in relation to God in which the differences in kind between any one ultimate subject of predication and any other are all relative rather than absolute. In some of its expressions, this understanding takes the form of a panpsychic or psychicalist metaphysics, for which not only the self but any other thing comparably concrete and singular is an instance, or an individual sequence of instances, of mind or sentience in a completely generalized sense of the words. But even in such expressions of process theology as voice serious reservations about this or any other form of categorical metaphysics, there is no basis for dualism either metaphysical or ethical; for one can say even in strictly transcendental terms that anything concretely and singularly real in the full sense of the words is an instance of real, internal relatedness to others and, therefore, of intrinsic and not merely instrumental good. Consequently, all expressions of process theology are able, as hardly any other kind of theology seems to be, to overcome homocentrism both metaphysically and ethically. Without in the least questioning the important relative differences between the level of becoming occupied by the self and its fellow selves and all lower, less conscious levels of becoming, they can nevertheless stress the relativity of the differences and urge an indefinite extension of the scope of the second commandment. Because anything concrete and singular is insofar intrinsically good, and is fully accepted as such by God, the neighbors we are to love as ourselves include not only all our fellow selves but also all the others at every level of becoming who can in any way be affected by our own acceptance and action.

But, surely, if there is any point where process theology is different from the Wesleyan witness, it is here. Beyond any question, Wesley everywhere takes for granted an understanding of self and the world that is homocentric when viewed from the standpoint of process theology. One reason for this, presumably, is that he could still assume a cosmology as well as a natural history of life and humankind that was in many respects prescientific. And yet it is also clear, I think, that his explicit metaphysics is sufficiently classical at this point, as at most others, to accept the traditional dualism between matter and spirit— so much so, in fact, that he can subtly confuse our only truly ultimate end in God with our unique enjoyment of this end as spiritual beings (Ogden, 1978).

But if recognizing this serves to remind us that there are indeed differences as well as affinities between the Wesleyan witness and process theology, we may still need to look closely if we are not to exaggerate the differences. All thinkers, Whitehead suggests, enjoy insights beyond the limits of the systems that we are accustomed to associate with their names. And so it is, in my opinion, with at least some of the things Wesley has to say on this very point. This is particularly so if one reads a passage such as the following against the background of orthodox eschatology with its teaching of the final annihilation of all things other than spirits in the *consummatio saeculi.*

Perhaps we may go a step farther still: Is not matter itself, as well as spirit, in one sense eternal? Not indeed *a parte ante*, as some senseless philosophers, both ancient and modern, have dreamed. . . . But although nothing beside the great God can have existed from everlasting—none else can be eternal *a parte ante*; yet there is no absurdity in supposing that all creatures are eternal *a parte post*. All matter indeed is continually changing, and that into ten thousand forms; but that it is changeable, does in no wise imply that it is perishable. The substance may remain one and the same, though under innumerable different forms. It is very possible any portion of matter may be resolved into the atoms of which it was originally composed: But what reason have we to believe that one of the atoms ever was, or ever will be, annihilated? It never can, unless by the uncontrollable power of its almighty Creator. And is it probable that ever He will exert this power in unmaking any of the things that he hath made? In this also, God is not "a son of man that he should repent." . . . [The elements] will be only dissolved not destroyed; they will melt, but they will not perish. Though they lose their present form, yet not a particle of them will ever lose its existence; but every atom of them will remain, under one form or other, to all eternity (Jackson [ed.]: 6:191-92).

I shall not repeat the kind of question I asked earlier so as to suggest that one could do justice today to Wesley's clear intention only by breaking with all homocentrism as sharply as process theology does. But I do wish to claim that even here there is more than sheer difference and that, when this passage is considered together with the other evidence and argument of this paper, there can be no question about the affinities between process theology and the Wesleyan witness. With whatever differences, they are sufficiently many and sufficiently close that not only those of us who do process theology as Wesleyan Christians, but anyone else concerned with "Wesleyan theology and the next century" cannot afford to ignore them.

NOTES

Carney, Frederick S.
1978   "Theological Ethics." In *Encyclopedia of Bioethics*, Vol. 1, ed. Warren T. Reich. New York: Macmillan: 429-437
Cobb, John B., Jr., and Griffin, David Ray
1976   *Process Theology: An Introductory Exposition.* Philadelphia: Westminster Press
Cragg, Gerald R. (ed.)
1975   *The Works of John Wesley,* Vol. 2: *The Appeals to Men of Reason and Religion.* Oxford: Clarendon Press
Deschner, John
1960   *Wesley's Christology: An Interpretation.* Dallas, TX: Southern Methodist University Press
Habermas, Jürgen
1976   "Was heisst Universalpragmatik?" In *Sprachpragmatik und Philosophie,* ed. K.-O. Apel. Frankfurt: Suhrkamp Verlag: 174-272
Habermas, Jürgen, and Luhmann, Niklas
1971   *Theorie der Gesellschaft oder Sozialtechnologie—Was leistet die Systemforschung?* Frankfurt: Suhrkamp Verlag
Hartshorne, Charles
1967   *A Natural Theology for Our Time.* La Salle, IL: Open Court Publishing Co.
1970   *Creative Synthesis and Philosophic Method.* La Salle, IL: Open Court Publishing Co.
1979   "Beyond Enlightened Self-Interest." In *Religious Experience and Process Theology: The Pastoral Implications of a Major Modern Movement,* ed. Harry James Cargas and Bernard Lee. New York: Paulist Press: 301-22
Jackson, Thomas (ed.)
1958-   *The Works of John Wesley.* Grand Rapids, MI: Zon-
59   dervan Publishing House
Langford, Thomas A.
1983   *Practical Divinity: Theology in the Wesleyan Tradition.* Nashville: Abingdon Press
Ogden, Schubert M.
1969   "Present Prospects for Empirical Theology." In *The Future of Empirical Theology,* ed. Bernard E. Meland. Chicago: University of Chicago Press: 65-88
1975   "On Revelation." In *Our Common History as Christians: Essays in Honor of Albert C. Outler,* ed. John Deschner, Leroy T. Howe, and Klaus Penzel. New York: Oxford University Press. 261-92
1976   "Sources of Religious Authority in Liberal Protestantism." *Journal of the American Academy of Religion,* 44, 3: 403-16
1978   "Why Did God Make Me? A Free-Church Answer." In *Why Did God Make Me?* ed. Hans Küng and Jürgen Moltmann. New York: Seabury Press: 67-73
1981   "The Concept of a Theology of Liberation: Must Christian Theology Today Be So Conceived?" In *The Challenge of Liberation Theology: A First World Response,* ed. Brian Mahan and L. Dale Richesin. Maryknoll, NY: Orbis Books: 127-40
Outler, Albert C. (ed)
1964   *John Wesley.* New York: Oxford University Press
Pelikan, Jaroslav
1964   *Obedient Rebels: Catholic Substance and Protestant Principle in Luther's Reformation.* New York: Harper & Row
Runyon, Theodore (ed.)
1981   *Sanctification and Liberation: Liberation Theologies in the Light of the Wesleyan Tradition.* Nashville: Abingdon Press
Sugden, Edward H. (ed.)
1951   *Wesley's Standard Sermons.* 3rd ed.; London: Epworth Press

2. PROCESS THEOLOGY AND WESLEYAN THOUGHT: AN EVANGELICAL PERSPECTIVE

Paul A. Mickey

One goal of this working group is to explore the realities and possibilities of drawing upon conceptualities offered by process modes of thought toward developing a fuller appreciation and application of Wesley's theological contributions in several crucial areas of inquiry at the beginning of the third centennial of American Methodism. The Wesleyan spirit has been seminal for a number of theological traditions and perspectives, including evangelical theology. As one asked to present a paper from that Wesleyan-informed tradition, I need to state that the understanding of what I consider the possibilities for evangelical and process theologies working alongside each other in a Wesleyan spirit is mine; they are not excerpts from a Wesleyan evangelical orthodoxy. Both evangelicals and those who claim their theological orientation along different theological lines need to consider this paper as the contribution of one person who in a general sense is asked to represent evangelicals in general. To help orient you to relevant aspects of my perspective, the following introductory comments are offered.

Introduction

My father was ordained in the old Evangelical Church that merged to form the Evangelical United Brethren Church in 1946. He devoted his entire ministry to rural churches in Ohio. Gentle in spirit, cooperative in community and ecumenical efforts, he lived out the quiet vitality of his German piety. Devout in its practice of faith in church settings, around the family table, and in civic and educational activities, my family instilled in me a deep sense of the experiencing presence of God in the ongoingness of daily life: family and church; sunrise, sunset; the preparing, planting, tilling, and harvesting of crops; health and sickness; the pain and reality of World War II; births, marriages, and funerals in my father's congregations.

Before entering college I enlisted in the Air Force and became a chaplain's assistant, affording exposure to Russian Orthodox, Roman Catholic, Episcopal, Southern Baptist, Presbyterian, and Methodist traditions. As a Northerner in Greenville, Mississippi, during the Little Rock school integration crisis, who also was the first to bring a non-Caúcasian into a Southern Baptist worship service in Greenville, I drank deeply of the wellsprings of cultural, religious, and ethnic pluralism.

During an undergraduate course on developmental psychology I was illuminated by the criticism of Sigmund Freud's developmental scheme: Freud's attention is devoted exclusively to the child's dependence on the parent; nowhere does Freud suggest what if any effect the child has on the parent or adult caretaker. An obvious empirical aspect of parent-child relations carried significant theological implications: God is an experiencing center; there is a mutual responsiveness, a reciprocity, a ceaseless, vital activity between God and creation.

The above touches fleetingly on some of the intellectual, spiritual, and developmental epochs that drew me toward process modes of thought expressing formally the theological and psychological assumptions in my life and work as an evangelical. I hope this background excursus is helpful because I want it to convey why I believe evangelical and process perspectives, despite obvious difficulties, have much in common.

In thirteen sections of the paper, I want to consider areas in which process and evangelical thought share common ground for those in the Wesleyan tradition.

I. Political Theology

It is significant to begin with political theology not doctrine. Politics is how we live, how we do business, how the actual give-and-take of everyday life comes to experience the givenness and possibilities of life itself. In the Wesleyan perspective, I believe one's world view is pluralistic. We are one among many: many faiths, many peoples, many expressions of God's life. Wesley and his followers were always in a technical sense a minority: Wesley's Holy Club, the Fetter's Lane Society, his bands and societies driven from the churches and parishes of England, the Schools for the Poor; his relationship with the Church of England, the Anglican Church's struggle with the Roman Catholic Church; his missionary efforts among the American colonies; the *eccle-*

siola in ecclesia principle of church renewal. These factors and many more suggest that the reality of the power of the *other* for Wesleyans is ever present: the power of nature, economic forces, natural resources, political control, spiritual dominions, to name a few.

The pervasiveness of not being in central control for Wesleyans moves one toward cosmic humility. Preoccupation with one's cosmic minority status could lead to a self-depreciating, low self-esteem. But whatever else is gained or lost in this perspective, one is in touch with one's finitude and the passive modes of relating. Wesley's appeal to the commoner, his preaching in the fields, his revivals among the miners and those caught in the poverty of the industrial revolution, especially in the urban centers like Bristol and London, drew the economically dispossessed and hopeless toward Christ but also produced a political theology that was a practical corrective for the *hubris* that inspired the French Revolution. Similar social conditions existed in England, but the political, industrial, and economic transition that accompanied the Wesleyan Revival was not only less violent but preserved the energy of a people for a more constructive vision of the future. Perhaps the influence of his parents' "shared" responsibilities, his large family, the awareness of the fragility and resilience of life contributed to Wesley's political theology, the sense that he and his movement were but one among many occasions of God's work within the world in which God's aims were being realized. I believe that evangelicals and process theologians share with Wesley that cosmic humility.

In the Wesleyan tradition one does not characteristically find the triumphalism that surfaced in Reformed traditions in the United States. Wesley did not accept a doctrine of election that would give a philosophical guarantee of the final outcome of any adventure—political or faithful. Wesley's is a vision shared with process thinking that the one thing necessary is the certitude of the emergent reality—not the final outcome. Few of the evangelicals in the Wesleyan tradition have subscribed to theological triumphalism. In the United States, and certainly in contemporary United Methodism, evangelicals are in a political minority position or at least self-consciously understand themselves to be one of many minority groups in the denomination. The major splits in the Wesleyan tradition have focused on the principle of including the ones less able: slaves in the South, poor people in the North who had to pay pew rent, the down-and-out in the cities.[1]

The ethos of the Evangelical United Brethren Church was a Wesleyan-oriented German pietism practiced by immigrant dirt farmers locating in the mid- and southwest. Farmers constantly are reminded that life is beholden to nature: humanity may be stewards of nature, but certainly we do not control. The piety of those German immigrants continues in its daily being reminded of the frustratingly finite limits of human control over nature. Human beings are under authority, always responsible to another power. The forces of God, nature, weather, economics, of being Germans in an "Allied" country during both world wars reinforced the relativity of life and underscored the ambiguity and ever changing alliances that constitute the radical newness that each tomorrow brings.[2]

God is no respecter of persons: German immigrants, Americans, Christians, Wesleyans, whomever. The influence of my Evangelical United Brethren background is more on the here and now, the present realities and what they may afford. In the closing months of World War II my father was appointed to follow a woman pastor in a small rural parish. Never once do I recall him showing anything but full respect for his female colleague in ministry. He always spoke of her as "Reverend" in the same respectful way he referred to the bishop. It was clear in the congregation itself that his predecessor had distinguished herself, and my father had "a hard act to follow."

Proponents of civil religion and triumphalism in the United States are not Wesleyan evangelicals. Such proponents come from the Reformed and Anabaptist side of the Reformation. Theirs is a world view more radical than the pluralism of a Wesleyan witness to the political realities of life. For example, the Moral Majority movement in this country, when analyzed theologically and philosophically, does not draw its energy from Wesleyan evangelicals. True, some Wesleyans may be involved, but there has been no formal effort nor success in recruiting United Methodist evangelicals to the ranks of this recent manifestation of triumphalism.[3]

II. Sacraments

The evangelical tradition of the Evangelical United Brethren nurtured more of an anabaptist quietism than did Wesley's Anglicanism. The Evangelical United Brethren held tightly to infant dedication, although Baptism in the Wesleyan tradition was offered as an option. The congregation was expected to nurture children in the faith. Confirmation—such as it existed—was more strictly a time of instruction, but it was not Confirmation as one finds it in Methodist, Lutheran, or Roman Catholic traditions. After joining the Duke Divinity School faculty, I visited a small black church in rural North Carolina, pastored by a seminary student; it was then that I was introduced to the high liturgy and high view of the sacraments among Methodists. A similar surprise occurred at the general board meetings of the Good News movement. The sacraments were highly valued by these evangelicals—black, white, and Latin. My Evangelical United Brethren background focused more on Word than sacrament. The subtle yet powerful balance between Word and sacrament achieved by my United Methodist evangelical friends continues to be impressive. Preaching and the sacraments are physical events, specific actual occasions in which God's objective presence is claimed. The sacraments objectify God's presence and God's aim. As specific emergent occasions, they are efficacious for me, but not causative. Their intent claimed by evangelicals is to invite response not to cause salvation. The grace extended in Baptism and Communion is an invitation emergent in God's real presence; it is a gracious lure by which we can begin to make sense of the past, especially the cross, *and* respond to the future.

The sacraments emphasize the nearness and accessibility of God.[4] It is the community, whether large or small, that helps to form the infant's or communicant's future. This theological vision reinforces—in a positive way—that one is but one among many. The high view of the sacraments among Wesleyans brings theological and personal balance to the passive/active dimensions of life: passive, in that we are to be quiet and know who God is and respond to the grace offered, not to produce a faith demanded; active in that one responds to the call to the Lord's Supper or to the baptismal font or that one shrinks from a public witness of one's declared intention to receive grace and walk in newness of life. The sacraments represent for the evangelical the epitome of the derived ("relational") life *and* the free (*causi sui*) life.[5]

III. Anthropology

Perhaps the hallmark of Wesleyan thought is its acknowledgment of the profound ambiguities in human experience. "Potential" is perhaps the best word to describe Wesley's anthropology. His stress on potential and growth was always counterbalanced by a rigorous emphasis on the *realities* of original sin.[6] Only his process perspective on human nature could hold Wesley's insistence on the curse of original sin *and* the glorious possibilities for growth in grace in workable tension. The causal efficacy of the Adamic curse for Wesley was pervasive, and in this he shared with the other Reformers the claim for the radical work of grace in effecting salvation. But the passivity that attends the curse of original sin, Wesley is able to understand as provisional and objective, to be certain, but not final. The actuality of the pervasiveness of original sin in individual and corporate realities clearly was accepted by him. But the reality of God and God's lure for the future can modify the effects of the past in the present, emergent occasion. The world is not cursed to repetition. God's ceaseless activity, in evangelical terms, through the prevenient work of the Holy Spirit, urges the individual to aim for novel response to what is given to one. Wesley's intuitive belief in the power of God's initial aim to break the conformal feelings of original sin is essential to his anthropology and the optimism structurally that attends it. Those responsive to this aspect of Wesley's thought do not think of God "back there"—in the garden. Rather God is powerfully active in each present moment, struggling with each, new emergent occasion that it might enjoy its highest potential. Whitehead of course said it, "God confronts what is actual in the world with what is possible for it."[7] Along with Wesley, the evangelicals have neither gloried nor despaired in the doctrine of original sin. It is a statement of what theologically "is actual in the world." The radicality of Wesley's process perspective was precisely in his unflinching belief that novelty, birth, the emergent occasion are radically different from the past life of the societies that constitute the human personality. The belief in the *causa sui*, self-creating aspect of human experience is the basis for Wesley's radical optimism toward novelty, change: the power of the subjective aim of each "believer." This optimism is further evidenced in his unalterable demands for discipline, group accountability, prayer, fasting, worship, and so on. Each moment is an occasion for novelty and enjoyment, and Wesley wanted to make certain that the band, society, prayer meeting, and the attendance of public worship all would be components in God's initial aim to effect—as an efficient cause—the individual with the enjoyment of going on to perfection. But Wesley was fully aware that his insistence on potential carried with it the possibility that one could go off half-cocked, falsely but creatively, in occasions of backsliding, living as though one's subjective aim is both resident in the believer and is at the same time God's initial aim. Therefore in Wesley's stress on holiness one's *causi sui* would do better to veer away from self-centeredness toward

God's lure and aim toward holiness, good works, and care for the poor.

The evangelical emphasis on the sinfulness of life, stated as the theological starting point, flows from this Wesleyan/process view that the *fait accompli* of the past is met *continuously* by the power of God's lure for the future, active yet graceful in the succession of present moments that constitute who we become and what we offer to the future. A bellwether of those who do not hold a Wesley/process view is their weak approach to a doctrine of original sin. If one locks onto only the future, potential, growth, and positive optimism is claimed; but the future will become anything but positive and harmonious. For example, Robert Schuller's treatment of self-esteem[8] is directed not so much at Wesleyans but Calvinists whose doctrine of election does not draw in the full range of the ambiguities of human nature and the vitality of God. An anthropological base on a doctrine of election inevitably witnesses to the pervasive heaviness of the past without experiential hope because Calvin did not understand God's relation to the world and human potential as a continuous struggle and interaction in which God's energy is in part the burst of energy that helps constitute each new, emergent occasion. The obsessive claims of "possibility thinking," of the "human potential movement," and of "changing social structures" are indications that the free and relational nature of human beings and the active, massive presence of God is understood from a perspective other than the Wesleyan/process/evangelical one.

Wesley's insistence on group accountability in worship, prayer, confession, exhortation, and his "demands" for good works, for fruits of the spirit reveals an important anthropological balance that lies at the heart of the evangelical motivation for piety and missions. Wesley understood in the fullest sense of the term the "internal relatedness" of life: the local society, the annual conference, and the cosmos. Likewise, his "reformed subjectivism" always anchored his piety in actuality, in history, in specific acts that show forth the workmanship begun by Christ in the believer. Wesley's process radicality was evidenced in his assertion that if there is a lack of or a deficiency in "fruits of the spirit," one has primary evidence that salvation is not being effected; it is only a subjective excursus in original sin.

IV. The Holy Spirit

Wesley's emphasis on the Holy Spirit is what I call the focused manifestation of the work of God in God's initial aim. The power of the past to effect repetition and conformal feelings is massive. However, the fact that God in God's ceaseless activity is ever present in each emergent occasion offers luring possibilities that the subjective aim of the occasion—or individual—might respond in the "intermediate phase" of the occasion's development so that it might enjoy the possibilities that God offers. In Wesley's doctrine of original sin, sin is so pervasive that if one is left to one's own power and ability, the rich possibilities that God offers in salvation are simply not integrated in the unrepentant sinner's sheer capacity to determine his or her own aim. In that sense the devil's gotcha! Wesley developed the notion of prevenient grace as that special work of the Holy Spirit that so floods the coming together of one's emergent moments of experience that as the sinner reaches forward for what he or she will become, the human aiming will include some aspect of God's grace. Specifically, God's wooing and convicting grace is offered as a powerful contrast to the teleological power of original sin which will not in fact lead to eternal bliss, joy, and harmony, regardless of how well the immediacy of the present moment might objectify itself in what the unrepentant sinner offers him or herself and the world for the future. Only the Holy Spirit as an exemplification of the Godhead has the power in the initial aim of prevenient grace to break the powerful oppression of the conformal feelings of original sin so that one's new aiming will become more responsive to divine lures for a faithful and graceful life.

Wesley's commitment to a process-oriented anthropology is seen in his reliance on the concept of prevenience not irresistible grace to express God's relation to the world. God, at the initial stages of creation both in genesis (*"creatio ex nihilo"*) and in personal and corporate salvation (prophet, priest, and king in the Old Testament and the anointed one, Jesus Christ, in the New Testament), works cooperatively, to woo, create, lure, convict, and challenge the emergent occasion to be responsible to the possibilities for becoming so that it will contribute the highest harmony possible for the future.

Calvin especially did not share this "cooperative" understanding of God and/in the world. Therefore on the contemporary evangelical scene, Robert Schuller's popularity in large measure denies original sin because he has to maneuver around irresistible grace which simply does not permit the quality if not the substance of human freedom occasioned by a thorough-going belief in the human capacity of *causa sui*. His possibility thinking is an effort to affirm the subjective aim of which Whitehead speaks. However, Schuller's thought is not Wesleyan and denies the connectedness of all of life, the past to the future, sin and possibility, corporate and individual harmony, and creates a genuine disunity. When one considers that the setting for *Hardcore* and Amway products both find themselves in Schuller's hometown of Grand Rapids, one can appreciate the difficulties with which those who do not historically share in a doctrine of prevenient grace must struggle.

Many pentecostal groups have come out of the Wesleyan tradition, and the most organized, energetic charismatic renewal group in the United States is a United Methodist group, "Renewal Support Services Fellowship." Why? In the Wesleyan tradition the work of the Holy Spirit begins in the earliest activities of creation, in the wooing and convicting of the believer in good works and is understood in a process perspective: the principal work of the Spirit is in providing and offering the eternal objects of God's "will" (lure) for the moment-by-moment emergence of the actual world. The struggle for the evangelical Wesleyans is not to tie up the initial aim associated with the Holy Spirit with the subjective aim of the individual in such a way as to lapse into subjectivism. Whitehead and his interpreters are quite clear about the objectification of the final phase of each moment. Each experience and its efficacious objective existence is a "gift" to what the future might become. Wesley's concern for this subjectivism was to continuously stress the need for *evidence* of fruits of the spirit. Wesley knew willy-nilly that the inner life, the internal relatedness, has external manifestations. That our lives are objectified is assumed without question by Wesley. The question is only What kind of objectification? What is the quality of the believer's moral life, witnessing, social responsibilities? One cannot hide in the spirit; there is no Spirit in which to hide. The Spirit is what and who contributes to what we become in the final phases of each experience.

V. Christology

Less innovative in his Christology than his pneumatology, Wesley's traditional Christology stressed that Jesus was truly man (humanity in the fullest sense of the word) and truly God. The ambiguity and tension with substance/essence vis-à-vis becoming/emergence is seen in Wesley's Christology. The evangelical Wesleyan claims Jesus as preexistent and locates Jesus' one nature with the primordial nature of God (truly God).

No adoptionism here. The other nature of Jesus, that like God the Godhead, is located incarnationally as the consequent nature, God's supreme manifestation of how human life influences and effects what God becomes. The incarnation means precisely that, with all its ambiguities, paradoxes, conflicts. The Whiteheadian understanding of the two natures of God, primordial (unchanging) and consequent (responsive), provides a conceptual aid in understanding how God is related to the world, and specifically in the incarnation of Jesus. No doubt the principal transitions about which Robert Chiles writes of Methodist thought in the United States ("revelation to reason," "sinful man to moral man," and "free grace to free will")[9] have prompted an evangelical defensiveness over the need to preserve the deity of Jesus. If the Chiles thesis is remotely accurate, there has been a shift from 1790 certainly to 1935, and quite arguably continuing further, that stresses human reason, the human capacity for moral act—and possibility thinking—and an optimism over the predictable capacity of human beings to exercise their free will in decision making for the good of all. This theological stress in American Wesleyan circles swings toward the human side of one's religious experience. Therefore understandably Wesleyan evangelicals have, as a corrective effort, asserted the truly God, or deity aspect, of Jesus' incarnation. Replete with dangers of subjectivism, gnosticism, spiritualism, this effort is not self-intended to be undercutting the humanity and responsiveness of God in Christ. Rather, among the evangelicals in its best light this claim is perceived as a corrective to the excesses of so-called humanism in which the dual nature, the two natures, of the work and person of Jesus are not held in the creative tension suggested in the earlier discussions here about the work of the Spirit.

That the spirit of the evangelical Wesleyans is oriented toward a process perspective is suggested by the relative attraction toward Niebuhr's radical monotheism and tentativeness toward Barth's "Christomonism." The full trinitarian activity of God needed to flesh out a process perspective moves away from an exclusively theological preoccupation with Jesus. Jesus Christ is seen for the evangelical principally relationally. His priestly mediatorial intercessory function wherein he participates both as the representative of the whole human race and as the Son of God in his tasting death for every creature is God's reconciling gesture to the world.[10] The process notion of the "dipolar" nature of God is most fully exemplified in the incarnation of Jesus, the active one, the passive one, the sinless one, the sinful one.

VI. Conversion

The evangelical stresses the need for a conversion experience. The emphasis on the practical, the actual, the temporal are influences historically to which the evangelical appeals in calling for the need for acts of repentence and the asking for forgiveness. Rejected are universalism and the ubiquitous redeeming qualities of environmental nurture. The combining of active and passive models of relatedness in conversion is symbolized in the need to point to a specific act or a series of internally related acts by which one confessionally witnesses to the personal historical experience of receiving Christ. Universalism is too abstract for the Wesleyan evangelical as is the process stress on the positive, luring, noncoercive use of God's power in motivating people. Wesley's notion of fleeing the wrath to come is more than a "scare 'em" tactic. It is a christological claim that in Jesus the past with its causal efficacy flowing from sin need not be experienced as a linear extension of that sin into the indefinite future. In the conversion experience the believer objectifies the newness of life in Christ and thereby breaks the tyranny of a linear extension of the past. That past may be culturally perceived as immoral and sinful. Or it may reside in the insidious reflections of the rich farmer who tore down his barns following the bumper crop or the high tech missile defense system that is deemed impenetrable: life will extend itself in unbroken positive contrasts that every day in every way the agribusiness or defense contracting is getting better and better. The future cannot be seen as a direct extension of the past except in a pervasive monopolar passivity, a sheer acquiescence framework. The call to conversion in order to flee the wrath to come as witnessed to in the Wesleyan tradition is a witness against the poverty and the self-aggrandizement of the human spirit.

At the same time Wesley and his followers were cognizant that not everyone will respond positively to the gospel. That orientation makes for a more aggressive proclamation but offers the possibility of preaching for decision for Christ in a less defensive posture because individuals in the actual occasions of their decisions are free, *causa sui*. It is Wesley's appeal to the activity in the human decision making capacity that empowers his emphasis on conversion: salvation is a historical event, and therefore it is more than sheer becoming. It is the overcoming of evil with good that is focused on the originating actualities of the transforming conversion experience.

VII. Growth: Call to Discipline

Because of his high anthropology and its affirmation of the power and dignity of the free, *causa sui*, self, Wesley realized that creativity, freedom, energy needed to be harnessed. His institution of the Rules of the United Societies and the Rules of the Bands[11] were not repressive but liberating measures designed to promote discipline, mutual accountability, love among the followers, and the development of a process perspective on the essential relational nature of humanity and divinity. Not allowing the converts to drift into isolation as detached, unrelated beings, Wesley demanded that a relational understanding of the Christian life be envisaged. Of the societies he claimed, "a company of men having the form and seeking the power of godliness, united in order to pray together, to receive the word of exhortation, and to watch over one another in love, that they may help each other to work out their salvation."[12]

The significance of the power and enabling qualities of the discipline of group process had not been formally understood until the emergence of "group process" in modern psychotherapy, management relations, and sensitivity training. The anthropological assumptions in contemporary group process technique are remarkably similar to the dynamics and results envisaged by Wesley. Both Wesley and modern social scientists suggest that individuals are not entities related to others solely by accidents of incidental group membership. The individual is not a container into which the experience is poured; rather one is one's experiences. Wesley perceived this aspect of human experience with a profundity not recognized formally until modern group process analysis. Therefore the classes, bands, and prayer meetings that characterized the evangelical constituency in the Wesleyan tradition need to be seen in a more significant ontological light rather than dismissed as recessive pietism. The discipline of the group and its continual claims for vulnerability, exhortation, and affirmation constitute a theological and anthropological recognition of the relational, emergent nature both of the convert's life as well as that of the Godhead. Foolish indeed would be an insistence on mutual formation and accountability among the believers in Wesley-spawned groups if the participants did not firmly believe the correlate that God too is responsive to the affirmation, exhortation, and confession of those seeking maturity in their Christian experience.

The scriptural claim of James 5:16 that the fervent, effectual prayer of the righteous availeth much certainly reflects a process understanding of the capacity of the believer to effect real change in God. Wesley's emphasis on the discipline of prayer, fasting, group accountability, and mutual stimulation in the faith rings hollow except as it is seen in a process perspective. Thus, evangelicals who stress personal, family and group devotions, table grace, bedtime prayer, and pastoral visits that offer the peace of prayer operate from a process perspective in their self-understanding of what constitutes the emergence of the mature spiritual life, especially the inner life. Claiming the inner, spiritual aspects of life in a process perspective is compelling because one's interior life lends itself more readily to acceptance of the subjective aspects of internal relatedness of the spirit. Affirming the power and efficacy of the structures of internal relatedness that are manifestly social is at least psychologically, if not theologically, more difficult. The failure by evangelicals to engage in consistent generalization of Wesley's principle of spiritual internal relatedness to all of life is precisely the point of the criticism that evangelicals are not interested in, committed to, or empathetic toward the broader social realities of life. The fundamental misinterpretation of Wesley's process perspective by some evangelical groups has led them to a myopic focus on the "religious feelings" of their faith while denying the necessary objectification of that faith in offering its efficacy to the larger society and the future.

VIII. Temporality

The Wesleyan insistence on discipline in faith and practice coupled with his belief in the perfectibility of one's walk with God cannot be adequately understood unless one ascribes to Wesley a prototypical process perspective on temporality. Perfection can be meaningfully understood only as one can accept the temporal nature of God as well as of the believer. Wesley's intention has fallen prey to the limits of language all too frequently. Traditional theological language especially stressed the formal monopolar nature of God and is inadequate to convey the richness of the operational conceptions in the Wesleyan movement. Had the Wesleys not been prolific hymn writers, preachers, pastors in day-by-day mundaneness of the Revival movement, formal language alone would not have been adequate to convey the spirit and intent of the Wesleyan movement. Perhaps it was a saving grace that Wesley was not a systematic theologian. Above all he was a practitioner: he was energetic in advocating his perspective in multiple modes of theological expression. The cumulative effect was to impart theological vision that today would be called process perspective. Wesley stressed that all moments of life are organically connected, having both immediate and accumulated significance. His envisagement of Christian perfection in a thoroughly temporal framework acknowledges that time is actual not vacuous. No empty moments for God or for the believer who by faith strives to be more Christlike in the daily hope of experiencing more completely the holiness of God in the believer's emergent life. While Wesley at times taught the instantaneous quality of Christian perfection or sanctification, it never was for him sheer becoming or vacuous status. For Wesley perfection was internally related to one's psychological development, the cultural milieu and historical relativity of one's society or band, and the ecological coterminouses of one's relative position among all the orders of nature.

Wesley's notion of perfection does not lend itself to a mathematical model of purity; nor may it be conceived of as unchanging spiritual substance; nor may one conceive of perfection as a rigid container filled by the fundamental wisdom of some fixed measure of spiritual blessing. To so believe is to misrepresent the fundamental wisdom of Wesley's temporal notion of perfection. If perfection is cast in terms other than temporal and social, it becomes detached from the ongoingness of life, which is precisely where Wesley himself located holiness. When the focus of perfection is the intention, the harmony, the responsiveness, and openness of the believer, one travels with Wesley. Otherwise claims for holiness and perfection are stolid examples of theological and psychological defensiveness because in this instance one wrongly interprets holiness as absolute not relative.

A brief example may be helpful despite its sensitivity. Historically Wilmore, Kentucky, is the institutional center of the holiness movement in The United Methodist Church. This small, midwestern-Appalachian town in the north central part of the state stands safely on the distant outskirts of Lexington. Railroad tracks coming from urban centers originally brought students away from city corruption to a place of spiritual safety. The town in 1983 lived as if time stood still; the ethos of a pleasant 1930s or early post-World War II lingers. Only now, after long years of an embattled isolationist witness, is the

Wilmore complex beginning to open itself to the kind of radical social transactions comparable to Wesley's own. The notion of instantaneous holiness or perfection has maintained its conceptual purity in this single location; life is experienced normatively as an unchanging moment. Now the opening of the new E. Stanley Jones School of Evangelism signals the true magnificence of the Wesleyan witness put in a larger context. As this evangelical enclave of the holiness movement begins to take time seriously, it will, I believe, begin to show a responsiveness to the actuality of time that will make it truly Wesleyan in ways that have been denied for epochs. For Wesley time was relational: it provided contrasts, moments of completion, beads and pulses of experience; it was understood as developmental stages not as the fixed substances of an instantaneous perfection. When the modern evangelicals are able to move into the "absolute relativism" of Wesley's concept of time, their understanding of both God's perfection and human holiness will more accurately reflect the intent of Wesley.[13]

IX. The Trinity and Sociality

Wesleyan evangelicals adhere to a thoroughgoing Trinitarianism. Not committed to a Christomonism or a theistic univeralism, and generally steering away from the spiritualism of pentecostalism, the theological function of a high doctrine of the Trinity is the best way available in traditional theological categories to express their conception of God as a social and temporal being. Evangelicals struggle with how to conceptualize the responsiveness of God to the human situation; yet the affirmation that God is responsive and is affected by the contributions of human need, pain, suffering, sin, and intercessory prayer to the life of God is firmly declared. The reality of this give-and-take, this dialectical vision of God's relation to the world outdistances the ability of most in the evangelical camp to conceptualize this experience without feeling they are doing theological violence, especially in the light of Scriptures that clearly refer to the unchangeableness of God: God, the same yesterday, today, and forever; God, the one in whom there is no variableness, nor shadow of turning. When the "two natures of God" language as employed in process conceptualities is offered into the discussion in a witnessing, not an argumentative, fashion, generally the "gut" or intuitive response among evangelicals is positive. Thus, the high view of the Trinity is an effort to express in traditional theological language the affirmation that process theology postulates about the temporal and relational nature of God.[14]

X. Ecumenism and the Catholic Spirit

A. *Ecumenism.* Generally evangelicals have been willing if not eager to work harmoniously with other Christian groups in cooperative activities, especially where the intention or the subjective goal of the effort aims to increase the instrumental effectiveness of the larger society. These efforts occur most frequently at low levels or lower orders of abstraction. For example, evangelicals are most active in cooperative summer Bible schools, union Thanksgiving and prayer services, work in the projects of humanitarian rehabilitation such as soup kitchens, clothing closets, "meals-on-wheels," transportation, community cleanup, and the like. Evangelicals are not inclined toward monolithic organizational unity. Aware of the diversity and pluralism of the universe (i.e., ecological politics) and the always mixed nature of reality, Wesleyan evangelicals are more likely to express a willing spirit if the ecumenical effort is related to practical problems.

The traditional contribution of evangelicals in the World and National councils of churches has not been substantial because the evangelicals historically are not persuaded that all peoples, underneath their theological language and cultural milieu present or represent the same theological or sociological reality. Therefore their cooperative spirit will focus on actual problems to be overcome. Evangelicals do not share the ambivalence of other religious orientations toward denominations. Denominations are affirmed as a fundamental concrescence in the upbuilding of the kingdom of God that cannot be bypassed or abandoned. In this sense they employ the practical cooperative spirit of Wesley's "catholic spirit."

B. *The Catholic Spirit.* Controversial in current debate within The United Methodist Church, and in larger church councils as well, is the evangelical interpretation of Wesley's famous sermon, "Catholic Spirit." Taking his text from II Kings 10:15, Wesley distinguishes between "opinion" and "essential truth." Moderns tend to sentimentalize imagery of the heart, whereas for Wesley it refers to the deeper strata of life and stands in distinctive contrast to thought or opinion. Matters of the heart are soul deep, opinions are more like conceptual feelings, primarily derived, not originating impulses. Wesley is clear in subparagraph 12 that having one's heart right with God is not simply a warm emotional feeling. Rather it necessarily includes the following beliefs/experiences of the depths of one's own being.

> Dost thou believe his being and his perfections, his eternity, immensity, wisdom, power, his justice, mercy and truth? Does thou believe that he now "upholdeth all things by the word of his power" [cf. Heb. 1:31], and that he governs even the most minute, even the most noxious, to his own glory and the good of them that love him? Hast thou a divine evidence, a supernatural conviction, of the things of God? Dost thou "walk by faith, not by sight," looking not at temporal things but things eternal [cf. II Cor. 5:7; 4:18]?[15]

These matters are resolved in the depths of one's being—the heart that is one's subjective aim that determines *how* one responds to *what* is given. This synthesizing capacity is constitutive of the heart of which Wesley speaks.

Therefore the statement, "Is thine heart right, as my heart is with thy heart?" does not appeal to psychology or the social skills of getting along well with people. Rather Wesley refers to the physical feelings or prehensions of the heart—the deep religious experiences of faith (quoted above) objectified and confirmed as beliefs. *Then* and only then may the becoming of acceptance, tolerance, goodwill, and mutual camaraderie emerge. If one is uncertain about the deep actualities of the heart of faith, offering the handshake of goodwill is fundamentally open to misinterpretation. In recent theological discussion in The United Methodist Church the evangelicals are concerned over appeals to the "catholic spirit" of Wesley in the lively debate about theological pluralism. Their reservation reflects Wesley's fear that the offering of the hand is not merely "*practical* latitudinarianism."[16] The conditions specified by Wesley: (1) love me, (2) pray for me, (3) stir me up to love, and (4) love me in the depths of truth,[17] are hallmarks of true pluralism, a pluralism that contemporary Wesleyan evangelicals would, I believe, affirm.

The physical prehensions of the deep matters of the heart and soul may not be confused with the conceptual feelings, opinions or intellectual talk. If relational and ontological priorities are understood, physical prehensions are seen as antecedent to conceptual feelings. Granted that then gladly is the heart of true faith and religion offered to and symbolized through the hand of ecumenical and pluralistic efforts that mutually stir up to good works.

C. *Doctrinal Purity.* All in the Wesleyan tradition tread a thin line of practical indifferentism on matters of doctrine. Wesleyans preeminently are people of action, of deed, of practical expression of their faith.[18] Not wanting to become entangled in endless doctrinal disputes that attended other groups to spring from the Protestant Reformation, Wesleyan folks want to get on with the building of the God's kingdom. The vitality of the sacraments, the benefits of the small group and personal discipline, the pull to engage in humanitarian service, and the mutual spiritual stimulation of one another prompt Wesleyans as a group to proclaim that they care less about the content of one's belief and more about how it works. Truly this is a process orientation, if ever there was one. This propensity to action, from the evangelical perspective, tends to be misinterpreted passively by the charismatics, on the one hand, who indicate little concern for political and ecological theology *and* by the social activists, on the other, who it seems join in a similar theological chorus: it doesn't really matter what you believe, just what you do. Yes, Virginia, it does matter; enough that we don't forget or neglect the proper instruction and discipline in matters of the heart—things spiritual—but not enough that we become paralyzed in doctrinaire squabbles such that the kingdom of God falters, waiting upon a pharisaical crossing of the *t or dotting of the i.*

XI. Growth: Call to Good Works

The focus of the discussion in section 7 on personal perfection, which may not ultimately be separated from good works that have a more manifestly social dimension to them. Wesley's appeal to Matthew 22:37-38 and the Great Commandment claims the singleness of intent to *love*: God, self, and neighbor as self. One cannot be fully related to any one entity without being related to others. The contemporary psychological and cultural obsession with self-fulfillment is an empty-hearted appeal of sorts to locate the depths of one's being in a purely internal psychological essence—a self-fulfillment substance. A radical critique of this subjectivism, gnosticism—if you will—narcissism must be and is being made.[19] Christians are called to offer a more rigorous critique of the blatant subjectivism of self-fulfillment as people discovering and living out life as a "new creation" in Christ: those called to do good works (Eph. 2:10) as a witness to internal and external fulfillment. The good works claimed in the Wesleyan tradition are not a superficial "show and tell" of cultural "blessings." The ongoingness of one's life in Christ is an objectifying witness of the transforming power of Christ's redeeming power as initial aim, but one is also called to join in the "downward pull of the gospel" (Phil. 2:5-11).

> We often think that service means to give something to others, to tell them how to speak, act, or behave; but now it appears that above all else, real, humble service is helping our neighbors discover that they possess great but often hidden talents that can enable them to do even more for us than we can do for ourselves.[20]

Good works are intended to show forth a spirit of gratitude and thankfulness, actions born of humble service. Having the mind of Christ is to endeavor to become more congruent with the persuasive lures offered as initial aims that the objectification of the moments of our experience will be more Christlike in offering an envisagement of potentiality to others.

XII. Scripture, Tradition, and Community

From its beginning the Good News movement, a self-acclaimed evangelical renewal group within the United Methodists, declared its principal concern one of theological witness. Its task force on doctrine, named in April 1973, began to formulate a statement on this United Methodist renewal group's distinctive beliefs. Was their theological perspective in contrast to any theological position that might be affirmed within the ranks of the larger denomination actually unique? The "Junaluska Affirmation" was the outcome. Adopted by the board of directors of Good News in 1975, it declared in the preamble, "We offer to the United Methodist Church this theological affirmation of Scriptural Christianity." It was an effort to state in contemporary language the intent both of Wesley's Thirty-Nine Articles and the Evangelical United Brethren Confession of Faith. Of note for the occasion is the section in that statement on the Scriptures.[21]

As chairman of that task force, I recall that only one topic in addition to the Holy Scriptures prompted as much internal debate. That related to the decision to choose "humanity," not the traditional "man," to title the discussion of theological anthropology. "Humanity" was selected as more appropriate both in its historic inclusiveness and in the light of the criticism of "man" as a generic term in the contemporary setting. Recall that this debate in the councils of Good News occurred in the early 1970s. Back to the other significant internal debate: How did the group want to express its commitment to an adequate expression of the doctrine of the inspiration of Scriptures? Rejected finally was the use of the terms "inerrant" or "infallible."

Selected as more fitting for Wesleyans was the term "accurate." Later in a commentary on the "Junaluska Affirmation" entitled *Essentials of Wesleyan Theology*, I explained this preference.

> The positive axis of *accuracy* conveys the pastoral and caring component in the writing of Scripture alongside the component of precision. . . . The small prefix *in-* introduces into the actual usage of *inerrant* and *infalliable* a defensive posture. When pressed, this negative axis of *in-* or *non-* locates the actual locus of importance of God's written Word, not on the relationship between God and creation—including the biblical authors—but a life of its own independent from its being a means of expression of its divine and human authors.[22]

In an earlier discussion in this section on the faith and practice, I expressed concern about the abandonment of the vitality of the emergent nature of the Bible's witness and Wesley's emphasis on the practice of piety, not scholasticism.

> Evangelicals, too, allowed the method of their theology to be controlled by secular scientism. They held tenaciously to *sola Scriptura*. But in their preoccupation to retain the pure orthodoxy of the biblical *content*—the Scripture alone is the authority for matters of salvation—they overstepped the essential principle of classical, orthodox Christianity. . . . This change began with the welcomed inclusion of scientific methodology but quickly transformed the theological vision of the evangelicals into a defensive, historical positivism.[23]

Throughout the discussion the affirmation offered a critique of any notion of mechanical verbal dictation, a key position implied though denied by Harold Lindsell's view on inerrancy.[24] His perspective is a clear violation of the hermeneutical spirit of Wesley. A theme clearly followed, both in the *Commentary* itself and perhaps more importantly during the deliberative processes of the task force, was a refusal as Wesleyans to be drawn into the scholasticism of the Princeton Theology and its philosophical assumptions that stand influencially behind the current inerrancy position.[25]

In an effort to further explicate the process modes of thought evident both in Wesley's position on Scripture (and perhaps more significant for current discussion), I presented a paper at the 1979 American Academy of Religion, "A Process Perspective as an Option for a Theology of Inspiration." Free in this context to explore more fully the relational aspects of the Scriptures, and how through the ongoing persuasive vitality of God the Scriptures continue to enliven

Christian faith and practice, the Wesleyan use of a practical process perspective in its views of divine and human interaction in the "co-authoring" of the Bible was explored.[26]

For Wesley clearly the Scriptures were the apex of the objective response by the communities of faith to God, although they too stand as witnesses. In the 1972 *Discipline* statement of the Wesleyan quadralateral the evangelical renewalists were not concerned to introduce a Wesleyan scholasticism, but rather they needed the reassurance that of the four components that constitute Wesleyan theological methodology, Scripture would be retained in a preeminent position.

One may speak of the Bible as "never alone" since it is always read with the help of the community, tradition, the congregation. There is a never-ending interaction between the Bible as written word and the tradition of the contemporary community in its struggle for self-understanding. An appeal for openness to the Holy Spirit to illuminate the *intent* of the biblical witness may not be lost in the present community of faith. The witness of the biblical writers, the "Fathers" of the faith in the broad and narrow context of tradition, of the local congregation, fellowship, or denomination, and of the current existential crises of faith within an historical community of faith flow together in a vital, ceaseless interaction that is at least practically self-evident. Tradition, the teaching office of the congregation, and the sermonic efforts of the pastor feed off the Scriptures. The appeal within the Wesleyan tradition to "Scriptural Christianity" appropriately is an aim to objectify one's reading of God's written Word, aided by a prayerful imploring the continuing luring, inspiring work of divinity to enliven the scriptural witness in its relevance for the church's future.

The precise hermeneutic to be used within this perspective that aims to be guided by the relevance and creative contrasts of the Scriptures for the contemporary situation is not clear, even to the so-called contemporary evangelicals. However the Wesleyan, process, and Roman Catholic perspectives may in fact and practice be closer than we have dared think.

XIII. Evangelicals and Process Modes of Thought: A Wesleyan Kinship

1. *"Process World View."* Evangelicals share with those committed to process modes of thought a stress on the actuality of human experience. Experience is not sheer becoming but moves through a series of actual occasions that are linked as societies of actual occasions. Each momentary experience has its initial, integrative, and final phases. God is active in each and every moment and structure of life. Human beings are both free and derived (relational). Neither God nor the world can be conceived of as rigid containers into which experience or time is poured. Rather we are our experiences.

2. *Grace.* Grace has both radically active and passive aspects. The penitent sinner gladly receives God's grace, but the transforming power of Christ and the Holy Spirit, while continuing to support the passivity needed to be responsive to God's continuous offering of grace, transforms grace into a vigorous faith, active in showing forth the workmanship of Christ in what the believer offers the larger world. The dipolar orientation of process thought and of Wesley allows the radical juxtaposition of grace and faith, active and passive, sinner and saint, certitude and searching to be brought as closely together as they are in this tradition. This tradition is, I would argue, unique in its ability to relate contrasts and discover their relevance for the future.

3. *Growth and Development.* The Wesleyan stress on discipline and growth in one's faith experience stresses singleness of intention, a valuing of time, as essential to God's and the believer's nature. They have a power over the tyranny of the past—sin. And in their affirmation of the radical openness of the future they are essentially relational or process categories.

4. *Absolute Relativity.* The emphasis in Wesleyan thought on the humble place of human life in the cosmos and the rich possibilities for new relations reflects a process orientation. The doctrine of original sin for Wesley evoked this humility, the potential both for growth and backsliding, the daily need of discipline, prayer support, exhortation, and witnessing yield an anthropological vision that, while optimistic about the potential of the human spirit, keeps it radically relative to the larger realities of the universe.

5. *Kinship Struggles.* Evangelical Wesleyan thought and process thought share genuine kinship. I would suggest that the philosophical and cultural differences are less real than traditionally imagined, and the closeness and incompatibilities would benefit from further exploration; that, in fact in the next bicentennial of Methodism that kinship will have become more explicitly a shared tradition in Wesleyan circles.

One of many lingering problems is the struggle with process theology's use of its theory at a level of abstraction just above the best capacities of the local church people to make comfortable connections back to their real life. Therefore unnecessary confusion results, and consequently distrust and alienation are induced. The use of mathematical models in Whitehead tends to perpetuate this abstractness, which nonetheless is gradually being translated into workable imagery for the average nonphilosopher. I share Bernard Loomer's concern that the second, and now the third, generation of Whitehead scholars, not lapse into a process or Whiteheadian scholasticism.

Perhaps ecology and economics are areas of common and heretofore unexplored mutual concern. Process thought is coherent, to be sure. The next major task is to make process categories more workable for the circumstances of the "lower ranks of people," if that can be done. Wesleyan evangelicals border on a holiness scholasticism and need more directly to translate their constructs into the broader public policy dimensions of the witness of contemporary and future United Methodism.

Wesley lived at the dawn of the industrial revolution and was indeed optimistic about the future. His optimism was expressed less in systematic theology than in the lower orders of abstraction: preaching, hymns, revivals, exhortations, debates, visiting. These indeed are low orders of abstraction. The challenge I see is to make the connections between the more systematic view offered by process modes of conceptualization and the practicalities of Wesleyan evangelicalism. Both groups and their intellectual traditions are different sides of the family. Each will need to give up absolute conceptual control and unflinching logical coherence for the sake of the family. Little will be lost, much gained.

The areas of most fruitful immediate discussion among the process and evangelical folks who come out of a Wesleyan tradition will be the cosmological and anthropological assumptions extant in the contemporary cultural milieu. And this discussion, whatever its eventual outcome, would be encouraged by Wesley.

NOTES

1. Donald Dayton, *Discovering an Evangelical Heritage* (New York: Harper & Row, 1976), chap. 9.
2. John B. Cobb, Jr., *Process Theology as Political Theology* (Philadelphia: Westminster Press, 1982), chap. 6.
3. During my tenure as chairman of the national board of directors of Good News, from January 1978 through May 1980, *no* contact was ever made with me by any person associated with what is commonly understood as the Moral Majority. Never in the history of Good News has any item ever come before the board that would suggest any contact, liaison, or collaboration with representatives of the Moral Majority. Further, during my tenure as chairman there was never any conversation with me by anyone about Good News becoming involved in civil political activities.
4. David C. Steinmetz, "Scripture and the Lord's Supper in Luther's Theology," in *Interpretation*, vol. 37, No. 3 (July 1983), pp. 253-65.
5. Bernard M. Loomer, "The Free and Relational Self," in *Belief and Ethics: Essays in Ethics, the Human Sciences, and Ministry in Honor of W. Alvin Pitcher*, ed. W. Wilick Schroeder and Gibson Winter (Chicago: Center for Scientific Study of Religion, 1978), pp. 69-88, esp. pp. 71-72.
6. John Wesley, "Original Sin," in *Works*, vol. 6, pp. 54-64.
7. Gordon E. Jackson, *Pastoral Care and Process Theology* (Washington D.C.: University Press of America, 1981), p. 49; and Alfred North Whitehead, *Religion in the Making* (New York: Macmillan Company, 1930), pp. 159, 205.
8. Robert Schuller, *Self-Esteem: the New Reformation* (Waco: Word Books, 1982).
9. Robert E. Chiles, *Theological Transition in American Methodism: 1790-1935* (Nashville: Abingdon Press, 1965), chaps. 3-5.
10. Robert Burtner and Robert E. Chiles, *John Wesley's Theology* (Nashville: Abingdon Press, 1982), pp. 78-80.
11. Albert C. Outler, ed., *John Wesley* (New York: Oxford University Press, 1964), pp. 177-81.
12. Ibid., p. 179.
13. Schubert Ogden, *The Reality of God and Other Essays* (New York: Harper & Row, 1966), pp. 56-70; Steve Harper, *John Wesley's Message for Today* (Grand Rapids: Zondervan, 1983), p. 93.
14. Ogden, *Reality of God*; Charles W. Hartshorne, *The Divine Relativity: A Social Conception of God* (New Haven: Yale University Press, 1948) and *Reality as Social Process: Studies in Metaphysics and Religion* (Boston: Beacon Press, 1953).
15. Outler, *John Wesley*, p. 97.
16. Ibid., p. 102.
17. Ibid., p. 101.
18. Harper, *John Wesley's Message*, p. 124; Thomas A. Langford, *Practical Divinity* (Nashville: Abingdon Press, 1983), esp. chap. 12; Paul A. Mickey and Robert L. Wilson, *What New Creation?* (Nashville: Abingdon Press, 1977), chap. 5. Throughout the interviews by Mickey and Wilson in preparing *What New Creation?* executives of other denominations were uniform in their admiration of the Methodists' ability to get things done; if someone wanted denominational leaders to do a project, Methodists were most frequently called upon and responsive to the challenge.
19. Daniel Yankelovich, *New Rules* (New York: Random House, 1981).
20. Donald P. McNeill, Douglas A. Morrison, and Henri J. M. Nouwen, *Compassion: A Reflection on The Christian Life* (Garden City: Doubleday & Co., 1982), p. 27 ff.
21. "The Junaluska Affirmation," adopted by the Good News board on July 20, 1975. The task force membership included Riley B. Case, local church pastor, North Indiana Conference; James V. Heidinger, local church pastor, East Ohio Conference; Charles W. Keysor, founder and editor of *Good News*, North Illinois Conference; Dennis F. Kinlaw, president of Asbury College; Paul A. Mickey, professor, Duke University Divinity School; Lawrence H. Souder, layman, Cherry Hill, NJ; Frank Bateman Stanger, president of Asbury Theology Seminary; Robert J. Stamps, campus chaplain, Oral Roberts University.
22. Paul A. Mickey, *Essentials of Wesleyan Theology* (Grand Rapids: Zondervan, 1980), pp. 115, 116.
23. Ibid., pp. 111, 112.
24. Harold Lindsell, *The Battle for the Bible* (Grand Rapids: Zondervan, 1976), see esp. chap. 1 and chap. 8.
25. Jack B. Rogers and Donald K. McKim, *The Authority and Interpretation of the Bible* (San Francisco: Harper & Row, 1979), "Introduction," chaps. 6 and 7.
26. Paul A. Mickey, "A Process Perspective as an Option for a Theology of Inspiration," unpublished paper, presented at the 1979 American Academy of Religion.

3. THE IDEA OF PERFECTION IN A FUTURE CHRISTIAN THEOLOGY

Carl Bangs

"I cannot be perfect; it is hopeless; and God does not expect it."—It would be more honest if one said, "I do not want to be perfect: I am content to be saved." Such ones do not care for being perfect as their Father in heaven is perfect, but for being what they call *saved*. —George McDonald.[1]

The Title and the Topic

The title is a paraphrase of the classic study by R. Newton Flew on the theme of perfection in Christian theology.[2] It is intended to indicate that something more needs to be said on the subject. Flew's work remains an impressive work of historical theology. It is only with tongue-in-cheek, with what I hope will be taken with some sense of humor, that in brief time and brief compass I suggest an "improvement" on it or any peculiar ability to speak about the future. At the same time, Flew's work still stands for some as the last word on the subject. But that last word has some very time-bound elements, some of which are to be appreciated, others not.

One thing that I appreciate is a phrase in his subtitle, "for the present life." That is modest. My title is immodest, "a *future* Christian theology." My boundless self-confidence has been tremendously chastened, however, as I have been trying to find a way to go beyond some basic problems that I see in Flew's work. If there are inadequate presuppositions underlying his work, all the historical work he has done needs to be redone. That task I cannot attempt here. Nor am I primarily interested in criticizing Flew. More modestly, I seek for an opening to the development of a future doctrine of Christian perfection that takes into account some new understandings with which we must deal.

Flew, publishing his work in 1934, was a man of his theological times. The language of the title of his book, "the idea," and of the subtitle, "the Christian ideal," is consonant with the temper of the idealism of late Protestant liberalism. His opening chapter on "The Teaching of Jesus" reveals considerable confidence in the ability to recover "the historical Jesus," and the conviction that the teachings and the religious and moral accomplishments of Jesus are both identifiable and necessary as a basis for Christian life and thought. Jesus teaches "the Kingly rule of God" as an "Ideal" (p. 25), and "The Kingly Rule of God is present in Jesus Himself" (p. 31). "The main elements in the doctrine of any ideal for the present life are still those of the teaching of our Lord, as recorded in the first three Gospels" (p. 415). Flew makes passing references to certain difficulties raised by I. Kant but is satisfied that F. D. E. Schleiermacher and A. Ritschl have overcome them.

Flew's presuppositions have been severely challenged, on many fronts, in the nearly fifty years since his book appeared. It is necessary, then, to open up a future for the doctrine of Christian perfection unless it is to be merely enshrined as an eighteenth-century monument or seen as just another way of expressing the convictions of Protestant liberalism.

A Methodist Subject and Task

Flew wrote as a Methodist, and although he surveyed the broad scope of Christendom, he did raise his voice when he came to John Wesley. The question arises anew for us, however, as to the propriety of regarding this as a peculiarly Methodist question.

A present task arises out of the past and looks to the future. In the denominations with rootage in the life and thought of John and Charles Wesley the past is marked by a central emphasis on Christian perfection. The United Methodist Church is one of these denominations. From that fact, at least, one can say that Christian perfection is a "Methodist subject." As Flew's work so admirably pointed out, however, it is not a Methodist monopoly. There is probably some kind of concern for Christian perfection in every major Christian tradition.

For the Methodists, however, the past provides a particularly heavy concern for the subject. For the Wesleys, Christian perfection was not one doctrine among many but a central theme for all doctrines and one by which Wesleyan thought was distinguished from other major traditions, particularly those of the continental Reformation. We may choose to move into our theological future without any special concern for the subject, but to do so is to move toward a theological amnesia that is already a possible cause of theological forgetfulness (dare I say dimwittedness?) among us.

It is not merely that two Englishmen and their friends, long ago, cared about Christian perfection. It was the central message of the founders and early leaders of American Methodism as well—Francis Asbury, Freeborn Garrettson, and Nathan Bangs, for example. This fact is strangely absent from the historical materials on American Methodism currently in use among us.[3] This is only a part of a general silence in the church on the subject. While there are pockets of vigorous and productive interest, the theme is not characteristic of current publications, curriculum, convocations, or pulpits. Even the hymnody is relatively silent. When Franz Hildebrandt brought out a collection of Wesley hymns, the theme of Christian perfection was markedly muted. Currently, *The Book of Hymns*, while historically and theologically deepened by a recovery of Wesley hymnody, is still slanted by its selections and deletions away from a sense of the centrality of Christian perfection for the Wesleys.

There are many reasons for this, and it is not new. Methodism has long been assuming the character of a "community church," comprehensive, embracing all, a form of Protestantism-in-general that reflects a religious consensus fairly interchangeable among major denominations. And so the "Methodist" character of the question of Christian perfection is debatable from two sides. On one side, Methodism may be deciding that it is no longer bound to its particular history but must simply attempt to meet the needs of a broad spectrum of religious traditions and convictions in the midst of a fast-changing society that has little patience with the past. On the other side, Methodists have no monopoly on any facet of Christian truth and experience, and hence no invitation or obligation to develop something that may at one time have been their special burden and joy.

And yet—we are the only denomination that asks its clergy whether they are going on to perfection, and whether they expect to be made perfect in this life. That quaint and, to some, embarrassing vestige of John Wesley's conferences we have not yet been willing to discard. It is a sign that the question is still with us. We can ignore it at the peril of an ahistorical superficiality or even of personal and corporate dishonesty. But the path is forward as well as backward. I believe that our unusually gifted and sometimes revered Father-in-God John Wesley is still our rich resource in the matter, and at the same time the warning of A. N. Whitehead is to be considered—that a science that is slow to forget its founder is doomed. Within that tension I find myself, as a United Methodist, trying to think about the future of the idea of perfection in Christian theology.

The Teaching of the Wesleys

Among theologians it is scarcely necessary to recount the teachings of the Wesleys and scarcely possible to reconcile all the divergent ways of doing so. I will evade direct responsibility by summarizing what Flew said was the Wesleyan teaching on Christian perfection, and then perhaps add a note or two.

Christian perfection is the "Great Salvation" that follows the experience of conversion (p. 316). It is a gift (p. 317), connected with the thought of the death of Jesus (p. 318).[4] It is communicated by those who already have it, it is usually preceded by distress and earnest seeking, and it is more than mere feeling (p. 318). It is followed by ethical results (p. 320). It is necessary for Christians to aim at perfection, a perfection of love that includes keeping all the commandments and freedom from sin (pp. 324-25). A distinction is made between voluntary and involuntary transgressions; freedom from sin is from the former (p. 326). The reception of the experience of Christian perfection is instantaneous (p. 327) and accompanied by assurance, the "testimony of the Spirit" (p. 328). It is a possibility for "ordinary human life" (p. 330), and it is not merely individual but social and missionary in nature (p. 331).

Much more could be said, but it is not the purpose of this paper to expound Wesley. I would add two points, however, that are central to Wesley. One is the distinction between the believer's "relative perfection" and the "absolute perfection" of God.[5] The other, not merely one among many, is that perfection is perfection in love, "loving God with all our heart, mind, soul and strength," so that "no wrong temper, none contrary to love, remains in the soul and that all the thoughts, words and actions are governed by pure love."[6]

This review must now stand in reserve as attention is drawn to some factors that can be identified as the "modern problem."

The Modern Problem

Since Kant, the idea of perfection has been just that, an *idea*, really the Idea of God, which serves as a heuristic principle whereby one can think about what perfection would be if there should be any perfection. This first of all with respect to divine perfection itself, or absolute perfection (as Wesley called it), or the divine itself. God, for Kant, is an Idea whereby we may think, or speculate, about what we would know if we could grasp the totality of all outer and inner sensations, synthesizing them completely into perceptions, and the perceptions into objects of knowledge, not only into objects of knowledge but into the *totality* of objects of knowledge. We are frustrated in both directions, however. Behind the sensations nothing can be said. The objects of knowledge, out of which the Idea-questions emerge, are finite. The Ideas are a sign of the finite limitation: beyond the Ideas nothing can be said. We are caught in the realm of experience.

It is even more problematical, since Kant, then, to talk about an "experience" of perfection. Experience is by definition finite, synthetic, subjective, incomplete, and in later language "ideological." What would an experience of perfection be? A grasp of the divine perfection? How would one be assured of such a grasp? By a perfect experience? But experience by definition is imperfect. Not only the knowledge of perfection but any knowledge at all is synthetic and incomplete.

The culture of Wesley's day was already infected by the skepticism of the modern mind that we trace from Descartes, Spinoza, and Leibniz through the British empiricists, to Kant and beyond. Wesley drew on Locke. Was he aware of the skepticism permeating Locke's epistemology? He would not have been aware of Kant's devastating disturbance of dogmatic slumbers in epistemology, scarcely published before Wesley died, but it occurs to me that Wesley's frequent (albeit unsteady) insistence on the doctrine of assurance was already in the strain of those revisionist theologies, following Kant, that would attempt to find some cranny in the phenomenal that would allow one to peak at the Thing-in-Itself, to speak, with assurance, of God and the soul, and of the perfection of both. And it was in this early dawn of the modern mind that Wesley developed his doctrine of Christian perfection.

In continuing alliances, formal and informal, conscious and unconscious, between Methodist theology and the broader currents of post-Kantian theology there can be discerned at least three responses to the problem of modern skepticism. One was to dismiss, by deliberation or by mere inattention, the matter of perfection as of no interest. Thus it was by no means uncommon for Methodist writers to ignore what for Wesley had been the very *raison d'etre* of the movement. Witness the long gaps of inattention in middle to late nineteenth-century issues of the *Quarterly Review*s and the *Christian Advocate*s, leading from time to time to outright editorial opposition.

A second response was to emphasize the *experience* of perfection, the "second blessing," the palpable guarantee of having attained the goal of Christian faith and life. There is a parallel to Schleiermacher's feeling of absolute dependence, that total and immediate grasp of God at the base of human experience that is elicited in the community that admires the sanctified consciousness exemplified in Jesus Christ. Some advocates of the second blessing acknowledged a kinship with Schleiermacher; others were unaware of it.

A third response was to interpret perfection ethically, giving rise to selected personal asceticisms and self-disciplines, on the one hand, and selected public concerns for social and civic righteousness, on the other. "Spreading Scriptural holiness throughout the land" could mean the promotion of abstinence from personal vices coupled with an intensified piety, and it could mean also the purification of public order through abolition of social and civic evils and the organization of works of mercy, education, and mission. Here the parallel, but by no means the entire dependency, is to A. Ritschl and his popularizing disciple, A. von Harnack. In some cases, Flew being one, the kinship was acknowledged and the dependency explicit.

This is to say that in the milieu of post-Enlightenment thought it was tempting to take flight from the hard question by recourse to a romanticist confidence in experience or to ethical rigor and activism. The hard question remained that of perfection itself, which is to say, of God, and the material content of that question is Christology. Other developments, within Christian scholarship itself, were to have the effect of leading to the same question.

Using the Bible

The advent of a critical approach to Scripture is another factor that calls for recasting the doctrine of Christian perfection. This has been tried from time to time. William E. Sangster, for instance, in *The Path to Perfection*, identified John Wesley's "thirty texts" (I have never been able to determine which thirty they were), and he judged them, in the light of critical scholarship, acceptable supports for Wesley's doctrine. But that approach is adequate neither for Wesley nor for the present situation in biblical studies.

Wesley himself could believe that he had derived his doctrine from the Bible, and to his credit it must be acknowledged that he and his brother Charles were so steeped in Scripture, in the original languages, and in the King James Version, that concordances in hand would have been unnecessary baggage for them. John Wesley's everyday speech, as seen in the *Journal*, reveals his practice, indeed his ingrained habit, of talking about almost anything in a pastiche of words and phrases from all over the Bible.[7] In some respects it could seem, then, that Wesley's theology was a paste-up of proof texts. Such a view, whether held even by Wesley or defended by Sangster, is somewhat beside the point, however, because in itself it does not get at the historical-theological reasons for Wesley's interest in perfection.

Wesley's concern for perfection was integral to the Anglican and anti-Calvinist piety and theology in which he was nourished and which he fostered. Life lived in the fullness of the perfect love of God was something more than forensic forgiveness. Wesley's message, as Sangster observed, was that God could do more about sin than forgive it. The concern for Christian perfection for Wesley was a way of getting at the quality of Christian life, the state as well as the standing, the obedience as well as the trust, life in time as well as life in eternity. If Wesley was pre-critical in his use of Scripture, he was not spiritually undiscerning as to what made sense theologically. The "man of one book" was (at his best) not a biblicist.

The rise of critical biblical scholarship, with which Wesley could scarcely have been acquainted, was related to something that had been central to Wesley, namely Christology. One of the first manifestations of this would be the Jesus-of-history movement. Wesley's Christology was traditional and orthodox, seeing Scripture through the faith of the "primitive church" (meaning the New Testament and the first five centuries, especially in the Greek writers). While he assumed that he knew about the "historical Jesus," that term, and the skepticism inherent in it, was unknown to him. Wesley's fellowship was with the Christ he encountered in the apostolic witness, while his Christology was classical orthodoxy's "from above." He saw no conflict between them.

The "from above" theme in the Charles Wesley nativity hymns is consistently clear: "Suffice for us that God, we know, / Our God, is manifest below." "God the invisible appears . . . And Jesus is His name." "See the eternal Son of God / A mortal Son of Man."

"Being's source begins to be, / And God himself is born!" "Our God contracted to a span, / Incomprehensibly made man." But at the same time there is the theme of friendship with Jesus, following in his ways: "God . . . shows Himself our Friend." "Jesus is our Brother now." "Into Thy love direct our heart, / Into Thy way of perfect peace." And the nativity hymns go one step farther, to link friendship with and following of Christ who is "God contracted to a span" with our perfection, indeed, in the style of the Greek writers, with our divinization: "He deigns in flesh to appear, / Widest extremes to join; / To bring our vileness near, / And make us all divine." "Made perfect first in love, / And sanctified by grace . . . Then shall His love be fully showed, / And man shall then be lost in God."

From the nativity hymns I get some clues that seem to help me move forward. To speak of Christian perfection is to speak of Christ. To put it negatively, Christian perfection is not to be defined in terms of perfection-in-general (although it may turn out that Christian perfection will illuminate the idea of perfection itself). And if Christian perfection is christological, something is lost or misdirected when the focus is put on human potentiality, on very special religious experiences, on ethical rigor, on social betterment, or even on the "absolute perfection" which Wesley ascribed to God alone. It may very well be that these will be illuminated by Christology, but they are not substitutes for it.

This is related to the matter of biblical studies because it has to do with what we are to look for when we read the Bible. It also has to do with the general or philosophical presuppositions with which we operate.

The Hard Part: Trying to Move Forward

Flew made a number of criticisms of the Wesleys' teaching on Christian perfection. I have not reviewed them here. The difficulties are more critical, I feel, than those he set forth. The problem has to do, on the one hand, with the "modern mind" of Kant and most post-Kantians, for whom talk about perfection (read: God) is at best speculation in the realm of ideas, or at worst not any real talk at all, there being no way, as they say, of empirically verifying the objective referent of God-talk. If, on the other hand, as Christians we are to say that Christian perfection is rooted in Christology, what Christology is possible for us if the quest for the historical Jesus is itself a futile effort to get behind the phenomenal (the biblical witness) to the noumenal (the "real" Jesus)?

Appeals to authority are tempting, and, since Kant, many have been tried. Christians since Kant, in a panic of uncertainty, have sought anchorage in something that they hoped would provide assured access to the perfect. Infallible Bible and infallible pope were only two such hopes. Sacramentalism, confessionalism, religious experience, systems of Christian idealism, social reconstruction, attempts to harmonize religion and science, biographical depictions of the nobility of the man Jesus, promotion of the social and personal utility of faith as positive thinking, the claim to understand the immanent dialectic of history, or the testimony that revelation seizes us vertically from above—all these have been tried. Perfection still eludes us.

When I get to this point, I am reminded of William Booth's famous book, *Darkest England, and the Way Out*. There were probably many people in Britain who could have written the first part. Booth is remembered because he wrote both parts. I hope now to find the clues that can direct us to the future, "the way out," even though I shall not hope to be acclaimed as a theological Booth.

I have held back from talking about the biblical studies of Bultmann and the post-Bultmannians, partly because I have not immersed myself in the literature, but mostly because I am deeply indebted to a colleague in theology who has done so, and who, in my opinion, helps me see something of "the way out." I refer to Professor Schubert Ogden, who combines, not only his deep involvement with the world of Bultmann and the post-Bultmannians, but also an awareness of the philosophical issues that cannot be avoided. It was one passage, at first, in his book on Christology that began to tie things together for me. "An answer to the question of God," he says, "expresses an understanding at once of what alone is ultimately real and of what we ourselves are therefore given and called to be."[8] In that passage I see the tie for which I have been looking between the divine perfection, "what alone is ultimately real," and our destiny, "what we are given and called to be."

Ogden makes another step for which I have been looking, the link between "what is ultimately real" and Christology. Without attempting to summarize his entire case, and absolving him from any responsibility for any misunderstanding I have of it, I bring forward some of his key statements. For one, "The question christology answers can be understood not simply as a question about Jesus, but also and at the same time as a question about the meaning of ultimate reality for human existence."[9] For another,

getting closer to what he understands to be possible in Christology, referring to passages in Acts and Mark, Jesus "is asserted to be the one through whom God is decisively revealed."[10] The New Testament witness is not "that he perfectly actualized authentic self-understanding," but that "he is the explicit primal source that alone can authorize any such self-understanding."[11]

Behind this is Ogden's rejection not only of the quest for the historical Jesus but also of the "new quest." In the place of the "empirical-historical" answers that these seek, Ogden finds in the New Testament witness the "existential-historical" answer that is needed religiously and theologically. The apostolic and Christian witness is that in Jesus we find "who we are given and called to be by the mysterious ultimate reality determining our existence as human beings."[12]

What are the implications of this for understanding Christian perfection? One, as the Wesleys have told us, is that it is love. Not just human love, not just love as an attribute of God, but the love which is God. "Thy nature and Thy name is Love" ("Wrestling Jacob"). This is to say, metaphysically, that ultimate reality is love, connectedness instead of conflict, community instead of isolation, integration instead of fragmentation, life instead of death. Is this confidence warranted in a post-Kantian age? To put it negatively, I find it no more problematical than the Cartesian skepticism and "rugged" and isolated individualism that was the underpinning of both continental rationalism and British empiricism. Kant could find no answer because his questions were wrong. He, and his heirs, had inherited two bankrupt traditions. The Wesleys, in proclaiming love as the very nature of God and therefore as the destiny for people living in time, ran against the temper of their skeptical time, but they knew that faith in Christ implied no less.

Some corollary observations come to mind. One is that a distinction between the "absolute perfection" of God and the believer's "relative perfection" is probably not helpful because it introduces a non-christological, speculative element that confuses and discourages. The terms are unclear at best. If relative perfection is the perfection we can know in relatedness, it is the only relevant perfection. Absolute perfection would probably be not very useful, or enjoyable. It would be like Aristotle's Unmoved Mover, about whom someone once observed that such a God could not be praised with a "Holy, Holy, Holy," but only with a "Circle, Circle, Circle." John Wesley sometimes had to "tone down" the exuberance of the poetic metaphorical perfectionist language of his brother Charles, probably because both of them entertained vestiges of Platonic notions of perfection and were not sure what to do with them. At their best, the Wesleys knew that Christian perfection was the fundamental category for talking about the Incarnate Love of the apostolic witness.

Christian perfection, then, is not something added to Christian faith as a special monastic "superabundance" or as an especially intense religious experience, or as moral rigor. It is at the heart of the faith, which is Jesus Christ as he is made real to us in the witness of the church. The notion of a "second blessing" can obscure the centrality of Christology, especially if it has the effect of transferring Christian perfection from Christology to a separate category of "pneumatology." At the same time, the "secondness" may be a way of saying that the continental Reformation was deficient or one-sided in its understanding of Christology, limiting the "benefits of Christ" to the removal of guilt.

If Christian perfection is to be termed an "experience," it must be seen in a metaphysics that does not assume the inability of experience to be in contact with God. Otherwise, the "experience" becomes sheerly subjective, on one hand, or, on the other, magical or "supernatural," a development that I think I see where a doctrine of Christian perfection is grafted on to a sheerly supernatural world view, calling for "supernatural phenomena" as evidences of the "blessing." The French Roman Catholic theologian Lucien Laberthonnière warned that "supernatural" is not necessarily "good." There is also *un surnaturel de pacotille*, supernatural trash.[13]

An old question inevitably arises and will not be put down. Is it not presumptuous to claim such a perfection? Does not the claim negate it?

The issue has been long debated. It is observed that Wesley seemed to make no such claim for himself. His grounds for claiming it for others seem problematical to us ("they rejoice evermore, pray without ceasing, in every thing give thanks"). Claims have been made that did not impress us. Perhaps we have been disappointed in our own. The question lies elsewhere. Have we been touched by the perfect, which is to say, have we been loved? If we have shut out the love which comes to us, or if we have failed to acknowledge the "ultimate reality" of it, the witness of the first Christians calls us farther. We are called in Christ to a different destiny, to the love that "alone is ultimately real," to "what we ourselves are therefore given and called to be."[14]

To link this with "destiny" and "calling" sets before me another task which is opened up by the new situation in biblical studies and new possibilities in metaphysics, the linking of the idea of Christian perfection with biblical and Reformation themes of "destiny" and "calling." Methodism, in its early polemical bouts with Calvinism in Britain and in New England, leaned heavily toward free will, freedom of choice. But there is one thing better than being free to choose, and that is to be chosen. The new understanding of predestination set forth in our century by Pierre Maury (followed by K. Barth) has stressed the *christological* character of predestination. Christ is the Chosen One, the true object of "predestination," and "in Christ" we find our calling. It is this emphasis that has enabled the Dutch Reformed Church and the Remonstrant Brotherhood in Holland to reach a formal accord on the issue which led to their separation in the seventeenth century and which has prompted the theologians of the Christian Reformed Church to issue a new translation of the Canons and Decrees of Dort to show the link between Christology and predestination. J. Arminius, in the early seventeenth century, had made some cautious but unclear moves in this direction, but they were overlooked by his followers, including the Methodists.[15]

In Sum

Methodism in its beginning bore witness to Christian perfection as the very purpose and content of Christian faith. The Wesleys interpreted it as a central affirmation of Christology, not as an option for those "who like that sort of thing." In the intervening decades Methodism has been uncertain about what to do with its historic witness. "It hasn't been nice to its Granddad," as a distinguished Lutheran historian of doctrine observed to me once. There is an opportunity now, in the light of new (and indeed "radical") biblical studies and in the context of a recovery of a metaphysics of love, to move forward to claim what ought to be our expectation, "to be made perfect in this life." Apart from that, what is the use of being "saved"?

NOTES

1. George McDonald, *Unspoken Sermons*, in C. S. Lewis, ed., *George McDonald, An Anthology* (New York: Macmillan Company, 1947), p. 28.
2. R. Newton Flew, *The Idea of Perfection in Christian Theology: An Historical Study of the Christian Ideal for the Present Life* (New York: Humanities Press, [1934] 1968).
3. The admirable work of Frederick A. Norwood is a case in point. In both his *Story of American Methodism* (1974) and his *Sourcebook* (1982), the topic is treated almost exclusively with reference to the later holiness movement.
4. Here I must already demur, for Flew omits the close

relationship of the gift to the birth of Christ, as expressed in the Charles Wesley nativity hymns, about which more later.

5. In *A Plain Account of Christian Perfection*, 1766.
6. John Wesley, *Thoughts on Christian Perfection*, c. 1759, rev. by Wesley, 1787; in Albert C. Outler, ed., *John Wesley* (New York: Oxford University Press, 1964), p. 284.
7. For a pastiche drawn from the pastiches of Wesley, see Carl Bangs, *Our Roots of Belief* (Kansas City: Beacon Hill Press of Kansas City, 1971), chap. 3.
8. Schubert M. Ogden, *The Point of Christology* (San Francisco: Harper & Row, 1982), p. 39.
9. Ibid., p. 87. Ogden develops and applies this point throughout the book.
10. Ibid., p. 76.
11. Ibid., p. 79.
12. Ibid., p. 42.
13. This point is developed in his *Le Réalisme Chrétien et l'Idéalisme Grèc* (Paris, 1904), a book still relevant for the development of a metaphysics of love.
14. Ogden, *Point of Christology*, p. 39.
15. See Carl Bangs, *Arminius: A Study in the Dutch Reformation* (Nashville: Abingdon Press, 1971), pp. 350-55 *et passim*.

4. WESLEY, PROCESS AND LIBERATION THEOLOGIES: A TEST CASE

Ignacio Castuera

Several concerns inform the writing of the present paper. A sense of rootedness impels me to pay attention to my Wesleyan heritage. A fascination and admiration for process thought categories compel me to test ideas over against this background. A passion for justice has made liberation theologies extremely appealing. And lately, as a district superintendent in the Los Angeles District, a concern for evangelization and ecumenical cooperation has forced me to deal almost on a daily basis with the question of how the theological influences in my life can be brought to bear upon decisions which affect the lives of the pastors and congregations under my supervision.

Los Angeles today is without any doubt the most cosmopolitan city in this nation and in the world. A recent article in *Time* refers to this city as the "new Ellis Island." Diversity and pluralism are the distinctive marks of Los Angeles. This diversity is extended beyond ethnicity to economic and life-style expressions. Los Angeles contains within its city limits the third largest concentration of homosexuals in the world. Only San Francisco and New York have a larger concentration of gay men and lesbian women. At the most recent Gay Pride Parade ninety thousand people showed up. Most serious politicians are astutely courting the gay and lesbian community for votes and financial support. Unfortunately at the very same time the church I love, The United Methodist Church, seems to be heading in a direction which will make it harder, if not impossible, to evangelize and attract to our congregations members of this much maligned community.

I love the city, Los Angeles in particular and the modern urban complex in general. The modern city is the haven of people who do not feel at home or accepted in their original settings. This brings richness and peril to the modern city, but there is the place where I want to live and continue my ministry. I attended seminary during the years when Harvey Cox's *Secular City* was in vogue, and my training included theologizing *in situ* among Hippies, revolutionary radicals, and the homophile communities in San Francisco and Los Angeles. What Bishop Paul Moore, Jr., once said about New York applies equally to Los Angeles and to the majority of the populous cities in the world:

> In New York we are not ministering to the ideal American nuclear family. Instead our churches are full of divorcees, alcoholics, the aged, homosexuals, poor Blacks, Hispanics, Asians, Haitians, immigrants—in a word the dispossessed. These are our people, God's children, the poor beloved of Jesus of Nazareth.[1]

It was among the dispossessed, wherever he found them, that John Wesley's ministry was first carried out, and it is in the spirit of our founder to continue ministering and theologizing with our newer tools in the midst of the city. Process thought and liberation theology are two of the best theological tools we have available, and we must use them to speak to our church in general and to our General Conference delegates in particular about the many issues which affect the lives of congregations in the large cities, beginning with the issue of participation of gay and lesbian people in all levels of our church life.

We are gathered here as theologians who have been summoned to speak about the issues which the church needs to address theologically in the next century. We would be derelict to our responsibility if we did not say something, however tentative, about this "hot" issue. We cannot expect other bodies in the church to address this matter dispassionately. Strong emotions are generated when religion and sex mix. I am not even sure that we can be dispassionate here (I know I will not be), but I happen to believe that we can speak the truth to each other in love much better here than in places where clever manipulations with Robert's Rules of Order will limit debate to an hour and speeches to one minute.

In his book, *A Disturbed Peace*, Brian McNaught states "No one should have expected the bishops to issue a public statement reversing 2000 years of procreative theology. If such a reversal comes, it will begin with theologians."[2] I can easily imagine a United Methodist saying the same and simply adding "or with the General Conference." If such a reversal is to happen in United Methodism, if we expect to hear statements informed with compassion and understanding, we as theologians must take the risk first.

I cannot go back to Los Angeles with confidence to speak about evangelization among gay men and lesbian women unless at the same time I challenge my theologian friends to start addressing this issue. This paper is therefore a witness and a summons for all of you to turn the light of intellect upon the dark scene of pure opinion. I address this issue in particular not because I feel that other matters are less important, but because I see in the irrational fear of homosexuals the vortex where all irrational fears have come together. "Homophobia" is the last of the aversions which can be publicly expressed without much fear of reprisal. Women and ethnics cannot be made the butt of jokes as easily as in the past (although this battle is hardly over). And all the accumulated anger against women and ethnics is surfacing with great force against homosexual persons. The real "phobia" then is not "homophobia" but "heterophobia," fear of those who are different. I am "hetero" enough to be concerned. Also my reading of history tells me that the persecution of any marginalized group is—if not checked—followed by the persecution of other identifiable minorities. Witness, for example, the fact that homosexuals and communists were among the first to go to the concentration camps and the ovens in Hitler's Germany.

Liberation Theology and Homosexuality

Generally liberation theologians have been occupied with the issues of racism, sexism, and economic oppression, and have neglected to write or speak of the issue of homosexuality. Yet when one starts out with a concern for justice, sooner or later the issue of the oppression of a group which has a love for persons of the same sex must be addressed. It is already evident that women who have identified themselves with the feminist perspective have also begun to use their categories for thinking for the issues of gay and lesbian liberation. More will be said about this later. For now it suffices to state that there are no structural or other reasons to assume that liberation theology will be antagonistic to the concerns of gay men and lesbian women.

Process Theology and Homosexuality

When one looks in the direction of process theologians, one immediately finds that the issue of homosexuality has already been addressed in a sympathetic—if not advocating—manner. David Griffin defended in front of the Disciples Convention the right of openly gay and lesbian persons to be ordained. (His statement was later printed in *Encounter*.)

Arvid Adell, from Millikin University in Decatur, Illinois, also has suggested that process thought can help the church move in the direction of a more compassionate and grace-full attitude toward homosexuals. Again, later in the paper it will be necessary to show more specifically how process theology can be a significant tool for the task, but it is important to acknowledge that United Methodist process theologians are by no means blazing an untrodden path. Others courageously have started ahead of us.

Among those who have addressed squarely the issue before us is the British Anglican theologian Norman Pittenger. Pittenger uses the categories of process theology to advocate before the majority community for understanding and openness, and before the homosexual community for an ethical life-style; within their particular gender and sex preference, which becomes the gospel. *Time for Consent* was Pittenger's plea to accept homosexuality as a part of the created order and not as a sin or an aberration, or even an illness. It is important to note that he was the first theologian of note to write in this manner at a time when churches here and in his native England were rather oblivious to the issue. Coincidentally United Methodists were among the first major denominations to say anything positive. Don Kuhn from Glide Memorial United Methodist Church wrote the final report of a consultation sponsored by the Board of Christian Social Concerns, now called Board of Church and Society, on the church and the homosexual. This consultation took place in 1965, and Edward Hansen, then a student at the School of Theology at Claremont doing an internship with Glide, was one of the prime movers and organizers of this event. Hansen and Kuhn are both United Methodists, and both find the categories of process theology very supportive of gay and lesbian persons in their struggles for justice. Pittenger's book appeared in England in 1967. Since then he has written abundantly on the subject, appealing to process thought categories as foundational in his work.

It is not surprising to me that both United Methodists and process theology exponents were among the first to come out in defence of homosexual persons. Wesley's passionate involvement with the dispossessed in his day and Whitehead's clear challenge and correction of traditional conceptions of God, nature, humanity, and so on, combine naturally to present a formidable approach to the possible solution of a problem which has plagued the Christian church for centuries.

Narrowing the Scope

In addressing the subject before us, myriad issues arise, and it is extremely important to focus clearly on two or three of those issues. Bishop Moore listed in his address to the 1977 Convention of the Episcopal Diocese of New York several, but by no means all, the subjects which need to be addressed when dealing with this issue:

Let me reiterate, we are dealing with a most complex problem. It includes the issues of the authority of the Church, the authority of Scripture, the nature of the Bishop's office, the doctrine of sacrament, the theology of ordination, the nature of man [sic], the place of psychiatric theory in the Church, the relation of the Church to the world, the dynamics of sexuality, the interpretation of Church history, and the role of the standing committees, to name a few.[3]

Indeed to name a few! As it must be evident, a paper for our consultation could not possibly touch on all the issues enumerated by Bishop Moore. I wish to make a few comments about two or three of them and concentrate on three areas where I believe that Wesley's thought and action, process theology and liberation movements in the church, have a more significant contribution to make: namely, the doctrine of God, Christian anthropology, and the nature of ordained ministry.

On the Authority of Scripture

I do not intend to sidestep the issue of scriptural authority. A United Methodist thinker dare not do that! My personal expertise in biblical studies is relatively limited, and I must rely on other scholars. However, in general my attitude toward the traditional interpretation of the few instances in which homosexuality is mentioned in Scriptures is colored by the historical critical method and the demythologization project of Bultmann and his followers. Cultural influences certainly must be taken into account when dealing with those texts which appear to have clear denunciations of homosexual behaviour. Our appropriating of valid and valuable teachings from our past is never wholesale, and as we well know, there are three other parts in the "quadrilateral".

Fred Craddock and Walter Wink have provided us with two concise statements on homosexuality and the Bible. Craddock concentrated on the New Testament texts and cautiously, yet firmly and convincingly, disagreed with negative statements which had emerged from misreadings in the past.[4]

Wink dealt mainly with Old Testament texts and concluded, more boldly than Craddock, that the Bible does not contain a sexual ethic, but only a "love ethic which is constantly being brought to bear on whatever sexual mores are dominant in any given country, or culture, or period."[5]

Process theology will, I am sure, help provide an adequate hermeneutic to deal with all the texts which appear to be flat condemnations of homosexual persons. A creative dialogue has already begun between process theologians and biblical scholars. One effort worth mentioning in this setting is that of William Beardsley.[6]

Since we are interested in what is happening in United Methodist circles it is important to mention that at Iliff, Kent Harold Richards has shown great interest in the way process thought and biblical scholarship can be creatively brought together. I would more than welcome an article or lecture on "A Process Hermeneutic on Biblical Statements on Homosexuality."

For me the bottom line remains that responsible use of the Bible demands that we do not limit ourselves to proof-text production but that we look for the way in which the Bible, as a living document, addresses the question of the nature of God, humanity, the church, and so on. As Gerhard Ebeling has correctly stated, "our duty is not limited to insist on one definite interpretation which we have inherited, but rather, to insist on a never ending interpretation of the Gospel."

Religion and the Sciences

Bishop Moore lists the question of the place of psychiatric theory in the church as an issue which those interested in speaking about homosexuality must address. That question is part of the larger question of the relationship between faith and science. The Christian faith has had a schizophrenic posture before the sciences. On the one hand, it has seen the sciences as "daughters" and encouraged scientific exploration, while on the other hand, it has seen in the sciences a threat. Process theology has been on the side of those who view the sciences positively; we have no other choice! Whitehead's thought is in itself scientific. Process theologians have encouraged and participated in dialogues with scientists. John Cobb and Charles Birch cooperated in a book in which theology and science produce a magnificent amalgam. All this is to suggest that at the very least psychiatry must be a conversation partner in the church when one deals with issues such as homosexuality, where psychiatric theory can illuminate the subject under discussion. This, of course, does not mean that psychiatry has the last word, but the church dare not pronounce that last word without consulting psychiatry. It is extremely important to remember before we proceed further that the American Psychiatric Association has removed homosexuality from its list of illnesses and that while the discussion is far from finished, the consensus in the scientific community is moving decidedly in the direction of viewing homosexuality as a condition within the varied range of human sexuality, a condition which does not involve after a certain early age the element of "choice." John Money, among others, has suggested that the question of social conditioning versus inherited or genetic determination of sexual preference is a moot one since physiologically the nervous system is not equipped to discriminate between impulses generated by one or the other cause. As it should be obvious by now, I operate from the perspective that homosexual persons do not have a choice in the matter of being homosexuals. However, my reasons for believing this, while informed by psychiatry, are determined more by sociology and by my personal acquaintance with oppression and marginalization. To suggest that a person would "choose" to be a homosexual in the midst of a "homophobic" society is as absurd as to suggest that a person would choose to be black or Hispanic in the midst of a racist society.

One more thing ought to inform the way in which we understand the issue of homosexuality. As process theologians we ought to follow Whitehead's advice to use our own personal experience to inform the way in which we view other experiences. Our own sexual passion ought to indicate or suggest that sexuality is not something anyone chooses; rather, sexuality is a mysterious, wonderful force designed by God and nature to bring people closer together as well as to insure the procreation of the human race. Ethical choices must still be made, and a homosexual ethic can and must be shaped by the church in conversation with homosexual persons, but the worst place to start is in condemnation and accusation. Violating somewhat the principle of not proof-texting, I wish to remind us that before Jesus said to the woman caught in "the very act of adultery" "Go and sin no more," he first stated, "Neither do I condemn you." I

said that I violated my suggested rule "somewhat" because in that text, which some members of the church found embarrassing enough to omit from many of the better manuscripts, we find Jesus at his best, proclaiming the indicatives of love long before the imperatives of that same love are enunciated.

Doctrine of God and Homosexuality

I suggested before that Wesleyan, process, and liberation conceptualities would have a positive contribution to make on the subject of homosexuality and Christian theology at the point of a concept of God, or a doctrine of God. Many of the people who make vituperative and derogatory statements about the role of homosexuals in the church would be horrified when shown what such statements say about their own concept of God. The Christian God, even in our most traditional formulations, has retained love as a central or, pardon the expression, essential component of deity. To suggest that a loving God would will homosexuality on approximately 10 percent of humanity, knowing that such a condition was an aberration, is to suggest that the God we know through Jesus Christ is some kind of a cosmic masochist who might as well also will or permit (take your choice) the slaughter of innocent children or the condemnation of the majority of the human race and the salvation of a few "elect."

John Wesley rebelled against suggestions which would have God playing macabre games of "win and lose." That is precisely what Wesley saw "Calvinists" doing in his time and against them he wrote:

> O that God would give unto you who thus speak [about predestination] meekness of wisdom! Then would I ask, What would the universal voice of mankind pronounce of the man that should act thus? that being able to deliver millions of men from death with a single breath of his mouth, should refuse to save any more than one in a hundred, and say, "I will not, because I will not!" How then do you exalt the mercy of God, when you ascribe such a proceeding to him? What a strange comment is this on his own word, that "his mercy is over all his work!"[7]

Explanatory note: In all quotations I am leaving intact the language which the authors used even though I disagree with the exclusive use of male gender nouns and pronouns. I find it too awkward to write *sic* after every instance where such language appears. I shall attempt to avoid sexist language in all my own text but will leave the quotes in their original patriarchal forms.

The statement by Wesley is fascinating because not only does it address the issue under discussion, that is, the nature of God, but also because it exemplifies the method which Wesley used to argue against misreadings of Scripture. It is rather obvious that the Bible does contain some texts which will lead a person to postulate a naïve doctrine of election. Wesley does not merely pit one verse against another—"His mercy is over all his works"—but appeals to reason and common experience. "What would the universal voice of mankind pronounce . . . ?" Here the universal voice of mankind appears to have more authority, when put together with "his mercy is over all his works," than whatever other text or texts Wesley's opponent may be using.

Now looking more closely at the subject of the concept of God which Wesley favors, it becomes apparent that mercy is the dominant character which he wants to preserve over against or above any other attribute. Wesley is consistent on this matter, and in spite of using such traditional categories as omnipotence and omnipresence, he comes back to the tender elements of mercy and love as central to the divine nature. In almost all the quotations which Burtner and Chiles use to show how Wesley spoke about God, the element of love is dominant and they take careful note of that.

Wesley orients his formulations of the doctrines of God, Christ, and the Holy Spirit about one central theme, the salvation of men's souls. Hence there is little philosophical speculation about the divine nature, while the love of God in saving grace is alluded to countless times. This love is basic to an understanding of the divine life; it is also the high calling of all men who are in Christ. It leads to a complete denial of the rigorous predestinarian doctrines of later scholastic Calvinism. God's love is poured out on all men who will be made whole by its power. *Any conception that implicitly or explicitly denies this distorts Christianity. Salvation by grace through faith does not permit views of God's sovereignty and justice which are not consonant with his mercy and love.*[8]

Liberation theologians—like Wesley—have not had the luxury of "philosophical speculation about the divine nature." Many critics, sympathetic and antagonistic alike, have pointed out this lacuna in much of liberation theology. However, the implied nature of God seems to indicate a dominance of love and mercy also. Granted, unashamedly the majority of liberation theologians would argue in favor of a "preferential option for the poor" (the position which the

bishops of CELAM assumed in Puebla in 1979), but they would add that this in turn also is good news for the oppressors who need to be liberated from the enslavement to all the excesses and vices that seem to accompany their position of privilege. William K. McElvaney understood this well and wrote a book with the fascinating title *Good news is bad news is good news . . .*[9] The action of God in history on behalf of the oppressed is also on behalf of the oppressors. The oppressors' perceive the good news to the poor as bad news for the wealthy, but in reality it is also good news for them. The fact still remains that liberation theology requires a God whose primary attribute is love.

Process theology provides both Wesleyan theology and liberation theology with the philosophical tools needed to undergird the pronouncements they make about the nature of God. First of all, process theology rejects the traditional notions of God as cosmic moralist, God as the unchanging and passionless absolute, God as controlling power, God as sanctioner of the status quo, and God as male (I am sure everyone here recognizes these headings as coming from Cobb and Griffin's *Process Theology: An Introductory Exposition,* pp. 8-10). Earlier Whitehead had started his attack against the God who is fashioned after caesar in favor of the God we know in the Galilean beginnings of Christianity, who is more akin to the tender elements of the universe. On the positive side process thinkers like Pittenger have referred to God not only as love but as the Lover:

I am absolutely convinced that a Christian must begin all of his thinking, as he must seek to govern all of his acting, with the assurance that the grain of the universe runs with, and is, nothing other than Love. I capitalize the word, because I am saying that in the light of all that Jesus of Nazareth was and did, meant and still means, we are given the disclosure, in concrete human and historical fact, of God as cosmic Lover, as Love itself but as Love in a personalized—and a personalizing—form. Whatever else we may feel it necessary to say about God must of necessity be understood as adverbial to the active verb, "to love," which is God himself—for God, in biblical understanding, is no "substance" of a static sort but a living, active, dynamic reality whose "being" is identical with his "doing."[10]

I quoted Pittenger, but I could have just as easily found similar statements written by just about any theologian who is influenced by process philosophical categories. It is important to note Pittenger's rejection of "essentialist" thinking. One of the reasons why traditional categories were problematic is because of their dependence on such essentialist thinking. It took all kinds of mental pirouettes to keep all "essential" attributes in balance. Process thought allows us to proclaim more firmly and convincingly God's grace.

When God is seen primarily as love or lover and not as cosmic moralist, it becomes a much easier task first to see judgmental statements in Scripture about homosexuals—or anybody—as culturally conditioned. Then following Wesley's methodology, we can use "the universal voice of mankind" plus process thought, plus other portions of Scripture that are congruent with God's love—like "His mercy is over all his works"—and state boldly that God's love for homosexual persons should be the guideline used by the church in treating God's creatures who happen to be of a homosexual persuasion.

Bishop Paul Moore may or may not be influenced by process thinking, but he is surely influenced by a theology which sees God's love as primary and all other "attributes" as subordinated to the Deity's grace.

> We Christians believe that the Spirit of God can and does work through the confusions of history to bring about His will. We are never sure at the time what His will may be, but looking back to the Old Testament history of the people of Israel, the life of Jesus and His followers in the New Testament, and the life of the Church ever since, certain patterns do emerge. Great movements occur which later generations tend to agree are providential even though, at the time they occurred, conscientious Christians or Jews battled to the death on either side. . . .
>
> The criteria by which I try to test the validity of change in doctrine are: Does this change give us a larger understanding of God and bring us closer to an understanding of Him as revealed in Scripture? Does this change liberate our spirit to become more fully human and nearer to the image of Christ? Does it reflect more clearly the image of God in which we are made? Therefore, does this change make us more compassionate, more just, more loving, and more free? If the change in thinking or practice accomplishes these goals, it is of God.[11]

"More just, more compassionate, more loving, more free." These are goals which the God which process theology can affirm can energize human beings to become. It is a concept of God which enriches Wesleyan and liberation theologies and which ought to enable the church to incorporate into all levels and roles of the life of the community of saved sinners those who find it imperative to disclose their sexual preference for the sake of a clear witness of love to the gay and lesbian communities. The task is not easy, especially because those who need to have a change of mind need also a change of heart and will not be convinced simply by cogent arguments and brilliant reasoning. However some will be converted when reminded that in the Christian church we are obligated to proclaim the primacy of grace.

Christian Anthropology and Homosexuality

The influence which essentialist thinking has had on Christianity can be partly blamed for the present situation vis-a-vis homosexuality. In addition, a view of nature as closed and ordered with a pyramidal structure having a perfect God at the top and lesser perfections in descending order further cooperates to create a climate in which homosexual persons are seen as "less than the ideal," or abnormal or unnatural. Attempts have been made to argue against such views, but generally they have failed to get to the central issue which is the "fixed" or "essential" categories used to refer to humanity and to the whole created order (even the use of terms like *created order* are atavistic!).

Existentialism in several of its forms began to mount the most formidable attack on essentialist views of humanity. Influenced by this thinking, people like Ross Snyder could assert "There is nothing more stupid or menacing than the argument we're often given that we should do something because 'It's natural'! Everything a man does is nature interfused with culture."[12]

Wesley was not able to transcend completely the cultural and ideological ethos of his time. This makes his statements on Christian anthropology appear awkward and inconsistent. But Wesley's view of humanity is so thoroughly subordinated to his view of God as grace that he allows for the "human condition," or "human nature," to be open for growth and change under the loving influence of God. The human condition, whatever that was, is only the beginning point, the changeable, overcomable, part of what it means to be human. Those who have studied Wesley's anthropology in relation to liberation theology have noted the affinity between Wesley's views and those of liberation theologians on the topic of human nature. The interesting part for me here is that this emphasis on humanity's openness for change (by God, of course, but through the human activity of faith!) has been labeled an "optimistic anthropology." However, the best way to label this position is to refer to it as an optimistic "theology"!

Liberation theologians have also rejected essentialist thinking through the Marxist influences on them. Humanity is best perceived as "project," and no fixed human nature is accepted. However, this view places too heavy an influence on persons' necessity to act and "change the world." While this changing of the world need not be seen as drudgery, it certainly carries with it the notion of obligation. To change the world almost becomes the new "essence" of humanity. *Homo faber* is presented as the *sine qua non* of personhood.

Wesley's anthropology resembles the liberationists' perspective, as Ted Runyon has already pointed out: "We note in Wesley's anthropology, therefore, some strong formal parallels with Marx. Human life is seen fundamentally as activity; as work which is teleological, always directed toward some purpose."[13]

Process theology can provide liberation theology and Wesleyan thought with conceptuality to support and enhance the perspectives advanced on human nature. Human beings are indeed *faber*, but are not only *faber*. And while much human activity is teleological and purposeful, some human activity can be adequately labeled nonpurposive. We are not only *homo faber*, but also *homo ludens*.

One of the sad realizations which liberation theologians came to after the fall of the Allende government in 1973 was how much they had ignored the playful side of their humanity. Only after the painful events of defeat and exile were many of them able to recapture their playful nature. Only after this were they able to really appreciate what Harvey Cox was trying to say in *The Feast of Fools* and Rubem Alves in *Tomorrow's Child*, that, fantasy, imagination, and play were integral elements in the process of liberation.

It is precisely here that process theology provides a necessary corrective.

> While Whitehead shares the existentialist stress on decision and responsibility, it is not for him the dominant note. Also decision is not so heavily freighted with moral considerations. The decision is directed toward a "satisfaction." The occasion "enjoys" its own immediacy. It attains some measure of "harmony," "intensity," "truth" and "beauty."[14]

While these statements are written in reference to existentialism, one could substitute for that term "liberation theology," or other schools of thought which have neglected the esthetic and playful elements in their definition of humanity.

Human sexuality has been seen for many centuries in the Christian church as primarily a "purposive" or even "teleological" function. Procreative views have dominated much of what the church has had to say about sexuality. *Homo faber* and not *homo ludens* is engaged in sexuality to change the world. A more comprehensive view of humanity, such as the one which process thinking allows us to have, will lead us to see sexuality more adequately as joyful, beautiful, intense, harmonious, and truth-full activity. This in turn may also lead us to realize that all sexual activity, and not only heterosexual, procreative activity is normal and good.

It should be evident that for process thinking, as for all theology, what one says about humanity must connect with what one says about God. And since process theology sees God as creative, responsive love, or as Pittenger puts it, as Cosmic Lover, human beings are seen as reflecting, however incompletely, that image. Sin mars that reflection, but in Christian theology justification and sanctification are seen as the ways in which that image can be restored. This is true for all human beings, homosexual or heterosexual.

Ordination and Homosexuality

None of the theologies under consideration would suggest the exclusion of anybody from ordination and expect to be consistent with their views of God, humanity, and church. This statement obviously implies that persons may be excluded from ordination on the basis of not meeting the basic requirements of call, confirmation of call by a community or congregation, educational competence, and the like. No person should be excluded *a priori* on the basis of race, sex, handicapping condition, or sexual preference. The battle cry of women who were struggling for ordination in the Episcopal Church applies equally to homosexual persons in our denomination: "Start ordaining them or stop baptizing them."

United Methodists share with the greater tradition of the Reformation the concept or—better yet—the doctrine of the "priesthood of all believers." Historical reasons, all too well known to us, forced Wesley—and in America, Coke and Asbury—to use lay persons in ministerial functions. Consequently our doctrine or theology of ordination has gravitated in the direction of functionality rather than sacramentality. Some attempts are made from time to time to reverse this trend and move us into a "catholic" or sacramental perspective, but those attempts have so far failed to gather any momentum or support.)

Our ordained clergy are not in the "sacerdotal" tradition. This is not to imply that the priestly role is absent from our concept of ministry, but rather to indicate that the "purity" and "perfection" demanded in Old Testament traditions and adopted to a large degree in Roman Catholic, Orthodox, and other traditions do not form part of our central interest. Recently the issue of ordaining people with handicapping conditions has forced us to reiterate our perspective that we are willing and ready to ordain those who could be considered in some traditions incapable of performing the sacerdotal functions because they are physically "less than perfect." Consequently, even if homosexuality were to be considered an ailment, or a deficiency of sorts, this alone should not bar any homosexual person from ordination.

Rather than go on and continue writing along these lines, let me simply refer you to the magnificent paper by David Griffin in *Encounter*, and state that my perspective is exactly the same as Griffin's. I will simply add that as someone who has been impacted by liberation theology, the issue of the human and religious and civil right of a homosexual person to be ordained is something I would want to insist on. Liberation conceptuality, in addition, would require consistency of application and not exclusion of persons from ministry or priesthood simply because of their homosexual condition. Finally let me remind you that the central issue is, in fact, not the ordination of homosexual persons, but rather the ordination of those homosexual persons who have taken the courageous step of declaring their homosexual orientation.

Ironically, The United Methodist Church finds itself in the strange position of encouraging mendacity and punishing candor. Homosexual persons have been ordained in the past and continue to be ordained. They have served us, and continue to serve us, in all levels of the church. If somehow we could honestly disclose here, in private, the identities of some of those gay brothers and lesbian sisters, we could all agree that they are among our brightest and our best. Unfortunately our "homophobia" will force them to remain silent and to "hide their light under a bushel", a light which other homosexual persons in the church and in society need to behold.

Homosexuality and Christianity

Some homosexual persons, following the example of some feminist theologians, are suggesting that Christianity is essentially homophobic, nay, that homophobia has been initiated and encouraged by Christianity, and they are leaving the church and asking other gay and lesbian Christians to do the same. John Cobb's response to Mary Daly applies equally here:

This raises the issue as to what Christianity is; for if Christianity can be defined in terms of the forms it has embodied thus far, then the case that liberated women [here we could insert "or radical gay and lesbian persons"] must leave is a strong one. My view is that any such definition of Christianity is false, in spite of the fact that it is characteristic of most theology, including my own past efforts. If we were forced to define Christianity in terms of its past forms it would certainly not be women alone who would have to leave. . . .

Against every definition of Christianity in terms of the forms it has embodied in the past, I urge that we recognize it to be a process. What Christianity is today at its growing edges is profoundly different from what Christianity was at its growing edges in the first, third, sixteenth, of nineteenth centuries. Undoubtedly there are certain forms that can be found in all these periods but that does not mean that the essence of Christianity consists in those forms. . . . There is no reason to suppose that those forms which survived intact through the nineteenth century will survive the twentieth. Nor is there reason to suppose that the displacement of received forms is faithlessness to the tradition. I would argue, on the contrary, that unwillingnesss to surrender what proves false or oppressive in a new context would be faithlessness. . . . Christianity will survive as long as living out of its history and its community is felt as grounding self-criticism and radical change appropriate to new situations and new understanding. Christianity dies when it attempts to defend what it has been."[15]

If we accept Cobb's definition of Christianity as a process whose identity through time is based on *the way it deals with its past tradition*, then it obviously follows that homosexual Christians and those who understand their struggle are called to remain in the church in its growing edge, helping it to shed one more *form* which needs to be discarded. Homosexuality and Christianity are not inevitably pitted against each other forever. Wesleyan Christians who are acquainted with the process of shedding outmoded and oppressive forms must actively be part of the movement to make homophobia in the church a thing of the past.

Reviewing Our Theological Task: A Concluding Plea

At the beginning of this presentation, I referred to Brian McNaught's confidence that the task of reversing two thousand years of procreative theology should begin with theologians. This is the closest thing we have for now to approximate the organization which Roman Catholics have of theologians, the Catholic Theological Society of America. We would be derelict if we chose to be silent on this most volatile issue. We have some bishops present at this gathering, and they, along with the whole Council of Bishops, need to hear what our best judgment on this subject, at this time, may be. This may be the last opportunity we have, as a group, to address the General Conference delegates, sharing with them our tentative answers. I am very much aware that bishops and delegates need not follow our counsel, but we dare not avoid giving it. I am aware of what has happened in other denominations and confessions with papers presented by individual theologians or teams of theologians. I know what Paul VI did with the theologians' report on contraception in 1968; I know how bureaucratic red tape and other delaying tactics are de facto shelving an excellent report of the Commission to Study the Church's Position on Homosexuality in the Archdiocese of San Francisco. I know how the hierarchy in the Roman Catholic Church has ignored the study commissioned and approved by the Catholic Theological Society of America (*Human Sexuality: New Directions in American Catholic Thought*). But I also know that theologians have *in fact* addressed themselves to the issue.

This group is composed in its majority by some of the most avant garde theologians, not only in United Methodism, but, I would dare say, in all Christendom. Part of the "growing edge" of the Christian faith is gathered here. Can the bugle sound an uncertain note?

The Roman Catholic report mentioned above suggests, among other things, two significant shifts: to move from an "act-oriented" ethics of sex to a "person-oriented" sexual ethics; and consistent with the first shift, it provided a list of criteria for a "humanized sexuality" instead of a list of approved or disapproved acts (note the different direction in which the Board of Higher Education and Ministry is moving by suggesting "fidelity in marriage," etc., etc.). United Methodism was already moving in the same direction Roman Catholic theologians are suggesting. Nearly twelve years ago paragraph 71 in *The Book of Discipline* was talking about sexual persons and an ethics of relatedness. Clever floor tactics of the conference manipulators succeeded in tacking onto this humanized perspective an "act-oriented" statement.

In other areas of human behaviour we had already moved in a humanized direction. In 1968 we removed specific "acts," like smoking and drinking, in favor of an ethics of relatedness. The long footnote to paragraph 404 is an attempt to document this humanized ethics stance. To allow the cleverly added statement in paragraph 71 to snowball into a regressive, past-form-preserving, act-oriented ethic, without a single word from the theological community, would be tantamount to dereliction of duty. Could we not at least affirm and make our own the criteria which our Roman Catholic brothers and sisters have hammered out? The list seems to be taken out of a text in process theology: "A humanized sexuality is one that promotes 'creative growth toward interaction.' It contains the capacity for personal affirmation and mutuality at the same time. It is 'self-liberating, other-affirming, honest, faithful, socially responsible, life-serving and joyous.' "[16]

The list of criteria could and should apply equally to heterosexual and homosexual persons. No "preference" or "orientation" would be labeled *a priori* "sin." The worth of human beings would be respected, the idea of God as love, or Cosmic Lover, would consistently apply.

As I finish this paper, I reflect on some of the sadness surrounding people who have taken up the cause of their gay brothers and lesbian sisters and evoked and provoked from otherwise respectful and loving church-goers vituperative and loathsome statements. Bishop Paul Moore in the Episcopal Church and Bishop Melvin Wheatley in our denomination have shed bitter tears over the church's inability and unwillingness to recognize the very face of Jesus in the persecuted homosexual Christians. The hate and negative emotions in general, generated by the issue of homosexuality, surpass anything either one of these "holy" men had faced before. Bishop Moore states in his book that having been through the racial struggles in the 60s and the antiwar events of the early 70s, he could now assert that the anger generated by his stance on homosexuality was far greater than the two other issues combined! Such raw emotion can only be named a phobia, homophobia.

I have not exactly been spared the pain. It has not been easy standing up to my bishop and opposing the "cabinet"-initiated leave of absence of the Rev. Morris Floyd. It has not been easy defending my position on the floor of the conference during executive session. It has not been easy being the only Chicano (perhaps the only ethnic minority) to assume this particular stance. Some of my close ethnic friends have suggested that taking a strong stance on this issue will render me worthless to the ethnic cause. "You should be addressing 'our' issues." Yet this is "our" issue for as I suggested earlier it is not so much homophobia that frightens me as it is "heterophobia," the fear of *any* "other" of which homophobia is only the tip of the iceberg.

I am sure that some of you may feel that this paper is not "theological" enough and that I am misusing or even instrumentalizing this consultation to grind my own axe. That may very well be true. I am Freudian enough to know that I do not know all of my motives and Sartrian enough to know that *mauvaise foi* (self-deception) can disguise its presence in the most clever ways. I know that the flower of altruism too often has crooked roots. But what I really believe is that I cannot ignore my past. The causal efficacy of moments with Cobb, with Allan Moore, with Ed Hansen, and the homophile community in San Francisco, and above all of the Christ, which has been mediated to me through all these folks and others, is more potent now than it might have been in the original moment. This is an issue I cannot evade, and I hope the church does not evade it either through "consensus" or "democratic" majority.

Bishop Paul Moore inherited a rule of thumb from one of his predecessors, Bishop Dan Corrigan. This rule of thumb summarizes my plea, and I also believe a process-liberation stance: "Whenever you are faced with a difficult choice, go with the future, not the past." I wonder if Corrigan ever read Whitehead's statement that life refuses to be embalmed. We *are* faced with a difficult choice.

NOTES

1. Paul Moore, *Take a Bishop Like Me* (New York: Harper & Row, 1979), p. 72.
2. Brian McNaught, *A Disturbed Peace* (Dignity, Inc., 1981), p. 91.
3. Moore, *Take a Bishop*, p. 185.
4. Fred Craddock and Water Wink, "How Does the New Testament Deal with the Issue of Homosexuality?" *Encounter*, vol. 40, no. 3, pp. 197-208.
5. Fred Craddock and Walter Wink, "Biblical Perspectives on Homosexuality," *Christian Century*, Nov. 7, 1979, pp. 1082-86.
6. Beardsley's paper appears in *Encounter*, vol. 36, no. 4, Fall 1975.
7. John Wesley, as quoted by Robert W. Burtner and Robert E. Chiles, *John Wesley's Theology: A Collection from His Works* (Nashville: Abingdon Press, 1983), p. 50.
8. Burtner and Chiles, *John Wesley's Theology*, p. 43, emphasis mine.
9. William K. McElvaney, *Good news is bad news is good news . . .* (Maryknoll; Orbis Books, 1980).
10. Norman Pittenger, *A Time for Consent* (London: SCM Press), pp. 101-2.
11. Moore, *Take a Bishop*, pp. 30-31.
12. Ross Snyder, *On Becoming Human*, as quoted by Howard Rice in a lecture delivered at annual meeting of Pacific and Southwest Annual Conference Chapter of Methodist Federation for Social Action, June 1982.
13. Theodore Runyon, *Sanctification and Liberation: Liberation Theologies in the Light of the Wesleyan Tradition* (Nashville: Abingdon Press, 1981), p. 20.
14. John Cobb, Jr., and David R. Griffin, *Process Theology: An Introductory Exposition* (Philadelphia: Westminster Press, 1976), p. 84.
15. David R. Griffin and Thomas J. J. Altizer, eds., *John Cobb's Theology in Process*, pp. 172-73.
16. Rosemary Radford Ruether, "Time Makes Ancient Good Uncouth: The Catholic Report on Sexuality," *Christian Century*, August 3-10, 1977, p. 683.

5. FEMINISM, PROCESS THOUGHT, AND THE WESLEYAN TRADITION

Sheila Greeve Davaney

Preface

In order to elucidate the form and content of this paper, it is important to state something of the background that I bring to this task. In contrast to the majority of the presenters of papers and participants in this working group, I am not a United Methodist, nor have I been connected with the Wesleyan religious tradition in any way. Further, until this summer, my knowledge of John Wesley's theology was limited to the most cursory of historical information. The major reasons for my being invited to participate in this consultation consist, I presume, in the fact that (1) I am a woman (2) who, while not explicitly identifying herself as a process thinker, still has a strong attraction to many of the tenets of process thought, and (3) teaches theology in a United Methodist seminary. While I am not at all convinced that these factors add up to any real qualification for undertaking this task, they did apparently prompt John Cobb, ever a believer in the process of creative synthesis whereby seemingly incompatible components are transformed into new and richer possibilities, to ask me to write a paper on the Wesleyan tradition, process thought, and feminism.

In preparation for fulfilling this assignment, I have read a good deal of Wesley and of the secondary interpretations and debates that have responded to his work. I now have a slightly less cursory knowledge of this material, though still thoroughly inadequate for the present purposes. Thus recognizing my own inadequacy and the greater understanding of the nuances of the Wesleyan tradition on the part of other participants, I have chosen to limit my discussion of Wesley and concentrate instead on the process and feminist side of the proposed conversation. In particular, I hope to indicate areas that, while in continuity with certain Wesleyan concerns, also deal with dimensions of experience which Wesley either neglected or, in my view, inadequately understood. In order to carry out this purpose, I have divided the paper into five sections. Section 1 presents a statement of my own understanding of the theological task. I have included this statement primarily because I suspect my views on this matter differ substantially from other participants and believe that clarity on such methodological issues contributes to later discussion. Section 2 sets forth several central tenets of Wesley's theology. Sections 3 and 4 attempt to respond to perceived inadequacies in that theology by developing process and feminist perspectives on the body-self relation and the individual-society interconnection. And finally section 5 offers brief concluding comments.

I. The Theological Task

For many theologians the enterprise in which we engage is viewed primarily as an interpretive or hermeneutical task. Theology, in this mode, represents the attempt to translate or redefine claims from an earlier era into language and concepts appropriate for the present. There are, most often, two poles which delineate the perimeters of this task; the one being contemporary sensibilities and the other being some aspect of the past that has been given an elevated and hence normative status. Underlying this view of theology is the assumption that "truth" or its approximation has already been disclosed in the past, whether in revelation or tradition, a human figure or philosophical argumentation. Theology's task is then to appropriate that supposed truth and to present it in an acceptable contemporary form. Criticism and creative translation are not ruled out, but their purpose is to support, not challenge, the hermeneutical process and the presuppositions that undergird it.

This approach to theology, in a number of guises, has remained prevalent on the theological scene.[1] However, it has long been in tension with many of the presuppositions of the modern world and has, I believe, become an increasingly problematic, indeed untenable, way to view the theological task. A number of factors has contributed to the challenge to this mode of theological reflection. The recognition of the historical and hence relative character of all religious visions and theological claims has functioned, at least since the nineteenth century, to undermine attempts to isolate and elevate particular segments of the past as "ontologically" unique and thereby authoritative.[2] The growing understanding of pluralism is, with increasing intensity, presenting its own challenge to claims of exclusive or definitive "truth."[3] And the current-day movement known as deconstructionism has raised the uneasy question, though it has not answered it convincingly, of whether one can indeed "do" history at all.[4] Going along with these challenges has been the all-important insight that our various versions of the truth, our visions of the nature and purpose of reality, are profoundly connected with the power we hold or that we fail to hold. The connection between power configurations and interpretations of reality, secular and religious alike, have been the concern of a wide variety of diverse thinkers including Troeltsch, Feuerbach, Marx, the critical theorists Adorno and Horkheimer, sociologists of knowledge such as Mannheim and, currently, political and liberation theologians.

It is this latter insight, that our understandings of reality are not disinterested or objective but rather are thoroughly value-laden, reflecting the interests and commitments of their holders, that has had the most profound effect upon feminist thinkers. Our feminist analysis has suggested that there has been a real and oppressive connection between male control of the social order and the ideas of God, self, and world that have emerged within such male-dominated contexts. And while we have recognized the great variety of visions that have emerged and the deep-seated differences among them, feminists, at least of a more radical bent, are convinced that nonetheless these visions all bear, to some extent, the mark of their origins in male thought and power.[5] Hence to view the theological task as that of interpreting or translating past claims whose essential validity and adequacy are assumed, appears highly problematic to women who view those visions as part of the history that has oppressed us. Revision and reinterpretation are not, given the history of oppression, adequate responses to our present need to transform the social order.

While theology conceived as a heremeneutical task is still a widely accepted approach, there has, however, been emerging an alternative conception of the theological discipline that, I believe, is more attentive to the historical, time-and-place bound character of human life and thought, and might conceivably be more responsive to the need for a radical new visioning of reality and humanity's place within it. This view is best described in theology as construction.[6] Such a constructive approach is grounded in the recog-

nition that human beings are, in the most fundamental way, symbol-creating creatures who live and act within the networks of meaning that they themselves have created.[7] Embedded in this claim are two further assumptions. First, it suggests that such a symbolic framework is imperative for all human thought and action. Indeed, without some at least implicit vision of reality, of the over-all context within which life takes place, and of the human place within that cosmic scheme, human beings would not be able to function at all.[8] Second, this view assumes that such networks of meaning, such world views, are cultural and social creations. Our ideas of reality are not dispassioned photo images of the world but rather are imaginative conceptions, built up through history and culture, of what we take existence to be about and of our own human place within the cosmic context. Thus, this approach claims, all our world views, secular and religious, Jesus' as well as our own, Scripture's as well as Marx's, are all thoroughly human constructions and represent human attempts to express fundamental convictions about the nature and meaning of reality. Further, these visions grow out of, reflect, and often if not always, undergird their societal contexts, the values and power arrangements of those contexts. Hence, humans' visions of the nature of meaning of reality and of human life are not disinterested accounts of reality but value and interest-laden interpretations of life and its purposes.

Beginning with these convictions, I would argue for a reconsideration of the theological task. Instead of reinterpreting visions from an earlier era whose validity is assumed, the task of the theologian would be to participate in the development of world views that are adequate for today. That is, recognizing that we exist in webs of meaning that we ourselves have created, the theologian's task becomes the self-conscious construction of such symbolic frameworks. Our role as theologians is to contribute to the development of views of self and world which are more adequate to our time and place, and which enable and nourish more humane forms of existence for today and the future.

There are several elements of this approach that it is important to highlight. First, it suggests that we carry out theological reflection for a highly pragmatic purpose; we seek more adequate frameworks for life today. Hence our theological thinking is not an end in itself but rather seeks to serve the goal of a transformed human order. In the words of Gordon D. Kaufman, "The central problem facing the present generation is the construction of a genuinely humane order—lest we destroy ourselves completely. If theological reflection is to be justified in this crisis, it must contribute to this work. A theology that makes an essential contribution to our humanization is the *only* sort we can afford today."[9] If this pragmatic purpose is important for all engaged in the theological enterprise, it is of immense significance for those who have suffered oppression. For the oppressed, reflection that does not serve liberation is a luxury we simply cannot afford.

Second, if our major goal is a transformed order, the norms for carrying out this task must be primarily generated by our present context. Or put otherwise, the past cannot provide us with any *absolute* norms against which to judge our present efforts. This does not mean that we should ignore our history; we are products of our personal and corporate memories and to fail to recognize that rootedness in our heritage is, on the one hand, to miss its possibilities and, on the other hand, to continue to be its victims. However, in contrast to the view of theology as hermeneutics, this approach suggests that no historical form or vision or figure be given an absolute status. Instead, all history, that of other traditions as well as our own, should be scrutinized so that we might gain insight from its errors as well as hope from the possibilities that it has engendered. Our mode of interaction with the past should not be the attempt to conform to a supposedly adequate truth revealed in that past but an effort to dialogue with that thoroughly human heritage, learning what we can but recognizing that the ultimate responsibility for our visions of reality resides with us today.[10] While I do not think John Cobb would necessarily concur with all I have argued thus far, he does, in his book *Process Theology as Political Theology*, suggest a similar approach to history. While fully recognizing the extent to which the past constitutes the present, Cobb rejects any move to absolutize that past or some element within it. He states that "the prophets, Jesus, Paul, John and many others, have great authority for us today. But there is no one locus of *absolute authority*. . . . Finally, we must decide"[11]; and again, "From the perspective of process theology, a truly critical and a truly political theology must learn to do without absolutes."[12]

A third element of this understanding of theology as construction is the recognition that if we cannot absolutize the past, neither can we absolutize our present efforts. Our visions will be, just as were those to which we are inheritors, thoroughly human constructions, and as such, relative, conditioned, and value-laden. Our goal may be a liberated and liberating order, but what constitutes liberation or humaneness will continue to be open to debate. We, in turn, must be open, not only to the insights of our traditions, but to the criticisms of our fellow humans and, perhaps most of all, to the new dreams and visions that are emerging from the imaginations of those who were denied participation in the creation of the vision of the past. Hence, if we seek to avoid making an idol of the past, of Scripture, or tradition, or indeed, Jesus, we must also be ever vigilant against our own tendencies to see our position as *the* one, final vision instead of one more effort in the ongoing human attempt to create a meaningful and value-filled interpretation of reality.

Thus, in sum, I view theology as primarily a constructive endeavor that seeks to contribute to the creation of a more humane order of existence. Its resources are many; our own traditions and the traditions of others; the disciplines of modern thought—sociology, anthropology, physical and psychological sciences, and political theory; finally and perhaps most importantly, the insights and dreams of those who have been voiceless. Its loyalty is to the present generation and to the generations of a hoped-for-future. Its norm is humaneness though it is recognized that this norm must be ever redefined in ongoing conversation and debate. Its underlying presupposition is that its present formulations are conditional and provisional and will indeed be transformed, for better or for worse, by succeeding generations. And finally, its sobering recognition is that it is we who are responsible for our visions, it is we, in the words of John Cobb, who must decide.[13]

It is with this view of theology as construction that I approach the present task. I understand John Wesley and the proponents of process thought to be conversation partners in my own attempt to contribute to the transformation of the standing order. As such, I am less interested in whether Wesley was truly in line with the Reformers on the question of grace or was a bit too Catholic or whether one or the other of the current process thinkers is more faithful to Whitehead's position. While these are admittedly interesting questions, I am more concerned with what their insights might suggest for the creation of a humane order; that is, what forms of life do their theologies engender and nourish? With this concern in mind, I want first to turn to Wesley's theology of justification, sanctification, and the pursuit of perfection, and second, to a process-feminist interpretation of that pursuit in terms of the quest for liberating wholeness. In this latter attempt, I will refer interchangeably to feminists and liberationists, for while I clearly recognize the differences between such approaches, it is a central conviction of mine that the insights of feminists and other liberationists must be integrated if we are to create a vision adequate for today.

II. Comments on Wesley's Thought

John Wesley's thought assumes, in good Protestant fashion, that a state of profound alienation exists between God and humanity and within the human community. This condition of sin is both total, encompassing all human beings, and radical, unable to be redressed by humans but requiring divine initiative and action to overcome the sinful situation. God's action, in the form of undeserved and freely given grace, is a recurring theme of Wesley's writings and sermons. It is only on the basis of God's transforming presence that healing and growth are possible.

Thus Wesley echoes the Reformers' assertions concerning the extensiveness of sin, humanity's inability to rectify its own condition, and the necessity of God's gracious action. But while grace is an ever-present motif in Wesley's thought, what is perhaps most unique and interesting in his position is his vision of the repercussions of such divine activity. Divine grace, for Wesley, is a profoundly freeing and enabling gift. It does not, as for certain theologians, take the place of human action or destroy human choice. Rather it empowers human freedom and lays the foundation for a creative partnership between God and humanity.

This justifying presence of God hence provides the basis for ongoing, personal transformation (sanctification). It sets individuals free to pursue what Wesley came to call perfection. Several dimensions of this are important for our present discussion. First, Wesley continues to emphasize the necessity of God's ever-present action; humans are indeed partners with God, but such partnership is predicated upon God's initiative. Second, perfection is to be sought, at least for now, in our worldly context. Wesley's vision of God's enabling grace is that it frees humans for life in this world. While there is definitely an eschatological dimension of Wesley's thought, it is not emphasized to the neglect of life in the present context.[14] Third, perfection is not a passive state; Wesley calls for active, creative response to God's initiative, not passive repudiation of responsibility. Fourth, perfection, in the Wesleyan framework, is not achieved once and for all. Instead, it is an ongoing pursuit which denies any easy satisfaction with particular individual or societal states and which further engenders an active criticism of the conditions of this world. And fifth, perfection is, in essence, to be understood as love of God and neighbor. Thus while Wesley speaks often of perfection as right relationship with God, when this relationship is interpreted in terms of love, it cannot be separated from human deeds but, by necessity, must issue forth in actions characterized by such love.

It is possible to understand why a number of thinkers both from the process perspective and from the ranks of liberationists have perceived an affinity between Wesley's theology and their own commitments. In a manner that resonates with process thinkers, Wesley maintains that grace and human freedom are not opposed but rather are positively related; divine action bears its fruit in human responsibility and creative possibilities. Further, liberationists would concur with Wesley that holiness is not an other-worldly concern but a this-worldly commitment and that perfection speaks more of correct attitude and action—love—than proper creedal formulas; in the now famous dictum of liberation theology, orthopraxy is more important than orthodoxy. In general, Wesley proposes a dynamic vision of reality that fosters human potential while recognizing the impediments to such transforming experience and that portrays God and humanity as partners in the quest for a renewed creation characterized by mutual love.

But if there are elements of Wesley's thought that suggest continuities with present day movements, there are as well dimensions of his position that stand in contrast to the insights and emphases that are emerging in process thought and liberation perspectives, especially in feminist analysis. There are two such areas that I would like to highlight in particular. The first is the relation between the individual and society. While Wesley called for the pursuit of perfection in this world and referred to religion as "social," he nonetheless did not appear to have either a clear recognition of the social character of human selfhood or an understanding of the need for profound change in the structures of society. As a result, he places greatest emphasis upon the individual and his or her inward experience and fails to address adequately the social dimensions of human life and the systemic character of human alienation. In the words of Josè Míguez Bonino, "Wesley's anthropology seems to me incurably individualistic. . . . For Wesley, society is not an anthropological concept, but simply a convenient arrangement for the growth of the individual. It is the individual soul that finally is saved, sanctified, perfected."[15]

In contrast to this individualistic orientation, both feminist and process thought argue for the social constitution of the individual and for the recognition that both alienation and liberation are social phenomena.

A second area that is receiving a quite different interpretation from that offered by Wesley is that of the relation between self and body. In keeping with his time, Wesley appears to work out of a dualistic vision of the human self. At least in the state of alienation, there exists a profound division between body and spirit, with the spirit struggling against the sensual appetites that seek to imprison it. Thus while Wesley is indeed concerned with concrete sanctification and while he does not envision perfection in terms of disembodied spirituality, he nonetheless was not able to offer a vision that overcame the deep and alienating dualism of spirit and body. Once more in Bonino's words, "The instruments with which he worked concealed the corporeal and corporate nature of human life, and thus he was unable to see these dimensions as constitutive of the holy life and could only co-opt them in a peripheral and nonessential way."[16]

It is precisely in relation to these dimensions of "corporeal" and "corporate" life that both process thought and feminist analysis are beginning to concentrate significant efforts.[17] In the remainder of this paper, I would like to turn to these issues of body-self relations and the interconnection between individuals and society in order to see what insights contemporary process thinkers and feminists might offer toward the envisionment of transformed human existence. I am not sure whether these claims can finally be interpreted as contemporary developments basically in tune with earlier Wesleyan assertions, or as fundamental challenges to the Wesleyan tradition. I am, however, convinced that a central concern of Wesley's was the nature of transformed human life and that today we cannot speak of such transformation apart from the concerns for liberation of self and society. Thus in the following two sections of this essay, I will attempt to indicate, at least in part, the possible contributions that feminist theory and process thought might make to the discussion concerning liberated life, and by so doing, to simulate conversation with the Wesleyan perspective concerning these matters.

III. Liberation as Wholeness: Embodied Selfhood

For many theologians today, transformed or fulfilled or redemptive human life is being spoken of in terms of liberation. As the reality of the myriad forms of oppression has become clearer, the motif of freedom from alienation, fragmentation, and bondage has become a central theme in theological reflection.[18] However, quite often this idea of liberation has carried a primarily negative connotation; it has stressed the critical dimensions of the transforming process, indicating most clearly what we are liberated from and, with less clarity, the new form of existence which we seek. In the following discussion, I would like to develop the positive side of the liberating process by utilizing the metaphor of liberation as wholeness. I believe that this image of wholeness, while retaining the critical emphasis of liberation, also indicates the positive direction of such transformation; it stresses not only that we are moving away from oppressive structures/institutions/relationships, but that we are moving toward liberated and liberating connections. Further, I think that this image of wholeness is particularly appropriate for women who have mythically been identified with undifferentiated life while in reality being forced to live in alienation from our own bodies and from the societal contexts in which we have existed. Thus, I will first unpack the notion of wholeness in terms of embodiment, with special reference to women, and then in turn analyze the image in relation to the societal character of human life.

* * * * *

There has arisen in the West a profound dualism of spirit and body and the concomitant elevation of the former over the latter.[19] Through the complexities of historical and cultural development, the human spirit and body came to be seen, not only as distinct from one another, but as in conflict with each other. The spirit, connected with the notion of a thing-like soul, has been viewed as, at least potentially, free and immortal, while the body was understood as mortal, corruptible, and worse—corrupting. It was, in various forms, the spirit or soul or mind that signified human transcendence and was taken to be the locus of redeemed and fulfilled human existence. The body was seen as a hindrance to this transcendence and, as such, that which should be dominated, controlled, and repressed.

This dualistic tendency, while present throughout much of the Christian era, has found deeply alienating expression in the modern period. With the advent of the Cartesian split between mind and body, and the emergence of what has come to be termed technological thinking, the body and the sphere of nature in general have come to be understood as lacking in intrinsic worth, and as having instrumental value *only* in so far as they can be manipulated to the ends of technological reason. The prevalent model for interpreting the body and nature has been that of the machine, and the bywords for understanding the spirit's or mind's relation to them have been control, possession, and manipulation.

Now, as numerous feminist thinkers have pointed out, this dualism between body and spirit has not only been applied to individual human beings, but has also been reflected in the differentiation between males and females. Males have, in most of our Western traditions, been understood as the bearers of transcendent selfhood, cultivators of the spirit seeking autonomy and freedom. Females, in contrast, have been identified with the natural order and the body, especially its sexual functionings. Female experience has been interpreted, not in terms of creative, transcending activity, but along the lines of passive immersion into body and environment. Rather than being viewed as autonomous manipulators of self and world, women have been seen as slaves to body, sexuality, and nature, and as such, have been controlled, and used as well, for the "higher" purposes of the more transcendent male.

Women, seeking to be freed from the oppression of male domination, are searching for visions that overcome these alienating dualisms that have characterized so much of our experience. We are seeking for ways to reclaim our bodies as well as to participate in the creative possibilities of spirit. Put succinctly, we are seeking a wholeness that does not sacrifice or deny either transcending spirit or embodiment. We are aware, however, that in order to achieve such creative wholeness, we will need to redefine, in a radical fashion, our understandings of spirit and body and their relation to each other. The normative ideas of transcending spirit and dominated flesh to which we are heirs, simply cannot be integrated with one another; that is, transcending spirit, as it has developed thus far, has done so at the expense of our bodies and of those who have been identified with the "matter" end of the human spectrum. While great achievements have emerged in art, culture, reflection, and technology, they have done so at a terrible cost. Feminist theologian Sheila Collins, reflecting upon the dubious value of Western achievements, comments that "Western 'freedom' and affluence depend on the domestication of women and the exploitation of a low-paid labor base made up of minorities and women, as well as unlimited access to foreign sources of natural resources which are taken from the

ground without regard for the rights of the Earth or the people who live on the land."[20] This is to say, that thus far the self-transcendence of a relative few has been predicated upon the continued oppression and exploitation of the many. It is the goal of women to find a way to nourish our spirits without alienating our bodies and without oppressing our fellow humans and our earth.

While there has developed a certain unanimity in feminist circles concerning the goal of creative integration of spirit and body, what constitutes such wholeness is an issue of deep and, thus far, unresolved debate. At the center of the debate is the question of the role of sexuality in relation to identity, or stated otherwise, the connection or lack of it between biology and experience. There are a number of nuanced arguments that have emerged in this discussion, and it is impossible, in this limited context, to detail all of them. However, I would like to delineate the two positions that I understand to be setting the boundaries for this ongoing debate; the perspective that claims males and females are not fundamentally different and that the minimal differences which do exist are the result of cultural and societal factors, in contrast to the position that sees male and female physiology laying the foundation for distinctive experiences in men and women.

Proponents of the first of these perspectives, recognizing that certain characteristics, traits, and potentialities have been assigned to men and others to women, and that by such assignments, whole arenas of experience, power, and identity were denied the other sex, have argued that these sex-divided designations are aritificial and arbitrary, and reflect social and political ideologies, not true differences between women and men. According to this view, biological differences are minimal; men and women share the vast amount of physical existence in common, and the bodily differences that do exist do not, of necessity, create different male and female psyches.[21]

Going along with this assumption of minimal biological difference has been the claim that the characteristics attributed to females and males, and the roles assigned them, are not the result of innate biological differences, but are the outcome of sociological processes and psychological structuring. In that sense, they are cultural artifacts and can be changed. There is little, and certainly no necessary, connection between biological sex differences and societally determined gender roles and identities. Those who have tied sex differences to gender differences have done so by an ideological leap.

In sum, this perspective has minimized biological differences, and has argued that what distinctions exist do so primarily because of cultural and social organization, not innate distinctions. The vision of wholeness that has emerged from this view is one that, while not denying biological input, has limited its significance for personality and rejected its delineation along sexual lines. Whole human beings will indeed be embodied, but the fact that those bodies are male and female will, in a liberated context, have little to do with the individual personalities and roles that emerge. While rejecting the old dualism of body and spirit, this perspective nonetheless continues to stress the transcendence of spirit over body, while envisioning a more "cooperative" and less hostile relation between them. Feminist theorist Gayle Ruben captures this view well when she states that "the dream I find most compelling is one of an androgynous and genderless (though not sexless) society, in which one's sexual anatomy is irrelevant to who one is, what one does, and with whom one makes love."[22]

The above-stated vision of full humanity has been a powerful and pervasive ideal for many feminists. However, in recent years there has arisen an alternative perspective that suggests that biology and psychology/sociology cannot be entirely disconnected.[23] The women exploring this option are proposing that female and male experience will never be the same, that they are different, not only because of external, oppressive structures, but because of intrinsic physiological factors. Theologian Penelope Washbourn essentially takes this track when she asks whether there is something "specific, unique, and distinctive to female experience that is affected not by her socialization, but by the quality of her body experience?"[24] For Washbourn, the distinctively female experiences of menstruation, pregnancy, birth, lactation, and menopause open up a uniquely female way of experiencing reality. In a way, for this perspective, biology is indeed a part of destiny, but not a merely negative element closing off avenues of experience, but rather opening reality in a very particular way. Other feminists, including such diverse thinkers as Mary Daly and Elizabeth Dodson Gray, have stressed their conviction that the cycles of female life have enabled women to be attuned to the rhythms and cadence of the natural world in a fashion not available to men.[25]

The vision of wholeness that is emerging from this direction is one that entails the radical reclaiming of bodily experience. It proposes that liberation for women means neither becoming like men nor being "liberated from femaleness" to a nonsexual or disembodied "humaness." Instead it stresses an organic view of self and body, and proposes that wholeness entails liberation as women to the full potentialities of female nature including female sexuality. Thus, body and spirit are interpreted as inseparable, not only in the general sense that humans are corporeal beings, but in the more radical meaning that such embodiment gives distinctive character to our personalities and individual spirits. While the social and cultural dimensions of life are neither denied nor ignored in this view, its present stress has been upon the positive reclaiming of bodily experience. Yet finally, in a manner reminiscent of the culturally defined perspective, the proponents of this orientation reject the notion that there is or should be a connection between biological specificity and societal role assignment. These thinkers, no less than their culture-oriented counterparts, argue that embodiment and engenderment, that is, the social differentiation of roles and identities along sex-specified lines, are not and should not be the same. We are embodied creatures, but in this view the organic relation between body and spirit should not be used to set rigid role determinations, but to free both men and women to a multiplicity of creative and freely chosen individual identities.[26]

Thus, each of these perspectives can be seen to propose a different emphasis in the envisioning of wholeness. Yet while they are distinct from each other, they are one in their rejection of the male ideal of autonomous selfhood that seeks freedom from the constrictions of bodily and social environments. Instead, both recognize that humans are constituted in a profound manner by such environments, whether these be understood primarily in terms of the immediate environment of our physical bodies, or the natural sphere or the human constructed social milieu. The problem has not been that we are so constituted, but that our relationships to body, nature, and society have been oppressively structured. Hence both views suggest that liberation understood as wholeness does not entail the escape from or the mechanistic manipulation of these environments, but rather creative interaction with them predicated upon a deep and sensitive attunement to their processes.

From a process perspective, John Cobb has demonstrated great sensitivity to these issues, recognizing both their complexity and their importance for the feminist movement. In his article entitled "Feminism and Process Thought: A Two-Way Relationship," Cobb suggests that process thought might offer a mediating position that recognizes the constituting-character of natural, including bodily, and social environments, but which avoids the dilemmas of biological or social determinism.[27] Reflecting primarily on the relation of body to spirit, he argues that human beings are indeed composed of and constituted by the multiplicity of physiological happenings we call our bodies. However, the human person is neither an unorganized grouping of bodily events, nor merely the sum of such events functioning for the blind purposes of biological reproduction and survival. Instead the multiplicity of bodily experiences is unified in and given direction by a regnant moment of experience labeled, utilizing Whiteheadian terminology, "the dominant occasion," or for Cobb, as its character persists through time, "the soul." There are several elements of great importance in this view. First, the presiding occasion is organically related to the multiplicity of experiences that constitute the body. Thoroughly rejected in this interpretation is the dualistic notion that body and soul exist in isolation from each other; in the process view, it is precisely the multiplicity of events within the body that provides the raw material, so to speak, for the dominant occasion's experience. Second, while embracing the view that the body influences, indeed constitutes, the soul, Cobb argues that such influence cannot be conceived in the terms of mechanistic and materialistic determinism. Instead, the soul is, at any one moment, the *creative* unification of bodily experience that both emerges out of and transcends the events of the body. In particular, this presiding occasion, while dependent upon the body, is capable of pursuing goals that are distinct from the biological drive for survival and reproduction. It is on the basis of this ability to be self-determinative that human persons can be considered responsible for themselves and their actions. The best term for human selfhood, as it fulfills its creative and self-directing potential is, for Cobb, spirit.

Cobb proposes that this organic view of body and soul, or spirit, provides a way to understand both the profound influence of sexuality and the human ability to transcend any narrow sexual determinism. In this view, all bodily influences, including sexual ones, contribute to the human person. Hence being male or female does indeed make a difference—and for Cobb, a great deal of difference—in personal experience. However, how individual persons integrate that influence, whether they highlight it or play it down, live in harmony with it or exist in tension, depends a great deal upon the self-directing experience which is the soul. This view, Cobb suggests, responds both to the concerns of women who seek to reclaim their bodies in a positive manner and to those who fear that such reclamation will result in a new version of the biology-is-destiny trap of which women have been age-old victims; the dualism of self and body is replaced with an organic view which acknowledges in a positive fashion our embodiment while insisting as well on the creative and self-transcending reality of the human spirit.

As a feminist friendly to the process vision, I find much to commend in John Cobb's proposal. Where I differ, I suspect, it is more a matter of emphasis than of radical disagreement. My major difficulty is that I hear lurking in Cobb and in many other process proponents, the dualistic thinking whose ideal is *control* over the body. That is, while the organic relation between body and spirit is acknowledged, what finally is emphasized is the spirit's ability to transcend that body or to utilize it for its higher purposes; transcendence is, while more organically conceived, still envisioned primarily as freedom from and dominance over. Now for many years I found myself thinking in this manner. I envisioned liberation in terms of freedom from everything—the past, the environment, society, and my own body. While I recognized I was constituted by these factors, I sought to limit their control over me and to be the determining agent, manipulating them as resources for my own purposes. However, this vision of freedom as transcendence over or freedom from seems increasingly problematic to me, especially in relation to our physical and natural environments. In this sense, I find myself, to my own surprise, listening more intently to those women who are urging greater attention to our bodies. Succinctly put, they are suggesting that transcendence out of tune with the rhythms of body and nature has brought us to the brink of disaster. In order to redress such lack of attunement, they are proposing that we learn to let our bodies "control" us, and to live lives determined more by the cadences of nature. In this transcendence is not ruled out, but it is reinterpreted to mean creative interaction with and harmonious attunement to the physical world rather than freedom from it. I believe the process perspective not only permits, but perhaps demands, this understanding of transcendence, and I am sure that at least in part, Cobb would concur with this emphasis. I am less certain, however, how to conceive of the relation between attunement to our bodies, and the societal roles and identities that we pursue.[28] This connection between biology and social roles is, I believe, an issue that is not yet resolved, and one which will demand in the future far more nuanced reflection. It is my hope that process thought's organic vision will contribute to this debate in creative and mediating fashion.

IV. Liberation as Wholeness: Social Salvation

As I have been arguing, women, in our search for wholeness, have been deeply interested in our bodies and in the role these intimate, immediate environments play in the constitution of our female selves. But if we have been aware that we are embodied selves, we have with increasing intensity, become cognizant that these selves are also socially derived and circumscribed, not only in terms of how we view and value our female bodies and sexuality, but on every level of our existence. We are mindful that our own oppression is not merely the distortion of private or individual relationships between women and men, but the result of structural and corporate oppression that is embodied in every level of social, economic, and political life. And we further recognize that the dynamics of oppression and injustice are operating not only between men and women, but between races, classes, and nations. In sum, we are fully aware that the wholeness and liberation we seek is not an individual phenomenon that leaves intact social, political, and economic structures; instead women are increasingly convinced that the liberation of women and other oppressed groups is tied to the radical transformation of global society, indeed to the dismantling and thorough reconstitution of the social, political, and economic order.[29]

Third world proponents of liberation, especially those working out of the Latin American context, have been especially instructive concerning this issue of structural oppression. Focusing on class conflict, and economic and political injustice, they have contended that the oppression that pervades the third world is not a historical accident, nor merely the reflection of the "natural" conditions of social and political life (i.e., "the poor will always be with you"). Instead, they argue, such oppression is structural and institutional, resulting from a worldwide class system that both engenders and supports the possession of economic and political power by a few, and the lack of self-direction and creative potentiality for the many. Transformation, given these circumstances, cannot be limited to individuals, but must encompass the entire social order. Salvation, indeed, must be social; if it is not, it is merely one more embodiment of the global edifice of injustice.

I believe first world feminists are listening with increasing attentiveness to these insights of third world liberationists, even as we hope they perceive our emerging visions. On the one hand, we are with ever-growing clarity recognizing that the economic and political oppression of which they speak has as its major victims, women. When class or role oppression are combined with sexual oppression, the results have been devastating for women. When we speak of the horror of widespread starvation, we are, in fact, referring primarily to victims who are female. When we hear of displaced persons, once more the majority of adults are women. And when we speak of the denial of basic human rights of self-determination, we cannot but remember that women in most parts of the world are still refused rights in relation to their own bodies, much less freedom to participate fully in the economic and political process. On the other hand, many feminists from the first world are increasingly aware that we, too, have participated in and benefited from the class and race structures that have oppressed others. White feminists, in particular, have heard the indictment that while oppressed as women, we have, nonetheless, contributed to racial and class oppression, and that real transformation will include the loss of privilege that has been ours as members of racial and class elites. Thus, women are increasingly concurring with the insight that both oppression and transformation are social realitites, not private experiences, and are arguing that the liberating wholeness that we seek entails profound alteration of the social order into a more just and life-sustaining one for all, rather than the arena of creative potentialities and freedom for the few.

Various proponents of process thought have also been attentive to these perceptions concerning the social character of liberation and have suggested that the organic and social vision offered by process thought resonates well with many of the insights and commitments of liberationists, feminist, black, and third world alike.[30] Several areas in particular have emerged as fruitful topics for dialogue. First, the process perspective has argued that human beings are not only constituted by the immediate environment of the body, but also by the external social context; both our possibilities and limitations as individuals are greatly determined by the resources that are available from our world, and from the personal and corporate experience that is the heritage of our past. Autonomous individuality, unaffected by social reality, is ruled out by process thinkers. All individual experience is constituted, for better or worse, by its social environment. Experience, while individual, is never merely private. Hence, the oppressive structuring of society issues forth in the distortion and diminution of the experience of individuals.

However, process thinkers argue, such social determination, while real and constitutive of experience, is not total. Rather, just as human persons are not merely the sum of biological functionings, neither are we solely the outcome of social structuring. Instead, in each moment of experience the influences of the past, of body, society, and history are unified in a unique and possibly transforming manner, which, while reflecting those influences, also creatively transcends them. The degree to which such transformation is possible varies from person to person, and clearly depends, at least in part, upon the possibilities for creativity present in the social order. However, whatever societal conditions prevail, there exists the possibility, however slight, for creative and transforming interaction with these conditions. It is precisely because of this element of creative self-constitution that we human beings are not condemned merely to repeat our pasts or reiterate the imperatives of the social order, but can indeed be, in part, the creators of our own destinies.

Hence, the process perspective argues that social determination is real, but that the human person is also self-creating. It is this dialectic of determination and freedom, interpreted as creative interaction, that explains why change is so difficult, but also, why there can be hope that such transformation is possible. But for many process thinkers it is not only, or even primarily, the human capacity for self-constitution that is the source for radical transformation. Instead, God is envisioned in the process perspective as the source of novel and creative possibilities that lure humans, as well as the rest of reality, to new levels of experience and creativity. Divine action, in this mode, is the ground for radical change, or in religious terminology, conversion, or in Schubert Ogden's words, emancipation.[31] God's gracious presence is, in the form of ever new creative potential, the source of our hope that oppression can be overcome and that oppressive structures, while constitutive are not wholly determinative, but open to the transforming power of God's action. In all of this, the process perspective resonates strongly with both the liberationist and Wesleyan vision of a divine presence which does not stand in opposition to human freedom, but is the ground for increased self-determination and for a truly liberating partnership of God and humanity.

But if the process perspective concurs with the Wesleyan and liberation view of the character of divine action, I think it is far less confident about the outcome of that gracious presence. For while God's presence is indeed the source of hope, it is not, for many process thinkers, the guarantee of any ultimate victory, at least for the human race. God's presence permits, nourishes, and provides the ground for ever greater freedom. But with that increased freedom come new and greater risks of evil and tragedy. In Charles Hartshorne's words, "The risks of freedom are inseparable from freedom and the price of its opportunities."[32] Thus while God's presence provides hope that we can transform the social order, it does not provide any assurance that we will, or that such transformation will be liberating rather than creating a new and perhaps worse form of oppression.

I believe this process vision both resonates with liberationist and, to some degree, the Wesleyan tradition while offering several correctives as well. It offers, as do these other perspectives, a view of cosmic, or divine, reality that is supportive of human freedom and responsibility, and that lays the foundation for radical transformation of the personal and the social order. This process God is no guardian of the social and individual status quo. However, it suggests, along with feminist, black, and third world perspectives, that human selfhood is far more social than Wesley understood, and that its fulfillment not only takes place in the social arena but depends upon that context for its possiblity. Further, in contrast to many liberationist assertions especially from black and third world representatives, the process vision contends that while the future is open, and radical change is possible, there is no promise of final victory or certitude of a future social order where the risks of injustice will be no longer. Instead, there is only the hope that transformation is always possible, and the conviction that the accomplishments of freedom are worth its risks.

While liberationists have much to learn from process thinkers, the reverse is true as well. First, much process thinking, while claiming to recognize the social character of existence, has nonetheless emphasized the individual's transcendence over its environment. It has further elevated this individual freedom and its potentiality for creativity to its highest value. Even now, as process thinkers seek to open themselves to the concerns of liberationists, many seem uneasy with the liberationist claim that some persons', that is, the oppressors', freedom will be curtailed in the quest for a just order.[33] Yet women and other oppressed persons have argued strongly that the self-determination of the elite has been, up until now, dependent upon the oppression of the many, and we are convinced that while new forms of freedom and creativity will be available in a transformed order, certain prerogatives of oppression will no longer exist. Insofar as process thinkers do not recognize that certain forms of self-transcendence have been predicated upon oppression, they will fail to understand the radical nature of the liberationist proposals.

Second, process thought has continued to emphasize that individuals are the only true agents, and that institutions have agential impact only insofar as they are composed of such individual actors. The liberationist perspective, concerned with the structural and institutional forms of oppression, suggests that process thinkers need to explore how process categories can better elucidate the impingement of social structures on individuals. While process thought may be able to do this, it is a task that, for the most part, has not yet been carried out successfully in relation to the structures of oppression. (In a related matter, women need to reflect more seriously on the fact that while we are calling for greater attunement to our bodies, we continue to argue for the necessity of transcending—i.e., being free from oppressive social structures; that is, we tend to assume an innately positive quality to our bodies and nature that we reject in relation to society. Whether there are good reasons for such assumption or whether it is the result of a naive romanticism is a question that needs further discussion.)

Third, process thinkers have elevated aesthetic categories over moral ones, arguing that the former categories can incorporate and do justice to the latter moral ones, while at the same time being more cosmically applicable, and hence, metaphysically relevant. While once more this may be true, process thinkers will need to indicate in far more explicit fashion the moral repercussions of a process vision if they are to dialogue with those whose primary concern is the quest for justice.

Fourth, liberationist visions suggest that the connection between God's sympathetic and, hence, suffering participation in creaturely reality must be understood as more closely tied with God's creative presence in the world. That is to say, liberationists propose that God's love of the world issues forth, not only in pursuit of aesthetic enjoyment, but in the partisan search for a just order. James Will, articulating the need to define more clearly the relation between God's appropriation of an oppressed world and the divine offering of creative possibilities, states it well when he claims, "The crucial matter is not God's capacity to resolve the world's tragedy in the harmony of his consequent nature, but God's

suffering creativity in universally and continually providing the initial aims which will transmute that ongoing suffering into new opportunities for justice as the form of his love."[34] In short, while individual redemption in God's memory is important, for liberationists, the greater concern lies not in the preservation of the past, but in how such retention contributes to transforming the future.

And finally, I think process thinkers can take a clue from Wesley's vision of divinely inspired freedom. For him, humans are set free, are provided with "novel and creative possibilities" not so that we might pursue highly individual purposes. Instead, we are, through God's gracious presence, freed to love and enabled to enter into liberating and transforming connectedness. It is this notion of liberation, not from relationship, but to creative and liberating forms of connection that I believe the proponents of process thought might most fruitfully develop.

V. Concluding Remarks

In closing, I would like to reiterate that I believe the Wesleyan tradition and process and feminist perspectives can fruitfully dialogue on many issues. They share in general, if not always in detail, a complementary vision of divine activity and human freedom, a dynamic view of human transformation, and a commitment to the overcoming of alienation. However, these preliminary explorations have indicated as well that many issues remain unresolved; in particular, the role of sexuality in transformed human life and the relation between the social order and the pursuit of liberating wholeness. It is to these issues that I hope our discussions might turn.

NOTES

1. Examples of this mode of theological reflection include Tillich's method of correlation and, more recently, David Tracy's attempt to coordinate contemporary theological claims with themes of the so-called Christian classics. In a slightly different way, I think Schubert Ogden's theological norms of credibility (presentday sensibilities) and appropriateness (the apostolic witness) also represent the theology-as-hermeneutics approach though Ogden's work embodies a more critical sense of the circular character of many of the other hermeneutical theologies.
2. Edward Farley has recently offered a powerful attack on the theology's "house of authority," esp. in the form of the Scripture-principle, upon which much of hermeneutical theology has been based. See E. Farley, *Ecclesial Reflection: An Anatomy of Theological Method* (Philadelphia: Fortress Press, 1982), part 1.
3. Diverse theological thinkers such as John Hick, Gordon Kaufman, Wilfred Cantwell Smith, and John Cobb are, with increasing intensity, arguing that the question of pluralism must become central to the theological discipline; i.e., they are claiming Western Christian theology can no longer be done without consideration of the claims of other perspectives, but must fully move into the global context.

4. See the works of French philosopher Michel Foucault, and in this country, philosopher Richard Rorty and theologian Mark Taylor.

5. Many feminist theologians consider themselves as interpreters of the Christian tradition and have, to that end, often expended considerable effort in the search for a pristine, and hence liberating, essence of Christianity or of the Christian message. However, many others, myself included, have moved away from this revisionary mode of theological reflection.

6. The understanding of theology that follows is greatly indebted to the work of Gordon D. Kaufman for both its content and its title. However, I am convinced that many women, especially those who are attempting to develop a female specific vision of reality, are, in fact, carrying out a very similar program. See G. D. Kaufman, *The Theological Imagination: Constructing the Concept of God* (Philadelphia: Westminster Press, 1981).

7. This view is articulated with particular power by Clifford Geertz in *The Interpretation of Cultures* (New York: Basic Books, 1973).

8. Geertz emphasizes this claim in his assertion that "a cultureless human being would probably turn out to be not an intrinsically talented, though unfulfilled ape, but a wholly mindless and consequently unworkable monstrosity." Geertz, *Interpretation*, p. 68.

9. Kaufman, *Theological Imagination*, p. 184; emphasis mine.

10. Delwin Brown has recently stressed this dialogical approach to history in contrast to an approach that sees the past as that to which we must conform. See Brown, "Struggle Till Daybreak: On the Nature of Authority in Theology," unpublished ms.

11. John B. Cobb, Jr., *Process Theology as Political Theology* (Philadelphia: Westminster Press, 1982) p. 48.

12. Ibid. p. 48.

13. Ibid. p. 48.

14. Josè Míguez Bonino is not quite as certain about Wesleyan theology's ability to commit wholeheartedly to the present order. See Bonino, "Wesley's Doctrine of Sanctification from a Liberationist Perspective" in *Sanctification and Liberation: Liberation Theologies in the Light of the Wesleyan Tradition*, ed. Theodore Runyon (Nashville: Abingdon Press, 1981).

15. Ibid. p. 55.

16. Ibid. p. 63.

17. I believe that while process thinkers and feminists have dealt with these issues in the past, there is presently a far greater concentration on them and the greater recognition of their centrality to viable contemporary theology.

18. While freedom from bondage has always been a theme of theological reflection, the recognition of its corporate character and its embodiment in oppressive structures is receiving a new and quite distinct rendering. Going along with this has been the insistence by liberationists that there is a profound difference between oppressors and the oppressed, and that despite the fact that we may all be sinners, such universal sin cannot be used as the excuse to obscure the difference between oppressors and their victims.

19. This rendering of the development of the self-body dualism is highly superficial. Any adequate treatment would need to trace the differences between our Hebraic and Greek heritages and the eventual victory of the Greek vision. Further, I am using the terms "spirit" and "soul" interchangeably, although I recognize that distinctions have been and can be made between the two.

20. Sheila Collins, "The Personal Is Political" in *The Politics of Women's Spirituality*, ed. Charlene Spretnak (Garden City, N.Y.: Anchor Books, 1982), p. 363.

21. Rosemary R. Ruether has been, among women theologians, a leading proponent of this view. A recent book by sociologist Nancy Chodorow has offered one of the fullest and most persuasive arguments for this position. See N. Chodorow, *The Reproduction of Mothering: Psychoanalysis and the Sociology of Gender* (Berkeley: University of California Press, 1978).

22. Gayle Rubin, "The Traffic in Women," in *Toward an Anthropology of Women*, ed. Rayna R. Reiter (New York: Monthly Review Press, 1975) p. 204.

23. This claim of the distinctive character of female experience has brought together a strange combination of people, including Penelope Washbourn and Mary Daly. However, they argue to vastly different conclusions, with Washbourn sounding like she assumes the complementarity of the sexes while Daly argues for radical separatism and a lesbian embodiment of female sexuality.

24. Penelope Washbourn, "The Dynamics of Female Experience: Process Models and Human Values," in *Feminism and Process Thought*, ed. Sheila Greeve Davaney (New York: Edwin Mellan Press, 1981) p. 88.

25. See Mary Daly, *Gyn/Ecology: The Metaethics of Radical Feminism* (Boston: Beacon Press, 1978); and Elizabeth Dodson Gray, *Green Paradise Lost* (Wellesley, Ma.: Roundtable Press, 1979).

26. The question of whether sexual identity is or should be separated from gender identity is a major, and bitterly debated, issue with most feminists arguing for the dissolution of gender roles. In a much debated article, feminist Alice Rossi raised the question anew by suggesting that women may be physiologically better suited for parenting. See Alice Rossi, "A Biosocial Perspective on Parenting," *Daedalus* (Spring, 1977): 106.

27. John Cobb, Jr., "Feminism and Process Thought: A Two-Way Relationship," in *Feminism and Process Thought*, ed. Sheila Greeve Davaney (New York: Edwin Mellen Press, 1981). The following discussion is based upon this article.

28. Sociobiologists, among others, are arguing that there is a genetically grounded connection between biology and socially assigned roles. Most feminists, however, reject the sociobiologist arguments contending, among other things, that they have failed to account for why female roles are universally devalued.

29. There is, as on the question of body-self relations, no absolute unanimity among women on this issue. However, at least in theological issues, there seems to be a growing consensus of the necessity of radical social change and a movement toward more radical political options.

30. See Delwin Brown, *To Set at Liberty: Christian Faith and Human Freedom* (Maryknoll, N.Y.: Orbis Books, 1981); Schubert Ogden, *Faith and Freedom: Toward a Theology of Liberation* (Nashville: Abingdon Press, 1979); Cobb, *Process Theology*.

31. See Ogden, *Faith and Freedom*, for discussion of the notion of emancipation.

32. Charles Hartshorne, *Faith and Freedom*, "A New Look at the Problem of Evil," in *Current Philosophical Issues: Essays in Honor of Curt John Ducasse*, ed. Frederich C. Dommeyer (Springfield, Ill.: Charles Thomas, 1966), p. 208.

33. See W. Widick Schroeder, "Liberation Theology: A Critique from a Process Perspective," p. 236; and John B. Cobb, Jr., "The Political Implications of Whitehead's Philosophy," in *Process Philosophy and Social Thought*, ed. John B. Cobb, Jr., and W. Widick Schroeder (Chicago: Chicago Center for the Scientific Study of Religion, 1981), p. 27. The desire to extend the benefits of self-transcending freedom to all while not diminishing the freedom presently enjoyed by those in power is reminiscent of the failed strategies of "development" that imagined progress in the third world without radical changes in the first world.

34. James Will, "Dialectical Panentheism: Towards Relating Liberation and Process Theologies," in *Process Philosophy*, eds. Cobb and Schroeder, p. 250.

IV. Methodism and Biblical Authority

1. THE WESLEYAN QUADRILATERAL

William J. Abraham

The Wesleyan quadrilateral is in itself an unwieldy and awkward object of thought. The various elements roll off the pen easily enough, of course; most of us can talk or write about Scripture, tradition, reason, and experience. The problem is that we can talk *ad infinitum* if not *ad nauseam* about them. The realities these terms refer to or embody are exceedingly complex, so much so that there will always be a temptation to short-circuit the discussion by assuming that at the end of the day only one of them really counts in making decisions in theology. It is not difficult to find historical examples. Deists preferred reason; liberal theologians of the nineteenth century opted for experience; fundamentalists chose Scripture alone. Or so they all thought. The failure of these moves to deliver the theological riches promised should make us more patient. Perhaps Wesley captured something wholesome when he preferred a wider group of sources in his theological deliberations. As we explore this possibility further, let us begin by situating the current interest in the quadrilateral in its historical context.

Historical purists among us will no doubt hope that the current interest in the quadrilateral is an expression of the renewed desire to expound Wesley's theology simply for its own sake. Their concern is entirely legitimate; indeed it is crucial if a fully accurate account of the Wesleyan quadrilateral is to become available to us. However, it would be naïve to think that this alone explains the present interest. My own guess is that that interest is related to the wider crisis which confronts Methodism as a theological tradition.

What is conspicuous about modern Methodist theology, in America at least, is its pluralism. It has been quite honestly confessed that any consensus there may have been in the past has broken down. Diversity, disagreement, and division are central facts of our theological life. Thus a major attempt has been made to hold together within the one family a wide variety of positions. The natural way to do this is to attain as much agreement as possible on procedures. This is to be found in methods which will be fruitful and fulfilling in theological reflection and construction. But what methods will work? "The answer comes in terms of our free inquiry within the boundaries defined by four main sources and guidelines for Christian theology: Scripture, tradition, experience, reason. . . . Jointly they have provided a broad and stable context for reflection and formulation."[1] The quadrilateral therefore has a pivotal place in modern Methodist theology in America and is intimately related to the pluralism which has been officially adopted. Perhaps it would be fair to say that it serves to hold the line on the integrity of the tradition. If there can be no agreement on what to believe, it is implicitly said, then let there at least be agreement on the context or the criteria of Christian believing.

It is worth noting that there has been little if any interest in the quadrilateral within British Methodism. The official account of British Methodist theology, which covers from 1850 to 1950, makes no reference to it at all.[2] Not even an advanced state of decay has awakened British Methodists from their dogmatic slumbers. In fact the only significant discussion of the quadrilateral which I know of in the recent past is by the Oxford philosopher, Basil Mitchell.[3] Mitchell, an Anglican, skillfully uses the ingredients of the quadrilateral to chart the various options open to the modern theologian who is seeking secure foundations for Christian belief. Clearly the quadrilateral is not of sectarian interest. In its own right it focuses issues which any serious theologian must face, for there is a general crisis in theology. There are no longer any giants in the land; consensus has broken down; so there is considerable pressure to explore in greater depth the general canons of theological reflection.

This is clearly the case within what we might loosely call modern evangelicalism. Thus some conservative Wesleyans who have become dissatisfied for very good reasons with modern evangelical orthodoxy have been driven to take a fresh look at Wesley. This has not been easy, for Wesley has been presented within conservative circles either as just another good fundamentalist or as a hero to be accepted uncritically. Despite this, Wesley's ideas have proved invaluable in helping some conservative Wesleyans to challenge modern evangelical orthodoxy from within the evangelical tradition. More specifically, the very existence of the quadrilateral within Wesley's thought makes it clear that Wesley offers a very different vision of the evangelical tradition

119

than that currently canvassed by those who sought to repudiate elements of fundamentalism in the last generation. Hence the quadrilateral in this context can serve as a lever to create space for innovation and theological renewal.

Yet it must be said that so far there has been very little progress. The potential is there, but it is not clear if it will be realized. One looks in vain for a sustained attempt to develop an account of authority which will break new ground and provide a viable alternative to the standard models shaped predominantly by the Reformed tradition. At best what we have is a realization that much work needs to be done.

But does the quadrilateral really help us find a way out of our current difficulties? We might think that it will be "fruitful" and "fulfilling" in our doctrinal reflection. We might believe it provides a much better way of construing biblical authority. But how far is this pious waffle and sentimental hope? Are we not being complacent and self-serving in proposing that the quadrilateral really does helpfully illuminate the constellation of authorities which any adequate theology must employ?

In my view, there are at least four major questions which anyone seriously committed to the quadrilateral must answer. There is, first, the question of meaning. How are we to construe Scripture, tradition, reason, and experience? Second, there is the question of internal relations. How are we to characterize the relation between these four factors? Third, there is the question of justification. Why should these four considerations be seen as crucially relevant to deciding the truth of any particular theological proposal? Fourth, there is the question of practicality. Is it really possible for a modern theologian to draw together the combined force of the data provided by Scripture, tradition, reason, and experience and then use these to build an adequate theology?

It is not my intention in this paper to answer these questions in even a modest way. I shall be content if I can indicate that they are central issues which must be explored if we are to take the Methodist theological heritage at all seriously in our day. I propose to do this by outlining and evaluating some aspects of Wesley's thinking on these issues.

Interestingly, Wesley, as far as I know, never explicitly mentions the quadrilateral, although he does speak of a joint appeal to Scripture, reason, and experience in his essay on original sin.[4] I have no doubt however that Wesley was committed to the quadrilateral. A careful reading of the standard sermons reveals that Wesley characteristically appealed to Scripture, tradi-

tion, reason, and experience when he wanted to support or defend his theology. To be sure, Wesley did this in an informal manner, but this is the way he generally works, given the constraints that the sermon form imposed upon him as a writer.

What this means is that just as the seventeenth-century Anglican divines moved beyond the horizons of the continental Reformation, so Wesley moved beyond the horizons of Anglicanism. Anglicans like Hooker went beyond the austerity of the Reformers by making a deliberate appeal to reason as well as Scripture and early tradition; they thus abandoned the ambivalence, if not hostility to reason, that one finds in Calvin and Luther.[5] Wesley is simply a good Anglican therefore in his appeal to the triad of Scripture, tradition, and reason. What is distinctive in Wesley is the additional appeal to experience. This was a move which was exceedingly controversial and as we shall see led Wesley to develop a fascinating synthesis of empiricism and Christian Platonism.

If we can agree that Wesley was committed to the quadrilateral, what does he have to say about the first three of the four issues I raised earlier? That is to say, how does he construe the various elements, how does he relate them to each other, and how does he justify their role in theology? As the answers to these questions are closely related to each other, I shall take them together rather than artificially and mechanically work through them one at a time. Let us begin with the place of Scripture.

Wesley shares with the Reformers the view that Scripture means basically the canon of sixty-six books of the Old and New Testaments. These constitute for Wesley the fundamental criterion for all theological proposals. Consequently, none of the other elements in the quadrilateral can be viewed as a coordinate canon of equal standing with the Bible. Tradition, reason, and experience are therefore subordinate sources of theological reflection. One of their primary functions is to enable us to rightly interpret what Scripture says. So Scripture is the primary canon.

Wesley's warrant for this decisive weighting of the relations between the elements of the quadrilateral is a doctrine of divine revelation and divine inspiration. Indeed Wesley goes so far, as does Calvin, to develop a doctrine of divine dictation.[6] Not surprisingly he therefore speaks at times as a committed inerrantist. "How did he inspire the Scripture? He so directed the writers that *no considerable error* should fall from them. Nay, will not the allowing there is *any error* in Scripture shake the authority of the whole?"[7]

Broadly speaking, Wesley then is at one with Reformation orthodoxy on the warrants of the use of Scripture. Scripture is the product of direct, divine inspiration construed in terms of divine dictation and speaking, therefore it is the primary means of access to the divine will.

Tradition is an aid to interpreting what Scripture teaches. The tradition in mind here is that of the primitive church, both as found in the writings of the early Fathers and also as mediated by the cardinal documents of the Anglican tradition, that is, the Thirty-Nine Articles, the Book of Common Prayer, and the Homilies. Wesley's enthusiasm for the latter can be quite unbounded, for he tells us that he reverences the authority of the Anglican Church "only less than the oracles of God."[8] Wesley may appear to be inconsistent here for he seems to set the Anglican tradition above that of the Fathers, but I prefer to take these really as one, in that Anglicans have classically seen their own traditions as embodying the thought of the early Fathers. The warrants for this claim are well known. The closeness of the early Fathers to the Apostolic period, their agreement as part of one undivided church, and their purity have been generally cited as crucial considerations. One presumes that Wesley shared these general Anglican assumptions.

Wesley was also very much an Anglican in his appeal to reason. He devotes considerable attention to reason and makes it abundantly clear that he is fully committed to the use of reason in religion. Yet Wesley is also at pains not to overestimate what reason can actually achieve. His clearest statement on reason comes in the sermon, "The Case of Reason Impartially Considered." There Wesley defines reason very carefully following the Aristotelian tradition which had been brought to something of a climax at Oxford by Henry Aldrich. That tradition construed reason as a faculty of the soul which exerted itself in simple apprehension, judgment, and discourse. Simple apprehension is the operation of perceiving things distinctly and clearly, judging is the operation of correctly putting terms and words into intelligible propositions, while discourse is the operation of deduction or inference. Elsewhere Wesley construed reasoning more summarily as the art of inferring one thing from another. He does also allow wider notions of reason; for example, he construes it as the "eternal reason" or "the nature of things."[9] Wesley also construes reason in very broad terms when he takes it to mean argument generally. However, he does not take these very seriously and prefers to use the more technical account given above.

Thus understood, Wesley encourages the use of reason in the affairs of common life and in the whole circle of arts and sciences. Within religion reason is also invaluable in interpreting the essential truths of Scripture and in understanding and discharging the duties of common life. Wesley also makes it clear that by reason we can know that God exists. "As soon as we came to the use of reason, we learned 'the invisible things of God, even His eternal power and Godhead, from the things that are made.' From the things that are seen we inferred the existence of an eternal, powerful Being, that is not seen."[10] Wesley clearly stands at this point in the tradition of Aquinas rather than of Barth.

Yet Wesley was deeply disappointed in the results of natural theology. It left him with so many doubts at one stage in his experience that he contemplated suicide.[11] Moreover, reason could not produce faith and love, therefore it could not produce virtue or happiness. There are two reasons for this. First, there is the reality of sin and its effects. Due to our fallen nature our faculties are corrupted and therefore need to be healed by God. Second, reason cannot work independently of material content. Reason requires data which it cannot in itself supply, hence more than reason is utterly essential if the truth about God is to be known.

Wesley at this point follows the classical empiricist tradition which rejects the notion of innate ideas and insists that all knowledge must be mediated through the senses.[12] Once the senses supply the "ideas" then reason can set to work, apprehending, judging, and discoursing. The favored model here is a perceptual one. The world exists objectively; it impinges on the senses which transmit "ideas" to the mind; then reason can do its work. Wesley took this to be the case with the physical world. It was equally true of the spiritual world. For there to be the knowledge of God, that knowledge must be direct and immediate. It must be knowledge by acquaintance. It was not enough for God to be an inferred entity such as is the case in classical natural theology. God must act by "perceptible inspiration" to make known spiritual reality.[13] This corresponds to the objective reality of the physical world which must impinge on the physical senses. But the senses must be in good working order if the world is to be perceived; indeed a person must be equipped with senses in the first place. Equally in the case of our acquaintance with spiritual reality, we need to have spiritual senses in good working order, so to speak. Unfortunately, we do not by nature possess such faculties, or, if we do, they are so corrupted as to be useless. Thus our natural state is one of rank atheism.[14] The only way for there to be true knowledge of God, then, is for God to provide such adequate, inward, spiritual senses so that the things of the Spirit can be properly perceived. It was precisely this that took place in the new birth when the Holy Spirit gave that gift of faith which made it possible for one to have the evidence or conviction of things unseen.[15] Without this special work of grace in the soul one remained utterly blind and hence was quite incapable of reasoning correctly about the things of God.

It will be clear by now that experience had a crucial role in Wesley's theology. By experience here we mean something quite specific, if not technical. Spiritual experience is construed quite deliberately as analogous to normal sense experience. By means of spiritual faculties one tastes, sees, and perceives the things of God. Such experience involves firsthand, uninferred, immediate acquaintance with the divine world. Now to be sure, just as reason has a broader and narrower range of application so too does experience. Thus Wesley also uses experience to mean astute observation of life and things in general. It is to this kind of general experience that Wesley appeals in his treatise on original sin and in his suggestions about the importance of self-denial.[16] This wider appeal has a marked place in Wesley's thought, and we shall note its significance later. But for now it is vital not to confuse this with the very precise account of experience that Wesley insisted was vital to all true knowledge of God. I want to bring out the importance of this by noting how sophisticated Wesley was at this point and by noting how this narrow conception of experience posed two interesting problems for him.

Before that, it should be recognized that the appeal to experience is logically prior in Wesley to the appeal to Scripture. In this connection it is interesting that when Wesley was challenged about the possibility of presumption in religious experience he cannot settle the issue by appeal to Scripture.[17] Of course, he can try to show that the marks which accompany genuine experience of God are those which accompany the experience of God as documented in Scripture. But Wesley knows that this will not satisfy the really persistent critic for the latter wants to know what criteria enable even the biblical writers, like Paul, say, to distinguish the voice of God from a human or angelic voice. Wesley has no real answer to this and alternates between challenging the question, appealing to self-evidence, and attending to the change of character following the experience of God. At this level, appeal to Scripture itself depends on the appeal to the experience of the writers as agents who have been subject to divine inspiration. In fact it is interesting that the appeal to present experience is couched in the language of inspiration for, as we have seen, Wesley accepted that experience as involving "perceptible inspiration." Indeed the difference between the biblical writers and the believer was one of degree and not one of kind. Whereas the biblical writers were continuously inspired, the believer was only occasionally inspired.[18]

What is happening here is that Wesley is quite self-consciously facing up to the inescapable epistemological dimension to theological claims about knowing God. Wesley's philosophical skill at this level is intriguing and, in my view, not inconsiderable.[19] Notice to begin with that Wesley has brought together the language of Zion and the language of Athens in a remarkable synthesis. He has integrated the biblical references to the new birth, the witness of the spirit, faith, and the like, with a philosophical account of knowledge which gives pride of place to the senses and a subordinate role to reason. That philosophical account is in turn a marriage between classical empiricism and Christian Platonism. From the former Wesley takes the principle that all knowledge comes through the senses; from the latter he takes the material or ontological claim that God can make direct contact with the human soul. Thus Wesley insists that we can know God directly by acquaintance; indeed it is exactly this that is happening when God's Spirit witnesses with our spirits that we are children of God. Faith is quite literally a gift of God constituted by *evidence* of things not seen, hence it leads to *conviction* and assurance. Without this special kind of internal evidence, the traditional arguments for classical Christian belief are quite inadequate.[20]

This last point is, in my view, of considerable philosophical significance in the debate about the relation between faith and reason, yet Wesley does not really develop it very thoroughly. It is here that we meet the limitations of Wesley's philosophical vision. Thus he does not explore why religious experience might offer a deeper and firmer support for Christian belief than traditional natural theology or how both religious experience and natural theology might be integrated to support each other. In other words, Wesley does not really tackle the justification for his appeal to experience and reason. To put it mildly, this is a piece of unfinished philosophical business.

I think this helps explain why Wesley had serious difficulty coping with mysticism, on the one hand, and lack of assurance among believers, on the other. It is natural that Wesley should have been very attracted to Christian mysticism. Indeed he shared with the mystics the appeal to direct acquaintance with God. What troubled Wesley, as Thorvald Källstad points out, was the mystics' contempt for means of grace, good works, and reason.[21] Wesley is surely correct to reject any view that would set inward religion over against these. Yet Wesley's rejection of the mystics lacks any deep theological or philosophical rationale, taking the form of dogmatic repudiation. But if Wesley had pursued the issue more comprehensively we might be in a better position to understand the reasons for this repudiation. More importantly we might also understand how he could speak of a *direct, inward* experience of God which was yet *mediated* by *external* means of grace. As it is, this is left unexamined.[22]

Equally, it is worth asking whether Wesley's philosophical limitations do not explain why his treatment of lack of assurance is so unsatisfactory. The early Wesley is surely entirely consistent. Given that faith involves the giving of new senses with which to behold spiritual reality, it is correct to argue that assurance automatically follows. Compare the physical analogy. A blind person who is given new eyes can normally see the physical world. Analogously, the spiritually blind, given the eyes of faith in the sense specified by Wesley, will normally see his or her sins forgiven and will know God. Wesley, as is well known, drew back from this, but insofar as he does so, he must confess he is being inconsistent or he must look afresh at the whole nature of evangelical experience. As it stands, he modifies his account of assurance without providing a convincing, alternative framework of interpretation.

Thus far I have tried to indicate how Wesley construed Scripture, tradition, reason, and experience, how he related these to each other and to what extent he offered a justification for their role in theology. We have seen that two of the four elements, namely reason and experience, were given both a narrow and wide interpretation, with the emphasis falling on the narrow conception of these terms. We have also noted that within theology, it was Scripture that was treated as the primary norm, with the other three functioning as interpretive and confirmatory. Yet Wesley recognized that such an internal ordering within the quadrilateral required justification. That justification was rooted in a doctrine of divine inspiration, which on the human side involved a foundational appeal to the experience of the writers of Scripture. These were understood to have direct acquaintance with the things of God through hearing and

seeing what God had revealed to them by inspiration. All believers needed to have the same kind of experience of spiritual reality. For this to happen, God had to provide appropriate inner senses which would permit the believer to know God personally by acquaintance. The spiritual reality encountered in experience is, of course, the God revealed in the Scriptures, hence the experience is interpreted in categories drawn from the Bible and therefore cannot be construed as contrary to Scripture. Thus Scripture remains normative. However, the experience of the believer, like that of the apostle Paul, is itself seen as foundational. There can be no retreat beyond this to something more basic which would justify the appeal to experience. Likewise with reason. Wesley does not provide any rationale for his appeal to reason. This is surely wise for such a move would be question-begging: it would involve the use of reason to justify the use of reason. Here one either trusts to inference or argument, or one does not, just as one either trusts one's senses, or one does not. In this respect tradition differs from reason and experience, for it is possible to give a rationale for the appeal to tradition which does not itself rely on an appeal to tradition.

We are left then with our fourth and final question, What light does Wesley throw on the question of practice? What does his work show about our efforts to be faithful to the quadrilateral in our theological deliberations? As this involves substantial evaluation of the viability of the quadrilateral, I shall lead into it by making some critical remarks on the issues discussed so far. To keep matters within bounds I shall resort to a series of telescoped comments.

First, the basic attraction of the quadrilateral is surely that it captures in a convenient principle the need for the theologian to consult all relevant data and warrants before arriving at any particular theological proposal. Scripture, tradition, reason, and experience, these four cover the various fields to be consulted. It is difficult to see how any relevant considerations would be omitted if these were properly explored.

Second, in saying this, I am leaving open how tradition, reason, and experience are to be defined or construed. I see nothing objectionable *per se* in this. As we have seen in Wesley, reason and experience can be interpreted in both a narrow and a broad sense. So too can tradition, as Rupert Davies has shown.[23] All of these elements are bound to be contested, hence to look for some kind of agreed, univocal interpretation is to ask too much. What we need to do is what Wesley did, namely articulate and defend our own way of construing these categories and resources.[24]

Third, I think Wesley was correct to insist that Scripture has a unique place in the constellation of considerations to which he appealed. Wesley does not, of course, provide a very developed account of what this involves. There is no discussion of the many problems which arise when we try to make Scripture uniquely normative. For example, how can we appropriate material which is generally agreed to be morally offensive, as Wesley himself noted in the case of the imprecatory psalms? Or how do we deal with the Old Testament? Does it count as of equal value with the New Testament? If it does, how do we reconcile this with the finality given to Jesus Christ? There is clearly room for an extended treatment of the canon of Scripture which would begin to address such matters.

Wesley is stronger in his rationale for the unique place of Scripture in theology. Leaving aside the typically confused account of inspiration that he offers, I think that Wesley rightly saw that the appeal to Scripture requires an adequate doctrine of special revelation. This in turn must incorporate a commitment to divine intervention such as Wesley himself held. In our days, all this appears antediluvian, for it faces a whole battery of objections which have arisen since Wesley's day. Some of these arise from reason and experience broadly conceived, and hence they challenge the internal scope for further discussion.[25]

Fourth, if that discussion is to be profitable we must be prepared to follow Wesley into the realm of epistemology. Be it noted that the Wesleyan quadrilateral is an attempt to solve the issue of what canons we should rely on in theology. Over against the Reformed tradition, Wesley worked with a more subtle account of authority. However, beyond this there are deeper questions about how knowledge of God is possible which cannot be solved by appeal to Scripture carefully confirmed by tradition, reason, and experience. The appeal to the quadrilateral itself presupposes, for example, the reliability of reason and experience. Here we arrive at basic questions about the ultimate foundations for our claims to knowledge as derived from Scripture, tradition, reason, and experience. At this level Wesley, as we have seen, did not appeal to Scripture, nor indeed could he. Rather he developed a synthesis of empiricism and Platonism which gave pride of place to experience.

It might be wondered whether Wesley was ultimately consistent when he thus made experience utterly basic in his claims to knowledge. How can this be reconciled with the quadrilateral which makes experience subordinate to Scripture? There is a dilemma here, but I do not think it should worry us. Scripture has a special place precisely because the writers have access *in experience* to the things of God. Thus Scripture embodies special divine revelation given in the past to the people of God. So one reason for the appeal to Scripture is precisely that it embodies the experience of special revelation. What Wesley is claiming is that that revelation of God, given itself in experience, is confirmed by our own personal experience of God through the Holy Spirit. This is entirely legitimate and consistent.

Consider an analogy. Suppose I know the prime minister very intimately. Suppose further that she has revealed certain things to me which I incorporate in my autobiography. What the prime minister has made known to me has been mediated through the senses. It has not been given to me through innate ideas or intuition, nor has it been inferred from her public actions. Yet what I write may become normative in the sense that it is relied on in giving an accurate portrait of the prime minister. Indeed, if I were the only intimate friend of the prime minister it would have a very privileged position. Moreover, what I say may well be confirmed by your experience of the prime minister as mediated by your senses.

Likewise, certain people may have access through their experience to those special acts of God in the past which uniquely make known what God is like. Because of their unique position, their reflection has a privileged position as normative. Yet their reflection depends crucially, if Wesley is correct, on their experience. What they know is not given to them through innate ideas or intuition, nor is it inferred in any straightforward sense from nature or history. It is given through the senses and without the senses it would not be available. Yet their reflection may clearly be confirmed by our own personal experience of God, which too, if Wesley is correct, will be mediated through the senses. At the foundations there is an appeal to the senses, yet within that appeal to the senses, some experiences may have a privileged and normative position. This, in my view, is a plausible way to argue and it dissolves the appearance of inconsistency.

What I am suggesting in all this is that we need to distinguish between the question of canon in Christian theology and the question of the foundations of our knowledge, including our knowledge of God.[26] These two matters are related, but they are logically distinct. The latter issue is strictly epistemological, and we make our choices between, say, experience, intuition, innate ideas, reason, and so on. At this level it does not make sense to appeal to Scripture or tradition. Nor does it make sense to speak of being a Calvinist, a Wesleyan, or a Roman Catholic. Rather we are empiricists, rationalists, intuitionists, skeptics. The issue of canon is quite different and is, broadly speaking, theological. Here we make our choices between Scripture, tradition, reason, experience, and it makes sense to speak of being a Calvinist, a Wesleyan, a Roman Catholic. Clearly the concepts deployed overlap and commitments in epistemology will almost certainly have a bearing on commitments on the issue of norms, but nothing but confusion will result if we fail to distinguish the nature of the questions addressed here. If we take our cue from Wesley, then we shall not hesitate to pursue both the issue of canon and the issue of foundations. Hence we shall not hesitate to enter the field of philosophy with all its maddening complexity.

This leads very naturally to a fifth comment. As we have seen, Wesley put great emphasis on religious experience. Indeed, this had a key role in his doctrine of assurance. Yet he does not reject the appeal to reason as classically understood, as we saw in his guarded comments about natural theology. In my opinion, the time is now ripe for a careful reworking of a Wesleyan position which parallels what Alvin Plantinga is currently constructing within the Reformed tradition. In other words, I think it is possible to argue that Wesley's emphasis on evangelical experience can be integrated with an appeal to the classical tradition of natural theology in such a way that it is both religiously and philosophically satisfactory. Speaking historically, Wesley offers in embryonic form a third alternative to the fideism of, say, Tertullian and Barth, and the hard rationalism of, say, Aquinas and Swinburne. The development of this alternative in our terms and context represents one of the great challenges facing philosophy of religion in the post-Wittgensteinian era.[27]

Last, it is about time that I said something about the practicality of appealing to the quadrilateral in our theological reflections. I have deliberately left this to the end because it poses the most serious threat of all to the viability of the quadrilateral. If we take the quadrilateral and interpret its elements in the broadest terms possible, then it would seem quite absurd to think that it will work. There are very few issues which we can run through the gamut of Scripture, tradition, reason, and experience. There is just too much territory to be covered and too much data to be interpreted and absorbed. Only an

old-fashioned, out and out comprehensive rationalist could think otherwise. Wesley saw himself in such terms. He had enormous confidence in his intellectual endeavors and ransacked Scripture, tradition, reason, and experience in order to settle the issues which perplexed him or to counter the objections made against him. The end result is a motley body of literary remains which can still inform and inspire us. How far he was successful is something that is hard to judge if we apply his own norms as enshrined in the quadrilateral. Relatively speaking, I judge his work to be a remarkable feat worthy of sustained attention.

We, however, cannot share his confidence. The pluralism within Methodism as a whole bears witness to the explosion of information, disciplines, methods, opinions, and skills which have to be mastered if we are to appeal to the quadrilateral in any serious manner. One is reminded of the kaleidoscope: you shake it, and each time the same fragments of colored glass provide a different pattern or shape. Methodists have shaken the contents of Scripture, reason, tradition, and experience together in their heads, and the result is a rich welter of theological patterns which some call pluralism.

Others call it chaos and understandably seek refuge in a single norm or perspective which will somehow solve the dilemma by giving us the key to truth once and for all. So some turn to the Bible alone; some turn to the experience of political liberation; some look to the speculative metaphysics of process philosophy; some hide away in the depths of Barth's *Dogmatics*; perhaps some hope that a new biblical theology, or maybe even canonical criticism, will bring peace to our troubled theological souls. No doubt one can, if one tries hard enough, find seeds or warrants for many of these moves within Wesley himself. I suspect, however, that they all have one feature in common: they pay little attention to the complex demands which the quadrilateral lays upon us.

My own response to the problem of practicality is a mixed one. First, I am inclined to believe that the situation is not quite as grim as was stated earlier. Provided we can agree with the weighting that Wesley assigned internally to the various elements in the quadrilateral, then the data is by no means beyond control. The central elements of the faith as articulated in the early creeds do sum up accurately the teaching of Scripture, and these can be defended on the grounds of reason and experience. This it seems to me is what Wesley believed, and I think a tolerably reasonable case can be made out for it. At any rate, I certainly do not believe that such a project is beyond repair in modern times. This still remains a viable option which is worth pursuing with diligence.

Second, even if this seems more of a confession of faith than an established reality, the quadrilateral is still worth retaining as an ideal to chasten us in our endeavors. There is no holy grail to solve all our problems or answer all our critics. There is no philosophical school, no theory of hermeneutics, no personal or corporate experience of liberation of any kind, no great giant of the past, no method or conception of biblical study or research, which can save us theologically. Not even the pope in Rome can do it. In the last analysis we are thrown back on the Holy Scriptures, on the traditions of the past, on the deliberations of reason, and the content of personal and corporate experience. Boldly and creatively we must step out in faith, diligently seeking the truth about God and our salvation, joyfully hoping that when we make up our minds we shall not have wandered too far from that light which enlightens us all.

NOTES

1. *The Book of Discipline of The United Methodist Church* (Nashville: The United Methodist Publishing House, 1980), p. 68.
2. See William Stranson, "Methodist Theology 1850–1950," in *A History of the Methodist Church in Great Britain*, ed. Rupert Davies, A. Raymond George, Gordon Rupp (London: Epworth Press, 1983), vol. 3, pp. 182-231. John Stacey does refer to the ingredients of the quadrilateral but ultimately reduces them to a triad. See his *Groundwork of Theology* (London: Epworth Press, 1977), pp. 53-71.
3. Basil Mitchell, "The Intellectual Foundations of Christian Belief." Unpublished ms.
4. The full title runs, "The Doctrine of Original Sin: According to Scripture, Reason, and Experience."
5. Luther's outbursts against reason are well known. Calvin's commitment to reason is in my view somewhat exaggerated. One is reminded of Locke's analogy of the taxicab: reason is summoned but then dismissed when you get to your destination. One senses a deeper commitment on the part of Wesley.
6. I have argued this in detail in "The Concept of Inspiration in the Classical Wesleyan Tradition," in *A Celebration of Ministry*, ed. Kenneth Cain Kinghorn (Wilmore: Francis Asbury Publishing Co., 1982), pp. 33-47.
7. Wesley, *Works* (Oxford), vol. 11, p. 504.
8. Ibid.
9. This is a very strange notion. For Wesley's use of it, see op. cit., p. 55. In "The Case of Reason Impartially Considered," however, Wesley seems to reject this concept of reason as incoherent. See para. I.1.
10. John Wesley, "Original Sin," para. II.3. Care must be taken not to overlook this side to Wesley's thought, as happens in Colin W. Williams' *John Wesley's Theology Today* (Nashville: Abingdon Press, 1960), pp. 30-31.
11. John Wesley, "The Case of Reason Impartially Considered," para. II.2.
12. The evidence for this has been impressively presented by Mitsuo Shimizu in "Epistemology in the Thought of John Wesley," (Ph.D. dissertation, Drew University, 1980), chapter 5.
13. For Wesley's commitment to this concept see *Works (Oxford), vol. 11, p. 171.*
14. *See Wesley, Sermons, "Original Sin", para. 113.*
15. It is small wonder that Wesley fastened to the concept of faith deployed in Heb. 11:1. It suited his concerns admirably. Wesley's conception of faith is well laid out in *Works* (Oxford), vol. 11, p. 533. I quote it here in part.
    "The faith by which the promise is attained is represented by a power wrought by the Almighty in an immortal spirit inhabiting an house of clay, to see through the veil into the world of spirits, into things invisible and eternal; a power to discern those things which with eyes of flesh and blood no man hath seen or can see: either by reason of their nature, which (though they surround us on every side) is not perceivable by these gross senses, or by reason of their distance, as being yet afar off, in the bosom of eternity."
16. Sugden, *Sermons*, "Self-Denial", para. 3. The standard sermons often make use of this conception of experience.
17. Ibid., "The Witness of the Spirit", paras. II. 9-10.
18. Wesley, *Works* (Oxford), vol. 11, p. 504.
19. It would be exaggerated to make Wesley into a philosopher here. My claim is that he is covering his intellectual bases quite thoroughly.
20. See Wesley, *Works* (Oxford), vol. 11, p. 536, paras. 5-6.
21. Thorvald Källstad, *John Wesley and the Bible* (Stockholm: Nya Boforlags Aktiebolaget, 1974), chap. 8.
22. Wesley tells us that all inspiration, though by means, is immediate. See n. 13 above. This is thoroughly obscure.
23. See Rupert E. Davies, *Religious Authority in an Age of Doubt* (London: Epworth Press, 1968), p. 27.
24. I suspect that this itself suggests that it is unlikely that the quadrilateral can provide the stability suggested earlier as a solution to the problem of diversity. See above n. 1.
25. I have sought to address some of these in *Divine Revelation and the Limits of Historical Criticism* (Oxford: Oxford University Press, 1982).
26. I would like to treat the former as a *canonical* issue, the latter as a *normative* issue. But I am not sure if this way of marking the distinction will work.
27. I have sought to develop such a position in chap. 9 of my *Philosophy of Religion*, forthcoming from Prentice-Hall.

2. BIBLICAL THEOLOGY: ISSUES IN AUTHORITY AND HERMENEUTICS

Bruce C. Birch

Beginning with Wesley himself and extending to the Methodist societies established in this country over two hundred years ago, the Bible has been understood as the foundation for all Christian theology. In the so-called Wesleyan quadrilateral, which has come to be identified with theology in the Wesleyan tradition, Scripture has a distinct and preeminent place alongside tradition, experience, and reason. One of the results of this stress on the importance of Scripture was the early founding of Methodist theological schools in this country with curricula organized around the central focus of scriptural studies. Biblical scholars produced by or teaching at these schools have had significant impact on the course of biblical scholarship in the United States.

In spite of this interest the two hundred years since the Lovely Lane Conference have not produced a distinctive Wesleyan biblical theology or hermeneutics. The genius of the Wesleyan churches seems not to lie in the development of a biblical theology peculiarly their own. It lies instead in the ability of American Methodist and Wesleyan churches to participate in, contribute to, and benefit from the discussions and insights that take place on the cutting edge of biblical studies in every generation.

Thus, this paper will not try to describe approaches to biblical interpretation that are peculiar to our tradition, but will discuss issues on the cutting edge of contemporary discussions of biblical theology. My suggestion is that these are, once again, the frontiers where churches of the Wesleyan tradition can appropriate for themselves the most challenging and creative insights available to make the Scriptures live as a resource for our own time. As it happens, I believe that several of the most promising developments in contemporary biblical scholarship are especially congenial to elements of the Wesleyan theological tradition.

Ferment in Biblical Scholarship

In 1970 Brevard Childs argued that a broad-based consensus on the nature, method, and scope of biblical theology had collapsed during the 1960s.[1] He then called for efforts to create a "new biblical theology" and made some proposals in that direction. Although some have contested the existence of a coherent "biblical theology movement"[2] (as Childs termed it), most have agreed that biblical theology is now in a period of particular ferment, and that many previously held assumptions and widely shared methods have come under challenge.[3]

It was also in the early 70s that a cry of alarm went up over the deplorable lack of acquaintance with the Bible in the churches and the great gap which seemed to exist between the interests of the academy and the church in the study of the Bible.[4] The decade in biblical studies was characterized by the opening up of new conversations with related disciplines in the university curriculum such as sociology, literary criticism, anthropology, and history. Much of what was produced in biblical studies did not seem easily appropriable for use in the church. For its part the church did not seem aggressively interested in fostering biblical scholarship in its own behalf and often continued to produce materials for the church based on outmoded or inaccurate biblical assumptions.[5] Continuing tensions between the academy and the church in their concern for biblical theology led Brevard Childs recently to label such tension as "one of the main symptoms of a deep malady within the field.[6]

Adding to the ferment in current biblical theology has been the growing challenge to the historical critical method as the prevailing pattern of biblical exegesis and hermeneutics. This challenge has come from several different quarters and represents not so much an anticritical mood as a recognition of the limits of historical critical method and a challenge to some of the ways in which it has been used.

Walter Wink's pronouncement that the historical critical method was dead[7] was expressive of a sentiment shared by many that historical criticism as it had been used in much of biblical scholarship had led to a fragmentation and relativizing of the biblical text that either eroded biblical authority (the conservative complaint) or rendered the Bible irrelevant to and remote from contemporary issues of life and faith (the liberal complaint).

The development of strong liberation and feminist theologies has fostered a search for a hermeneutic appropriate to these theologies rooted in the experience of marginalization.[8] This search has necessitated a sharp, critical break with traditional models of historical critical exegesis and method, since this method claimed objectivity, yet the results of its scholarship had been largely in the service of white, middle-class, male perspectives. Biblical theology done from a self-conscious advocacy stance rooted in experience represents a clear departure from traditional critical exegesis, while at the same time making use of the critical tools of analysis. The rejection is not of the critical tools but of a framework for their use which stands exposed as possessed of its own ideology.[9]

Prevailing modes of historical critical exegesis have also come under criticism from those calling for renewed attention to the importance of the canon as the ultimate context of biblical theology. Brevard Childs first called for biblical theology done in the context of the canon in his 1970 volume as a corrective to exegetical method that "would imprison the Bible within a context of its historical past."[10] Childs followed this in 1979 with his monumental volume *Introduction to the Old Testament as Scripture* in which he describes the final form of the text as the only legitimate arena of biblical theology and heightens the challenge to historical critical method by referring to the present as the post-critical era.[11] His objection is that critical methodologies have focused on a set of concerns dealing largely with the prehistory of the text. This has produced a neglect of the text's own agenda seen in the final form of the text which became the Scripture of the community of faith. While rejecting what he sees as a prevailing method, Childs does not reject the critical tools *per se* as seen in this question he poses for himself, "Is it possible to understand the Old Testament as canonical scripture and yet to make full and consistent use of the historical critical tools?"[12]

The work of James Sanders[13] is equally identified with a concern for the canon but with some crucial differences of approach from Childs. Sanders places more stress and value on the canonization process which led to the final form of the text. He believes it is important to recognize the authoritative role played by the tradition in the communities which received and passed on the tradition until it was fixed in its final form. The result is a more dynamic view of canon than in Childs. Nevertheless, Sanders's work is also challenging to older patterns of historical critical exegesis that reduced or fragmented the text without seeing the work of the faith community in an ongoing process that produced the whole we call Scripture. The issues of tradition, authority, and canon raised by Childs and Sanders, and sharpened by their differences, are issues to which we must return later.[14]

The purpose in this paper to this point has been to briefly describe the state of ferment in biblical theology which forms our present context for discussion. Clearly we are in the midst of a search for new hermeneutical paradigms with a rich variety of voices claiming a hearing. The intent has not been to sound a pessimistic note. On the contrary, the profusion of recent articles and books on biblical theological themes bespeaks a renewed vigor in the field which should excite and challenge us, even if the shape of some new and broad consensus is not yet in sight.

In the remainder of this paper we will focus on three substantive issues under discussion in biblical theology that would seem to be of particular importance to those of us who work within the Wesleyan tradition and seek to remain open to the ever new speaking of God's Word from the words of Scripture.

The Role of Experience in Biblical Interpretation

In 1962 Krister Stendahl argued that the task of the biblical theologian is properly limited to the "descriptive," whereas the "normative" dimension of Scripture is the province of systematic theologians.[15] This represented the triumph in biblical studies of a view first introduced by Gabler in 1827 that descriptive theology must be sharply divided from the work of constructive theology.[16] At that time biblical scholars largely believed they were engaged in describing the history and faith of the communities of the Bible in an objective and value-free fashion through the use of historical critical methods. They viewed this task as detached from the claim of confessing communities that these materials were "Scripture" and somehow authoritative for modern faith.

This approach still dominates much of published biblical scholarship, and one still hears talk of "what a text meant" and "what a text means" as if the two were separable and one could legitimately choose to work only on the former.

Increasingly, biblical scholarship is acknowledging the important perspective represented by the interpreters' own experience and insights. An adequate hermeneutical model must take account, not only of the experience of individual interpreters and their contexts, but the experience of communities of faith that claim biblical texts as Scripture. It is clear that one can no longer divide sharply between what a text meant and what it means. The two questions interact and affect one another. Brevard Childs recently wrote,

> It is far from obvious that an appeal of objectivity will resolve the hermeneutical issues. Nor is it evident that the subjective presuppositions of the interpreter can only be regarded as a negative factor. . . . It is a false dichotomy which contrasts objective analysis with subjective presuppositions. The issue is rather the quality and the skill with which presuppositions are brought to bear on the biblical material. In sum, one of the major issues for developing a new biblical theology lies in rethinking the sharp distinction which Gabler first introduced into the field when he separated descriptive from constructive theology. The two aspects of biblical theology belong together.[17]

The most radical challenge to reassess the role of experience in biblical interpretation has come from liberation theologians (such as Juan Luis Segundo)[18] and feminist theologians (such as Elizabeth Schüssler Fiorenza).[19] These theologies from the perspective of marginated people recognize clearly the ideological bias of historical critical exegesis which claimed objectivity. Female presence and female images in the Bible remained invisible to "objective" scholarship because women were treated as invisible in the church which produced the scholars. The biblical concern for the poor and the oppressed was often spiritualized because of the cultural biases of comfortable, middle-class societies whose institutions supported the scholars.

For scholars like Fiorenza and Segundo the choice is not between the objective and subjective exegesis. The former does not really exist, and the latter implies an abandonment of critical judgment. The call is for an advocacy stance which clearly identifies, and thus can critically reflect upon, one's own socio-political and theological commitment. The advocacy stance of engagement for and with the oppressed is not an abandonment of critical reflection, but a refusal to let the necessary biases of every interpreter remain hidden and unexamined. To include the experience and vision of those working toward a more inclusive and liberating church in the processes of exegesis can give us new eyes and ears with which to see and hear the ancient word.

An enhanced role for the interpreter's own faith experience (and the experience of the interpreter's faith community) in the processes of exegesis ought to result in biblical theological work that is more readily accessible to the life of the church. After all, much of the church's preaching and teaching calls for an interaction between one's own story and the biblical story. Biblical scholarship seldom modeled this interaction in the past. Seminaries often taught a style of exegesis that was difficult to relate to the systematic theology class or the preaching practicum.

Those of us who work in the context of the Wesleyan tradition should find this emphasis on the role of experience especially congenial considering the strong position that Wesley himself gave to experience. William J. Abraham has reminded us that Wesley believed that the "revelation of God [in Scripture], given itself in experience, is confirmed by our own personal experience of God through the Holy Spirit."[20] This was a bold claim in Wesley's time, and we should be no less clear on its implications for our own. The claim for the authority of Scripture cannot be allowed to rigidify as if God were not present and active in our midst today. The hearing of the biblical word can only properly take place out of an awareness of our own experience of the presence and activity of God judging, liberating, and reconciling in the midst of our broken world.

The Issue of Canon and Authority

One of the liveliest discussions in biblical theology today is taking place around the question of the canon and its authority. Several positions are worth noting. Brevard Childs has reemphasized the importance of the canon and claimed the final form of the canonical text as the *only* normative basis for biblical theology.[21] On the one hand this is a welcome corrective to earlier reductionist exegesis which seemed to theologize only on the various discernible levels in texts and seldom on the whole. Nevertheless, Child's rather rigid focus on the final form of the text seems unnecessarily restrictive.[22] Is not Scripture a witness to God's activity with the biblical faith communities? To the degree that that experience is left visible in various levels of the final text, is that not a legitimate focus of study as long as one returns to the witness of the final text for the setting of each layer of tradition?[23]

Over against Childs stand a number of voices

which argue in some manner that canonization is but the final stage in the tradition-building process and not to be valued theologically more highly than any discernible stage in that process.[24] This position is difficult to translate into a useable understanding for the church, which claims the whole of the Bible as Scripture, since one can focus on the claims of any level of the tradition without being theologically obligated to measure its claims against the whole of Scripture.

James Sanders seems to occupy a somewhat mediating position.[25] He stresses the importance of the process whereby communities received and adapted tradition until it achieved its final fixed form. This process and the discernible evidence in levels of the text can, for Sanders, be the proper focus of theological interpretation, but he also stresses the need to set that reflection in the context of the final canonical form which the tradition took.

Another important perspective on canon is raised by feminist and liberation scholars who are rightly suspicious of a renewed stress on canon if it takes a rigid form since the final form of the canon in many places is problematic. Does this mean the fixing of patriarchal culture evident in much of the Bible as normative? Are texts that justify slavery and demean women as authoritative as texts which demand justice in God's name, simply because both are included in the final canonical text? Such problems have led some to reject the notion of canon outright as unhelpful or to proceed to the identification of a new canon.

Such approaches as these latter do not address the reality, for good or ill, that the canon exists in the churches which all still claim that the whole of Scripture is foundational for their faith. At least for those who wish to impact the life of the church the options cannot be limited to a rigid, dogmatic view of the canon, on the one hand, or a total devaluing of the canon, on the other.

Surely the real question to be addressed is how the canon is understood in the life of the church. Can the church be led to new and broadened understandings of the canon and its function which avoid the problems and pitfalls of some of the positions described above?

A beginning point would seem to be the recognition that whatever authority is to be ascribed to the canon is authority derived from God who alone is truly absolute. The Bible itself is authoritative, not in any absolute sense, but in the sense that it records God's self-disclosure to the biblical communities of faith. Authority refers to the revealing of God's will through the biblical witness. But God was not only active in relationship to the biblical communities. God's will has continued to be made known to the church in all succeeding ages, and God is still present, disclosing the divine will for the church and the world. The task of authentic biblical hermeneutics is to aid the church in discerning the divine will. This will require labor at the intersection of the biblical story with our story. What is authoritative in the biblical witness must be consistent with what the church knows from its experience with a living God. Thus, the Scriptures will not only reveal to us something of God's truth, but also something of the earthen vessels in which that truth is contained.

To speak of biblical authority in this way would lead to a much more multifaceted view of the biblical canon than has been common. Space will only permit a few suggestions on elements that might be included in such a multifaceted and de-dogmatized concept of canon.

1. The canon is the product of actual faith communities. Therefore, it reflects all the gifts *and* failures of those communities. For example, the New Testament contains, not only witness to the ethic of coequal discipleship rooted in the ministry of Jesus, but also the *Haustafeln* of Colossians 3 and Ephesians 5, in which that ethic was subverted due to pressure toward cultural acceptability.[26]

A canon which reflects the realities of actual community experience with God is necessarily pluralistic.[27] The canon does not speak in a single voice. This is both a witness to the variety of experience with God and a corrective to warn us against absolutizing any selection of the voices through which Scripture speaks. That the biblical communities themselves can be seen judging and reinterpreting and measuring the tradition against their own experience of God can be read as a support for similar activity on our part.

This will, of course, necessitate attention to every level of witness preserved within the text as well as to the final form as the ultimate shape given to the text by the biblical communities. The canon is a record, not only of a destination, but a record of the journey as well.

2. The canon is the source of life and death, liberation and oppression, hope and despair. Historical criticism has always tended to equate the clear analytical understanding of a text with our ability to appropriate that text as meaningful. But in many instances, our clear understanding of a text becomes the source of problems and impediments to our theological appropriation. For example, the clearer we have become about the patriarchal structures of biblical communities, the more difficult it has become for women in the church to claim the

traditions of these communities.[28] To claim that the word of God speaks to us through the Scripture is not to claim the cultural character of the biblical communities as automatically normative. It seems clear that the word of God is sometimes communicated to us in spite of the social and political bias, the narrow vision, and the participation in the brokenness of sin which we see in the biblical communities alongside witness to their faith. Indeed, to recognize this is sometimes to allow us to hear the word of God more clearly.

3. The canon is also the possession of the modern church. Thus, it is appropriate that it be received and interpreted only in conversation with our own experience of a living God and the demands of that God for faithfulness in our time. The goal is a canon in truthful dialogue with our own experience of faith, especially in terms of the particularities of our own social location for faith experience. The conversation will be as diverse as the canon itself, and to the degree that we can receive that diverse witness we will be enriched with new eyes and new ears for our own receiving of the biblical word. The dynamic relationship of canon and contemporary faith experience is two-way. As we come to see the pluralism of the canon's own witness, we become more attentive and receptive to the diversity of modern witness to what God is doing to bring liberation and reconciliation in our own time.

These suggestions are by no means exhaustive, but the questions of canon and authority seem especially crucial for a revitalized biblical theology in our time. The goal toward which we should strive is a de-absolutized canon which allows for the honoring of ancient witness to the degree that it reveals to us the basic truths of our faith while at the same time honoring the power and authority of our own experience of God. Only such a goal can do justice to the notion of a living God who speaks to us through a living word.

Scripture in the Confessing Community

Any successful biblical theology for our time will have to take seriously, not only issues raised by and appropriate to the academy, but will have to concern itself with the use of the Bible as Scripture in the church.[29] The Bible was produced by the confessing community, and it remains foundational for such communities in the present. It would be incorrect to imply that biblical scholarship has shown no recognition of the function of the Bible as the church's Scripture, but largely this has been seen as a matter of applying the results of exegesis to the life of the church. There has been little aware-

ness of how Scripture actually functions in its different uses in the life of the church. Few have ventured to suggest that different functions for Scripture in the church might affect the study of Scripture in the first place. Historical critical exegesis has seemed to imply a single, basic and appropriate model for the study of Scripture, but does this do justice to the radically different modes of perception involved in worship and its uses of Scripture as compared to a study group?

Fortunately, there appears to be some renewed interest in questions of biblical theology raised from the arena of the church. We can mention several areas in which there are some encouraging developments as well as additional work to be done.

The title of Phyllis A. Bird's excellent book *The Bible as the Church's Book*[30] symbolizes a renewed willingness on the part of biblical scholars to let awareness of the Bible as Scripture of the church become a more active and conscious element in the conduct of biblical scholarship. On the one hand this has resulted in a flurry of interest in the nature of Scripture and its authority *per se*. Recent books by James Barr, Paul Achtemeier, and Jack Rogers and Donald McKim[31] come quickly to mind. On the other hand, there has been an increase in the number of books on specific biblical themes which clearly and consciously position themselves at the intersection of the interests of the academy and the church. The entire series Overtures to Biblical Theology, published by Fortress Press, is a fine example of this. The journal, *Interpretation*, which has a long history of interest in fostering biblical scholarship in the church's behalf, has now launched a series of Interpretation Commentaries published by John Knox Press. The first two volumes by Walter Brueggemann on Genesis and Charles B. Cougar on Galatians[32] seem excellent beginnings toward filling a long-standing gap in the literature. They are commentaries which constantly address the theological interests of the church in this material without sacrificing the need for rigorous critical examination of the biblical text in its ancient setting.

It is increasingly important to study how biblical texts are heard and used in congregational life. Some helpful work is available here already. This includes studies on the role of Scripture in the church's theological life,[33] the relationship of the Bible to Christian ethics,[34] and a flurry of recent books by biblical scholars on the Bible in preaching.[35] Robin Maas has helpfully addressed issues of method and approach in lay Bible study,[36] and Mary Boys[37] has analyzed the influence of *heilsgeschichte* understandings of biblical theology on Christian education,[38] but the whole area of the role of the Bible in Christian education is one needing urgent additional attention.

A final concern for the church's use of the Bible may represent the special pleading of an Old Testament theologian. It would seem that we are overdue for some attention to the way in which the Old Testament is understood and used in the church, particularly in its relationship to the New Testament. Much of the church's attitude toward the Old Testament borders on an unconsciously held Marcionism. Biblical scholarship has moved beyond this relegation of the Old Testament to second-class status for the most part. There is a lively renewed interest in the Old Testament roots of the New Testament. Can we now assist the church to a whole view of its Scripture without imposing artificial organizing categories (e.g., Eichrodt's covenant) or subordinating one part to another as if it was not the same God to which the whole of Scripture witnesses?

As biblical theologians it seems to me that we live and work in a time filled with the excitement of new possibilities for God's word to break out afresh in our midst. It is fitting that we work in anticipation and openness as we seek the new shape God's word will take for our time. As those who stand in the tradition of John Wesley, we should not only hope for but expect that the word of God contained in Scripture will touch both head and heart once again making all things new.

NOTES

1. Brevard S. Childs, *Biblical Theology in Crisis* (Philadelphia: Westminster Press, 1970).
2. James D. Smart, *The Past, Present and Future of Biblical Theology* (Philadelphia: Westminster Press, 1979).
3. See Gerhard F. Hasel, "Biblical Theology: Then, Now and Tomorrow," *Horizons in Biblical Theology*, 4 (June 1982): pp. 61ff.
4. See James D. Smart, *The Strange Silence of the Bible in the Church* (Philadelphia: Westminster Press, 1970); and Elizabeth Achtemeier, *The Old Testament and the Proclamation of the Gospel* (Philadelphia: Westminster Press, 1973).
5. As an example, a good deal of Protestant and Roman Catholic church school curriculum was greatly influenced by the work of Ronald Goldman on teaching the Bible to children (*Religious Thinking from Childhood to Adolescence* and *Readiness for Religion* [London: Routledge & Kegan Paul, 1964, 1965]). Even a cursory glance at his understandings of biblical theology by someone conversant with recent discussions in the biblical field would quickly give evidence of a simplistic, reductionist, and Marcionite understanding of the Bible and its development. Yet, his work has deeply influenced many Christian educators and educational curriculum material.
6. Brevard S. Childs, "Some Reflections on the Search for a Biblical Theology," *Horizons in Biblical Theology*, 4 (June 1982): pp. 1ff.
7. Walter Wink, *The Bible in Human Transformation* (Philadelphia: Fortress Press, 1973).
8. The Liberation Theology Working Group of the AAR has been working for several years on liberation hermeneutic and feminist hermeneutic. Unpublished papers by members of this project will hopefully be published for broader circulation in the near future.
9. See Elizabeth Schüssler Fiorenza, "Toward a Feminist Biblical Hermeneutics: Biblical Interpretation and Liberation Theology," *The Challenge of Liberation Theology*, B. Mahan and L. Dale Richesin, eds. (Maryknoll: Orbis Books, 1981), pp. 108ff.; see Letty M. Russell, "In Search of a Critical Feminist Paradigm for Biblical Interpretation," unpublished paper for the Feminist Hermeneutic Project, AAR Annual Meeting, 1983.
10. Childs, *Biblical Theology in Crisis*, pp. 99-100.
11. Brevard S. Childs, *Introduction to the Old Testament as Scripture* (Philadelphia: Fortress Press, 1979), p. 16.
12. *Ibid.*, p. 45.
13. James Sanders, *Torah and Canon* (Philadelphia: Fortress Press, 1972); "Adaptable for Life: The Nature and Function of Canon," *Magnalia Dei: Essays on the Bible and Archaeology in Memory of G. Ernest Wright* (Garden City, N.Y.: Doubleday & Co., 1976), 531ff.
14. See my own article "Tradition, Canon and Biblical Theology," *Horizons in Biblical Theology*, 2(1980).
15. "Biblical Theology, Contemporary," *Interpreter's Dictionary of the Bible*, vol. 1. (Nashville: Abingdon Press, 1962), pp. 418ff.
16. Johann Philip Gabler, "*Oratio de iusto discrimine theologicae biblicae et dogmaticae regundisque recte utriusque finibus,*" *Kleine theologische Schriften*, ed. Th. A. Gabler and J. G. Gabler. Ulm, 1831, vol. 2, pp. 179-98.
17. Childs, "Some Reflections," pp. 5-6.
18. Juan Luis Segundo, *The Liberation of Theology* (Maryknoll: Orbis Books, 1976).
19. Fiorenza. see n. 9.
20. See William J. Abraham, "The Wesleyan Quadrilateral," the previous chapter in this book.
21. Childs, *Introduction*, pp. 76, 83.
22. The phrase itself is problematic. Which textual tradition is the final form? Does this mean Old and New Testaments together as the final canonical context, or can the Old Testament also be studied for its own witness before relating it to the New?
23. See my critique of Childs in "Tradition, Canon and Biblical Theology."
24. Hartmut Gese, "Tradition and Biblical Theology"; R. Laurin, "Tradition and Canon"; and Douglas A. Knight, "Revelation Through Tradition"; all in *Tradition and Theology in the Old Testament*, ed. D.A. Knight (Philadelphia: Fortress Press, 1977).
25. See n. 13.
26. Elizabeth Schüssler Fiorenza, "Discipleship and Patriarchy: Early Christian Ethos and Christian Ethics in a Feminist Theological Perspective," *Proceedings of the Society of Christian Ethics*, 1982.
27. See James Sanders, "The Bible as Canon," *The Christian Century*, Dec. 2, 1981.
28. See Sharon H. Ringe, "Positive Force for Justice or Benediction to Abuse?" *Engage/Social Action*, 11 (July/August, 1983): 26ff.
29. Childs, "Some Reflections," p. 6.
30. Phyllis A. Bird, *The Bible as the Church's Book* (Philadelphia: Westminster Press, 1982).
31. James Barr, *Holy Scripture: Canon, Authority, Criticism* (Westminster, 1983); Barr, *The Scope and Authority of the Bible* (Westminster, 1980); Paul J. Achtemeier, *The Inspiration of Scripture: Problems and Proposals* (Westminster, 1980); Jack B. Rogers and Donald K. McKim, *The Authority and Interpretation of the Bible: An Historical Approach* (Harper & Row, 1979).
32. Walter Brueggerman, *Genesis*; Charles B. Cougar, *Galatians*, Interpretation Commentaries (Philadelphia: John Knox Press, 1982).
33. David H. Kelsey, *The Uses of Scripture in Recent Theology* (Philadelphia: Fortress Press, 1975).

34. Bruce C. Birch and Larry L. Rasmussen, *Bible and Ethics in the Christian Life* (Minneapolis: Augsburg Press, 1976), and Thomas Ogletree, *The Use of the Bible in Christian Ethics* (Philadelphia: Fortress Press, 1983).

35. Leander Keck, *The Bible in the Pulpit* (Nashville: Abingdon Press, 1978); Donald Gowan, *Reclaiming the Old Testament for the Christian Pulpit* (Atlanta: John Knox Press, 1980); Reginald Fuller, *The Use of the Bible in Preaching* (Philadelphia: Fortress Press, 1981).

36. Robin Maas, *The Churches' Bible Study Handbook* (Nashville: Abingdon Press, 1982).

37. Mary C. Boys, *Biblical Interpretation in Religious Education* (Religious Education Press, 1980).

38. See the special issue of *Religious Education* on "The Bible and Religious Education," 77 (Sept.-Oct., 1982). Also W. Brueggemann, *The Creative Word: Canon as a Model for Biblical Education* (Philadelphia: Fortress Press, 1982).

V. Constructing a Feminist Theology
in the Wesleyan Tradition

1. TOWARD A FEMINIST THEOLOGY IN THE WESLEYAN TRADITION: INSIGHTS FROM NINETEENTH- AND EARLY TWENTIETH-CENTURY METHODISTS

Jean Miller Schmidt

In my plenary address at the Bicentennial Consultation at Drew, I focused on the problem of overcoming the public/private split, looking at four symbolic dates (1840, 1866, 1884, and 1919), and lifting up examples for each of these revelatory moments of Methodists who combined conspicuously well the spiritual and social dimensions of their faith. I tried to include in my survey the "Wesleyan denominations in America," that is, all those groups which regard the Christmas Conference of 1784 as in some way a part of their founding history.*

As we look at the nineteenth and early twentieth centuries for historical and theological insight into the possibilities of a feminist theology in the Wesleyan tradition, it seemed to me useful to look again at these same Methodist figures. If, as I have suggested, they were in fact pioneers and innovators, relating private faith to public order in a way not typical for their historical moment, then it is also likely that they were unusually sensitive to social evils such as racism and sexism. On what basis did they advocate an expanded role for women in both church and society?

The figures at whom we shall be looking are (1) Wesleyan Methodist Luther Lee; (2) Gilbert Haven, crusader for racial equality in the Methodist Episcopal Church who became a bishop in 1872; (3) three Methodist women in the 1880s: Frances E. Willard, president of the W.C.T.U.; Lucy Rider Meyer, founder of the Chicago Training School for City, Home, and Foreign Missions, and of the Methodist deaconess movement; and Belle Harris Bennett, key figure in women's home missions work and the struggle for laity rights for women in the Methodist Episcopal Church, South; (4) and in 1919, two men who, as bishops, led their respective denominations (A.M.E. Church and M.E. Church) in social gospel efforts responsive to the new industrial city, Reverdy Ransom and Francis J. McConnell.

Obviously it will not be possible in a brief "idea paper" and presentation to describe at length the thought and activities of these figures. In surveying them (rather than focusing on a single figure) the goal is to convey the range of ideas, the changing and developing rationale for the full and equal participation of women in society and church during the period from 1840 to 1939 (from the time when the Methodists became the largest Protestant denomination in America to the formation of The [reunited] Methodist Church).

Evangelical scholars like Donald and Lucille Sider Dayton and Nancy Hardesty have frequently stressed "the Evangelical roots of Feminism."[1] Donald G. Mathews's *Religion in the Old South* also makes clear the implicit egalitarian or "leveling" impact of evangelical religion and its consequent promise of liberty for women (and blacks) in the pre–Civil War South. With its stress on the conversion experience and the requirement of public profession of faith prior to church membership, evangelicalism provided women "psychological and social space," creating a "sense of release from prior restraints" and a new self-esteem.[2] Church membership itself afforded the supportive "intimate bonds of religious community"[3] in which women (especially through the development of exclusively female organizations) increasingly found opportunities for self-expression and exercise of leadership and a more public life. The evangelical revival of the eighteenth century gave women new roles in the church, but the evangelical impetus toward feminism and women's rights is properly associated with the new revivalism of Charles G. Finney and others in the nineteenth century, and is closely linked with the related abolitionist and holiness movements.[4]

The distinctively Wesleyan form of evangelical religion stressed not only the conversion experience, but also growth in grace, the actual transformation of the individual Christian toward entire sanctification or holiness of heart and life (referred to in the nineteenth century by various names such as "heart purity," "entire consecration," or "the baptism of the Holy

Spirit"). In this view, power and authority were conferred on women as well as men through the gifts of the Holy Spirit, quite apart from traditional sources of ecclesiastical authority. Thus in her massive work, *Promise of the Father* (1859), Phoebe Palmer defended women's right to preach on the basis of the gift of the Spirit to the church at Pentecost and the expectation that its female as well as male members would seek this endowment of power and exercise the gift of prophecy as the Spirit gave utterance. Palmer believed that "woman has her legitimate sphere" and was not arguing for "women's rights," but she insisted that women be permitted to pray and testify in the churches and even to preach Christ for the conversion of sinners.[5]

In 1853, Wesleyan Methodist pastor Luther Lee preached the ordination sermon for Congregationalist Antoinette Brown, probably the first woman to be fully ordained to the Christian ministry in an American denomination.[6] Lee's sermon, entitled "Woman's Right to Preach the Gospel," interpreted Galatians 3:28 to mean "that males and females are equal in rights, privileges and responsibilities upon the Christian platform" (i.e., in the church).[7] He went beyond Phoebe Palmer in identifying "prophetic charisms"[8] with historic ministry, claiming that prophecy and preaching were the same and that women therefore had the same right as men both to preach *and* to be ordained, or set apart to the work of Christian ministry. From the 1860s on, women preachers (many of them ordained ministers) played a prominent role among the holiness denominations.[9]

When we turn to the late 1860s, at least three factors ought to be mentioned as significant for our purposes: the aftermath of the Civil War, the assumption of woman's special sphere (the "cult of domesticity" or "true womanhood" that prevailed increasingly after the 1840s in Victorian America),[10] and the movement for woman suffrage, which became a central issue when constitutional amendments to enfranchise newly freed black males failed to include enfranchisement of women. Gilbert Haven, the New England Methodist preacher who became editor of *Zion's Herald* in 1867, was caught up in all three.

Northern Methodists made the centennial of American Methodism in 1866 a celebration of both the preeminence of their church and the peculiar destiny of the American nation. Although Haven shared their confidence in the coming of God's millennium, particularly after the Civil War had purged the "Model Republic" of the evil of slavery, he was aware of the contradiction of racism. The new order would be characterized by liberty, equality, and unity, and America's chosenness depended upon her willingness to cooperate with God in inaugurating this millennium. In Haven's view, it was the church's role to become a racially inclusive community in order to prod the nation toward an integrated and just society.[11] Haven's millennialism had important implications for the role of women in both church and society.

In a Thanksgiving Day sermon preached after the election of Grant to the presidency in 1868 (entitled "America's Past and Future"), Haven reviewed the long struggle against the sin of slavery, beginning with the fall! It was here that woman had become slave to her husband; the other children to the first-born:

> From the first sin, this principle has possessed the hearts of men; from the first sinner, it has found foothold in human society. "Thou shalt rule over her," was the estate into which one half of the race was plunged by the first transgressor. "Thou shalt rule over him," the first declaration made to Cain concerning Abel, cast a large portion of the other half into the same chains. . . . The law of sin was a law of bondage.[12]

Now that the victory over slavery was won, "the universality of suffrage and the equality of legal and civil rights"[13] must be secured, and prejudice against people of color must be abolished. Confident that the election of Grant was an important step in that advance, Haven saw the way open for further victories, including woman suffrage. He assumed the prevailing view of woman's special sphere, arguing for woman suffrage on the basis that women were (1) "always of equal intelligence, often of superior virtue to man," (2) "citizens of the Commonwealth, having equal rights with every other member," and (3) needed in order to establish God's kingdom of peace, unity, righteousness, and love.[14] "How can this be done," Haven insisted, "except by the cooperation of the best and most numerous members of that society? Only by woman's vote can the kingdom of God be completely established. When the next election comes may we see our sisters sitting by us, and transforming the dirty, smoky atmosphere of the voting-rooms into sweet and quiet parlors, full of pleasure and peace."[15]

Haven's egalitarianism was rooted in his millennialism and perfectionism. Although the evil of racism was always foremost in his view and commitments, he seems to have anticipated in significant ways the modern feminist vision of the church as the vanguard of a new and liberated humanity living in equality and mutality.[16]

138

In his role as editor of *Zion's Herald*, Haven supported both woman suffrage and ordination. After Maggie Newton Van Cott was awarded a preacher's license in 1869 (being the first woman in the Methodist Episcopal Church whose evangelistic work was officially recognized in this way), he spoke out in favor of her ministry and urged her admission to the New England Conference. (In April 1870, the New York *Christian Advocate* complained that *Zion's Herald* was abusing its editorial freedom by pushing for her ordination!)[17] He also wrote a glowing introduction to her biography, heralding her success as a preacher in winning "more souls to Christ than any of her brothers."[18] He had an important role in organizing the New England Woman Suffrage Association in 1868, and served for a time as president of the American Woman Suffrage Association, founded in November of 1869 by Lucy Stone, Julia Ward Howe, and others.[19] He was almost certainly the New England bishop referred to in Anna Howard Shaw's account of her ordination who promised to ordain her but died before she applied for ordination in April of 1880.[20]

During the 1880s, Methodist women initiated a whole range of activities that both constituted a pragmatic social gospel in its own right and resulted in a greatly enlarged sphere of influence for the women themselves. For the most part, women's movement into the world beyond home and church came through their creation of organizations "for women only."[21] The same year that Maggie Van Cott received her preacher's license, the Woman's Foreign Missionary Society of the Methodist Episcopal Church was formed to provide outlets for the ability and leadership of American women by sending and supporting female missionaries to evangelize and liberate the women in non-Christian lands. Its monthly publication, directed to all women in the denomination, was entitled *The Heathen Woman's Friend*. Part of the intention of this separate sphere for women in the church was the creation of a sense of sisterhood. As Jennie Fowler Willing put it, "If all men are brothers, all women are sisters. Let every lady who feels that she would be a missionary, go to work at home, and she may, by every dollar raised, teach her heathen sisters."[22] In the 1870s and 1880s, similar women's foreign missionary societies were founded in all the major branches of Methodism (and in other Protestant denominations as well).

Frances E. Willard was the means by which countless Victorian "ladies" left the sanctuary of their homes to support the causes of temperance and woman suffrage for the sake of "home protection." She was able to use the rhetoric of woman's "higher," more spiritual nature associated with the sphere of the home to urge upon women a mission to make the world (not just men, but male institutions as well)[23] more "homelike." Proclaiming itself "organized mother-love," the W.C.T.U. under Willard's "Do-Everything Policy" involved women in a wide range of social reforms, including prohibition, woman suffrage, social purity, concerns of labor, peace, and arbitration, welfare work among blacks and immigrants, temperance education, and health.[24] Under Willard's leadership, women gained an increased sense of their own power and learned the rudiments of political involvement. As the motto "for God and home and native land" suggests, W.C.T.U. women were urged to develop their gifts for the sake of the Christianization of their nation.

The same phenomenon of women beginning by extending the influences of the home and gradually increasing their involvement in the public sphere occurred in both the deaconess movement and the women's home missionary movement of the 1880s. The conviction of women like Lucy Rider Meyer and Belle Harris Bennett that women's response to the call of Christ must involve their usefulness in furthering God's kingdom and that usefulness implied training, led them to found the Chicago and Scarritt training schools. Methodist deaconesses were determined to transform the city by bringing their "womanly care" into tenement neighborhoods. They became a new breed of church women: trained for and consecrated to the order, they became experts in the field of Christian social service.[25]

When, in the 1880s, women began to challenge the church to ordain those women who felt called to the pastoral ministry and to grant women full laity rights, they used a range of arguments to justify their cause. Perhaps the dominant rationale was an elaboration of the biblically based theme that men and women have equal rights and privileges in the church (Gal. 3:28). In her appeal for ordination to the 1880 General Conference of the Methodist Episcopal Church, Anna Oliver set her obedience to God's calling her to pastoral ministry over against the laws and traditions of men, but there was never any real response to this line of reasoning.[26] Frances Willard's *Woman in the Pulpit* (1888) picked up a theme in Anna Oliver's plea for ordination—that the pastorate was "motherly work"—and once again used the sentiment of woman's special sphere to argue for an enlarged role for women. "The mother-heart of God," she urged, "will never be known to the world until translated into terms of speech by mother-hearted women."[27] Certainly another issue in all these struggles was women's realization of their powerlessness when forced to rely on "praying and pleading"[28] alone. Thus the W.C.T.U. women became converted in the 1880s to the need for woman suffrage to deal adequately with the liquor traffic. Similarly, the women of the Methodist Episcopal Church, South, launched the laity rights movement in their church (from 1906 to 1918) on recognizing that the suffrage issue was not only a question of representation, but more basically of self-determination.[29]

While insisting that men and women were alike created in the image of God and equal in Christ (i.e., in terms of their baptism and spiritual gifts), women in the 1880s still struggled with the Victorian view of separate spheres, often turning its rhetoric into a defense of women's expanded role in both church and world. It remained for others in the twentieth century to begin to move significantly "beyond separate spheres."[30]

Black Methodists in the 1880s and 1890s had to deal with two sets of challenges: those facing Christian America, and those confronting black America. Among the latter were the question of meaning and the death of hope that resulted from the failure of Reconstruction (the racial segregation, the lynchings, the end of civil rights), as well as the need for new leadership in the black Methodist churches, such as the A.M.E. Church, the massive movement of blacks into the cities, and the beginning of an autonomous black culture no longer under the tutelage of the A.M.E. or any other Protestant church.[31]

In 1919, Methodists were celebrating the centenary of the Methodist missionary enterprise with a financial campaign closely associated with the Interchurch World Movement. It was an important year both for Methodists and for the country as a whole: the Joint Committee of Reference was appointed to draw up a proposed constitution for a unified Methodist Church; both Prohibition and woman suffrage were approved as the Eighteenth and Nineteenth Amendments; black Americans commemorated the three hundredth anniversary of the coming of the first African slaves to Virginia, and the first widespread radical black urban resistance broke out in cities like Chicago and Washington. In 1919, Reverdy Ransom was editor of the *A.M.E. Church Review* (elected in 1912). He would be elected bishop in 1924 at age sixty-three, serving as bishop until his retirement in 1952! After the death of Bishop Turner in 1915, it was Reverdy Ransom who was most responsible for carrying forth under changed circumstances the A.M.E. Church's traditional concern for the formation of a black Christian culture.

In 1919, Francis J. McConnell was both bishop of the Methodist Episcopal Church and president of the Methodist Federation for Social Service (having held both offices since 1912). Only forty-eight years old, he had already earned the reputation for being an outstanding presiding officer and a prominent churchman vitally concerned about the industrial order in America. Doubtless for both these reasons he was chosen to chair the commission of inquiry investigating the U.S. Steel strike in 1919. The commission's report corroborated the grievances of labor and requested government intervention in the regulation of industry; the investigation itself seems to have been a decisive factor in the emergence of social gospel radicalism.[32]

Reverdy Ransom and Francis McConnell were both theological liberals and prominent social gospel figures. They were deeply influenced by the newer thinking in the social sciences that began to replace the Spencerian view: understanding the relationship between biology and culture/society in ways that stressed the "social self," cooperation, and interdependence instead of competition, the need for radical critique of the American social order (particularly the economic sphere), and the important distinction between social roles and biology in terms of "gender differentiation."[33]

Ransom's predecessors in the A.M.E. Church tended to share the view of woman's special sphere so prevalent among white middle-class Christians. Black women were seen as the principal bearers of Christianity and civilization through the home, and were to be pious, disciplined, and self-sacrificing.[34] In the mid-1880s, Bishop Turner had ordained a woman to the ministry, but this action was subsequently ruled contrary to church law, and the General Conference of 1888 was rigid in its reaffirmation of the prohibition against ordaining women.[35] In 1900, deaconesses were finally authorized in the A.M.E. Church, but they were to be pastoral assistants in the local church rather than engaged more independently in social service in the world. In his roles as editor and bishop, Ransom consistently encouraged expanded influence for women, supporting A.M.E. deaconesses and woman suffrage in the early years of these struggles, and in general moving away from the view of separate spheres.

Bishop McConnell wrote little specifically about women's appropriate role in church and society. Much of his attitude can be surmised on the basis of his behavior, as confirmed particularly by recollections of his daughter Dorothy.[36]

McConnell assumed that women would be active in leadership roles in the church as well as in public matters. A number of his closest friends were professional women involved in various areas of social service and reform. He recognized the crucial work done by the deaconesses of his church. In his labors for a more just and humane social order, he obviously expected to find women as equal partners.

When we turn to the years after 1919, we enter much less familiar ground with regard to historical and theological insight into the possibilities of a feminist theology in the Wesleyan tradition. Here it may be useful simply to suggest some possible avenues for future investigation. Both Ransom and McConnell remained active in leadership of their respective denominations into the 1950s. It would be interesting to know more about their actions as bishops in later years. For example, as women in the Methodist Episcopal Church pursued the struggle for full clergy rights from the 1920s (ordination as local elders, 1924), to the narrow defeat of full conference membership for women at the Uniting Conference in 1939, to eventual victory in 1956, what was Bishop McConnell's role and involvement? How actively did he pursue an advocacy stance? Recent scholarship has recovered the story of Winifred Chappell's leadership role (with McConnell and Harry F. Ward) of the Methodist Federation for Social Service from 1922 to 1936.[37] It would be revealing to explore further the relationship between this brilliant Methodist deaconess whose socialist orientation led her to espouse particularly the cause of women workers in industry and the two radical and courageous Methodist men with whom she worked in an executive capacity. What has happened to women's roles in the black Methodist denominations in the twentieth century? Bishop McConnell shared with women like Georgia Harkness theological training in Boston personalism. More should be done on Harkness's theological understanding of women and "women's place" and its implications for a feminist theology.[38] Finally, although well beyond the scope of this paper, it is important that more work be done on the Woman's Division of Christian Service, particularly on its historical and theological contributions in the years from 1940 to 1964.

It appears to me that advocates of the full humanness of women, and therefore of the equal participation of women in both church and society, still use many of the same arguments that were used in the late nineteenth and early twentieth centuries. Some assert that all humans, whether male or female, possess "a full and equivalent human nature and personhood,"[39] while others perpetuate gender complementarity in talking about the special gifts of women for ministry and for social reform. I have been greatly helped in thinking about this by the most recent work of Rosemary Ruether. In *Sexism and God-Talk* (1983), Ruether suggests that recent research on right- and left-brain capacities in relation to socialization of males and females, as we know it, both discloses the capacity of both sexes for psychic wholeness and explains why women *do* presently have insights and experiences of crucial importance for envisioning and actualizing a new and more human future.[40] We need to continue to move beyond separate spheres to recover "the fullness of redeemed humanity"[41] beyond gender stereotypes.

NOTES

* See Jean Miller Schmidt, chapter 6 in *Rethinking Methodist History*, Russell E. Richey and Kenneth E. Rowe, eds. Nashville: Kingswood Books, An Imprint of The United Methodist Publishing House, 1985.
1. See, e.g., Donald W. Dayton, *Discovering an Evangelical Heritage* (New York: Harper & Row, 1976), chap. 8: "The Evangelical Roots of Feminism"; Lucille Sider Dayton and Donald W. Dayton, " 'Your Daughters Shall Prophesy': Feminism in the Holiness Movement," *Methodist History* 14 (January 1976): 67-92; Nancy Hardesty, Lucille Sider Dayton, and Donald W. Dayton, "Women in the Holiness Movement," in *Women of Spirit: Female Leadership in the Jewish and Christian Traditions*, ed. Rosemary Ruether and Eleanor McLaughlin (New York: Simon & Schuster, 1979); Nancy A. Hardesty, "The Wesleyan Movement and Women's Liberation," in Theodore Runyon, ed., *Sanctification and Liberation: Liberation Theologies in the Light of the Wesleyan Tradition* (Nashville: Abingdon Press, 1981), pp. 164-73.
2. Donald G. Mathews, *Religion in the Old South* (Chicago: University of Chicago Press, 1977), pp.97-124; quotes on p. 104. (In his plenary address at Drew, Mathews discussed this in terms of the "liminal event." See Mathews, chapter 9 in *Rethinking Methodist History*.)
3. Mathews, *Religion in the Old South*, p. 105.
4. See, e.g., Dayton, *Discovering*, pp. 86-91.
5. Phoebe Palmer, *The Promise of the Father; or, A Neglected Specialty of the Last Days* (Salem, Ohio: Schmul Publishing Co., 1981). Paperback reprint of the 1859 ed. See pp. 1, 12-13 for disavowal of women's rights and discussion of woman's sphere.
6. The Wesleyan Methodist Connection was formed in 1843 (after secession from the Methodist Episcopal Church) on the basis of abolitionism and John Wesley's doctrine of Christian perfection. (As the pastoral address at the organizing conference explained: "It is holiness of heart and life that will give you moral power to oppose the evils and corruption in the world, against which we have lifted up a standard." See Donald G. Mathews, *Slavery and Methodism* [Princeton, N.J.: Princeton University Press, 1965], p. 231; Dayton, *Discovering*, chap. 7.) There is a new biography of Antoinette Brown: Elizabeth Cazden, *Antoinette Brown Blackwell* (Old Westbury, N.Y.: The Feminist Press, 1983).
7. Luther Lee, "Woman's Right to Preach the Gospel," in *Five Sermons and a Tract by Luther Lee*, ed. Donald W. Dayton (Chicago: Holrad House, 1975), pp. 77-100. Quote is on p. 80. Women benefited from abolitionist struggles with biblical interpretation.
8. The term is Rosemary Ruether's. See her new work, *Sexism and God-Talk: Toward a Feminist Theology* (Boston: Beacon Press, 1983), pp. 196-99.

9. Dayton, *Discovering*, pp. 91-98.
10. Historians Barbara Welter, Nancy F. Cott, Kathryn Kish Sklar, and others have described the cult of true womanhood and its historical development in America. For a comprehensive treatment, see Mary P. Ryan, *Womanhood in America: From Colonial Times to the Present*, 3rd ed. (New York: Franklin Watts, 1983).
11. William Gravely, *Gilbert Haven, Methodist Abolitionist: A Study in Race, Religion, and Reform, 1850–1880* (New York: Abingdon Press, 1973), pp. 117-18, 127.
12. Gilbert Haven, *National Sermons: Sermons, Speeches, and Letters on Slavery and Its War* (Boston: Lee and Shepard, 1869), p. 605.
13. Ibid., p. 620.
14. Ibid., pp. 626-7.
15. Ibid., p. 627. (Mary Ryan aptly refers to this as "social housekeeping." *Womanhood*, p. 198.)
16. See for instance, Ruether, *Sexism and God-Talk*, chap. 8: "Ministry and Community for a People Liberated from Sexism," pp. 193-213.
17. Janet S. Everhart, "Maggie Newton Van Cott: The Methodist Episcopal Church Considers the Question of Women Clergy," in *Women in New Worlds*, vol. 2, Keller, Queen, and Thomas, eds. (Nashville: Abingdon Press, 1982), p. 306.
18. Gilbert Haven, in John O. Foster, *Life and Labors of Maggie Newton Van Cott* (Cincinnati: Hitchcock & Walden, 1872), p. xxiii.
19. Gravely, *Gilbert Haven*, pp. 159-60.
20. Nancy N. Bahmueller, "My Ordination: Anna Howard Shaw," *Methodist History* 14 (January 1976): 127. There are a few problems in making this identification. Shaw claims that the bishop died before she graduated from Boston. That was in 1878; Haven died January 3, 1880. Also Haven was elected from the New England Conference, but he was assigned to Atlanta. In spite of these qualifications, he still seems to have been the New England bishop known to favor the ordination of women.
21. Rosemary Skinner Keller, "Lay Women in the Protestant Tradition," in Rosemary Radford Ruether and Rosemary Skinner Keller, eds., Women and Religion in America, vol. 1, *The Nineteenth Century* (New York: Harper & Row, 1981), pp. 242-43.
22. Rosemary Skinner Keller, "Creating a Sphere for Women," in *Women in New Worlds*, vol. 1, Thomas and Keller, eds. (Nashville: Abingdon Press, 1981), pp.246-60; quotes pp. 256-57.
23. Ruether refers to this as "reformist Romanticism." See *Sexism and God-Talk*, pp. 106-8.
24. On Frances Willard, see esp. Mary Earhart [Dillon], *Frances Willard: From Prayers to Politics* (Chicago: University of Chicago Press, 1944), chap. 9, "National President of the Union." Also Carolyn DeSwarte Gifford, "For God and Home and Native Land: The W.C.T.U.'s Image of Woman in the Late Nineteenth Century," *Women in New Worlds*, vol. 1, pp.310-37; Ida Tetreault Miller, "Frances Elizabeth Willard: Religious Leader and Social Reformer," Ph.D. dissertation, Boston University, 1978.
25. For biographies of Lucy Rider Meyer and Belle Harris Bennett, see Isabelle Horton, *High Adventure: Life of Lucy Rider Meyer* (New York: Methodist Book Concern, 1928); and Mrs. R. W. [Tochie] MacDonell, *Belle Harris Bennett: Her Life Work* (Nashville: Board of Missions, MEC,S, 1928). On Methodist deaconesses, the following are useful: Lucy Jane Rider Meyer, *Deaconesses . . . With the Story of the Chicago Training School for City, Home and Foreign Missions and the Chicago Deaconess Home*, 3rd ed., (Chicago: Cranston & Stowe, 1892); and Mary Agnes Dougherty, "The Social Gospel According to Phoebe," in *Women in New Worlds*, vol. 1, 200-16. The point about deaconesses as a "new breed" of church women is Dougherty's.
26. Kenneth E. Rowe, "The Ordination of Women: Round One; Anna Oliver and the General Conference of 1880," *Methodist History* 12 (April 1974): 60-72.
27. Nancy A. Hardesty, "Minister As Prophet? Or As Mother?: Two Nineteenth-Century Models," in *Women in New Worlds*, vol. 1, pp. 88-101; quote on p. 100. See also Frances E. Willard, *Woman in the Pulpit* (Boston: D. Lothrop Co., 1888.)
28. Carolyn D. Gifford, "Home Protection: The W.C.T.U.'s Conversion to Woman Suffrage," unpublished paper, December 1980.
29. Virginia Shadron, "The Laity Rights Movement, 1906–1918: Woman's Suffrage in the Methodist Episcopal Church, South," in *Women in New Worlds*, vol. 1, pp. 261-75.
30. Rosalind Rosenberg, *Beyond Separate Spheres: Intellectual Roots of Modern Feminism* (New Haven: Yale University Press, 1982).
31. David W. Wills, "Introduction," in David W. Wills and Richard Newman, eds., *Black Apostles at Home and Abroad: Afro-Americans and the Christian Mission from the Revolution to Reconstruction* (Boston: G. K. Hall, 1982); David Wood Wills, "Aspects of Social Thought in the African Methodist Episcopal Church 1884–1910," Ph.D. diss., Harvard University, 1975.
32. William McGuire King, "The Emergence of Social Gospel Radicalism in American Methodism," Ph.D. diss., Harvard University, 1977.
33. Rosenberg, *Beyond Separate Spheres*.
34. Wills, "Aspects of Social Thought," chap. 4: "Marriage, Family, and the Role of Women."
35. Jualynne Dodson, "Nineteenth-Century A.M.E. Preaching Women: Cutting Edge of Women's Inclusion in Church Polity," in *Women in New Worlds*, vol. 1, pp. 276-89. Amanda Berry Smith was the most famous of these "A.M.E. preaching women" between 1868 and 1900. Dodson makes it clear that in spite of the prohibition against ordination, A.M.E. preaching women's activities were not diminished after 1888. She suggests that the action of the 1884 General Conference to approve the licensing of women as local preachers is a tribute to their numbers and effectiveness; the conference thought it best to exert some control over these preaching women!

On Ransom, see Wills, "Aspects of Social Thought," chap. 6: "The Vision of Reverdy C. Ransom."
36. Interview with Dorothy McConnell by Joanne Brown, June 1983.
37. Miriam J. Crist, "Winifred L. Chappell: Everybody on the Left Knew Her," in *Women in New Worlds*, vol. 1, pp. 362-78.
38. But see Joan Chamberlain Engelsman, "The Legacy of Georgia Harkness," in *Women in New Worlds*, vol. 2, pp. 338-58.
39. Ruether, *Sexism and God-Talk*, p. 111.
40. Ibid., pp. 111-13. (Ruether emphasizes women's desire to "integrate the public and the private, the political and the domestic spheres," p. 113. Note the centrality of this concern to both my Drew address and this paper.)
41. Ibid., p. 114.

2. FEMINIST THEOLOGY AND THE WOMEN OF MR. WESLEY'S METHODISM

Earl Kent Brown

It is now just a bit over a century since the first Methodist scholar to seriously try to get an overview of the history of women in Methodism wrote what might well be the text for our present considerations together. "It may be doubted whether any section of ecclesiastical history since Mary, the mother of Jesus, is richer in female characters than that which records the Religious Movement of the Eighteenth Century called Methodism."[1] Abel Stevens spoke with the benefit of one hundred years of hindsight. His judgment confirms that of the biographer of Mrs. Pawson, who in 1813 wrote from his own memory and experience.

> Almost every large society in the Methodist connection can boast of women, whose faith, nourished by a lively expectation of the coming and the Kingdom of our Lord Jesus Christ, has prompted them to make every sacrifice to which they were called, and devote their time, their talents and their futures wholly to his glory. They have trampled on the varieties of conformity to the world, and regulated the whole of their life on the noble principle, to be approved and owned by God.[2]

It should come as no surprise to modern scholars in search of sources for a feminist theology to learn that the women of the eighteenth century addressed some of the issues this consultation will need to address. Sometimes their message is direct and clearly spoken to the points raised by modern feminism. When they are so, we should be grateful. More often their commentary is to be found by drawing inferences from comments directed to other topics. While one must always be aware in historical papers of imposing the agenda of our century on the thoughts of another, it seems quite appropriate to examine the body of writing by and about these eighteenth-century "women of the word" and adapt those aspects thereof that seem most useful to our purposes.

I shall divide my commentary into two main headings: Sources for a Feminist Theology; Confirming and Sustaining Feminist Activism.

I. Sources for a Feminist Theology

The women of eighteenth-century Methodism were in large part disciples of Mr. Wesley. It is natural that their sources for all theology, and thus of any feminist theology, looked firmly to the Wesley quadrilateral. Wesley turned to Scripture, tradition, reason, and experience as theological sources. So did the early Methodist women.

1. Scripture

There are many women whose doings and/or character are reported in the Old and New Testaments. Methodist women quite naturally took examples of the "Mothers of Israel" as their own models. Such models are of pious, hard-working, devout, serving women in large part. There are few examples in Scripture which might seem to justify women preaching, for example. However, as we shall note later, women of the evangelical awakening felt such a call, and they sought scriptural justification therefor. One way to do this was to generalize from general commands which the Scripture addresses to the whole Christian community. Thus Sarah Mallett urges that "all, both local and traveling preachers, think more on these words, 'quench not the Spirit. Despise not prophesyings.' "[3] The commands are clearly not limited to the Spirit in or the prophesyings of males.

Similarly, when called upon to preach the first time, Sarah Cox responded because she found the following biblical passages imperative and demanding, "Cry aloud, spare not, lift up thy voice like a trumpet (Isa. 58:1). Or again, "Gird up thy loins and arise and speak unto them all that I command thee" (Jer 1:17). The passages are not addressed to women specifically in the Scripture, but neither are they limited to men. Sarah resolved to speak and did so "with great acceptance and success" for several years in Leicestershire and Nottinghamshire.[4]

The real problem, of course, was not to find Scripture passages that might be interpreted to allow female preaching. Rather the problem was to deal with what appeared to be direct prohibitions in Scripture—particularly in II Timothy and I Corinthians. Wesley in 1765 was just skirting the edges of the difficulty when he argued that I Corinthians 14:35 is not a ban on women speaking in the bands. He argued that the word "church" in the passage referred only to the "great congregation," not to casual small religious meetings.[5] However, women were soon feeling the call to preach, even in the "great congregation."

In 1771 Mary Bosanquet met the prohibitions head-on. Writing to Mr. Wesley, she examined the Pauline texts carefully. II Timothy 2:12—"Let the women learn in silence"—she found to mean only that women should not take disciplinary authority over their husbands. Surely, she argues, it cannot mean "she shall not entreat sinners to come to Jesus." I Corinthians 14:34—"Let your women keep silence"—was, she argues, spoken in a "time of dispute" and means no more than does the Timothy passage. If it were taken literally, then what is one to make of I Corinthians 11:5, which allows women to prophesy if properly attired? How can one prophesy without speaking? To those who argued that the woman in I Corinthians 11 must have had a "particular impulse" in order for her speaking to be legitimate, she raises the question of frequency. How often may such a woman feel such an impulse? "Perhaps you will say two or three times in her life. Perhaps God will say two or three times a week or day." Again she speaks to those who argue that preaching is immodest and contrary to proper womanly behavior. Modesty, she argues, is a matter of purity and humility of mind and purpose. Surely it is not a function of being silent in public meetings. Was the Magdalene immodest when she told the disciples that Jesus had risen? If she was not, why are modern women called immodest when they proclaim the same message? Was the woman of Samaria immodest when she invited a whole city to be Christian? Surely not; nor was Deborah when she urged the men of Israel to get about the Lord's work. So she concludes that the study of Scripture reveals a number of "extraordinary calls" addressed to women to proclaim the word. Such, she insists, is her own call. "If I did not believe so, I would not act in an extraordinary manner."[6]

Mr. Wesley picked up the language of the "extraordinary case" from Miss Bosanquet and used it in his famous letter of June 13, 1771. This letter defined his mature view on women preaching.

I think the strength of the cause rests there—on your having an *extraordinary* call. So I am persuaded

has every one of our lay preachers; otherwise I could not countenance his preaching at all. It is plain to me that the whole work of God termed Methodism is an extraordinary dispensation of His providence. Therefore I do not wonder if several things occur therein which do not fall under the ordinary rules of discipline. St. Paul's ordinary rule was "I permit not a woman to speak in the congregation." Yet in extraordinary cases he made a few exceptions; at Corinth in particular.[7]

The citation to Corinth clearly refers to the cases of the charismatic women and prophetic women of I Corinthians 11. It may also be referring to Priscilla, who was native in that city. With her husband, Aquila, she "expounded" to Apollos, according to Acts 18. So it is that by 1771 Mr. Wesley and his lady supporters had found biblical precedents for the women preachers. In a sense they are using the same precedents used for permitting laymen who were uneducated and unordained in the Church of England order to preach. Preaching was appropriate in the "extraordinary case"—that is, when God calls a particular person despite his/her apparent lack of other qualifications and then blesses their efforts.

2. Tradition

The tradition of Christianity is rich with the names of women. Mr. Wesley calls on that tradition when appropriate, as do his female counterparts. Probably his most important educational endeavor for the man/woman of the pew was the *Arminian Magazine*, which he published from 1778 to his death. In the pages of this periodical one will find articles on Monica, the mother of Augustine, Mrs. Richard Baxter and various other women from the Christian tradition—including at least one he identifies as a witch. Even more important than the ancient tradition however, and certainly more productive of arguments for his purpose, is the recent tradition of the women of Methodism itself.

Between 1778 and his death in 1791, Mr. Wesley published something over 550 letters from his associates in the magazine. Well over a third of these were from women. Many take the form of a narration of the Christian experience of this or that person. Many others are in the form of personal testimonies. In the same issues of the magazine were dozens of obituaries of persons who had died in the faith and are for that reason worthy of study by contemporary Methodists. Forty-two such obituaries of women were printed during the last five years of Wesley's leadership. In these articles, letters, and death notices one finds a narration of the recent tradition of Methodist women and their role in church and society.

In later years, as some of these remarkable women came to their deaths and were discovered to have left extensive journals and/or letters, biographers sought to preserve the ladies' memories in studies that often are primarily in the women's own words. Other times what they write hovers on the borderland between hagiography and history. In all such cases, the intent is clear. The authors are calling on Methodist tradition as a source for models of the faith—"Mothers in Israel," to use their phrase—whose lives would teach the readers much about how the Christian life should be lived. Mrs. Fletcher's biographer spoke for them all when he hoped that this book might be an inspiration "for the pious females who labour in our sabbath schools, who visit the sick and dying, or who go from house to house, bringing messages of mercy to the ignorant and depraved."[8] Clearly the tradition was a prime source for feminist thinking about themselves. Modern Methodists who seek to recover the lives of notable women stand in a royal tradition.

3. Reason

We need not expound largely on the use of reason as a source of religious truth. Wesley's dependence upon it is substantial, and his use of it skillful and comprehensive. The irrationality of silencing or discouraging women in the face of God's obvious use of their ministry was clear to him and to his women friends. Mrs. Fletcher's scornful, "I do not apprehend that [II Timothy 2] means she shall not entreat sinners to come to Jesus,"[9] is essentially an appeal to reason.

One of Wesley's most cogent arguments for the legitimacy of preaching other than that done by ordained priests of the church is found in his 1750 sermon, "A Caution Against Bigotry." The sermon never mentions women preachers and was surely not written with them in mind. This early, Wesley's own mature attitude toward woman preachers was not yet formed. But the argument here formulated, rationalistic in character, lay ready for women to use effectively in later years. The argument runs something like this.

The sermon is based on Mark 9:38-39—the rebuke by John of the man who cast out demons n Christ' name, though he was not of the disciple group. Jesus in turn rebuked John, arguing that "he who is not against us is for us." Wesley argued that every preacher does, in effect, "cast out demons," when people are converted under his leadership. How do we know this to be the case? "Is there full proof (1) That a person before us was a gross open sinner? (2) That he is not now, and lives a Christian life? And (3) That this change was wrought by his hearing this man preach?"[10] These three being assured, the preacher does indeed cast out demons, for God acknowledges his labors. In such a case, Wesley is quite clear. "Forbid him not either by order or argument. Nay encourage him." The argument was elaborated originally in defense of male lay preachers. But once he has evidence that God was similarly acknowledging the labors of women, the logic of the argument applied to women lay preachers as well as to males.

4. Experience

The biographies of the early women are filled with wonderful tales of intense, glowing, and evolving religious experience. These experiences of God shaped their theologies and determined their actions in general and in detail. We have lengthy journals of some of these ladies which reveal women who sought to live in constant readiness to do the King's command whenever it was clearly given. Of the many whom we could discuss, I choose here to discuss Hannah Ball.

Born in 1733 to a family of moderate means, she had eleven siblings. Thinking back on her childhood, it seemed to her that she maintained her individuality by exercise of pride. "Restraint I could not brook,"[11] she later recalled. Fortunately she had parents and guardians who gave an attentive eye to her correction. She recalled particularly an aunt with whom she lived after her home was broken up at age nine. The lady encouraged a period of reading and prayer each evening. To Hannah's surprise, "After a short time it became a pleasing experience."[12] In her teens she began to keep house and do nursing for relatives in need of such service. From the age of twenty-six she lived with a widower cousin in High Wycombe and raised his four children. Though there was no outward evidence of sin in her life in this period, she recalled herself as much tempted. In 1762, when she was twenty-nine, there was a crisis experience during a violent thunder and lightning storm. The outcome was a deep fear of death and a dreadful apprehension about her likely fate should she die unrepentant. A period of illness followed, after which she entered into a covenant with God. "I promised the Lord that if he would restore me to health, I would, by divine assistance, seek true religion."[13] When she was well again, she found herself inclined to put such efforts off, however; and it was another twelve months before she seriously began the search.

She was discouraged at first, for the folk to whom she turned—friends, family, associates, the Church of England pastor—seemed to know little of heart religion. She says she prayed for divine direction to a people of true worship, and shortly thereafter the name of the Methodists came to her attention. What she heard was not all good however. When the thought occurred that God had intended her to become a Methodist, she replied, as she put it, "with displacency, 'Lord I cannot go with them.' So great was my aversion to that people, I once thought I would as soon go to hell as unite with the followers of John Wesley."[14] Somewhat later she read a sermon by Thomas Walsh which motivated her to seek opportunity to hear Methodist preaching. John Wesley's visit to High Wycombe in her thirty-second year provided that opportunity. She attended a 5:00 A.M. preaching service and heard him speak on the text, "Woman, great is thy faith; be it unto thee, even as thou wilt."

In succeeding weeks, she heard the local assistants preach and found aid and counsel from several Methodist women. She moved gradually toward a climactic experience of God's grace and her own assurance. She described the climax in a journal entry of June 3, 1765. "This day the evidences of divine faith were so clear and strong that all doubt of my acceptance with God was removed, and I knew my sins were forgiven."[15]

Class meetings proved most helpful to her.
This social conversation on the work of God in the souls of unfeigned believers is calculated to strengthen and confirm serious souls . . . for they find other Christians exercised with similar crosses, trials and difficulties, and happily delivered out of them. It is a confirming testimony to the divine record.[16]

She was aware of the need for further growth, and her journal records that that growth was not denied her. On April 9, 1769, we read:

For more than a year past I have been enabled to give God my whole heart. I still feel the necessity of earnestly seeking the Lord as much as ever; and the more so as I never saw my weaknesses as I have done since I entered into this liberty of the children of God.

Eight days later she wrote:

I feel a longing desire for more grace, to have the whole image of God stamped on my soul, and to be persuaded that all the promises of the Gospel are fulfilled in me.[17]

Her yearnings led finally to fruition. In 1773, she wrote:

Of late the Lord has graciously increased my little

stock of love; what was once as a parting stream, is now like Jordan's flood. I enjoy much greater peace and strength of faith; the light of heaven shines on my path, as I know my works are wrought of God.[18]

It was out of this kind of experience that the service activities arose. Her own experience caused her to "feel tenderly ever after for all young beginners in the way of salvation."[19] On the fifth anniversary of her conversion, she would write of the consequences of her religious experience.

I desire to spend the remaining part of my life . . . in labours of love to my fellow-creatures— feeding the hungry, clothing the naked, instructing a few of the rising generation in the principles of religion, and in every possible way I am capable, ministering to them that shall be heirs of salvation.[20]

In these words one finds the dynamic force that made her an indefatigable sick visitor and jail visitor. Here is the root whence sprang dozens of letters of spiritual counsel to friends and neighbors far and wide. It is this experience that caused Mr. Wesley to see her as the "chief support" of the society of High Wycombe.[21] Because of her experience it seemed natural to Wesley to write her concerning the spiritual condition and talents of the ministers on her circuit.[22] The repeated references to the younger generation make it no surprise that she founded one of the first Sunday schools in the world for their guidance.

Miss Ball apparently never felt the call to preach. But most of the women who did preach based their authority on an experience of the Divine. Some put it quite bluntly. Ann Gilbert writes of a service she attended where the preacher scheduled for the day did not show up. "Immediately I received such a manifestation of the love and power of God that I was *constrained* to entreat and beseech them to repent and turn to the Lord."[23] Sarah Lawrence spoke of the work she began among the miners at Coalport. "If ever I was called anywhere, I surely was to that place. It seemed at times, as if my whole soul were drawn out in their behalf."[24]

Sarah Crosby "heard" the Lord speak the following words to her heart: "Feed my sheep."[25] Still later she would write, "My soul was much comforted in speaking to the people, as my Lord has removed all my scruples respecting the propriety of acting thus publicly."[26] Margaret Davidson remarked, "It was mightily impressed upon my mind to pray with them when they assembled together, and I was likewise urged to it by my father."[27] Clearly the experiences of the

Lord's grace working within is a primary source for the early thinking about the role of women in the Methodist societies.

Any feminist theology "in the Wesleyan tradition" will need to take the doctrine of Christian experience seriously.

II. Confirming and Sustaining Feminist Activism

Nearly every woman minister and most laywomen with whom I have discussed their Christian activism in any depth get around eventually to the problem of support or confirmation. Women ministers speak of the lack of day to day undergirding from structures of a church largely staffed by men. Individual activists speak of their loneliness in their activities. It seems therefore appropriate to seek to discover where the ladies of early Methodism turned for sustenance and confirmation, as they sought the Lord's will to do it. It may suggest where today's feminists may expect to find support as they try to build a feminist theology in the Wesleyan tradition.

1. Worship

Many of the women sought sustaining/confirming experience in a variety of worship settings. These early women had a far more extensive and rationalized order of such opportunities than is characteristic of their modern sisters. One can get a more or less typical view of their worship practice by examining the schedule of Darcy Brisbane, Lady Maxwell—the mother-confessor of Scottish Methodism for forty years.

Every day of the week, it was her custom to attend the Methodist preaching/prayer meeting at 5:00 A.M. Later in the morning she led family prayers in her own household. In early days she had hired a chaplain, but she became convinced it was her duty as head of the house to lead in prayers. In addition, on Sunday she attended St. Cuthbert's or West Kirk of the Kirk of Scotland for sacrament and/or preaching in the morning and Methodist preaching in the evening. Monday there was normally an evening public prayer meeting, followed by band meeting at the chapel. Thursday evening the Methodist ministers and their wives in Edinburgh met at her home for a class meeting under her leadership. In addition, there were occasional meetings when Mr. Wesley or some other visiting preacher might be in town. She also led one or two other class meetings from time to time.[28]

Lady Maxwell and the early Methodist women partook of basically three types of public worship. First is the so-called objective worship of God through the sacramental services of the church. Second is the worship of *koinonia*, fellowship in the small supportive class or band of devoted seekers. Third is the worship of hearing the word in society meeting. The ladies knew that this is important business for which one hour on Sunday morning is not sufficient. They did not begrudge the time.[29] Modern Methodists might learn from their example.

All of the above is basically public worship. There were, of course, private devotions as well. Hannah Ball gives insight into her method.

> Whenever I find a fresh trial coming, as I find many, . . . I look to the Lord and beg he will give me strength to overcome. [I] am allway [sic] careful not to reason in a time of storm, but . . . I [appeal] to my God in earnest prayer and he assuredly abates the violence of the storm or else gives me strength adequate to the day.[30]

Both Miss Ball and Lady Maxwell fasted regularly on Friday, and both resorted repeatedly to private prayer and wrestling with the Lord. Lady Maxwell regularly formally "renewed her covenant" with God. Both women also kept journals, as did many of the early Methodist ladies. These writings provided an opportunity to articulate precisely what they had experienced of God on a given day, and thereby enabled them to understand their experience better. Meditation on the journal entries over a lengthy period of time also enabled them to sense growth in grace and understanding.

2. Divine Confirmation

Worship led perhaps naturally to a sense of divine confirmation of what they were doing. These women were enbued deeply with Wesley's progressive doctrine of salvation. Thus those who were justified endeavored to "go on to perfection," and even those who felt they had been sanctified were expectant of yet further progress. They lived in lively expectation of further spiritual experiences, and that fact may have played its role in their finding what they sought. However that may be, the ladies do testify to continuing and growing and confirming experiences.

After a preaching service which had required such extended travel that she had really dreaded to undertake it, Mary Bosanquet could testify as follows. "[As I rode home] I had a clear conviction God brought me to Yorkshire, and that I had a message for his people. . . . I was at present where God would have me." As it happened there were many financial difficulties in her living situation just then, and the future of her school looked quite dark. But the reassurance rising from this sense of God's approbation could enable her to say in her heart, "If I am but in His will I am safe; for where the Lord leads me, there he will be my light."[31]

When people made fun of her, called her "ridiculous" or even "vile" and "impudent" because of her activities, Miss Bosanquet often found need of confirming witness from her God. Others criticized her manner of preaching and her calling such occasions "meetings" rather than "services." Still others told her she really had a "Quaker call" and should leave the Methodists to become a Quaker. Her reply was, "I know the power of God which I felt when standing on the horse-block at Huddersfield."[32] This is written about six years after she began to preach, and five years after Mr. Wesley had given his approval of her "extraordinary call." Clearly the extraordinary witness had continued to undergird her.

Mrs. Crosby's diary reflects similar experiences. About six years after she began to preach, she wrote, "Full of faith and expectation I met the band. Jesus made me his mouth unto the people and poured the spirit of love, zeal and wisdom upon me for their instruction."[33] Again six years later she wrote, "I was so sensible when praying alone that I was doing my master's blessed will, in going among the people, that no outward voice could have strengthened the conviction."[34]

Hester Ann Roe kept a journal most of her adult life. The tone of that journal is established by her repeated expressions of joy and gratitude to God for this work in her and around her. On April 15, 1776, we read, "Glory be to God, he gives me constant communion with himself. I live by faith, committing my every care unto him, and he orders all things well."[35] Ten days later we read, "Blessed be God, he still keeps my happy soul in Perfect Peace."[36] Twelve days after that we find, "How wonderfully does the Lord listen to a poor worm."[37]

These ejaculations out of the way, the entry may go on to discuss her day, the needs of others, going to society, who preached what, troubles with "momma" or what have you. Here was clearly a life lived in expectation and fulfilled experience of the witness of God. Her life is an example of Mr. Wesley's dictum that it is impossible "to retain pure love without growing therein."[38]

Sometimes this type of interest was carried to the point of refusing to take certain actions without clear intimation in advance that God willed them. Elizabeth Ritchie noted, when a seemingly eligible man proposed marriage, that she did not feel that "particular conviction from God without which I cannot act in an affair of this kind." Then she continued. "I do not mean that I expect a particular revelation to be made to me on the subject; but I think that, whenever I am called to change my situation it will plainly appear to my understanding that by such a change I shall be likely to become more holy and more useful."[39]

Miss Bosanquet, an heiress in her own right, had many offers of marriage in the near two decades she ran the Leytonstone and Cross Hall schools. She reports her technique: "No sooner do I hear the offer, than a clear light seems to shine on my mind, as with this voice, 'You will neither be holier nor happier with this man.' "[40] With Mr. Fletcher, she felt differently; but he had not proposed. She set herself a seemingly unlikely series of conditions that must be achieved to indicate God's approval before she would consider Mr. Fletcher seriously—that Mr. Fletcher must recover from his illness in Switzerland; that he must take the initiative in renewing a friendship after fifteen years lapse of communication; that he must call on her in Yorkshire; that there must be a resolution for the problems of the school. One by one the conditions were met, and when he asked her, she said yes.

3. Ownership/Fruits

One of the prime means whereby the women were sustained in ministries and lives that were often discouraging in the extreme was the sense that somehow God had "owned" their labors and was sending fruit appropriate to those labors. The word "own" in this sense is frequently used by the early Methodists in something of the sense we use when we ask someone to "own up" to a given action. God "owns" our efforts when he blesses them with productive outcome and thereby identifies them as his own. Thus Ann Gilbert would continue to preach because of her strong sense that God "owned my poor labors in the conversion of many sinners."[41] Likewise, in the great controversy over women preachers following Mr. Wesley's death, Mr. Pawson defended the ladies in a letter to his friends at Dover. After citing Wesley's approval in the "extraordinary case" and the examples of Mrs. Fletcher and Mrs. Crosby, he comes to Mrs. Taft.

I believe the Lord hath owned and blessed her labours very much, and many, yea very many souls have been brought to saving knowledge by her preaching. Many have come to hear her . . . and have been awakened and brought to God. . . . I would therefore advise you by no means oppose her preaching, but let her have full liberty, and try whether the Lord will not make her an instrument of reviving his work among you.[42]

Wesley himself used the terminology of "ownership" when someone inquired of him, "Mr. Wesley, how is it that you encourage certain females in preaching?" Said he, "Because God owns them in the conversion of sinners, and who am I that I should withstand God?"[43]

The measure of the fruits in question usually was evangelical success. Margaret Davidson wrote of her early labors: "There were some that appeared to be awakened that testified their repentance by tears, and refrained their tongues from their customary swearing. Many of them, also, begged me to bring a [regular] preacher among them."[44] Eventually *vox populi* came to seem to her like *vox dei*, and she began to preach and itinerate herself. It was success, measured by the attendance of two hundred at her class meeting at Derby, that led Sarah Crosby to make her first essay at preaching. It was the same success that convinced Wesley that such activity was appropriate. Some ten years later she had 220 public meetings and over six hundred small group meetings in a single year. The people came in droves.[45]

Miss Bosanquet went to Leytonstone to found a school and naturally set aside a time for Bible reading and prayer for her pupils. A poor woman of the town asked to attend, and Thursday at 7:00 was set as a time when she and other guests would be welcome. Within a few weeks twenty-five were coming. Miss Bosanquet normally read a chapter and spoke from it—what she would call "expounding." At this point she and Mrs. Ryan interviewed each attendant privately on the state of their souls. Many "expressed conviction of sin," and a Tuesday evening class was set up for the serious-minded. Thursday remained a public meeting and continued to grow. They asked Wesley to send an itinerant, and the Methodist society of Leytonstone was in business with twenty-five members at the first meeting. Wesley exulted over this sign of God's ownership of the ladies' work. The good health of the society apparently also depended upon the women's leadership. When they removed to Yorkshire, the society declined distressingly. In 1774 Wesley reported to his *Journal* a visit to Leytonstone. "The society is shrunk to five or six members and will probably soon shrink to nothing."[46]

The ladies' evangelistic endeavors were addressed to those close to them personally as well as to their "flocks." Miss Ball clearly had designs on her brother's and her sister's souls. Hester Ann Roe earnestly sought the conversion of

"Momma" and "Uncle Roe." She was instrumental in the conversion of her beloved "Coz Roe," and sorrowed when his untimely death prevented his intended ordination. The Rev. Mr. Cousins was pleased to note that he had "married his mother [in the gospel, i.e.]."[47]

4. Mutual Ministry and Fellowship

The fellowship of other believers and the mutual nurture which was inherent in class and band meetings were yet another means of confirming the believers. This fellowship began naturally with Mr. Wesley himself and the other itinerants. The multiple letters between Mr. Wesley and his lady correspondents is abundant testimony to the support role he played in many women's lives. They played a similar role for him as well at times.

We have noted above the frequent letters, death notices and articles in the *Arminian Magazine* which Mr. Wesley published. His motive is quite clear. "As nothing is more animating to serious people than the dying Words and Behaviour of the Children of God, I purpose inserting, in each of the following magazines, one (at least) of these accounts."[48] These articles, letters, death notices, and reports of experiences were intended to strengthen and undergird the women of Mr. Wesley's Methodism with the fellowship of "the saints who from their labors rest."

For those who were married to Methodists, oftentimes support and mutual growth took place in the fellowship of the home. For a select few of the ladies, this meant functioning as a preacher's wife. They had to carve out a new role for themselves. But an itinerant's wife found the established role models of Anglican priest's lady did not fit her life-style. They moved annually, or at least biennially. Their husbands were often away from home on itineration. Where we have detailed reports of these marriages, the support the couple gave each other shines clearly in the record. There is a chapter in my forthcoming book, *Women in Mr. Wesley's Methodism*,[49] on the role of the minister's wife. Let me only say here that in the case of the Rev. and Mrs. Rogers, the Pawsons, and the Fletchers of Madeley, ministry was a partnership undertaking. All three of the husbands seem to have respected their wives as persons and to have trusted their spiritual insights and rejoiced in their evangelistic success. In each couple there is evidence of close interdependance and mutual help. When one reads Mrs. Rogers's report of their ministry in the Dublin revival, one cannot but be struck by the recurrence of the first person plural pronouns—that is, the "we" and the "our." "*Our* hands being thus strengthened by the Lord, *we agreed solemnly to devote ourselves and our all to this work.*"[50]

In another place I have written about the feminine support groups which existed in Mr. Wesley's Methodism.[51] These groups enabled women to give each other the support and encouragement each needed in her own spiritual quest. There is no need to repeat that material here, save perhaps to note that the early Methodist women were using the technique of "networking" long before modern feminists invented the term. Perhaps it is a universal method adopted by women across history when they tried to live productive fulfilled lives in a world which men often control. The Methodist women did it well and recommend their experience to women of a later era.

It may perhaps be argued that this paper has said too little about theology and too much about history to be an ideal paper in a workshop on "Constructing a Feminist Theology in the Wesleyan Tradition." On the one hand I might reply, "That is what you get for asking a church historian." More seriously I would accept this critique only if theology be defined very narrowly as systematic logical exposition of philosophical/theological points. There is a lot of theology implied and lived in the practice of the early Methodist women. I have tried here to describe that practice. It speaks loudly and clearly on the sources of theology—feminist or otherwise. The whole quadrilateral is affirmed, but the strongest emphasis is clearly on Scripture, experience, and Methodist tradition. We cannot construct a feminist theology without a clear understanding of the nature of religious experience—and the Wesleyan tradition with its progressive emphases is a good place to begin such a construction. In the second half of our paper we have found the women speaking loudly on the doctrines of God's works among the daughters of the faith, on the pragmatic emphasis on fruits as a test of valid feminist activism, on the doctrine of the priesthood of all believers and the communion of saints as evidenced in the eighteenth century, and on a theology/practice of worship. There is little systematic theologizing about the role, function, or place of women in the divine economy in these early women's writings. There is much testimony on the work of God in the lives of women. Surely that kind of emphasis is more appropriately Wesleyan.

NOTES

1. Abel Stevens, *The Women of Methodism* (London: Tegg, n.d.), pp. 2-3.

2. Joseph Sutcliffe. *The Experience of Mrs. Frances Pawson* (London: Cordeux, 1813), pp. 5-6.
3. I Thess. 5:19. See Z[echariah] Taft, *Biographical Sketches of the Lives and Public Ministry of Various Holy Women* (London: Kershaw, 1825), vol. 1, p. 85.
4. Ibid., pp. 72-74.
5. Conference minutes, quoted in John Simon, *John Wesley, the Master Builder* (London: Epworth Press, 1955), p. 293.
6. Taft, *Holy Women*, vol. 1, pp. 22-23.
7. John Wesley, *Letters*, vol. 5, p. 257.
8. J. Burns, *Life of Mrs. Fletcher* (London: J. Smith, 1843), p. 12.
9. Taft, *Holy Women*, vol. 1, p. 22.
10. Wesley, *Sermons*, vol. 2, p. 117.
11. Joseph Cole, *Memoir of Miss Hannah Ball of High Wycombe* (London: Mason, 1839), p. 2.
12. Ibid., p. 3.
13. Ibid., p. 5.
14. Ibid.
15. Ibid., p. 17.
16. Ibid., pp. 8-9.
17. Ibid., pp. 26-27.
18. Ibid., p. 110.
19. Ibid., p. 10.
20. Ibid., p. 71.
21. Letter to Hannah Ball, June 7, 1783 in Wesley, *Letters, v. vii, p. 180.*
22. See letters to Miss Ball on Apr. 12, 1774, May 9, 1787, Sept. 1, 1773 et al in Wesley, *Letters.*
23. Ann Gilbert. "Experience of Mrs. Ann Gilbert," *Arminian Magazine*, vol. 8 (1795), p. 44.
24. Taft, *Holy Women*, vol. 1, p. 46.
25. E[lizabeth Ritchie] M[ortimer], "The Grace of God Manifested in an Account of Mrs. Crosby of Leeds," *Arminian Magazine*, vol. 29 (1806):470.
26. Diary, Feb. 13, 1761, in Taft, *Holy Women*, vol. 2, p. 43.
27. Edward Smyth, ed. *The Extraordinary Life and Christian Experience of Margaret Davidson* (Dublin: Dugdale, 1782), p. 97.
28. John Lancaster, *Life of Darcy, Lady Maxwell* (London: Kershaw, 1826), *passim.*
29. Earl Kent Brown, "Early Methodist Worship Styles," *Religion in Life*, ca. 1968.
30. Manuscript letter to Miss Dickenson, Oct. 13, 1776, in Methodist Research Collection, John Rylands Library, Manchester, England.
31. Henry Moore, comp. and ed., *Life of Mrs. Mary Fletcher* (London: Wesleyan Methodist Book Room, preface dated 1817), p. 112.
32. Ibid., pp. 124-25.
33. Taft, *Holy Women*, vol. 2, p. 54.
34. Ibid., p. 75.
35. Hester Ann Roe Rogers, "Manuscript Journal" (unpaged), in Methodist Archives and Research Collection.
36. Ibid.
37. Ibid.
38. Letter to Adam Clarke, Wesley, *Letters*, vol. 8, p. 188.
39. Agnes Bulmer, *Memoirs of Mrs. Elizabeth Mortimer.*
40. Moore, *Life of Mrs. Fletcher*, p. 105.
41. Taft, *Holy Woman*, vol. 1, p. 50.
42. Letter in appendix to William Bramwell, *A Short Account of the Life and Death of Ann Cutler* (Whitby: Clark, 1819), pp. 40-41.
43. Cited in Taft, *Holy Women*, vol. 1, p. iii.
44. Smyth, *Experience of Margaret Davidson*, p. 98.
45. See my article in Rosemary Keller and Hilah Thomas eds., *Women in New Worlds* (Nashville: Abingdon Press, 1981), pp. 74-75, 80.
46. Wesley, *Journal*, vol. VI, p. 11.
47. Taft, *Holy Women*, vol. 1, p. 291.
48. *Arminian Magazine*, vol. 4, p. 153.
49. Forthcoming.
50. Hester Ann Roe Rogers. *The Experience and Spiritual Letters of Mrs. Hester Ann Rogers* (London: Mason, 1933), p. 68.

3. THE CONFLICT OVER SEXUAL ROLES IN PAULINE CHURCHES

Robert Jewett

Introduction

The large number of articles and studies on the question of feminine and masculine roles in early Christianity provide a serious dilemma for the interpreter. Hermeneutical theories of various sorts have been applied to try to overcome the discrepancies in the evidence. It seems to me that light is thrown on our current situation when we take seriously the fact that at least one branch of early Christianity experienced very modern-sounding conflicts over sexual roles in the first and second generations. The conflict in the evidence concerning the role of women in the church and the attitude toward feminine leadership reflect very real conflicts between groups and ideologies. In the Pauline churches in particular, these conflicts developed and an evolution can be traced from early to late stages of Paul's own development. The fact that Paul's own views of the role of women in the church and the language he used differed from his earlier to later letters, and the fact that his churches were the arena of some of the most serious conflicts over the issues raised by feminine leadership makes it feasible to concentrate on the contribution of Paul and the Pauline school. I would like to provide a brief summary of the major trends.

I. The Evolution of Paul's Perspective

In the article I wrote in 1979 for the supplement volume of the *Journal of the American Academy of Religion* entitled "The Sexual Liberation of the Apostle Paul" a case was made that when one takes the chronological sequence of Paul's references to women into account a remarkable evolution is visible. The first stage of this evolution is prior to the writing of his first letter to the Thessalonians around A.D. 49. It is clear from references in various letters to Paul's missionary colleagues at periods before the writing of his first letter that there was a practical equality in mission between male and female, at least for Paul's branch of the church. One piece of evidence pointing in this direction is I Corinthians 16:19, which refers to Prisca and Aquila, the married pair whom Paul met in Corinth and with whom he carried out close relations as a missionary colleague for a number of years subsequently. The fact that Prisca is mentioned first makes it fairly clear that she was the dominant partner, and some of the more recent studies of the sociology of early Christianity make it fairly clear also that Paul probably worked under their patronage in Corinth. That is, they became patrons of the house church which they had founded prior to Paul's arrival. Paul refers in Romans 16:3 ff. to Prisca and Aquila as "co-workers," a technical term for early Christian missionaries. It is clear that they are not in any sense subordinate to Paul. Paul views both of them as fully equal to himself in mission. This means that at least at the time of the beginning of the Corinthian ministry, that is, prior to the writing of I Thessalonians, Paul was working closely with at least one feminine leader in early Christianity.

We can push the evidence back even earlier than the Corinthian ministry, however, on the basis of Paul's reference in Philippians 4:2 ff. to two evangelistic colleagues, Euodia and Syntyche. Paul refers to them as "laboring side by side in the gospel," in language that reflects the technical references to early Christian missionaries. These two leaders are having a conflict at the time that Paul writes Philippians some years later, but on the basis of their importance for the congregation and the reference to their having worked with Paul while he was in the founding mission, which took place in A.D. 48 and 49, it is clear that we have evidence in this instance of a practice of equality in mission. This basic pattern is also reflected in the various references to women in Romans 16, which according to more recent studies is now clearly to be assigned as an original part of the Roman correspondence. Paul's reference to Phoebe in Romans 16:2 as a deaconess and sponsor, or patroness, of the church at Cenchraea probably reaches back to the time when the cities in the proximity of Corinth were being evangelized, that is, in A.D. 50-51. Phoebe is apparently a woman of independent wealth, and her traveling to Rome at the time of the Roman correspondence and Paul's request to give aid to her probably reveal that she was, in fact, acting as something of a patroness in Paul's mission to Rome. Paul refers to her having been a patroness to himself in times past and also to other early Christian missionaries. Four other women are mentioned in Romans 16:6 and 12, and it appears that they are also early Christian missionaries of some prominence whom Paul met in the Eastern mission field and who are now residing in Rome.

The evidence for equality in mission is all the more striking when one compares it with Paul's earliest references to the issues of marriage and feminine roles in his earliest letter. When one looks at I Thessalonians 4:1-8 it is quite striking that Paul's language reflects the patriarchal tradition of his Jewish background rather than this egalitarian pattern of the early Christian mission whose evidence we have just sketched. Paul refers to the problem of marriage in Thessalonica as if it were a problem of male rights only. Women are referred to in the passage as the "vessel," which is a literal translation of the Hebrew euphemism for a wife. The ethical admonition in the passage is addressed to males only, "that each of you take a vessel for himself in holiness and honor," which reflects the Pharisaic and general Judaic marriage ideal in which it is the male's sexual rights which are in the forefront. The warning in I Thessalonians 4:6 not to "overreach and defraud" each other refers to respect for the marriage contract of other people, in this case other males. The commercial terminology employed in this verse is consistent with the terms used in rabbinic references to marriage. It seems to me quite striking that this early stage of Paul's language is patriarchal and highly traditional. One can only infer that nothing has stimulated the evolution of Paul's language at this point and that there is no evidence that he was conscious of the striking contradiction in language and outlook between the patriarchal tradition of Judaism and the egalitarian mission strategy of early Christianity in which Paul had been a participant.

The next stage in the evolution of Paul's language is visible to us in a remarkable reference in I Corinthians 7:1 which, according to recent research, is one-half of a proverb that Paul had apparently taught while he was in Corinth. As reconstructed by recent research, it appears that this proverb which reflects the traditional Judaic sexual ethic ran something as follows: "It is well for a man not to touch a [strange] woman, lest he incur the wrath of God." Only the first portion of this saying is quoted in I Corinthians, but it is quite likely that Paul is being cited in this somewhat mutilated proverb and that the content of this sexual ethic is fully congruent with I Thessalonians 4:1-8. It addresses males only and views women as sex objects. Its origin and terminology and ideology are Judaic, and it clashes very much with Paul's egalitarian mission practice.

The evolution of Paul's perspective is evident in the materials written in the mid-fifties, after the writing of I Thessalonians in particular. Here we have an evolution toward "equality-in-principle," which I believe may in all likelihood reflect conflicts over sexual roles in Corinth. The first piece of evidence in this connection, chronologically speaking, is Galatians 3:28, the well-known reference to oneness in Christ between male and female. If Galatians was written in approximately A.D. 53 from Corinth, it seems quite likely that the effect of Corinthian Christianity and possibly the impact of Prisca and Aquila are visible here. The work on this verse that has been done in the last decade indicates quite clearly that we have a baptismal formula here which reflects Hellenistic Christianity and claims a transcendence over sexual, economic, and racial roles and expectations. The elimination of subordinate status, of being minors under the law, which is the thrust of Paul's argument in Galatians 3, seems consistent with this perspective. It is interesting, however, that the closing greeting, both in Galatians and in the earlier Thessalonian letters, still retains the term "brethren" in its wording: "The grace of our Lord Jesus Christ be with your spirit, brethren. Amen" (Gal. 6:18). There appears to be a residual kind of patriarchy, at least in the language of this closing greeting, which stands implicitly in contradiction with the radical egalitarian perspective of Galatians 3:28. The capstone in this evolution toward "equality-in-principle" between male and female in the church is visible to us in I Corinthians 11. In part our analysis of this chapter is dependent upon a redactional theory of the Corinthian correspondence, which I do not have time to lay out here in detail. It seems clear, according to this kind of redactional approach, however, that the first references to women in the Corinthian correspondence are in I Corinthians 11, the passage which has been widely debated. The passage itself has a series of references to traditional role definitions with the question of the uncovered head as a crucial issue. It is quite likely that the question of the "veil" and "uncovered head" in fact relate to hairstyles and that the debate is provoked by the emergence of androgynous impulses in the Corinthian congregation in which females are taking male hairstyles as a sign of their equality and/or their submerging themselves into an androgynous state on the basis of their early Christian experience. Paul responds to this situation in a highly dialectical manner, insisting in verses 11 and 12 on equality between male and female and the subordination both of male and female under God. This egalitarian line is held in tension with traditional references to role definitions, that is, to the acceptance of traditional hairstyles, both for male and female, that one sees in I Corinthians 11:3-7, 10, and 13-15. One thing is certain in this passage, however, and that is that I Corinthians 11:5 implies that women are, in fact, leading early Christian worship services, which is consistent with the strategy of equality in mission which is evidenced from earlier references in the Pauline corpus. When one adds up the sum of the argument in I Corinthians 11 it seems clear that Paul was attempting to maintain two seemingly contradictory points at the same time: sexual differentiation between male and female, on the one hand, and equality in honor and role, on the other.

The later phases of the Corinthian correspondence show a further evolution of the egalitarian attitude with what would have to be called the evolution of a consistent viewpoint. It surfaces in an early fragment of Corinthian letter B, II Corinthians 6:14–7:1, which features an explicit alteration of an Old Testament citation to include the word "daughters" as well as "sons" among the prophetic members of the early church. This reference in II Corinthians 6:18 is a clear indication that Paul affirms a tradition of feminist leadership in the early church. The very next section in this reconstructed Corinthian letter B continues a stress on sexual equality by dealing in I Corinthians 6:12-20 with a prostitute in a way that was completely unprecedented in the ancient world. In this passage Paul gives up the chauvinist language tradition of his Judaic background and refers the ethic both to male and female members of the church. The theme that "you are not your own, so glorify God in your body" (I Cor. 6:19-20), is addressed both to male and female. What is even more striking is that in this passage there is not a single reference to the marriage contract, and there is no stereotyping of the female sexual partner as a "vessel." Instead the argument is conducted on the basis of male and female becoming "one flesh," based on Genesis 2:24. Paul claims in this passage that the body, which is the basis of personhood, is the "temple of the Holy Spirit" and that sexual identity is therefore basic to personhood.

The final section of this letter includes a greeting which I think may well reflect this evolution toward a consistent view of equality. The greeting in I Corinthians 16:23 ff. is to "you all" rather than to the brethren. In the next phase of the Corinthian correspondence the eglitarian ethic evolves into a full statement of conjugal rights between male and female. First Corinthians 7:1b is a citation of the proverb that the radicals in Corinth had apparently mutilated in order to advocate an ascetic view of marriage. It appears that the line, "it is well for a man not to touch a woman," should be in quotation marks because it is what Paul counters throughout the entire chapter. This citation indicates that an antisexual movement was underway in Corinth advocating Platonic marriage and a resistance against members of the church entering into marriage contracts. Paul's argument is that each person, both male and female, should be married unless there is a particular "gift," as referred to in I Corinthians 7:7. Paul explicitly places the male and the female on an equal basis in this passage, particularly extending the range of sexual rights from the male to the female: "For the wife does not rule over her own body but the husband does, likewise the husband does not rule over his own body but the wife does" (I Cor. 7:4). This is connected with the idea of unique "gifts" which include sexual inclination of various types given to males and females. It is remarkable, furthermore, in this chapter that the free decisions both of males and females concerning marital partners are the underlying premise of the advice. Paul refrains throughout this entire passage from viewing women as subordinate or as mere objects of the actions of others. It is perhaps useful to wrap up our brief reference to the Corinthian correspondence by noting that the greeting at the end of II Corinthians also lacks the reference to the "brethren." Verse 12 of II Corinthians 13 refers to greeting "one another" with a holy kiss, and the final lines in verse 14 ask that "the grace of the Lord Jesus Christ . . . be with you all." This same egalitarian greeting is visible to us in Paul's later letter to the Romans. The greeting in Romans 15:33 and the one in 16:20 have the kind of inclusive language that is consistent with the Corinthian correspondence.

There are several possible ways to interpret this evolution in Paul's perspective, but I think that the impact of the Corinthian ministry is the most likely answer. It is clear that there were major issues in Corinth concerning sexual roles and that the women leaders in Corinth had evolved toward an explicit liberation campaign of their own, adopting male hairstyles and the like in a way that proved disruptive for the congregation. I think it quite likely that the impact of this situation led to the evolution of Paul's own views. But it would be wrong to conflate what was going on in Corinth in the first century with the liberation movements of the nineteenth and twentieth centuries. One of the features of the ancient liberation movement is the prominent role of androgyny.

II. The Rise of Androgynous Egalitarianism and Asceticism

We have referred already to the research that has been done on Galatians 3:28 indicating that we have in that verse a reference to an early baptismal formula which seems to imply that in Christ male- and femaleness are overcome in a fundamental manner. Given the important role of androgyny in the ancient world, Wayne Meeks has made a significant assertion, which many current scholars have accepted, that the baptismal formula was understood as a unification formula by some branches of the Greek-speaking church. In this context, Galatians 3:28 would have implied that sexual differentiation was in fact overcome and that females were incorporated once again into the original state which, in the imagination of the ancient world, of course, was a male state. The more recent work that has been done on I Corinthians 7 seems to confirm the line of this research that radical Christians who used the baptismal formula of Galatians 3:28 indeed believed that sexual differences were overcome in Christ. The difficulty that this Hellenistic conception caused in the early church we touched on already in reference to the debate over hairstyles in Corinth. The acceptance of male hairstyles by women as a sign of their having broken away from the subordinate status of women in the Graeco-Roman world is most likely to be understandable with an androgynous hypothesis. There is evidence in several locations in the letters of early Christianity, even during Paul's lifetime, of social disruption caused by this rejection of traditional sexual roles. I think in particular of the evidence in the Colossians letter of resistance against traditional sexual roles which correlates with a pattern that begins to evolve in some of the later New Testament letters. The tendency is to insist on subordinate status for women, and this insistence, which emerges in the later New Testament letters, seems to reflect a perceived problem on the part of conservative leaders with the expression of the radical equality of early Christianity. The line that is quite visible by the end of the first century has been traced by Elaine Pagels in her study, *The Gnostic Paul*, and also in her book, *The Gnostic*

Gospels. The preference for God the mother and the pattern of understanding salvation as incorporation into an androgynous state which transcends sexual differentiation was picked up in Gnostic Christianity and carried to its logical extreme. Part of the pattern that Pagels has noted is the dualism and the rejection of sexuality as such and the tendency toward asceticism and/or libertinism. The pattern toward the end of the first century and into the second century makes it quite clear that only one portion of the Pauline churches was able to keep the idea of radical equality intact, and they were able to do this only at the price of rejecting sexual differentiation as such. In this sense, the Gnostic theorists of the second and third century are a somewhat dubious resource for modern liberation movements since the equality was purchased at such a price.

III. The Development of Moderate Subordination In Pauline Churches

While Paul's own evolution was in the direction of egalitarianism, there are numerous indications that many of his coworkers, even during his lifetime, tended in the direction of a larger measure of conformity with the sexual stereotypes of the Greco-Roman world. While retaining equality in principle, the tendency was to limit it in practice. This pattern surfaces first in the letter to the Colossians.

The dating that I am following with the Colossian correspondence is supplied by Eduard Schweizer, who contends that Colossians was designed by Paul but drafted by one of his colleagues because of the imprisonment circumstance at the time. The Colossian letter has the first of the so-called "house tables" in chapter 3, in which the admonition "wives be subject to your husbands" is found. The likelihood is that this acceptance of a traditional subordination pattern for women by one of Paul's coworkers was directed against a movement of radical equality of some type which rendered marriage and other family relationships questionable. James Crouch in his study of the subordination material in Colossians has made the case that the author is reacting against spiritual excesses by people who believed that traditional obligations "in the flesh" were now overcome. We have, therefore, in Colossians, what one might call the development of "moderate subordination" because there is a strong emphasis in 3:19 on "husbands, love your wives and do not be harsh with them." Also it is important to take into account the fact that the closing greeting in Colossians is quite different from the greeting of a patriarchal letter such as I

Thessalonians. The simple "grace be with you" in Colossians 4:18 lacks any reference to the "brethren." It does not seem to me, therefore, that we have a full return to the Judaic pattern of the subordination of women in this writing.

A similar case, I believe, can be made concerning Ephesians, which appears to be the product of the next generation of the Pauline school. Once again there is a table of household laws, but it is started with the idea of mutual subordination in Ephesians 5:21. "Be subject to one another out of reverence for Christ." This means that husbands are to be subject to wives as well as children are to be subject to parents and parents subject to children. This idea of mutual subordination is quite different from the chauvinistic pattern of patriarchy, characteristic of Judaism in the ancient world, and of much of the Greco-Roman world as well. The sex ethic, however, just as in Colossians, articulates the admonitions differently for male and female and thus does not come up to the level of Paul's treatment in I Corinthians 7, which was completely egalitarian. It is also interesting to observe that the greeting at the end of Ephesians reverts to what was probably the traditional greeting of early Christianity, "Peace be to the brethren."

The material of I Peter, while not explicitly a product of the Pauline school, seems to fit into this pattern of moderate subordination for women in the early church. The household table of chapter 3 insists on wives being submissive to husbands but urges in explicit detail that husbands should "live considerately with your wives, bestowing honor on the woman as the weaker sex, since you are joint heirs of the grace of life." The traditional pattern of the exposed situation of women in the ancient world as the sex more weakly supported or defended by law is taken over here but is coordinated with the theme of being "joint heirs of the grace of life," which has a thoroughly egalitarian implication to it. First Peter does not come up to the level of I Corinthians 7 in its treatment of women, but it is certainly not on the level of the chauvinistic repression of some of the later New Testament writings with which it is often compared. It is also worth noting that the greeting at the end of I Peter lacks any sexist language: "Greet one another with a kiss of love. Peace to all of you that are in Christ" (I Pet. 5:14).

A final reference should be made to the role of women in the book of Acts. It has often been observed that Luke-Acts affords a prominent place for women and seems quite different from most Greco-Roman writings in depicting them in sympathetic ways. As far as the Pauline churches are concerned it is interesting that in some instances the role of women as converts is stressed. However, what is left out of account here in the book of Acts was the pattern of early Christian missionaries of the feminine gender. This may in part derive from the fact that most references to Paul's missionary colleagues are missing in Acts. The tendency is to make it appear that Paul the apostle was the heroic leader of the Gentile mission, whereas in fact he was one of a large number of traveling and stationary missionaries, both male and female, in the first generation of the Hellenistic branch of the church. I would not be inclined therefore to place Acts in the category of chauvinistic writings in the New Testament.

IV. The Rise of Sexual Repression in Early Catholicism

In the latter decades of the first century the stage is set for a full-blown conflict over the role of women in the church. It was highly unfortunate, I believe, that the conflicts between conservatives and liberals had so automatically negative an effect on feminine roles. The left wing of the Pauline churches, which were moving increasingly toward Gnosticism by the end of the first century, retained Paul's conception of equal roles for women but did so by denying the meaning of sexual differentiation. The conservative group reflected in the Pauline school toward the end of the first century moved toward traditional Judaic values and attitudes toward women and returned as well, at the same time, to the subordination patterns of much of the Greco-Roman world. One factor in this conflict between conservatives and liberals at the end of the first century was the arrival of immigrants from the conservative Jewish-Christian churches after the Jewish-Roman war which concluded in A.D. 70. But the sad consequence of this conflict was the eradication of feminine leadership from the public life of the church, at least in its orthodox branches.

Some of the earliest evidence about the trend toward sexual repression is visible from a study of the redaction of the Corinthian correspondence which apparently took place in the 80s or 90s of the first century. At least seven original portions of the Corinthian correspondence were woven together as two letters, and a study of the redactional processes indicates very clearly the hands of early Catholic circles of the Pauline school who had chauvinistic attitudes toward women. The most prominent evidence of this, of course, is the interpolation of I Corinthians 14:33*b*-36. This passage is so crucial for the discussion of the problem of sexual roles in the

Pauline churches that a case against the authenticity of these verses must be reviewed. That I Corinthians 14:33b-36 is an interpolation that does not derive from Paul is evident first of all in the break of the flow of the argument. Verse 37 joins very neatly with verse 33a, providing a transition which is far superior to the transitions which are currently in the canonical text. One might note in this connection that most modern translations place awkward paragraphs, in the middle of verse 33 and ending after verse 36, indications of a strange transition which conservative commentators have tried their best to clarify.

The second argument in favor of the interpolation theory of I Corinthians 14:33b-36 is their non-Pauline content. That women should "keep silence in the churches," I Corinthians 14:34, was clearly not Paul's pattern, as we have seen. It flatly contradicts I Corinthians 11:5 ff., which assumes that women are prophesying freely and openly in church services. It also contradicts the prominent role of women leaders in many other locations of early Christianity in the Pauline mission field. The language and reasoning of these verses is also non-Pauline with the term "permitted" in verse 34 used very uncharacteristically by Paul, and the term "the law" in verse 34 used in a positive way that assumes that in Paul's ethic the law is the final word. It violates not only much of the Corinthian correspondence but the central thesis of Galatians and Romans in a very flagrant manner. Paul's ethic is not legalistic. The business of women being subordinate to males and to their husbands and about church matters "at home" in verse 35, flatly contradicts the egalitarian ethic of I Corinthians 7. Finally, in verse 36, the questions about whether "the word of God" originated with you Corinthians or whether it, by implication, did not originate in a Jewish-Christian setting, has the argumentative force of making a female subordination pattern that was prevalent in Jewish-Christian congregations normative for all congregations. The thrust of the argument in verse 36 is that if women take a prominent role in the church this violates the original revelation of the gospel in Jewish-Christian settings. This implies that Pauline churches are dependent on Jewish-Christian traditions for their ethic. This is a line of reasoning that Paul flatly contradicts throughout the entirety of Galatians and Romans. His conception of the spiritual integrity of Gentile Christianity is completely contrary to the authoritarian logic of this passage.

A third line of evidence that reveals an interpolation has to do with textual criticism because some Latin versions and the Western text group place verses 34-35 in another location in chapter 14. They place it after verse 40. There are other minor variations which have led several of the most prominent text critics to conclude that these verses were originally written in the margin and penetrated into the text at a later point in its evolution.

I am particularly interested in the question of why these verses were inserted at the location in chapter 14 where we currently find them. I believe that it is related to the wording of verse 32, that "the Spirits of prophets are subject to prophets." This basic principle is that all who share the prophetic gift should exercise that gift with autonomy and that they are under self-control when they do so. This principle clearly allows no room for sexual discrimination because there were both prophets and prophetesses in the Hellenistic church and in the Pauline churches as well. With the insertion of verses 33b-36, however, women are explicitly excluded from this role. This has an impact also on the interpretation of verse 37, in that the appeal to those who consider themselves "a prophet or spiritual" would explicitly exclude females. The "command of the Lord" in this verse is thus not that they exercise their gifts responsibly, which had been the thrust of Paul's original argument, but that they be silent.

When one takes the location and content of this interpolation into account the proximity both in ideology and language to the Pastoral Epistles is very prominent. Only in places like I Timothy 2:11-12; 5:13; and Titus 2:2 can one find a similarly explicit anxiety and irritation about the participation of articulate females in early Christian worship. Interpolation, therefore, links the redactor of I Corinthians very closely to the group responsible for the Jewish and the Pastoral Epistles.

The creation of the Pastoral Epistles by the Pauline school at the end of the first century or the very early part of the second century marks a climactic stage in the rise of sexual repression in early Christianity. Given the content of I and II Timothy and Titus, it seems clear that one of the primary goals of these letters written in the name of Paul was to stifle feminist roles in the church. We need to study this legacy in detail because it has had such a negative impact on the question of sexual roles in the Christian community.

First Timothy 2:8-15 limits public leadership in worship to men and insists that women should be not only modest but subordinate in their actions. Verse 11 is crucial, "Let a woman learn in silence with all submissiveness. I permit no woman to teach or to have authority over man; she is to keep silent" (I Tim. 2:11-12). The proximity to the language of I Corinthians 14:33b-36 is very striking in this instance. Here is a flat rejection of the role of women in early Christianity under the authority of Paul. The rationale for this, which flatly contradicts what Paul argued in I Corinthians 7, argues that since Adam was formed first and Adam was not deceived that women should be subordinate. There may be a redeeming element in I Timothy 2:15, but the pattern of subordination remains dismally clear. This pattern reflects itself further in the rules and regulations for "widows" in chapter 5. The role of women in the Pauline churches is here defined as a matter of serving other people in the church, "washing the feet of the saints," and helping the poor. The role of women here is explicitly taken away from the political leadership category, and the qualification of women to be supported by the church in carrying out such roles is sharply delineated.

In II Timothy 3:6 we have an allusion to women in a negative way, reflecting the prominent role of women in the communities competitive with the early Catholic circles of the Pauline school, namely, the gnostic communities. It is quite clear from gnostic materials that the historical references dug out by Elaine Pagels and others, that the pattern of patroness figures supporting the community of Christian gnostics was probably carried over from the very first generation of the Pauline churches. There is a highly stereotyped implication in the polemical wording of II Timothy 3:6 which lists among people to avoid such heretics as "make their way into households and capture weak women, burdened with sins and swayed by various impulses." The wording of this verse is vastly different in its attitude toward women than that reflected in the Pauline letters. That women are simply "captured" because of their "weakness" is light years removed from Paul's reference to the missionary partners and colleagues and patronesses with whom he had worked during his lifetime.

A summary of the subordinationist ethic of the Pauline school is provided in the third of the letters that were written in his name. Titus 2:3-5 is a summary of ethical guidelines for women which confirms their subordinate status. "Bid the older women likewise to be reverent in behavior, not to be slanderers or slaves to drink; they are to teach what is good, and so train the young women to love their husbands and children, to be sensible, chaste, domestic, kind, and submissive to their husbands, that the word of God may not be discredited." The reduction of the feminine role to the household and the concern that prominent feminine leaders might look scandalous in the Greco-Roman world are characteristic here. It is clear that this subordinate definition of the feminine role in the church is the one that has been dominant through most of Christian history.

Conclusion

When one surveys the historical evidence of this conflict over sexual roles in Pauline churches one is struck with the volatile legacy of the Pauline theology. It emphasizes an equality of role between male and female, with sexual identity retained and kept distinct between male and female. But this volatile legacy which finally crystallized in mature Pauline letters broke apart after his death. It seems quite clear that the left-wing branches of the Pauline churches retained the stress on equality between male and female and continued to encourage female leadership and sponsorship of congregations. But given the Greco-Roman tendency toward dualism in the first century and the affinity of these groups with gnostic theology, the inevitable result was that the egalitarian tradition moved into androgyny. The meaning of sexual identity was dropped, and the unspoken assumption of the recovery of an androgynous nature, especially for women, was dominant. The trend toward asceticism or libertinism, the opposite ends of the gnostic sex ethic, remains a characteristic of this tradition.

It was the conservatives in the Pauline tradition, represented by the early Catholics, who created the Pastoral Epistles, who were able to retain Paul's doctrine of sexual differentiation. They made excellent use of his arguments that women should retain different hairstyles than men, and so forth, but in the process they rejected the egalitarian legacy that he had laid down. They submerged the authentic references to equal prophets and prophetesses with explicit commands written in Paul's name to eliminate the feminine role in the public life of the church.

It seems to me that there are several aspects of this volatile legacy that bear on our discussion of *the role of women in the Wesleyan tradition.* While Paul came from a highly chauvinistic tradition of Judaism, he was evidently capable of moving in a liberationist direction, first in practice and then in theory. Several features of his theology could be mentioned as possibly encouraging an evolution in this direction. Each of these features has its counterpart, interestingly enough, in the Wesleyan tradition. The idea of salvation by faith alone, evoked by a charismatic gift of grace, tends to transcend sexual and social differences. The stress on charismatic leadership in Pauline

157

theology tends to undercut social stereotypes about who should and should not exercise this kind of a role. The emphasis on freedom from the law and the evolution of a charismatic ethic of love tends to relativize the social stereotypes that one finds in the legal tradition of Judaism. The apocalyptic urgency of Pauline theology, with its vision of a new age breaking into history, was correlated with an emphasis on a radically transformed community that would reflect the standards of the new age rather than the chauvinistic values of the old. Each of these theological commitments of Paul's own theology is consistent with an egalitarian structure of religious and family organization.

It is interesting to observe that a very different set of theological principles emerged among the early Catholic inheritors of the Pauline tradition. These principles are much less friendly to egalitarian ideals. In the Pastoral Epistles and the interpolation of I Corinthians 14:33b-36 there emerges a set of principles that one can identify in many later periods of chauvinistic Christianity. In place of an emphasis on the Holy Spirit as the key to church leadership, there is a stress on apostolic succession and authority. Faith in these writings tends to be reinterpreted as a set of beliefs inculcated by tradition, so that its socially transforming character is fundamentally altered. In place of a perfectionist ideal of a community reflecting the values of a new, egalitarian age, there is a tendency to urge conformity to societal expectations. In place of Paul's idea of charismatic gifts shared by all Christians, there is in these later New Testament writings a limitation of leadership gifts to male clergy, the bishops and elders. In place of freedom from the law, there arises an emphasis on the law of the Old Testament as the standard to be enforced in the church, with the result that male leadership is institutionalized.

I am just in the beginning phase of thinking through the implications of these observations. It is at least clear that social conflicts between leaders and groups in the early church were closely correlated with theological values, and that certain of these values have a tendency to encourage growth in the direction of equality. In the evolution of early Christianity, none of the groups deriving from the Pauline tradition was able to preserve these values in their entirety by the end of the first century. The distinctive Pauline legacy that combines the values of sexual equality with those of sexual differentiation fell apart in part because of a changed social environment and in part because of the loss of the charismatic, apocalyptic, perfectionist, and transformationist elements of Pauline theology.

It seems to me that part of the challenge of the Wesleyan movement is to recover this theological legacy and provide the substantial underpinning of an egalitarian ethic that Paul himself was moving toward in the last decade of his life.

REFERENCES

(Derived from Jewett article, "The Sexual Liberation of the Apostle Paul," *JAAR* Supplement 47 (1979), 55-87)

P.E.B Allo, *Saint Paul Seconde Epître aux Corinthiens* (Paris: Gabalda, 1956).

D.L. Balch, "Backgrounds of I Cor. VII: Sayings of the Lord in Q; Moses as an Ascetic Theios Aner in II Cor. III." *NTS* 18 (1973-74): 351-364.

J.P.V.D. Balsdon, *Roman Women: Their History and Habits* (London: Bodley Head, 1962).

Heinrich Baltensweiler, *Die Ehe im Neuen Testament: Exegetische Untersuchungen über Ehe, Ehelosigkeit und Ehescheidung* (Zurich: Zwingli Verlag, 1967).

Otto Bangarter, *Frauen im Aufbruch: Die Geschichte einer Frauenbewegung in der Alten Kirche: Ein Beitrag zur Frauenfrage* (Neukirchen: Neukirchener Verlag, 1971).

Michael L. Barre, "To Marry or to Burn: *Purousthai* in I Cor. 7, 9." *CBQ* 36 (1975-76): 193-202.

Charles Kingsley Barrett, *A Commentary on the Epistle to the Romans* (New York: Harper & Row, 1957).

———, *A Commentary on the First Epistle to the Corinthians* (London: Adam & Charles Black, 1971).

Markus Barth, *Ephesians 1–3; 4–6* (New York: Doubleday & Co., 1974).

R. Beauvery, "*Pleonektein* in I Thess. 4.6a," *Verbum Domini* 33 (1955): 78-85.

Jürgen Becker, *Der Brief an die Galater* (Göttingen: Vandenhoeck & Ruprecht, 1976).

Georg Bertram, "*sunergos, sunergeō*," *TDNT* 7 (1971): 871-76.

Ernest Best, *A Commentary on the First and Second Epistles to the Thessalonians* (London: Adam & Charles Black, 1972).

Hans Dieter Betz, "2 Cor 6:14–7:1: An Anti-Pauline Fragment?" *JBL* 92 (1973): 88-108.

———, *Galatians: A Commentary on Paul's Letter to the Churches in Galatia* (Philadelphia: Fortress Press, 1979).

Richard and Joyce Boldrey, *Chauvinist or Feminist? Paul's View of Women* (Grand Rapids: Baker Book House, 1976).

Udo Borse, *Der Standort des Galaterbriefes* (Cologne: Peter Hanstein, 1972).

Madeleine Boucher, "Some Unexpected Parallels to I Cor 11:11-12 and Gal 3:28: The New Testament and the Role of Women," *CBQ* 31 (1969): 50-58.

Bernadette Brooten, "Junia . . . Outstanding Among the Apostles (Romans 16:7)," in *Women Priests: A Commentary on the Vatican Declaration*, eds. L. and A. Swidler (New York: Paulist Press, 1977).

Charles Henry Buck, and Greer Taylor, *Saint Paul: A Study of the Development of His Thought* (New York: Scribner & Sons, 1969).

Walter Bujard, *Stilanalytische Untersuchung zum Kolosserbrief als Beitrag zur Methodik von Sprachvergleichen* (Göttingen: Vandenhoeck & Ruprecht, 1973).

G.B. Caird, "Paul and Woman's Liberty," *BJRL* 54 (1972).

Jerome Carcopino, *Daily Life in Ancient Rome*, ed. H.T. Rowell, trans. E.O. Lorimer (New Haven: Yale University Press, 1940).

David Cartlidge, "I Corinthians 7 as a Foundation for Christian Sex Ethic," *JR* 55 (1975): 220-234.

J.F. Collange, *Enigmes de la Deuxieme Epître de Paul aux Corinthiens. Etude exegetique de 2 Cor. 2:14–7:4.* (Cambridge: Cambridge University Press, 1972).

Hans Cozelmann, *Der erste Brief an die Korinther* (Göttingen: Vandenhoeck & Ruprecht, 1969).

James E. Crouch, *The Origin and Intention of the Colossian Haustafel* (Göttingen: Vandenhoeck & Ruprecht, 1972).

Alan Cumming, "Pauline Christianity and Greek Philosophy: Study of the Status of Women," *Journal of the History of Ideas* 34 (1973): 517-28.

Ernst von Dobschütz, *Die Thessalonicher-Briefe*, Reprint of the 1909 edition (Göttingen: Vandenhoeck & Ruprecht, 1974).

J.K. Elliott, "Paul's Teaching on Marriage in I Corinthians: Some Problems Considered," *NTS* 19 (1972-73): 219-225.

E. Earle Ellis, *Paul's Use of the Old Testament* (Grand Rapids: Eerdmans, 1978).

———. "Paul and His Co-Workers." *NTS* 17 (1970-71): 437-452.

———. *Prophecy and Hermeneutic in Early Christianity* (Grand Rapids: Eerdmans, 1978).

Morton Scott Enslin, *Christian Beginnings* (New York: Harper, 1938).

A. Feuillet, "La signe de puissance sur la tête de la femme (I Cor 11, 10)," *Nouvelle Revue Theologique* 105 (1973): 945-954.

———, "L'homme 'gloire de Dieu' et la femme 'gloire de l'homme' (I Cor. xi, 7b)," *RB* 81 (1974): 161-182.

———, "La dignite et le role de la femme d'apres quelques textes Pauliniens: Comparaison avec L'Ancient Testament," *NTS* 21 (1975): 157-191.

Elisabeth Schüssler Fiorenza, "The Apostleship of Women in Early Christianity," in *Women Priests: A Catholic Commentary on the Vatican Declaration*, eds. L. and A. Swidler (New York: Paulist Press, 1977).

———, "Women in the Pre-Pauline and Pauline Churches," *USQR* 33 (1978): 153-166.

James A. Fischer, "Paul on Virginity," *Bible Today* 72 (1974): 1633-1638.

———, "I Cor 7:8-28—Marriage and Divorce," *BN* 23 (1978): 26-36.

Gottfried Fitzer, *"Das Weib schweige in der Gemeinde." Ueber den unpaulinischen Charakter der mulier-taceat-Verse in 1. Korinther 14* (Munich: Chr. Kaiser, 1963).

Joseph A. Fitzmyer, "A Feature of Qumran Angelology and the Angels of I Cor xi. 10," *NTS* 4 (1957-58): 48-58.

———, "Qumran and the Interpolated Paragraph in 2 Cor. 6, 14-7, 1." *CBQ* 23 (1961): 271-280.

Werner Foerster, *"exestin, exousia, exousiazō, katexousiazō,"* *TDNT* 2 (1964): 560-575.

J. Massyngberde Ford, "The Rabbinic Background of St. Paul's Use of *huperakmos*," *JJS* 17 (1966): 89-91.

———, "Biblical Material Relevant to the Ordination of Women," *JES* 10 (1973): 669-694.

Patrick Ford, "Paul the Apostle: Male Chauvinist?" *BTB* 5 (1975): 302-311.

Cecil L. Franklin, "Sexuality and Gender in the Bible: A Brief Survey," *Iliff Review* 35 (1978): 19-28.

Gerhard Friedrich, *Der Brief an die Philipper* (Göttingen: Vandenhoeck & Ruprecht, 1976).

———, *Der erste Brief an die Thessalonicher* (Göttingen: Vandenhoeck & Ruprecht, 1976).

Victor Paul Furnish, "Development in Paul's Thought," *JAAR* 38 (1970): 289-303.

———, *The Moral Teaching of Paul: Selected Issues* (Nashville: Abingdon Press, 1979).

Gamble, Harry, *The Textual History of the Letter to the Romans* (Grand Rapids: Eerdmans, 1977).

Charles H. Giblin, "1 Corinthians 7—A Negative Theology of Marriage and Celibacy?" *Bible Today* 41 (1969): 2839-2855.

J. Gnilka, "2 Kor. 6, 14-7, 1 im Lichte der Qumranschriften und der Zwölf-Patriarchen-Testamente," *Neutestamentliche Aufsätze: Festschrift für Prof. Josef Schmid*, eds. J. Blinzler et. al. (Regensburg: Pustet, 1963): 86-99.

R.W. Graham, "Women in the Pauline Churches: A Review Article," *LTZ* 12 (1976): 25-34.

W. Grossouw, "Over de echtheid van 2 Cor. 6.14–7.1," *Studia Catholica* 26 (1951): 203-206.

R. Gryson, *The Ministry of Women in the Early Church*, trans. J. Laporte and M.L. Hall (Collegeville: Liturgical Press, 1976).

Robert H. Gundry, *Sōma in Biblical Theology with Emphasis on Pauline Anthropology* (Cambridge: Cambridge University Press, 1976).

Barbara Hall, "Paul and Women," *Theology Today* (1974), 50-55.

Anthony T. Hanson, *Studies in Paul's Technique and Theology* (Grand Rapids: Eerdmans, 1974).

Jean Hering, *The Second Epistle of Saint Paul to the Corinthians*, trans. A.W. Heathcote and P.J. Allcock (London: Epworth Press, 1967).

William Hewett, "A Possible Link in the Development of St. Paul's Teachings on Marriage," *Bellarmine Commentary* 4 (1966): 23-30.

E. Hoads, "Prisca (Priscilla), St." *New Catholic Encyclopedia* 11: 789.

M.D. Hooker, "Authority on Her Head: An Examination of I Cor. 11:10," *NTS* 10 (1963-64): 410-416.

W.E. Hull, "Woman in Her Place: Biblical Perspectives," *Rev Exp* 72 (1975): 5-17.

John C. Hurd, Jr., *The Origin of I Corinthians* (New York: Seabury, 1965).

James B. Hurley, "Did Paul Require Veils or the Silence of Women? A Consideration of I Cor. 11:2-16 and I Cor. 14:33b-36," *WTJ* 35 (1973): 190-220.

Annie Jaubert, "Le Voile des Femmes. I Cor. XI, 2-16," *NTS* 18 (1971-72): 419-430.

Paul K. Jewett, *Man as Male and Female* (Grand Rapids: Eerdmans, 1975).

Robert Jewett, "The Epistolary Thanksgiving and the Integrity of Philippians," *Nov Test* 12 (1970a): 40-53.

———, "Conflicting Movements in the Early Church as Reflected in Philippians," *Nov Test* 12 (1970b): 363-390.

———, "The Agitators and the Galatian Congregation," *NTS* 17 (1970-71): 198-212.

———, *Paul's Anthropological Terms: A Study of Their Use in Conflict Settings* (Leiden: Brill, 1971).

———, "Enthusiastic Radicalism and the Thessalonian Correspondence," *SBL Proceedings*, Vol. 1. Ed. Lane C. McGaughy (Missoula: Society of Biblical Literature, 1972), 161-232.

———, "The Redaction of I Corinthians and the Trajectory of the Pauline School," *JAAR* 44 (1978): 389-444.

———, *A Chronology of Paul's Life* (Philadelphia: Fortress Press, 1979).

Raphael Jospe, "The Status of Women in Judaism: From Exemption to Exclusion," *Iliff Review* 35: (1978) 29-39.

Else Kähler, *Die Frau in den paulinischen Briefen: Unter besonderer Berucksichtigung des Begriffes der Unterordnung* (Frankfurt/Zurich: Gotthelf Verlag, 1960).

Robert J. Karris, "The Role of Women According to Jesus and the Early Church," *Women and Priesthood: Future Directions, a Call to Dialogue*, ed. C. Stuhlmueller (Collegeville: Liturgical Press, 1978), 47-57.

George W. Knight, III, *The New Testament Teaching on the Role Relationship of Men and Women* (Grand Rapids: Baker, 1977).

Johannes Lähnemann, *Der Kolosserbrief: Komposition, Situation und Argumentation*, (Gütersloh: Gerd Mohn, 1971).

Franz Leenhardt and Fritz Blanke, *Die Stellung der Frau im Neuen Testament und in der alten Kirche* (Zurich: Zwingli, 1949).

Johannes Leipoldt, *Die Frauen in der antiken Welt und im Urchristentum*, 2nd ed. (Leipzig: Kohler & Ameland, 1955).

Hans Lietzmann, *An die Korinther I-II* (Tübingen: Mohr, 1931).

Stefan Lösch, "Christliche Frauen in Korinth," 127 (1947): 216-261.

Raphael Loewe, *The Position of Women in Judaism* (London: SPCK, 1966).

Loewen, H., "The Pauline View of Women," *Direction* 6 (1977): 3-20.

Gerd Lüdemann, *Paulus der Heidenapostel. I. Studien zur Chronologie* (Göttingen: Habilitationsschrift, 1977), publication in the FRLANT series anticipated.

Wilhelm Lütgert, "Die Vollkommenen in Philipperbrief und die Enthusiasten in Thessalonich," *BFCT* 13: (1909): 547-654.

Charles Masson, *Les Deux Epitres de Saint Paul aux Thessaloniciens* (Neuchâtel: Delachaux et Niestlé, 1957).

Christian Maurer, *"Skeuos,"* *TDNT* 7 (1971): 358-367.

John L. McKenzie, *Did I Say That?* (Chicago: Thomas Moore, 1973).

————, "St. Paul's Attitude Toward Women," *Women Priests: A Catholic Commentary on the Vatican Declaration*, eds. L. and A. Swidler (New York: Paulist Press, 1977), 212-220.

Wayne A. Meeks, "The Image of the Androgyne: Some Uses of a Symbol in Earliest Christianity," *HR* 13 (1973-74): 165-208.

John P. Meier, "On the Veiling of Hermeneutics (I Cor 11: 2-16)," *CBQ* 40 (1978): 212-226.

J. Hugh Michael, *The Epistle of Paul to the Philippians* (New York: Harper and Brothers, 1928).

Virginia Ramey Mollenkott, *Women, Men and the Bible* (Nashville: Abingdon Press, 1977).

Winfred Munro, "Patriarchy and Charismatic Community in 'Paul,'" *Women and Religion*, eds. Plaskow and Romero (Missoula: Scholars Press, 1974), 189-198.

Jerome Murphy-O'Connor, "The Non-Pauline Character of I Cor 11:2-16?" *JBL* 95 (1976): 615-621.

————, "Corinthian Slogans in 1 Cor 6:12-20," *CBQ* 40 (1978): 391-396.

Kurt Niederwimmer, "Zur Analyse der asketischen Motivation in I Kor 7," *TLZ* 99 (1974): 241-248.

Grant R. Osborne, "Hermeneutics and Women in the Church," *Journal of the Evangelical Theological Society* 20 (1977): 337-352.

Elaine H. Pagels, "Paul and Women: A Response to Recent Discussion," *JAAR* 42 (1974): 538-549.

Constance F. Parvey, "The Theology and Leadership of Women in the New Testament," *Religion and Sexism: Images of Women in the Jewish and Christian Traditions*, ed. R.R. Ruether (New York: Simon & Schuster, 1973), 117-149.

Sarah B. Pomeroy, *Goddesses, Whores, Wives and Slaves: Women in Classical Antiquity* (New York: Schocken, 1976).

A. Van Roon, *The Authenticity of Ephesians* (Leiden: Brill, 1974).

Ruether, Rosemary Radford, *Religion and Sex: Images of Woman in the Jewish and Christian Tradition* (New York: Simon & Schuster, 1974).

————, "The Subordination and Liberation of Women in Christian Theology: St. Paul and Sarah Grimke," *Soundings* 61 (1978): 168-181.

David Saperstein, *The Role of Women in Judaism* (New York: Committee on the Centennial, Union of American Hebrew Congregations, 1972).

Heinrich Schlier, *Der Brief an die Galater*, 12th ed. (Göttingen: Vandenhoech & Ruprecht, 1962.)

Walter Schmithals, *Gnosticism in Corinth*, trans. J. Steeley from the 3rd ed. (Nashville: Abingdon Press, 1969).

Wolfgang Schrage, "Zur Frontstellung paulinischer Ehebewertung in 1 K 7, 1-7." *ZNW* 67 (1976): 214-234.

Eduard Schweizer, *Der Brief an die Kolosser* (Zurich: Benzinger: Neukirchen: Neukirchener Verlag, 1976).

————, "The Letter to the Colossians—Neither Pauline Nor Post-Pauline?" *Pluralisme et oecumenisme en recherches theologiques: Hommage zu R.P.S. Docks*, ed. R. Hoeckman (Gembloux: Editions J. Duculot, 1977), 3-16.

Robin Scroggs, "Paul and the Eschatological Woman," *JAAR* 40 (1972): 283-303.

————, "Paul and the Eschatological Woman: Revisited," *JAAR* 42 (1974): 532-549.

Derwood C. Smith, "Paul and the Non-Eschatological Woman." *Journal of Religious Studies* 4 (1976): 11-19.

Graydon F. Snyder, "The *Tobspruch* in the New Testament," *NTS* 23 (1976-77): 117-120.

Evelyn and Frank Stagg, *Woman in the World of Jesus* (Philadelphia: Westminster Press, 1978).

Krister Stendahl, *The Bible and the Role of Women: A Case Study in Hermeneutics* (Philadelphia: Fortress Press, 1966).

Hermann Strack and Paul Billerbeck, *Kommentar zum Neuen Testament aus Talmud und Midrasch* (Munich: Beck, 1922-28).

Alfred Suhl, *Paulus und seine Briefe: Ein Beitrag zur paulinischen Chronologie* (Gütersloh: Gerd Mohn, 1975).

Leonard Swidler, "Greco-Roman Feminism and the Reception of the Gospel," *Traditio-Krisis-Renovatio aus theologischer Sicht*, eds. Jaspert and Mohr (Marburg: Elwert, 1976), 41-55.

Leonard and Arlene Swidler, eds., *Women Priests: A Catholic Commentary on the Vatican Declaration* (New York: Paulist Press, 1977).

Margaret E. Thrall, "The Problem of II Cor. vi. 14 - vii. 1 in Some Recent Discussion," *NTS* 24 (1977-78): 132-148.

W. Vogel, "*Eidenai to heautou skeuos ktasthai*. Zur Deutung von I Thess. 4, 3ff. im Zusammenhang der paulinischen Eheauffassung," *Theologische Blätter* 13 (1934): 83-85.

William O. Walker, Jr., "1 Corinthians 11:2-16 and Paul's Views Regarding Women," *JBL* 94 (1975): 94-110.

Johannes Weiss, *Der erste Korintherbrief* (Göttingen: Vandenhoeck & Ruprecht, 1910).

Heinz Dietrich Wendland, *Die Briefe an die Korinther* (Göttingen: Vandenhoeck & Ruprecht, 1968).

Kathleen O'Brien Wicker, "First Century Marriage Ethics: A Comparative Study of the Household Codes and Plutarch's Conjugal Precepts," *No Famine in the Land: Studies in Honor of John K. McKenzie*, eds. J.W. Flanagan and A.W. Robinson (Missoula: Scholars Press, 1975), 141-153.

Robert L. Wilken, "Collegia, Philosophical School, and Theology," *The Catacombs and the Colosseum: The Roman Empire as the Setting of Primitive Christianity*, eds. S. Benko and J.J. O'Rourke (Valley Forge: Judson Press, 1971), 268-291.

4. SO THAT HEART PURITY
MIGHT RULE THE LAND

Joanne Carlson Brown

Many people living in the nineteenth century believed that it was God's best century. They set out to proclaim that belief in word and deed, spurred on by a strong and growing belief in perfection. God had chosen America. America was God's final and best hope. This belief also inspired a quest for holiness, in which all of nineteenth-century America seemed to be involved. "Revivals of Religion have been gradually multiplying, until they have become the grand and absorbing theme and aim of the American religious world."[1] This movement and this quest for holiness grew as the century progressed. Far from causing a mystical turning inward, this holiness quest propelled people outward to bring this inward conviction to society at large so that it, too, could be converted, turned toward its true destiny of perfection by which the millenium would be brought about. This inward search for perfection was the driving force of many nineteenth- and early twentieth-century people.

This is particularly true of the women in American Methodism. Laced throughout their articles, speeches, sermons, and by-laws of organizations was the firm conviction that faith put into action could, and indeed would, bring about a change in the world. They were working to bring about the kingdom of God and this could only be accomplished if everyone had "heart purity," sanctification, Christian perfection.

One such woman was Jennie Fowler Willing, a commited Methodist and reformer. She was active in almost every major reform movement in which Methodist women were involved in the late nineteenth century. She is a good representative to examine because of the great amount she wrote and because she was acknowledged during her lifetime as a spokeswoman for Methodist women.

Willing was born January 22, 1834, in Canada but was raised in Illinois after her family fled Canada following her father's involvement in the Papineau rebellion. She married William Crossgrove Willing, a Methodist preacher in 1853. They served charges in the Genesee and Rock River conferences including four terms as presiding elder. Willing died in New York City October 6, 1916, after years of work at the New York Evangelical Settlement House and Train-ing School which she founded and ran in Hell's Kitchen.

Jennie Fowler Willing was driven by her complete devotion to God and to God's causes in which she felt deeply called to participate. Her primary identification would probably be as a church woman. She was a faithful member of the Methodist Episcopal Church and attended services regularly. In addition to Sunday attendance, Willing was a worker in her local churches, serving as an officer of local church societies and as a pair of hands when there was work to be done. She served the general church through her activities as an organizer for the woman's missionary societies and the temperance unions. She was also a clergy wife and as such saw herself with a special role to play in the church.

Willing was a woman who saw herself as being involved in ministry. She argued for and upheld the concept of lay preaching. "Lay preaching has been the driving wheel of Methodist machinery."[2] And it was a woman, Susanna Wesley, who preserved this activity in Methodism. In the literature examined, Willing never speaks of Susanna without mentioning this fact. Women and lay preaching were linked in Willing's mind.

The atmosphere created by the revival aided this idea. Lay leadership and participation was coming to the fore, as the ideal of individual "entire sanctification" contributed to the superseding of clerical predominance and special spirituality.[3] Willing, catching on to that supersession, held up the gifts of the Holy Spirit and not clerical recognition or sex of the preacher as being the determining factor in whether a person could "prophesy" or not.

> Prophecy, according to Paul, is a gift of the Holy Spirit. "He that prophesieth, speaketh unto men unto edification, and exhortation, and comfort." That the pronoun "he" is used in its generic sense, and means woman, as well as man, is shown in I Corinthians 11:5, in which he directs how women, in that corrupt age, should dress when they prophesy.[4]

Willing carried out her theories by speaking and leading devotional exercises all across the country without benefit of formal recognition from her church but with the recognition of many of her hearers. Edward Eggleston in an article entitled "Methodist Women and the Ministry," written in 1870, wrote of Willing, "We know the wife of a western Methodist presiding elder, who is a woman of rare ability, who virtually preaches every week of her life. We still live in hope of hearing that Mrs. Willing has been licensed."[5] That vocational direction had been paved by Maggie Van Cott, who in 1869 became the first woman to be licensed to preach by the Methodist Episcopal Church. Willing followed suit, and in 1873 was licensed to preach by the Rock River Conference—the first woman engaged as an evangelist in Illinois.[6] She was encouraged to do so, not only by her outside admirers, but also by her husband. William was the presiding elder of the Joliet District at the time she was licensed in that district. As he had done in many of her causes, he encouraged and strengthened her to take the final step.

Far from being an embarassment, her status was promoted by the institutions and causes in which she worked. Elizabeth Cady Stanton raised the fact when writing of Willing's involvement in the Illinois Suffrage Association.[7] Illinois Wesleyan University prominently mentioned her licensed status in their announcements of her joining the faculty.[8] She was apparently very effective in that capacity. Bishop Simpson wrote that "she is earnest and useful in conducting religious meetings."[9] She was in great demand on the camp meeting circuit, particularly the temperance camp meetings. Announcements of her appearances as speaker occur monthly in the *Union Signal*.[10] *The Guide to Holiness* reported that Willing spent her vacation in 1901 "in the West, chiefly among her old friends in Illinois, visiting the camp meetings."[11] The records of the annual meetings of the Woman's Foreign Missionary Society often mention Willing leading the devotional exercises or "seasons of prayer" for a specific concern or thanksgiving. "Mrs. Willing proposed prayer and thanksgiving to God that so many thoroughly qualified young ladies had been willing to accept the responsible position of a foreign missionary. A short and fervent season of prayer followed, led by Mrs. Willing."[12] Despite this effectiveness and the admiration of leading church people, Willing, along with all licensed women, lost her license to preach by action of the 1880 General Conference of the Methodist Episcopal Church.

That was a conference of joy and pain for women working in temperance. Their temperance speaking and work had come to fruition in their church. The 1880 General Conference mandated the use of the "unfermented juice of the grape" in communion services, but attempted to silence the very voices which had helped to bring such a "victory" to pass. Willing never spoke to the conference action directly in the surviving literature. Rather she wrote and spoke against the prejudice which blocked women's God-given place in church work. However, Frances Willard, in the wake of her own rejection as a lay delegate to that same body eight years later, made these remarks in her annual report to the National Woman's Christian Temperance Union Convention.

A church that officially declines to license such women as Mary T. Lathrop, Jennie F. Willing, Sarah O. Robinson, and Maggie Van Cott, has surely taken a long step backward, and the earnest women of its great membership must join hands with the growing element of progressive minds among its men, to regain ground already lost, and win a fair footing throughout its wide domain.[13]

Many nineteenth-century feminists such as Elizabeth Cady Stanton and Matilda Joslyn Gage considered religion and the Bible as the chief elements in holding women under bondage.[14] But others viewed religion and the Bible as liberating forces for women. Through revivals, missionary movements, and social reform, women enlarged their "sphere" by following what they perceived as their call from God to serve God and God's people. Jennie Fowler Willing was one of those nineteenth-century women who deeply identified with the church and its doctrines. It was her Protestant (even Wesleyan) Christian tradition that strengthened her resolve and provided the arguments for her reform activities. Willing used her faith and her religion in all its strength as a sustaining ideology for protest. Willing chided those of her own time for railing against the church and the Scriptures. By doing so, they were bringing failure upon themselves. The religion of Jesus Christ had liberated women and this liberation should free women to work for all the reforms demanded by their only Lord, Jesus Christ.

In viewing this question in the light of the centuries, we find that in no land or time in all this sorrowful world has there ever been hope or heart for women except as the religion of the Lord Jesus Christ has borne sway. Women never had and never can have a firmer, better friend than the Son of Mary. Of all the systems of philosophic and religious thought none has given her the place accorded to her by Protestant Christianity. They who strike at the Church because some of its limitations are faulty and irksome, are like the Ancient Mariner who shot the albatross. They will bring down upon themselves a doom more bitter than death, that of the abominable old sensualisms. The Bible is woman's Magna Carta, and it is worse than suicide for her to set aside its pure, high truths.[15]

This was Willing's guiding principle. She was an example of religion strengthening a resolve, motivating to reform and enabling women to stand and claim the position of equality their Creator had originally intended and the freedom won for them by their redeemer and only Lord, the Son of Mary.

Willing was not blind to the historical and potential repressiveness of the religion she so strongly advocated. These restrictions and oppressive activities she attributed to weak and imperfect men who had misunderstood the divine message down through the ages. She had a great esteem for Paul—her favorite text being Galatians 3:28: "There is neither Jew nor Greek, there is neither bond nor free, there is neither male nor female, for ye are all one in Christ Jesus." She saw the epitome of Paul's belief in this one sentence. Any other interpretation of Paul or his words on the woman's question "have been wrested by the unlearned and unstable to the destruction of thousands of souls."[16] The Galatians passage was the key to the whole of Christianity, not only the salvation of women, but also of the church and, indeed, society. "When the Christian Church cuts down through gloss and prejudice to the core of the meaning of that utterance we may look for the millenium."[17]

And look for the millenium she did, but she also worked for it and urged others to that work. Willing encouraged women to enter all aspects of the life of the church, as she did herself. Willing was commited to the church and working in it to correct the twisting and misapprehension of God's laws and God's call. She strove for perfection, but far from driving her out of the church, it settled her in deeper. Women were called by God and had to respond with their all. Nothing should be allowed to stand in their way. Examining her theological convictions can give a better understanding of this driving force.

Theologian

Willing was an effective evangelist all through her life. She used her skills, not only to convert people herself, but even more importantly to teach others to be workers for Christ in a field that was ready for the harvest. She was sustained and strengthened in the work by her faith. She taught others this faith through her constant use of theology, even if not done in the traditional sense of the word. She was not a systematic theologian. Her theology has to be gleaned from her writings primarily directed at other things. By examining her theology, a better understanding can be gained of Methodist theology of the nineteenth century, as Willing placed herself firmly in that tradition. Willing is particularly helpful in understanding the idea of entire sanctification and how it has evolved in America since Wesley propounded it.

Willing divided her estate between the Woman's Christian Temperance Union and the evangelistic training schools for women of the Methodist Episcopal Church. The will states: "The students in all these training schools must be taught to teach and preach the truth of the Bible as they are set forth by the theological authorities of the Methodist Episcopal Church at this date."[18] Willing directed that if the conditions were not complied with, her estate was to go to the Salvation Army. It was not specified who was to judge the compliance. Just what were the "truths" she perceived the Methodist Episcopal Church to be teaching? In the October 1905 edition of *The Open Door* Willing laid out what the "essential doctrines of our religion" were: immortality of the soul, divine inspiration of the Scriptures, existence of God, Trinity in unity, divinity of the Lord Jesus Christ, personality of the Holy Spirit, atonement, duty of all to love and worship God, justification by faith and sanctification by faith.[19] These doctrines were held not merely through emotion but through intellect. Those who denied the intellectual process in religion had fallen to the level of Romanists.

They are consecrated men and women who are ready to pray and praise indefinitely, and to do anything that will give a good, active tone to their feelings, but who seem to think it cold and heartless to pay any attention to the spiritual use of intellect. . . They bring their emotions to the happiest condition, but leave their power to think upon the tremendous questions pertaining to the spiritual life all unused and weedy, like a fallow field. The result is a character, one-sided, weak, superstitious, bigoted, liable at any hour to be warped out of all form and comeliness by the arch enemy, and always unfit for the heaviest, strongest work.[20]

Of particular interest for our discussion here is Willing's understanding of sanctification. Willing identified herself with the holiness movement, which she saw as a revival of Wesley's true doctrine. Holiness of heart was for her, the watchword of the Wesleys. "They and their followers experienced it, lived it, prayed it, preached it, wrote it, sung it, shouted it, and died in the fullness of glory."[21] The next generation, however, lowered the standard. God raised up people to revive this doctrine. Chief among these for Willing were the Palmers, particularly Phoebe Palmer. That this movement and this doctrine were not popular was apparent to Willing. "A resurrected doctrine is usually received as Ulysses after his long absence. . . . The revival of Christian holiness half a century ago was no exception to this rule. The Palmers found that out to their cost; but they obeyed the Lord, and the result was glorious."[22] Willing described the inward process of salvation. It depended on union with God. The original life of the soul was forfeited by sin. Grace finds us dead in trespasses and sins, and renews in us the life of God. We live this life more or less affluently in proportion to our submission to the divine will, and our trust in the atonement. When, in the maturity of our Christian knowledge, we accept the will of Christ in all things, he will lead us to completed spiritual life.[23] For Willing sanctification was that change of nature that fits a soul for heaven. It was brought about when the faith of the believer gives the Holy Spirit the opportunity to remove all original sin, or depravity, by the blood of Christ, he himself, filling the soul with perfect love to God and humanity. It has to be preceded and followed by growth in grace. Sin is limited by knowledge. One must never have less than a complete choice of God's will, and a sure confidence that the atonement avails to save from all known sin. Sanctification, says Willing, is possible at any time after one is justified.[24]

Willing argued with the objections to this doctrine. To those who argued that sin inheres in matter and that we are not free from sin until death, Willing answered that this view makes necessary an after death purgatory, for nothing unholy is allowed to enter heaven. The concept of purgatory was totally unacceptable to her. It is not death that frees us from sin but the blood of Jesus which cleanses us from sin. We know this because God promises it.[25] There were many who argued that sanctification was merely salvation through good works. Willing, correctly countered with the Wesleyan understanding that all grace is received by faith. The whole process of sanctification is the work of the Holy Spirit, who convicts, points out areas of deeper need, and who—in response to consecration and faith—provides the dynamic to meet those needs. The graces of the Spirit are for perfection of character, but they are not earned. Grace is always a free and abundant gift of God.[26] Even between those who accepted the idea of sanctification, there were disagreements. These stemmed from how and when sanctification occurred. Wesley asserted that it was won by faith

and to delete the possibility of instantaneous sanctification was to cancel the experience of gradual sanctification as well. Thus, Wesley left the possibility open for both, as did Willing. To counter those who affirmed that sanctification was reached by growth she made the distinction that we grow *in* and not *into* grace. Its advance is not a question of time or growth, but of obedience and trust. As soon as this is perfect and complete one is sanctified. This could occur at any time.[27] Many people misunderstood Wesley's idea of sinless perfection. Once one had attained sanctification, one did not consciously sin. If one did, then the sanctification would be lost. This total life in the Spirit was maintained on a moment by moment basis. Willing used this active living in grace as the basis of her argument against those who held that after believers are sanctified, no matter what they do, they cannot commit sin. Willing affirmed that all people's wills are free, and in fact, one could make a wrong choice and fall from any state of grace.[28] Willing was all too painfully aware of the possibility of losing grace as she reported both she and William lost their sanctification during the controversy in the Genessee Conference.[29]

The key to full salvation is whole-souled, unconditional surrender. You must yield perfectly to God. One can glimpse Willing's idea of the process by her guidance of William back to perfect love. First, a person must surrender without reserve or conditions. Then believe that when you do your part, God does his. When one gives all into God's hands, and asks God to cleanse her from all sin, and truly believes when she asks, then God hears; and when God hears then the petition is granted. One must pay no attention to feelings. The just live by faith. The question to ask yourself is, not do you feel differently, but do you believe differently.[30]

An essential element of self-surrender is the will. The will must choose God in all things for all time. This must be as complete as we know how to make it. Every suggestion of possible service or suffering must be met with, "Yes, if it be God's will, I will do it." One must trust God to keep one out of fanaticism and unnecessary self-mortification. One must simply put the conduct of one's life into God's hands and never worry about it again.[31] This attitude was clearly born out in Willing's life. Every decision for service she had to make was made through prayer and even over her own objections of insufficient time, talent, or energy. This complete surrender, and hence sanctification, is not a matter of time. Many old Christians are as much fettered as they were the day of their conversion. It is not simply a matter of growth. Many who have grown a great deal in knowledge, and more or less in grace, since their conversion, are still very far from giving Christ the entire control of their lives. For Willing there are only two things necessary for this result, submission and trust. They can be done as soon after conversion as one is able, through the Spirit's help, to apprehend the need. They are very simple when one honestly seeks to do them. In this connection Willing will begin to talk about assurance.

Assurance, too, is a part of a process. One gives oneself over to the Lord—body, soul, and spirit, for time and eternity—that God's will may be done and God's alone, as far as one is able to find out that will. God is asked to cleanse from all sin, to eliminate the element of disobedience from the soul. If one submits and trusts in this manner, it will not be very long until one will know beyond question, that the blood of Christ has cleansed her, and that he has supreme control of her life.[1] But this assurance does not free anyone from temptation. Willing replied to another of the misunderstandings of sanctification this way. "Tempted? Why I thought you people who profess to be fully given to the Lord were away beyond all that. If you think, my friend, it is possible to get out of reach of temptation, this side of the world of glory, you can't have read your Bible to very good purpose."[33] It is in fact essential that people not be removed from temptation. It would be much easier to completely surrender if people could suffer one pang and be done with it, or if in submission they lost their free agency so to be perfectly safe from ever drawing back into sin and death. But it is part of God's plan that people shall present their bodies as a living sacrifice complete in their restored image of God.[34]

Willing's account of her complete surrender is lengthy but worth quoting in its entirety as it serves concretely to illustrate all the theories she propounded.

I shall never forget the hour when I made that surrender. One afternoon when the Holy Spirit sent His light into the depths of my soul, I discovered, hidden away, like the wedge of gold in Achan's tent, a determination to work, and study, and make something of myself. Not that I might win the wealth and honors of the world, but I would make for myself a dainty, little snuggery into which I would bring a few fine books and pictures, some good music, and a coterie of choice friends. The loud, rough, coarse old world might wag its way, and not a whit would I care for its tinsel and show, nor its troubles, either,—do you see? The Lord in kindness threw a picture upon the canvas that day, that gave me to see how wickedly selfish was my little scheme. I saw myself in a hospital with scores

of people who were dying, and there was no one to give them their medicine, or even a cup of cold water. I had been sent there under orders to help all whom I could possibly reach; and there I was, planning to fit up my exquisite little room, in one corner, its walls padded to shut out the groans, and to shut in the delicacy and beauty that I hoped to gather around me. I saw that selfishness like that could never get into Heaven. . . .then I saw that, I was enabled to say, "I give it all up. Henceforth for me, only thy will, and thy work." The pain of the surrender was so severe that a knife seemed to pierce my heart, and the tears leaped from my eyes. Let me add that all these years, just in proportion as I have held myself loyal to that surrender, has God given me richly to enjoy the things that I put aside to accept His will.[35]

Willing was a firm believer in humanity's co-worker status with God. Although she may not have used the word per se, the idea is all through her writings. God works salvation, but only through people's efforts as well is it totally accomplished. If they would have God lift them up, they must do what they can to lift themselves. For Willing it was essential to have a combination of faith and work. Nothing could be accomplished if emphasis was placed only on one side or the other. This attitude even comes through Willing's strong reliance on prayer. "Now prayer is always appropriate, but it is not the only thing to be thought of. We may cry to God till our voices fail. He will not do for us, what we ought to do for ourselves."[36] One needs to keep one's will in harmony with God's will. If all people would say "thy will be done" and mean it, this world would become Paradise again.[37] People are responsible beings, endowed with this responsibility/freedom by God. They must do their best, do all they know how to do to bring a result and then put the case entirely in God's hands. People have been given the power to cooperate with the divine will and must begin to use this power to the fullest extent possible. "Either God's will can be done, or it cannot. If it is done arbitrarily, we are free from responsibility, and there is nothing for us, but the moral helplessness and imbecility of perpetual babyhood."[38] It is here that Willing places herself fully in the Wesleyan tradition of faith and holy living and, like Wesley, removes herself from the other Protestant traditions. They are inextricably bound by their emphasis on faith, but the idea of sanctification will pose a block to Willing's full acceptance of other traditions, even the Reformed one in which she grew up. For Willing it was essential that one go to *work* with a hearty faith—when this was done all things were possible.

But the glory does not belong to people. If they

begin to think so, they will fail miserably. It cannot be all human. Willing did not fall into the either/or trap. Willing stressed a balanced effort of God and God's people. To those who maintain that people can do nothing, that God does all, she replied that people's weakness was not a bar to successful effort. God would not succeed without us, but neither would we succeed without God.

> God always uses means utterly inadequate to the result to be produced, that it may be thoroughly understood that the excellency of the power is not of humanity, but of God. Then needy souls will know that to Him alone they must look as the source of help and strength, and not to the servants of His bidding.[39]

One does this faith and work in a Christian life. Willing enumerated characteristics of what she called the "normal Christian life."[40] A Christian life was one of total consecration, whose one thought and purpose was to get all with whom they have contact, and whom they can reach with any sort of influence, back to their allegiance to God. Christianity, for Willing, was based upon self-giving, which included one's possessions. There were things and attitudes which had to be done away with in order to be living a Christian life. Prime among these was egotism. It is most easy to slip into while doing the best work for God. One must watch out for self-trust.[41] All must be submitted to God including the conduct of life. This is often the last to be surrendered. Willing never said that the Christian life was an easy life. "It adds to the difficulty to know that for the sake of discipline and development God will probably lead us to just the work we most dislike and hold us back from the things that we prefer."[42] Total surrender and faith in God can turn one around. It acts at the conversion but continues to do so all through one's life. Willing rarely spoke of herself, but she was not reluctant to do so if it could provide an example—even if it was a negative reflection on herself. She used one personal incident to show how a total Christian life must be lived.

> For many years I lacked the spiritual insight to see that I must "speak evil of no man." I drew the line at the harm it would do. Alone with my wise husband who would "treat them just the same" and "never tell," I might speak my mind, especially when they were despicably mean and annoying. I would take good care to say kind things of them everywhere else. I thank God I have put away that "childish thing." My lips are sealed to the faults of others, unless opened by a clear conviction of duty.[2]

Willing believed that God radically converts

people, they become co-workers with God, and then through the transformation of individuals, a transformation of the entire society and world would occur. This is evident in all of Willing's reform efforts. She wanted as many people as possible to be converted to the cause, to be involved with the work, for only through them will the society be transformed into God's new community. Christians desire most the renovation of society which will only come about by the regeneration and spiritual culture of all people.[44]

This idea of sanctification led Willing to become what is classified as a religious reformer. Religious reformers were those whose actions and words stemmed from a strong conviction of God leading them in their cause. Often these religious reformers were what could be classified as holiness people, those folk who had a sense of the importance of sin, had experienced conversion in their own lives, and who were convinced that if people were brought to recognize their sin and shown what God's will was in the matter, they would mend their ways and join the work to eliminate the evil from the world.

Perfectionism was a powerful element in the makeup of the religious reformer. This perfectionism fit in very well with the ideas of progressive nationalism. Religious reformers were interested in conversion, yes, but just as important was a person's conduct after conversion—this was the reform part of the religious reformer. They were motivated by God's love and will to work toward perfection as individuals and as a society. Paired with the sense of social idealism which was prevalent in the country, this was a mighty force to do battle with the liquor trade, the slumlords, the vice purveyors, slaveholders, and male supremacists. "The nineteenth century quest for holiness was turned into avenues of service, instead of the byways of mystic contemplation."[45] God was to establish the Kingdom on earth. It was not a believer's role to sit back and wait with joyful anticipation. God required action of all people who would work to achieve this Kingdom.

Not all holiness people fit in with this description. Indeed, Frederick Norwood identifies two lines of development of this movement in the Methodist Episcopal Church. The one described above is the religious reformer, combining revivalistic perfectionism with social concern for the Christianization of society. Norwood includes in this group Charles Finney and Asa Mahan. The second group divorced the two factors. The solution to the social ills lay exclusively with the conversion of individuals. This group affirmed that committed Christians seeking perfection stayed out of politics and avoided entanglements with worldly issues. Norwood places Phoebe Palmer in this group.[46] While Jennie Fowler Willing was an ardent admirer of Mrs. Palmer and wrote for *The Guide to Holiness*, she must be classified as a member of the first group.

Willing drew her strength and her convictions from her assurance of God's love and will. She worked long and hard for the conversion of individuals. But to be genuine "heart purity" had to manifest itself in action. Willing's life is the best proof of that belief. Perry Miller identifies the strong links between revivals and various reform movements. Revivals provided the impetus and methods of organization for the religious reformers.[47] This is a sentiment with which Willing agreed. While speaking of the founding of the Women's Foreign Missionary Society she gave example of just this idea.

1870 was famous for the grand on-moving of Evangelism. . . . America has been a battle ground as certainly as France. We believe God's cause has been the gainer, as not before for many a long year. Vital godliness, "Scriptural holiness," has taken the initiative, grandly and victoriously.[1]

She went on to say that "good people" regarded this woman's missionary movement as a millennial sign. Willing provided the concrete measure of Miller's links between revivals, missions, millennium, benevolence, and reform.[49] Willing was a religious reformer on an individual and a societal basis.

Willing believed that all reformers had to have a clear conversion. It was through this "heart purity" that the reformer would be able to discern God's will and gather strength from which to act. In fact it was impossible not to respond to needs once one had been "awakened." Willing used the parable of the good Samaritan to illustrate the principle.

The lesson of social obligation taught in this parable may be formulated something in this way: the knowledge of need and the ability to meet it lay upon one a responsibility commensurate with his power to serve. It is not optional with us to help those who need our aid. There is an obligation upon us as sacred and binding as it is possible for any to be, because it is one that grows out of the nature of our relation to others, and it is laid upon us by God himself.[50]

But this work was not to be done alone. Willing was a firm believer in organizations. People banding together give each other strength and provide a united stance in the face of evil. Willing

demonstrated this idea vividly in her concept of the Sisterhood of Prayer. In discussing its merits she showed the close link between religion and reformer.

The pledge to band praying women together, helps all concerned. . . . The women who have joined hands for special prayer, bearing one another's burdens, are freer to pray for those to whom they are not personally related . . . we never get greater blessings from God, than when we are trying to help others walk more closely with him. All social reforms are wrought by that rule.[51]

Willing called on all reformers to rely on God. In fact that is where the strength of conviction came from. Without a conversion experience of God's love and will a person would not be strong enough to pull for the long haul. They and their movement would fail. For Willing, all reformatory power was vested in the Lord Jesus Christ.[52]

For Willing a reformer was one that knew the need of self-sacrifice. One had to follow the central truth of Christianity—an infinite self-giving for the salvation of the lost. In her books and articles she often had characters who, though they called themselves Christian, did not truly understand what being a Christian meant. Often these people were clergy and their wives.

The scoffers said of the dying Christ, He saved others; himself he cannot save. This was false upon the surface, yet true in its deeper meaning,—and true of every Christ-like soul. If we would help others, we cannot save ourselves from pain and loss in the labor, though the soul is strengthened and enriched by the service.[53]

But this self-sacrifice was not a fatalistic kind of notion. Willing, in fact, held fatalists in special contempt. The world could be made a better place. God has called all people to the task of helping usher in the Kingdom. God gives to all who ask the strength to persevere. Willing was fond of quoting a poem to which she did not attribute an author. It expresses her belief in the power of God for reform and our ability to answer.

Not in dumb resignation
 We lift our hands on high,
Not like the nerveless fatalist,
 Content to do and die.
Our faith springs like the eagle's,
 Who soars to meet the sun,
And cries exulting unto thee,
 O, Lord, Thy will be done.

Thy Will! It bids the weak be strong;
 It bids the strong be just;

No lip to fawn, no hand to beg,
  No brow to seek the dust.
Wherever man oppresses man
  Beneath the liberal sun,
O, Lord, be there, thine arm made bare,
  Thy righteous will be done! [54]

In fact, Willing's view of a reformer was identical with that of her view of a Christian. For Willing, the two were inseparable.

Willing had strong views on what a reformer was not also. She criticized organizations and individuals who used "devious" means to obtain money for their work or for any advancement. In *The Only Way Out,* Willing criticized a character in the book for her methods. Mary, upon reaching thirty, began to play the role of a charming member of Boards of Charity. She was used like a floral display whenever a pretty face was needed to loosen the purse strings of potential benefactors who were swayed by "skillfully managed aesthetic influences" rather than by the merits of the case. Willing contrasted Mary with her sister Josephine. Josephine disdained this "unwomanly maneuvering." Josephine gave of her own money—even to the last penny, and she personally worked attacking wrongs that should be put down.[55] One should not use trickery or social prejudices to gain reform. These methods only furthered the need not the solution. One should be personally involved in all aspects of the work—raising and giving money, support for workers and for the needs in prayers and in actions. Perhaps Willing's most powerful statement on reformers comes from her book of essays, *Diamond Dust.* In her description of the role of a reformer she presages much of what liberation theologians of today speak about.

> The subject race must be made to comprehend its own dignity. The principle violated in human servitude is the inherent greatness of humanity, and they who are under can be trusted to rise to equality or superiority only as they apprehend this principle. Without that apprehension, a change of position would be only a change of tyrannies. To lift up a man or a race, one need not trouble himself to make the oppressor understand the worth of the slave. Let him teach the slave his own dignity and trust him to make his master comprehend that lesson. The liberator must also see so plainly the tremendous import of human life, that he will go down among the oppressed and share the obloquy of their wrongs, sustained by his belief in the intrinsic human royalty.[56]

Willing lived out these convictions. She and her husband left their teaching post at Illinois Wesleyan to work in the missions of Chicago. From there they felt the stronger cry from New York City. When William died, Jennie started the New York Evangelical Training School and Settlement House in the area of New York known as Hell's Kitchen. There she lived and worked and fought for the kingdom of God. She was part of the large group of people talking about and working for "Christian socialism."

Willing was a Christian socialist, but of her own brand. She combined conservative theology with a vision of far-reaching social reforms. She believed in personal sin and the need for personal regeneration. It was through these regenerated persons that the world and society would be transformed. So, in a sense, she worked for both individual and societal regeneration, but the emphasis was on the individual. Willing preached to the rich to examine their comfortableness and rely completely on God. She was not content with their money. She wanted their souls. She did not glorify involuntary poverty, nor did she blame the poor for their condition. They were not poor because God was punishing them. True, God taught lessons through personal disasters; but this could not cover whole classes of people. Willing attacked the materialism of the rich and the superstition of the poor. Possibly her ideal was a character she created in *The Only Way Out.* Gideon Strong was a poor boy who worked his way up with the help of a generous rich family. He was a success in business because of his strong personal faith and complete reliance on God's guidance and precepts. He worked at the Water Street mission after work and on weekends. He gave to charity. He maintained an orphan girl in a good home and set up industrial schools where girls could go to learn cooking and sewing and housekeeping and earn better wages as better trained workers and also make better homes for themselves and their families. Finally he succeeded in converting members of the rich family which first befriended him. He lived simply but well, gave of his money and his time. He was a success in business and in life.

Willing firmly believed that people needed physical and spiritual care. Success would not come if only one was present. People needed food and clothes and jobs, but they also needed someone to care about them personally and to bring them the love of God in Christ through their beings. Willing in her stories had pictures of peaceful happy people in poverty, but these were to contrast with the tortured rich. The role basis for this was to show the peace which came with accepting Christ. This did not imply accepting one's condition. In fact, it was just the opposite. One's being was transformed for action to transform society.

We have been unable to find any direct reference to Rauschenbusch, Sheldon, or any other prominent social gospel people in Willing's writings, even though they shared many of the same concerns and solutions. Willing did not rely as heavily as many social Christians on governmental action to cure the social ills. There were specific areas where laws were needed—the right of women to vote, outlawing polygamy, outlawing the liquor traffic. We have found no direct reference by Willing to what could be termed labor laws--wages, hours, conditions, or welfare. This she believed should be enacted by employers voluntarily under the influence of heart purity. She should not be classified with political conservatives. While she did push for heart purity it was a state which transformed peoples' lives *and* showed in their outward actions—faith leading to good works. Willing was a good Wesleyan, and that led her to the convictions and actions of a Christian socialist.

Willing prayed and worked and lived to bring in the kingdom of God on earth. She saw society as a potential not reached, as possibilities lost, and dreams unfulfilled. All that would change if everyone were a true Christian; if everyone had heart purity and accepted, trusted, and relied solely on Christ. Willing had a vision of a new heaven and a new earth. She wrote books and articles exhorting people to change their ways, holding up this vision as a real possibility for which to work. She lived the life of the oppressed and understood and worked for them to understand their own dignity and worth as God's free and valued children. She fought the evils, spiritual and physical, that were holding the world in the kingdom of evil. Willing worked and prayed for reform, and lived her creed, and stood up for her convictions. Aided by her God and her sisters and brothers in the faith, she was a reformer. It was a vision she made real for many American Methodist women. It is a legacy passed down to us and upon which we can build as theologians and re-formers—making all things new.

NOTES

1. Calvin Colton, *History and Character of American Revivals of Religion* (London: Frederick Westley and A. H. Davis, 1832), p. 59.
2. Jennie Fowler Willing, *Heathen Woman's Friend*, May 1870, p. 92.
3. Timothy Smith, *Revivalism and Social Reform* (Gloucester: Peter Smith, 1976), p. 80.
4. Jennie Fowler Willing, *The Open Door*, January 1909, p. 9.
5. *The Independent*, 21 July 1870, p. 4.
6. Elizabeth C. Stanton et al., *History of Women Suffrage* (Rochester: Charles Mann, 1881), vol, 3, p. 579.
7. Ibid.
8. *Alumni Journal of the IWU*, January 1874, p. 3.
9. Matthew Simpson, *Cyclopedia of Methodism* (Philadelphia: Louis H. Everts, 1881), p. 953.
10. See *Union Signal*, 1883–1890.
11. *The Guide to Holiness*, August–September 1901, p. 79.
12. *Heathen Woman's Friend*, June 1878, p. 272. See also July 1881, p. 4, or any other report of the annual meetings found in the *Heathen Woman's Friend*.
13. *Annual Report of the National Woman's Christian Temperance Union*, 1888, p. 46.
14. See particularly Elizabeth Cady Stanton et al., *The Women's Bible* (New York: European Publishing Co., 1898); and Matilda Joslyn Gage, *Woman, Church and State* (Watertown, Mass: Persephone Press, 1980; reprint of orig. 1893 ed.).
15. Jennie Fowler Willing, *Diamond Dust* (Cincinnati: Walden & Stowe, 1880), p. 87.
16. Ibid., p. 85.
17. Ibid.
18. *The New York Times*, 27 October 1916, p. 2.
19. Willing, *The Open Door*, October 1905, p. 28.
20. Willing, *Diamond Dust*, p. 64.
21. Willing, *The Guide to Holiness,* April 1894, p. 119.
22. Ibid.
23. Willing, *Diamond Dust*, pp. 128-29.
24. Willing, *The Open Door*, October 1908, pp. 42-43.
25. Ibid., p. 42.
26. Ibid., p. 43.
27. Ibid.
28. Ibid.
29. Jennie Fowler Willing, *A Prince of the Realm* (Cincinnati: Cranston and Curts, 1895), p. 17.
30. Ibid., pp. 23-24.
31. Willing, *Diamond Dust*, p. 32.
32. Willing, *From Fifteen to Twenty-five*, pp. 37-38.
33. Willing, *The Guide to Holiness*, November 1867, p. 138.
34. Willing, *Diamond Dust*, pp. 127-28.
35. Willing, *From Fifteen to Twenty-five*, pp. 75-77.
36. Willing, *The National Sunday School Teacher*, February 1870, p. 36.
37. Willing, *The Open Door*, May–June 1909, p. 25.
38. Ibid., p. 36.
39. Willing, *Diamond Dust*, pp. 12-13.
40. Ibid., p. 209.
41. Willing, *From Fifteen to Twenty-five*, p. 135.
42. Willing, *Diamond Dust*, p. 122.
43. Willing, *The Guide to Holiness*, June 1894, p. 174.
44. Willing, *The National Sunday School Teacher*, March 1873, p. 85.
45. Smith, *Revivalism*, p. 178.
46. Frederick Norwood, *The Story of American Methodism* (Nashville: Abingdon Press, 1974), p. 293.
47. Perry Miller, *The Life of the Mind in America* (New York: Harcourt, Brace & World, 1965). These ideas are prevalent all through book one. See especially chap. 3, "Pentecost and Armageddon."
48. Jennie Fowler Willing, *Heathen Woman's Friend*, January 1871, p. 79.
49. Miller, *Life of the Mind*, p. 80.
50. Willing, *Diamond Dust*, p. 159.
51. Willing, *The Open Door*, March 1910, p. 7.
52. Jennie Fowler Willing, *The Only Way Out* (Boston: D. Lathrop & Co., 1881), p. 166.
53. Ibid., p. 166.
54. *The Open Door*, October 1905, is just one example of a place she used it.
55. Willing, *The Only Way Out*, pp. 33-34.
56. Willing, *Diamond Dust*, p. 114.

5. TOWARD A WESLEYAN-FEMINIST CHRISTOLOGY: CAN A DISEMBODIED CHRIST HELP ANYBODY?

Jean C. Lambert

I. Prologue

Rosemary Radford Ruether, whose 1976 "occasional paper" for the United Methodist Board of Higher Education and Ministry inspired my imitative title[1], makes a provocative observation in another article:

> Feminist liberation theology starts with the Church (liberation community) as the context for discussing questions of . . . creed or action. Without a liberation community, all such questions . . . are meaningless . . . . Conversion to a new humanity beyond sexism points toward the entrance into a body of people who share this commitment and support each other in it.[2]

She concludes with a question: "Where does one find such a community?" Her question, in combination with another of my own asking, might — I think — lead us toward a genuinely Wesleyan, genuinely creative, human theology, particularly concerning the meaning of Jesus Christ for those twentieth-century humans whose calling it is to be Christian and feminist. The second question is this: "How can we do theology on the basis of communities of liberation in such a way that our articulated thinking is truly *ours*, ever increasingly ours?"

Several presuppositions and begged questions need comment before I can proceed. I adopt an eighteenth-century pattern.

Q. Why should a particular community be the basis for a particular theology?

A. A theology reflects a particular situation, and if our theology is not to be trapped by the sexism of our culture we need to do it in the context of a community intentionally struggling against that sexism.

Q. Why can't we depend on reading books and journals by other feminists and experience a "liberation community in dispersion"?

A. We have been, and this is a model much of the church has always followed in order to be in communication with its forbears in faith as it reads scripture and traditional texts, as well as corresponding with and holding occasional conference with its historical contemporaries. By the mediation of the Spirit there is a kind of presence we have with each other even when we are—humanly speaking—mostly absent.

Q. Then what are you suggesting that is more than this? And why? are you suggesting that our ways of being put limits on the Spirit of God?

A. Whether we can finally thwart the Holy Spirit I am not competent to judge. Scripture constrains us from thinking so. While Paul urged us not to quench the Spirit (I Thessalonians 5:19), the psalmist knew the Spirit as ubiquitous (139:7) and prophets have assured the people, offering the presence of the Spirit of God as an unshakable resource (Haggai 2:5). Nevertheless, Paul's advice suggests human resistance can impede God's work among us, so it seems likely that human cooperation might allow or assist that working, at least by noninterference.

Q. What, then, happens in a face-to-face community of believers, or a liberation community, that does not happen when one reads the writing of another believer?

A. In their communion the believers become open to the Spirit in a way different from their openness when they are solitary. They can be empowered to think together, rather than independently, or dependently; dominatingly or submissively; traditionally or fantastically.[3]

Q. What do you mean by "genuinely Wesleyan"? and "genuinely creative"?

A. By "genuinely Wesleyan" in this context I mean living out, and acknowledging that we live out, and encouraging each other to live out the growing in grace that Wesley envisaged when he spoke of perfection or of sanctification. Such living out includes incarnation in transformed social institutions. By "genuinely creative" I mean to use 20th century language that gathers up Wesley's meanings about sanctification, in history, and that adds to them (or clarifies if this is indeed what Wesley meant) the dimension of transition from destruction of the old to emergence of the new, and the sense that this transition is always a selective weaving together of many threads.

Q. Is that related to the way you repeated the word "ours"? What do you mean? "Ours" rather than whose?

A. I would signify those who struggle together in liberation community. I would contrast it with "mine," or "yours," or "his," or "hers," though I value my own theologizing, and yours, and that of our sisters and brothers. Without denigrating those values, I want also to find a way to a theology that is truly *ours*. Especially when we talk about Jesus Christ, it seems to me that his body ought to be taught to speak, so that it can speak wholely. I am presupposing that the Holy Spirit present in the gathered community *is* the being-with-us of the choice of God for human life, for human love, for human empowerment to transform human society.

I do not claim to have special information about this, but am extrapolating from the church's common inheritance. It is time for us to envision a way past head, heart, or shoulder-to-the-wheel theology, past women's or ethnics' theologies, and past individuals' theologies. We probably are not yet ready to take that step. We cannot take a detour around the struggles of our history; there I agree with the left-wing Hegelians. I merely suggest that we need to nurture a vision of how such whole steps may one day be taken. Without a vision of alternatives, we repeat the oppressive systems and the oppressing theologies arising from their contexts.

Q. Did the church ever have a theology that was "ours"?

A. Some have credited previous ages of the church with genuinely common theology, which they called "catholic." Something common existed, but I doubt it was ever catholic theology. Always there have been individual perspectives, and the pseudo-catholic dogma that was the institutional line ignored or disvalued such differences, even when it did not overtly persecute them. "Our" theology should be both common and embrace—as a positive value—the reality of individual, class, sexual, racial, personality, age, life-style, cultural, and political differences. The Body of Christ is not simpleminded, and has rich experience. I look to the embodied Christ for help. I recognize that it is not only those who "name the Name" who participate in genuinely liberating community. I do not believe Christ is *absent* from any place where people seek liberation from

oppression. It seems to me such confidence is the foundation of even the most fundamental versions of the Christian gospel.

II. Liberation Community

How does one find a liberation community? How could a liberation community theologize so as to give birth to a genuinely Wesleyan and genuinely creative common theology?

In this discussion-inviting paper I do not want to develop further those two questions or to propose practical routes to answers, except to say that I think we cannot "find" such community but rather must make contexts in which people can cooperate with the Spirit in creating it. To this purpose, though, I will apply some reflections on history. They support an observation that seems promising to me as a step toward a feminist Christology in the Wesleyan tradition. After making the observation and offering the historical reflections, I will move to a possibility and some evidence from recent theology that suggests the possibility is not totally unrealistic.

First, the observation: Once Wesleyanism had a way of building liberation community. So also did Feminism. I refer to classes and bands, and to consciousness-raising groups. Both have waned. Like Methodism in the nineteenth century, the new wave of feminism has made the shift from "movement" to "institution" with similar spiritual losses, losses—that is—to the reality of liberation community.

I refer to the shift away from commitment of Christian believers to the spiritual friendship, encouragement, and discipline of the Wesleyan "class" and "band" of the earliest days of the Methodist movement, and to the shift of contemporary feminists away from the "consciousness-raising groups" that characterized the first years of the "second wave" of feminism in the 1960s. Methodism has become a family of denominations; Feminism has become a sorority of self-help and social critique/change organizations.[4] Methodism has become an approach to religious and societal involvement sufficiently "establishment" in orientation to be described, however inadequately, by an American president as the faith of the American people. (Or is that apocryphal?) Feminism has become a perspective on society indistinct enough for the mass media to identify it with dressing for success, proabortionism, antiabortionism, lesbian separatism, and equality of opportunity according to strict constructionist standards vis-à-vis the United States Constitution.

The course of this shift is easier to trace with reference to Wesleyan bands and classes than with reference to feminist consciousness-raising

171

groups. The inheritors of Wesleyanism seem to continue his penchant for procedures and record-keeping.

It is clear that from the beginning of Wesley's public activity the people called Methodist were appointed to "bands" in which their growth in Christian perfection was to be stimulated, guided, challenged, and kept alive. Bands were introduced in 1739[5] and their procedures formalized by rules published in 1791.[6] The classes, which Ahlstrom describes as "far more important," began in 1742,[7] as an accident of history in response to a need in Bristol for a way to collect funds. The class system soon became normative in the young Methodist movement; a directive of Wesley stated:

> All members shall have their names entered on a Classbook, shall be placed under the pastoral care of a class leader, and shall receive a Quarterly Ticket of Membership.[8]

Both bands and classes were far more important in England than in the United States, the bands (being for those who had found the way of salvation and were engaging in discipline so as to persevere) and the classes (being for those seeking salvation, guided by the leader and helping each other to find it) together being normative for membership in Methodist societies. A strict test of membership in England, the classes were never that in the United States, though they were taken seriously well into the late 19th century, apparently in both places.[9]

The fellowship of these meetings was bracing to say the least. I quote from the pamphlet by James D. Nelson in the *Spiritual Formation Resource Packet* published in 1983 by the Board of Higher Education and Ministry:

> The questions which were asked of each member at the weekly meetings by the layperson in charge reflect the rigor of the society's efforts.

> 1. *What known sins have you committed since our last meeting?*
> 2. *What temptations have you met with?*
> 3. *How were you delivered?*
> 4. *What have you thought, said, or done of which you doubt whether it be sin or not?*
> 5. *Have you nothing you desire to keep secret?*

Utter frankness was the norm for all conversation in such a group.

New members were asked:

> *Do you desire to be told your faults? . . . Consider! . . . Is it your desire and design to be, on this and all other occasions, entirely open, so as to speak everything that is in your heart without exception, without disguise, and without reserve?*[10]

Bracing and rigorous though it was, it must also have been a discipline welcomed and in some sense enjoyed by its participants. A quotation from the *Cyclopedia* of 1882 indicates the regard in which at least that writer held the class meeting:

> The character of the class meeting cannot be lowered, or the gracious soul-refreshing and powerful vitality of the church will cease to exist.[11]

Perhaps he was already sensing the change. One hundred years later an American doctoral student, William Dean, in *Wesleyan Historical Society Proceedings*, comments on the significance of the decline of this innovative factor in Methodist life. I find his reflections on this decline theologically suggestive, both because of the way he identifies the value of the class meeting itself, and because of the explanations he offers for its loss of favor and practice among Methodists. I will therefore comment on his article in some detail.

The early phase of Methodism was characterized, Dean says, by an "emphasis on the quality of personal relationships among Methodists as *the chief evidence of the work of God.*" (Emphasis mine.) He uses the terms "warm informality" and "direct mutuality" to describe the "original form" of the class meeting.[12]

The relational quality was not valued primarily as a bonding mechanism of the movement, as an evangelistic asset, or even as a mollifying counter-energy to the strict discipline of thought and action the class demanded. The relational quality was prized as "evidence of the work of God."

But what happened? Dean notes that a definite shift happened in the mid-nineteenth century, although the phenomenon had continued—apparently with strong commitment—for a century. One explanation offered by Robert Currie is that a liberalizing trend rendered discipline unpopular among those in chapel who sought entertainment rather than rigorous religious exercises.[13] Another view is expressed by Henry Rack, who believes classes withered from unpopularity, a result of the boring and repetitive character of the testimonies, stories told and help requested.[14]

Dean, in contrast, takes a clue from Ernst Troeltsch and notes that damage to the early fervor had already happened by 1850, and cites diary and journal evidence. He theorizes: the original function of the class—to evangelize and to conserve new converts in their commitment—had eroded due to a web of historical circumstance leaving the class without purpose except as an entry to society membership.

What were these circumstances? They were, basically, three: (a) a change in manner of conversion; (b) public "success" of the Methodist movement; and (c) public acceptability of the movement, such that it ceased being persecuted.

(a) Whereas conversion had formerly been a long, soul-searching process, nurtured by a particular guide and supported by a covenanted group, instantaneous conversion became the norm as revivalism spread. The prayer-meeting that followed the preaching service—what many of us probably experienced as "the season of prayer in the pastor's study," or "praying through at the altar rail"—this replaced the weeks of struggle and reflection typical of the class. Prayer meetings also continued, but these lacked the person-to-person confrontational discipline of the earlier class meetings.[15]

(b) As the revival eroded the evangelising function, its "apparent success" eroded the conserving function. The revivals resulted in "the Victorian cultural synthesis of the 19th century." One characteristic of the sect, its uncompromising ethical standard, requires contrast with the broader social environment. When that environment adopts the sect's outward style, so to speak, it steals its thunder. So the need to keep strong in face of "worldly" erosion diminished.[16]

(c) As for the third eroder of the class, Dean's observation about loss of persecution may need a bit of expansion. Compared with the tortures suffered by Mennonites, Jews, and witches, the persecutions suffered by Methodists may appear tame, at least to us. For the persecuted, however, "egging, stoning, destruction of property, physical abuse, and social ostracism" probably seemed strenuous enough. In any case, as the nineteenth century progressed, such hazards of being a Methodist diminished, and with them the cohesion among the members of classes that had been strengthened by harrassment.[17]

Dean relates all three circumstances I have just detailed to the institutionalizing of Methodism. He says it "shifted the center of attention from Wesley's emphasis on the quality of interpersonal relationships . . . to the public, more impersonal, and less demanding. . . ."[18]

I will leave it to a historical theologian to trace whatever correlations there may be between the demise of the classes and bands, and the course of Wesleyan theological development. As I indicated at the outset, I am following a hunch and am struck by the similarity between these "classes" and feminist consciousness-raising groups, and between the demise of the classes and a similar demise some of us older feminists have witnessed. Many have noted that Wesleyanism has shifted from a disciplined and cohesive body to one whose connectional coherence is not matched by doctrinal awareness or commitment among laity. Not only pluralism characterizes 20th century Wesleyanism, but general neglect among laity and clergy of sacraments, piety, and social action toward justice and peace which are clear marks of its earlier century.

Likewise, the sisterhood and clarity about purpose for self-development, sisterly aid, and deep societal change that marked the feminism of the 1960s, was replaced by trashing, pluralism, separatism, ecumenism, and confusion as the 80s move along.

Perhaps modes of conversion contribute to how the changes emerge. In the late 1960s and early 70s one became a feminist by "having one's consciousness raised." Though there has certainly never been a prescribed orthodoxy about this, the most common route involved weeks of struggle with a small group of women who met to speak painful truths to each other about our experiences. Many groups seem to have used a set of discussion-starting questions in order to guide their self- and other-examination. I know we did. Though no authority dictated a particular set, many women's groups used questions of similar nature. I cannot find our list, but suspect it must have been a source for or may have drawn upon the same sources as this untitled one published by the American Baptist Convention in a women's resource packet during the early 1970s.

> What are my dreams for life? . . . How might sex and age oppress me and limit my relationships? . . . How was womenhood presented to me as a child? What expectations was I supposed to fulfill? . . . Must I sacrifice my integrity to be in this relationship (that I currently am in)? . . . Do I treat little girls differently than little boys? . . . What kind of work do I do for a living? . . . Do I think I could get a better job? . . . What work do I do in my family? Is it equitable? Inevitable? Shared? . . . Do I pretend to have an orgasm? . . . Do I value women's opinions? . . . Do I compete with women?[19]

There is no superficial similarity between these questions and those asked in a Wesleyan class. Nonetheless, I cannot help noting the similarity in their implication that one ought to be growing and changing, that one needs to examine oneself, that one must act on one's discoveries, and that the place to work on these tasks is in a small, committed group. Indeed the anti-quietistic emphasis is explicitly stated in this same guide's instructions for conducting consciousness raising groups.

> The actions we will take . . . will reflect our individual needs, but . . . it is important we become involved. . . . Consciousness without action is not really consciousness.[20]

The guides church women's groups circulated enumerated many goals for consciousness-raising groups. Their major functions, however, were analogous to those of classes. They provided a context in which women could come to awareness of the ways in which sexism oppressed them and how they internalized the oppression, and in which they could make a decision to pursue liberation. And they supported women in the growth toward that liberation. Indeed, the typical label for groups in the 1970s, if I recall correctly, was "consciousness-raising/support group," but perhaps this was a local phenomenon. One might say that these combined for feminism the function of classes and bands for early Methodism.

For those of us who struggled through to some new awareness in such settings, they were truly "communities of liberation." In the last decade, however, there has been a change. Feminism has lost its separate identity in the public awareness. People of diverse approaches to life—even men—speak of being feminists. Yet one rarely hears a feminist of any variety speak of her consciousness-raising group in the present tense. Some of us claim support groups, or long to find or to build one.

I would note here, too, the sense among self-acknowledged feminists that not all of us are alike. Carol Christ, in *Womanspirit Rising*, differentiates between reformist and radical; Ann Belford Ulanov in *Receiving Woman*, distinguishes between hard and softer; Ruether— more carefully, I think, than both—identifies a range of types in *Sexism and God-Talk*.[21] Pluralism sometimes is expressed as separatism, and some of the criticism from even virulent anti-feminists is echoed by self-acknowledged feminists; many would probably agree that the women's movement has lost its critical edge, or, to change to a more traditionally feminine metaphor, we might say that the pattern of our weaving is becoming so complex it is sometimes difficult to differentiate a feminist vision from mere "piece-of-the-pie revisionist capitalism."

What has happened? I suggest that like nineteenth-century Methodism we have become institutionalized. The ways differ from the denominational institutionalization of the Wes-

leyan movement, but they correlate to some extent with the three circumstances Dean cited for the demise of the Wesleyan classes.

(a) Rapid "conversions" to feminism have occurred. Catalyzed by women's studies courses, by mass-media interpretations, and by concerts of "women's music" among other influences, women and some men have arrived at genuine "a-ha!" experiences whose insights have been nurtured in broad-brush ways by the same large-scale processes that prompted them.

(b) A superficial, popular concurrence with some of the externally visible ethos of feminism has created the illusion that the struggle is largely successful, and only a few minor issues need to be cleared up. This is particularly characteristic of new feminists, though not only chronologically young ones. Those of us who teach women in seminaries, I suppose, share recognition of what I would call "first-year opacity" and "the great awakening of the second year." Perhaps the timetable differs in other curricula than ours. I refer to the transition from "I think we should work together to benefit *everyone*," to "*Now* I see what those third-year women were talking about. You know what happened to *me*?"

(c) And third, the relative lack of persecution *at some levels* has watered down the tough, critical, compassionate sisterhood some of us credit not only with our feminist consciousness but with our sanity during the years of the late sixties and early seventies. Admittedly, not all of us white feminists were dealing then with racism as we ought to have been. But much of what we learned then has direct application now to these more sensitive times. It is well for feminists to criticize other feminists for political and personal narrowness of all oppressing types. Yet we need to remember the terms "queen bee," "trashing," "horizontal violence." We can learn from the subtle analyses of black feminist Bell Hooks, rather than shrugging off woman-to-woman violence with "that's politics." Or, "What did you expect?"[22]

Of course, women's virtue is not undiluted, and the near-total subjectivity of some early phases of consciousness-raising threatened to doom the movement to naval-gazing and bourgeoisie ignorance of all who were not white and middle class. Yet I also am convinced that the spiritual center of feminism, the sisterhood in oppression and in being mutually, gradually liberated together as our consciousnesses were raised, has weakened perceptibly. We who are white, middle-class feminists are always in danger from the sexism we don't any longer expect in our somewhat sensitized subculture, and from the blindness of ourselves as we

174

overlook and thereby contribute to the oppression of sisters in lower classes and of various colorful ethnic groups.

So, to conclude this first section, I restate from the observation with which I opened: Like Methodism in the nineteenth century, the new wave of feminism has made the shift from "movement" to "institution" with similar spiritual losses, losses, that is, to the reality of liberation community.

I have sketched this because I think that if we seek to find or to build liberation community we had better listen hard to these historical phenomena and learn what we can from them. And, of course, I do think that we had better seek to discover or build such communities. This leads me to my promised comments about a possibility.

III. Christological Visioning

I suspect that the reinvention of *loci* of Christian accountability, friendship, and encouragement may go hand in hand with the emergence of a Christology that can address this decade with the power for humanizing and sanctifying transformation of persons and social institutions that Wesley's unique Arminianism offered the eighteenth century. I suggest that ecclesial creativity and theological creativity are in fact the poles of the same dynamic. That is, developing authentic and new church forms may go hand in hand with a genuine and new Christological interpretation.

Let me share first a theological vision, and then I will offer some already extant manifestations from theology and from ecclesial praxis that suggest the vision is more than a midsummer night's dream.

Suppose that there were a network of liberation communities that were both Christian and feminist. (I would like them to be consciously anti-racist, anti-ageist, anti-body-cultist, and so on, but this is subject matter for another paper.) Such communities would include both men and women. They would enact the obvious feminist commitments, such as inclusive language, equal distribution of all community work along lines of giftedness, with encouragement for each member to develop gifts hitherto unused because of internalized sexism. Beyond this, though, they would embody shared initiating and responding, criticizing and encouraging, in such a way that engrained hierarchical patterns would deliberately be challenged, broken, and left behind as new forms emerged or were rediscovered. Such communities would enact obvious Christian commitments. They would worship a holy presence thoroughly free to empower persons and groups for a present-transcending future. They would affirm the call to love each other redemptively, their inability and unwillingness to do so adequately, and their need to confess their failures honestly to each other, ask for, and offer forgiveness and restoration to each other. They would share a hope for justice, bread, peace, freedom, and fresh respect and liveliness toward all creatures; and they would rejoice in the struggle of putting flesh on these hopes. Their joy would evoke celebration of that holy and free spirit present among them, empowering them. Together they would remember a man, Jesus, who in some way authentically embodied a faith they share, and even authored it, and as they told stories about him and by him, and shared meals in solidarity with him and those with whom he identified—the poor, the alien, the oppressed—they would experience something *that only they could talk about.*

Little more can be said about such a Christology from this side of such an as-yet-to-be-experienced liberation community. I personally believe, experience, and want to say more than this about Jesus. Yet I begin to sense that now is not the time for individual assertion. Rather, I am suggesting the possibility that we may find a healing, invigorating, and faithful Christology, as feminists in a Wesleyan tradition, when we find ourselves— no, rather, find each other—in liberation communities that embody the living Christ about whom we purport to speak.

Putting this negatively, I would say I doubt that any one of us will be able to articulate solo a faithful or adequate Christology. Such a Christology must, I think, be "our" Christology in a way as different from an ecumenical committee document as the planet Earth is from a computerized satellite or even a "humanned" space shuttle. Only an embodied Christ can help us; I am visioning the possibility, merely, that a fallible, sinful liberation community could nevertheless be the body of Christ, and could articulate, as it were, Christ's self-understanding in a Christology appropriate for its own time.

We have not seen such a Christology. But we have crumbs, some nourishing, good-sized chunks, in fact, that the half-orphaned children, Hansel and Gretel, who are our sisters and brothers, have dropped along the way. I don't imagine that in the reflections that follow I will have plucked up the best or most valuable necessarily. They are three chunks that seem promising to me.

Gregory Baum critiques the God/Christ who is "extrinsic" to ourselves. Isabel Carter Heyward critiques the God/Christ who is "unique Lord" of human experience. The community-toward-liberation in Solentiname critiques the God/Christ who is captive to the oppressive interests of the economically, racially, and sexually dominant elite. They all offer explicitly or implicitly an interpersonal, relational, historically powerful and historically vulnerable Christ.

In his 1970 book subtitled *God in Secular Experience* Gregory Baum explicitly rejected the notion of a God external to human life and history.

> God is redemptively present in human life . . . There is no human standpoint from which God is simply . . . over-against. . . . Once man is defined in terms of his own powers and resources, God becomes an outsider and it is impossible ever to get him back in again. But if man comes to be in a process of dialogue and sharing, then he is an historical, open ended being in which, by definition, more than he himself is involved. If man comes to be in a process of listening and responding, in which his freedom is creatively engaged, then it is possible to see how God, summoning and freeing man, enters into the very constitution of who man is and will be. . . . This dynamic understanding of human life is implicit in the new Spirit-created experience of the Gospel and hence in the doctrinal development of refocusing the Gospel. It is equally implicit in the first principle of reinterpreting the doctrine of God.
> God is . . . present in man and includes him in his own mystery. . . . Every sentence about God can be translated into a declaration about human life. . . . The Good News tells us that God's presence to human life is God as he is in himself. [So] it should be possible to speak about this God by clarifying certain dimensions of human history. . . . [To say] God exists . . . means that wherever people are something new happens.[23]

I included this too-lengthy excerpted quotation because it illustrates what "our" theology will probably *not* be, as well as offering a useful crumb. The almost exclusively cognitive language is too dessicated to communicate the living Christ embodied in real groups of real people in history. And, it is masculinist.

Nevertheless, Baum "locates" God, so to speak, completely immanently. Not, as he explicitly states, pan-theistically, for as he sees it that would deny the human reality in its terrible freedom, but nonetheless Baum interprets God in a thoroughly non-transcendent way. Second, I notice that he introduces Christology as a mediating dimension, not as a content-giving dimension. That is, he speaks explicitly about *God*; God is the content of revelation and of theologically important knowledge. Jesus Christ is the *mediator* of that knowledge; Baum's image for this is "the Good News."

The other individual whose work suggests likely directions for "our" Christology is Isabel Carter Heyward, whose dissertation, *The Re-*

demption of God, was deposited a decade after Baum's work was published. I find her central concept similar to Baum's, though she develops it radically differently.

A clue to her direction lies in her first chapter title, "In the beginning is the relation." Nothing is by itself alone, she suggests; whatever has power to be and act has it in virtue of relations, from which it cannot be severed without loss of its own being. Her theological vision is intimated in the near slogan-quality *credo* she offers at the beginning of the book: "I believe that God is our power in relation to each other, all humanity, and creation itself."[24]

Heyward has an odd way, as do many of us now, of insisting that God is not a being, of putting personal pronominal referents to God in quotation marks, and then going on to express hope that we may "experience God incarnate as friend and lover."[25] She quotes Martin Buber approvingly when he says, "That you need God more than anything you know at all times in your heart. But don't you also know that God needs you—in the fullness of his eternity, you?"

"If God loves us," she continues, "God needs us. A lover needs relation—if for no other reason, in order to love."[26] God as non-personally personal?

Any God-language at all for Heyward is incarnational, or better, intercarnational, so why be explicitly Christological? She indicates it is partly in recognition of Jesus' human uniqueness. It also is partly because he is the figure about whom the Church has claimed that meaning-unlocking mystery—incarnation—which she understands to be the essential character of relations among all persons.

> We need to act differently, not in order to uphold Jesus, but rather in order to uphold—support—ourselves. Only in this way does incarnation—God's active presence in and with the world, the flesh, humanity—make sense.
>
> Relational theology is incarnational.[27]

The Christological significance of Heyward's book, as I look toward "our Christology," is not so much what she says about Jesus of Nazareth or about Jesus as the Christ. Rather, it is what she *does* by retelling the Jesus story, re-imagining it, she calls it, so as to sharpen its function for empowering, challenging, and calling the human hearer/reader to fully responsible life. For her, this involves rejection of Jesus' unique Lordship[28] because it lifts him above human experience and strips us of our responsibility to make God incarnate in the world. But her book is more than an ideological critique. It is a treatment of the stories themselves that makes them freshly reflection-able and action-able for those who would accept her script for human responsibility. They powerfully challenge the ordinary Christian explanation of who Jesus was and how Christ is related to God. But her point is much the same as mine, I think, though she says it differently: Christology that is true is not merely a more or less accurate metaphysical description, an account of the structure of being. Rather, a true Christology is an authentic articulation of the living Christ, embodied in the liberation community, acting, changing, accomplishing salvation together for each other, and in and for the world.

I want to lift up a third nourishing chunk along this route toward "our" Christology. Most of us have at least read in the multivolume *Gospel in Solentiname* by Ernesto Cardenal. For those who have not, I describe what he does. Meeting regularly with a small liberation community on an island in a lake in Nicaragua, this priest worked with them in reflection on gospel stories. The simple pattern, as it emerges in his offering of those sessions in his "gospels," is that after someone read a text aloud without comment, the members of the community—sitting together—told in a free and informal way what the text said to them. Sometimes, apparently, they heard a person's comment, and then went on. Sometimes they voiced agreement, disagreement, and correction or elaboration on what had been said. The priest participated but—in the published version of the talks—he did not *appear* to dominate or even lead. The group tended often, it seems to me, to give him the last word, however. (I would love to know what instructions he gave them, and to what extent the published versions express the actual conversations rather than Father Cardenal's editing.) However accomplished, the result is a rich and shaggy wrestling with the gospel, in which—from my perspective—the living Christ seems clearly to have been present and active.[29]

It was no part of that group's purpose to generate a Christology. I introduce these books, their experience, here because it is to communities somehow like theirs that I look for the Christology that is genuinely Wesleyan, genuinely feminist, truly "ours," to emerge.

I do wonder what it means that all three examples I chose were from the catholic—Roman or Episcopalian—side of our Christian tradition? I wonder what it means that I, a free-church theologian whose roots are deep in the conventical movement of the nineteenth-century pietist revival in Sweden, am making

these observations. I leave that speculation to someone else.

My intuition suggests that a Christology that is truly "ours" may inherit from these afore-cited "crumbs," and will more clearly than they bear the imprint of a corporate origin.

For one thing, its mode of expression is likely to be less linear and to convey a less settled or completed or decided atmosphere even than these innovative approaches. I would guess it will be a Christology with built-in "outward swinging doors" that recognizes that our Christ is the Christ of a liberation community more inclusive than has yet been built. Hans Küng's use of questions in *On Being a Christian* is one such including method.[30] So also are parabolic stories, as Sallie McFague has amply shown,[31] and as Marjorie Suchocki has illustrated to the great refreshment of readers of process theology.[32] The packet-form of corporate theological expression is another example of inclusive communication; Grailville's seminary quarters, as well as denominational women's divisions, have pioneered such modes of theological expression.[33]

"Our Christology" will not fear negation. Christian thought has a long tradition of rejecting error, though recent Wesleyan theology, at least of the predominant Methodist type, has not been willing to reject much explicitly. Thor Hall's survey, *The Evolution of Christology*, which I found a wonderful and including thesis, is nearly mute as regards what—if anything—he would reject.[34] As feminists and as Wesleyan theologians generating "our Christology," we will need to take authority from the Christ embodied among us, I suspect, to reject among other formulations the imperial Lord—as Heyward does—and the model-for-imitation Jesus, no matter how scripturally warranted these images may be.

Moreover, the necessary rejecting of some images will—in our Christology—be done in a mode radically different from that of the anathematizing clauses in the Nicean Confession of 325. It will also differ from wholesale rejection of viewpoints and viewers with whom we find fundamental disagreement. Because the purpose of our Christology is ever more adequate, ever more faithful, ever more true expression of the living Christ embodied in the liberation community, the negations of our Christology must be stated so as to leave open doors.

IV. Moving Toward Our Christology

Throughout this exploration I have not addressed the presuppositional questions of those who affirm the critique from radical feminists, who find the specific claims we make about Jesus Christ no more oppressive than the fact that we make any claims at all. They deplore *any* religious significance in this male, sometimes Lordly, sometimes self-sacrificing macho wimp who seems to command self-denigrating attitudes for those who relate to the Holy through him, and to pretty effectively prevent responsibility-taking in this world in ways that would humanize and restore the planet to creaturely livability. They rage in quite appropriate anger, it seems to me, against the horrors committed in Jesus' name against our fellow women who practiced the craft, against Jews, against nonconformers of all types. Our Christology will need to wrestle with that too.

One way we might fruitfully take a step in that direction is to listen to a practitioner of ancient women's wisdom as she and her coven have sought to reclaim it in this century. Though many of us are probably not ready to hear much of her religious system with appreciation, I think she can offer us wise guidance concerning the human dimension of communities of liberation.

In the sixth chapter of her book, *Dreaming the Dark*, Starhawk offers experientially informed counsel about building community and facilitating the life of groups so that genuine connections with each other can be forged within them that recognize each person's worth and promote critical self- and other-valuing. For her, the power of life is best named Immanence.

> Immanence means that each of us has inherent worth—yet we cannot feel self-worth because we believe it as a theological doctrine. We feel it when we connect with another person, when we can comfort someone in distress, ease someone's pain, do work that means something to us. We feel our own worth when we help shape the choices that affect us.
>
> To call forth power-from-within, to free ourselves, we must be willing to move beyond self-interest, to cease grabbing for the carrot and flinching from the stick. We must be willing to give away.[35].

I include this quotation because it expresses the paradox that outsiders miss when we hear about witch covens, often at least. We hear their advocacy of self-affirmation and of power-from-within, and we may interpret that—within our still-dualistic system—as meaning the design is self-absorbed, self-exalting, and other-ignoring. In studying Starhawk's book I find much to appreciate, and I commend it to us as we seek a whole, an embodied, Christology, specifically for the sound help she offers as to *how* to work in groups—what I have called communities of liberation in this paper, following Dr. Ruether's

cue — how to work in them so as to keep them creative at the points where both the Wesleyan classes and the feminist consciousness-raising groups bogged down and lost their sense of direction.

A moment ago I alluded to the image of Hansel and Gretel dropping crumbs to lead us on this journey toward our Christology. What about the cottage in the woods? What about the witch? Is it significant that I hope to find unexpected help in a twentieth-century practitioner of *wicca*?

In his theorizing about the demise of Wesleyan classes, Dean suggested that prayer groups had become a kind of pale substitute for classes and bands. In a similar sense I suggested that the softer notion of support groups had replaced the more disciplined challenge of consciousness-raising for feminists. And there is clearly an upsurge of growth and creativity in the arena of women's spirituality, in efforts to recover ancient goddess religions, in the popularizing of ritual witchcraft, and in practicing traditional women's ritual witchcraft and in practicing traditional women's wisdom. I do not suggest causal links, but must observe that the rise of interest in women's spirituality coincides roughly with the loss of direction and strength in consciousness-raising groups as entry points for feminist conviction and commitment.

I do not at all regard the rising interest in witchcraft as a wasted diffusing of energy, however, or as a trivializing of the impetus of some pure, original feminist vision. Rather, I see it as an effort—in Starhawk's version, at least —to focus the energy of feminism and guide it toward purposes the consciousness-raising groups had begun to explore. Besides the personal and spiritual work, feminists have been undertaking political action in a variety of modes, seeking to transform our culture in much the same way that eighteenth-century Wesleyans transformed theirs.

What if Wesleyan Christians who have had our particular thicket in our social woods cleared (razed) by a feminist consciousness could articulate our faith in the Holy in an embodied and continuously incarnate-able Christology? Then we might have a word to say about Jesus in the world that even a witch could hear as a sisterly communication of love.

NOTES

1. My title imitates the title of an article by Rosemary Radford Reuther, "Christology and Feminism: Can a Male Savior Help Women?" *Occasional Papers*, United Methodist Board of Higher Education and Ministry, I:13, 12-25-76.

2. Ibid., "Feminist Theology and Spirituality," *Beyond Domination: New Perspectives on Women and Philosophy*, Carol Gould, ed., (Totawa, N.J.: Rowman and Allanheld, 1984).

3. This is a statement in which my own faith interprets my own experience. I value the concurrence with such a statement by others. I do not offer it as dogma but as witness.

4. Here I think of social action organizations such as the National Organization for Women, the National Abortion Rights Action League, and the NOW Political Action Committee, and of publications such as ISIS, *Daughters of Sarah*, and ANIMA.

5. "Band Meetings," *Encyclopedia of World Methodism*, Nolan B. Harmon, gen. ed., vol. 1 (Nashville: United Methodist Publishing House, 1974), p. 212.

6. Ibid.

7. "Class Meetings," Elmer T. Clark, *Encyclopedia of World Methodism*, pp. 519-20.

8. "Methodist Churches," *Oxford Dictionary of the Christian Church*, Second Edition, F.L. Cross and E.A. Livingston, eds. (Oxford: Oxford University Press, 1974), p. 909.

9. I base this conclusion on the 1882 *Cyclopedia of Methodism* articles "Classes," and "Class Meetings," indicating class membership was still then a test of membership in Britain, and indicating no criticism of American Methodism for deviation from this, though noting that they were "not so strictly a test" as in England (p. 228). "Classes," in vol. 1, pp. 227-9 (Philadelphia: Louis H. Everts, 1882).

10. James D. Nelson, "United Methodist Heritage," Section I, paper C of the *Spiritual Formation Packet*, Nashville: Division of Ordained Ministry, Board of Higher Education and Ministry of The United Methodist Church, 1982, quoting from John Wesley, *J. Wesley, Sermons on Several Occasions*, ed., Albert Outler (London: Epworth Press, 1980), p. 181, and pp. 180-81.

11. "Classes," "Class-Leaders," "Class Meetings," *Cyclopedia of Methodism*, pp. 227-29.

12. William W. Dean, "The Methodist Class Meeting: Signs of its Decline," *Proceedings of the Wesleyan Historical Society*, 12/81, vol. 47, p.46.

13. Robert Currie, *Methodism Divided*, 1968, cited by Dean, op. cit., p. 43.

14. Henry Rack, "The Decline of the Class Meeting and the Problem of Church Membership in Nineteenth-Century Wesleyanism," *Proceedings of the Wesleyan Historical Society*, 273, vol. 39, p. 12 ff.

15. Dean, op.cit., pp. 43 ff.

16. Op.cit., p. 46.

17. Op.cit., p. 47.

18. Op.cit., p. 48.

19. "The Process of Consciousness Raising and the Formation of Support Groups," Untitled women's packet, American Baptist Convention, undated (approx. 1976), pp. 3-4.

20. Ibid., p. 2.

21. Carol Christ and Judith Plaskow, "Introduction," *Womanspirit Rising, A Feminist Reader in Religion* (San Francisco: Harper & Row, 1979); Ann Belford Ulanov, *Receiving Woman, Studies in Psychology and the Theology of the Feminine* (Philadelphia: Westminster Press, 1981); Rosemary Radford Reuther, *Sexism and God-Talk* (Boston: Beacon Press, 1983).

22. bell hooks, *Ain't I a Woman* (Boston: South End Press, 1982).

23. Gregory Baum, "Man Becoming: God in Secular Experience," in *Contemporary American Theologies, II*, ed., Deane William Ferm (New York: The Seabury Press, 1982), pp. 316-27.

24. Isabel Carter Heyward, *The Redemption of God, a Theology of Mutual Relation* (Washington, D.C.: The University Press of America, 1982), p. 6.

25. Ibid., p. 7.

26. Ibid.

27. Ibid., p. 31.

28. Ibid., p. 33.

29. Ernesto Cardenal, *The Gospel in Solentiname*, tr. Donald D. Walsh, 4 vols. (Maryknoll: Orbis Books, 1976, 1978, 1979, and 1982).

30. Hans Küng, *On Being a Christian*, tr. Edward Quinn (Garden City: Doubleday and Company, Inc., 1976).

31. Sallie McFague, *Speaking in Parables, A Study in Metaphor and Theology* (Philadelphia: Fortress Press, 1975), and *Metaphorical Theology, Models of God in Religious Language* (Philadelphia: Fortress Press, 1982).

32. Marjorie Hewitt Suchocki, *God, Christ, Church, A Practical Guide to Process Theology* (New York: Crossroads, 1982).

33. Packets of Grailville material may be obtained in many seminary libraries or from The Grail, Loveland, Ohio. Denominational women's divisions can supply their literature.

34. Thor Hall, *The Evolution of Christology* (Nashville: Abingdon Press, 1982).

35. Starhawk, *Dreaming the Dark* (Boston: Beacon Press, 1982), p. 96.

6. THE WOMEN PIONEERS
OF
EARLY METHODISM

Paul Wesley Chilcote

When Humphrey Clinker, the Methodist footman-preacher of Smollett's last and more mellowed novel, addressed a coach-house gathering, Melford and his uncle reacted with predictable hostility: "But if we were astonished to see Clinker in the pulpit, we were altogether confounded at finding all the females of our family among the audience . . . and all of them joined in the psalmody, with strong marks of devotion."[1] The gentlemen's shock, however, is only symptomatic of the great concern among the critics of Methodism who interpreted the movement's particular appeal to women as a revolutionary attack against a precariously stable society at its most vulnerable point.[2] In their minds, it was but a short step from the evangelical proclamation of freedom in Christ to the feminist plea for emancipation in society.

A common charge, leveled early against the Methodist women, therefore, was the neglect of domestic responsibilities. As early as 1740, the Rev. James Buller indicted Wesley for keeping the women in his Bristol society so busy with religious duties that they could not supplement their husbands' incomes during a period of great economic depression.[3] The early Methodists were also susceptible to the same criticism which had been leveled against the Quakers of the previous century, namely, that their societies consisted mainly, if not exclusively, of women. In 1741 William Fleetwood summarily dismissed these so-called perfectionists, observing that "for the most part, their attendants are silly *Women*."[4] In a scurrilous attack upon the character of Wesley and particular developments within Bristol Methodism, an anonymous critic estimated that three-quarters of Wesley's adherents were women.[5] Toward the end of the century a London bookseller, James Lackington, caustically wrote of his former spiritual leader: "I believe that by far the greatest part of his people are females; and not a few of them sour, disappointed old maids, with some others of a less prudish disposition."[6]

The fact which the adversaries of Methodism suggested in their diatribes against the movement becomes obvious when the evidence is closely examined. The Methodist societies were, for all intents and purposes, organizations of women. On Sunday, November 11, 1739, Wesley preached his first sermon in the ruins of an old foundery in London, which he had secured for the use of those who sought his spiritual direction. The following summer when dissension over Moravian quietism finally ruptured the Fetter Lane Society, Wesley noted the important consequences:

Our little company met at *The Foundery*, instead of Fetter Lane. About twenty-five of our brethren God hath given us already, all of whom think and speak the same thing; seven- or eight-and-forty likewise of the fifty women that were in band desired to cast in their lot with us.[7]

A little more than two years later, in April 1742, Wesley drew up the first list of the Foundery Society's sixty-six leaders, and in this significant group, women outnumbered the men forty-seven to nineteen.[8] A list of Select Society members in February 1744, containing the names of those Methodists who had received remission of sins and whose faith had been tested and proved, reflects a similar proportion of fifty-two women to twenty-five men.[9] The example of the Foundery Society with its two-to-one ratio of women to men is typical of early Methodism as a whole, both in its beginnings and throughout the eighteenth century.[10] There can be no doubt that women wielded tremendous influence during these formative years wherever Methodism was planted and flourished.[11]

Of even greater significance than the preponderance of women in the membership of the societies, however, is the fact that as Methodism began to expand, women were conspicuous as pioneers in the establishment of new societies. The proliferation of these Wesleyan cluster-groups was often the direct consequence of the activity of a woman or group of women. Women invited and hosted the preachers, founded prayer groups and societies on the basis of their own initiative, and propagated and maintained the faith. This fact profoundly affected the general attitudes of Wesley and his adherents concerning the place of women in the movement.

When Wesley was visiting the neighborhood of Halifax in the summer of 1742, Mrs. Holmes of Smith House, Lightcliffe, invited him to preach at her home.[12] Subsequently, Smith House became a chief center for religious revival and greatly contributed to the establishment of Methodism in that general vicinity. About the same time, Wesley honored the request of a poor widow named Goddard and made Chinley a resting-place for his itinerants who began regular preaching there.[13] Mary Allinson was the first to open her house to Methodist preachers in Teesdale;[14] the aunt of Mary Denny introduced Methodism to Maldon;[15] Mrs. Hosmer procured a room for preaching in Darlington;[16] and preaching was reinstated at Normanton only by means of an unnamed woman's persistence.[17]

The initial adherents to the evangelical message preached by Wesley and his itinerants, moreover, were very often women. The famous stone-mason preacher of the north, John Nelson, described the events leading to the introduction of Methodism to Leeds: "Now the people from every quarter have flocked to Bristol on the Sabbath, but as yet there came only three from Leeds—Mary Shent and two other women."[18] Converted under the first sermon they heard, these "three Marys," including Mary Weddale and Mary Maude, formed the nucleus of the first band established in that strategic industrial town, probably before the end of 1742.[19] Across the channel, Eliza Bennis, who later became a devoted correspondent and useful advisor to John Wesley on Irish affairs, was the first Methodist in Limerick, converted under the preaching of Robert Swindells, in 1749.[20]

Some women took the initiative in the actual formation of societies with no other authority than their own determination and sense of divine calling. Several years before Wesley's first visit to Macclesfield, Mary Aldersley opened her home called Shrigley-fold for religious services and was accustomed to meeting with her friends for prayer, reading of Scripture, and religious conversation.[21] In 1746 Elizabeth Blow crossed the Humber from Grimsby where she had been one of the earliest members and pioneered the founding of Methodism in Hull.[22] Mrs. Martha Thompson, a wealthy widow who possessed a considerable estate at Rufforth, not only opened her own home for preachers, but used her influence to obtain their admission into the cathedral city of York.[23]

Another Martha Thompson, of strikingly dissimilar background and circumstances from her namesake, is credited with the foundation of Methodism in Preston.[24] With the assistance of Sarah Crosby, who would shortly thereafter become the first woman preacher of Methodism, Mrs. Dobinson of Derby became the "principal instrument in introducing our preachers into that town."[25] And this she did in the face of much opposition and discouragement. In this pioneering work, a servant girl, a textile worker, or a housewife, was no less acceptable than a woman of social position and influence.[26]

Wealthy women, however, were able to commit not only their lives, but their resources, to the subsequent development and consolidation of the Methodist societies. The building of chapels was one such contribution. In Macclesfield, Elizabeth Clulow, together with George Pearson, secured a small preaching house for the infant society, and when expansion necessitated a larger chapel, Mrs. Clulow payed for its construction.[27] Mrs. Henrietta Gayer, wife of the clerk to the House of Lords for the Irish Parliament, was converted in 1772. She set apart a room in her house known as the "Prophet's Chamber" for the preachers, secured the erection of the first chapel in Lisburn in 1774, was instrumental in planning the construction of the Donaghadee chapel, and after her husband's death devoted the totality of his estate to Christian work.[28]

The first Methodist in Sevenoaks was Mrs. Amy George who had walked to Shoreham in order to invite Wesley to preach at her home, subsequently designated the "Pilgrim's Inn." She built a chapel at the back of her business premises which Wesley opened on December 12, 1774.[29] He was impressed with the great hall which Miss Harvey had built in her hometown of Hinxworth in Hertfordshire.[30] She had taken a lively interest in the prosperity of Methodism and built several other chapels at her own expense in Baldock, Stevenage, and Biggleswade, all of which she settled on the Methodist plan. At her death she left a legacy of three thousand pounds to support the Methodist cause.[31] Wesley maintained an intimate contact with these pioneers and patrons who were greatly respected within their societies. It was not uncommon for him to place reliance on such leaders who had proved themselves worthy of his trust, even in those areas traditionally dominated by men.[32]

The pioneering work of Mrs. Dorothy Fisher illustrates the formative influence exerted by a woman at all the various levels of a new society's development.[33] While her story comes from the last quarter of the eighteenth century, it is representative and serves as an example of how Methodism grew in its early days and how women quite often stood on the cutting edge of its expansion. Dorothy was converted under Wesley's preaching in London and joined the society there in 1779. About the year 1784 she moved to Great Gonerby in Lincolnshire, opened her house to preaching because of the great accommodation it afforded, and in 1786 purchased a small stone building to be fitted up for a chapel, principally at her own expense. A small group of Methodists at Sturton had heard of Dorothy's piety and thought that the state of religion in Lincoln could be immeasurably improved if she were to make her residence there.

The prime mover of this missionary venture, Sarah Parrot of Bracebridge, walked twenty-seven miles to Mrs. Fisher's home, placed the proposition before her, and Dorothy, concluding that it must be a call from God, consented, settled her affairs, moved to Lincoln, procured a suitable residence, and invited the traveling preachers to take the city into their round at the close of 1787. The following January, Wesley wrote to Lancelot Harrison expressing his hopeful expectations:

I am glad sister Fisher is settled at Lincoln, and that you have begun preaching there again. Hitherto it has been

A soil ungrateful to the tillers' toil;
But possibly it may now bear fruit.[34]

A small society was formed in an old lumber-room near Gowt's Bridge, consisting of four women, Mrs. Fisher, Sarah Parrot, Hannah Calder, and Elizabeth Keyley. The newly planted society did bear fruit, and Dorothy subsequently built a chapel with an adjoining residence which was later entrusted to the care of the Methodist Conference. Thus Methodism was established in that cathedral city, as it had been planted in many other places throughout the British Isles. The extent to which women were permitted to assume the initiative in the societies and function as pioneers and sustainers of the Methodist cause, often gave them a working equality with their male counterparts. The atmosphere created by their activities and witness became more and more conducive to the expansion of their roles.

NOTES

1. Tobias Smollett, *The Expedition of Humphrey Clinker* (Harmondsworth: Penguin Books, 1978), p. 169.
2. See Donald Henry Kirkham, "Pamphlet Opposition to the Rise of Methodism: The Eighteenth-century English Evangelical Revival Under Attack." Ph.D. dissertation, Duke University, 1973, pp. 217-28.
3. James Buller, *A Reply to the Rev. Mr. Wesley's Address to the Clergy* (Bristol: S. Farley, 1756), p. 25. See similar criticisms in *The Mock-Preacher: A Satyrico-Comical-Allegorical Farce. As it was Acted to a Crowded Audience at Kennington-Common, and many other Theatres With the Humours of the Mob* (London: C. Corbett, 1739), pp. 15-16; [Samual Weller], *The Trial of Mr. Whitefield's Spirit in Some Remarks upon his Fourth Journal, Published when he staid in England on Account of the Embargo* (London: T. Gardner, 1740), pp. 35-36; and *A Plain and Easy Road to the Land of Bliss. A Turnpike set up by Mr. Orator- - - - -; On which a man may travel more miles in one day, than on any other highway in forty years. With a dedication, such as never was, or will be, in vogue* (London: W. Nicholl, 1762), p. 65.
4. William Fleetwood, *The Perfectionists Examined; or Inherent Perfection in this Life, no Scripture Doctrine, To which is affix'd, the Rev. Mr. Whitefield's Thoughts on this Subject, in a Letter to Mr. Wesley* (London: J. Roberts, 1741), p. 2.
5. An Impartial Hand, *The Progress of Methodism in Bristol: or, The Methodist Unmask'd*, 2d ed. (Bristol: J. Watts, 1743), p. 20.
6. James Lackington, *Memoirs of the Forty-five First Years of the Life of James Lackington, the Present Bookseller in Finsbury Square, London. Written by Himself . . .*, new ed. (London: By the Author, 1794), p. 123. Cf. James Bate, *Quaker-Methodism; or A Confutation of the First Principles of the Quakers and Methodists. . . . In a letter to the Author, Concluding with an Address to the Free-Thinkers* (London: John Carter, [1740]).
7. July 23, 1740, Wesley, *Journal*, vol. 2, p. 371. On March 13, 1740, in a letter to Zinzendorf, the Moravian James Hutton wrote: "John Wesley and Charles Wesley, both of them, are dangerous snares to young women; several are in love with them. I wish they were once married to some good sisters, but I would not give them one of my sisters if I had many" (Ibid., 2:338). This proved to be a perennial problem for the dashing and well-educated itinerant priests. John was particularly concerned about the problematic consequences of such attractions. While this attraction of women to the Wesleys as men does in part explain the phenomenon of female preponderance, it is but a minute factor in the unfolding of events.
8. These earliest extant society lists are recorded in George J. Stevenson, *City Road Chapel, London, And Its Associates* (London: George J. Stevenson, [1872]), pp. 28-39. It is important to note that Stevenson incorrectly refers to these lists as "class lists" when in fact they are clearly "band lists." Prior to 1743 there were no "class lists." Many errors have sprung from this misnomer. When spoken of as "society" records, these lists properly refer to the "select society," i.e., the grouping together of the members of the "band societies."
9. The bands, at this time generally composed of six or seven members, were separated into four categories: single men, married men, single women, and married women. Fifty-seven of the eighty-five leaders in the list of band members for June 1745 were women.
10. The strength of this claim becomes increasingly evident upon examination of the extant society lists from this period. Early records of the society in Bristol afford corroborative evidence, a spot check of Wesley's manuscripts, dated September 29, 1770, revealing a total membership of 901 in 54 classes, composed of 592 women and 309 men, all illegible or questionable names being counted as men. The earliest list for the Frome Society, that of June 1759, contains the names of 25 women and 13 men. The occupations of the working women included card-setters (4), spinners (4), scribbler (1), shoe-maker (1), and map maker (1). [Stephen Tuck, *Wesleyan Methodism in Frome, Somersetshire* (Frome: Printed by S. Tuck, 1837), p. 35.] The earliest records extant, not merely for the Glamorgan Circuit, but for Methodism in Wales, are lists for the eleven societies formed in

that region prior to Wesley's death. Dated 1787, these lists include the names of 101 women and 49 men. The seven members of the Newport Society were all women. Idwal Lewis, "Early Methodist Societies in Glamorgan and Monmouthshire," *Bathafarn* 11 (1956): 57-59. Likewise, another Newport Society, on the Isle of Wight, was composed of only women according to the records of 1762. John B. Dyson, *Methodism in the Isle of Wight: Its Origin and Progress Down to the Present Time* (Ventnor, Isle of Wight: George M. Burt, 1865), pp. 60-61. Earlier that same year, on May 26, 1762, Wesley recorded that ". . . in the afternoon we got well to Galway [Ireland]. There was a small society here, and (what is not common) all of them were young women" (Wesley, *Journal*, 4:505). While exclusively female societies were rare, and there were exceptions to the general preponderance of women, such as the religious revival at Everton in 1759 which, according to Wesley, attracted three times as many men as women (*Journal*, 4:317-18) or the exclusively male societies of the Bradford area (W. W. Stamp, *Historical Notices of Wesleyan Methodism in Bradford and Its Vicinity* (Bradford: Henry Wardman, n.d.], pp. 62-63), the general impression of a large female majority in the membership throughout the British Isles remains. It is interesting also to note that Donald G. Mathews' examination of the old South revealed that about 64 percent of each congregation was female, a statistic which nearly matches that of early Methodism in Britain. See *Religion in the Old South* (Chicago: University of Chicago Press, 1977), pp. 102-24.

11. One must be cautious so as not to fall into a dangerous trap when analyzing and evaluating statistics regarding sex ratios within the Methodist societies. While records show that the membership of early Methodism was then (as possibly now) on a proportion of two women to one man, such numerical preponderance does not *necessarily* imply twice the influence. Despite the socio-religious impediments of the eighteenth century, however, the influence of women within Methodism, more often subliminal than apparent, was certainly pervasive. It is noteworthy, e.g., that Wesley's diaries throughout this early period indicate that he spent much more time with women than with men, and necessarily so. Whereas, in the balance, women *may* not have exerted an influence greater in proportion or quality to that of Methodist men, the great value which was placed upon their presence within the societies (in contrast to the general cultural attitude) carried with it an inherent power of affecting others.

12. June 2, 1742, Wesley, *Journal*, vol. 3, p. 16; cf. vol. 6, p. 16, 102; and vol. 3, p. 297 for a picture of this stately residence. James Everett says that "Mrs. Holmes was then apparently the only person in that neighbourhood, who ventured to brave the obliquy and hostility of the times." *Wesleyan Methodism in Manchester and Its Vicinity* (Manchester: Printed by the Executors of S. Russell, 1827), p. 52. Cf. *W.H.S.* 7 (1910): 169-73; John Simon, *John Wesley and the Methodist Societies* (London: Epworth Press, 1923), p. 76; and Schmidt, *Wesley*, vol. 2, p. 74.

13. Wesley, *Journal*, vol. 3, p. 142 n.

14. Anthony Steele, *History of Methodism in Barnard Castle and the Principal Places in the Dales Circuit* (London: George Vickers, 1957), p. 41.

15. Leslie F. Church, *The Early Methodist People* (London: Epworth Press, 1948), p. 40. Cf. Wesley, *Journal*, vol. 4, pp. 249, 289.

16. George Jackson, *Wesleyan Methodism in the Darlington Circuit* (Darlington: Printed and sold by J. Manley, 1850), p. 17. Cf. George Smith, *History of Wesleyan Methodism*, 2d ed., rev., 3 vols. (London: Longman, 1862), vol. 1, pp. 279-80.

17. Thomas Cocking, *The History of Wesleyan Methodism in Grantham and Its Vicinity: With Preliminary Observations on the Rise . . . of the Connexion* (London: Simpkin, Marshall, & Co., 1836), pp. 173-74, regarding the influence of Mary Kerry; cf. *Methodist Magazine*, 37 (1814): 188. For a representative selection of references to women who invited or hosted Methodist preachers, see Wesley, *Journal*, vol. 5, pp. 435, 447, 450, 473, 479; vol. 6, pp. 40-41, 52, 66, 283, 286. For the influence of Mary Carey of Donaghadee in the establishment of Irish Methodism, see C. H. Crookshank, *History of Methodism in Ireland*, 3 vols. (Belfast: R. S. Allen, Son & Allen, 1885), vol. 1, pp. 46-47; cf. vol. 1, pp. 200, 241, 252, 297, 407-8; vol. 2, pp. 44, 114-15.

18. Thomas Jackson, ed., *The Lives of the Early Methodist Preachers. Chiefly Written by Themselves*, 4th ed., 6 vols. (London: Wesleyan Conference Office, 1875), vol. 1, p. 60.

19. J. E. Hellier, "The Mother Chapel of Leeds," *Methodist Recorder Winter Number* 35 (Christmas 1894): 62-63; John Lyth, *Glimpses of Early Methodism in York and the Surrounding District* (York: William Sessions, 1885), p. 24; George West, *Methodism in Marshland* (London: Wesleyan Conference Office, [1886]), pp. 21-22; Smith, *History of Methodism*, vol. 1, p. 221. A similar society of three women was formed by Wesley in the village of Gamblesby between 1749 and 1751. See G. H. Bancroft Judge, "The Beginnings of Methodism in the Penrith District," *W.H.S.* 19, 7 (September 1934): 153-60. Cf. the account of the three women who formed the first society in Gonersby, in Cocking, *Methodism in Grantham*, pp. 143-44. For Ruth Blocker, the pioneer of Methodism in Briestfield, see John R. Robinson, *Notes on Early Methodism in Dewsbury, Birstal, and Neighbourhood* (Batley: J. Fearnsides & Sons, 1900), pp. 32-33.

20. C. H. Crookshank, *Memorable Women of Irish Methodism in the Last Century* (London: Wesleyan-Methodist Book-Room, 1882), pp. 20-30; Wesley, *Letters*, vol. 4, pp. 82, 220-21, 228; vol. 5, pp. 6, 24, 56, 137, 142, 150, 188, 190, 193, 242, 268, 283, 290, 298, 314, 321, 337, 343; vol. 6, pp. 6, 16, 23, 40, 55, 68, 76, 79, 243. Cf. Crookshand, *History of Methodism in Ireland*, vol. 1, pp. 48 and 240-41, 287; vol. 2, pp. 153-54 concerning other women pioneers.

21. Benjamin Smith, *The History of Methodism in Macclesfield* (London: Wesleyan Conference Office, 1875), pp. 17-19.

22. See *Methodist Magazine*, 60 (1837): 885-99, where a full account of the early history of Hull Methodism is given. Cf. J. H. Grubb, "The Conference Town," *Wesleyan Methodist Magazine*, 121 (1898): 483-94; George Lester, *Grimsby Methodism (1743–1889) and the Wesleys in Lincolnshire* (London: Wesleyan-Conference Book-Room, 1890), p. 48; Wesley, *Journal*, vol. 4, p. 20n; and John Simon, *John Wesley and the Advance of Methodism* (London: Epworth Press, 1925), p. 228.

23. Lyth, *Methodism in York*, pp. 53-54. Cf. *Arminian Magazine*, 6 (1983): 471, and Wesley, *Journal*, vol. 4, p. 66n. Lyth further notes that it was to the zeal, determination, and consistency of Hannah Harrison and Ruth Hall in particular that "the successful establishment of Methodism in this locality is greatly indebted" (p. 64). These two women later emerge in Methodist history as influential women preachers.

24. John Taylor, *The Apostles of Fylde Methodism* (London: T. Woolman, 1885), pp. 8-17; J. W. Laycock, *Methodist Heroes of the Great Haworth Round, 1734–1784* (Keighley: Wadsworth & Co., The Rydal Press, 1909), pp. 198-200; W. Pilkington, *The Makers of Wesleyan Methodism in Preston* (London: Charles H. Kelly, 1890), p. 14; W. F. Richardson, *Preston Methodism's 200 Years* (Preston: n.p., 1975), pp. 9-15; and Maldwyn Edwards, *My Dear Sister: The story of John Wesley and the women in his life* (Manchester: Penwork (Leeds) Ltd., n.d.), pp. 45-50.

25. A. Seckerson, "An Account of Mrs. Dobinson," *Methodist Magazine*, 26 (1803): 557-66. Cf. 24 (1801): 274; 53 (1830): 786.

26. See Wellman J. Warner, *The Wesleyan Movement in the Industrial Revolution* (London: Longmans, Green, and Co., 1930), pp. 264-65.

27. Smith, *Methodism in Macclesfield*, pp. 45-46, 149-50. Cf. Tyerman, *Wesley*, vol. 3, p. 8. This chapel was completed

in 1764, and it is important to note that the society placed its trust in the judgment and integrity of this woman. The deed was transferred to Martha Ryle from her husband on December 30, 1780, with a trust deed properly executed soon thereafter.

28. Crookshank, *Memorable Woman,* pp. 36, 116-24; and *History of Methodism in Ireland,* vol. 1, pp. 286-87.
29. Thomas Brackenbury, "Methodism in Sevenoaks," *Methodist Recorder, Winter Number* 41 (Christmas 1900): 91-93; Wesley, *Journal,* vol. 3, p. 265; vol. 6, p. 53. The appellation "Pilgrim's Inn" became a familiar epithet designating houses of hospitality for the Methodist itinerants. See F. F. Bretherton, *Early Methodism in and around Chester, 1749–1812* (Chester: Phillipson & Golder, 1903), pp. 62-65, regarding the home and hospitality of Mrs. Mary Lowe, and her memoirs in *Methodist Magazine,* 32 (1809): 187-91, 229-39.
30. Wesley, *Journal,* vol. 6, p. 362; vol. 7, pp. 35, 40, 216, 337.
31. *Wesleyan Methodist Magazine,* 52 (1829): 289-92; cf. Wesley, *Journal,* vol. 6, p. 362 n. According to Bretherton, Mrs. Mary Bealey of Radcliffe near Manchester "built at her own expense what was considered to be at the time the prettiest Chapel in Methodism" (*Methodism in Chester,* pp. 194-95). It was not uncommon for a woman of means to erect a chapel at the scene of her conversion, as did Miss Richardson of Ryefield. See Crookshank, *History of Methodism in Ireland,* vol. 2, p. 160; cf. *Wesleyan Methodist Magazine* 67 (1844): 633-35.
32. In 1777 Wesley entrusted the building program of the chapel at High Wycombe to his faithful correspondent Hannah Ball. See Wesley, *Letters,* vol. 6, p. 258; and Joseph Cole, *Memoir of Miss Hannah Ball, of High-Wycombe, in Buckinghamshire. With Extracts from Her Diary and Correspondence,* rev. & enl. by John Parker (London: Published by John Mason, 1839), pp. 137-48.
33. Abraham Watmough, *A History of Methodism in the Neighbourhood and City of Lincoln* (Lincoln: Printed by R. E. Leary, sold by J. Mason, 1829), pp. 21-25; Cocking, *Methodism in Grantham,* pp. 217-26. Cf. Wesley, *Journal,* vol. 7, pp. 412-13; *Letters,* vol. 7, pp. 326-27; and *Wesleyan Methodist Magazine,* 48 (1825): 290.
34. Ibid., p. 24. This letter of January 18, 1788 apparently escaped the attention of Telford in his edition of Wesley's letters. The original was in the hands of Harrison's daughter, Mrs. Belton of Walkeringham, when Watmough produced his history.

7. CONTEMPORARY ISSUES AND IMPLICATIONS FOR WOMEN IN LAY AND CLERGY MINISTRIES

Mozella G. Mitchell

Much has been studied, written, and discussed orally about the historical situation of women and the new trends in feminist theology and ministry in general. Practical application of findings, theories, and solutions in specific religious groups and denominations naturally seems to be the next stage. This application in Methodism will no doubt proceed from the local church situation to the district and regional and national organizations of the denominations or church communions (or vice versa), and, perhaps, spread throughout Methodism in general. Although the fundamental issues and problems facing women in theology and ministry in the church are the same (confronting the patriarchal set-up and overcoming the obstacles it has created), the manifestations of these issues and problems are different even in the various Methodist church bodies (A.M.E., U.M.C., A.M.E.Z., and C.M.E.); and the solutions, therefore, must necessarily be determined by the peculiarities of the situation. I would like to approach the issues and problems in Zion Methodism (A.M.E.Z.) from my perspective as a pastor and student and teacher of religion and consider the application of some of the theories and solutions offered by various feminist ministers, scholars, and leaders.

As a black church in the Wesleyan tradition, Zion Methodism has much to be proud of, including rich spiritual and organizational and governmental resources. This it has in common with other Methodist bodies, as well as many problems and difficulties concerning women in ministry and other leadership positions. As is true of other Methodist bodies, it is a strongly patriarchal society, and patriarchy in it, as in other black churches, takes on a peculiar flavor. One might say that it is more crucial to the very fabric and survival of this branch of the church than most others. The first woman was ordained deacon in the A.M.E.Z. church on May 20, 1894 (Mrs. Julia A. Foote); and the first woman ordained elder was Mary Jane Small on May 23, 1898.[1] Yet the patriarchal system naturally perpetuates a very low key role of women in the church and ministry.

Within the last decade trained women minis-ters and pastors and lay leaders have increased tremendously (at least two women presiding elders have been appointed and two general officers and a national lay council president elected.) However, along with this progress in the leadership function of women, which is tokenism at most, goes the intensification of obstacles and problems faced by women in the patriarchal system. The effectiveness of women's leadership is inhibited by the patriarchal struc-ture of the church, locally and nationally, and the attitudes instilled by both the organizational structure and the language of liturgies and litanies and general church disciplines (almost all of which are drawn from the Wesleyan tradi-tion).

After serving as assistant and associate pastor for ten years in four conferences (Western New York, Virginia, Georgia-South Georgia, and South Florida), I was appointed to pastor a small congregation. From my previous experiences and from insights gained from serving in that position for almost two years, I have discovered that, as Rosemary Ruether and others so well state, being accepted in token numbers in a highly patriarchal set-up creates a tremendous strain on women in both lay and clergy leader-ship positions. Trying to measure up to stan-dards controlled and set by patriarchal symbols of dress, decorum, and performance; and trying to function in the hierarchical relationship dominated by male authority figures are unnec-essarily draining and psychologically damaging to women. A cultural gap exists here. It is like black people trying to practice religion in a white church according to the worship styles of white religion, or vice versa. Unless some fundamental changes are made to undermine the completely patriarchal structure of the church, women leaders will not continue to survive in it, nor will the church prosper.

Some of the innumerable questions raised in my mind concerning the church are: How do women minister to an overwhelmingly female church? How do women overcome the sexual dependencies that usually accompany the pater-nal role played by male pastors? How do women overcome the numerical imbalance of women over men in the church? How do we retain men and women in an equitable relationship in the church (or how do we achieve this)? How do we overcome the lack of faith in women's leadership? How can lay and clergy women develop their ministries in partnership rather than in partisanship?

I am convinced that the answer to most, if not all, of these questions, and many others not listed here, lies largely in modifying the traditional language and organizational structures of the church. In relation to Zion Methodism, I have reference to the language of liturgies and church discipline concerning membership, baptism, beliefs; and organizational structures such as class leaders, stewards, stewardesses, trustees, deacons, deaconesses, and the like. Revision of these patterns is necessary for the accommodation of full humanity in the Wesleyan church tradition.

Certain solutions offered by some feminist scholars and ministers seem highly desirable and would probably work in particular churches or among particular groups, but would be hardly viable in the black church of the Wesleyan tradition. Yet other suggestions among various feminist religious professionals, with some modification, may be found quite helpful in bringing about the needed changes in the patriarchal church structure for the accommodation of more effective participation of both women and men in leadership functions in the church.

Before getting into any of these suggestions, I would like to point to certain pecularities of the black woman minister and lay leader's situation in regard to the black church. In spite of the almost relentless patriarchal leadership of the black church, it has in it intrinsically a tradition of spiritual and physical liberation upon which the black woman minister or lay leader can depend and from which she can draw strength for her mission. As the black church has always found the good news of the gospel of Jesus Christ "liberating from every societal binding," so the black woman minister or lay leader easily appeals to this tradition in the church for liberation from the patriarchal binding. Leotine Kelly is right in asserting that "there is no way for a black woman to have understood the Christian witness of her people, who received the message of salvation from the very persons who enslaved them, without affirming her personhood sexually as well as racially."[2] Kelly, of course, has reference to the aware black women in the church. Naturally, all were not aware of this tradition.

Furthermore, the black church, whether in the Wesleyan or other traditions, is the lifeblood of the black community. "The social dimension is clear: God is a God of love and justice. Jesus is the liberating word of God. The preaching then relates itself to social and political issues. That which is 'too controversial' for white pulpits is imperative for the Black church."[3] Thus, the black woman minister or lay leader finds her sustenance here, and though she must confront and destroy the evils of patriarchy in the church in order to establish a viable leadership, she must not destroy the fiber of that institution. It is very intricately interwoven with family structure, social prestige, and community development and stability. Therefore, it is a very delicate situation both psychologically, economically, and socially. Any sudden overturning of practices and procedures based upon this structure would be disastrous to both the black woman seeking acceptance and authenticity as a religious authority and to the church and community in general.

Rosemary Ruether offers some penetrating and valuable insight into the process of depatriarchalization of the church. She speaks of transforming local churches into liberation communities where "women pastors or women and men in team ministry share a vision of the Gospel as liberation from patriarchy" and where feminism is integrated into the understanding of being church, and where this is reflected in language, ministerial form, and social commitment.[4] These are excellent suggestions and are already being carried out by some persons.[5] They may also be workable to an extent in the black church.

However, Ruether's suggestion of creating autonomous feminist base communities, which serve as a vehicle for developing a community of liberation from sexism, may cause insoluable problems for the black church and community. The effect may be alienating and completely disruptive. And whereas the notions of mutual empowerment, the dismantling of clericalism and ecclesiastical hierarchy as a means of liberation from patriarchy make perfect sense, these would be extremely difficult, and perhaps detrimental, to the black community if they were attempted in any radical sense.[6] Black people have learned too long and too well their dependency upon the patriarchal system. The process of change would be very slow at best.

On the issue of clerical hierarchy, I find myself torn between Ruether and Patricia Park, who claims that "authority is necessary in the institutional church. In liturgy of any kind, one must feel that he or she serves in a capacity of representation in order for the liturgy itself to have authenticity."[7] I am afraid that this is the way most black church persons feel, and it would be murder to tear them away from such a notion. I am also impressed by Park's insight that, finding it difficult to establish her own source of authority with the institution, over the years she sees that it has come from the lay people of the church and their affirmation of her ministry and from her own faith. This may take a long time, and perhaps we cannot wait for it, but it must be more genuine and satisfying. But the question is, Does it undermine patriarchy? Probably not.

I am very much impressed by the practiced approach of Lora Gross.[8] She works successfully as co-pastor of a Lutheran church and co-director of Lutheran Metropolitan Ministries in her city. Along with Ruether and others, Gross rejects patriarchal institutions as being "ordered along hierarchical 'chain of command' or 'lines of authority' rather than being communal, as being exclusive rather than inclusive." In them is "a conscious or unconscious belief in the basic superiority of men and inferiority of women" which "inevitably affects the convictions we hold about the meaning of community, about nature, the mission of church to society, issues of justice, perceptions of God and the divine purpose" (p. 139). No one can deny the truth of this insight, and numerous ways can be cited by which it is proven in our experience.

Explaining the damaging effects of that system on both men and women and on the society, Gross draws from her experience in working in dual ministry with a male to demonstrate the positive results of an alternative to the patriarchal practice—"equalitarian balance in female-male teams" of service. Through her experience she envisions an "empowerment which comes through an embodied maleness and femaleness as a means by which we seek each other not as opposites but as sisters and brothers coming together as human neighbors."[9] If successfully tried, her model would overcome the unhealthy situations of powerless women seeking identity through powerless men, powerless men seeking identity through empowered women, powerless women seeking identity through empowered women, and replace these with empowered women and empowered men in reciprocal interchange. In the same manner, female-female competition and rivalry may be overcome and "authentic affiliation between women and women" can take place, resulting in empowered women in "reciprocal interchange" with one another.[10]

I find Gross' model highly encouraging for the local church in terms of developing shared lay offices, as well as ministerial, between men and women as against the sharp distinctions in male and female roles built into the offical structure of Zion Methodism derived from the Wesleyan system. All of the lay and ministerial offices in traditional Methodism were conceived and designed for men, except the office of deaconess, which was designed expressly for women. These include elders, deacons, exhorters, class leaders, stewards, trustees, and so on. Class leaders, for instance, were described as "men of sound, fervent, enlightened piety." Stewards were described as "men of solid piety and sound judgement."[11] Later methods created another office for women called stewardesses. All of this was done in a strongly patriarchal setting in which male-female superiority-inferiority status was acceptable and normative.

But today's church can no longer function with these offices as defined. The church is predominantly, and in some cases overwhelmingly, female, which means that women must fill these traditionally male roles, often along with or instead of men, in a situation which in the long run may be psychologically damaging. Either these traditional offices must be reconceived today to encourage a male-female equitable relationship of service, as Gross described, or abolished and replaced by new equitably conceived offices where men and women may serve in team relationships with one another and develop their leadership autonomously.

Similarly, the language of liturgies and disciplines must be changed to be inclusive of both genders. The titles "deaconess" and "stewardess" must be abolished and the positions revised to allow for the equal participation of men and women. These are changes that must be instituted at the General Conference level and filtered down through annual and district conference, into the local churches. Once women begin to get the feel of being included in the language structure describing disciplines and functions, they will gradually abandon the sense of role differentiation. Eventually, they will feel empowered and no longer find difficulty in assuming "provocative leadership outside their traditional roles and relegated areas."[12] Similarly, male members of congregations will be led to abandon the sense of exclusive male prerogative and positions of authority. Consequently, the problem will resolve itself where presently female ministers who attempt to develop their own leadership styles run the risk of "threatening male leadership and authority, and in some cases even a man's concept of his masculinity."[13]

To conclude, only this week I have been confronted with an incident at my church which has convinced me more thoroughly than ever of the perversity and aberrations resulting from the system of patriarchy in the church. A self-styled male "evangelist," an unemployed drifter who refuses to work, claiming that he is the "prophet of God" who is supposed to be fed and clothed and housed by church members in obedience to God's word, has been stalking our congregation and accosting them on occasion about their refusal to "obey God" and give him assistance. Before he exposed all of this about himself, several months back I convinced my people to give him $15 and a meal or two to help him on his way. Later he returned and has since been trying to convince me and my congregation that God has sent no women to preach or pastor. He has been in jail numerous times for trespassing.

Recently, finding no place to stay, he moved in on the screened-in porch of our education building and refused to leave because he was "told by God" to come there. Still he has been constantly condemning the people and their woman pastor. He has destroyed all sympathy for himself among my people, and he has made it plain that he will certainly not "hear" anyone but God. Clearly, he is insane, and we have had to have him arrested, and we padlocked the door. But this is an extreme case of the perversion of patriarchy, for this man carries a big Bible, patterns himself much after the prophets of old, and quotes the passages of Scripture that support his antifemale position and boosts his male ego. Needless to say, this man is an embarrassment to the whole church, both male and female. But the sickness that has obsessed him is present in varying degrees throughout the church membership worldwide. Even one of the policemen who came to arrest him for trespassing on our property agreed with him that "God didn't necessarily send no woman to pastor a church," but he said, "This lady here is given the authority to ask you to vacate the premises."

It is clear that we have an enormous task before us, and we have begun none too soon.

NOTES

1. W. J. Walls, *The African Methodist Episcopal Zion Church: Reality of the Black Church* (Charlotte, N.C.: AMEZ Publishing House, 1974), pp. 111ff.
2. Leotine Kelly, "Preaching in the Black Tradition," in Judith L. Weidman, ed., *Women Ministers: How Women are Redefining Traditional Roles* (New York: Harper & Row, 1981), pp. 67-76.
3. Ibid., p. 74.
4. Rosemary Ruether, *Sexism and God-Talk: Toward a Feminist Theology* (Boston: Beacon Press, 1983), pp. 201-2.
5. See Lora Gross, "The Embodied Church," pp. 135-57; and Linda McKreinan-Allen and Ronald J. Allen, "Colleagues in Marriage and Ministry," pp. 169-82, in *Women Ministers* (New York: Harper & Row, 1981).
6. Ruether, *Sexism and God-Talk,* pp. 205-10.
7. Patricia Park, "Women and Liturgy," in *Women Ministers,* pp. 76-87.
8. Gross, "The Embodied Church," pp. 135-57.
9. Ibid., pp. 144-46.
10. Ibid., pp. 146-53.
11. James Porter, *Compendium of Methodism,* rev. Daniel Dorchester (New York: Eaton and Mains, 1897), p. 327.
12. Gross, "The Embodied Church," p. 152.
13. Ibid., p. 150.

8. A BLACK FEMINIST CRITIQUE
OF FEMINIST THEOLOGY

Emilie M. Townes

On one of our visits to Daytona Beach I was eager to show my daughters some of my early haunts. We sauntered down the long street from the church to the riverfront. This had been the path of the procession to the baptismal ceremony in the Halifax River, which I had often described to them. We stopped here and there as I noted the changes that had taken place since that far-off time. At length we passed the playground of one of the white public schools. As soon as Olive and Anne saw the swings, they jumped for joy. "Look, Daddy, let's go over and swing!" This was the inescapable moment of truth that every black parent in America must face soon or late. What do you say to your child at the critical moment of primary encounter?

"You can't swing in those swings."

"Why?"

"When we get home and have some cold lemonade I will tell you." When we were home again, and had had our lemonade, Anne pressed for the answer. "We are home now, Daddy. Tell us."

I said, "It is against the law for us to use those swings, even though it is a public school. At present, only white children can play there. But it takes the state legislature, the courts, the sheriffs and policemen, the white churches, the mayors, the banks and businesses, and the majority of white people in the state of Florida—it takes all these to keep two little black girls from swinging in those swings. That is how important you are! Never forget, the estimate of your own importance and self-worth can be judged by how many weapons and how much power people are willing to use to control you and keep you in the place they have assigned to you. You are two very important little girls. Your presence can threaten the entire state of Florida."[1]

All theologies of liberation are theological reflection on the assignation of place. They attempt, from a particular context, to critique society as well as the church and traditional theology. This critique is designed to be a more faithful witness to the kingdom of God.

Feminist theology attempts to articulate this faithful witness through a call for the re-imaging of the roles of men and women in the church as well as in secular society. This witness does not accept the place we either allow ourselves to assume due to social mores and strictures or to which we may be assigned by those same forces. Feminist theology, at its best, attempts to be nonsexist, nonracist, nonclassist, nonhomophobic.

However, as a black feminist theologian/minister/ethicist, I find much of feminist theology lacking when placed within the context of the struggle for survival by black people, and particularly when placed within the context of black women.

Perhaps the most disturbing feature of feminist theology is that it lacks praxis. For a theology of liberation, this is a major methodological error. To be born a woman, or born black or of any other ethnic/racial group, does not insure that the woman will either explore her experience or articulate it. Further, it does not insure that the woman has an experience which lends itself to inclusivity in theological reflection.

An example of this flaw in feminist thought is Mary Daly. Although she now considers herself a post-Christian feminist, her latest book, *Gyn/Ecology*, has influenced a great deal of feminist theological reflection. The following is an excerpt of an open letter to Daly written by Audre Lorde:

> When I started reading *Gyn/Ecology*, I was truly excited by the vision behind your words, and nodded my head as you spoke in your first passage of myth and mystification. Your words on the nature and function of the Goddess, as well as the ways in which her face has been obscured, agreed with what I myself have discovered in my searches through African myth/legend/religion for the true nature of old female power.
>
> So I wondered, why doesn't Mary deal with Afrekete as an example? Why are her goddess-images only white, western-european, judeo-christian? Where was Afrekete, Yemanje, Oyo and Mawulisa? Where are the warrior-goddesses of the Vodun, the Dohomeian Amazons and the warrior-women of Dan? Well, I thought, Mary has made a conscious decision to narrow her scope and to deal only with the ecology of western-european women.
>
> Then I came to the first three chapters of your second passage, and it was obvious that you were dealing with non-european women, but only as

victims and preyers-upon each other. I began to feel my history and my mythic background distorted by the absence of any images of my foremothers in power. Your inclusion of african genital mutilation was an important and necessary piece in any consideration of female ecology, and too little has been written about it. But to imply, however, that all women suffer the same oppression simply because we are women, is to lose sight of the many varied tools of patriarchy. It is to ignore how those tools are used by women without awareness against each other.

To dismiss our black foremothers may well be to dismiss where european women learned to love. As an african-american woman in white patriarchy, I am used to having my archetypal experience distorted and trivialized but it is terribly painful to feel it being done by a woman whose knowledge so much matches my own. As women-identified women, we cannot afford to repeat these same old destructive, wasteful errors of recognition.

When I speak of knowledge, as you know, I am speaking of that dark and true depth which understanding serves, waits upon, and makes accessible through language to ourselves and others. It is this depth within each of us that nurtures vision.

What you excluded from *Gyn/Ecology* dismissed my heritage and the heritage of all other non-european women, and denied the real connections that exist between all of us.[2]

It is more accurate to state that the praxis utilized in feminist theology belies the larger issues of racism and class bias. Both forms of oppression are operative in feminist theology.

Too much of feminist theological reflection of late, does not include the struggle feminists in the church have among themselves on the issue of race. Feminist theology is moving toward a prescriptive stance without adequately acknowledging and critiquing *and* eradicating the chauvinism within itself.

Black and white feminists often talk past one another. Elements of romanticism, guilt, anger, insensitivity, and pain are not dealt with. Dialogue, the little there is, is stunted. The particular concerns of women of color are often ignored in a drive to articulate the roles of men and women.

Black women *begin* at a different point from their other sisters of color and white women. The milieu of the black church and larger black secular community is different. Black women are the oppressed among the oppressed. The layering that black women in the church must cut through requires a different stamina, a different analysis, a different feminist theological methodology.

Coming from the black community and the black church (and the pulpit) means that black women understand the need for clarity in their speech, action, and thought. Feminist theology has said and continues to say little to us. Too much of feminist theology is caught up in academic semantics that have absolutely no relation to the actual battle to survive black women are engaged in and called to lead their churches in.

Often, the reply black women hear is "It is not my experience as a white woman, so I do not wish to offend you by presuming to understand what it is like to be a black woman." The experience of participating in maintaining a racist society *is* the experience of white women as well as all of us. Feminist theological reflection that does not take into account the individual's participation in maintaining sinful structures, ceases to be theological reflection.

Feminist theology must begin to take seriously the need to build coalitions within the women's community. More black women have not joined the feminist movement, because it is not serious about unity within diversity. We do not acknowledge our divisions, or if we do, we allow them to be divisive.

Women of color have much to gain from white women's learnings of dealing with a male power structure. But, black women refuse to join any movement which does not allow us to articulate the plight of black women in a multilayered society in which we are at the bottom. We begin from different places. There are differences in how we look at society and the paths of mobility open to us. To admit that we are not all the same is not to say that we are not all of the body.

The task is to be self-critical in our inclusivity. As Jacqueline Grant so eloquently states:

Having a stake or an investment, black women (and other black Third World women) stand in a unique position to demand the self-criticism of the various perspectives and groups in order to insure wholistic analysis.[3]

Further she cites a poem by Lucille Clifton and writes,

In this poem, Clifton draws attention to the continuity between Miss Ann of the nineteenth century and the first half of the twentieth century and Ms Ann of the contemporary women's liberation movement.

The prophetic church will meet this situation head on rather than ignoring the pains and wounds of black women in hopes that the problem will magically go away by invoking some false sense of reconciliation.[4]

To be sure, black women and all women of color need to begin to put their theology in writing. Too often we are caught up in the doing of theology and forget the importance of writing down our thoughts, strategies, and actions. All of us—black and white—need to take seriously the diversity among us and confront (face together) the systems that oppress us as well as those in which we are oppressors.

The goal is liberation. Our paths may be separate, but through meaningful coalition-building we can acknowledge, understand, and celebrate our differences then move, together, toward our common goal, each with her own experience and each from the experience of her sister.

NOTES

1. Howard Thurman, *With Head and Heart* (New York: Harcourt, Brace & Jovanovich, 1979), p. 97.
2. Audre Lorde, "An Open Letter to Mary Daly," in *This Bridge Called My Back: Writings by Radical Women of Color,* ed. Cherrie Moraga and Gloria Anzaldua (Watertown: Persephone Press, 1981), pp. 94-95.
3. Jacqueline Grant, "Tasks of a Prophetic Church," in *Theology in the Americas: Detroit II Conference Papers* ed. Cornel West, Caridad Guidote, and Margaret Coakley (Maryknoll: Orbis Books, 1982), pp. 139-140.
4. Ibid.

9. THE TRANSFORMED LIFE IN JESUS CHRIST: TOWARD A FEMINIST PERSPECTIVE IN THE WESLEYAN TRADITION

Rosemary Keller

"Theology for John Wesley," writes Thomas Langford in *Practical Divinity: Theology in the Wesleyan Tradition*, "was intended to transform life. Always in the service of presenting the gospel, theology was to underwrite the proclamation of the grace of God given in Jesus Christ for the redemption of all people."[1]

Throughout his ministry of preaching and teaching, John Wesley sought that converts experience new life, indeed that their lives be transformed through Christ's saving power. The reception of grace and the experience of redemption express the essence of new life in Christ in the powerful and compelling way which Reformation thinkers such as Wesley saw as essential.

New and transformed life on earth is also the goal of feminist theology, approximately a decade old in its "classic" formulations. It seeks to set women and men free from binding and constricting roles which society and religion have prescribed for them for centuries. To be freed from the sins of sexism, in Letty Russell's words, would be "steps on the road toward a *human liberation of people*, becoming free in conformity with the authentic humanness of the Son of Man."[2]

The transformed life is central to the thought of both John Wesley and feminist theology. Their formulations of its meaning are quite different, however. A study of both theological perspectives raises these questions: How do they compare and contrast? Are they mutually exclusive or complementary? Would it be possible to hold a feminist perspective in the Wesleyan tradition? Has there actually been such a perspective, even though unnamed, within the United Methodist past? What are the implications of a feminist viewpoint for the denomination as we enter the third century of United Methodism?

This paper will respond to some of the above questions. It seeks to define the meaning of the transformed life in Jesus Christ as it emerges in both theological disciplines, focusing on the sermons of John Wesley and the work of some contemporary feminist theologians. It advances speculations of what might be incorporated into a feminist perspective in the Wesleyan tradition. The primary purpose of the paper is to stimulate our corporate thinking in order that the emergence of feminist theology might bring us to a new place in theological construction within United Methodism and expand our opportunities to formulate a critical tradition and envision a future of faith and action.

I. A Wesleyan Perspective

In the 1746 preface of his *Sermons on Several Occasions*, John Wesley states that his purpose is to bring together "the substance of what I have been preaching for between eight and nine years last past."[3] The forty-four sermons in the volume contain all points of doctrine on which, in his own judgment, he had expounded, sometimes numerous times each day, throughout those years.

Through these sermons, Wesley is identified foremost as an evangelical preacher. The "essentials of true Religion" come together in a highly focused central message of "plain truth for plain people."[4] One sermon after another reads as a variation on the theme of transformation of human life on this earth. His primary concern is for persons to respond to God's gift of grace in Jesus Christ by making a personal choice for the way of God in Christ over the ways of the world—and then proceeding to live out a life of holiness in accord with that commitment. The decision called for is between being an almost Christian or an altogether Christian, being asleep or awake, being a "natural man" or experiencing new birth, being a dead Christian or being born again in Christ. One lives either in the spirit of bondage or the spirit of adoption, is spiritually dead or spiritually reborn, commits him or herself to the love of the world and earthly values or to the love of God and neighbor.

Wesley's understanding of transformation is rooted in the personal relationship of the individual to God in Christ. Its fundamentals are spelled out in the sermon on "The New Birth."[5] The central message is conveyed in the five words of his text: "Ye must be born again" (John 3:7).

The grace of God, which is always primary, comes to human beings through the experiences of justification and salvation or new birth. As doctrines, they convey what God did *for* us, forgave our sins, and what God does *in* us, gave us new life. The Christian must be born again to be restored to God's image, primarily a moral image of righteousness and holiness, whereby the new being exemplifies God's loving nature of justice, mercy, and truth in all relationships.

One must be born again to put on the image of God because all descendents of the first Adam came into this world spiritually dead. Though made in God's image, God gave Adam and all heirs the ability to stand on their own feet. Thus, their fall was real, issuing in a state of sinfulness caused by "man's" pride and self-will. To cast off this image of the devil, which we bear both corporately and individually, new birth is essential. Spiritual rebirth is vividly described as analogous to natural birth: one's spiritual senses are within him or her but are locked up, just as one has eyes and ears but cannot see and hear until the actual event of physical birth. Wesley sums up the transformation of new birth:

> From hence it manifestly appears, what is the nature of the new birth. It is that great change which God works in the soul when He brings it into life; when He raises it from the death of sin to the life of righteousness. It is the change wrought in the whole soul by the almighty Spirit of God when it is 'created anew in Christ Jesus'; when it is 'renewed after the image of God in righteousness and true holiness'; when the love of the world is changed into the love of God; pride into humility; passion into meekness; hatred, envy, malice, into a sincere tender, disinterested love of all mankind. In a word, it is that change whereby the earthly, sensual, devilish mind is turned into the 'mind which was in Christ Jesus.' This is the nature of the new birth: 'so is every one that is born of the Spirit.'[6]

While the transformed life is understood, first, through the unequivocal either/or decision, Wesley also delineates the spiritual and psychological changes which result in new birth through three stages of conversion: the natural, legal, and evangelical "man." His three sermons, "The Spirit of Bondage and of Adoption," "Awake, Thou That Sleepest" (the only sermon of Charles Wesley's included in the forty-four), and "The Almost Christian" are particularly helpful in understanding these distinctions.[7]

The natural man exists in a deep sleep of the soul, characterized by darkness, blindness, and false peace and security, born of ignorance of one's real condition. Insensible to his or her fallen nature, the "poor unawakened sinner . . . sees *no necessity* for the *one thing needful*: even that inward universal change, that 'birth from above,' . . . full of disease, as he is, he fancies himself in perfect health. . . . He says, 'Peace! Peace' while the devil, as 'a strong, man armed,' is in full possession of his soul."[8]

In the natural state, he or she may convey the form of godliness, being quiet, rational, or inoffensive, esteemed by the world. The person's condition is like that of the Pharisee, as he justifies himself to God and labors to be righteous. The outward cup is clean while the inside is filthy. One sins willingly, dreaming of worldly happiness and fearful to ever question the state of the soul.[9]

Before experiencing new life, "the almost Christian" awakens to consciousness of the inward sinful state and enters the second or legal stage. Under the law, one realizes the inward state of sin, characterized by Wesley as pride, anger, evil desire, self-will, and envy. Made sensible of the lost and fallen condition, seeing the painful light of hell, one realizes the deadness of his or her personal life. One sins unwillingly, unable to cast off bondage to sin, guilt, and fear, as the person begins to realize that only an infusion of God's grace can bring new and real life.[10]

In this way, God makes the soul ready for the reception of grace to awaken the new born Christian from the dead, that he or she may receive the spirit of adoption and become "the altogether Christian." Entrance into the third stage of new birth does not necessarily entail a Damascus Road experience. However, the evangelical Christian knows it to be the decisive, transforming step.

> 'If ye will hear His voice to-day, while it is called to-day, harden not your hearts.' Now, 'awake, thou that sleepest' in spiritual death, that thou sleep not in death eternal! Feel thy lost estate, and 'arise from the dead.' Leave thine old companions in sin and death. Follow thou Jesus, and let the dead bury their dead. 'Save thyself from this untoward generation.' 'Come out from among them, and be thou separate, and touch not the unclean thing, and the Lord shall receive thee.' 'Christ shall give thee light.'[11]

Primarily, the transformed being knows that his or her old life has been crucified with Christ: "Nevertheless I live; yet not I, but Christ liveth in me." Dead to pride and ambition for worldly approval and gain, one's whole heart is given to the love of God and neighbor. The new being thus takes on the servanthood of Christ, seeking only the neighbor's good and salvation. The evangelical Christian gains life by giving it for others: "And is this commandment written in your heart, 'That he who loveth God love his brother also'? Do you then love your neighbour as yourself? Do you love every man, even your own enemies, even the enemies of God, as your own soul? as Christ loved you?"[12]

To answer yes to these questions, not by outward appearances, but from inward conviction, is to experience salvation, enter the life of holiness, and begin the walk of perfection. Wesley recognizes that one will not always, perhaps not even usually, experience the evangelical state as purely separated from that of the natural or legal stages. Conversion and the transformed life do not constitute a "pure" state in this life, but they provide a radical new orientation, commitment, and loyalty, enabling one to perceive reality, measure success, and discipline life in a totally new manner.

To Wesley, "Christianity is essentially a social religion; and that to turn it into solitary religion, is indeed to destroy it." In the social situation, the converted Christian's life is primarily characterized through new kinds of relationships to the neighbor. First and foremost are new attitudes toward personal acquaintances on a one-to-one basis, a disposition of meekness, peacemaking, merciful concern for others. In sum, the Christian gives unmeasured outward service motivated by inward purity of heart.[13]

Wesley also recognizes the national and worldly scope of social sins and mourns for the ungodliness of the land, the whole earth. The promise is that one day "Christianity will prevail over all, and cover the earth." The reign of Christianity will result from the correction of sins: "oaths, curses, profaneness, blasphemies, the lying, slandering, evil-speaking; the Sabbath-breaking, gluttony, drunkenness, revenge; the whoredoms, adulteries, and various uncleanness; the frauds, injustice, oppression, extortion, which overspread our land as a flood."[14] In calling the Christian to rebirth in the spirit, Wesley clearly understands new life in three concentric circles: within the individual, spreading from one person to another and covering the earth. Characteristic of thinking of his day, Wesley did not delineate between what we term individual and systemic expressions of sin. Further, though he did not address the necessity and means of systemic change, his

vision is of a new and transformed earth growing out of love of neighbor, broadly and deeply interpreted.

> Can Satan cause the truth of God to fail, or His promises to be of none effect? If not, the time will come when Christianity will prevail over all, and cover the earth. Let us stand a little, and survey (the third thing which was proposed) this strange sight, a *Christian world*. . . .
> Suppose now the fullness of time to be come, and the prophecies to be accomplished. What a prospect is this! All is peace, 'quietness and assurance for ever.' Here is no din of arms, 'no confused noise,' no 'garments rolled in blood.' Destructions are come to a perpetual end': wars are ceased from the earth. Neither are there any intestine jars remaining; no brother rising up against brother; no country or city divided against itself, and tearing out its own bowels. Civil discord is at an end for evermore, and none is left either to destroy or hurt his neighbour. Here is no oppression to 'make' even 'the wise man mad'; no extortion to 'grind the face of the poor'; no robbery or wrong; no rapine or injustice; for all are 'content with such things as they possess.' Thus 'righteousness and peace have kissed each other'. (Ps. lxxxv:10); they have 'taken root and filled the land'; 'righteousness flourishing out of the earth'; and 'peace looking down from heaven'.[15]

II. A Feminist Perspective

My own perceptions regarding feminist theology grow primarily out of the work of scholars such as Rosemary Ruether, Letty Russell, Marjorie Suchocki, and Virginia Mollenkott—persons committed to reforming the church from within in terms of a radical critique of traditional structures.[16] With such theologians as my mentors, I propose that an understanding of the transformed life in Jesus Christ, as Rosemary Ruether states it from a feminist viewpoint

> must reach for a continually expanding definition of inclusive humanity—inclusive of both genders, inclusive of all social groups and races . . . women cannot simply reverse the sin of sexism. . . . Women cannot affirm themselves as *imago dei* and subjects of full human potential in a way that diminishes male humanity. . . . Feminist theology reaches for a new mode of relationship, neither a hierarchical model that diminishes the potential of the "other" nor an "equality" defined by a ruling norm drawn from a dominant group; rather a mutuality that allows us to affirm different ways of being.[17]

From a feminist perspective, the dominant streams of Christian theology within Orthodoxy, Catholicism, and Protestantism have been unable to contribute a viable theological doctrine of the transformed life because they have failed to take specific account of the condition and humanity of women. These traditions are sexist in that they have accepted as normative the principle of hierarchy in God's relationship with human beings and in men's and women's relationships with each other. Yet these traditions also give credence to mutuality and equivalence of human beings growing out of concepts of God which affirm alternative relationships between the divine and human and between human beings. A theology of transformation, from a feminist perspective, is rooted in the biblical tradition of the prophets and Jesus Christ, as well as of St. Paul (in his theological positions which transcend cultural limitations), which envision a radical reordering of human relationships and social structures as the new reign of God on earth growing out of God's partnership with humanity.

The saving action and living work of Jesus Christ provides the model for transformed humanity. The paradox of Christian faith was in Jesus Christ's choice of lordship in the form of servanthood. By freely giving his life to restore human nature, Christ shed all vestiges of Messiahship in terms of traditional visions of hierarchical rule. Jesus' consciously chosen servanthood represented a reversal in human conceptions of divine redemptive action and of a model for disciples to follow. As servants of God, we are freed from all bondage and subservience to human beings and liberated for service to all.[18]

The relationship to "neighbor" is focused in theology in new models of mutuality between men and women exemplified in Jesus' life-style. The humanity of Jesus is key, in one sense, because it demonstrates a transformed model of living for males. Virginia Mollenkott points out that Jesus Christ needed to be a person who possessed power in order to demonstrate its proper use: to be free in a slave-owning society and to be male in a sexist society. In giving up power, Jesus freely became vulnerable, but he did not become a victim.[19]

His servant role is central to exemplify new humanity, not sexuality. Embodied in Jesus Christ, servanthood becomes the highest model of service, stripped of its traditional identification with subordination. As a vindicator of women, and others who were marginalized and oppressed in society, Jesus elevated servanthood to the most valued function one can render to others out of love of God. For both men and women, Jesus' actions symbolized the overthrow of patriarchal order and the transformed humanity of service and mutual empowerment.[20]

Transformation, in feminist theology, focuses on radical either/or choices for both women and men of how they will relate to other human beings on this earth. The initial choice is between whether persons assume traditionally sanctioned hierarchical roles of superiority and subordination or whether men and women caste off cultural prescriptions in favor of Jesus' transforming model of servanthood.

Through this decision, one chooses between sin and salvation, as stated in traditional categories. Sin, as Rosemary Ruether puts it, is the distorted I-Thou relationship which violates the integrity, humanity, and full selfhood of both sexes. Men and women have fallen into sin by accepting culturally assigned spheres of psychic capacity and social roles—for males the ascription of rational being whose identity is centered in the public order; for females, the designation of the feeling and caring person encased in the domestic world. Relegation of sexes almost exclusively to opposite spheres has limited the nature of full personhood for both men and women.[21]

This sinful distortion for males, following society's prescription of domination by their sex, has resulted primarily in pride. For women, who have acquiesced to a socially sanctioned subordinate status, sin has been their self-abasement and lack of self-esteem. While pride and self-abnegation cannot be categorically ascribed only to one sex or the other, feminist thought has gone significantly beyond classical Christian theology in recognizing that a universal definition of sin as pride does not describe the basic violation of personhood in all people.

Instead of using the term "salvation," feminist theologians speak of new life as humanization and conscientization. While men and women must make a conscious choice of humanization, they are seldom able to sustain such an individual decision without participation in a community, hopefully the church, which supports them over against group ego pressures. "New beings" are beginning to emerge whose lives reflect integration of psychic functions and social roles, beyond women simply moving into public positions and men sharing household responsibilities. Such transformed images of humanness point toward redeemed humanity, the reconstitution of human nature in the image of God. The new age of God's reign will be one in which separate spheres of men's and women's roles will be broken down. The gifts of the spirit which God has given to persons, not sexuality, will be the primary determinants of what people do in society, in the domestic or public arena, or in both. The recovery of such lost human potential demands a social revolution. It cannot simply amount to "one-on-one" relationships. Further, the capacity for rationality will no longer be a tool for competitive relations, and the means of relationality will no longer be used for manipulation of others and abnegation of self.[22]

The experience of transformation can also be understood in a three-stage process of change, which includes spiritual, psychological, and social dimensions, as well as in terms of an either/or decision. The three stages, from a feminist perspective, I will label as cultural conformity, affirmative action, and liberated humanity. They may be evaluated in comparison to Wesley's stages of the natural, legal, and evangelical consciousness.

In the first stage of cultural conditioning and conformity, both men and women accept unquestioningly the roles which have been assigned to them by society and sanctioned by the traditional religious order. Neither recognize their sins of domination or self-abnegation because they have been so long and strongly ingrained into them. When such prescriptions are challenged, a woman's initial reaction may be, "I've never been discriminated against," while a man may respond, "It's a man's world. My wife wants me to be the president and she the vice-president." With no skills or experience in public life, women have an unconscious fear of questioning their long-held life-style. They may find it inwardly impossible to be supportive of women whose worlds are expanding, holding such an attitude as, "I couldn't be ministered unto by a woman." Christianity has so long supported woman's role of selflessness and emptying self for her family that even considering self-interest results in guilt. It cannot be expected that men would initiate such change because, initially at least, it appears that they have everything to lose.

In the second stage of affirmative action, women, first, and then men, begin to be awakened to the reality of sexism. Emerging consciousness characteristically blends with a sense of "ought" and gives rise to various manifestations of a legal response. Women begin to get in touch with their own inner anger and recognize sexism in highly concrete forms within their own household, as well as in broader cultural and historical contexts, which provide a massive undergirding system, deemed impossible for anyone to confront. Their general reaction is to become the Superwoman, feeling that "I want to be myself, but I must be responsible to everyone for everything."

In this stage some men become conscious of the reality of sexism both from the female and the male standpoint. Affirmation of women's expanding role comes primarily out of a sense of legal right. Male clergy, for instance, may vote for one female "colleague" to be a member of the General Conference delegation (but because the ballot is secret, who knows!). Men may also begin to realize, and perhaps admit, that "professionalism isn't all that it looks to be from the outside." On the other hand, male clergy may resent women "moving up" outside the established career advancement pattern, which means a closing out of some of their own dreams for the future. Their feelings are highly ambiguous. The man recognizes the public world as oppressive and constrictive to him and wishes to give more of himself to his family. His thought may be that there is more to life than work, but the threat of articulating such feelings to his wife or to male colleagues is enormous. A man may realize that it will set in motion changes that he knows not where will end.

The final stage of liberated humanity is more difficult to describe because few of us are really that far along yet! Certainly, it means that men and women affirm the journey and the struggle together: their humanity and fulfillment are inseparably linked. Reflection on the age-old question, "What does it mean to love my neighbor as myself?" may provide some vision. The neighbor in God's *oikonomia* may be someone we do not know, or it may be our enemy or God's enemy. But neighbor implies friend. We receive the friend as an equal and a confidante. Neighbor implies community, of two or countless more. Community means support and mutual caring, not isolation and insulation. To love my neighbor "as myself" is to affirm my own inestimable value in God's eyes and purpose. We do not manipulate or use our friends. We do not compete with friends. We genuinely desire and seek their good—that God's will may be done on this wide earth in all of our lives.

The social dimensions of transformation from a feminist perspective are expansive. The vision is of redeemed and liberated humanity and earth. A strength of the feminist perspective is its interpretation of "humanity" in specific terms of both sexes and of all races and classes. Further, redemption addresses both the bodily and spiritual realities of peoples' lives and requires elimination of physical oppression as well as release of one's spiritual and psychic resources. "Wholeness" means redemption of both the inner and outer conditions of persons' lives. Further, systemic change of social structures is essential to relieve the oppression of sexism, racism, and classism. Patriarchy as the sanction of domination of any person, group, or class by another must be abolished. Community is necessary to support, embody, and model change. The church stands as the foremost community to be the social pioneer both in modeling mutuality and partnership of equivalence and in advocating a parallel vision in other social structures. Feminist theology, finally, recognizes that transformation of human life in its inclusiveness calls for faithful and responsible care of the earth as God's creation. The perfect ordering of all life under such a vision will be beyond actualization on this earth, but it remains the call, both in Wesleyan and in feminist theology, upon those who wait upon the Lord.

> We await that massive repentance of all humanity, that great *metanoia*, in which all humans decide to disaffiliate from violence and cooperation with violence. This would deprive the whole system of power and make possible a complete redemption. This is the future that eludes us, not because it is not within our power as *humans*, but because it is not within our power as *individuals* or small groups. It demands the conversion of all, not only as individuals, but as a collective system. Although the transformation of the whole, or what theology has called the Shalom of God, eludes us, we can make a beginning. In making a beginning, we can discover that the power of sexism has already been disenchanted. It has begun to be defeated "spiritually," that is, it has lost its authority over our lives. We can begin to act differently.[23]

III. Recovering a Usable Past

After placing side-by-side summary statements of the transformed life in Jesus Christ from John Wesley and from contemporary feminist theologians, the next likely step could be an attempt to compare and contrast and to synthesize the viewpoints into one perspective—hopefully acceptable to both disciplines. Such an approach could presume that a feminist perspective in the Wesleyan tradition had not existed before.

My own vision of a feminist perspective in the Wesleyan tradition has not emerged over the past few years through theological construction, however; rather, glimmerings of what such a "discipline within disciplines" might encompass have emerged less systematically through my more primary studies in American history and the history of women. By examining the experience of women and their relationship to men in the Wesleyan tradition, a usable past of a feminist perspective in the United Methodist heritage has begun to unfold. This academic and faith journey suggests that a feminist viewpoint has been a part of the Wesleyan tradition since its beginnings, obviously without being so labeled.

The two volumes of *Women in New Worlds: Historical Perspectives on the Wesleyan Tradition* provide the basic published resource available at this time for study of women in the United Methodist past.[24] The forty articles in the volumes also include essays on early English roots and background to the two centuries of the American heritage. In order that the ministries of women may be more fully incorporated into theological and historical studies of United Methodism, I shall focus on particular issues as they emerge through these volumes which contribute to a feminist perspective in the Wesleyan tradition in understanding the transformed life in Jesus Christ. While the essays convey much that has been sexist in the tradition, they also suggest an alternative vision of inclusiveness by all persons in Jesus Christ based upon mutuality and equivalence of sexes, classes, and races.

The overarching theme that emerges through these volumes is the spiritual empowerment of women in the Wesleyan tradition and the effect which that empowerment has had on their roles and on men in the church, on structures of the denominational heritage, and on movements for reform in society. The transformation in the lives of women surrounding John Wesley and the changes in his own views of women in church and society provide an essential background for the experience of women in the United States.

The traditional view of females in England during the sixteenth and seventeenth centuries is reflected in the restricted and conventional female relationships with men which society expected of Anglican clergy wives. The pattern of subjection and obedience to husbands, which characterized their lives, did not provide an adequate model for Wesley's own mother or for the women of "Mr. Wesley's Methodism."[25] Susanna Wesley, who grew up in the family of a dissenting Puritan clergy and was married to an Anglican minister, was a woman of immense spiritual and intellectual stature. Her own self-conscious and well-articulated understanding of her life made her an example to her family of piety and spiritual commitment. It also led her, for a period of time, to conduct large religious meetings in the rectory during her husband's absences at convocation in London. John Wesley described his mother as a minister of righteousness in her own right, just as were male members of his family over several generations.[26]

Mutual empowerment characterized John Wesley's relationship to women throughout his active ministry. The correspondence of Wesley with women richly describes their personal conversions, sharing of spiritual concerns, mutual encouragement in the faith, activity in class meetings, and preaching in public gatherings. The conviction of women's personal witness expressed in letters and their effectiveness in class meetings led Wesley to conclude that God was owning the ministries of these women with a harvest of souls. No longer laboring distinctions between testimony, exhortation, and preaching, he permitted women to preach in extraordinary cases because they were effective in converting sinners to Christ. Wesley did not go so far as to appoint women to the itineracy, though a number "travelled the connection" with him, often at the invitation of laity, and were received eagerly.[27]

Wesley's contact with Selina, the Countess of Huntingdon, wealthy upper-middle-class reformer, illustrates similar mutual empowerment. In mid-life, through a spiritual conversion and insight into her role as a woman, Selina forged a new personal identity, leading to remarkable independence and authority for an eighteenth-century woman. She enabled other women to do likewise through their participation in missionary and prayer groups which she led. A unique colleagiality with Wesley and Whitefield grew, which led the countess to wage an assault on her own class to convert the elite and channel their resources into assistance for the poor, evangelization of the Indians, and church development.[28]

New disclosures in the John Wesley–Sophy Hopkey interlude indicate that Wesley may have pioneered a tradition of enlightened relationships between men and women that was firmly grounded in his personal integration of the Christian faith. Wesley related to Hopkey, not as if she were a possession of her uncle before marriage or of her husband after marriage, but as an individual responsible for her own salvation, with a right to spiritual and intellectual independence. The tension, however, between Wesley's liberated ideas on relationships between men and women and the social prescriptions which provided little freedom for women outside pastoral, pedagogical, or marital relationships, could not be resolved.[29]

As the trans-Atlantic connection of Methodist movements developed during the nineteenth and twentieth centuries, conflicts between ideology and practice are key to an analysis of transformation in women's and men's lives.

During the nineteenth century, as antecedent branches of United Methodism changed from frontier movements to institutionalized churches, prescriptions of women's roles became increasingly constrictive. Periodicals of the church, including Sunday school literature, *The Christian Advocate*, and the *Southern Lady's Companion* appear to advocate women's religious conversion as a means of social control in a turbulent, mobile society. Revivalists found their ripest converts among women, and the church promulgated an ideology that the transformed life was meant to be only an inner experience which made women morally superior to men, endowed with the task of redeeming a fallen, disreputable mankind and social order. Obviously, that task was to be performed within the home.[30]

Official public roles in the church were never naturally or automatically opened to women. Many of the major struggles of the church during the last two hundred years revolve around issues of admitting women into membership in established church structures—ordination, laity voting rights, mission board membership, and mission field work were areas of bitter controversy. The general pattern was that women who pioneered in opening these doors understood new life in Christ to apply both to their private lives and spiritual natures and to their public roles and Christian service. Often their arguments for admittance into mainline structures of the church involved interpretation of Scripture along radically egalitarian lines. Phoebe Palmer, powerful and influential evangelist of Methodism and the holiness movement in the mid-and-late nineteenth century, based her convincing argument for women's right to preach on the fulfillment of the prophecy at Pentecost, "Your sons and your daughters shall prophesy." Frances Willard, on the other hand, who received "entire sanctification" at the hands of Phoebe Palmer and became the second president of the Women's Christian Temperance Union, used conservative, more socially acceptable ideology with equally determined conviction to expand women's role in church and society. Building on the "cult of true womanhood" argument, she contended that women should be ordained and enter social reform work in order to extend their mothering role into society and make the whole world more home-like. In fact, however, Willard was one of the most effective women in the late nineteenth century in actually transforming woman's role from one limited to the domestic scene to involvement in all conceivable areas of social reform and to gaining voting rights as laity in the Methodist Episcopal Church.[31] Her actual practice was more radical than was the ideology which she used to justify it.

A few women, such as Georgia Harkness and Mary McLeod Bethune, seem to have experienced a transformed life in Christ in the public sphere as well as in a personal way without female support networks to advocate for them. Harkness stood out as an individual female scholar surrounded by male professors of higher education, while Bethune became a lone pioneer black woman in several areas of public responsibility in church and society.[32] This was not the case for women who sought ordination and lay voting rights in the late nineteenth century. Until support movements developed, mainline institutional offices were denied women. It took over seventy-five years from the time women first sought ordination in the Methodist Episcopal Church before full clergy rights were granted. One level of transformation of the institution is admittance of women to full and equal rights and responsibilities. What effect the presence of women in the ordained ministry will have on the structural nature of the church remains unclear even today.[33]

Alternative structures "for women only" within the church have often been developed by women because established structures were closed to them. Such was the case regarding origins of women's missionary societies and the deaconess movement.[34] Quite often both in ideology and practice, these organizations advocated radical ʾroles of "the new woman of Methodism," which provided public empowerment of personal spiritual convictions. Deaconesses were often the first single female missionaries to venture into national and world mission stations in which it was considered impossible for women either to survive or to be able to serve effectively. Such women developed a highly conscious ideology of their servanthood function growing out of "service not sexuality." Further, while they sought to evangelize the world in the name of Jesus Christ, they also knew that their specific responsibility was to perform "Women's Work for Women." Female missionaries often became the first liberators of their sisters throughout the world, evangelizing, educating, and morally uplifting women on the "dark and heathen continents."[35]

Women's entrance and contributions to social reform often paralleled their involvement in missionary society organizations, deaconess societies, and mission field work. Out of inward religious motivation, women began to enter every area of social reform in the nineteenth and twentieth centuries, including antilynching, temperance, industrial reform, and movements for national independence.[36] Generally, such areas were out of bounds for female activity before the entrance of women who saw social reform as their evangelical mission. Idealistic as was their vision of a new order, it was their religious commitment to Christian servanthood which enabled them to sustain momentum over long hauls.

The stories related through *Women in New Worlds* are primarily those of women's inward spiritual journeys and their movement into service in church and society growing out of religious convictions. However, the United Methodist tradition in its two-hundred-year heritage in the United States demonstrates the same realities of the transformed consciousnesses of men as in the case of John Wesley. Many instances reveal relationships of men and women, such as of the Rev. John Goucher and Mary Goucher, whose marriage was a genuine partnership of equality. It was the spirited and independent Mary Goucher whose rising consciousness opened her husband to new understandings of equality of women and men as they together became major philanthropists of the Methodist Episcopal Church.[37] In other cases, men such as Bishop John Thoburn of the Methodist Episcopal Church realized the need for single women missionaries in the foreign field and recruited his sister, Isabella, to be the first single female missionary to India. Similarly, the Rev. Young J. Allen, superintendent of the China District of the Methodist Episcopal Church, South, envisioned the need of women missionaries to minister to the women of China and commissioned Laura Haygood for that task. More often, the story is a more complex one of conflict, sometimes followed by resolution and reconciliation, and sometimes not between women and men, regarding admission to ordination, laity rights, or the power of the purse in distributing mission dollars. In every case, the structures of the church are expanded or contracted as vision is tested and living faith seeks to respond creatively to God's new day in history.[38]

IV. A Feminist Perspective in the Wesleyan Tradition

Historically, a feminist perspective of the transformed life in Jesus Christ has been a part of the two-hundred-and-fifty-year heritage of women in the Wesleyan tradition in England and

America. It cannot be analyzed in a neat line of progression or of steadily expanding structures of church and society. However, issues have been raised and tested which provide the beginnings of a more systematic construction of a feminist perspective in the Wesleyan tradition. An effort toward such a constructive task is made primarily to critique the past and present, and to envision a more human existence for all God's people on this earth. The following paragraphs are included simply to begin dialogue on the subject.

Theologically, a feminist/Wesleyan viewpoint has been grounded most basically in the experience of conversion, a radical change in lordship and loyalty, both in individual and corporate accountability to Christ, leading to personal appropriation of grace and institutional responsibility for the human and created order. Historical analysis demonstrates that radical implications of conversion have effected women's relationship to the church both in terms of personal spirituality and social responsibility.

The ideology growing out of women's personal spirituality has often been used in a reactionary way to restrict women to the home on the claim that females are spiritually superior to males. On the other hand, alternative visions raised by women and men over two and a half centuries have held females to be spiritually equal to men and have thus been a primary means of justifying their admittance into institutions of church and social reform. In this way, a feminist viewpoint has been effective in overcoming the spirit-body dualism which has traditionally circumscribed women's proper function to the domestic sphere.[39] The strong emphasis in the Wesleyan tradition, and of a feminist perspective within that tradition, on the work and gifts of the Holy Spirit provides a fruitful focus for constructive theology. If gifts are given as an expression of God's grace for service in Christ, and not as an attribute of sexuality, then they become the natural means of freeing both women and men for wholeness of life. Questions of the private or public sphere no longer have any relevance.

Similarly, conversion has radical implications for social responsibility through a feminist perspective in the Wesleyan tradition. Conversion is no longer understood simply as an individual experience leading to salvation. Women within the Wesleyan evangelical heritage of nineteenth-century America moved toward an understanding that institutions themselves must be converted. Their efforts to enter mainline structures of the church were threatening because their admittance often carried with it consciously laid programs that necessitated reconstruction in terms of mutuality and partnership of women with men. Alternative structures "for women only" became the earliest effective training ground for women in any type of social organization. This historical precedence lays the basis for the church to function as social pioneer today, as a converted institution committed to reordering itself within to be a witness and model for other structures of society.

NOTES

1. Thomas Langford, *Practical Divinity: Theology in the Wesleyan Tradition* (Nashville: Abingdon Press, 1983). p. 24.
2. Letty Russell, *Human Liberation in a Feminist Perspective—A Theology* (Philadelphia: Westminster Press, 1974), p. 13.
3. John Wesley, *Sermons on Several Occasions* (London: Epworth, 1944: first printed 1746), p. v.
4. Ibid.
5. Ibid., pp. 514-26.
6. Ibid., pp. 519, 520.
7. Ibid., pp. 11-19; 20-32; 96-110.
8. Ibid., pp. 20, 21.
9. Ibid., pp. 13, 20, 21.
10. Ibid., pp. 97-110.
11. Ibid., p. 27.
12. Ibid., pp. 18, 19.
13. Ibid., pp. 237, 238.
14. Ibid., p. 30.
15. Ibid., pp. 41, 42.
16. Among the works of these authors are Rosemary Ruether, *Sexism and God-Talk: Toward a Feminist Theology* (Boston: Beacon Press, 1983) and *New Woman, New Earth: Sexist Ideologies and Human Liberation* (New York: Seabury Press, 1975); Letty Russell, *Human Liberation* and *The Future of Partnership* (Philalphia: Westminster Press, 1979); Marjorie Suchocki, *God, Christ, Church: A Practical Guide to Process Theology* (New York: Crossroads, 1982); and Virginia Mollenkott, "'You Shall Receive Power': Whole Persons in a World," in Roberta Hestenes and Lois Curley, eds., *Women and the Ministries of Christ* (Pasadena: Fuller Theological Seminary, 1979), pp. 111-20.
17. Ruether, *Sexism and God-Talk*, p. 20.
18. Ibid., p. 121.
19. Mollenkott; see note 16.
20. Russell, *Future of Partnership*, pp. 61-77; Ruether, *Sexism and God-Talk*, pp. 29-33, 119-122.
21. Ruether, ibid., pp. 160-183.
22. Ibid., p. 113.
23. Ibid., p. 183.
24. Rosemary Keller, Louise Queen, Hilah Thomas, eds., *Women in New Worlds: Historical Perspectives on the Wesleyan Tradition*, 2 vols. (Nashville: Abingdon Press, 1981, 1982).
25. Anne Barstow, "An Ambiguous Legacy," ibid., vol. 2, pp. 97-111.
26. Frank Baker, "Susanna Wesley," ibid., vol. 2, pp. 112-131.
27. Earl Kent Brown, "Women of the Word," ibid., vol. 1, pp. 69-87.
28. Mollie Davis, "The Countess of Huntingdon," ibid., vol. 2, pp. 162-175.
29. Alan Hayes, "John Wesley and Sophy Hopkey," in ibid., vol. 2, pp. 29-44.
30. Joanna Gillespie, "'The Sun in Their Domestic System,'" ibid., vol. 2, pp. 45-59; James Leloudis, "Subversion of the Feminine Ideal," ibid., pp. 60-75; Suranne O'Donnell, "Distress from the Press," ibid., vol. 2, pp. 76-93. Clergy wives make a significant case study of the

way in which women sought to expand this revivalistic role to the public scene and its relationship to their own role identification: Julie Jeffrey, "Ministry through Marriage," ibid., vol. 1 , pp. 143-160; Rosa Motes, "The Pacific Northwest," ibid., vol. 2, pp. 148-61.

31. Nancy Hardesty, "Minister As Prophet? or As Mother?" ibid., vol. 1 , pp. 88-101; Janet Everhart, "Maggie Newton Van Cott," ibid., vol. 2, pp. 300-17; Susan Lee, "Evangelical Domesticity," ibid., vol. 1, pp. 295-309; Carolyn Gifford, "For God and Home and Native Land," ibid., vol. 1 , pp. 310-27.

32. Clarence Newsome, "Mary McLeod Bethune As Religionist," ibid., vol. 1, pp. 102-116; Martha Scott, "Georgia Harkness," ibid., vol. 1, pp. 117-140; Joan Engelsman, "The Legacy of Georgia Harkness," ibid., vol. 2, pp. 338-358.

33. James Will, "Maggie Van Cott," ibid., vol. 2, pp. 300-17; William Noll, "Laity Rights and Leadership (Methodist Protestant)," ibid., vol. 1, pp. 219-32; Donald Gorrell, "A New Impulse (United Brethren in Christ & Evangelical Association)," ibid., vol. 1, pp. 233-45; Rosemary Keller, "Creating a Sphere for Women (Methodist Episcopal)," ibid., vol. 1 , pp. 246-60; Virginia Shadron, "The Laity Rights Movement (Methodist Episcopal South)," ibid., vol. 1 , pp. 261-75; Jualynne Dodson, "Nineteenth Century A.M.E. Preaching Women," ibid., vol. 1 , pp. 276-89.

34. Besides the essays referred to in note 33, see also Virginia Brereton, "Preparing Women for the Lord's Work," ibid., vol. 1, pp. 178-99; Mary Agnes Dougherty, "The Social Gospel According to Phoebe," ibid., vol. 1, pp. 200-16; Catherine Prelinger and Rosemary Keller, "The Function of Female Bonding," ibid., vol. 2, pp. 318-37.

35. Keller, "Creating a Sphere for Women," ibid., vol. 1, pp. 246-60; Frederick Norwood, "American Indian Women," ibid., vol. 2, pp. 176-95; Joan Brumberg, "The Case of Ann Hasseltine Judson," ibid., vol. 2, pp. 234-39; Adrian Bennett, "Doing More Than They Intended," ibid., vol. 2, pp. 249-67; Sylvia Jacobs, "Three Afro-American Women," ibid., vol. 2, pp. 268-80; Carol Page, "Charlotte Manye Maxeke," ibid., vol. 2, pp. 281-89.

36. Alice Chai, "Korean Women in Hawaii," ibid., vol. 1, pp. 328-44; Mary Frederickson, "Shaping a New Society," ibid., vol. 1 , pp. 345-61; Miriam Crist, "Winifred Chappell," ibid., vol. 1 , pp. 362-78; Anastatia Sims, "Sisterhoods of Service," ibid., vol. 2, pp. 196-210; Arnold Shankman, "Civil Rights, 1920–1970," ibid., vol. 2, pp. 211-33.

37. Emora Brannon, "A Partnership of Equality," ibid., vol. 2, pp. 132-47.

38. The several articles previously referred to on missionary societies and mission field work, ordination, laity rights, and deaconess orders may be studied here.

39. See Sheila Davaney's paper, "Feminism, Process Thought, and the Wesleyan Tradition," in this volume.

VI. Black and Ethnic Religion and the Theological Renewal of Methodism

1. THE APPEAL OF METHODISM TO BLACK AMERICANS

William B. McClain

Introduction

The creation of the Wesleyan wing within the Church of England meant that the faith moved from those associated with the established church to a new group which was being marginalized under industrialization. This took place first within the existing church, and then as a separate church. In the main, it represented the movement of the faith across class and vocational barriers.

Although the founder, John Wesley, and his brother Charles, the poet of Methodism, could hardly be considered as lower class, the Methodist movement which they started was rooted in a passionate and enthusiastic concern for the poorer classes. Wesley preached a gospel of salvation to the miners and day laborers, to those who worked in the factories at Bristol and inhabited the gloomy and dingy slums of London and other large cities of England.

John Wesley was a graduate of Oxford and bore its ineffaceable stamp, and attracted to the Methodist movement as its initial leaders those of similar background and learning: George Whitefield, a graduate of Pembroke College, Oxford, acclaimed as one of the most powerful preachers of all times, joined the Wesleys and became one of the Oxford Methodists. Dr. Thomas Coke, a university man like the Wesleys and Whitefield, and a Welshman of considerable means, became Wesley's chosen spokesman and crossed the Atlantic no fewer than eighteen times at his own expense to give leadership to the fledgling Methodist movement. And then there was Francis Asbury, who accompanied Coke. Although, unlike Wesley, he was not a university graduate, like him he was well-read and believed in education. He is reported to have had a fixed rule to read one hundred pages daily. He made himself a scholar and mastered Greek, Latin, and Hebrew. These middle-class leaders established a church of the poor in England that later blossomed in the latter part of the eighteenth century on the frontier and plains of America, as the circuit riders rode across this land, finding lodging in the rough cabins of the pioneers and making tracks through shadowy and virtually untrodden forests and into the urban areas along the Atlantic sea coast to proclaim a simple gospel of salvation to all who would listen.

The poor and the disinherited, the unchurched and the uneducated listened gladly to the call to repentance under the threat of damnation. The Methodist preachers told of a Christ that Wesley had discovered at Aldersgate who gives an inner assurance of love and causes the heart to feel strangely warmed. This simple message was good news to the hard-working, God-fearing common people who populated the perimeter of colonial America, and they responded with enthusiastic emotionalism to the Methodist evangelical vision of Christianity. Group after group were brought into the church because of a loving acceptance which could prevail over the rejections found elsewhere.

It used to be said that the Episcopal priests waited for the trains with velvet-covered seats to go West, while the Presbyterian clergy went in covered wagons with the migrants before the railroads were built. The Methodist preachers, by contrast, rode on horseback ahead of the people and greeted them as they arrived. Despite allowances for exaggeration by Methodists, there is some truth to that saying as it appears in an emblem associated with the United Methodist denomination which features a circuit rider seated on a horse, reading a book.

By the time of the first annual conference in 1773, these itinerant preachers had penetrated the settled coastal regions and were keeping abreast of a population that was threading its way westward through the Appalachian barriers and along the rivers that led to out-of-the-way and isolated places. At that first annual conference, appointments of preachers were made for a region extending from New York City southward to Norfolk and Petersburg in Virginia, and westward to Philadelphia. Joseph Pilmoor had volunteered to come from England to America, and had made a preaching excursion from Philadelphia to Savannah. Richard Boardman, his English comrade, had gone as far north as Boston to stake out the claim for Methodism in New England.

Among the poor and disinherited who listened and responded to the gospel message of the Methodist preachers were the black slaves who had been brought to America in chains. They joined the Methodist "classes" and "societies" and attended the preaching events and camp meetings. Perhaps, "for the slave," as Harry V. Richardson points out, "becoming a Christian represented a complex of aims and hopes in which his soul's salvation was only one."[1] In any case, the black diaspora from the African motherland responded. There was immediate and rapid growth among the black Methodists. In some cases, the number of black people equalled or exceeded the white people. Thomas Rankin, a white Methodist preacher in Virginia, reports the response to his preaching in 1776:

> At four in the afternoon I preached again. . . . I had gone through about two-thirds of my discourse, and was bringing the words home to the present *now*, when such power descended that hundreds fell to the ground, and the house seemed to shake with the presence of God. The chapel was full of white and black, and many were without that could not get in. Look wherever we would, we saw nothing but streaming eyes and faces bathed in tears; and heard nothing but groans and strong cries after God and the Lord Jesus Christ.
>
> Sunday 7. I preached at W's chapel, about twenty miles from Mr. J's. I intended to preach near the house, under the shade of some large trees. But the rain made it impracticable. The house was greatly crowded, and four or five hundred stood at the windows, and listened with unabated attention. I preached from Ezekiel's vision of dry bones: "And there was a great shaking." I was obliged to stop again and again, and beg of the people to compose themselves. But they could not; some on their knees, and some on their faces, were crying mightily to God all the time I was preaching. *Hundreds of Negroes* were among them, with tears streaming down their faces.[2]

Freeborn Garrettson, another of the Methodist itinerant preachers, describes the response of the slaves to his preaching in North Carolina:

> In September I went to North Carolina, to travel Roanoak circuit, and was sweetly drawn out in to the glorious work, though my exercises were very great particularly respecting the slavery, and hard usage of the poor afflicted negroes. Many times did my heart ache on their account, and many tears ran down my cheeks, both in Virginia and Carolina, while exhibiting a crucified Jesus to their view; and I bless God that my labors were not in vain among them. I endeavored frequently to inculcate the doctrine of freedom in a private way, and this procured me the ill will of some, who were in that unmerciful practice. I would often set apart times to preach to the blacks, and adapt my discourse to them alone; and precious moments have I had. While many of their sable faces were bedewed with tears, their withered hands of faith were stretched

out, and their precious souls made white in the blood of the Lamb. The suffering of those poor out-casts of men, through the blessing of God, drove them near to the Lord, and many of them were amazingly happy.[3]

It is the experiences of these black people who joined the Methodist movement from the very start, who found their spiritual home in the Methodist Episcopal Church and who have remained a part of this body throughout its social metamorphosis and its changing structure and its checkered history that I want to focus on.

Present throughout this unfolding drama, beginning with the first organized Methodist Society at Sam's Creek in Frederick County, Maryland, and continuing through the last General Conference of The United Methodist Church, is a perennially present and all-too-familiar question, What shall we do with the blacks? That question has received several clumsy, compromising, tentative, and uncertain answers. The question black Methodists may have to answer for themselves, along with other ethnic minorities, is whether they are a saving remnant or a sedimental (and perhaps sentimental) residue.

The Appeal of Methodism to Black Americans

There are numerous accounts of black Americans responding to the evangelistic message of the Methodists. Letters were sent back to Wesley in England in abundance by the preachers he sent to America. They told of the dramatic conversions of hundreds upon hundreds of blacks who accepted Christianity in emotional and celebrative rejoicing. These were sincere and profound religious experiences, as the black slaves heard of a good and loving God who knew the sufferings of his children, even his sun-baked sons and daughters who found themselves in chains in a strange land. Richard Allen, one of the early converts under Methodist preaching and later the founder of the African Methodist Episcopal Church, recorded his personal conversion of 1777 in his memoirs many years later that seems to be typical of such dramatic conversions:

> I was awakened and brought to see myself, poor, wretched and undone, and without the mercy of God must be lost. Shortly after, I obtained mercy through the blood of Christ, and was constrained to exhort my old companions to seek the Lord. I went rejoicing for several days and was happy in the Lord, in conversing with many old, experienced Christians. I was brought under doubts, and was tempted to believe I was deceived, and was

206

constrained to seek the Lord afresh. I went with my head bowed down for many days. My sins were a heavy burden. I was tempted to believe there was no mercy for me. I cried to the Lord both night and day. One night I thought hell would be my portion. I cried unto Him who delighteth to hear the prayers of a poor sinner, and all of a sudden my dungeon shook, my chains flew off, and, glory to God, I cried. My soul was filled. I cried, enough for me—the Saviour died. Now my confidence was strengthened that the Lord, for Christ's sake, had heard my prayers and pardoned all my sins.[4]

On November 4, 1769, Richard Boardman wrote to John Wesley telling of the blacks attending his meetings and how their response affected him:

Our house contains about seven hundred people. About a third part of those who attend get in, the rest are glad to hear without. There appears such a willingness in the Americans to hear the word as I never saw before. They have no preaching in some parts of the back settlements. I doubt not but an effectual door will be opened among them. O! May the Most High give his Son the heathen for his inheritance. The number of blacks that attend the preaching affects me much.[5]

And as blacks became members of the new Methodist movement they became faithful in their devotions and sincere in their commitment to worship. Abel Stevens describes how one such incident led to the conversion of the plantation owner:

Henry D. Gough, wealthy planter, heard Asbury preach. He was deeply impressed and burdened. He could no longer enjoy his accustomed pleasures.

He became deeply serious and, at last melancholy, and was near destroying himself under the awakened sense of his misspent life; but God mercifully preserved him. Riding to one of his plantations, he heard a voice of prayer and praise in a cabin, and, listening, discovered that a negro from a neighboring estate was leading the devotions of his own slaves, and offering fervent thanksgivings for the blessings of their depressed lot. His heart was touched, and with emotion he exclaimed, "Alas, O Lord, I have my thousands and tens of thousands, and yet, ungrateful wretch that I am, I never thanked thee, as this poor slave does, who has scarcely clothes to put on or food to satisfy his hunger. The luxurious master was taught a lesson, on the nature of true contentment and happiness, which he could never forget. His work-worn servants in their lowly cabins knew a blessedness which he had never found in his sumptuous mansion.[6]

The *Discipline* of The United Methodist Church attempts to account for the response of black Americans to Methodism. In its discussion of "Black People and Their United Methodist Heritage," it asserts the following: "Methodism won favor with the black people for two main reasons: (1) its evangelistic appeal; (2) the Church's attitude toward slavery."[7]

While these two reasons are certainly true in summary, and need further explanation, perhaps there were some other factors that also need to be included.

The Wesleyan evangelical message was a simple gospel of salvation, designed to awaken a godly experience of the conscious fellowship with God in its hearers. Emphasizing the love of God and the way of redemption, it sought to bring into the lives of poor benighted sinners the message of a Father who cares for his children—all of his children. This conscious acceptance with God issues forth in daily growth in holiness. Christians could have as their dominant motives the love of God and of their neighbor and these could free them from sin. Poverty was no barrier to membership; the poorest were made most welcome. Religion, for these early Wesleyans, was not a perfunctory, ritualistic faith, nor a mere cultural expression, but rather an "experience" of faith through which one responded to the love of God. It was a clarion call to righteousness in this world in order to escape eternal damnation in the world to come.

These evangelists never left their hearers and congregations with any doubts about the living reality of the divine mercy. In almost every sermon this eternal mercy was assured; it was sung in the Charles Wesley and Isaac Watts hymns; the theme ran like music through all occasions. Even though hell in all of its terrors was graphically pictured, the preachers never forgot to proclaim the offer of divine mercy that was wider than the sea. The sufferings of hell were made realistic in order to make the way of salvation even more glorious.

The Wesleyan revivalists were Arminian in theology as opposed to strict Calvinism. They held that Christ died for all, that salvation is by faith alone, that those who believe are saved, that those who reject God's grace are lost, and that God does not elect particular individuals for either outcome. Strict Calvinism held that before God had created the world God had decreed who should be saved and who should be damned. It was this issue over which Wesley and Whitefield split and perhaps it accounts for their differences on the issue of slavery. Whitefield was a strict

Calvinist who believed in predestination. Obviously, for Whitefield, God had not elected black people, and therefore they could easily serve as slaves and be the "hewers of the wood and drawers of the water now henceforth and forever." And Whitefield provided the spurious and devastating theological and biblical bases for slavery out of his Calvinism, and did not scruple to buy some fifty slaves when his orphan-home was at stake.

The Arminian tradition, however, prevailed in its emphasis upon prevenient grace, that is, God bestows will as well as the grace that is willed and that grace is sufficient to effectually impel belief. And the Methodists preached such a grace that breaks every barrier down.

As Walter G. Muelder points out, there was in this simple message a revolutionary potential for the unwanted poor and uninterested destitute who were excluded through social stratification from the "morally soft and spiritually dead churches of the well-to-do." It is evident in one of the now-famous letters of the Duchess of Buckingham to Lady Huntington:

> Their doctrines [those of the Methodist preachers] are most repulsive and tinctured with impertinence and disrespect toward their superiors, in perpetually endeavoring to level all ranks and doing away with all distinctions. It is monstrous to be told that you have a heart as sinful as the common wretches that crawl the earth. This is highly offensive and insulting.[8]

Blacks were attracted to such a simplistic and sincere message, as were the poor white farmers, and those who were the outcasts and the *declassé* masses. Great numbers flocked to hear this good news, and expressed their feelings with cries, screams, shouts, tears, prostration, physical convulsions, and other physical and emotional responses, including sometimes falling insensible.

John Thompson, born as a slave in Maryland in 1812, draws the clear distinction between this revivalist preaching and the more ritualistic and staid approach of the established church:

> My mistress and her family were all Episcopalians. The nearest church was five miles from our plantation and there was no Methodist church nearer than ten miles. So we went to the Episcopal Church, but always came home as we went, for the preaching was above our comprehension, so we could understand but little that was said. But soon the Methodist religion was brought among us, and preached in a manner so plain that the wayfaring man, though a fool, could not err therein. This new doctrine produced great consternation among the slaveholders. It was something which they could

not understand. It brought glad tidings to the poor bondsman; it bound up the broken-hearted; it opened the prison doors to them that were bound, and let the captives go free. As soon as it got among the slaves, it spread from plantation to plantation, until it reached ours, where there were but few who did not experience religion.[9]

Second, the slaves responded to the Methodists because these early evangelists were opposed to slavery. John Wesley was uncompromising and unalterably against slavery and furiously attacked it. He saw it as an institution to satisfy the greed of men. He denied that it was necessary in the economic operation of the colonies. And even if it was, he insisted that prosperity purchased at so great a price was an offense against God. From the view in South Carolina until the last letter to Wilberforce on his death bed, Wesley believed that slavery was a deep-rooted evil that must be destroyed. But Thomas Coke, Francis Asbury, Freeborn Garrettson, and most of the early Methodist evangelists—with the notable exception of George Whitefield—were opposed to slavery. This eventuates in the seventeen Methodist ministers at a conference in Baltimore taking up the question of slavery and deciding that itinerant preachers holding slaves had to promise to set them free. They declared, "Slavery is contrary to the laws of God, man and nature—hurtful to society; contrary to the dictates of conscience and pure religion, and doing that which we would not others should do to us and ours." This was not the end of Methodists' dealing with slavery and the question of blacks. But let it suffice here to say that Methodism began in America with its leadership opposed to slavery and were evangelical in that stance—to which the slaves responded.

Harry V. Richardson points out the fact that "despite their enslaved condition, the blacks come in large numbers to attend the meetings, hear the Gospel, and seek conversion made all the more poignant the inhumanity of slavery and the sin of it."[10] Asbury found himself moved by the antislavery leadership of the Quakers to write in his Journal in 1778: "I find the most pious part of the people called Quakers, are exerting themselves for the liberation of the slaves. This is a very laudable design; and what the Methodists must come to, or, I fear the Lord will depart from them."[11] Freeborn Garrettson upon his conversion in 1777 is reported to have immediately emancipated his slaves on religious grounds. He declared: "It was God, not man, who showed me the impropriety of holding slaves." He joined the ranks of those early Methodist preachers who fought slavery.

Perhaps the clearest evidence of how the slaves felt about the Methodists and their stance on slavery is seen in the account of the Gabriel Prosser slave revolt. Prosser, convinced on religious grounds—perhaps the influence of the evangelical Methodists—that slavery should be over-turned and that he had been chosen by God to be a deliverer of his people, planned a rebellion. A young man of twenty-five with impressive physical and mental capabilities, and also a student of the Bible, Gabriel felt that he was to follow the model of Samson against the Philistines. Perhaps this possibility seemed even more likely to him in 1800.

Toussaint L'Ouverture had recently completed a successful revolution against slavery in Haiti and had taken command of the entire colony of Santo Domingo. Gabriel's plan was to destroy Henrico County and lead the slaves to the establishment of a new black kingdom in Virginia, with himself to be the crowned king. The plan called for killing all the whites who accosted his followers, seize arms and ammunition from the arsenal in nearby Richmond, loot the treasury, and, if possible, arrive at an agreement with the remaining slavemasters for the freedom of all slaves. It was a well-planned plot in which Gabriel's testimony declares he had ten thousand men ready to go into battle. The insurrection failed because of logistical problems, slave informers, and a serious storm. Gabriel and a number of other slaves were hanged. But Gabriel's instructions concerning the two Christian groups he believed to be on God's side against the practice of slavery were clear: *All Methodists and Quakers were to be spared.* He also included Frenchmen, presumably because France had recognized the new nation L'Ouverture had established on the Island of Hispaniola.

Clearly, Gabriel knew of the Methodist witness against slavery. Some would maintain that it was through the itinerant ministers who went back and forth from church to church that information was transmitted to the insurgents.[12]

In addition to black Americans responding because of the evangelical, simple message of salvation of the Methodists, and the attitudes of the early Methodist leaders toward slavery, there are at least three other factors that account for the appeal of Methodism to black Americans. These are: (1) the preaching and worship style of the Methodists appealed to blacks; (2) blacks were allowed to serve as lay preachers; and (3) Methodism was adaptable enough to fit their own situation so that they could make it their own.

The stress of the evangelistic Methodists as well as the Baptists and, perhaps to a lesser degree, the Presbyterians, was on the *conversion experience* itself. While the Methodists had a concern that the conversion experience ought to issue forth in daily growth in holiness and Christian conduct, even "moving on toward perfection," *after* the conversion, it was the *experience* of conviction, repentance, and regeneration which primarily occupied the attention of the preacher. The more established clergymen of the Anglical Church tended to concentrate on teaching doctrines and moralizing. Their preaching style reflected this didactic preoccupation. They were concerned that the slaves learn to recite the Ten Commandments and the Lord's Prayer and the Apostle's Creed. They expected the slaves to be able to give the correct answers to the catechismal questions. One of the missionaries for the Society for the Propagation of the Gospel in Foreign Parts gives us an account of this emphasis:

Upon these gentlewomen's desiring me to come and examine these negroes . . . I went and among other things I asked them, Who Christ was. They readily answered, He is the Son of God, and Savior of the World, and told me that they embraced Him with all their hearts as such, and I desired them to rehearse the Apostle's Creed and the 10 Commandments and the Lord's Prayer, which they did very distinctly and perfectly. 14 of them gave me so great satisfaction, and were so desirous to be baptized, that I thought it my duty to baptize them and therefore baptized these 14 last Lord's Day. And I doubt not but these gentlewomen will prepare the rest of them for Baptism in a little time.[13]

But the evangelical Methodist preacher was concerned about the experience of conversion and exhorted the slave by visualizing, personalizing, and dramatizing the nature of sin and salvation, picturing the darkness of sin and the glorious light of salvation. He helped them to see the beauty of the Father seeking after the son who is the prodigal. He helped them to feel the weight of sin, to picture in their minds the threats of Hell, and to accept Christ as their only Savior. Like an artist, he drew a picture on the canvas of the minds of the hearers. This was an emotional and appealing word for the converted heart; a reminder of the day and hour when the dungeon shook and the chains flew off. And it filled the heart with gladness and rejoicing. For those who had never heard the message of salvation, it made the soul feel happy as they "came out of de wilderness, leaning on de Lord." One of the slaves who experienced hearing both contrasts the preaching:

> The preaching [Episcopalian] was above our comprehension. . . . But soon the Methodist religion was brought among us, and preached in a manner so plain that the wayfaring man, though a fool, could not err therein. . . . It brought glad tidings to the poor bondsman.[14]

These preachers' style was dictated both by the message and the overriding passionate goal: to help the poor sinner make a decision for heaven rather than allow their souls to be consigned to hell. And the preachers exhorted this fiery message of salvation as hope with personal, emotional appeal and enthusiasm which often triggered responses of groans and shouts that become infectious and spread throughout the meeting place. It was not just the message but also the manner in which it was delivered.

Thomas Rankin, one of the revivalists, reports his experience on the Baltimore Circuit:

> Near the close of the meeting I stood up and called upon the people to look toward that part of the chapel where all the blacks were. I then said, "See the number of Africans who have stretched out their hands unto God!" While I was addressing the people thus, it seemed as if the very house shook with the mighty power and glory of Sinai's God. Many of the people were so overcome that they were ready to faint and die under his Almighty hand. For about three hours the gale of the Spirit thus continued to breathe upon the dry bones; and they did live the life of glorious love! As for myself, I scarce knew whether I was in the body or not; and so it was with all my brethren . . . Surely the fruits of this season will remain to all eternity.[15]

As Raboteau comments, "The revivalists, moreover, tended to minimize complex explanations of doctrines. The heightened emphasis on conversion left little room for elaborate catechesis."[16] For their spiritual nurture the converts were organized into societies, and these were subdivided into classes with a class leader. This was part of the organizational genius of Wesley. With such minimal organization, slaves could be taken into the movement and fully participate more easily than in a settled and established church. It must be remembered that Wesley's interest was not to start a new church, but a drive for renewal, revival, and piety within the established church. However, these societies did become churches, in the fullest sense in 1784, as Thomas Coke is dispatched by John Wesley, over the objections of his brother Charles, to form the new church.

The other aspect of the worship that attracted and appealed to the slaves was the singing. The Methodists became known for their vigorous and spirited singing of hymns and psalms. John Wesley had emphasized singing from the very beginning of the movement. He was a hymn-writer himself and translated some of the early hymns of the German Reformers and the early church into English. During his brief stay in America, his volume, *A Collection of Psalms and Hymns*, published at Charlestown, South Carolina, in 1737, became one of the first hymnals in the English language prepared for use in public worship.[17] His concern for the publishing and singing of hymns continued until his death. Before breathing his last breath, he is said to have sung one of his favorite hymns: "I'll praise my maker while I've breath."

In Wesley's preface to *Sacred Melody* in 1761, he developed some seven specific directions for singing, which are printed in the current *Methodist Hymnal*. One of these admonishes the Methodists: "Sing lustily and with good courage. Beware of singing as if you were half dead, or half asleep; but lift up your voice with strength. Be no more afraid of your voice now, no more ashamed of its being heard, than when you sung the songs of Satan."

But it was really Charles Wesley who was the poet and hymn-writer of Methodism. In all, he wrote more than six thousand hymns, many of which are among the great hymns of the Christian church. He is considered by most hymnologists, both in quantity and quality alike, the great hymn-writer of all ages. He is rivaled only by Isaac Watts, the Dissenter of the previous century, who had become the father of the modern hymns by setting the metrical psalms to poetical form. But Charles Wesley's list would carry many more of the favorite hymns that became part of the heart and center of the Methodist worship and would account for the popularity and the appeal of Methodism to the black slaves. Singing also revolutionized the concept of worship and influenced the camp meetings and the revivals which blossomed into the Second Great Awakening. The circuit riders carried a simple message of the gospel and an informal service of worship, consisting primarily of extemporary preaching, extemporaneous prayer, and hymn-singing, across the fields and plains of America and into the backwoods and towns and hamlets.

There was something in the vigorous singing of the hymns of the Methodists that awakened a familiarity in the Africans, perhaps half-forgotten and half-remembered, but nevertheless still there, in the recesses of their being. Even with the absence of African gods and the replacement of the Christian god, the African heritage of singing was brought back to mind by the Methodist meetings. The ancient African dictum, "The spirit will not descend without song," was made manifest. And, "the still white notes of the Wesleyan Hymnal"[18] notwithstanding, it was a far cry from the Gregorian chants and plainsong.

Francis Asbury commented that the African slaves sang "in cheerful melody."[19] Perhaps it was the sound of their kinsmen joining in song that would lead hundreds of slaves to the sites of these evangelical meetings. The Rev. Greene gives a detailed description of how the hymn-singing spread into the cultural life of the black slave quarters.

> At night, especially in the summer time, after everybody had eaten supper, it was a common thing for us to sit outside. The old folks would get together and talk until bedtime. Sometimes somebody would start humming an old hymn, and then the next-door neighbor would pick it up. In this way it would finally get around to every house, and then the music started. Soon everybody would be gathered together, and such singing! It wouldn't be long before some of the slaves got happy and started to shouting.[20]

It is, therefore, not surprising that Charles A. Tindley, for more than thirty years the black Methodist pastor of East Calvary Methodist Episcopal Church of Philadelphia (now changed to Tindley Temple in honor of him), and a former slave, was to become a prolific writer of gospel hymns and the forerunner and father of modern gospel music.[21] His songs became a "profound universal appeal to the human heart with words of hope, cheer, love, and pity." Commenting on the contribution of this one-time slave and hod carrier, Dr. J. Jefferson Cleveland comments: "He bequeathed to all Methodism and to Christianity a legacy that will live on through his hymns."[22]

Another reason why blacks were attracted to Methodism was that the slaves were, early in the movement, allowed to preach and were licensed as local preachers and later as traveling preachers. As opposed to the Presbyterians, Congregationalists, Disciples, Lutherans, Episcopalians, Moravians, and other mainline Protestant denominations, Baptist and Methodist churches had black preachers. There was an exception here and there; for example, the Presbyterians licensed George M. Erskine, a slave in east Tennessee in 1818, and Hiram Revels, later to be elected to the United States Senate, left the African Methodist Episcopal Church to organize a Presbyterian Church in St. Louis in 1855, which was subsequently closed.

If the slave had a converted heart and a gifted tongue and showed talent for exhorting, he exhorted, and not merely to black congregations. There was an elite group of black Methodist preachers, including "Black Harry" Hosier, who traveled with Bishop Francis Asbury; Henry Evans, a free-born black of Virginia, who is credited with establishing Methodism among both blacks and whites in Fayetteville, North Carolina; and John Stewart, who ministered in Ohio among the Wyandotte Indians and gave birth to the home missions enterprise in the Methodist Church.

Raboteau points out that among the Methodists many black men served as lay preachers. While "they could not celebrate the sacraments" [nor could white lay preachers], they were allowed to preach and discipline black members "within a certain locale."[23] Even when the laws were passed forbidding such a practice, the Methodists sent out black assistants with their itinerant preachers. The Methodists skirted the law by creating a preaching category, "exhorters." In the strictest sense, black exhorters were really black preachers. And these so-called exhorters were known to act as pastors of their own people.[24]

Few have really assessed and appreciated the importance of these black preachers for the conversion of slaves to Christianity and the spread of Methodism among both blacks and whites. Following the Revolutionary War and into the early decades of the next century, they became the critical link between Christian belief and the experiential world of the slaves. It was these black preachers who saved their soul and sanity with an interpretation of the humanity of God's children and the fatherhood of God. He gave realism and substance to things hoped for and a taste of things not seen. He was a part of the travails of the people, for whatever happened to the people happened to him also. Wherever they were, he was there, too. Kneeling on the cold dirt floor of a slave hut . . . Picking cotton in the long, hot, dusty, and endless rows . . . Making his way along the long and lonely wilderness trails to get to his church and his people to fulfill his calling and keep his charge. He stood between the inexhaustible storehouse of hope and the depleted lives of his beleagured and bewildered flock and shouted a word to keep them going: "Walk together, children! Don't get weary!"

And he preached a fiery gospel with a pastor's

heart and proclaimed himself a steward of a mystery that offered to the oppressed slaves salvation and hope and an escape from earthly woes.

A correspondent to Georgia expressed her amazement at the eloquence of these preachers to the editor of the *American Missionary*:

I listened to a remarkable sermon or talk a few evenings since. The preacher spoke of the need for atonement for sin. "Bullocks c'dn't do it, heifers c'dn't do it, de blood of doves c'dn't do it—but up in heaven, for thousan and thousan of years, the Son was saying to the Father, "Put up a soul, put up a soul, Prepare me a body, an I will go an meet Justice on Calvary's brow!" He was so dramatic. In describing the crucifixion he said: "I see the sun when she turned herself black. I see the stars a fallin from the ski, and them old Herods comin out of their graves and goin about the city, an they knew 'twas the Lord's Glory."[25]

But the black slaves who heard these preachers often were used to such eloquence, and preferred its experiential, dramatic, and picturesque message. And they responded to him and his message with tears of sorrow and shouts of joy and committed lives. They were converted in great numbers, and black congregations sprang up wherever they were allowed.

It is at this critical juncture that a bicultural synthesis begins to take place. The Afro-American culture has its beginning as these black leaders nurture the birth of these Christian communities and become the initiators and prime movers of a culture that persists unto this day.

The University of Chicago sociologist, the late Robert Park, has commented on these men and their movement.

With the appearance of these men, the Negroes in America ceased to be a mission people. At least from this time on, the movement went on its own momentum, more and more largely under the direction of Negro leaders. Little Negro congregations, under the leadership of Negro preachers, sprang up wherever they were tolerated. Often they were suppressed, more often they were privately encouraged. Not infrequently they met in secret.[26]

Methodism was extended and black people responded to it in greater numbers because of these black sons of thunder who moved across the pages of history almost unnoticed by historians, but who made an indelible impression on the lives of black people, and thus began a continuing line of splendor. And the Christian faith was refashioned by this new breed to fit their own situation.

But before looking at the third factor in black people's response to Methodism, a word must be said about how the hierarchical structure viewed these men. Even though a number of black preachers served regular stations and circuits as well as in missions, and were licensed as exhorters and local preachers, there were severe limitations. They were licensed by the quarterly conferences and had no voice in their own annual renewal, nor did they vote for one another. As John Dixon Long, a white Methodist minister, put it: "Even in the midst of their brethren, they are made to feel they are not one in Christ Jesus."[27] Determinative control and power lay far beyond the reach of these men whose flaming ambition was to be faithfully on their errand as good servants of Jesus Christ.

The third factor in blacks' being attracted to and responding to Methodism was that it was adaptable enough to their own situation so that they could make it their own. They refashioned the Christian tradition as introduced by the zealous Methodists into a religion that served their needs and their situation. E. Franklin Frazier, in his penetrating study of *The Negro in America*, accounts for this factor:

But there were even more fundamental psychological factors in human nature which offer an explanation of the response of the slaves to the religion of the Methodists and Baptists. The slaves, who had been torn from their homeland, from family and friends, and whose cultural heritage had disintegrated or had lost its meaning in a new environment, were broken men. The bonds of a common tradition, of religious beliefs and practices, had been broken and the Negroes had become "atomized" in the American environment. Here was an appeal, emotional and simple, that provided a new way of life and drew them into a union at first with whites, but later formed a stronger bond with members of their own race.[28]

Without yielding Frazier's analysis in total that the Africans were completely "atomized,"[29] there is adequate evidence that the new religion creates a bond of social cohesion and influences what develops. But what emerges from the creative genius of these African slaves who became Methodists and Baptists is not merely a replica of the white religion or the white church. It is a dual process in which the blacks accept Christianity and the peculiar evangelical interpretation, and at the same time make it their own. They did not merely become Christians; they fashioned a Christian tradition to fit their own situation.

They created a faith that met their own needs as blacks experiencing a particular kind of oppression in America.[30]

One can even say they fashioned something new in the same sense that Shakespeare's plays were new. The themes and plots were not, for almost all of his stories were borrowed from chronicles, biography, prose tale, or Greek myths and tales. But the way that they were woven together and expressed was new. For he unerringly seized upon the dramatic elements and revealed life in its full richness and movement. What the black Methodist did with the Western Christian religion was to take on the outward appearance of Christian conversion, and take from it whatever was efficacious for easing their burdens in captivity, whatever offered hope in facing their earthly woes; and they seized its prophetic tradition for moral reform in a specific societal context and paid little attention to the rest.

The difference was not always apparent to the slavemaster, nor even to the white evangelical preachers and missionaries. A white Methodist minister who had preached to black Methodists at Charleston belatedly discovered the dichotomy and reflected this new knowledge in his report:

There were near fourteen hundred colored communicants. . . . [Their] service was always thronged—galleries, lower floor, chancel, pulpit, steps and all. . . . The preacher could not complain of any deadly space between himself and congregation. He was positively breast up to his people, with no possible loss of . . . rapport. Though ignorant of it at the time, he remembers now the cause of the enthusiasm under his deliverances [about] the "law of liberty" and "freedom from Egyptian bondage." What was figurative they interpreted literally. He thought of but one ending of the war; they quite another. He remembers the sixty-eight Psalm as affording numerous texts for their declaration, e.g., "Let God arise, let his enemies be scattered"; "The Chariots of God are twenty thousand"; "The hill of God is as the hill of Basham"; and especially, "Though ye have lain among the pots, yet shall ye be as the wings of a dove covered with silver, and her feathers with yellow gold." . . . It is mortifying now to think that his comprehension was not equal to the African intellect. All he thought about was relief from the servitude of sin, and freedom from the bondage of the devil. . . . But they interpreted it literally in the good time coming, which of course could not but make their ebony complexion attractive, very.[31]

The black Methodists may have been, by and large, uneducated, but they were not fools. They knew that a religion that talked about justice and

righteousness and oneness in Christ, but failed to ordain their brothers and husbands and fathers and insulted the black Christians by seating them in separate areas, and oppressed the black sons and daughters of a just God by forcing them to remain slaves had something wrong with it. It had to be reinterpreted and refashioned to meet their needs. There was nothing wrong with the message: there was something wrong with the messengers and those who sat in the choicest seats.

NOTES

1. Harry V. Richardson, *Dark Salvation* (Garden City, N.Y.: Anchor Books, 1976), p. 47.
2. Nathan Bangs, *A History of the Methodist Episcopal Church* (New York: The Methodist Book Concern, 1838), vol. 1, pp. 111-12.
3. *The Experience and Travels of Mr. Freeborn Garrettson* (Philadelphia: Parry Hall, 1791), pp. 76-77.
4. Richard Allen, *The Life Experience and Gospel Labors of the Rt. Rev. Richard Allen* (Nashville: Abingdon Press, 1960), 2nd Ed., pp. 15-16.
5. Letter to John Wesley, quoted in Abel Stevens, *History of the Methodist Church* (New York: Carlton and Porter, 1866), vol. 1, p. 103.
6. Ibid., p. 236-37.
7. *The Book of Discipline of The United Methodist Church*, p. 14.
8. Quoted by Walter G. Muelder in "Methodism's Contribution to Social Reform," *Methodism*, ed. William K. Anderson (Nashville: The Methodist Publishing House, 1947), p. 193.
9. John Thompson, *The Life of John Thompson, A Fugitive Slave* (Worcester, Mass., 1856), pp. 18-19. Quoted by Albert J. Raboteau, *Slave Religion* (New York: Oxford University Press, 1980), p. 133.
10. Richardson, *Dark Salvation*, p. 52.
11. Ibid.
12. See Gayraud Wilmore's discussion of this point in *Black Religion and Black Radicalism* (Garden City, N.Y.: Anchor Books, 1973), pp. 77ff.
13. Quoted in *Classified Digest of the Records of the Society for the Propagation of the Gospel in Foreign Parts* (London, 1893), p. 16. Cited by E. Franklin Frazier, *The Negro in the United States* (New York: Macmillan Company, 1949), p. 337.
14. John Thompson, *The Life of* . . . Quoted in Raboteau, *Slave Religion*, p. 133.
15. Stevens, *History*, p. 44.
16. Raboteau, *Slave Religion*, p. 133.
17. See "Preface" to *The Methodist Hymnal* (Nashville: The Methodist Publishing House, 1964), p. v.
18. A pejorative description of the Wesleyan hymn often used by Imanu Amiri Baraka (LeRoi Jones).
19. See Richardson, *Dark Salvation*, p. 48.
20. *God Struck Me Dead* (Philadelphia: Pilgrim Press, 1969), pp. 87-88.
21. He is described as the "father of gospel music" by Thomas A. Dorsey and the late Mahalia Jackson, a modern gospel singer.
22. See J. Jefferson Cleveland, ed., *Songs of Zion* (Nashville: Abingdon Press, 1981), pp. 4-6.
23. Raboteau, *Slave Religion*, p. 136.
24. See Donald G. Matthews, *Slavery and Methodism: A Chapter in American Morality, 1780–1845* (Princeton: Princeton University Press, 1965), pp. 64ff. Also see his explanatory notes in ibid.
25. *American Missionary*, 8 (April, 1864): 100. Quoted in Raboteau, *Slave Religion*, p. 235.
26. Robert E. Park, "The Conflict and Fusion of Cultures with Special Reference to the Negro," *Journal of Negro History*: 4:2 (April, 1919): 120.

27. E. A. Andrews, *Slavery and the Domestic Slave-Trade in the United States* (Boston: 1836), p. 37. Quoted in Raboteau, *Slave Religion*, p. 207.

28. Frazier, *The Negro*, p. 339.

29. Raboteau's discussion, summary and evaluation of the age-old Herskovits-Frazier debate is refreshingly illuminating. See Raboteau, *Slave Religion*, pp. 48ff.

30. See Gayraud S. Wilmore, *Black Religion and Black Radicalism* (Garden City, N.Y.: Anchor Books, 1973) pp. 1-19. Raboteau, *Slave Religion*, pp. 152-210, esp. pp. 207-10. Peter J. Paris has a well-developed argument that there is a distinct "Black Christian Tradition" that has developed in America "as a non-racist appropriation of the Christian faith" which challenges racism in all spheres of its influence: social, religious, moral. See his essay, "The Moral and Political Significance of the Black Churches in America" in *Belief and Ethics: Essays in Honor of Alvin Pitcher* (Chicago: Center for Scientific Study of Religion, 1977), pp. 315-29.

31. A. M. Chreitzberg, *Early Methodism in the Carolinas* (Nashville: Methodist Book Concern, 1897), pp. 158-59.

2. BLACK METHODISTS
AND THE
METHODIST ROMANCE

C. Eric Lincoln

Few churches can compare with Methodism in the richness and fruitfulness of its heritage. It is a religion ordained by the times and the circumstances which witnessed and responded to its birth, yet it has in a mere two centuries matured into a faith for all seasons and all conditions of the human experience. Born of the most parochial interests, the Wesleyan tradition has become in two hundred years as near a universal faith as mankind is likely to develop. The circuits of its busy, indefatigable ministry touch and reinforce each other wherever in the world the cry for the sponsorship of God and the fellowship of man has been heard. In Methodism, there has never been a question of Whom shall I send? or Who will go for us? but merely Does the bishop know there's anybody out there? He'll send somebody!

Fortunately, there is always somebody to send, for the men and women who comprise the clergy of the Methodist Church are as dedicated and selfless as they are confident of their mission and certain of their calling. They are a unique breed, a peculiar people.

Undoubtedly, the distinctiveness of Methodists and the uniqueness of Methodism derive in large part from a body of tradition and belief which over the years has defined the prism through which Methodists see themselves. I was tempted to say "the body of tradition and convention which constitute the mold in which they were originally cast." But the notion of a mold is too rigid. A mold can only produce clone-like replications of a prototype, allowing no latitude for growth or modification, whereas a prism refracts reality in terms of the source, the angle, and the intensity of the light it receives. Such a metaphor best describes Methodism, I believe, for like all mature religions, Methodism changes with each experience of new light, yet that light is always refracted through a body of faith which is itself unchanging. It is a dynamic, living religion, always struggling to remain what it must be; always endeavoring to become what it ought to be. That, I take it is the principal reason for this consultation: to assess where we've been,

to better understand how we got to be where we are, that we may better employ our endowments to move on toward where we ought to be.

One very critical index of our progress, or lack of it, has to do with how we as a universal church and as morally responsible individuals who claim for ourselves the spiritual comforts of the Wesleyan tradition, have dealt with the problem of race and ethnicity. While it is true that such a problem could not exist in the ideal church, we are not yet that church, though we struggle according to our light to become it.

This section of this consultation addresses itself to the troublesome dilemma of being "inclusive" in doctrine but less certain in performance. The dilemma is all the more disquieting because our notable successes so often illustrate our less joyful failures. Certainly we have had a long time to resolve the dilemma—longer than the church has been in existence, for blacks have been part and parcel of Methodism since its inception. John Wesley, himself, while serving in Georgia, denounced slavery (and by implication every form of racism in 1739), and baptized the first black Methodist in 1758. In 1766, blacks were represented in the very first congregation of American Methodists. From 1782 to 1810—thirty-two years, Rev. Harry Hosier, or "Black Harry" as he was called, traveled with Bishop Asbury. Hosier was such a notable preacher that it is said that the people gathered from miles around to "shake hands with the bishop and to hear Black Harry preach." Dr. James Rush, the sage of Philadelphia, called Hosier the greatest orator in America.

There was something about Methodism that was uniquely attractive to black Christians. Blacks helped to found—and to finance historic John Street Methodist Church in New York, and large numbers of black Methodists held membership in St. George's in Philadelphia. When in 1791, the Rev. Richard Allen was asked by the Free African Society (he founded) to assume the leadership of the first black Episcopal Church in America, Allen declined the honor. For said he, "I could not be anything but a Methodist, as I was born and awakened under them." He also said of Methodists, their "plain and simple gospel suits best for the people; for the unlearned can understand, and the learned are sure to understand." Since Allen and a number of other black Methodists had been pulled from their knees for inadvertently praying in a section of the gallery reserved for whites at St. Georges, one cannot help but be impressed by the tenacity with which his faith in Methodism was secured. Predictably, when Allen did found a church three years later, it was a *Methodist* church: Bethel African Methodist Episcopal Church, the mother church of the largest denomination of black Methodists in the world.

Many other illustrations of the black romance with Methodists and Methodism could be mentioned, but one more instance must suffice. In 1780, Henry Evans, a devout Methodist preacher, born free in Virginia, and licensed to preach in Stokes County, North Carolina, passed through Fayetteville, on his way to Charleston where he hoped to ply his trade as a shoemaker. Appalled by the absence of any Christian training for blacks in the Fayetteville area, he decided to stay on there to preach to them, but he was whipped for his impudence and forbidden to hold services. Undismayed, he formed an underground church that met clandestinely in the forests and the sandhills. So determined was he that on three occasions in the dead of winter he broke ice to swim the Cape Fear River to be with his converts. Eventually, the plantation owners were so impressed with the improved behavior of their slaves that they stopped harrassing Evans and permitted him and his flock to build a crude church where they could meet under the watchful eyes of the slavemasters.

In a short time, so many whites attended his services that the walls of the church had to be knocked down so that adjoining sheds could be built for the slaves. In 1805, Evans's church, now with a controlling white congregation, became a part of the Methodist Episcopal Church, and he became official pastor to the first Methodist Church in that section of North Carolina. He retired in 1808, and his grateful congregation pensioned him and built living quarters for him behind the church he founded. Thereafter white pastors were assigned until the church reverted to black leadership after the Civil War. By that time, Methodism counted well over 150,000 black members, most of them in the South, and despite the fact that the Methodist Church would flounder and split over the issue of slavery, it is interesting to note that when Gabriel Prosser mounted his abortive insurrection in 1800, he gave explicit instructions to the desperate men who rode with him: "Do not harm any of the people called Methodists." In retrospect, we may well struggle with the rationale of Prosser's dictum for it is our contemporary understanding that whoever sullies God's image and compromises man's humanity by wantonly and selfishly taking away the freedom of an individual does so at his peril, and is entitled to the chastening the reciprocation of his sentiments will induce. Why then such an anomalous, such an apparently inordinate concern about Methodists—especially those who had strayed so far from the moral principles and the theological precepts of John Wesley? Just who are these "Methodists," and what is this "Methodism"? And what are its prospects for the revitalization of its founding principles and its significant humanitarian traditions? These are the questions to which this consultation must address itself, or our efforts here may someday be dismissed as a week-long review of two centuries of Methodist romance, signifying nothing palpable in the human predicament.

VII. Wesleyan Mission and Evangelism in Global Context

1. PROPHETIC EVANGELISM: THE GOOD NEWS OF GLOBAL GRACE

David Lowes Watson

I. Social Justification: Toward an Expanded Evangelism

It is an aspect of our Methodist heritage often taken for granted or overlooked, that Wesley developed his strategy for evangelizing the British Isles by doing it, thus obliging him at an early stage in his work to contextualize the gospel. The account he gives us of his first venture into field preaching indicates that it was a cultural confrontation of the first order; yet it became the pattern of Methodist outreach throughout the country, cutting across social and ecclesial lines, and, to a larger degree than has yet been researched, surmounting linguistic barriers.[1] If we are to draw on our tradition for a theology of evangelism, therefore, we must take note of Wesley's theological principles as he applied them in the field. Our questions must be honed, as were his, in the interface between gospel and hearers, and not, as so often happens, in the more limited interface between theology and worldview, where the language of discourse is usually academic and restricted by very particular dialogical referents. Authentic evangelism must be forged in the praxis of taking the gospel to ordinary men and women, and thereby having to find the appropriate form and method for its presentation.

Wesley's directive in this regard is quite clear. He quickly found that the cutting edge of the gospel is the confrontation of human sin, and that the love of God cannot be proclaimed with meaning until this has become a point of conviction. His method for evangelism was thus from law to gospel, from the bondage of sin to the adoption of grace. Much though he stressed the building up of faith and the working out of discipleship, the necessary first step was this critical challenge, made by the evangelist and met by the believer in repentance and conversion.[2]

It is at this point that the evangelist who studies Wesley is often placed at a disadvantage by the theologian who studies Wesley.[3] On the tacit assumption that Wesley's method for evangelism is appropriate and efficacious, the theologian will argue that the new birth is *only* the beginning, and that Wesley's doctrine of sanctification is far more important in the overall perspective of Christian discipleship. We cannot evangelize merely by proclaiming personal salvation from sin, not least because the doctrine of justification has been over-personalized by our evangelistic tradition. We must focus on the changed life which results from Christian commitment, and on its social implications. Indeed, to proclaim personal salvation from sin is a weighty error if the need for a changed life and a changed world is not integral to the message. Grace is not cheap, and the cost of discipleship should always be made clear at the very outset.[4]

The disadvantage in this for the evangelist is not lessened by the fact that the argument is valid. Wesley himself affirmed the necessity of preaching Christ in all his offices, as prophet as well as priest,[5] and from the very beginning of the Methodist movement he stressed the necessity of good works in the *ordo salutis*.[6] Moreover, there are just enough examples of cheap grace offered by contemporary evangelists to persuade the theologian that evangelism as a whole needs a greater sensitivity to social sin.[7] The problem is that this insight of itself gives very little help to the evangelist who, being in the field, is only too aware of social sin. The evangelistic question is how to address this social sin in terms of the gospel; for, as any practised evangelist can readily testify, to proclaim what ought to happen in human society without any promise of how it can be brought about, is to proclaim a message without power. It is to preach only the law; whereas, the whole point of the law in evangelism is to provide a cutting edge for the redemptive grace of the gospel.

It is no surprise, therefore, to find the field of evangelism wrestling with two perspectives which should provide a synthesis, but which usually prove antithetical. On the one hand, there is the proven evangelistic method of proclaiming the gospel by law and grace, challenging human sin and offering forgiveness and reconciliation. On the other hand, there is the proven theological analysis that human sin is

Reprinted by permission of the *Perkins Journal*.

broader than the individual and reaches into oppressive systems from which people also need to be saved. The challenge of contemporary evangelism is how this wider perspective, the gospel for sinners *and* sinned against, might be incorporated into an evangelistic message which goes beyond personal conviction, repentance, forgiveness, and regeneration, to a global hope and vision: a message for human systems as well as human beings; a hope for human history as well as human souls.

The theologies most frequently employed to substantiate this expanded gospel are those of liberating praxis, and we are fortunate to have a volume of essays from the *Sixth Oxford Institute for Methodist Theological Studies* which breaks some important new ground in linking them to Wesley's doctrine of sanctification.[8] By contextualizing Wesley's praxis for the contemporary church, the essays show that the personal regeneration fostered by the societies, classes, and bands, had inescapable social implications. Notwithstanding their lack of conceptualization in Wesley's own theology, these issues emerged in the nineteenth century at the vanguard of social reform. The point is argued perhaps most cogently by Theodore Runyon's major essay of the volume, which correlates Wesley's emphasis on the necessity of transforming good works with Marx's analysis of social alienation. Liberation from unjust systems is thus a corollary of personal sanctification, a necessary working out of God's salvation.[9]

Once again, however, the evangelist is left at a disadvantage. If we accept Wesley's guidelines for evangelistic proclamation, then it becomes clear that the pivotal doctrine for evangelism is not sanctification, but justification. This is not to deny the importance of sanctification in proclaiming the gospel; but the cutting edge, the point at which people will respond to the *evangel*, is the conviction of sin and the offer of forgiveness and reconciliation. For Wesley, justification was essentially the response to God's offer of salvation: an acceptance by the sinner of God's pardon, and an acceptance by God of the sinner, warts and all. It was a liberation for joyful and obedient service, in the assurance that the best one could do was now good enough for God.[10]

It is this which the evangelist often finds lacking in theologies of liberating praxis—any real development of justification as a social doctrine alongside that of sanctification. Social and systemic sin is well analyzed, and the hope of the New Age is well advocated. But social redemption cannot be proclaimed as an *evange-listic* message without the liberating power of present pardon. In the same way that justification by faith for the individual is not only conviction of sin and repentance, but also the acceptance of God's forgiveness and reconciling love, so the extension of evangelism to the censure of social sin entails the correlative acceptance by God of sinful systems as the condition of their regeneration. Only thus can the evangelist contextualize the gospel for a post-Marxian, as well as a post-Freudian, age.

The theological groundwork for this broader doctrine of justification lies first of all in a self-contextualizing of Protestant thought, and a significant resource in this regard, one which should prove consequential for Western theological understanding, is the volume of Robert E. Cushman's collected essays, *Faith Seeking Understanding*.[11] In the introduction, Cushman traces the course of Western theology which has brought us to the isolation of man as the *de facto* starting point for theological understanding. Christian wisdom, as the witness of faith, was the standpoint mediated by Augustine to the Latin West from the Greek and Latin Fathers. It was reversed by the Aristotelianism of the High Middle Ages from *fides quarens intellectum* to *intellectus quarens fidem*, with the consequent conception of a two-fold truth in which faith perfected reason. The reaction to this in the fourteenth and fifteenth centuries was a radical resurgence of faith under Scotist and Occamist influences, which virtually eclipsed the role of reason in Christian wisdom, and provided the context for the Reformation thinking which dominates us to this day.

This [resurgence of faith] was conjoined with, as it was also dependent upon, an awesome doctrine of God—the doctrine of absolute divine sovereignty. In provenance it was Augustinian, but, on grounds peculiar to itself, it incurred the extinction of any intelligible connections between nature and divine grace or between man and God. These were now at the absolute determination and, therefore, inscrutable will of omnipotent fiat. It was this philosophical background against which Reformation theology of the European continent was formulated and which it reflects. Consequently, as may be seen, it was formulated upon the urgently needed and near universally espoused premise of Luther's spiritual ordeal: salvation by grace *alone* through faith *alone*. Since there is no way at all from man to God, Scripture *alone* shows an opened way from God to man. The *Deus absconditus* becomes, for Luther, *Deus revelatus*.[12]

Cushman proceeds to argue that this has

conditioned Protestant theology to a view of God's creation "no longer conceived as in any sense God's established order of due process according to *inherent* secondary powers of nature or natures, . . . thereby depriving human nature of *inherent* dignity."[13] The result has been the "orphaning of man along with the dissolution of the *inherent structures* of the created order of due natural process," leading to a newly discovered and insistent subjectivity.

> Perhaps the scales were tipped in favor of a pervasive subjectivity by the Reformation, but not by it alone; Occamism had a wider patronage. In its secular form, the tireless preoccupation of man with the universe of his ego-self—having explored through the Enlightenment all the resources of "reason alone"—reemerged at the start of the 19th century in the vein of Romanticism. In the domain of religion, it took the form of what we usually speak of as "modern Protestant theology." And, at this point, Christian faith, in the New Testament sense, was successively translated into some species or other of the human self-consciousness. With Kant, it was the moral-consciousness, or the God-consciousness (Schleiermacher), the value-consciousness (Ritschl), the religious *a priori* (Troeltsch), religious experience (Wm. James), ultimate concern (Tillich), authentic self-understanding (Bultmann).[14]

These are, as Cushman concedes, broad strokes in which to plot the pedigree of modern Protestant thought. But his scholarship is sure, and his purpose is salutary: to contextualize Western theology for what it is, a heritage with Occamist rootage "left standing at its inception and, even now, largely unexamined," but which, once examined, shows that "the watchwords of the Reformation—*sola* gratia, *sola* fides, *sola* Scriptura—are valiant but, withal, deceptive. . . . [For] behind their bold program, including "their enthronement of the Word of God,"

> is a counterproductive philosophy of Reality, present but unacknowledged. It is a philosophy according to which there are no ways to comprehend significant relations between the Creator, his world, the creatures and man—save as by "special providences." In such a world, faith there may indeed be, but it can hardly advance to understanding. And, in such a world, the divorce of nature and grace persistently fosters the breaching of Christianity and culture and invites the progressive secularization of the work-a-day world. So, in spite of itself, this philosophy robs God of the glory. It does so in sundry tendencies on "imputed righteousness," to multiple instances in our time that refer to the Kingdom of God as beyond history.[15]

This masterly piece of theological traditioning demonstrates why contemporary evangelism and contemporary theology so often conflict without resolution of the conflict. The pietism which so offends the theologian and the theology which so confounds the evangelist are but two horses from the same stable. Neither has the capability of criticizing or complementing the other, since both spring from a philosophical framework which has not been adequately analyzed. And while the political theologies which draw their philosophical framework from Marxian views of history are one alternative—and an important one, since they have brought eschatology back to the fore of missional outreach —they fail to diagnose the real problem of Western Protestant theology, which is to acknowledge that it is governed by philosophical criteria peculiarly Western in origin.

This is not the place to argue the point further, but the inference is inescapable: that the tension between first and third world theologies will remain obstructive rather than creative as long as Western theologians fail to undertake this fundamental self-contextualization.[16] As a minimal gesture, for example, it could be agreed that "systematic" theology be more accurately styled "Western" theology. It happens to have been forged systematically, and often with marked brilliance, but in fact it is particularly, and even parochially, a product of Western thought, and should be recognized as such. This, rather than further praxis-abstract confrontations, might begin the liberation of a theology for evangelism. It would also provide an appropriate corrective to the theologies of history, political and liberationist, which, as we have suggested, offer an *evangel* of global hope without an adequate doctrine of justification. These theologies have done much to counter the spiritualized eschatology which, among other trends identified by Cushman, has placed the kingdom of God beyond history.[17] But without the necessary evangelistic dynamic of forgiveness and reconciliation, this proclamation of future hope merely engenders a deep cognitive dissonance among Christians between what the world is and what the world ought to be. Those who respond to the vision and the expectation of the New Age find in such a message no present power of grace out of which to proclaim it with assurance, no catalyst to energize the tension. The world is confronted with its sin, but is offered no *immediate* hope of its salvation.

As an example of this confrontation, we can turn to a collection of essays by John Howard Yoder, one of the most significant contemporary prophets of peace. In *The Original Revolution,* written for the most part during the sixties in the context of emerging theologies of liberation, Yoder argues convincingly for an eschatology of God's fulfilling work in history as opposed to an apocalypticism which renders God remote from human affairs.[18] Adopting Oscar Cullman's analogy of D-Day and V-Day, he argues that, since the old and new aeons overlap in history, history perforce is the sphere of the church's work.[19] Without this eschatological impetus, there is paganization of the church and demonization of the state, with the state usurping God's causes.[20] A noneschatological history, he continues, is unprotected against subjectivism, and the realism of the Constantinian church, given much substance by Schweitzer's questionable eschatology, concedes to politics a largely free hand.[21]

So far so good. But as Yoder propounds the social sanctification for which the theologies of hope and liberation contend, he qualifies it by stating that prophets can never offer a positive solution to the problems of the state, since the state is always imperfect. It is a mistake, he suggests, for Christians to try to define the state positively when their agenda, pending the eschaton, must always be corrective.[22] The *evangel* can offer present justification for the individual in history, but not for social structures.

Significantly, among the perspectives which Yoder regards as inadequate for this Christian worldview, is the notion, found in the Anglican tradition, that the Incarnation constitutes a divine sanction of all human concerns. It is deceptively incomplete, he suggests, to assume that "our work and our family, the total fabric of our society—economics and warfare, have been bathed in the light of God's presence. . . . When God came among men He did not approve of and sanction *everything*. . . . He did not make of *all* human activity, not even of all well-intentioned human activity, a means of grace."[23]

In referring to the Anglican tradition, Yoder has rightly identified the most important exception to the nominalist framework within which Protestant theology has functioned. For it was the refusal of Henry VIII to permit continental influences to dominate English theology which allowed the Anglican *via media* to develop as an alternative theological method, generating in turn the *Ecclesiastical Polity* of Richard Hooker, the Oxford Rationalists, the Cambridge Platonists, Jeremy Taylor, Richard Baxter, to Wesley himself. And, perhaps not surprisingly, Wesley again holds the answer.

As with most of his theology, Wesley's doctrine of creation is not well developed, being subsumed by his overwhelming concern with evangelistic outreach. Nor yet did he have a developed political theory. But there are places where he makes very clear that he gave little attention to the broader questions of creation and society precisely because he appropriated his doctrine of both from the Anglican tradition.[24] Rather than view the state as chronically deficient in God's grace, he saw it as being acceptable to God as an ordained structure; imperfect of course, and sinful, but reformable under God's justice, rather than reprobate. Just as persons are convicted of sin, repent, are reconciled to God, and then grow in grace, so does the rest of God's creation.[25]

This has profound implications for our evangelism. To begin with, it calls us to accept God's grace, not only in persons, but in societies and systems. It calls us to be prophets, not only against injustice and oppression, but for the working out of God's salvation in the world. It means regarding the question of power, not merely as that of identifying its abuse, but also of its redemption by God for the New Age. And more, it means being ready to accept this redemption when it actually occurs.[26] The enlargement of our evangelistic vision must have as full a gospel message for systems as for individuals. Communities, cities, nations, conglomerates, must not only be analyzed as sinful, but must be called to repentance, and can *be expected to repent*. Their salvation, along with that of individuals, is to be nurtured and brought to fulfillment by the love and the grace of God.

Without such a theology of social justification, "traditional" evangelism will continue to evince an overpersonalized gospel, and theologies which call us to a global vision of hope will remain powerless. For if the gospel which challenges the systems in which they live and work is seen to lack the redemptive grace of the gospel which challenges them personally, then people will continue to distinguish their salvation from that of the world. But if the *ordo salutis* can be discerned in a social and global setting as well as an individual setting, subject to the sovereignty of grace at every level, then well-established evangelistic methods can indeed be expanded to a global vision.

The following model is an attempt to establish practical guidelines for just such an evangelism.

II. A Model for Prophetic Evangelism

1. Theological Foundations

Prophetic evangelism is the form of evangel-

allocate specific responsibilities to its members:

** Someone should be assigned to read the newspapers every day, and clip out any items of interest.
** Periodicals should likewise be assigned: *Time, Newsweek,* and more specialized magazines of social interest.
** Religious publications should be covered as representatively as possible.
** Denominational periodicals are of special interest, since preliminary interpretative work has often already been done.
** At least one person should be assigned to biblical and theological research on relevant issues — and this should *not* be the minister.
** Political literature should be covered, propagational as well as informational.
** Local and national political events should likewise be covered. Visiting speakers to the community should be evaluated.
** Cultural affairs should be noted — movies of interest or controversy, for example.
** The task force should consult regularly with members of the community beyond the church, particularly those engaged in social work.
** They should also consult regularly with other church members for their insights.

At the weekly meetings, the most important task is to collate all of this data, and engage in an "editorial conference" to determine the evangelistic relevance of what is available.

The following questions should be asked:

*** Is the justice, power, freedom, peace, or love of God discernible in this happening or insight?
*** If so, in what ways?
*** How can it be interpreted as a sign of the New Age of Jesus Christ?
*** How should this interpretation be communicated? Verbally? In written form? Visually? One-to-one? Collectively?
*** To whom should it be communicated? To the church membership? Beyond the church? To the community? Beyond the community?
*** How can this interpretation make clear the invitation of the gospel to be part of the New Age of Jesus Christ? Is the church ready to receive those who do respond?

or

*** Is the injustice, tyranny, oppression, self-centeredness, or hatred of the world discernible in this happening or insight?
*** If so, in what ways?
*** How can it be interpreted more clearly as an impediment to Christ's coming *basileia*? How can it be branded as *out of date*?
*** How should this interpretation be communicated? Verbally? In written form? Visually? One-to-one? Collectively?
*** To whom should it be communicated? To the church membership? Beyond the church? To the community? Beyond the community?
*** How can this interpretation make clear the invitation of the gospel to repent and be reconciled as part of God's new creation? Is the church ready to deal with a response to this invitation?

4. Implementing the Work of the Task Force

To ensure that the task force maintains a truly representative role in the life of the congregation, there should be a regular process of consultation over any statements or actions which go beyond the church membership. Examples of these might be:

** A letter to the local or national press.
** A regular newsletter delivered to every home in the community, consisting of evangelistic interpretations—and *not* church news!
** Radio or television spots of 15, 30, or 60 seconds at most. This use of mass media is often much less expensive than imagined, and permits the use of air time in a direct and focused format.
** Advertisements in the local press.
** Photographic essays, utilizing the insights of the task force through the camera and appropriate captions.

On those occasions when no direct action is envisaged beyond the church membership, the task force should ensure that all church members receive the benefit of its work by preparing regular reports or information sheets, passing on the interpretative editing which has taken place. The purpose of the information sheets should be made clear: they are not merely to inform, but to provide a means for each person in the church to communicate the gospel prophetically. A sample information sheet might read as follows:[27]

allocate specific responsibilities to its members:

** Someone should be assigned to read the newspapers every day, and clip out any items of interest.
** Periodicals should likewise be assigned: *Time*, *Newsweek*, and more specialized magazines of social interest.
** Religious publications should be covered as representatively as possible.
** Denominational periodicals are of special interest, since preliminary interpretative work has often already been done.
** At least one person should be assigned to biblical and theological research on relevant issues — and this should *not* be the minister.
** Political literature should be covered, propagational as well as informational.
** Local and national political events should likewise be covered. Visiting speakers to the community should be evaluated.
** Cultural affairs should be noted — movies of interest or controversy, for example.
** The task force should consult regularly with members of the community beyond the church, particularly those engaged in social work.
** They should also consult regularly with other church members for their insights.

At the weekly meetings, the most important task is to collate all of this data, and engage in an "editorial conference" to determine the evangelistic relevance of what is available.
The following questions should be asked:
*** Is the justice, power, freedom, peace, or love of God discernible in this happening or insight?
*** If so, in what ways?
*** How can it be interpreted as a sign of the New Age of Jesus Christ?
*** How should this interpretation be communicated? Verbally? In written form? Visually? One-to-one? Collectively?
*** To whom should it be communicated? To the church membership? Beyond the church? To the community? Beyond the community?
*** How can this interpretation make clear the invitation of the gospel to be part of the New Age of Jesus Christ? Is the church ready to receive those who do respond?

or

*** Is the injustice, tyranny, oppression, self-centeredness, or hatred of the world discernible in this happening or insight?
*** If so, in what ways?
*** How can it be interpreted more clearly as an impediment to Christ's coming *basileia*? How can it be branded as *out of date*?
*** How should this interpretation be communicated? Verbally? In written form? Visually? One-to-one? Collectively?
*** To whom should it be communicated? To the church membership? Beyond the church? To the community? Beyond the community?
*** How can this interpretation make clear the invitation of the gospel to repent and be reconciled as part of God's new creation? Is the church ready to deal with a response to this invitation?

4. Implementing the Work of the Task Force

To ensure that the task force maintains a truly representative role in the life of the congregation, there should be a regular process of consultation over any statements or actions which go beyond the church membership. Examples of these might be:
** A letter to the local or national press.
** A regular newsletter delivered to every home in the community, consisting of evangelistic interpretations—and *not* church news!
** Radio or television spots of 15, 30, or 60 seconds at most. This use of mass media is often much less expensive than imagined, and permits the use of air time in a direct and focused format.
** Advertisements in the local press.
** Photographic essays, utilizing the insights of the task force through the camera and appropriate captions.

On those occasions when no direct action is envisaged beyond the church membership, the task force should ensure that all church members receive the benefit of its work by preparing regular reports or information sheets, passing on the interpretative editing which has taken place. The purpose of the information sheets should be made clear: they are not merely to inform, but to provide a means for each person in the church to communicate the gospel prophetically. A sample information sheet might read as follows:[27]

Task Force on Prophetic Evangelism
Report to Church Members

Item

At the last three meetings of the task force, we have considered ways of communicating the Christian message to our community.

At each meeting we have also been confronted by the quadrennial emphasis of The United Methodist Church on world hunger. The member assigned to denominational literature found something new each week to make us mindful that every two seconds someone in the world dies of hunger.

The task force found this increasingly disturbing, because our church is at present holding $1,000 in reserve to purchase a new carpet for the sanctuary. It was unanimously agreed that this was a conflict of objectives.

Evangelistic Interpretation

Jesus Christ announced and inaugurated a New Age, the *basileia*, in which there is no room for hunger and suffering.

The New Age is not yet here in its fullness, not least because some people in the world have the bad manners to eat in plenty while *at the same time* people die from starvation. The command is very clear. The good news of the gospel will not be heard by those with empty stomachs.

Our $1,000 carpet fund is therefore *out of date* and an impediment to the New Age.

Recommendations

Even though our annual budget is only $7,200, and even though people have contributed to this fund over several years, the task force recommends that the church give away this money immediately to UMCOR.

Further, that we send a letter to all present and past members, informing them why we have done this. That we also request our decision be published in the conference newspaper in the hope that the *evangel* might prompt others to similar action. Giving of the same proportion conference-wide would result in an immediate donation to UMCOR of $3,051,252.

NOTES

1. Wesley, *Journal*, vol. 2, p. 172. The point about language barriers should not be regarded lightly. As the visitor to contemporary Britain quickly apprehends, regional accents and dialects render the English language incomprehensible in many parts. And since dialect is closely linked to social and economic caste, it can safely be assumed that not least of the innovations of Wesley's outdoor preaching was the sound of an educated accent in direct communication with common speech. See W.]

Doughty, *John Wesley, Preacher* (London: Epworth Press, 1955), pp.146ff.

2. Wesley, *Letters*, vol. 3, pp. 79-82; *Minutes of the Methodist Conferences, from the First held in London by the Late Rev. John Wesley, A.M., in the year 1744*, vol. 1 (London: Conference Office, 1812), p.20; *Wesley's Standard Sermons*, ed. Edward H. Sugden (2 vols.; London: Epworth Press, 1921), vol. 1, pp. 178-98.

3. Indeed, the point can be made much more generally, in that dialogue between evangelism and theology throughout the church is rarely interdisciplinary or properly collegial. Evangelists and theologians alike permit theology to exercise a disproportionate influence over evangelism. This is not to suggest that evangelism should not rely on theology for clarification of the message and criteria for its proclamation; but it is to say that theology is seldom tested by its applicability to the proclamation of the gospel.

For example, it is well established that contemporary theology is richly pluralistic. It would thus seem appropriate for evangelists to select from available theologies the ones most appropriate for evangelism, as increasingly is the accepted practice in other areas of ministry, such as church education, pastoral care, and social action. In evangelism, however, this point of collegiality has yet to be established. Disputes in the field continue to stem primarily from theological polemics, especially in soteriology and eschatology; and theologians, instead of working through these issues and leaving the evangelists to utilize the fruits of their work, still expect evangelists to be accountable to their own particular theological criteria. This of course permits the theologian to question the appropriateness of evangelism indefinitely, since the criteria for appropriateness are those of critical reflection, and the evangelist is a practitioner.

The result is a deep confusion over the church's evangelistic mission in the world. There are some ministers and laity who try to meet the criteria of the theologians for appropriate evangelistic outreach, and who find this such a demanding exercise that they have little time or energy left for practising evangelism. There are others who find the lack of collegiality so frustrating that they reject theological dialogue altogether, and thereby develop evangelistic practices which most certainly should be questioned theologically.

The danger in this for evangelism, in the United States and throughout the world, is that strategy and theology are increasingly perceived to be alternative rather than complementary criteria; and in an age of advanced communications technology, this is leading to new and troubling divisions in missional outreach. The answer lies in a genuine dialogue between evangelism and theology through a mutual recognition of priorities: the theologian providing critical criteria by which to measure the proclamation of the gospel in the world; and the evangelist discerning the judgment of ordinary people on that theology as the message is taken into the world. At very least it means affirming, in the midst of theological pluralism, that some theologies are more useful for evangelism than others.

The Working Group on Evangelism at the *Seventh Oxford Institute for Methodist Theological Studies* explored this question in some detail. See pages 138-71 in the published version of those papers, *The Future of The Methodist Theological Traditions*, ed. by M. Douglas Meeks (Nashville: Abingdon Press, 1985).

4. This is a very different from the point being made by Roy Sano, that salvation from sin is not a full salvation as long as people remain oppressed by the usurpers of divine sovereignty. It would of course be a tautology to stress costly discipleship for the oppressed.

5. Wesley, *Sermons*, vol. 2, pp. 76, 444-45.

6. *Minutes*, pp.4ff. Cf. *The Works of John Wesley*, 3rd ed. (14 vols.; London: Wesleyan Methodist Book Room, 1872), 8:275ff.

7. See, e.g., William K. McElvaney, *Good news is bad news is good news . . .* (Maryknoll: Orbis Books, 1980); James Armstrong, *From the Underside: Evangelism from a Third World Vantage Point* (Maryknoll: Orbis Books, 1981); John Walsh, *Evangelization and Justice: New Insights for Christian Ministry* (Maryknoll: Orbis Books, 1982).

8. *Sanctification and Liberation: Liberation Theologies in the Light of the Wesleyan Tradition*, ed. Theodore Runyon (Nashville: Abingdon Press, 1981).

9. Ibid., pp.39ff.

10. The early *Minutes* sum this up well, pp.21ff,. Cf. Wesley, *Works*, vol. 8, pp. 287ff.

11. Robert E. Cushman, *Faith Seeking Understanding: Essays Theological and Critical* (Durham, N.C.: Duke University Press, 1981).

12. Ibid., p.xii.

13. Ibid., p.xiii.

14. Ibid., pp.xiii-xiv.

15. Ibid., p.xv.

16. In this regard, the work of Jurgen Moltmann has of course been pivotal; though he was foreshadowed, to a much larger degree than is often acknowledged, by the early work of the World Council of Churches, including Hans Margull's remarkable book, *Hope in Action*. For an application of these theological insights to contemporary evangelism, see Alfred C. Krass's foundational study, *Five Lanterns at Sundown: Evangelism in a Chastened Mood* (Grand Rapids, Mich.: Wm. B. Eerdmans, 1978).

17. John H. Yoder, *The Original Revolution: Essays on Christian Pacifism* (Scottdale, Pa.: Herald Press [1971], 1977).

18. Ibid., pp.50,60-61.

19. Ibid., pp.60ff.

20. Ibid., pp.70-71.

21. Ibid., pp.75f.

22. Ibid., pp.111-12.

23. Runyon, *Sanctification and Liberation*, pp.46-47.

24. This is nowhere more explicit than in his short essay, *Thoughts Upon God's Sovereignty*, where Wesley enjoins upon God's absolute decrees the further quality of immutable justice. Both characteristics, he insists, are to be found in the divine nature, and neither can be confused with the other. In one brilliant stroke, he shatters the nominalist framework of Protestant theology, uniting Creator and creation under a sovereignty of grace. See Wesley, *Works*, vol. 10, pp. 361-63.

25. So Daniel Jenkins, *Christian Maturity and Christian Success*, Laity Exchange Books. (Philadelphia: Fortress Press, 1982), pp.40-44. "The most substantial work of theology published in the last decade or so which deals with (the relation between Christian faith and politics) is the trilogy of Jurgen Moltmann, *The Theology of Hope; The Crucified God;* and *The Church in the Power of the Spirit*. Although he has much to say that is illuminating, at no point does he grapple with the complex implications of the possibility that some of those who are sustained by the hope of which he so eloquently speaks in his first volume may actually find their hopes realized" (pp.43-44).

26. I have attempted to explore the implications of this major adjustment in "The Church as Journalist: Evangelism in the Context of the Local Church in the United States," *International Review of Mission* 72:285 (January 1983):57-74.

27. The information sheet is based on an actual case study. The recommendations were presented to an open church meeting, and approved. The check was paid to UMCOR the following week, and the conference newspaper carried the item. This material was used for a case study in *Mission and Evangelism as an Ecumenical Affirmation: A Study Guide for Congregations*, ed. Jean Stromberg (Geneva: WCC, 1983).

2. METHODIST SOCIETIES IN THE EIGHTEENTH CENTURY AND CHRISTIAN BASE COMMUNITIES IN THE TWENTIETH CENTURY

An Exploration of the Wesleyan Heritage from a Latin American Perspective

Mortimer Arias

William Cook, in his doctoral dissertation on the "Christian Ecclesial Communities" of Brazil, and their missiological implications for Protestantism,[1] points to the fact that there are in Protestantism important precedents of these grass-roots Christian communities, one of the most impressive phenomena taking place in Latin America today. It is estimated that there are more than eighty thousand such communities in Brazil alone, and a similar combined total in the other Latin American countries. Dr. Cook believes that there is a notable precedent in the case of early Methodism.

If this is so, this fact is also very important for our concerns with mission and evangelism today, because the Methodist societies were the specific evangelistic tool of the Wesleyan movement.

In order to explore this promising vein, I have widely and freely used two doctoral dissertations of the last decade by Methodist scholars on this area of the religious societies related to the Wesleyan movement. (Some of these ideas I shared with our colleagues in a Consultation of Latin American Methodist Theologians, held in Costa Rica in February 1983.)

The first one is Richard Paul Heitzenrater's *John Wesley and the Oxford Methodists, 1725–35*,[2] presented to Duke University in 1972, based on the journals of the Oxford Methodists that he has been able to translate in full, thanks to his discovery of the clue for their shorthand writings. The second study is David Lowes Watson's dissertation on *The Origins and Significance of the Early Methodist Class-Meetings*,[3] also presented to Duke University in 1978. Watson spends the first half of his dissertation on the Wesleyan theological dialectics, in the context of the Anglican "middle way," especially in relation to the doctrines of justification and sanctification. I am going to draw mainly from his second half, where he deals with the Wesleyan synthesis of the *ecclesiola in ecclesia*.

I. *Ecclesiola in Ecclesia*: The Wesleyan Synthesis

Let us begin with what Watson calls the Wesleyan synthesis in chapter 4 of his dissertation, namely, the concept of *ecclesiola in ecclesia*, the underlying principle in all that Wesley thought and said about the church.

It is an acknowledged fact that Wesley stood for the Protestant definition of the church, as the community of believers, where the Word of God is faithfully preached and the Sacraments are duly administered, as formulated in the Anglican Articles of Religion (No. 19; No. 18 in our present version of the Articles of Faith). Wesley also accepted the Protestant principle that no church has preeminence above the others. The Anglican Church was for him the visible church for England, but he was not ready to exclude the other churches, the Roman Catholic Church or congregations where there might be some errors in preaching or sacraments.

Wesley was constantly arguing that his societies were legitimate inside the doctrine and the law of the church. His rules had to do with discipline, not with doctrine. He was insisting all the time on the duty to participate in the sacraments and the public worship of the Anglican Church, and he remained an Anglican all of his life, and while he lived he would not allow the Methodists to become a separate church. He defined schism as inherently evil and a distraction from the essentials of faith.

But, as Watson contends, Wesley went even farther: the order in the church is not an end in itself, it must be at the service of mission. As he says in his letter to John Smith: "What is the aim of any ecclesiastical order? Is it not to snatch souls from the power of Satan for God and to edify them in the love and fear of God? Order, then, has value only if it responds to these aims; and if not, it is worthless."[4] Both the experience of Wesley's evangelistic movement and his readings of works on the early church, supported Wesley's pragmatism in relation to church structures.

Wesley was adamant on this point: the ecclesiastic structure, whatever it may be (episcopal, presbyterian, or independent), must be judged by its efficiency for mission. Power and authority in the church rest on the free consent of its members; without it there is no authentic pastoral function in the church.

Watson's contention, then, coincides with Dr. José Míguez Bonino's analysis of Wesley's ecclesiology some years ago:

We find in Wesley a classic Protestant ecclesiology with some Catholic elements strongly underlined (the objectivity of the Church, the importance of the sacraments). But the whole of his ecclesiology is put in the context of an evangelistic and missionary passion. In a historical situation where "authority" was the most outstanding trait of the Church, this Wesleyan missionary thrust inevitably had to originate conflict. In this crisis, Wesley calls the Church to enter into a fundamentally new era, as a force for evangelization, announcing the forgiveness and power of the gospel. Wesley puts the totality of the constitutive elements of the Church—correct doctrine, sacramental practice, and above all ecclesiastical order—at the service of the evangelistic proclamation. In this sense, he is proclaiming in fact the instrumentality of the Church for mission[5].

So, maintains Watson, the Methodist class meetings have to be seen, not merely as a pastoral expediency, but as a solid base for Christian discipleship, a real implementation of the ecclesiastical order, based on tradition and accountable to Christian theology. In sum, the Methodist class meeting is the typical Wesleyan form of the *ecclesiola in ecclesia*.

At this point, already, we can find some amazing parallels with the Christian Base Communities inside the Roman Catholic Church in Latin America. They are grass-roots cells, mainly lay groups with some clergy inspiration and assistance at large, quite independent of the hierarchy of the church. They were not started by the hierarchy of bishops, but they had to be recognized as an ecclesial reality. Already in the Latin American Episcopal Conference of Medellín, in 1968, they were endorsed by the bishops as "a basic cell of the Church, a nucleus for evangelization, and a motor for human advancement." Pope Paul VI on his "Apostolic Exhortation on the Evangelization of the World Today" (*Evangelii Nuntiandi*) points to the "Basic Ecclesial Communities" as "a hope for the Church."

In this movement of church renewal, evangelization, and human promotion, with a strong element of social involvement, it has been very clear from the beginning that (as Wesley wanted for his societies) they do not question the doctrine of the church, they do not intend to leave the church or to provoke a schism, and they constantly protest their respect for their bishops and the pope. But, as happened with the Wesleyan movement of *ecclesiola in ecclesia*, the subordination of the authority and the structures of the church to its mission leads to conflict with the hierarchy. Some Catholic theologians, like Leonardo Boff from Brazil, call this phenomenon an *ecclesiogenesis*, a reinvention of the church from below, from the people, "the Church born of the people."[6] And this is exactly what makes the bishops nervous and defensive. While confirming the unique value and potential of the Basic Ecclesial Communities, the bishops in their Conference of Puebla in 1979, were sounding warnings about the risks of a "parallel magisterium," the sectarianism of the movement, and the need to be attached to the proper magisterium and authority of the church. They denied that the church can be born from below, it is born from above, from the Spirit of God, and under the authority of the hierarchy. They specifically rejected the terminology of a "Church of the People" (Iglesia Popular), especially when it implies the commitment to the struggles of the poor in the Latin American countries. It has been a pathetic thing to watch the vows of loyalty and the eager expectations of these popular communities in Central America in relation to the pope, and his implicit and explicit rejection of them in his recent visit to Central America. John Paul II did not mention the Basic Ecclesial Communities one single time in his seventy-nine speeches in the area, which came to a dramatic anticlimax in Nicaragua.

The tension in this case is clearly political and ideological—it reflects where the Christian masses are and where the majority of the hierarchy is—but the tension is already built into the concept of *ecclesiola in ecclesia* itself. Though the Roman Catholic grass-roots communities, and their theologians, do not use that expression in general, the reality is there.

The *ecclesiola* is the natural form of the incarnation of the gospel in a given social group, or a historical situation, a nucleus for evangelization—an attempt to find a way to live, to incarnate, and to propagate the gospel authentically. It is a discipleship and a missionary structure. But it tends to question, to challenge, sometimes to confront, the institutional church in its search for authenticity and mission. On the other hand, the *ecclesiola* may also tend to become *ecclesia*.

Of course, the question is relevant for Protestant churches, and for the contemporary Methodist churches, which are no longer *ecclesiola in ecclesia*, but *ecclesia*. As we say in the United States: "an inclusive church" and "a complete church"![7]

But let's not press the point too far, now. I think it is helpful to look at the whole phenomenon of "religious societies" in eighteenth-century England, and the "Methodist societies," as they took shape in that context. Maybe there is here something to learn about structures for mission today.

II. The Context of Religious Societies:
An Established Church and a Revolutionary Society

Both Watson and Heitzenrater do not deal in detail or in depth with the social context of the religious societies. Watson concentrates on the interpersonal psychology and group dynamics, while Heitzenrater sticks to his monographic historical work of the Oxford Methodist diaries. They give, however, a few suggestive brush strokes.

For Heitzenrater the eighteenth century in England is one of contrasts: extreme poverty and extreme wealth, in politics the monarchists (Jacobites) and the republicans, virtue and immorality. It is also a century of stability at any cost. After so many religious or politico-religious wars (the Reformation, the Glorious Revolution, the Restoration, the Commonwealth), the English are paralyzed by the fear of extremism. They are yearning for a middle way. "The status quo seemed to represent the last word of divine wisdom. They were ready to accept the world as it was and to respect the order as the incarnation of eternal laws." Anybody wanting to go beyond this formula was called an "enthusiast" (today we might call them extremist, or even worse, terrorist). Those clergy and laity who were looking for a revitalization of Christian standards, to overcome the pervasive apathy and religious decadence, according to Heitzenrater, tried the way of religious societies inside the Anglican Church (pp. 1-8).

It is interesting again to point the obvious similarity with J. Míguez Bonino's description of the period:

The XVIII century man is looking for tolerance and tranquility, and was ready to listen to anybody who tells him that he can reach those aims by the use of his reason and freedom, and not by submitting to a religion than sunk Europe in a blood bath. The political authority receives the credibility that the ecclesiastical authority has lost

People expect the government to be strong and stable, able to control the fighting religious factions, a truly sovereign state. The age of the established Church, with a granted authority for the Christian religion, is gone. Man has liberated himself from the religious tutelage.[8]

It is important, it seems to me, to realize that the religious societies movement took place inside an established church, in intimate relationship with the political and economic power, a church that was unable or unwilling to do any social criticism. The clergy were the object of satire by the blossoming intellectuals and writers of the time. The German Methodist historian Martin Schmidt, concludes that

the history of the Church in Great Britain from the end of the middle ages presents a classic example of ecclesiastic politics. Almost in no other country the ecclesiastical affairs were so strongly determined by the events of the political sphere or by the action of the state authorities.[9]

We need to remember that bishops were members of the House of Lords, that the allocation of priests was done by the state, making the clergy dependent on the official favor in order to secure a place in the restricted job market of available parishes. Meanwhile, the church was totally alienated from the masses.

Watson reminds us that the social English context was one of agitation, of questioning of the established order, of migrations from the fields to the cities, of replacement of the artisans guilds by manufacturing centers, and great commercial expansion abroad. "The rapid increase of the poor was inevitable," in this situation, which is one of "dehumanization." Summarizing the studies by Robert F. Wearmouth, "discontent was prevailing, disorders were frequent, and the way to deal with these symptoms was a wild Penal Code that solved nothing" (Watson, p. 357).

Beyond Watson and Heitzenrater, however, we need to remember that the religious societies, and particularly the Methodist societies, were born in the midst of the Industrial Revolution with its two faces: in the rural areas and in the cities. As Franz Hinkelammert has reminded us in the Costa Rican Consultation, the development of textile industry, based on sheep's wool, produced a radical change in the rural areas. Food production was replaced by wool production, great landowners transformed their estates for that purpose, and they began to take the communal lands and to push out the landless peasants who were no longer necessary, and who began to crowd the cities to form a floating, uprooted population (the textile manufacturing industry did not absorb them). Unemployment and vagrancy are widespread. The answer to that social problem was repressive laws, repressive actions against "vagabonds."[10]

So, it may well be as William Cook says in his dissertation about the origin of religious societies:

The Christian grass-roots communities tend to appear at the beginning of the process of revitalization or breaking with the former situation which is perceived as institutionalized. . . . *The Communitarian movements of any type have proliferated in times* of severe social tension, which goes along the transition towards *a new order.* . . . The base movements proliferate in times of change from a socio-political paradigm to another. . . . A radical contextualization, often emerging from an instinctive need of cultural disaffiliation, and as a sign of social protest, besides the religious factors, play a very important role in the birth and development of ecclesial communities at the base, in the history of the Church.[11]

According to Cook, this is true of the original base communities in European Protestantism, particularly true of the Methodist movement, and he concludes, "A comparative study would show that the socio-economic, political and religious contexts, are very similar to the ones in Latin America today."

Two elements of the situation in England in the eighteenth century have a bearing on the present situation in Latin America, where the emergency of the Basic Ecclesial Communities is taking place. One is the fact that it is happening inside the established church. The Roman Catholic Church has been a state church in most of the Latin American countries for more than four hundred years, practically until the present century. Even after the independence in the 1820s. In those countries where there was a nominal separation of church and state, the church was very active behind the scenes, in alliance with the political powers or providing religious sanction to society structures. In the last twenty years, however, while the church was in the process of post-Vatican renewal, and the states became increasingly repressive, there has been a widening of the gap between the church and the political powers, and a growing approach by the church to the masses, siding with the poor and oppressed in many ways. The Basic Ecclesial Communities have been a decisive factor in, as well as a product of, this new situation.

The other element to be taken into account is the prevalence of repression, conflict, the crisis of former models of society, politicization and polarization, economic disasters and impoverishment of the vast majority of the population, in short, a revolutionary, or at least a prerevolutionary situation. It can be called dehumanizing, as Watson called the situation in England; or it can be termed "a situation of sin," of "institutional violence" as the bishops called it in Medellin. Economists will call it a situation of dependence in relation to the global capitalistic system, and Christian activists will call it a situation of oppression that calls for liberation. Anyway, the Basic Ecclesial Communities are a response to that situation.

III. The Religious Societies in England: *The Search for Moral and Spiritual Renewal*

Heitzenrater summarizes the emerging of the religious societies as "an interesting and quite spontaneous fusion of moralism and devotionalism, cemented by an strict adherence to the structure and the liturgical forms of the Church of England." (p. 8) They represent a quest for moral and spiritual renewal, which was achieved to a certain extent. A closer look at the variety of these societies, suggests also that they performed as well a subsidiary function of indirect or direct social control.

1. First we have the *apologetic and catechetical societies.* The first ones were created by Dr. Anthony Horneck, a German Lutheran minister at the service of the Anglican Church and the royal house. It was in 1678, during the reign of Charles II, that a small group of young people over sixteen, from middle-class families, came together, seeking to lead a holy life, holding weekly meetings where they read the Scriptures, talked about their religious needs, and tried to edify each other. They prayed for their sanctification and committed themselves to raise the moral and religious standards of their country. The "director" should be a "pious and orthodox minister" of the Anglican Church. All discussion on "controversial issues of theology" or about the Anglican Church or the government should be avoided (Watson, pp. 251ff and references). Apparently there was an apologetic, somewhat ideological, purpose: "to combat the increasing papism in the high spheres and an effort to win the public mind." The objective of the meetings, however, was clearly catechetical and devotional, including a "religious discourse." There were appointed "stewards" to guide the discussion, the singing, and the liturgy of the day that was not exclusive of the clergy. In the absence of the minister, these lay stewards proceeded with the meetings. Self-examination was a basic condition

for membership, and the entrance was strictly regulated.

As we can see, these societies were pretty elitist in composition and intention, though in the long range they strengthened the lay participation. They were viewed askance and attacked as suspect of papism or schismatic intentions. The effect, however, was that the societies became an auxiliary arm of the church and many people came back to it through these societies.

This model was kept and developed in the following years, as we can see in the classic work by Josiah Woodward, first published around 1700. He says that the societies had reached a number of one hundred in London and Westminster. There was a partial collapse of the societies in the reign of James II, and also under William and Mary. In the reign of Anne the societies greatly prospered, and during this time Woodward's book was written.

The emphasis remained devotional, aiming at the holiness of heart and life, including works of charity, especially schools for poor children, and abstention from play-houses and taverns, and the catechizing of "young and ignorant people." But the social and political implications are openly there in Rule XI:

> That they often consider (with an awful dread of God's wrath) the sad height to which the sins of many are advanced in this our nation; and the bleeding divisions thereof in Church and State. And that every member be ready to do what, upon consulting with each other, shall be thought advisable towards the punishment of public profaneness, according to the good laws of the land, required to be put in execution by the Queen's and late King's special order (Anne and William III). And to do what befits them in their stations in order to the cementing of our divisions.[12]

2. There were also *moralist societies*, and religious societies with a strong moralistic emphasis, responding to the common concern with "immorality and irreligion." They attacked the problem of immorality on strictly personal and individualistic bases. As Heitzenrater puts it:

> This was not a program to reform England in one stroke. The strategy for transformation of society was to change one at a time . . . and through the development of a life of personal piety. . . . In some aspects the program of the religious societies can be compared with the development of the terciary orders of lay people in the Roman Catholic Church (p. 10).

To reach the aim of moral renewal, says Heizenrater, they had the positive method of mutual support and the negative method of mutual vigilance. The rules for members of these societies were taken from biblical quotations on regular prayer, fasting, taking the Communion, self-examination; being patient, humble, compassionate, and helping each other.

There were, however, other specific moralist societies, such as the "Societies for the Reformation of Manners." They should not be confused with the religious societies, but there was overlapping of members (they had been started also by distinguised members of the Anglican Church), and they had the endorsement of church authorities. They started in 1690, under Queen Anne, with the purpose of suppressing the prevailing "impudent vices and impieties." They collected an abstract of penal laws against vice and profaneness and drew up rules for the conviction and prosecution of offenders. They organized themselves in groups of informants, to denounce the violators and to enforce the law against profanity and vagrancy. They were practically a voluntary police, a committee of vigilantes!

Starting in the famous Tower of London area, they were multiplied through branches over England and Ireland. Spies were everywhere. In 1735, the last year they functioned, the total number of actions taken for debauchery and profanity (drunkards, blasphemous, profaners of the Lord's Day, clients of the "houses of disorder"), in London and Westminster only reached the considerable figure of 99,380.[13] Watson describes the social stratification inside the societies themselves, from the top financing club, to the merchant making the charges, down to the informants.

Suddenly in 1735, the Societies for the Reformation of Manners fell into rapid decadence, then death. Maximin Piette asks why? The answer is simple: There was no more money for the informants, and to be a spy was no longer profitable. As soon as the courts and the police didn't pay attention to denunciations, they died a natural death. Besides, they had failed. Repression did not produce the change of lives.[14] In their fall the spies pulled down the religious societies as well, because both were rightly or wrongly associated in the public opinion.

3. Finally, we have the *societies of philanthropic and educational* emphasis. Most notable of all was the "Society for the Promotion of Christian Knowledge," founded in 1698, which has survived to our days. This society was born under the assumption that vice and immorality are caused by the ignorance of the Christian principles, and that education and literature are the remedy. The program consisted of creating schools for the poor children, libraries, instruc-

tion programs for the prisoners, and disseminating pious literature and catechisms. The society was also supporting the missionary work in the American "plantations" and the functioning of small religious societies in the parishes. Samuel Wesley, John's father, was one of the founder members. In 1701 the Society for the Propagation of the Christian Gospel in Foreign Parts was born.

Again, the philantropic, educational, and missionary motivation of these societies had social implications also, as suggested by this intriguing comment from Heitzenrater:

> The intention of the religious societies in working with the poor was not so much to raise their standard of living in the economic aspect, as to improve their moral aspect. The fear of Eighteenth Century England that these movements might cause drastic changes in the economic structure of society, forced the religious societies to assume an apologetic posture for the support of such charity schools. They were very careful to point that these schools were not attempting to teach the poor children to be discontent with their situation in life, but rather to "instruct them carefully on the duties of servants and the submission to their superiors." (p. 14).

Now, here we have quite a few implications for evangelization through religious societies! Let's start recognizing the importance of these religious societies for the future Wesleyan movement. Watson has summarized at least six elements that will appear in the future: (1) the admission procedure; (2) the supervision of the private and public behaviour of its members; (3) the weekly meetings; (4) the limit of twelve members; (5) the "society" and "steward" terminology; (6) the increasing role of the laity.

John S. Simon begins his book on *John Wesley and the Religious Societies*, with a quotation from a letter of John Wesley in the *London Magazine* in 1760:

> About thirty years ago I met with a book written in King William's time, called *The Country Parson's Advice to His Parishioners*. There I read these words: "If good men of the Church will unite together in the several parts of the kingdom, disposing themselves into friendly societies, and engaging each other, in their respective combinations, to be helpful to each other in all good Christian ways, it will be the most effectual means for restoring our decaying Christianity to its primitive life and vigour, and the supporting of our tottering and sinking Church." A few young gentlemen, then at Oxford, approved and followed the advice. They were all zealous Churchmen, and both orthodox and regular to the highest degree. They were soon nicknamed Methodists. . . . Nine or ten years after

many others "united together in the several parts of the kingdom, engaging, in like manner, to be helpful to each other in all good Christian ways." Their one design was to forward each other in true Scriptural Christianity.[15]

This is an interesting witness. Here we see how the Oxford Methodist movement and the Methodist class meetings were the continuation of the religious societies described by that book written just two years after Horneck began his first society. But, even more important, by this testimony of Wesley himself, we can have in retrospect a hint of what kind of evangelization he had in mind: no more and no less than the "one design to forward each other in Scriptural Christianity," inspired by the challenging task of "restoring our decaying Christianity to its primitive life and vigour and the supporting of our tottering and sinking Church." This was precisely formulated in the first annual conference in 1744, "to reform the nation, especially the Church, and to spread biblical holiness across the land."

Meanwhile, there is food for thought about the relationship between certain forms of evangelism and the support of the status quo, what we today might call "the ideological function of religion." And what is even more touchy, how evangelism may become an instrument of repression, the propagation of a repressive type of religion and ethics, which in the long range or in the short range, may become the negation of good news from God, in order to adapt people to the bad news from man—and society—the denial of the ultimate human right of knowing and receiving the liberating gospel of Jesus Christ.

There is a lot for us to think about in Latin America, where religion has been for such a long time an instrument of repression, where the conflict between the churches and repressive states has come about precisely because the churches are refusing to play a police role. There is a lot to think about some forms of "evangelism" without any prophetic voice with regard to the violations of basic human rights—stressing individual vices and guilt, but not touching on the social structures and powers, not mentioning some notable born-again dictators who have translated their repressive ethics and understanding of the gospel into summary executions of supposed terrorists, and the scorched-earth policy for some Indian communities because of their supposed connivance with the guerrilla fighters. There is a lot to think about the open war against the theology of liberation, not only from other theologians or from hierarchies, but from intelligence services from the north and the south of the hemisphere, by the think-tank of President Reagan in the famous document of Santa Fe, pointing to liberation theology as the enemy.

And here, in the United States, there is a lot to think about the repressive evangelism of the new religious right and the prime time TV preachers; the open holy war of Carl MacIntire against liberals, ecumenicals, and liberation representatives at home and abroad; or the ideological undergirding of some "grand designs" of "Here Is Life, America—I Found It," and the evangelization of the world in this generation through a billion dollars to be gathered from the top financial and technological circles. And so on, and so forth. And yet this type of evangelism, stressing the individual sins, vices, and salvation, the devotional practices and pious terminology, is what may be demanded, with the best of intentions (or with second ideological intentions) from our own Methodist ranks. Is there anything in our Wesleyan heritage, and Wesley times, that can help us find the way to trust recovery of "Scriptural Christianity" today?

We can look now at the Methodist societies.

IV. The Oxford Methodists:
The Search for Total Holiness

In 1725, just graduated from Oxford and accepted as a fellow in Lincoln College, John Wesley decided to initiate the road toward ordination in the Anglican Church. Inspired by Jeremy Taylor's and Thomas á Kempis' works, Wesley embarks on an intense and persistent quest for total holiness. He begins to write his diary and the daily practice of self-examination. His goal: "to have the mind of Christ" and "to walk as he walked." The Dominican, Piette calls this Wesley's first conversion. It is still an individual quest, together with a small group of friends and colleagues that will become a Christian base community at the university. But it was not until 1729 that he started with his brother Charles and two others the "Holy Club." They met in the evenings to read Greek and Latin classics, the New Testament in Greek, and other works of theology and spirituality. Frequent communion was at the top of their priorities. This communitarian experience, says Heitzenrater, helped Wesley to go beyond the eremite tradition of individual search for saintliness (p. 86). He had developed a method of study and devotion and had attracted a small group of young people. Wesley was happy and ready to spend the rest of his life in Oxford.

Not far along the way, and by the initiative of several members of the group, they were developing a concern for others and taking some concrete steps of commitment to the neighbor. They started visiting prisoners in the jail every Saturday afternoon. John Wesley extended the visits during weekdays and preached there for the next four and a half years. They also visited sick people and poor families, with whom they shared their faith, taught them to read and write, and gave them money from their own incomes, and later on from other contributions. While the original motivation was their personal spiritual development, reality was pointing them to the route of the neighbor. In trying to justify himself before his friends, John Wesley appealed to Matthew 25:31-46, saying: "Shouldn't we imitate the one who came doing good?" (Conversion to Christ in the neighbor is one of the crucial emphases of the theology coming from the Basic Ecclesial Communities.)

But John Wesley was not satisfied just with good actions, and he pursued, with pathetic persistence, the inner holiness through reading of the Scriptures, through prayer, and through unmitigated self-searching. He attracted a few but raised the hostility of others who criticized his way of using time and money, his long hair, and called him "singular, capricious, formal." Ten years of titanic effort did not give him the fullness, "the holiness of heart and life" he was looking for.

Heitzenrater summarizes this decade of experience as follows:

> Wesley had exhausted the possibilities of the thought forms and structures of the societies that had developed in his time, and he was unsatisfied. Actually, the very intensity of his attempt to combine the perfection of the pietists, the devotion of the mystics, and the moralism of the puritans, inside the doctrinal frame of the Church of England and the structural organization of the religious societies, made his unsatisfaction even more desperate (p. 423).

However, Heitzenrater concludes that there is a positive side to the experience:

> Although the dynamic element of later Methodism was missing, the Oxford years established a pattern of intellectual, spiritual and social interest that will continue to be a distinctive mark of the Wesleyan movement throughout the Eighteenth century and beyond (p. 427).

We do not need to enter into Wesley's experience as a missionary in Georgia, except to remember that he was not able to evangelize the Indians as he had hoped, and that he was not very successful in his pastoral efforts with the colonizers. However, he considered his modest beginning of a small society in the parsonage in

Savannah, as a "second rise of Methodism." So, we see that the base community is a constant pattern both in his search for holiness and in his efforts for mission.

V. The Moravian Bands: *Intimacy and Communion in the Evangelical Experience*

The experience of the warmed heart in Aldersgate, May 24, 1738, has been called by others Wesley's conversion. In any case it could be his "second conversion": the experience of assurance, the evangelical personal experience of salvation, the Reformer's "inner witness of the Holy Spirit." His preaching of this new emphasis cost John Wesley access to the English pulpits.

The Aldersgate experience was intimately related to the Moravians and their particular brand of religious societies. Both in Georgia and in London, J. Wesley had been in close touch with the Moravian leaders Spangenberg and Peter Bohler, the last one being his practical guide toward the interpretation of his experience of faith as assurance. Just a few weeks before Wesley felt his heart "strangely warmed," he had participated in the organization of a new society at Fetter Lane, following very closely the pattern of the Moravian bands. Watson indicates that Fetter Lane was halfway between an Anglican religious society and a Moravian band. Wesley joined it with great hopes and expectations as a community for support and growth.

The two basic rules of this society were to share in prayer and confession in their weekly meetings and to accept as members those who had the same purpose. The society was then divided in bands of five to ten persons, according to their mutual affinity, and their level of instruction and spiritual development. Watson affirms that "Wesley owed to the religious societies the discipline of Methodism, but he owed to the Moravians the concept of spiritual cultivation and the guidance of faith towards its maturity" (p. 272). Among the Moravian practices were the prayer vigils and the love-feasts (agapes). In the band, each one had to "speak as freely as he could, simply and concisely, about the true state of his heart, including recent temptations and victories since the last meeting." They had to be "totally open, with no reservation at all." Candidates had to enter as members in a probationers' band, "assisted" by other members for several months before final admission. There were detailed general questions and rules of bands and societies to help in this process of self-examination and witness, in their search for intimacy and communion. For instance: "What sin have you committed since last meeting? What temp

tations? What victories? Do you want to keep anything in secret? Have you God's forgiveness of your sins? Have you the witness of the Holy Spirit to your spirit? Do you wish your faults to be talked about? Do you want us to go to the marrow and to explore the very bottom of your heart?"

It was not, however, in Fetter Lane, but in another small society in Aldersgate Street, that Wesley reached the experience of the warmed heart. His former associations and the decisive influence of the Moravians, and his characteristic thoroughness, surely were factors in John Wesley's decision to make a personal pilgrimage to the very center of Moravian spirituality, Herrnhut, in Germany, just two weeks immediately after Aldersgate. The Moravian community in Herrnhut, fleeing from religious persecutions and religious wars in former years, had taken refuge in the lands of Count Zinzendorf. They were descendants of the old communities of followers of John Hus, known as the *Unitas Fratrum*, which took shape also under persecution and repression.

The Moravian community was under the authority of Count Zinzendorf, though formally attached to the territorial parish of Bethelsdorf, as an *ecclesiola in ecclesia* (Watson, p. 289). The community was submitted to an internal discipline, almost as a monastic order, divided by sex, marriage status, and age into obligatory groups called choirs. There were also voluntary groupings of two or three persons, called bands. In addition, people were in subgroups according to their spiritual state as "dead," "ignorant," "awakened," or "in progress."

John Wesley appeared to be "extremely consoled and strengthened" by that "delightful people," and he went back to England "more fully determined to dedicate his life to witness to the gospel of the grace of God." Wesley may have been deeply motivated to witness to the gospel of grace by the example of the Moravians, but their band structure would prove inappropriate for evangelistic purposes.

Wesley had second thoughts about the absorbing authority of Count Zinzendorf, the environment of secrecy in the community, and the lack of mutual responsibility and maturity (Watson, p. 298).

Precisely, this was one of the areas of conflict in the Fetter Lane Society that entered into a crisis in the following year. Wesley did not agree with the subdivision in bands under an appointed monitor, which he considered unnecessary and counterproductive: "Each person in my band is my monitor, and I am his, otherwise there is no use in being in a band." But it was the Moravian emphasis on stillness, as it took shape in Fetter Lane, that finally led Wesley to withdraw from the society and to start his own in the Old Foundery in London. Moravian quietism did not fit to the situation of the emerging Methodist movement, especially in Bristol. That sort of intimacy, inner discipline, and introversion might be possible in an isolated community in Herrhut but not for the masses of people at the crossroads of the world in Bristol and London. Once again, as on other occasions, Wesley's pragmatism would save him from the wrong path and lead into new ways. This is Watson's evaluation of the Fetter Lane crisis:

One of the most important contributions Wesley made to the Christian tradition was that, being confronted with the alternative of looking for doctrinal and behavioural absolutes, or to accept pragmatically human behaviour in its social reality, he accepted the last with no doubt. (pp. 105-106).

Wesley had reached the conclusion that Christian fraternity was essential, and Christian discipline fundamental, but, as the ecclesiastical order of tradition, it had to be at the service of mission: "the propagation of Scriptural holiness across the land." The Moravian bands were too enclosed in themselves for that purpose.

Of course, this experience in the long Wesleyan pilgrimage may help us in the assessment of similar movements today and their relevancy for mission in our context: the place and role of monastic orders, selective spirituality groups, charismatic cells, the secularized pietism of awareness and therapy groups, and the orientalized practices of transcendental meditation, and the like, to say nothing of the contemporary fever for physical fitness and aerobics. How do these movements help or hinder the motivation for the sharing of the good news of Jesus Christ, in the propagation of biblical holiness across the land? Are their central motivations and their structures adequate for holistic evangelization today?

VI. Methodist Societies and Class Meetings: *Structures for Discipleship and Mission*

Bristol 1739: this is the crucial year in Wesley's development, in the emergence of the Methodist movement, and in the shaping of the particular Wesleyan form of the *ecclesiola in ecclesia*: the Methodist society with its class meetings.

Bristol was not Oxford, nor Georgia, and least of all the bucolic isolation of Herrnhut. It was rather the epicenter of the Industrial Revolution and the rural crisis, with its dislocated peasants, its coal miners ("colliers"), its factory workers, its merchant class with all the constellations that g

with a seacoast center of the British Empire in the eighteenth century.

It was in Bristol that Wesley had one of his providential encounters with his Lord. It was through the circumstance of Whitefield's request to go there and replace him. Whitefield was leaving for North America. Whitefield had started a real mass movement through his effective evangelistic preaching to large audiences in the city of Bristol and surrounding centers of population. He knew that John Wesley was the man for the job: "Many are ready here for the bands. I leave this entirely in your hands. I am only a novice; you are familiarized with the great things of God. Come, I beg you; come soon. I have promised not to leave this people until you or somebody else come to take my place."[16] After personal and community searching Wesley went to Bristol. That short trip marked the beginning of the Methodist Revival.

Albert Outler, in his little masterpiece, *Evangelism in the Wesleyan Spirit*, suggests that what happened to Wesley in Bristol was a third and more decisive conversion (the first one being in Oxford 1725, and the second in Aldersgate 1738). Without this experience, even "twelve months after Aldersgate, his name would not rate a footnote in the history books." "Aldersgate had warmed his heart but had not taught him to communicate the gospel or how to guide men into holiness." What happened?

There is a mystery here that I don't pretend to understand—but there are also some important aspects of this transformation from barren to fruit-bearing evangelism that can be analyzed and that might be relevant to our concerns with evangelism. The first of these was Wesley's conversion from passion to *com*passion as a dominant emotion, his change from a harsh zealot of God's judgement to a witness to God's grace, from arrogance to humility.

How did it happen? Again, Outler has no formula, but he points to a sign:

The sign-event of this remarkable conversion—not its cause, else we could duplicate his results simply by adopting his methods—was Wesley's embarrassed descent into field preaching on 2 April 1739. This was an even more decisive event for the Revival than Aldersgate—although, of course, without Aldersgate, *this* could scarcely have been possible. In any case, it was a shattering experience for the Oxford don who had hitherto cared so much more about "delivering his own soul" than about the needs and disposition of other people.

His passion for truth had been transformed into compassion for persons.[17]

This experience of going out to the people, identifying with them and preaching to them, not only made him finally "an assured believer" but also an effective evangelist. He was evangelized in the process of evangelizing. As Outler remarks: "The gospel is not truly preached until it has been truly heard." 'Preach faith until *you* have it' had been Peter Bohler's prescription, but it hadn't worked like that. Instead, "Wesley had preached faith until *others* had it—and that was what broke the drought in his own spirit."

But it was not only field preaching that took Wesley toward the people; his pastoral work in Bristol involved him more significantly with them. Again, responding to specific and practical needs, he took the next step of starting the class meetings. They emerged from the demand of the people who wanted to be strengthened in their faith, and relate it to their problems and situations. He tried to meet them once a week to provide this kind spiritual and pastoral service, but the people were too many. So, he had to organize them in small groups of twelve and put them under the care of a lay guide. Initially, the guide's function was to visit the members of his class to collect the weekly penny for the poor, and gradually he became a sort of pastor for his people. Then the weekly meeting was the natural outcome. As David L. Watson says: "What began as a financial expediency soon presented itself as an opportunity of pastoral supervision" (p. 315). Wesley tells the story and concludes matter-of-factly: "This was born, without any previous design from our part, what later on was going to be called a *society*, a very common and innocent name." The class meeting became a dynamic fellowship of disciples and an instrument for mission. Wesley pointed out that their members began to carry each others burdens, "speaking the truth in love and growing in everything in the one who is the Head, Christ." The class meeting, with its guides and stewards, was later integrated through local preachers and itinerant preachers, with societies, circuits, and annual conferences, to become the basic cell of a growing network known as the Connexion. Revival had found content and structure. As Watson puts it: "It had just been born, the ecclesial Methodist model: an inclusive concept of salvation, in which persons participated with responsibility, and a format of Christian fraternity based on the realities of the world: 'the class meeting (p. 313)'. ("An inclusive concept of salvation" and "a format of Christian fraternity" could be pretty appropriate descriptions of the Basic Ecclesial Communities).

This model was open and inclusive: "The only condition to enter into the societies was the desire for salvation and to flee from the wrath to come."

But it was also demanding and exclusive: in order to remain in the society, its members had *to show* in practice the reality and efficacy of the fundamental desire, in their worship of God and their service to people, in very practical specifics of everyday life, abstaining from anything that might do harm to the body, mind, or soul of their neighbors, and to do good in the same holistic understanding of human life and needs.

Now Methodists would have an evangelistic, all-inclusive goal: "to reform the nation, and particularly the Church, and to propagate biblical holiness across the land." And for that purpose, the Wesleyan movement had what was called in the first Annual Conference a prudential means of grace, namely, the class meeting.

VII. Wesley's Evangelism—And Ours

Was this Wesleyan evangelism? Yes, there is nothing else. Although, we must remember that John Wesley never used the word "evangelism" in all of his life and writings. The word didn't seem to be known at all during the eighteenth century.

From this we come to a strange realization: If this is Wesley's evangelism, it was not the evangelization of pagans in far away lands or the growth of church membership, but it was an effort to incarnate the gospel in a "Christian" land! To put it otherwise, it was not so much to church the unchurched, as to evangelize the churched. His main target was a holistic understanding of the gospel, "the whole gospel, for the whole person, for the whole of society," under the themes of Scriptural Christianity and biblical holiness, and with the intention to *reform* the nation, particularly the church, to save "a decaying Christianity" and "tottering church."

Wesley's evangelism then was *ad intra*, the evangelization of the church itself ("from the form of piety to the power of piety"). Of couse, this *reform*, which is the effect of true conversion and holiness, will issue into the most powerful evangelistic and missionary movement of the eighteenth century, with no frontiers.

So, I believe Watson is right when he defines the Methodist class meetings as "structures for discipleship and mission." But discipleship first. The societies, as Albert Outler also says, were a way to make the gospel *visible*, not only *audible*. This company of lay witnesses for Christ was not a stage *beyond* evangelism, it was rather, the evangelistic enterprise itself in its natural unfolding. For Wesley understood, as we seem to have forgotten, that it is the *Word made visible* in the lives of practicing, witnessing lay Christians that constitutes the church's most powerful evangelistic influence."

No wonder, so many times, when we look at our heritage, we look at these societies and class meetings, base communities, with nostalgia. Bishop Francis Ensley in his little book on *John Wesley, Evangelist*, published twenty-five years ago, was already saying that the churches today need to find the contemporary equivalent of the Methodist societies and class meetings.[18] Dr. Albert Outler, in his Harry Denman lectures, ten years ago, was commending the grass-roots societies as "the church's most powerful evangelistic influence," and that precisely because these societies combined the personal and the social, the audible and the visible aspects of the gospel.

My point is that evangelism must issue in visible and social effects or else its fruits will fade and wither. Christian proclamation must take on visible form, and the Christian community must be committed to social reform, or else it will stultify our Lord's prayer that God's righteous will shall be done *on earth*—here and now, in justice and love and peace— as always it is being done in heaven. Outward witness in daily living is the necessary confirmation of any inward experience of inward faith. The Word made *audible* must become the Word made *visible*, if men's lives are ever to be touched by the "Word made flesh."
For Wesley, the essence of faith was personal and inward, but the evidence of faith was public and social.

So, the incarnation of the gospel is not only in the individual Christian but in a Christian community. As Outler says:

In and through the Methodist societies, however, the Word made audible was also made visible and thus became more effective, as the societies became evangelistic agencies in their own right. Thousands of men and women who may never have heard Wesley preach (or only on rare occasions) were attracted to the Christian life and were actually evangelized (converted, born again, nurtured and matured) by the outreaching and ingathering influence of the local Methodist people. It was not only their preaching that made its impact in the world but also their lives—on the job, in the marketplace, in their redemptive involvement in the social agonies of the times.
Wesley had somehow grasped the secret of the Word made social, and of the faith that works by love not only in the heart but in the world as well.

But Outler stresses the other essential aspect of the Methodist societies: they were part of a lay movement.

For Wesley organized his converts into societies with rules and rituals, with programs of self-direct-

ed nurture and with lay leadership that was locally responsible, along with and often in spite of his overall autocratic supervision. Generally speaking—and this is my main point here—he left the local societies largely on their own. . . For the greater part of any given year, it was the Methodist laypersons who were the most visible exemplars of Evangelical Christianity in any given local community; *they* were the actual sponsors of the Revival, the real martyrs for Christ at the grass-roots level.[19]

In this interpretation of Wesleyan societies, I seem to be hearing a description of the role and meaning of the Christian base communities in Latin America. The gospel made visible in the life, not only of individual Christians, but of grass-roots communities in the midst of the social agonies of the times. A people's movement, a people's church, living in tension inside a hierarchical church with autocratic leaders. The only difference is that this time it is happening, not in a Protestant church, but in the Roman Catholic Church. And it is not happening in the same way among the majority of middle-class Methodist churches in Latin America.

There is another aspect of the Wesleyan movement that has not surfaced in Outler's interpretation, but which is very significant for our re-reading of our Wesleyan heritage in Latin America, and this is the fact that the Wesleyan movement took root and caught fire among the poor and the marginal of his society. This is an aspect that has not been adequately treated in European and American Wesleyan scholarship. We still need to write and read history from the underside, history from below, not from the winners but from the losers. Not the official history of those who kept control of the Wesleyan movement in Great Britain in the nineteenth century, but maybe a history written by the defeated Primitive Methodists, who found in the gospel preached and incarnated in the Wesleyan movement a strong motivation to engage in the struggles of workers and the work of unions and politics in the very center of the capitalistic system. Official Methodism took the route of neutrality and nonparticipation in politics and social struggles, a deviation from its original thrust (if I understood Watson's own commentary on the point). Elsa Tamez, the young Mexican theologian from the Latin American Seminary in Costa Rica, was also calling on the Oxford Institute last year to look for "the Wesley of the poor."[20]

This point is absolutely relevant for any consideration of evangelization today. Those who press all the time "to reach the unreached," the almost three billion of nonevangelized people on earth, need to be reminded that that huge mass of the unreached are the poor of the earth. How are the rich peoples and the rich churches going to make meaningful the good news to the wretched of the earth, who are on the seamy side of the global system of exploitation of resources and concentration of profits which the rich Christian minorities of the world control? It is certainly relevant for us in Latin America, where 110 million are living below the level of the most elementary needs, the poorest among the poor. And they are Christians as well! And the painful question for us Methodists, mostly from middle class or moving toward it, is how can we participate (not dream of initiating it) in the movement of the poor. The Christian base communities are movements of the poor, from the poor, the church of the poor, the poor are the church. And the question may be even more painful for churches in an affluent society, accustomed to seeing the poor "out there" or "down there" and relating to them as occasional donors or helpers. Such folks do not dream of receiving something from the poor, nothing less than "the good news of the Kingdom." As the Melbourne Conference on Mission and Evangelism said: "There is a missionary movement taking place among the poor, . . . Christ is moving into the periphery and from the periphery."

Where are the poor in our Methodist churches today? Where are we in relation to the thirty-four million who are under "the poverty line" in the United States? Where are we in relation to the new moving populations of the so-called ethnic minorities, and the increasing numbers of migrants. What about the so-called undocumented, the millions who are marginal and underground, one of the most fertile mission fields, and one of the most needed sectors of our society? Is The United Methodist Church going to become a structure for mission and put all its strength in the formation of new churchesm among the poor, with leadership from the poor, who are not able to support a professional ministry, working at different levels of culture and formal education? Will our structures be at the service of mission with people where they are, or will they be a hindrance?

Our church, with other mainline churches, has been suffering and complaining about decline of membership. During these same years, the Church of God in Christ increased its membership from 425,000 in 1965, to 3,284,661 in 1981. Guess in what sector of the population they have been working? If we are serious about evangelization today how can we go on with business as usual without any serious strategy in relation to the poor and peripheral? Do we think that we can

still put structures at the service of mission as in the Wesleyan movement, or have we reached a stage similar to that of the Anglican Church of the eighteenth century, except for official establishment?

Howard A. Snyder, a dedicated student of the Wesleyan heritage, who belongs to the Free Methodist Church, has also called for a contemporary equivalent of the class meetings which, according to him, Wesley considered the cornerstone of Methodism. He comments:

> The implication here for the modern church seems obvious: the recovery of some functional equivalent of the class meeting with intimacy, mutual care and support, and discipline is essential. Such a rigorous structure naturally goes against the grain in our lax, individualistic, live-and-let-live society.[21]

And yet, it does not seem that the many attempts to develop spiritual cells and discipleship groups have gone very far during these years. The problem is, What do we mean by "functional equivalent"? The Basic Ecclesial Communities in Latin America seem to be that because of their variety in Bible study, catechetical instruction, celebration, fellowship, social engagement, commitment to the transformation of society, and more. But what would be the functional equivalent in the United States, in this huge religious supermarket with 138 million church members, with so many denominational structures at all levels functioning as complete churches, with so many millions under the spell of the electronic church? Sometimes I wonder if the task forces, coalitions, and networks are not in some ways functional equivalents of grassroots communities, in spite of their ad-hoc nature and their sometimes elitist composition? Shouldn't we look at them as alternative, or perfectable structures for discipleship and mission? Their efforts to be consistent Christians in a world of so many problems and challenges, to commit themselves to an area of human need and Christian witness, and to express their solidarity with the poor at home and abroad, are some signs of the incarnation of the gospel in persons and communities. Addressed toward the world, this belongs to the essence of the holistic evangelism in the Wesleyan tradition.

So, it looks like we have been more successful in keeping one aspect of our evangelistic heritage, namely, "an inclusive salvation," or what we might call today a holistic gospel: for the whole of persons, for the whole of society, for the whole world." But we are having difficulty discovering the contemporary equivalent for what has been the special aspect of the Wesleyan genius for evangelization: "The format of a

Christian fraternity for discipleship and mission."

If Watson is right, and the Wesleyan synthesis was the *ecclesiola in ecclesia*, where do we stand now that we have become an *ecclesia*, "an inclusive church," "a complete church"? Are we going to stimulate or tolerate or foster or lodge new *ecclesiolas* under the the umbrella of the church? Are we already in the same situation as the Anglican Church in the eighteeenth century, unable to recognize the movement of the Spirit and unable to put structure at the service of mission? Can we attempt that task of renewal for mission, or is that passing to other churches? Can we discover in our ecumenical times room for special vocations, particular witness, varieties of the incarnation of the gospel in a given context, while sharing a common witness in the one church of Christ?

One thing appears clear to me as permanently valid from our Wesleyan heritage: evangelization has to be holistic and incarnational. Another thing should be clear: we cannot repeat or imitate in our times what Wesley and his movement did. The question is Can we find the way to make the gospel *visible* (in persons, communities and society), among the agonies of our time?

NOTES

1. A. William Cook Jr., *The Expectation of the Poor: A Protestant Missiological Study of the Catholic "Communidades de Base" in Brazil*, Fuller Theological Seminary, School of World Mission, Ph.D. 1982 (Ann Arbor, Mich.: University Microfilms International), pp. 5-6, 372ff.
2. Richard Paul Heitzenrater, *John Wesley and the Oxford Methodists*, Duke University, 1972 (Ann Arbor: University Microfilms International).
3. David Lowes Watson, *The Origins and Significance of the Early Methodist Class Meetings*, Duke University 1978 (Ann Arbor: University Microfilms International).
4. Wesley, *Letters*, vol. 2, pp. 77-78.
5. J. Míguez Bonino, "La Eclesiologia Wesleyana", Lecture Notes from "semana Wesleyana," San Paulo, Brazil: Facultade Teologia, 1969, vol. 2, 3-4, 10-12, mimeo.
6. Leonardo Boff, *Eclesiogénesis: Las Comunidades de Base Reiventan la Iglesia*, Santander, Espana: Sal Terrae, 1980. (Original in Portuguese, Petropolis: Vozes, 1977).
7. John G. McEllhenney, ed., *Proclaiming Grace and Freedom: The Story of United Methodism in America* (Nashville: Abingdon Press, 1982), pp. 1-5.
8. Bonino, vol. 1, 5.
9. Martin Schmidt, *John Wesley* (London: Epworth Press, 1962), p. 31.
10. Franz Hinkelammert, "The Socio-Economic Conditions of Methodism in England in the Eighteenth Century", *La Tradición Protestante en la Teologiá Latinoamericana: Lectura de la Tradicion Metodista*, Jose Duque, ed. (San Jose: DEI, 1983), pp. 21-29.
11. Cook, *Expectation of the Poor*, p. 374.
12. John S. Simon, *John Wesley and the Religious Societies* (London: Epworth Press, 1955), p. 14.
13. Maximim Piette, *John Wesley in the Evolution of Protestantism* (London: Sheed & Ward, 1937), p. 189.
14. Piette, p. 190.
15. Simon, p. 9.
16. Luke Tyerman, *The Life of the Reverend George Whitefield*, 2 vols. (New York: Randolph and Company, 1877), I, 193; Wesley, *Works*, I, 176; Watson, *op. cit.*, pp. 301-302, n. 4.
17. Albert Outler, *Evangelism in the Wesleyan Spirit* (Nashville: Tidings, 1971), pp. 18-20.
18. Francis Gerald Ensley, *John Wesley, Evangelist* (Nashville: Methodist Evangelistic Materials, 1958).
19. Outler, *Evangelism*, pp. 25-28.
20. Elsa Tamez, "El Wesley de los Pobres", in Duque, ed., *La Tradicion Protestante*, pp. pp. 219-236. See also brief reference in Howard A. Snyder, *The Radical Wesley and Patterns for Church Renewal* (Downers Grove: Inter-varsity Press, 1980), pp. 31.
21. Snyder, p. 149.

3. A THEOLOGY OF EVANGELISM

Roy I. Sano

Foundations and Their Development

The Spiral of Action-Reflection. There are two moments in the development of a biblical and theological foundation for evangelism. One is *action* and the other *reflection*. Some suggest that a *sequence* is required, when they urge we move *from* action *to* reflection. Others suggest a *circle* is involved when they say action generates reflection, which in turn leads back to action. A circle, however, suggests a movement on the same plane. We certainly hope that when we return from reflection to action we will be on a different level. For that reason, I prefer speaking of a procedure which moves like a *spiral* from action through reflection and then to better action, and that in turn will prompt improved reflection and even better action, and so forth.

Practical and Systematic Theology. To the extent that we reflect on action, this theological approach stays in touch with specific practices and particular experiences. Hence, I will use biographical material related to evangelistic ministry which I hope will prove illuminating for people to reflect on their own efforts and encounters.

In this session, however, we are doing theology in a narrow sense of the word. The distinction we can draw between practical theology and systematic theology helps us delineate what characterizes this presentation. Practical theology asks what personnel and programs, and the qualities and spirit which infuse both, are appropriate for evangelism in a particular setting. Evangelism can be understood as a *distinct program* as well as an *ingredient of other functions.* Hence we can ask whether and in what way evangelism can be conducted through our church schools, worship services, Bible studies, prayer meetings, as well as social, cultural, and recreational programs. We can also look beyond programs to principles. We can ask how the principles of self-propagation, self-government, and self-support can promote evangelism. Improving the efforts and the leaders in evangelism as a separate function and a dimension in other functions will rightly occupy us here.

These questions concerning techniques, programs, personnel, qualities, and principles should not, however, exclude the additional reflections associated with what I am momentarily calling systematic theology.[1] Without such questions we become functionaries and hucksters. At some points, we must raise questions about our faith. Thus, if practical theology, as I am using the phrase at the moment, asks where we enlist people into the ongoing work of the church, systematic theology asks whether such involvement means they are participating in God's drama of salvation. We can, after all, substitute busy-ness in church programs for religious experiences, as John Wesley frequently reminded us.[2] We cannot automatically assume some emotional high authenticates that a particular person has had an experiential knowledge of God's grace. Thus, while developing a theology of evangelism will inevitably be done in conjunction with considerations about appropriate practices and concrete experiences, we also ask *whether people are participating in God's drama of salvation, beyond their involvement in the church's programs or encounters with evangelistically skillful persons.*

Practical theology and systematic theology cannot, in the end, be divorced. To speak of practical theology already acknowledges that a certain amount of theology in the narrower sense is operating; to say the doing of theology involves two moments, action and reflection, also acknowledges that practical elements have slipped into theory. While the two are connected, emphasis on either action or reflection distinguishes practical and systematic theology. In this presentation, while practice and experience will be mentioned, more time will be spent on reflection.

Resources for Reflection. If theology in the narrower sense asks whether evangelistic efforts mean people are participating in God's redemptive process, and not simply socializing themselves into a congenial fellowship or the institutional church, what resources have been used?

Four have become prominent for me. I will discuss them in couplets. On the one hand, the biblical witnesses and the theological traditions help us in our query whether incorporation of people into the church means participation in the divine story of salvation. The second couplet, the social and cultural considerations, help us reflect on the adequacy of that participation in God's redemptive work. Once the biblical and theological resources are consulted and once the social and cultural factors are considered in our critical reflection on action, we can contextualize a theology of evangelism for Pacific and Asian American ministries.

Rather than prolong my analysis of the procedure, I will illustrate them by practicing them. I will demonstrate that much of the United Methodist heritage in evangelism serves us well, and, at the same time, how adaptations are necessary if we are to contextualize evangelism among Asian Americans and Pacific Islanders.

Adopting the Good News in Our Heritage

Personal Experiences. My personal experiences bear witness to the authenticity of much of the evangelism I have come to associate with the United Methodist heritage. I grew up in a warm Christian home where my parents with their faith as first generation converts shaped our whole lives. We attended a wonderful local church in Brawley, California, which ministered to the wide ranges of our human needs. To this day, people who participated in that church recall those rich experiences five decades after the fact.

It was not until I became a teenager, however, that this largely secondhand faith and hand-me-down fellowship, this witness and this service, started to become more my own. What happened in the 1940s changed my life. World War II disrupted our family. We were hauled off to a concentration camp. After some time, Quakers sponsored us in a resettlement program. They found housing and employment in Media, Pennsylvania. The Methodist Church there had an active youth group, a vigorous Bible class with boys and men ages fourteen through sixty-five meeting together, an effective choir, and much more. While many fond memories are associated with coeducational softball games, weekend conferences, and moving moments in choir practices, two experiences are particularly prominent in my memory.

One was my call to the ministry, which I answered at a youth conference at Blair Academy, in Blairstown, New Jersey. The second occurred at a summer camp meeting, replete with a makeshift altar rail, wooden pews, and a sawdust covered aisle. I responded to the invitation to accept Christ as my personal Savior and Lord. I walked forward with several others in the youth group. I was overwhelmed with a

sense of relief. I cried profusely as I knelt at the altar. As I walked the half mile through the fields from the bus stop to our farm house, the night hardly seemed dark. My body was so invigorated, I felt I could run all night and not tire.

Biblical and Theological Reflections. I am convinced that I am yet to uncover all that started happening through that camp meeting. I am sure those experiences in Sunday school classes, youth fellowship, the choir, camping trips, and many other programs contributed something to my readiness to answer that invitation. My pastor's preaching, his musical skills, his pastoral visits, fellowship hours for youth in the parsonage, and his compassionate altar call—all had their part as well. Reflecting and learning from such programs and persons are all very necessary in thinking about the evangelism we practice today. Such questions are entertained appropriately in workshops on evangelism and in courses in practical or functional theology at seminary.

There are also legitimate theological questions we can raise. What actions of God are these programs participating in, if any? What was God doing in and through these events? I have found the insights of the biblical witness and the theological tradition very helpful in mining the rich treasures of those formative experiences as a young teenager and the rich events which they made possible.

I will illustrate the way the biblical witness and the theological traditions help us detect what God is doing. Thereby, we can decide whether a particular experience is spurious or authentically Christian, whether we have only joined a congenial fellowship or are part of the body of Christ. Later, I will illustrate the way social and cultural considerations move us along the road toward indigenization of evangelism.

Because my spiritual experiences in the summer of 1947 reversed the usual story which moves from conversion to call, I suffered turmoils of doubt about the state of my soul. After I returned to California, I was told in my circles that a person could not hear God's *call* without first having a relationship to God in *conversion.* It never occurred to me to ask them how such a Catch 22 situation could ever make conversion possible! That is, how can one talk to God, which is part of conversion, if one does not have a previous speaking relationship with God which conversion made possible. Years later, I heard a radio evangelist say that dating our rebirth was not as important as knowing whether we live in God now. He likened it to our physical state. People do not need a conscious memory of their birth to know whether they are alive or not. We take our bearing from the present. In the same way, we examine our life today to see if God is in it and whether we are in God.

Biblical stories are particularly useful in depicting the way God works. If we have encountered analogous experiences, we find in these narratives pointers to our participation in God's drama of salvation, whether they are the stories of Paul's conversion or Peter's continuing struggles. Such biblical stories explained the renewal of that experience in the altar call.

Theological symbols and categories frequently compress these stories into a single word or phrase. Hence, consulting abbreviated summaries of these stories alongside the biographies of an Augustine, Luther, or John Wesley illuminates theological statements about justification.

To the extent that this theological heritage and the biblical witness declared God forgiving sins or *justifying us* in the sense of looking on us, "just-as-if-I'd-never-sinned," they described my experiences. I trusted these words and the God they pointed to. I do not take this as proof, but at least a pointer which makes sense out of that conversion experience and many times subsequently of being at peace with God. Such words as I John 1:9 became very important to me. "If we confess our sins, God is faithful and just, and will forgive our sins and cleanse us from all unrighteousness." In my devotional life the Psalms became my prayer book.

Bless the Lord, O my soul;
 and all that is within me,
 Bless God's holy name!
Bless the Lord, O my soul,
 and forget not all of God's benefits,
 who forgives all your iniquity, . . .
 so that your youth is renewed like the eagle's.

The Lord is merciful and gracious,
 slow to anger and abounding in steadfast love.
God will not always chide,
 nor will God remain angry forever.
(Ps. 103, adapted.)

The Pauline epistles became my first textbook for theology.

But now the righteousness of God has been manifested apart from law, although the law and the prophets bear witness to it, the *righteousness of God through faith in Jesus* for all who believe. For there is no distinction; since *all have sinned* and fall short of the glory of God, they are *justified by his grace as a gift*, through the redemption which is in Christ Jesus, whom God put forward as an expiation by his blood, to be received by faith. . . . We hold that (we are) justified by faith apart from the works of the law. (Rom. 3:21-28, adapted, emphasis added)

Thus, in a King James Version of the Bible, which was a constant companion when that initial experience at the altar was being developed along these lines, the onion-skinned pages of the Bible became clothlike in the Psalms and the Pauline epistles because I used them regularly.

That initial experiential knowledge of salvation had another quality beyond forgiveness of sins and justification by grace through faith. Beyond relief of guilt there was *regeneration*, a deliverance from the grip of sin through *sanctification* or rebirth. I had some inkling of the restoration of the image of God that night in 1947 when my senses seemed so alert and my body so invigorated. Later when I was introduced to II Corinthians 5:17, I could appreciate it. "If anyone is in Christ, s/he is a new creature. The old is passed away; behold, the new has come." The Appendix collects several of the key United Methodist theological statements on justification, regeneration (or rebirth), and sanctification.

The sanctifying operations of God have continued crucial through the years, as the initial momentary trust was renewed again in personal devotions, interactions with others in study or worship, and in engagements of the world in mission. They suggest yet other ways in which we are brought into touch with the sanctifying work of God, although the initial task of this action of God came at the altar for me.

While these reflect on a particular experience through the use of the biblical and theological heritage, albeit sketchy for this presentation, I want to illustrate how additional theological resources as well as social history and cultural heritages, introduce adaptations of the heritage. This version of a mild adaptation will uncover the way such considerations point to a recovery of a fuller understanding of justification. More fundamental changes will be proposed later.

With the passing of the years, an interpretation of the justifying work of God which I had previously resisted, has come to make sense to me. At first, I found Paul Tillich's restatement of justification by grace through faith as "accepting the fact that we are accepted," a shallow treatment. However, as I came to reflect on the rejection so central to our experiences of racism and particularly recalled the acceptance received in Media, Pennsylvania, I have come to appreciate his reformulation.

I can see that as an impressionable adolescent,

the war-time hysteria cut very deep. The denunciation of us Japanese Americans, the hostility ventilated against us, and the inhuman incarceration, all had an impact on me. Thus, compassionate gestures to the contrary were crucial to my well-being. They were my salvation. As the psalmist wrote,

The floods have lifted up, O Lord,
  the floods have lifted up their voice,
  the floods lift up their roaring.
Mightier than the thunders of many waters,
  mightier than the waves of the sea,
  the Lord on high is mighty!

(Ps. 93:3-4)

Praises be to God! Two situations illustrate the point. One occurred in Arizona, the second in Pennsylvania.

I remember the kindness of a white woman missionary who left Japan on one of the last ships returning United States citizens before the outbreak of the war. She came and lived with us in the Poston, Arizona concentration camp and taught a class I attended. When our family was leaving camp she was still remaining to teach. She called me to the front of the room and announced to the class I was moving to Pennsylvania. Then she hugged me and I broke down crying. All I could remember of that moment as a youth was the embarrassment she "inflicted" on me. As time has passed, however, I know now the importance of that gesture and why I was overcome. Here was an acceptance, quiet and gentle, miniscule and frail, when compared to the wholesale rejection of Japanese Americans during the war. The fact that she lived with us in prison, when she could have been employed elsewhere, shouted down all that fearsome hatred which a society gripped by war-time panic could hurl at us. That was the miracle of her witness!

Later, when we moved to Pennsylvania, I experienced the same acceptance which counteracted the rejection which had assumed such a dominant role in our consciousness. Those Christians in the Media church communicated the love of God through their programs and personal interactions. Thus, when I went forward and knelt at the altar, I believe it was a young man saying in his way, "I acknowledge publicly that I yield my life to this island of acceptance in an ocean of rejection." That acceptance poised against the war-time hysteria and hate pointed an impressionable adolescent to a deeper reservoir of acceptance which no human rejection could erase.

In the intervening years I have recognized that

John Wesley himself found acceptance crucial in his pilgrimage. He did not commit any gross sins and was not seeking a clear conscience. He was looking for that inner witness of the Spirit that he was a child of God (Rom. 8:16). In any case, this society had made us into "enemy aliens," "national security risks," "beasts of burden," and much more—anything but a child of God! The Christians in Media communicated an acceptance of us as people that made it possible to hear an inner witness of the Spirit with our spirits that we are children of God. Eventually, in our Pacific and Asian American caucus struggles, we found that I Peter 2:10 articulated it for us.

Once you were no people but now you are God's people;
Once you had not received mercy but now you have received mercy.

Thus, justification by faith as forgiveness of sins, and accepting the fact that we are accepted, articulate the sanctity in those gracious gestures of love. This is only a more generalized way of saying that a divine presence and a saving action were experienced. That is what our Euro-American theological tradition acknowledges and confirms.

While this eventual interpretation of that initial experience at the altar appreciates the Wesleyan and the biblical acknowledgment of the role of the inner witness of the Spirit, I suspect something else is operating in this heightened appreciation of acceptance which Tillich fostered.[3] Culturally speaking, the heritage of a shame-culture shaped largely by Confucianism is operating. We feel the eyes of the world are upon us sanctioning and censuring us.[4] If we proclaim the message of God's love among persons influenced by this cultural force, acceptance in their social and psychological terms should be explored. The hallowedness and the sanctity of God's mercy can certainly be expressed in and through this shame-culture as it has been in a guilt-culture. Incidentally, some claim guilt-culture has atrophied the meaning of justification by restricting it to forgiveness of sins and that shame-culture can help us reappropriate a fuller meaning of divine grace.

Conclusions: Adopting our United Methodist Heritage. I would whole-heartedly adopt the witness of the saving work of God to which our tradition testifies. First, the forgiveness of our sins which is an integral element in the justification by the grace of God through faith is indeed an illuminating description of the good news. Second, the regeneration and restoration of the image of God central to the sanctifying work of

God describes very well another element in the good news. Third, further reflections have helped me appreciate Tillich's restatement of justification as accepting the fact that we are accepted, despite rejections we experience. In moving in this direction we have detected how a person from shame-cultures may be appropriating a fuller meaning of divine justification. This suggests that the Wesleyan focus on forgiveness of sin may need expanding. More of this emphasis on adaptation is forthcoming in the next section.

Theological tradition and the biblical witness have helped detect God's forgiveness, santification, and acceptance (fuller understanding of justification) operating in evangelistic programs, persons, and techniques. Because these theological and biblical symbols have clarified the sanctity which saves us amidst the sacrilege committed against human lives, I find myself appreciating that part of our heritage which describes the good news of God's saving acts. Amidst our own sins and evils, over and above the damnable manipulations which distort the image of God, there is a gracious and mighty God bent on reclaiming the created order and all that is within it. Amen!

Adaptations in the Good News

Personal Experiences. I wish to move in a different direction with further reflection on a theology of evangelism, or a review of the good news we can proclaim. These reflections grow out of the interfacing of action and reflection. I cannot cite a single revelatory and life-changing moment in this case as in my conversion, although there are many clusters of events which are particularly illustrative. One appears in the issue of race, and the other is related to neocolonialism. Both were among the most important events which led me back, for the last decade, to the Bible and the theological tradition, to social analysis and cultural heritage, concerning God's saving work.

Racial struggles occurred at Mills College, Oakland, California, in the late sixties and early seventies where I was working. Many strikes and demonstrations occurred on that campus and others in that period. One in particular is memorable because it was so closely tied to my pilgrimage in the faith. The Chinese kitchen help went on strike. As a chaplain at the college and as an Asian American, I joined their efforts. As a chaplain, I was also an administrator who supposedly had access to the president while being answerable directly to him.

During the course of the strike, the president broke a regulation prohibiting management from meeting with workers. Arbitrators, after all, were the negotiators at that point. The president delivered an offer and threatened to fire eventually those who would not cooperate. A meeting with the Chinese kitchen workers was denied when students asked about it.

This triggered a deep response. I became aware that this stirring was not simply a personal bias or a racial animosity, though those were mixed in. I saw this stirring as a religious experience, a call of God. Eventually, I joined the students when they invited me to move with them into the president's office and occupy it. His work was disrupted until certain concessions were gained. Amidst the complex turn of events, however, we were upstaged despite the gains we thought we had made. I remember, however, how I was willing to think of the stirrings as a presence of God.

The same sense of encountering God occurred in contacts with religious promoters of human rights whom I met in Korea in the early 1970s. I prayed with them and sang hymns at meetings where there were known informants. As I walked out of one of these gatherings, I saw hundreds of riot police who were waiting for them to come out. I knew I was encountering a divine presence in the face of repressive measures. I had not known it in such situations before those days, and if God was present in similar situations, I was not prepared to acknowledge it because my theological training in some circles reduced these struggles to secular concerns. What profanity! No doubt many others have come to similar discoveries. A surge of energy carried them into an act as they happened to do some task. For me, this moment was loaded, weighted with sanctity, making it *kairotic* or holy moment. A good part of my theological pursuit since the early 1970s has been an attempt to make biblical and theological sense out of what was happening in these events. I have, therefore, stated to those who guided me into those experiences that they could only be compared to my conversion and calling.

Reflections. Reflections have uncovered additional moments in the story of salvation. The good news of God's gracious and mighty deeds now include *redemption and reconciliation*. I have come to see justification and sanctification as two aspects of reconciliation. As a working hypothesis, I have assumed that ever since the fourth-century Constantinian recognition of Christianity as a legitimate religion in the Roman Empire, the story of salvation was reduced from two events to one. We moved from a story with redemption and reconciliation to simply one of reconciliation. The United Methodist understanding of salvation has fallen heir to this truncated version of the fuller story. Hence a reading of the key documentary summaries of our faith in the Articles of Religion and the Confession of Faith, as well as that normative collection of John Wesley's sermons, reflect this tunnel vision. Readers may review them in the Appendix.

The great contribution of the Wesleyan reformation and revivals is a revitalization of reconciliation as justification and sanctification. This eighteenth century movement and its heirs in the nineteenth and twentieth centuries have made the abstract doctrines a vital experience, an experiential knowledge. That is no small gain, but it still remains a recovery of the partial story!

We must look elsewhere for suggestions of redemptive work of God which retell the fuller story and keep reconciliation from degenerating into appeasement. By redemption, I have in mind the deliverance from the reign of pretenders to God's throne. Because they are not God, or willing agents of God, these pretenders can only produce half-truths of consumerism or outright lies of censorship in place of the truth which will pervade God's reign. They can only create rampant poverty alongside gluttonous plenty, not the fullness and wholeness of God. In place of the reign of trust, they inflict the reign of terror in martial laws and their variations.

In our struggles against racism and neocolonialism we uncovered a reign of principalities and powers which manage and manipulate the wealthiest. These hosts of lords outmaneuver and outwit the most highly educated and the best intentioned. As the Holy Spirit convicts us of sin, righteousness, and judgment when we experience salvation as reconciliation, I believe the Holy Spirit raises consciousness of people about the reign of the usurpers who make the faithful into their servants no matter how much they may be pious and ostensibly dedicated to God. At best, they may become *people* through reconciliation, but they are not people *of God* so long as they are not redeemed from the reign of the hosts of lords. They are owned, managed, manipulated by the "elemental spirits of the universe" (Gal. 4), no matter how much they are delivered from the grip of personal sins. Those who restrict themselves to the narrower evangelism for reconciliation are like crown jewels, colorful and brilliant, even precious, but they only decorate the crown of the rapacious reign of lesser gods.

The biblical drama of salvation which moves from the Exodus to the covenant help us see this fuller story. First deliverance or *redemption* from pharaoh must happen (Exod. 1–18) before *reconciliation* with God or others is created through the covenant. The story reappears in Revelation. Until the reign of other gods and lords is overturned, we do not see a God who makes a dwelling with humankind (Rev. 17:1–21:1-4).

A theological model of this biblical story occurs in two periods of our history. While some feel a compulsion to reject civil religion, I find in it elements of truth worth recalling. We came into existence as a colony when we got out from under the archbishop of Canterbury and the king (redemption), and then we created the Mayflower Compact before we landed on the New England soil (reconciliation). In our origin as a nation, the same twofold story is told. We were delivered from the domination of the heartless king and the unrepresentative parliament in the Revolutionary War (redemption), and then we made a covenant and were united in the Constitution (reconciliation). In both instances, we find redemption from the domination of principalities and powers before reconciliation occurs.

Research into the history of theology suggests this twofold story of salvation appeared in Reformed theology and other antecedents. Suffice it to say, if we agree in some measure about our social situation of racism, neocolonialism, classism, and sexism which prevails, we need this fuller story of salvation. Only in this way do we become people of God. Without enabling people through our worship, education, pastoral counseling, and social service to participate in these saving works of God we are only offering half a loaf for the bread of life. A stubborn constriction of salvation to reconciliation in justification could mean we become false prophets who preach, peace, peace, when there is no peace! We could make our ministers and members into snow-job artists. They would not be bearers of the good news of the mighty and gracious acts of God which we can know experientially, even if that knowledge in history is only a partial pointer to consummate redemption and reconciliation.

I do not see evangelism in this broader sense undercutting the narrower practices. The black religious experience and the Christians in human rights struggles have helped me sense something of the divine presence in both redemption and reconciliation. As people proclaim these fuller stories, they too raise consciousness as earlier there was conviction of sin. Such stories of God's great work also call for a decision of trust, commitment, and yielding. Because the larger story is good news and has helped people enter God's actions and through it has created the body of Christ in mission in this earth, I see this as a part of evangelism which must be learned by our authentic but narrow heritage.

Conclusions

I offer a summary of the message this exploratory statement suggests, and trace some implications for practice.

The Message. The recollections of saving experiences and reflections on them with the biblical and theological heritage urge us to adopt the heritage of *authentically saving experiences of reconciliation* which we have appropriated by joining The United Methodist Church.

Additional saving experiences and meaningful struggles have prompted further reflections on the biblical and theological tradition, as well as on our social locus and our cultural heritage. They have pushed us to uncover a fuller story of salvation which asks whether our enlistment of people into the programs of our church in evangelism is adequate. I would suspect that much of the *redemptive action of God's saving work* is already being experienced but has not surfaced in lucid proclamations and concrete programs because our heritage of a truncated salvation story has prevented it. Thus, our reflections on our experiences and actions *urge us to adapt* our United Methodist heritage and bring it in line with a fuller story we find in the biblical witness and the theological heritage. That fuller story calls for redemption and reconciliation (justification, regeneration, and sanctification) if the salvation we experience through persons and programs of evangelism is to be both authentic and adequate.

Practices. Three implications can be traced for evangelistic efforts. First, to the extent that a program or evangelistic person facilitates experiences of *reconciliation,* which includes justification, regeneration, and sanctification, we should pursue such ventures. Individual persons and groups should continue experimenting and developing those practices, programs, and qualities which enable them to work with this reconciling ministry. Even if people enter their pilgrimage with God in these reconciling experiences, however, our reflections suggest we cannot stop there if we are to be more fully the people of God.

Thus, the second implication for practice is that a fully evangelistic program will invite people to participate in the *redemptive work of God.* We are hearing more and more how people in liberation struggles, such as in human rights, have been led to acknowledge the redemptive work of the God known in Christ. Because redemption is part of God's saving work, we can speak of their "saving knowledge of God," if we are to use such traditional phrases.

Many of these people had found the church repulsive because Christians had restricted their witness to reconciliation which had degenerated into demeaning appeasement without redemption. As evangelism which is focused on reconciliation eventually opened many of us up to the redemptive work of God, so too, one hears of the way people who enter the faith with glimmerings of redemption also have had a foretaste of reconciliation.

The third implication for practice is that the range of possibilities of enabling people to participate in the saving actions of God through redemption and reconciliation is limitless. The possibilities are shaped by temperament or geographical location of individuals or groups, as well as national ancestry and ministry specialties. The important point to bear in mind is to work at developing those gifts and graces which God has endowed us with. We are called to release the saving actions of God in the created order—in individual lives, the processes of history, and even in the cosmos. Because of God's decisive work in Christ and the presence of God as Holy Spirit, all is now ready. The "harvest is ripe." Praises be to God for this high calling and privilege. Amen.

NOTES

1. In Albert C. Outler's *Evangelism in the Wesleyan Spirit* (Nashville: Tidings, 1971), he treats the question of *personnel* in chap. 1, "Wesley the Evangelist" and chap. 4, "A Church of Martyrs and Servants." The question of *techniques* and *programs* appear in chap. 3, "A Third Great Awakening?" The *message*, the focus of this presentation, is studied in chap. 2, "Wesley's Evangel."
2. See, e.g., John Wesley's comments about "The Almost Christian," *Sermons*, pp. 11-15.
3. See Paul Tillich's justly famous sermon, "You Are Accepted," in *Shaking of the Foundations* (New York: Charles Scribners Sons, 1949). "In the picture of Jesus as the Christ, which appeared to him [the Apostle Paul] at the moment of his greatest separation from other men [sic], from himself and God, he found himself accepted in spite of his being rejected. The moment in which grace struck him, and overwhelmed him he was reunited with that to which he belonged, and from which he was estranged in utter strangeness. Do we know what it means to be struck by grace? . . . Grace strikes us when we are in great pain and restlessness. . . . Sometimes at that moment a wave of light breaks into our darkness, and it is as though a voice were saying: 'You are accepted. *You are accepted*, accepted by that which is greater than you, and the name of which

you do not know. Do not ask for the name now, perhaps you will find it later. Do not try to do anything now; perhaps later you will do much. Do not seek for anything; do not perform anything; do not intend anything. *Simply accept the fact that you are accepted!*' If that happens to us, we experience grace. . . . In that moment, grace conquers sin, and reconciliation bridges the gulf of estrangement" (pp. 160-62).

4. See, e.g., Ruth Benedict, *Chrysanthemum and the Sword*

(Boston: Houghton, Mifflin, 1946) More recently, themes mentioned in the following cast light at various points on this topic: Takeo Doi, *The Anatomy of Dependence* (Tokyo: Kodansha, 1971); Chie Nakane's *Japanese Society* (Berkeley: University of California Press, 1970); and David K. Reynolds, *Morita Psychotherapy* (Berkeley: University of California Press, 1976), esp. pp. 92-116 on "Japanese Character."

APPENDIX

The Good News in The United Methodist Heritage

The following quotations illustrate the points made in the presentation above. One can read them for evidence of the good news in the United Methodist heritage which *focuses on justification and sanctification*, the latter beginning in new birth or regeneration. It has been claimed, above, that these are moments in the reconciling work of God.

The reader will note that these summaries of God's saving work do not include what has been called redemption as it is used in the presentation.

The first set of quotations, entitled, "Doctrinal Summaries," come from the documents brought to the union of churches in 1968. The Articles of Religion, from the Methodist Church; The Confession of Faith from the Evangelical United Brethren. Both appear in the *Discipline*.

The second set of quotations are "Passages from John Wesley's Sermons" which the "Model Deed" established as one of the norms for preachers in England in 1773. It was adopted in the United States in 1784.

Doctrinal Summaries

1. *Articles of Religion*
   IX - Of the Justification of Man
   We are accounted righteous before God only for the merit of our Lord and Saviour Jesus Christ, by faith, and not for our own works or deservings. Wherefore, that we are justified by faith, only, is a most wholesome doctrine, and very full of comfort. (1980 *Discipline*, p. 57)

   Of Sanctification
   Sanctification is that renewal of our fallen nature by the Holy Ghost, received through faith in Jesus Christ, whose blood of atonement cleanseth from all sin; whereby we are not only

delivered from the guilt of sin, but are washed from its pollution, saved from its power, and are enabled, through grace, to love God with all our hearts and to walk in his holy commandments blameless. (A "legislative enactment" and "not part of the Constitution." 1980 *Discipline*, p. 62)

2. *The Confession of Faith*
   VIII - Reconciliation Through Christ
   We believe God was in Christ reconciling the world to himself. The offering Christ freely made on the cross is the perfect and sufficient sacrifice for the sins of the whole world, redeeming man from all sin, so that no other satisfaction is required. (1980 *Discipline*, p. 65)

   IX - Justification and Regeneration
   We believe we are never accounted righteous before God through our works or merit, but that penitent sinners are justified or accounted righteous before God only by faith in our Lord Jesus Christ.

   We believe regeneration is the renewal of man in righteousness through Jesus Christ, by the power of the Holy Spirit, whereby we are made partakers of the divine nature and experience newness of life. By this new birth the believer becomes reconciled to God and is enabled to serve him with the will and the affections.

   We believe although we have experienced regeneration, it is possible to depart from grace and fall into sin; and we may even then, by the grace of God, be renewed in righteousness. (1980 *Discipline*, pp. 65-66)

   XI - Sanctification and Christian Perfection
   We believe sanctification is the work of God's grace through the Word and the Spirit, by which those who have been born again are cleansed from sin in their thoughts, words and acts, and are enabled to live in accordance with God's will, and to strive for holiness without which no one will see the Lord. (1980 *Discipline* p. 65)

Passages from John Wesley's *Sermons*

Justification as Pardon

The plain scriptural notion of justification is pardon, the forgiveness of sins. It is that act of God the Father, whereby, for the sake of the propitiation made by the blood of His Son, He "showeth forth His righteousness" [or mercy] "by the remission of the sins that are past." ("Justification by Faith," vol. 5, p. 53.)

Concerning Justification and Rebirth (First Step of Sanctification)

If any doctrines within the whole compass of Christianity may be properly termed "fundamental," they are doubtless these two, — the doctrine of justification, and that of the new birth: the former relating to that great work which God does *for* us, in forgiving our sins; the latter, to the great work which God does *in* us, in renewing our fallen nature. In order of *time*, neither of these is before the other; in the moment we are justified by the grace of God, through the redemption that is in Jesus, we are also "born of the Spirit"; but in order of *thinking*, as it is termed, justification precedes the new birth. We first conceive His wrath to be turned away, and then His Spirit to work in our hearts. ("The New Birth," No. 39, p. 514)

VIII. The Ethics of Character and the People Called Methodist

1. CHARACTERIZING PERFECTION: SECOND THOUGHTS ON CHARACTER AND SANCTIFICATION

Stanley Hauerwas

I. What Is Right and Wrong About Wesley

My attempt to use Wesley's account of sanctification to recover the importance of character for the moral life is but an aspect of my general admiration for Wesley's insistence on the empirical character of Christian convictions. Christianity, for Wesley, is about changed lives and any belief that does not serve that end held little interest for him. Moreover, this "turn to the subject" was not an attempt on Wesley's part to avoid questions of the truth of Christian belief, but rather an attempt to locate the right context to ask the question of truth. For example, in "A Plain Account of Genuine Christianity," Wesley says, "If, therefore, it were possible (which I conceive it is not) to shake the traditional evidence of Christianity, still he that has the internal evidence (and every true believer has the witness or evidence in himself) would stand firm and unshaken." Still he could say to those who were striking at the external evidence, "Beat on the 'sack of Anaxagoras,' but you can no more hurt my evidence of Christianity than the tyrant could hurt the spirit of that wise man. I have sometimes been almost inclined to believe that the wisdom of God has, in most later ages, permitted the external evidence of Christianity to be more or less clogged and encumbered for this very end, that men (of reflection especially) might not altogether rest there, but be constrained to look into themselves also and attend to the light shining in their hearts."[1]

Wesley's attack on halfway Christians, on lukewarm belief, was not only an attempt to upgrade the morality of Christians but involved basic questions of the truth and falsity of Christian convictions. His insistence on integrity between what Christians believed and what they did was uncompromising because any temporizing on the part of Christians betrayed the character of their belief.[2] Christians, for Wesley, are a pilgrim people undertaking an arduous but fulfilling journey. It is, therefore, unthinkable that those on that journey would not manifest some predictable and observable empirical change. Wesley's doctrine of perfection, for all of its difficulties, at least rightly denotes that there is an inherent contradiction to claim to be a Christian without that claim making a difference in our lives and how we live. The affirmation of such a change after all is not a statement about our ability but the sovereignty of God's grace over our sinfulness.

The difficulties with Wesley's doctrine of perfection are well known—as how sin remains in the "perfect," what it would mean for the perfect to sin in a manner that is not "deliberate,"[3] and the inherent temptation to works righteousness always present in such a doctrine. Yet in spite of these difficulties I continue to think that Wesley was right to hold that the peculiar contribution of Methodists to the church universal lies in our struggle to recover the centrality of holiness as central to the Christian life. I must admit, however, I often wish that Wesley might have hit upon a less troublesome notion than "perfection" in order to express his convictions about the necessity of continued growth in the Christian life.[4] Perfection unfortunately conveys too much of a sense of accomplishment rather than the necessity of continued growth that was at the heart of Wesley's theological account of sanctification. Thus Wesley says, "Yea, and when ye have attained a measure of perfect love, when God has circumcised your hearts, and enabled you to love him with all your heart and with all your soul, think not of resting there. That is impossible. You cannot stand still; you must either rise or fall; rise higher or fall lower. Therefore the voice of God to the children of Israel, to the children of God, is, 'Go forward!' 'Forgetting the things that are behind, and reaching forward unto those that are before, press on to the mark, for the prize of your high calling of God in Christ Jesus'!"[5]

Not only do I think Wesley was right to stress the centrality of such growth for any truthful account of Christian convictions, I think such an emphasis remains particularly significant for today. For we live in the world that was just beginning to be born in Wesley's time—a world that no longer assumes that a religious, or in particular, a Christian, account of life is necessary for decent and upright living. What difference, if any, it makes to be a Christian becomes even more pressing in such a world. No account of the truth or falsity of Christian convictions can or should avoid that question, not because it is the question asked by the world, but because it is a question, as Wesley saw, that is at the heart of Christian faith.

Yet it does not seem possible for us to speak with the same confidence about perfection as Wesley. The fragmentation of our world, and the correlative fragmentation of our lives, makes us less sure than Wesley that we are in fact continually being sanctified. We are happier thinking of ourselves at best as troubled sinners and certainly not as righteous saints. Moreover, Wesley thought he could say in no uncertain terms in what the real change consisted. Thus those that walk after the spirit "show forth in their lives, in the whole course of their words and actions the genuine fruits of the Spirit of God, namely, 'love, joy, peace, long-suffering, gentleness, goodness, fidelity, meekness, temperance,' and whatsoever is lovely and praiseworthy."[6] Moreover, we are a bit embarrassed that Wesley thought the demands of "perfect love" involved questions of what to wear, how to eat, how we are to entertain ourselves, and so on. Theologically it seems we are in a no-win situation. Like Wesley we feel the necessity to claim that being a Christian makes a difference, but we are less sure how to characterize perfection without resorting to vague generalities about "being loving" or appearing overly moralistic by being too specific. For we have become acutely aware that "the pious" too often lack the substance that makes their piety authentic.

In *Character and the Christian Life* I was intent to show that character might be a way of displaying perfection that might avoid these difficulties. For Wesley was not any less conscious than we of the hypocrisy of being a halfway Christian. If anything, he was even more concerned with the problem since he lived in an age when what it meant to be a "better sort of person" was assumed equivalent to being a Christian. His doctrine of perfection was an attempt to challenge this assumption by insisting on the necessity of "purity of intention" or "a single eye" for the life of the Christian.[7] To be so determined meant that everything we are and do derives from a wholehearted devotion to God that precludes any ulterior motive—that is, what we do and do not do springs from our character as people devoted to God. By developing the notion of character I tried to suggest a means of characterizing concretely the subject and form of such wholeheartedness.

Yet I have never felt completely happy with that attempt, as character remains far too abstract a notion. I think part of my difficulty has to do with Wesley's way of characterizing

perfection. For even though Wesley's account of sanctification is inherently teleological,[8] he was unable to find the appropriate means to suggest how our being on a journey also requires results in the particular kind of singleness characteristic of Christians.

In this respect I think his problem was similar to the difficulty Alasdair MacIntyre has recently called to our attention in respect to the virtue of constancy. According to MacIntyre constancy is a relatively recently identified virtue displayed in its most compelling form in the novels of Jane Austen. Constancy is that quality that allows us to reaffirm the unity of the self across and through our many different loyalties and actions.[9] It is akin to the Christian virtue of patience and the Aristotelian virtue of courage, but it is not the same as either. For constancy results from the recognition of the particular kind of threat to integrity presented by the modern world, a recognition patience does not require. Moreover, constancy requires a sense of self-knowledge based on a recognition of the necessity of repentance since the constant person is acutely aware that the generally agreed upon manner of behavior, which is quite right in itself, can also be a snare that only gives the illusion of constancy.

It would be fascinating in itself to explore in what ways Wesley's sense of perfection is like and unlike MacIntyre's (and Austen's) sense of constancy. Certainly I think it is no accident that novelists and theologians at that time seemed equally concerned to explore the difference between those that are genuinely moral and those who have but the appearance of morality.[10] Yet equally interesting for our purposes is MacIntyre's observation that constancy is quite different from other virtues such as justice, patience, courage, and so on. Such virtues can be spelled out in reference to concrete practices, but constancy cannot be specified "at all except with reference to the wholeness of human life."[11] So unless there is a "*telos* which transcends limited goods or practices by constituting the good of a whole human life, the good of a human life conceived as a unity, it will both be the case that a certain subversive arbitrariness will invade the moral life and that we shall be unable to specify the context of certain virtues adequately."[12]

I think that MacIntyre's point about the difficulty of characterizing constancy is almost exactly parallel to Wesley's stress on perfection. To adequately characterize perfection requires a "reference to the wholeness of a human life," but that is obviously no easy matter. It is, moreover, made even more difficult when you are attempting, as Wesley was, to remain faithful to Reformation insights concerning justification and yet maintain the priority of a teleological understanding of Christian existence. For example, Gilbert Meilaender has recently noted that there are in Christian tradition two pictures of the Christian life which are not necessarily irreconcilable, but are certainly not easily harmonized—namely, that of life as a journey and as a dialogue.[13]

When the Christian life is pictured as a dialogue, ethics becomes but an attempt to explicate the divine verdict on human life by exposing our status as sinners. In these terms it is very difficult, Meilaender observes, to make sense of notions of progress in righteousness. In contrast, when the Christian life is pictured as a journey, "as the process by which God graciously transforms a sinner into a saint, as a pilgrimage (always empowered by grace) toward fellowship with God,"[14] progress is an essential element of the Christian life. Righteousness is not just a right relation with God, but becoming the sort of person God wills us to be. Meilaender suggests that the tension between these two pictures of Christian existence cannot be overcome, nor should we try to overcome it.[15] Yet Wesley did try to overcome it by clearly making his teleological framework primary and then making justification but one step along the road.

As a result he fell into the unfortunate language of "stages" in an attempt to characterize perfection. Thus in his sermon, "The Scripture Way of Salvation," he enumerates the stages of justification and sanctification as: (1) the operation of prevenient grace; (2) repentance previous to justification; (3) justification or forgiveness; (4) the new birth; (5) repentance after justification and the gradually proceeding work of sanctification; and (6) entire sanctification.[16] The problem with his scheme, of course, is that it is too neat, for Wesley was acutely aware our lives can hardly be laid out with such exactness. Stages overlap and we regress.

But even more troubling, the language of stages is simply insufficient to characterize the kind of telos that Wesley was attempting to reclaim through his insistence on perfection.[17] For if perfection can be characterized only by "reference to the wholeness of *a* human life" then the language of stages is far too abstract. Rather what is required is the actual depiction of lives through which we can be imaginatively drawn into the journey by being given the means to understand and test our failures and successes. That such is the case, moreover, reflects the kind of journey that Christians are asked to undertake. For the telos of the Christian life is not a goal that is clearly known prior to the undertaking of the journey, but rather we learn better the nature of the end by being slowly transformed by the means necessary to pursue it. Thus, the only means to perceive rightly the end is by attending to the lives of those who have been and are on the way.

In order to develop this point I want to call our attention to a work well known to Wesley, namely William Law's, *A Serious Call to a Devout and Holy Life*. It is generally acknowledged that in spite of his differences with Law's account of the atonement and his later mysticism, Wesley was deeply influenced by Law's view of Christian perfection.[18] I certainly have no reason to challenge that assumption as I think my analysis of Law can only substantiate Law and Wesley's common vision. Yet I want also to suggest that Wesley missed what was perhaps the most important aspect of *A Serious Call to a Devout and Holy Life* by his failure to learn from Law's character studies what was crucial to his account of perfection. For as I shall try to show, those character studies are not simply "examples" that can be left aside or ignored, but are essential to the substance of Law's account of Christian perfection.

By pursuing this line of inquiry, moreover, I hope to indicate perhaps some of the kind of work we need to do if we are to be worthy heirs of Wesley's heritage. My calling attention to Law is not meant as a fundamental criticism of Wesley, but rather to suggest the means to work out Wesley's own best insights in a different, but I think compatible, direction. In the process I hope to show that Wesley and Law's account of the Christian life is particularly significant today if we are to meet the challenge of saying what difference being a Christian might make—and thus why it is we believe our faith to be true.

II. The Structure of *A Serious Call to a Devout and Holy Life*

In order to understand the place of characterization in *A Serious Call* it is necessary to have a sense of the structure of the entire book. Law obviously thought a great deal about how the book should be shaped, as he was intent on the book's becoming an exercise that might put one on the path to holiness. The book begins, therefore, with a general claim that devotion signifies a life given or devoted to God, not just in performance of certain religious duties, but in all the ordinary actions of our life. Indeed the problem is that so many Christians are "strict as to some times and places of devotion, but when the service of the Church is over, they are but like those who seldom or never come there. In their way of life, their manner of spending their time and money, in their cares and fears, in their pleasure and indulgences, in their labor and diversions, they are like the rest of the world. This makes the loose part of the world generally make a jest of those who are devout, because they see their devotion goes no further than their prayers, and that when they are over, they live no more unto God, till the time of prayer returns again; but live by the same humour and fancy, and in as full an enjoyment of all the follies of life as other people."[19]

According to Law, however, it is absurd to suppose holy prayers without a holiness of life as to suppose a holy life without prayers. Either "reason and religion prescribe rules and ends to all the ordinary actions of our life, or they do not: If they do, then it is as necessary to govern all our actions by those actions, by those rules, as it is necessary to worship God" (5).[20] Thus if self-denial or humility is essential to our salvation then they must be made part of every aspect of our lives.

For Law the problem is how to explain how it has come to pass "that the lives even of the better sort of people are thus strangely contrary to the principles of Christianity"(11). His answer is quite simple. It is not that they want to live a life of devotion, but due to the frailty of the flesh, fail to do so. Rather it is that they plainly lack the intention or desire to live a holy life. Thus some will say "that all people fall short of the perfection of the Gospel, and therefore you are content with your failings. But this is saying nothing to purpose. For the question is not whether Gospel perfection can be attained, but whether you come as near it as sincere intention and careful diligence can carry you" (19). Not to pursue perfection is not only irreligious but irrational if, as the Scripture makes clear, "our salvation depends upon the sincerity and perfection of our endeavors to obtain it"(20).[21]

Moreover it is not possible to distinguish between states of life, excusing some from holiness because they are involved in worldly pursuits. Holiness is required by all, clergy, businessman and women alike. Indeed most of the employments of life are by their nature lawful so long as we engage in them only so far, and for such ends, as are suitable to beings that are to live above this world. "This is the only measure of our application to any world business; let it be what it will, when it will, it must have no more of our hands, our hearts, or our time, than is consistent with an hearty, daily, careful preparation of ourselves for another life"(32).

The man of the world is no less required to be truthful and honest in all his dealings than those concerned more directly with "spiritual" matters.

The same is equally true of humility as it must become a "general ruling habit" extended to all our actions and designs. For Law observes that though we

> sometimes talk, as if a man might be humble in some things, and proud in others; humble in his dress, but proud of his learning; humble in his person, but proud in his views and designs. But though this may pass in common discourse, where few things are said according to strict truth, it cannot be allowed when we examine into the nature of our actions. It is very possible for a man that lives by cheating to be very punctual in paying for what he buys; but then everyone is assured that he does not do so out of any principle of true honesty. In like manner, it is very possible for a man that is proud of his estate, ambitious in his views, or vain of his learning, to disregard his dress, and person, in such a manner as a truly humble man would do. (38-39)

Christian perfection, therefore, is exactly the attempt to extend a "regular and uniform piety" (40) to all the actions of our common life. What is crucial, therefore, for Law and Wesley is the singleness of intention, the constancy of character, that makes our behavior consistent with a life devoted to God.

Law next turns to those who are free from the necessity of daily toil by the owning of estates and fortunes, suggesting they must consider themselves devoted to God in even a higher degree. It is not enough that they do occasional acts of humility, devotion, or justice, but rather they must live by habitual exercise of charity to the utmost of their power (55). Those with such advantages, however, are particularly tempted to have their soul destroyed by the misuse of innocent and lawful things.

> What is more innocent than rest and retirement? And yet what more dangerous than sloth and idleness? How lawful and praiseworthy is the care of a family! And yet how certainly are many people rendered incapable of all virtue by a worldly and solicitous tempter? Now it is for want of religious exactness in the use of these innocent and lawful things that religion cannot get possession of our hearts. And it is the right and prudent management of ourselves as to these things that all the arts of holy living chiefly consist. Gross sins are plainly seen, and easily avoided by persons that profess religion. But the indiscreet and dangerous use of innocent and lawful things, as it does not shock and offend our consciences so it is difficult to make people at all sensible of the danger of it. (60-61)

For more people are kept from a "true sense and state of religion by a regular kind of sensuality and indulgence than by gross drunkenness"(65).[22]

In the context of discussing the special responsibilities of those with a secured living Law treats especially the role of women. But in doing so he continues his theme of the need to bring every rule and action under the intention to live completely devoted to God. Thus, it is not enough to be but a little vain for to be vain in one thing means we are vain in all things (76). Like the good high church Puritan he was Law does not refrain from treating the place and use of clothes.[23] To be sure, as he admits, such matter can be trivial, but it is nonetheless as impossible "for a mind that is in a true state of religion to be vain in the use of clothes as to be vain in the use of alms or devotions" (77). To be plainly and soberly dressed is but to manifest the plainness and simplicity of the gospel. That Law would take the time to deal with such matters denotes the thoroughness of his concern to bring all our behavior under the single rule of the gospel.

Having argued for the necessity of forming all our behavior in accordance to our devotion to God no matter what our state of life, turns Law next to counter the objection that such a life cannot help but be dull and lifeless. On the contrary, such a life is the only true and interesting one for true piety rightly directs our passions to their true good. When that is missing we are beset by trouble and uneasiness that is founded on our mistaken want of something or the other (103).

> The man of pride has a thousand wants, which only his own pride has created; and these render him as full of trouble as if God had created him with a thousand appetites without creating anything that was proper to satisfy them. Envy and ambition have also their endless wants, which disquiet the soul of men, and by their contradictory motions render them as foolishly miserable as those that want to fly and creep at the same time. (104)[24]

But the challenge that Christian holiness is life-denying cannot be countered just by showing the inevitability of worldly desires. Rather what is required is a depiction of the life of holiness that is compelling and attractive. And it is to that task that Law turns in the second half of his book. His discussion is shaped around the times of our daily prayers with a corresponding virtue associated with each time. The result is a comprehensive account of the Christian life seldom equalled.

He begins by countering all objections that it is not possible to take the time for such a regular devotion by suggesting it is impossible not to take the time if we truly believe we have a destiny beyond this world. For devotion is "nothing else but right apprehensions and right affections toward God," and, as such, we void life of interest and adventure if we fail to develop such affections through devotion (162).[25] Not only would we engage in daily devotions, but we should have some fixed subject which is our chief matter of prayer at that particular time of day. Thus "as the morning is to you the beginning of a new life, as God has then given you a new enjoyment of yourself and a fresh entrance into the world, it is highly proper that your first devotions should be a praise and thanksgiving to God as for new creation; and that you should offer and devote body and soul, all that you are, and all that you have, to His service and glory" (155).

Indeed Law insists that we ought to chant our prayers for singing unites the soul and body in a manner nothing else can do. For the "soul has no thought or passion but the body is concerned in it; the body has no action or motion but what in some degree affects the soul" (169). Since we are neither all soul nor body; and seeing that we have no habits that are not actions both of our souls and bodies; "It is certain that if we would arrive at habits of devotion or delight in God, we must not only meditate and exercise our souls, but we must practice and exercise our bodies to all such outward actions as are conformable to these inward tempers" (171).

At nine o'clock Law suggests the subject of our prayers ought to be humility. He devotes more space to his discussion of humility than to any of the virtues he treats in the last part of the book. He does so because "a humble state of soul is the very state of religion," but it is essential we rightly understand the nature of humility. For humility does not consist in having a worse opinion of ourselves than we deserve, "but as all virtue is founded in truth, so humility is founded in a true and just sense of our weakness, misery, and sin. He that rightly feels and lives in this sense of his condition lives in humility" (183).

Humility, for Law, comprises nothing less than the Christian taking a stance against the spirit and temper of the world. For the world is built on false assumptions that fuel envy, pride, and power which the Christian cannot help but reject.[26] It is no accident that it is in this context that Law makes appeal to the life of Christ, and in particular his cross. For it "was the spirit of the world that nailed our blessed Lord to the cross, so every man that has the spirit of Christ, that opposes the world as He did, will certainly be crucified by the world some way or the other. For Christianity still lives in the same world that Christ did; and these two will be utter enemies till the kingdom of darkness is entirely at an end" (199). The fact that many assume that the world has become Christian, according to Law, only makes the world a more dangerous enemy by having lost its appearance of enmity. "Its outward profession of Christianity makes it no longer considered as an enemy, and, therefore, the generality of people are easily persuaded to resign themselves up to be governed and directed by it. There is nothing, therefore, that a good Christian ought to be more suspicious of, or more constantly guard against, than the authority of the Christian world" (201).

The subject of our prayer at noon is universal love. But before treating that subject directly Law returns to his contention that all people, those in business, those of "figure" or dignity, must engage in the practice of daily prayer.

> For it is the very end of Christianity to redeem all orders of men into one holy society, that rich and poor, high and low, masters and servants, may in one and the same spirit of piety become a "chosen generation, a royal priesthood, an holy nation, a peculiar people," that are to show forth the praises of Him Who hath called them out of darkness into His marvelous light (I Pet. 2:9). (242)[27]

It is natural that he should return to this theme in the context of stressing the significance of universal love, for his account of such love is uncompromising. The "greatest idea that we can frame of God is when we conceive Him to be a being of infinite love and goodness, using an infinite wisdom and power for the common good and happiness of all His creatures" (243). And since we are to live in the image of such a God, it is our duty and privilege to look upon all people in the same manner. There are other loves that may be tender and affectionate, but unless they derive their source from this kind of love they lack piety—they are loves of "humor, and temper, or interest, or such a love as publicans and heathens practice" (244).

Law readily admits that our power of doing external acts of love and goodness are restrained, but we must do what we can to heal the sick, relieve the poor, and be a father to the fatherless. For the love required by God is not any natural tenderness, which is more or less in people according to their constitutions, but that larger principle of the soul, founded in reason and piety, which makes us tender, kind, and benevolent to all our fellow-creatures, as creatures of God, for His sake. It is this love of all things in God, as His creatures, as the images of His power, as the creatures of His goodness, as parts of His family, as members of His society, that

becomes a holy principle of all great and good actions (247-248).

Only on the basis of such a love can we rightly learn to love ourselves. For while we must detest and abhor many of our past actions and honestly admit our folly, we must nonetheless not "lose any of those tender sentiments toward ourselves" as we are required to love ourselves as God has loved us. For even though we cannot do all we need to do as lovers of ourselves and others, we can still pray for others thus forming a universal friendship with ourselves and others in God's life. It is because we can so pray that Christians have been raised to a state of mutual love that "far exceeds all that had been praised and admired in human friendship" (256).[28]

At three o'clock our prayers should be concerned with resignation to God's will. For the "whole nature of virtue consists in conforming to, and the whole nature of vice in declining from, the will of God" (272). Resignation is the great enemy of all our fears and envies for it requires us to learn to see that nothing that has happened in our lives is without value.[29] There can be no room, therefore, for envy since we know that we have lacked nothing that is necessary for our salvation.

Finally at evening prayer we are to confess all our sins for it is necessary to repent of our sins as otherwise the guilt of unrepentent sins will continue with us. Such confession requires the most stringent self-knowledge. Thus, as every man has something particular to his nature, some stronger inclinations to some vices than others, it is necessary that these particularities should never escape a severe trial at evening repentance (89).

Through his discussion of daily prayer Law has attempted to provide an account of the virtues necessary for Christian living.[30] For the "singleness" the "purity," the constancy that is the soul of Christian living is formed by humility, love, resignation, and repentance. The interrelation and interdependence of these virtues are just what is necessary for Christian perfection. For they give the means and skills for constant self-examination that provides the means for us to be less subject to the sins of pride, envy, and disregard of others.

For Law as for Wesley love is the crucial and central virtue—love that loves all as God loves. Yet love of itself is not sufficient to bring all our behavior under a single principle unless it has the humility that derives from our recognition and repentance of our own sinfulness. But humility is not sufficient unless it results in a recognition that God has given us everything we need to make our lives our own, to be content with our calling in life. For it is just such contentment, such resignation, that is the necessary condition for our being at home with who we are, our character, that makes possible the singleness of life called perfection.

The analysis I have provided of Law's *A Serious Call to a Devout and Holy Life* may seem to add little to Wesley's account of perfection. Certainly Law's account is more systematic that Wesley's occasional sermons, but almost everything Law has said can be dug out of Wesley in one place or another. Yet there is an added dimension to Law's account that I have as yet to expose—namely, his constant use of character studies to enliven his account of the Christian life. For it is insufficient to only assert the interrelation of humility, love, resignation, and repentance, the way they interrelate to form holy lives must finally be depicted.

III. Law's Characters

Most of *A Serious Call to a Devout and Holy Life* involves Law's portrayal of a large cast of characters meant to illumine negatively and positively the nature of the Christian life. Thus we soon learn to know Penitens, Calidus, Serena, the two unforgettable sisters Flavia and Miranda, Fulvius, Coelia, Flatus, Succus, Octavius, Cognitus, Negotius, Classicus, Comecus, Paternus, Matilda, Eusebia, Claudius, and Ouranius. Their names alone are enough to indicate that Law wants to do no more than draw certain stereotypes that are easily recognized, but yet these "stereotypes" often take on unexpected life due to Law's acute insight into character.[31] Moreover, the liveliness of these characters is crucial to the depiction of perfection that Law is trying to elicit in his readers.

The basis for such a claim finally rests on the total effect of Law's book and a discussion of each character. I obviously cannot attempt to show how Law's depiction of each character fits into the total purpose of his book, but I want to take at least a few examples to illumine how he is working. Many of Law's characters are negatively drawn. For he tells us,

Examples of great piety are not now common in the world; it may not be your happiness to live within sight of any, or to have your virtue inflamed by their light and favour. But the misery and folly of worldly men is what meets your eyes in every place, and you need not look far to see how poorly, how vainly men dream away their lives for want of religious wisdom. This is the reason that I have laid before you so many characters of the vanity of a worldly life, to teach you to make a benefit of the corruption of the age, and that you may be mad

wise, though not by one sight of what piety is, yet by seeing what misery and folly reigns, where piety is not. (128)

Thus Law introduces us to Flavia as part of his discussion of the problems of those who have the benefit of an estate. Flavia is the wonder of all her friends because she manages so well a moderate fortune. She is more genteel than ladies with twice her fortune. She is always in fashion and in every place where there is a diversion. She is very orthodox and is often in church and at the sacrament. She once thought highly of a sermon against pride and vanity as she was sure it was directed at Lucina, who she takes to be finer than she needs be. She is charitable if she likes the person making the request, but when she gives her half-crown she tells him that if he knew the milliner's bill she just received he would know what a great deal it is to her. Thus, when she hears a sermon on the necessity of charity she is sure the man preaches well since she applies nothing to herself remembering her half-crown. As for the poor themselves, she will accept no complaints from them thinking them all cheats and liars. She buys all the books of wit and humor, but will read a book of piety only if it is short and written well and she can know where to borrow it. Law suggests that Flavia would be a miracle of piety if she were half as careful for her soul as her body. The rising of a pimple in her face, the sting of a gnat, can make her keep to her room for two or three days. She is so over-careful of her health she has the misery of never being able to think of herself as really well. As a result she must spend a great deal on sleeping-draughts, drops for the nerves, and so on. And yet Flavia is considered by herself and all as a paradigm of a Christian, being especially careful to allow no work on Sunday. She even turned out a poor old widow from her home for mending her clothes on Sunday night (61-63).

Flavia is obviously presented in an unsympathetic light, but she is no less real for that. We have met Flavias, and we know the Flavia that is in each of us. And as a result we are stung by Law's judgment that Flavia's whole life is in opposition to the tempers and practices necessary for our salvation. For Flavia, according to Law, is suffering from her good fortune as it has filled her whole life with indiscretion, and "kept her from thinking what is right, and wise, and pious in everything else" (64). She is the paradigmatic example of that "regular kind of sensuality" that ultimately corrupts our lives by leaving us with the illusion that we are living rightly.

Or then there is Flatus, whom Law treats as a

257

counter to the claim that a life of holiness is a life devoid of interest and desire. Flatus is rich yet always uneasy and always searching for happiness. Each time you meet him he has some new project in his head, and it, at that time, is always what he has really been looking for. At first his great interest was in fine clothes, and he spent hours seeking out the best tailors, but this ultimately did not answer his expectations and he turned to gaming. This satified him for a while, but by the fate of play, he was drawn into a duel where he narrowly escaped death, and thus he no longer sought happiness amongst gamesters. Next he gave himself over to the diversion of the town, and you heard him talk of nothing but ladies, drawing rooms, and balls. But he unluckily fell into a fever, grew angry at strong liquor, and took his leave of the happiness of being drunk. Next he tried hunting, building new kennels, new stables, but soon learned to hate the senseless noise and hurry of hunting. Anyway, his attention was drawn away to rebuilding his estate, and he spent much time with architects endlessly discussing details, but the next year he left his house unfinished, complaining of masons and carpenters. Flatus goes through other interests such as scholarly pursuits, living on herbs, and so on (118-119).

Law has told us that a life not directed by holiness is hollow, but we cannot see that hollowness nearly so well without the life of Flatus. For we need his depiction to be able to see that pattern of his life that may be more or less reflected in our own lives. Though Flatus is certainly overdrawn, Law suggests his mode of life is "one of the most general characters in life; and that few people can read it without seeing something in it that belongs to themselves. For where shall we find that wise and happy man who has not been eagerly pursuing different appearances of happiness, sometimes thinking it was here and sometimes there?" (122)[32] The major difference between most of us and Flatus is that, whereas Flatus is continually changing, most of us become satisfied with one form of false happiness, such as heaping of riches or seeking of status. But in fact we are no better and just as silly as Flatus.

Or consider the opposite to Flatus, Succus, who having realized the vanity of most of our desires tries to secure happiness by living a well regulated dispassionate life. His greatest happiness is a good night's rest and a good meal when he gets up. He undertakes no business that may hurry his spirits or interfere with his rest or eating. He talks coolly and moderately on all subjects and is as fearful of falling into a passion as of catching cold. He is very loyal, and as soon

as he likes any wine he drinks the king's health with all his heart. All hours not devoted to repose or nourishment are looked at by Succus as waste. In the morning you always see him at the same place in the coffee room, he next plays cards to take up the time. In the afternoon he is afraid to sleep because he has heard it is not healthy, so he waits patiently for his supper, after which he engages in discussions praising the English constitution. At eleven he bids us good night looking forward to going to the coffee-house the next morning.

Succus, to be sure, is not anxious in the manner of Flatus, but that is just his problem. Rejecting the demands and interests commensurate with the Christian way, he is left with the dullness of a life devoid of any significant desires. Against such a life the "tedious and tiresome" nature of continual exercise of charity, devotion, and virtue is anything but dull. Rather it is the life of ultimate interest, as in it we are put on the road of true desire and passion.

Characters such as Flatus and Succus are perhaps too obvious in their lack of devotion. But Law was acutely aware of this, and most of his characters are more "realistically" drawn. For example, consider Negotius, a temperate and honest man. He is the master of a great trade and has grown wealthy at it. According to Negotius what is good for trade is good for life. As money has come to him he has often let it go to various charities, and he is almost always ready to join in any public contribution. Thus he has given a "fine ring of bells" to a church, as Negotius has a generous spirit and does nothing in a mean way. Moreover, Negotius is free from all scandalous vices because they are simply inconsistent with his trade. He thus views the pleasures of debauchery and piety with the same indifference, since neither of them is consistent with that turn of mind necessary for the multiplicity of his business which is his true happiness. If Negotius were asked what drives his life he would be at a loss for an answer. For though he is always doing something, he cannot tell you of any one end of life that he has chosen that is truly worthy of his labor and pains. Most people when considering Negotius would think him a paradigm of goodness and happiness since he is sober, prudent, rich, prosperous, generous, and charitable (135-137).

Yet for Law, nothing could be farther from the truth. For a life of such business is as poor and ridiculous as any that can be invented. "For if the temper and state of our soul be our whole state; if the only end of life be to die as free from sin and as exalted in virtue as we can; if naked as we came, so naked are we to return, and to stand a trial before Christ and His holy angels, for everlasting happiness or misery; what can it possibly signify what a man had, or had not in this world?" (137)

Law not only portrayed negative characters, however, but spent equal time depicting people that we can and should admire. That he did so is not accidental, for he must show that the life of piety is more attractive and interesting than its opposite. That is no easy matter since generally sin makes a better story than virtue, but Law was suprisingly successful in portraying the virtuous. That he saw he must do so results, at least partly, from his understanding of the close interrelation of soul and body. For he knows that our souls must be reached through the body as our imaginations must be stirred if we are to live rightly. Thus, he recommends in light of the fact that our imaginations have great power over our hearts and can affect us greatly with their representations, that "at the beginning of your devotions, you were to imagine to yourself some such representations as might heat and warm your heart into a temper suitable to those prayers that you are then about to offer unto God" (177).[33]

Law's depictions of virtuous characters are meant to serve just that purpose. They are meant to stir our imaginations so that we might envision as a real possibility the life of perfection. Thus, in contrast to Flavia he depicts Miranda, the sister of Flavia, who seeks to live as a sober and reasonable Christian. Though her mother forced her to be genteel, to live in ceremony, to be a fashion, to be in every polite conversation, to hear the profaneness of the playhouse, she now remembers that life only as a way to atone for by contrary behavior. She does not divide her duty between God and neighbor, but considers all due to God. She thus has divided her fortune between herself and several poor people. But she does not give foolishly, as she will not give a poor man money to go see a puppet show since she will not allow herself to spend money in the same manner. For she thinks it foolish for a poor man to waste what is given to him on trifles when he wants food and clothes. So she holds herself to the same disciplines as if she were equally poor.

She eats well but simply, and she keeps her body neat and clean. She observes one rule as to dress, which is to be always clean and in the cheapest things. She rejoices in the beginning of every day for her day is structured by devotions to God. She thus never finds herself bored. She is constantly at work, either doing something necessary for herself or others who want to be assisted. Her charity is as common as the next day, and she has saved many a poor tradesman

and educated several poor children. She does not refuse to aid the reprobate, but wisely waits for a time of adversity hoping such aid may help provide a new way of life.

Miranda's charity extends even to common beggars. She sends none away simply because he may be a cheat, but relieves them because they are strangers and unknown to her. For she takes seriously the words of the Savior, "I was a stranger, and ye took me in." She knows that it may be said that she gives alms to those that do not deserve it or may make ill use of them, but her response is What of it, for is this not the very method of divine goodness? For just as God makes his sun rise on the evil and the good, we plainly see that the merit of a person is no rule of our charity. Or it may be charged she encourages people to be beggars, but the same thoughtless objection can be made against forgiving enemies or clothing the naked (68-75).

Law commends Miranda's life to us, not because of its good effects, but because of its constancy. For "there is nothing that is whimsical, trifling, or unreasonable in her character, but everything there described is a right and proper instance of a solid and real piety. It is as easy to show that it is whimsical to go to Church, or to say one's prayers, as that it is whimsical to observe any of these rules of life. For all Miranda's rules of living unto God, of spending her time and fortune, of eating, working, dressing, and conversing, are as substantial parts of a reasonable and holy life as devotion and prayer" (76).

Yet Miranda does not quite come to life for us because she is simply too good to be true. But Law does not hesitate to depict his characters' struggles with envy and pride. Thus in discussing the demands of universal love he portrays Ouranius, a priest, who labors in a small country village.[34] Every soul under his care is dear to him as he prays for them as well as himself. He never thinks he can love or do enough for his flock, and he visits everyone in his parish with the same piety with which he preaches to them.

But when Ouranius first became a priest it was not so. For he had a haughtiness in his temper that bred a contempt for all foolish and unreasonable people. But slowly and surely he has "prayed away this spirit. Now rude, ill-nature, or perverse behavior on the part of any of his flock, rather than betraying him to impatience, only brings in him a desire to pray to God for help. It would strangely delight us to see, Law alleges, "with what spirit he converses, with what tenderness he reproves, with what affection he exhorts, and with what vigour he preaches; and it is all owing to this, because he reproves, exhorts, and preaches to those for whom he first prays to God" (259).

Such a spirit has invaded his whole life, for when he first came to his little village every day was disagreeable to him since such a parish did not seem worthy of his talents. The parish was too full of mean people who were unfit for the conversation of a gentleman. He stayed at home and wrote notes on Homer and Plautus, but devotion had got the government of his heart. Now rather than his days being tedious, he wants more time to do the variety of good for which his soul thirsts. He has come to love the solitude of the parish because he now hopes that God has placed him and his flock there to make their way to heaven. He now, not only converses with poor people, but attends and waits on the poorest kind of people. For it now means more to him to be considered a servant to all than a gentleman.

Enough has perhaps been said to suggest the importance of such characters for Law's overall project. They are not just "examples" of what can be said more abstractly about perfection. They are necessary exhibits of perfection exactly because becoming perfect is such a nuanced affair in which we are constantly tempted to self-deception. We cannot simply decide to love universally and will ourselves thus free of envy. We need to be drawn from our envy by the skills we can learn from others. For perfection requires the "wholeness of a human life" for us to properly have sense of it. Law tried to supply that "wholeness" through his characterizations.

To be perfect requires knowledge, but it is not knowledge like that embodied in a rule or principle. Rather, it is the kind of knowledge we know as judgment—that is, a sensitivity to particulars and their implications that cannot be taught by a general theory. Knowledge of what is valuable and worthy involves such judgments (303). But we can acquire that knowledge only by attending to those that have paid the price for it. Thus Law provides us with characters to inspire our imagination that we might learn the skills to have selves capable of being perfected.

IV. Characterizing Perfection

It is now appropriate to ask where has all this got us. I have tried to show why Law's use of characterization of perfection is superior to Wesley's use of the language of stages. It is so because the journey of the self denoted by perfection requires display by concrete lives that adequately reflect the ambiguity as well as accomplishment of those seeking well-lived lives. For the "singleness" that perfection demands is

no easy matter, as the closer we come to embodying it, the more we are beset by temptations that deny its character. By attending to good lives we develop those skills necessary to ridding our lives of envy and pride and rendering them more accessible to love, and this makes possible the repentance necessary to being perfect. Yet what are the implications of this for how we do Christian ethics today? As I suggested at the beginning, I think the Wesleyan emphasis on the empirical character of religious belief as well as the theme of perfection has particular relevance in our own time.

Perfection maintains a teleological focus that any adequate account of the Christian life requires. Moreover, it places that emphasis rightly for the teleology is not one of moral decisions or justifications, but of the self.[35] It may be the language of perfection is archaic, but I think little will be gained by trying to translate it into more contemporary idioms, such as "maturing" or "wholeness." What is required is not the "updating" of the language, but rather the imaginative endeavor to learn how to characterize perfection in a manner quite similar to Law's.

Such characterization can be accomplished, however, if we are able to identify those who are in fact living the life of perfection. And in that sense our task is quite different from that of Law or Wesley. For their problem was how to distinguish authentic holiness from counterfeit in a polite age where everyone could at least claim to be if not look like a Christian. Our task is to locate within the anarchy of endless "life-styles" that kind of life characteristic of Christians. For even though Christians will differ from one another in what they do, they are nonetheless a people on the same journey, one that requires the same virtues and character of all. We know in fact that many are on that journey. What we lack is the courage and ability to depict their lives for our and the world's benefit.

Little has been said to this point about the communal context of a life of perfection, but the demand to locate and characterize lives of perfection is fundamentally a communal task. For the journey that Christians undertake is the journey of a people. The growth of their individual lives, which certainly is also a journey, is intelligible only within the movement we call the church. It is perhaps one of the church's most important tasks to identify those people who in a compelling manner embody in their lives that larger journey. I suspect that this is constantly done in churches in an informal manner. I am simply suggesting that at least part of the humble service of ethics to the church might be to learn to do this in a more formal manner so that we might have the benefit that comes from learning to characterize perfection.

NOTES

1. John Wesley, *A Plain Account of Genuine Christianity* in *John Wesley*, ed. Albert C. Outler (New York: Oxford University Press, 1964), p. 192. Hereafter cited as Outler.

2. See, for example, Wesley's sermon, "The Almost Christian," in his *Forty-Four Sermons* (London: Epworth Press, 1964), pp. 11-19. It is interesting that in this sermon Wesley says that sincerity is impossible for an "almost Christian." Indeed without a "real, inward principle of religion, from which these outward actions flow," it is not possible to be even a honest heathen (p. 14). But sincerity is not sufficient to be a Christian since that requires love of God and neighbor. Thus Christian sincerity is formed by a different set of presuppositions than that of heathen honesty.

3. Wesley, *A Plain Account of Christian Perfection*, in Outler, p. 286.

4. William Cannon plainly states that "Perfection is a weasel word in Christian theology," since it at once sets a standard too high for attainment but yet maintains it is a possibility as a temporal goal. "John Wesley's Doctrine of Sanctification and Perfection," *Mennonite Quarterly Review*, 35 (April 1961): 5-9. He is of course right as long as perfection is construed in the language of a "goal." The matter becomes quite different, however, once perfection is understood as a qualification of our character as I have tried to show in my *Character and the Christian Life: A Study in Theological Ethics* (San Antonio: Trinity University Press, 1975), pp. 179-228.

5. John Wesley, "Sermon on Faith" quoted by Harald Lindstrom, *Wesley and Sanctification* (Nashville: Abingdon Press, 1946), pp. 118-19.

6. John Wesley, "The First-Fruits of the Spirit," in *Forty-Four Sermons*, p. 87.

7. See, for example, my *Character and the Christian Life*, pp. 198-99. Though Wesley often used the language of "internal" to talk about the subject of perfection, in fact the "intention" that is purified is everything we are and do. Thus contrary to our assumption, Wesley's sense of "internal" was in principle public.

8. For example, Lindstrom suggests "In regarding love to God in this aspect of man's reunion with Him, Wesley has logically to make Him ultimately the sole object of human love. All else becomes a means to this end. Further, as love is considered a gradual growth, it follows that love to God as well as already involving fellowship with Him must also be seen as a progress towards an ever more perfect fellowship with Him" (p. 189). Or again, "The Christian, as in William Law and the mystics, is above all (for Wesley) a pilgrim, his life on earth a journey, the destination Heaven. And the path he must travel to reach his goal is the path of sanctification, of real empirical change in man" (p. 218).

9. Alasdair MacIntyre, *After Virtue* (Notre Dame: University of Notre Dame Press, 1981), p. 225.

10. It would be particularly interesting to pursue this theme by comparing and contrasting Wesley's concern for perfection and the concerns of the "realistic" novelist of the nineteenth century. For the latter were acutely concerned with the problem of integrity or constancy as the hallmark of the moral man. For one attempt at developing this point see my "Constancy and Forgiveness: The Novel as a School for Virtue," *Notre Dame English Journal* (Forthcoming).

11. MacIntyre, *After Virtue*, p. 189.

12. Ibid.

13. Gilbert Meilaender, "The Place of Ethics in the Theological Task," *Currents in Theology and Mission*, 6 (August 1979), p. 199.

14. Ibid., p. 200. I think Meilaender's account of dialogue is a little too Lutheran for me. After all, a dialogue can be an ongoing conversation in which one can certainly make progress.

15. Ibid., p. 210. Meilaender in good Lutheran fashion wants to maintain that these two emphases should always be kept in dialectical tension, though he hints that, at least for dogmatic theology, the journey metaphor is primary. I think he is right about that, but I would go even farther and suggest that the metaphor of dialogue only makes sense as a necessary and continuing part of the journey. In that sense I think Wesley and the whole sanctificationist tradition are more nearly right. The problem, however, is that when either justification nor sanctification becomes an independent theological notion something has gone wrong. Thus "perfection" displays justification and sanctification not vice versa. For a more extended argument defending the secondary nature of justification and sanctification see my *The Peaceable Kingdom: A Primer in Christian Ethics* (Notre Dame: University of Notre Dame Press, 1983). I think part of the difficulty with the last chapter of *Character and the Christian Life* was my concentration on justification and sanctification as abstracted from any account of what kind of journey Christians are asked to undertake.

16. Lindstrom, *Wesley and Sanctification*, p. 113.

17. In an interesting way the same difficulty of "stage" language is reappearing in much of the literature influenced by Kohlberg. For example, much of the work being done by James Fowler is an attempt to restate Wesley's emphasis on perfection in a new idiom. But I think Fowler's own best insights often are constrained by his commitment to Kohlberg's stages. In his fine book, *Stages of Faith* (San Francisco: Harper & Row, 1981) his analysis only comes alive when he begins his insightful and nuanced account of Mary's pilgrimage. Though he uses that account to substantiate his earlier analysis of the stages, in fact his own narrative of Mary's pilgrimage is a nice illustration of why narrative rather than stages is a more fundamental category for illuminating spiritual growth. I suspect the language of stages is useful because we cannot help but construe them narratively.

18. For what remains one of the best treatments of Law's influence on Wesley, and in particular their differences concerning the atonement, see Lindstrom, *Wesley and Sanctification*, pp. 55-60. Also see Lindstrom's discussion of how closely Wesley followed Law's account of perfect love, pp. 161-83.

19. William Law, *A Serious Call to a Devout and Holy Life*, with an introduction by Geoffrey Bromiley (Grand Rapids: Wm. B. Eerdmans, 1966). All page references to this work will appear in the text in parentheses. There are several editions of *A Serious Call*, the most recent being in the Classics of Western Spirituality, edited by Paul Stanwood (New York: Paulist Press, 1978). I have used Bromiley's edition because I find his notes most helpful.

In the last chapter of *A Serious Call* Law returns to his theme claiming "because in this polite age of ours we have so lived away the spirit of devotion, that many seem afraid even to be suspected of it, imagining great devotion to be great bigotry; that it is founded in ignorance and poorness of spirit, and that little, weak, and dejected minds are generally the greatest proficients in it: It shall here be full shown that great devotion is the noblest temper of the greatest and noblest souls, and they who think it receives any advantage from ignorance and poorness of spirit are themselves not a little, but entirely ignorant of the nature of devotion, the nature of God, and the nature of themselves" (299).

20. Though Law and Wesley were often identified as religious enthusiasts that had no use for reason, both maintained that everything they advocated was based on rational grounds. Thus Law says, "If we had a religion that consisted in absurd superstitions, that had no regard to the perfection of our nature, people might well be glad to have some part of their life excused from it. But as the religion of the Gospel is only the refinement and exaltation of our best faculties, as it only requires a life of the highest reason, as it only requires us to use this world

as according to reason it ought to be used, to live in such tempers as are the glory of intelligent beings, to walk in such wisdom as exalts our nature, and to practice such poetry as will raise us to God; who can think it grievous to live always in the spirit of such a religion, to have every part of his life full of it, but he that would think it much more grievous to be as the angels of God in heaven?" (47-48).

21. Of course, it was this kind of language that made Wesley shudder as it had an unmistakable Pelagian ring. Yet Wesley was not far from a similar view, even though he explicitly rejected Law's view that Christ's atonement was a representational act in the name of mankind that still requires our own mortification. Once a theological view of salvation is accepted, I think it is very hard to avoid something very much like Law's account of the matter. To do so in no way undermines the priority of God's grace, but rather it is a reminder that God's grace is a form of forgiveness that graciously gives us a way to go on—that is, grace is just the invitation and opportunity to take part in the journey of God's people.

22. Though we tend at best to regard Law's and Wesley's concern with dress, how we eat, and our modes of entertainment with embarrassed bemusement, I think we do so by sacrificing a certain kind of seriousness. Law is perfectly right that it is the small habits that finally corrupt, not our large sins. Moreover, he was by no means narrowly moralistic about such matters, thinking they could be clearly determined by a general rule or practice. His concern was not that all Christians dress alike, indeed he explicitly criticized such an assumption, but that our dress denote a simplicity that marks the simplicity of our character.

23. As a non-juror and with his high view of the sacraments, Law obviously appeared as the very opposite of the Puritans, but one cannot help being impressed by how much his understanding of the Christian life parallels classical Puritan presentations such as Bunyan's.

24. Samuel Johnson, who acknowledged Law's influence, interestingly gives as one of his examples of the lengths men will go to avoid boredom the attempt to fly. See his *History of Rasselas, Prince of Abyssinia* in *The Selected Writings of Samuel Johnson*, ed. with an introduction by Katharine Rogers. (New York: A Signet Classic, 1982), pp. 170-73. Indeed, I suspect Law's influence on Johnson was not only profound in terms of Johnson's own views of religious life, but also in the style in which he wrote. For anyone familiar with Johnson's *Rambler* and *Idler* cannot help but be struck by Johnson's use of character studies that imitate closely Law's method in *A Serious Call*. Moreover, it is my suspicion the moralist tradition, represented by Taylor, Law, and Johnson, found its ultimate home in the eighteenth- and nineteenth-century novelist. For their development of character, realistic though it is, is never without moral purpose. Indeed, Trollope could not resist, which he might well have done, calling his minor characters by stereotypical names—e.g., Lawyer Too Good in *The Last Chronicle of Barset*. Moreover, central to Austen, Eliot, and Trollope was the problem of how true vision requires repentance and forgiveness—themes at the heart of Law's and Wesley's concern with perfection.

25. The significance of this should not be overlooked, for Law never understood holiness as consisting of the denial of the passions, but rather as the passions finding their true end.

26. For example, Law argues that envy is built into our educational system so that it unavoidably becomes our way of life, even though "envy is acknowledged by all people to be the most ungenerous, base, and wicked passion that can enter into the heart of man. And is this a temper to be instilled, nourished, and established in the minds of young people? I know it is said that it is not envy but emulation that is intended to be awakened in the minds of young men. But this is vainly said. For when children are taught to bear no rival and to scorn to be out-done by any of their age, they are plainly and directly

taught to be envious. For it is impossible for any one to have this scorn of being out-done, and this contention with rivals, without burning with envy against all those that seem to excel him or get any distinction from him. So that what children are taught is rank envy, and only covered with a name of a less odious sound" (207-8). Part of Law's great power was his ability to locate and reveal our vices that we have learned to call by less odious sounds.

27. While I could not take the time to do it in this paper, it would be fascinating to study Law's and Wesley's understanding of church and society. For each, almost in spite of himself, shares with certain forms of sectarian Christianity than the church type to which they were both so explicitly loyal. The relationship between Wesley and the Anabaptists has often been suggested, but never subjected to rigorous analysis. There is certainly no doubt, however, that Wesley's (and Law's) understanding of regeneration was very similar to that of Menno Simons and many other of the early Anabaptists. See, for example, Harold Bender's and Franklin Littell's articles in the special edition of the *Mennonite Quarterly Review*, 35 (April 1961) that was specifically directed to explore the relation between these two traditions. I suspect the most determinative difference is that the Anabaptists never lost sight of the fact that, scripturally, the kind of perfection required was non-violence and forgiveness. Yet Law and Wesley were uncompromising in their insistence that perfect love particularly required love of the enemy, though they did not draw the same implications about violence as the Anabaptists. See, for example, Wesley's sermon "The Marks of the New Birth," in *Forty Four Sermons*, p. 170. I am indebted to the Rev. Michael Cartwright for suggesting some of the similarities between Wesley and my views of the church.

28. Though he does not develop a conceptually explicit argument, it seems clear Law believes that only on the basis of such a love it is possible for our lives to have the kind of singleness required for living as a Christian. Yet while perfection requires perfect love, it is not identical with perfect love since it also requires humility, resignation, and repentance. Nor is perfection simply the combination of these virtues, though we cannot be perfect without them. Law does not attempt to account for the interrelation of these virtues in a conceptually satisfying manner. Yet, as I hope to show, that is not a major difficulty as instead he attempts to display characters who exhibit perfection by their formation by these virtues.

Another issue Law does not treat is the tension between universal love and our more particular loves and duties. He is simply not alive to that alleged tension because he understands "universal love" as loving as God loves. Thus any tension between our concrete loves and our love for all people is resolved by intercessory prayer.

29. Law's relatively brief treatment of resignation should not be taken as a sign of its lack of significance or his lack of insight about it. Indeed, I think it is one of best parts of his book. For example, I think he is right to employ the notion of resignation rather than the usual, "conforming our life to God's will." For he sees that our lives are not so much lived prospectively by our conforming to a prior command of God. Rather, resignation is the virtue by which we learn to look back upon our lives and affirm in all that we have done and that has happened to us that God is present. By that means we can learn to praise God as much in our suffering as in our success and thus to be able to make sense of—that is to narrate—our lives.

30. By treating the matter in this way I do not mean to suggest that Law's insistence on the actual practice of prayer is secondary to the development of these virtues. Certainly, because of my own lack of such practice, I am tempted to interpret Law in that manner, but that would not only be unfair to Law, but I suspect would undervalue the practice of prayer for living the moral life of the Christian.

31. Certainly Law's characterizations never came close to those of the great novelists of the eighteenth and

nineteenth centuries. But then Law could not take the time to develop the narratives that are essential to the complexities of character. His studies are like the first introduction of a character in a novel without the subsequent story required for the development of character—developments that often require us to reassess our first impressions. Of course, it was just such reassessments about which Jane Austen was so concerned with in her novels, since she also was fascinated by the moral problem of distinguishing true virtue from the appearance of virtue in a society where everyone was taught the outward skills of a gentleman.

32. Johnson's *Rasselas* is but an entended commentary on this point. Thus the book concludes, after a fervid search for the choice of life that can bring happiness, with Rasselas's sister concluding, "To me the choice of life is become less important: I hope hereafter to think only on the choice of eternity" (p. 256).

33. In the light of his understanding of the moral significance of the imagination, it is a bit of a puzzle why Law (as well as Wesley) had such a negative attitude toward art and, in particular, the novel. I suspect it has much to do with the fact that they were acquainted with the worst examples—thus Law's antipathy to opera because it portrayed non-serious love.

34. Bromiley suggests that Law probably drew more heavily on autobiographical insights for the presentation of Ouranius than any other of his portrayals (p. 269).

35. For a very helpful analysis of various kinds of theological ethics see Frederick Carney, "On McCormick and Teleological Morality," *Journal of Religious Ethics*, 6 (Spring 1978), pp. 81-107.

2. THE PHYSICS OF TRUE VIRTUE

Robin W. Lovin

I. Introduction

John Wesley was an Englishman of the eighteenth century. His life extended through eight decades of it, and his habits of thought were in many ways typical of the educated man of that time and place. When we set out to understand his distinctive ideas and opinions, we will find it helpful to consider them against this background, which includes not only a history of theological reflection, but a more general philosophy about human knowledge and about social and political communities. These wider philosophical presuppositions are especially important when we come to consider Wesley's ethics and attempt to identify his ideas in systematic or theoretical terms that make sense to us today.

The master idea of this intellectual world of the eighteenth century was *empiricism*: "Our ideas," Wesley states, "are not innate, but must all originally come from the senses."[1] The mind, in Locke's memorable image, is a *tabula rasa*, a blank slate which acquires its contents by receiving, combining, and recombining the impressions that the world makes on our senses. To be sure, even Locke allowed that a few fundamental ideas, such as causality and mathematical relationships, are intuitive, rather than empirical knowledge. A number of philosophers, notably Richard Price, held for intuitionism in ethics on the grounds that sense knowledge simply is not reliable enough for such important considerations. Nevertheless, the main current of opinion after Locke was for empiricism, and this current grew stronger as the century progressed.[2] If one wanted to make plausible claims about moral knowledge or the motives to right action, one had to put these claims in terms that showed their experiential foundations. What the age understood by sense experience was, moreover, quite materialistic. Sense impressions were conceived as physical interactions between organ and environment, tiny particles in the ether conveying motions from objects and exciting motions in the sense organs, motions which not only register the presence of an object on the mind, but also excite the subtle movements of desire and aversion that contribute the affective dimension of every experience. This mode of explanation tended to be analytical, breaking complex experiences down into simpler units, and mechanical, reducing physiology, and even psychology, to physics. Moral choice and the habits of virtue were explained less in terms of ideas than in terms of the intensity of certain feelings, the power of one set of motions to cancel the effects of another and exert a causal force sufficient for the overt, external motions that mark human choice and action.

Wesley was no exception to this empiricist temper of the times. Empiricism was one of his habits of thought, as it was for other educated people in his day, including a broad range of Calvinist, Arminian, Anglican, and Nonconformist theologians.[3] These divines continued to argue free will versus predestination, the effects of grace, and the marks of Christian living; but the terms of those debates were subtly altered by the empiricist framework of their thought, so that Calvinist and Arminian opponents in Wesley's day had perhaps more presuppositions in common than either of them shared with seventeenth century predecessors. Our task in this essay, then, is first to understand Wesley's ethics against this background broadly shared and then to consider the relationship between the empiricism of the eighteenth century and Wesley's distinctive emphasis on sanctification. We will find at almost every point a subtle dialectic between the empiricists' physics and traditional theology, a dialectic which recasts the theological positions, but which also pushes against the limits of the mechanistic explanations available in the physics. What emerges in Wesley's case is an idea of virtue that emphasizes affection and will over pure intellect, but which also insists on the immediacy and reality of God's power in individual lives.

II. True Virtue and Splendid Vices

Empiricism in moral philosophy leads to an emphasis on the affective basis for choice and action. The Scholastic model of right reason overcoming the distractions of the passions and guiding the will to the morally correct choice, a model which dominated Anglican theology after Hooker, was decisively set aside, for in the empiricist scheme, the will can be moved only by that which has the power to excite the affections. However the intellect may assess the conditions and consequences of a proposed course of action, action will ensue only if the affections are engaged. "Deliberation" on this account is less a methodical weighing of reasons than an attentiveness to the variety of fears, sympathies, desires, and aversions that sway us in any situation of difficult choice. In the end, it is the strongest and most immediate affection that will guide the action. The appeal of an ethics of character or virtue to an age with these ideas is obvious: once we are caught in the grip of a situation of choice, appeals for calm and reason are by and large useless. The most important thing we can do to sway actual choices is to cultivate the sympathies and sensitivities that will give larger play to the benevolent and socially useful affections when the choice is upon us.

The emphasis on affection should also caution us against making too much of the notion that this was an age of reason, or of Wesley's repeated appeals to reason in particular. Reason, as Wesley briefly observes, is simply "the nature of things: the nature of God and the nature of man with the relations necessarily subsisting between them."[4] To be reasonable is to understand those relations precisely, avoiding superstition or popular misconceptions. Among other things, that means recognizing that in human nature, it is the affections and not the intellect that determine will and action. The empiricism of the eighteenth-century moralists generally blurs the distinction between *explanation* and *justification* in accounts of human action. Providing reasons amounts to helping the reader understand how the action in question follows from one or another affective motivation.

Just how to incorporate theology into these explanations of human experience was one of the great problems of the century. In moral philosophy, the great argument was whether the emotions of approval and disapproval that are the starting point for moral judgment are special, disinterested *moral* affections, or whether they are simply our usual, self-interested responses, modified by a sympathetic effort to put ourselves in the place of others who are affected by events that do not touch us directly. The former *moral sense* theory was maintained especially by Francis Hutcheson, the latter theory of *moral sentiments* by Adam Smith and David Hume. The argument between these theories was protracted, but at least the question was empirical. It could, in principle, be settled by increasingly refined introspections. How this human moral experience could be understood in relation to God's will was another matter. Indeed, as Hume cautiously pointed out, insofar as the only will and moral judgments we can experience depend on human affections, it is hard to know how we can meaningfully speak of God's will and God's judgments at all.[5] When he looked at the physics of ordinary moral experience, Hume found it hard to see how he could get to a reality that would include the reality of God.

The theologians started in a different place. Because God is real and known to us, there must be a mechanism in experience through which this knowledge is acquired. We may now set Wesley's avowal of empiricism, quoted above, in its full context:

> And seeing our ideas are not innate, but must all originally come from our senses, it is certainly necessary that you have senses capable of discerning objects of this kind—not only those which are called "natural senses," which in this respect profit nothing, as being altogether incapable of discerning objects of a spiritual kind, but *spiritual* senses, exercised to discern spiritual good and evil.[6]

Theology can be empirical, then, but it has to begin with the right questions. Instead of arguing by analogy from human experience to God's experience, the task is to identify and explain the effects of God in human experience. The unmistakable realities of religious affections, the experiences of conversion, assurance, and perhaps even of Christian perfection, must be accounted for by mechanisms analogous to those of the ordinary, natural senses. By these mechanisms, too, the impact of these religious experiences on human choice and will can be understood and explained.

Not every theologian developed this notion of a special, spiritual sense. The chief alternative, elaborated by Bishop Berkeley, was to make the will of God the actual cause behind every apparent physical experience, but that idealism flew in the face of the commonsense realism that was implicit in most empiricist philosophy. Besides, if *all* experiences depend in the same way on the reality of God, the special religious experiences that were of more interest to the evangelical theologians and preachers would still go unexplained. So for a very large number of them, including minds as diverse as Jonathan Edwards and John Wesley, this notion of a special spiritual sense, activated by God and conveying an experience of reality unavailable to the natural man, provided a way to integrate a Christian theology of grace into an empiricist account of human knowledge.

So understood, Christian character is far more than a resolute determination to see things one way and not another or to act in one way and not another. Indeed, one's own resolution cannot make it possible at all. Christian character depends on a distinctive experience, which one either has or not, as God's grace provides. To be a Christian is not to act in a particular way, but to act on particular motives, affections which simply are not felt by those who live by the natural senses alone. Because a full account of any action in empiricist terms must trace it back to the affections that initially set it in motion, our theologians could be quite sure that any similarity between the choices and actions of Christians and those of their ordinary good neighbors was merely superficial. Insofar as they must spring from different motives, they cannot be the same action.

Characteristically, those theologians who stress God's presence in experience through the medium of spiritual senses also adopt the Augustinian position that natural virtues are "splended vices." Neither in Roman Africa nor in Georgian Britain could one deny that non-Christians often behaved themselves remarkably well, but when God's grace is made the source of Christian action, it becomes essential to deny that the virtues of the pagans really correspond to the Christian virtues at all. Wesley adopts this position and argues that good works done before justification cannot be pleasing to God, and he defends himself against charges that this is an intolerant and demoralizing doctrine by pointing, somewhat illogically, to the strong Augustinian tendency in the Articles of Faith of the Church of England.[7] Wesley's answer to critics is that the "splendid vices" doctrine is above all Anglican. Whatever faults it may have, his opponents are saddled with it too.

Nevertheless, the Augustinian tradition is significantly modified by its appearance in the empiricist context. Augustine, for all his emphasis on the importance of what one loves, objected to the *ignorance* of the virtuous pagans.[8] They knew what to do, but they had no clear idea about the full reality within which their actions were set. Hence their virtues were likely to become prideful self-assertions. For Wesley, the issue was not knowledge, but affection. Wesley had a high regard for what the ancient pagans knew, and most of the pagans he could see around him were not distinguished from the Christians by their professed beliefs.

What Wesley and his theological compatriots had to maintain was not a distinction between the true beliefs of Christians and the false beliefs of the unconverted, but the distinction between what they called "notional" knowledge and knowledge based on real experience. Here again, the analogy between ordinary sense experience and religious experience is important. Those without a real experience of God's grace were not precluded from reading and understanding Christian theology. They might even give intellectual assent to what they read in books or heard from the pulpit. Mere notions, however, could not be the starting point for a genuine understanding of the things of God.

To use the trite instance: as you cannot reason concerning colours if you have not natural sight—because all the ideas received by your other senses are of a different kind, so that neither your hearing nor any other sense can supply your want of sight, or furnish your reason in this respect with matter to work upon—so you cannot reason concerning spiritual things if you have no spiritual sight.[9]

Different theologians made different assessments of this "natural" or "notional" knowledge which they thought many of their contemporaries were trying to substitute for genuine experiences of faith. Wesley is here quite disparaging of the accuracy and adequacy of notional knowledge as a foundation for reasoning. That is not simply a reflection of his polemical tendencies; it relates to the distinctive emphases of his doctrine of sanctification, as we shall see. Other writers of a more Calvinist bent might rather stress the capacity of the notional ideas to provide an accurate shadow image of what could only be known by grace, so that the unconverted who had to rely on notional knowledge of God might have a quite accurate idea of what they were missing.

The important point for ethics on which all the evangelical theologians were agreed, however, was that notional awareness cannot possibly be motivating. Though one might by the natural senses have a shadowy awareness of the reality of God and acknowledge intellectually that the will of this divine being would be worthy of respect, only a real experience of God could have an impact on the affections sufficient to determine the will on religious grounds. In the absence of that experience, the will would simply be determined by some other affection. No mere notion of divine command would be powerful enough to overide the effects of real experiences of more immediate, natural realities.

Explaining why the unconverted by and large conform to the requirements of Christian morality—or at least appeared to do so in the eighteenth century—requires a rather extended chain of cause and effect. It may be argued, for example, that because God in his concern for human welfare has ordered the world so that right action leads over the long run to human happiness, the powerful motive of self-interest will combine with an intellectual apprehension of one's long-term good to produce a pattern of action not very different from that pattern motivated by love for God.[10] One might even concede that a notional awareness of God as a being powerful enough to mark his displeasure with an eternal punishment would effect a rather drastic revision of one's calculation of long-term self-interest, producing a conformity to God's will that would be remarkably attentive, though unmotivated by any experience of love.[11]

By the end of the century, this theological utilitarianism had prevailed (at least at Cambridge), and it set the theme for the equation of Christian ethics and prudent self-concern that characterized the Victorian era. Christian virtue and the good behavior of men and women who were comfortably situated and not concerned to rise above their stations could not be sharply distinguished. The eighteenth-century evangelicals, however, would have none of this. Common virtues were splendid vices because anyone who understood how motivation and choice work could see that in the end, these utilitarian virtues were merely selfishness in a useful disguise. The experiential foundations that could make these habits of action true experiences of love for God and God's world, rather than prudent efforts at self-love, simply were not present. The best that reason could do with the experience of the natural senses might be elaborated into a socially useful scheme of correct behavior, but for these theologians, that was not enough.

Wesley's ethics is an ethics of character, then, not because he surveyed the alternatives and decided to work that way, but because of a set of assumptions about knowledge and action that he shares broadly with his educated contemporaries and specifically with those theologians of the evangelical revival who stressed the importance of religious experience.

Wesley did not stress particular normative choices or methods of moral decision making. He was, of course, a rigorist in his application of moral standards, but he made the plausible assumption for his age that people know what they ought to do and that the moral problem is to get them to do it. For that purpose, the important consideration is the immediacy and the affective power of what they know about what they ought to do. Mistakes in judgment will occur, but these are few and far between compared to the defeats

of weak apprehensions of long-term self-interest by more powerful affections of fear, greed, lust, or laziness. For these, the only antidote is an immediate and powerful awareness of the love, presence, and power of God.

The evangelicals' claim that natural virtues are only splendid vices did not impugn the choices that ordinary good people make for ordinary moral reasons, but it did have the effect of making their virtues seem rather less reliable. An act that is motivated by a lengthy chain of reasoning about self-interest seems less certain than one actuated by an immediate religious experience. Theologians might concede the extent and regularity of systems of natural virtue, as Jonathan Edwards did in a cryptic comment on the family life of "American savages,"[12] but no one who thought in the terms we have set out here could find these virtues as reliable as the actions motivated by a religious experience so immediate and powerful as to overwhelm all other motives and leave the Christian quite literally incapable of any act except the one that God's love requires.

III. Sanctification vs. The "Patrons of Sin"

An understanding of religious experience that integrated it into an empiricist theory of reason, will, and action was widely shared among British and American theologians in the eighteenth century, but their theological interpretations of this physics of true virtue differed widely and occasioned sharp conflicts. For some, the irresistible motivating power of God's grace for those who had it and the utter absence of experiential knowledge of God for those who did not echoed Calvinist doctrines of predestination and provided the basis for an up-to-date account of theological determinism. For others, probably the majority of British theologians, the possibility of a coherent explanation of God's action on the soul and a reasoned appeal to those who truly sought a more immediate experience of God opened the way to a theology which, while still insisting that the experience is God's gift, resembled more closely the Arminian view of human will.

Wesley, of course, was an Arminian. This is not the place to sort out completely the eighteenth-century theological controversy between free will and determinism. From our point of view, an empiricist account of motivation, will, and action establishes such mechanical connections between these terms that even the Arminian position looks rather deterministic.[13] The point of this section is to set Wesley's emphasis on sanctification in a context broad enough to allow its distinctive theoretical features to emerge. What is unique to Wesley appears most clearly in controversy with the Calvinists. His emphasis on sanctification, while offensive to many moderate Arminians, was a consistent application of the principles that separated all of them from the Calvinists, and his insistence on the possibility of actual moral change is his major implication for our work in ethics today.

Jonathan Edwards, whose work Wesley knew and admired, exemplifies the possibilities and problems that empiricism offered to Calvinist theology. If on the one hand, the empiricist model of all experience lends itself to predestinarian interpretations, the "sense of the heart" that grace awakens does not neatly fit into any of the earlier accounts of what grace is supposed to do to nature. Empirical senses are quite discrete channels of connection between the mind and the external world. They have no hierarchy. Add one or take one away, and the operations of the rest are little affected. So one cannot say that addition of a spiritual sense in any way completes or perfects nature. The natural senses go on writing on the mind's blank slate the same messages as before. For the same reason, one cannot say that conversion or religious experience replaces nature, though we might expect a Calvinist to want to say that. The separation of the senses that marks all empiricist psychology prevails even when one of these senses is a special, spiritual sense.

Thus understood, the theologian's emphasis on rebirth—there is, after all, a new sense, a new realm of experience unavailable before—is apt to be joined with a cautious reminder of the persistence of the Old Adam. The senses that aroused the lusts and errors of unconverted life remain intact and operative. In fact, this is the position we find in Edwards's systematic writings on motivation.[14] We can account for the effect of grace in securing a general disposition to act rightly, but we can never be certain that another motive will not triumph in the event. In his practical advice, too, Edwards has a sense of the liveliness and power of the natural motives that continue to compete with love for God even in the experience of the redeemed.

> Sin is of a deceitful nature, because, so far as it prevails, so far it gains the *inclination* and will, and that sways and biasses the judgment. So far as any lust prevails, so far it biases the mind to approve of it. So far as any sin sways the inclination or will, so far that sin seems pleasing and good to the man; and that which is pleasing the mind is prejudiced to think is right.[15]

Just as the Calvinist must take care not to claim for oneself the credit that rightly goes to God's grace for the first impulse to virtuous action, so one must not disclaim the lapses and faults because they originate in competing motives that are not of God. The key to accountability is the recognition that in a world of cause and effect, every action is *both* the result of a motive that originates outside the self *and* an outcome of one's own choices. "In efficacious grace we are not merely passive, nor yet does God do some and we do the rest. But God does all and we do all. God produces all, and we act all. For that is what he produces, viz., our own acts. . . . We are in different respects, wholly passive and wholly active."[16]

What the Calvinist expects from the life of virtue, then, is not an utter exclusion of wrong choice and action. That would be unrealistic. The point is rather to acknowledge in each action both the sovereignty of God and one's own accountability. Norman Fiering notes the provocative similarity between this theological determinism and some modern psychoanalysis. "The patient and the seeker both accept that they are justly suffering for who they are by admitting in the end that the most despised elements in their personalities are, in effect, the product of deliberate choice *as well as being at the same time* the result of outside forces. By this process of humiliation and remorse, health and salvation may be gained."[17] The persistence of mixed motives and the powerful attraction of occasional temptation suggest that purity of heart is unavailable, even to the redeemed. For the Calvinist, however, that is irrelevant. The aim is not purity of heart, but a vindication of the justice of God.

Set against this Calvinist position, we have Wesley's Arminianism, which shares the emphasis on religious experience, but simply refuses to admit the deterministic implications of the prevailing empiricism. "It is not easy for a man of common understanding, especially unassisted by education, to unravel these finely woven schemes, or show distinctly where the fallacy lies. But he knows, he feels, he is certain, that they cannot be true; that the holy God cannot be the author of sin."[18] Wesley's position on these matters is summed up by his introduction to Edwards's *Treatise on Religious Affections*. The work, Wesley tells us, is a "dangerous heap, wherein much wholesome food is mixed with much deadly poison."[19] His way of dealing with the heap is indicative of his theological method. He simply excised the Calvinist portions of Edwards's work and published the rest as an aid to the experiential piety of his Methodists.

We cannot say that Wesley offers us a consistent, complete, and well-thought-out alternative to Calvinist determinism. Albert Outler has summarized the strengths and limits of his pastoral approach to theology by saying:

It cannot be claimed that Wesley's efforts here come even close to matching the scope and learning of his opponents. They do succeed, however, in exhibiting the folk-theologian in reaction to a theoretical menace to the Christian message. His presupposition is that if the conclusion of an argument cancels either the premises or the consequences of the gospel, something is wrong with the argument.[20]

The key to Wesley's theology of sanctification will not be found in the subtle details of his psychology of perception, but in the broad outlines of his account of religious experience, for he would always find a theology that matched that experience, and he would always demand that philosophy provide the connections he had to build or to break to get the job done.

I am not careful, therefore, about the flowing of my blood and spirits, or the vibrations of my brain—being well assured that, however my spirits may flow or my nerves and fibres vibrate, the Almighty love of God can control them all, and will (unless I obstinately choose vice and misery) afford me such help as, in spite of all these, will put it into my power to be virtuous and happy forever.[21]

The experiential foundation of Wesley's theology of sanctification is the immediacy and vivacity of the experiences we acquire through the spiritual sense. He holds to the sharp empiricist separation of the different forms of sense experience, as we have seen. Sight is not hearing, hearing is not taste, and no physical experience is like the spiritual. Nevertheless, the discrete senses inhere in one subject, who can make qualitative distinctions between them. The testimony of Christian experience is that the spiritual sense is more immediate and compelling than any of the attractions presented to our natural senses. Moreover, even the person who has no Christian experience can make qualitative judgments about the experience he or she does have. The starting point for an appeal to "men of reason" is not an argument for the existence of God or a future state of reward and punishment. It is the simple question: "Are you *now* happy?"[22]

In contrast to the seductive power of lust and sin which Edwards portrays as able to convince through sheer pleasure that wrong is right and bad is good, Wesley finds the world vain and boring. He believes and preaches the terrors of hell, but that is not the basis for his appeal to his educated contemporaries, nor is it, one suspects, the salvation for which he himself is most thankful.

"By this faith we are saved," from all uneasiness of mind, from the anguish of a wounded spirit, from discontent, from fear, and sorrow of heart, from that inexpressible listlessness and weariness, both of the world and of ourselves, which we had so helplessly laboured under for many years, especially when we were out of the world and sunk into calm reflection. In this we find that love of God and of all mankind which we had elsewhere sought in vain.[23]

All experience motivates, activates, energizes. That is the given of empiricist psychology. Wesley simply insists, on the basis of his own experience, that religious experience does that better than any other kind. Sense experience awakens needs and desires that can move us to action, but the multitude of desires and the ambiguity of their satisfactions quickly reduce us to a state of self-doubt and contempt for those other striving, grubbing creatures that saps our will to any action whatsoever. Languor, not lust, was the temptation John Wesley knew best. The love of God impelled him to action, and he expected no less of anyone else who had the same experience. "I *do* preach to as many as desire to hear, every night and morning. You ask what I would do with them. I would make them virtuous and happy, easy in themselves, and useful to others."[24]

Wesley's theology of sanctification, his insistence that perfection in Christian love is a real possibility in this life, is simply an extension of this account of Christian experience. The Calvinists, with their insistence on the darkness of the human soul and the inevitable mixture of motives at war in any act of human will, had to rely on grace both to explain the gift of spiritual experience and the fact of its triumph over other motives to human choice. For Wesley, the experience was indeed a gift of grace, but its power was not at all mysterious. Once the growth of virtue and happiness is begun, these characteristics have no real competitors, and there is no reason why they should not grow until they do indeed control every act of will and choice.

That may well be the consistent conclusion of the Arminian position, but Wesley was among the very few who followed it that far. If the evidence of spiritual experience testifies to the transforming power of God's love, everyday inductive generalizations testify that this is not going to happen always, or even very often. Wesley never denied that, but he refused to emphasize the scarcity of perfected Christians by making excessive claims for the motivating power of transgression. In his sermon on Christian perfection, he awards the ironic title, "patrons of sin" to those who insist that Christians cannot be perfect.[25] We need not ignore the reality of sin, Wesley suggests, but we should avoid doing it too much honor.

The possibility of real personal change must appear quite lively to an empiricist who believes that character, no less than knowledge, is all the product of experience. This conviction Wesley shared with the evangelicals of his century generally, and the common background of empiricism in their thought helps to explain why religious experience occupies so much of the theological foreground. The durability of these personal changes and the extent of the transformation of character would depend, in an empiricist's physics of virtue, on the continuity of the new experiences and on their liveliness being sufficient to overcome consistently the power of other motivations. On this point, Wesley's doctrine of Christian perfection underscores the distinctive features of his account of Christian experience. Like most other theologians, he trusts God, once God has given the experience of grace, to continue these impressions on our spiritual senses; but he is unique in the extent of his confidence that once the experience is received, its energizing, gratifying power cannot be seriously contested by any of the duller pleasures that characterize natural human experience.

IV. Change and Will

For Wesley, personal transformation is the key to moral problems. Because he believes these transformations are possible, he can set aside many of the institutional issues that arise when society tries to deal with intractable personal characteristics. Prisons, workhouses, and slums were the scenes of his ministry, but they do not figure in the intellectual landscape of his ethics. The main feature of that landscape is individual will, will shaped by affective experiences and will shaping a pattern of life that marks Methodists as "virtuous and happy, easy in themselves and useful to others." It is a picture of the moral life that is too simple for our contemporary psychology, but in this simplicity some truths stand out which are obscured by the rococo realism of today's Christian ethics.

Wesley's premise that real change is always possible implies a straightforward approach to the behavioral and relational problems of personal ethics. If, as Norman Fiering suggests, the Calvinist theology of predestination approximates the Freudian psychologist's therapeutic aim that the patient take responsibility for who he or she has necessarily become, Wesley's views come closer to those of contemporary behavioral therapists. These counselors typically avoid the psychoanalytic exploration of hidden dynamics in the personality in favor of self-awareness and understanding of more overt behaviors, the coping mechanisms, strategies of relationship, and risk-avoidance devices that make for success or failure at work or in family life. Their goal, not unlike Wesley's, is to make people happy and useful. Their presumption is that character traits that do not work toward those ends can be identified and changed. Most modern practitioners of these therapies—a group which would include many Methodist clergy—would claim somewhat less for them than Wesley did. Not every problem can be solved this way. Nevertheless, a very large number of people who find themselves unhappy and useless are that way because of character traits that could be changed. For them, the real problem is not living with matters as they are, but change. A Wesleyan insistence that these changes are possible may produce devastating guilt if it is pushed on those for whom a more sophisticated psychology warns that change is *not* possible, but where the underlying problem is one of will to change, the Wesleyan tradition warns us against settling for a listless (or even medicated) acquiescence in the way things are. "Are you *now* happy?" is a bold question for any minister or counselor to ask. It not only invites an honest answer; it implies that things can be recognizably better *now*. It claims that we have more to offer than a way to bear one's burdens patiently.

Insistence that real change is possible has a place in social ethics as well, though Wesley's witness here is more complicated. Wesley resisted carrying the democratic, egalitarian implications that others saw in empiricist ethics into the political realm. At one point he denounces those who talk of political consent for excluding the disenfranchised majority of men, let alone women and children, from the moral basis on which they say society must be built; but we discover at once that this is not an argument for universal political rights. He regards it as a *reductio ad absurdum*: because a political system based on consent would imply giving everyone a say, those who talk about the importance of consent cannot really be serious.[26] For some, the empiricist moral philosophy gave powerful reasons for electoral reform. For Wesley, it apparently argued for a rather sharp line between ethics and politics. His own politics were nicely summed up by the Authorised Version of I Peter 2:17: "Fear God. Honour the King."

The problem here, I think, is that Wesley could not appeal to a normative political consensus that was as widely shared as the eighteenth-century British consensus on personal morality and social order. From the time of the Glorious Revolution, there was great complaint in Britain about moral laxness in society as a whole.[27] Wesley's own comments on current events fit readily into that literature.[28] An appeal for moral rigor works, however, only when people are rather generally convinced that they know what they ought to do, and that the real problem is that they (or their neighbors) are finding it hard to do it. In that case, a solution that rests on strengthening the moral will is called for, and eighteenth-century options were provided by the moral sense theorists, who wanted to strengthen natural benevolence, and by the evangelicals, who relied on a new experience of divine grace.

Controversies over electoral reform and American independence and the persistent Tory rejection of the contractual legitimation of parliamentary democracy gave regular reminders that no normative political consensus existed that could be compared to the consensus on personal morals. In those circumstances, the possibility of real change on which Wesley based his moral appeals solved few problems. What change? Toward what goals? Guided by what ideals? Those remained the major questions, and Wesley was perhaps wise to maintain an unusual reticence to speak up on them. The distinctive things he had to say simply did not answer the political questions.

The dominant Christian realism of twentieth-century Protestant ethics also minimizes Wesley's social relevance, though for different reasons. Realism is suspicious of any attempt to achieve ideals in political life. Even when a normative political consensus exists, as it did, say, in America during the Second World War, the realist finds the business of ethics not in promoting the possibilities for real change, but in taking full account of the obstacles to change and in puncturing any illusions about how far we have already come.

The need for a prior normative consensus and the tendency toward unreserved enthusiasm for the ideals we do have are both genuine weaknesses in Wesley's ethics, weaknesses, which along with his Tory politics, limit our application of his thought to social ethics today. Neverthe-

less, the fundamental Wesleyan message of the possibility of real change and the link between these changes and the will and the affections is worth rethinking and incorporating into whatever ethical system we find more adequate on the whole. Wesley calls our attention to the points at which justice and human welfare in society depend, not on our ideas, but on our will to do what is clearly possible. He reminds us that motivation remains an issue, not only in the shaping of personal choices, but in the political order as well.

To use just one prominent example, arms control today is clearly as much a matter of political will among the superpower leadership as it is a matter of technical questions about the balance of forces and the verification of compliance. Experts continue to propose new plans in hopes of a conceptual breakthrough in negotiations, but Wesley, with his emphasis on will and motive might well come up with a simpler, yet more penetrating analysis. Leaders on both sides are haunted by visions of nuclear destruction and by their own political stakes in gaining or maintaining the upper hand in any negotiations. As long as the fear of electoral defeat (or whatever its equivalent may be in the *arcanum* of Soviet politics) is stronger than love for humanity and commitment to the future of unborn generations, no one is likely to run the risks that serious negotiations involve, no matter how good the proposals that the experts may draft. Wesley reminds us that there simply are those points in human affairs at which more ideas will not help. Only a new will, based on new affections, will move the situation forward.

An arms control agreement is a very complicated matter, of course, and I do not imply that the ideal agreement already exists, wanting only a set of signatures to make it a reality. On this subject, as on so many others, we lack the normative consensus that would make Wesley's emphasis on will *alone* an adequate explanation of our problem. But even the attempt to create a normative consensus requires an initial act of will, requires a lively sense of common humanity and common future with those who must join the consensus, and requires a perception that the old pattern of prevailing by bluff and power offers no satisfactions comparable to the joys of real agreement. "Are you *now* happy?" becomes a profound political question as the peoples of NATO and the Warsaw Pact realize that the roundabout way of achieving security by balancing unacceptable risks has not worked. Ideas alone will not move us from where we are to the place we dimly see that we would like to be.

1. John Wesley, *The Appeals to Men of Reason and Religion*, in *Works* (Oxford), p. 56.
2. For a general study of ethics in this period, see D. D. Raphael, *The Moral Sense* (Oxford: Oxford University Press, 1947).
3. Although we tend to think of empiricism as a skeptical philosophy, it was typical of orthodox British thinkers through most of the eighteenth century. The intuitionists, by contrast, tended to be Unitarians under the leadership of Richard Price. Perhaps our contemporary association of skepticism and empiricism reflects too heavily the influence of Hume, who enters the scene as a major figure with a popular following rather later in the eighteenth-century story.
4. Wesley, *Appeals*, p. 55.
5. See Hume's letter of March 16, 1740, to Francis Hutcheson, in D. D. Raphael, ed., *The British Moralists: 1650–1800* (Oxford: Oxford University Press, 1969), vol. 2, p. 110.
6. Wesley, *Appeals*, p. 56.
7. Ibid., p. 113.
8. Augustine, *City of God*, xix. 25.
9. Wesley, *Appeals*, p. 57.
10. On this point, see Butler's "Dissertation on the Nature of Virtue." Butler makes a strong case against this prudential argument, but the vigor of his polemic suggests that it was a popular idea. See Raphael, *British Moralists*, vol. 1, p. 385.
11. See William Paley, *Principles of Moral and Political Philosophy* (Houston: St. Thomas Press, 1977), pp. 58-59.
12. Jonathan Edwards, *The Nature of True Virtue* (Ann Arbor: University of Michigan Press, 1960), p. 60.
13. It is probably true that the most consistent, rigorous thinkers among the empiricist theologians were determinists, and their system lends itself more readily to a consistent theoretical explanation. See, for example, Arnold S. Kaufman and William K. Frankena on Jonathan Edwards in their introduction to Jonathan Edwards, *Freedom of the Will* (Indianapolis: Bobbs-Merrill, 1969), pp. ix-xxxviii.
14. Norman Fiering, *The Moral Thought of Jonathan Edwards and Its British Context* (Chapel Hill: University of North Carolina Press, 1981), pp. 305-13.
15. Jonathan Edwards, "Christian Cautions, or the Necessity of Self-Examination," in *The Works of Jonathan Edwards* (Edinburgh: Banner of Truth Trust, 1974), vol. 2, p. 175.
16. Edwards, "Concerning Efficacious Grace," *Works*, vol. 2, p. 557.
17. Fiering, *Moral Thought*, p. 320.
18. John Wesley, "Thoughts on Necessity," in Albert C. Outler, ed., *John Wesley* (New York: Oxford University Press, 1964), p. 480.
19. John Wesley, "To the Reader," *The Works of John Wesley* (Grand Rapids: Zondervan, 1958), vol. 14, p. 270.
20. Outler, ed., *John Wesley*, p. 474.
21. Wesley, "Thoughts upon Necessity," ibid., p. 491.
22. Wesley, *Appeals*, p. 60.
23. Ibid., p. 47.
24. Ibid., p. 51.
25. John Wesley, *Sermons on Several Occasions: First Series* (London: Epworth Press, 1944), p. 469.
26. John Wesley, "Thoughts Concerning the Origin of Power," *The Works of the Rev. John Wesley, A. M.*, ed. John Emory (New York: Hunt and Eaton, n.d.), vol. 6, p. 272.
27. Dudley W. Bahlman, *The Moral Revolution of 1688* (New Haven: Yale University Press, 1957).
28. John Wesley, "An Estimate of the Manners of the Present Times," *The Works of the Rev. John Wesley, A. M.*, vol. 6, pp. 347-52.

IX. Spirituality, Perfection, and the Human Vocation: Wesley and Human Development

1. AN EMPIRICAL STUDY OF EARLY METHODIST SPIRITUALITY

Thomas R. Albin

One might well ask: Is it possible to make an empirical study of Christian spirituality? How can one quantify or measure spiritual realities? "The wind blows where it wills, and you hear the sound of it, but you do not know whence it comes or whither it goes; so it is with every one who is born of the Spirit" (John 3:8, RSV).

At the outset, let us acknowledge that many aspects of Christian spirituality are impossible to quantify or to measure objectively (sincerity, degree of commitment or sanctification, etc.). At the same time, it is possible to measure others (time, place, date, age, social environment, etc.), just as it is possible to measure the direction, force, and physical effects of a windstorm or tornado.

One primary function of a quantitative study of a significant sample is that it provides a more objective standard by which popular theories might be tested. What follows are some tentative observations based on a study in which I am presently engaged. This study takes as its sample the accounts, for the most part autobiographical, of the spiritual lives of 555 early British Methodists, drawn from the pages of the *Arminian Magazine* and other early sources.

Evident in these accounts is the tendency on the part of the writers to stylize their spiritual journey around definite stages: (a) the workings of prevenient grace resulting in conviction of sin; (b) the experience of justification and new birth resulting in the sense of forgiveness and peace; and (c) the quest for holiness of heart and life, often culminating in the experience of entire sanctification. The following account by John Barritt can be taken as typical of the literature and illustrates the stylization and flavor of the sources with which my study deals.

I was born in the year 1756 at a place called the Hallet-Hall in the Lordship of Fouldrige and parrish of Colne in Lancashire. My parents were members of the Church of England. 1773, when I was about 17 years of age I providentially heard a Methodist preacher, namely Mr. Bardsly. His text was Isaiah 3:10. "Say ye to the righteous, it shall be well with him for he shall eat the fruit of his doings. Woe to the wicked. It shall be ill with him for the reward of his hands shall be given him"

I went home weeping and continued to weep and pray for near a month. Praying that the Lord would save me from hell, for at that time I was ygnorant of the plan of salvation by faith in Christ. I went to hear again and the preacher was Mr. Thomas Taylor. He preached from the evidence given to Job by his friends. "Acquaint now thyself with him, and be at peace and thereby good shall come unto thee." In his discourse he told us that all by nature were unacquainted with God and had no true peace. He proceeded to preach to us how we might become acquainted with the Lord so as to find pardon and peace.

I was much enlightened by his discourse and joined the society, and the first time I met in class my knowledge of the plan of salvation through Jesus Christ was much increased. I prayed at all opportunities, in the house, barn, and fields; and I soon found peace with God and sang:

> Ah, wherefore did I ever doubt,
>   Thou wilt in nowise cast me out.
> A helpless soul that comes to thee
>   With only sin and misery.

1774

Then I went on my way rejoicing. Perhaps a year after this we had Mr. William Brammah on our circuit. He frequently preached on the subject of sanctification; and by hearing him I began to understand that it was my privilege to advance in the divine life, and I got Mr. Wesley's thoughts on *Christian Perfection* and read it carefully over. I began to see something of it in my Bible, especially in reading the following words: "If we confess our sins, he is faithful and just to forgive us our sins and cleanse us from all unrighteousness." I recollected we prayed to the Almighty at church to cleanse the thoughts of our hearts by the inspiration of his Spirit and I began to think that these words and similar expressions must mean something. When I heard Mr. Brammah preach from such passages as the following:

> O for a heart to praise my God
>   A heart from sin set free.
> A heart that always feels thy blood
>   So freely shed for me.

On sabbath days I went to Padiham and heard Mr. Brammah preach from these words. "Except I wash thee thou hast no part with me." I prayed, "Lord, wash me," and I found the Lord speak to my heart, "I will, be thou clean." I said, "Lord, thy will be done" and I found a glorious change and my soul was filled with love to God and man.[1]

Definitions, Sources, and Methods

John Barritt's experience is one of the 555 early British Methodists included in a quantitive study done at the University of Cambridge using the Statistical Package for the Social Sciences (SPSS).[2] For the purposes of this study an "early Methodist" was defined as any person in Great Britain who consciously identified himself/herself with the movement led by John and Charles Wesley during the years 1725-90. This definition includes everyone who joined the society and others who date their significant religious experience within the period and attribute it in some way to the Wesleys or their followers.

Every person included in this quantitative study (QS4)[3] meets two or more of the following criteria:

—significant information available concerning spiritual experience(s);

—mentioned in more than one source;

—clearly identifiable name or dates;

—resources for study exceed a brief obituary notice.

Table 1 at the end of this chapter provides the reader with a detailed evaluation of the major data source for each person in QS4. In 78 cases or 14.1% of the 555 individuals included in QS4, a manuscript provided the majority of the information. By far the largest single resource for the study of early Methodist spiritual experience was the *Arminian Magazine* and its successors (285 persons or 51.3%). When one adds Jackson's *Lives of the Early Methodist Preachers*, which is largely derived from the *Magazine*, the total comes to 323 or 58.2%. Therefore, a further word concerning the *Arminian Magazine* is in order. Where the original manuscript materials exist to compare with the version printed in the *Magazine*, one finds that the texts have been faithfully reproduced with only minor editorial changes.[4] However, there are not enough significant manuscript documents available at the present time to provide an adequate test for editorial bias in the spiritual biographies and autobiographies published in the *Arminian Magazine*. All one can say is that at the present time the evidence would suggest that material printed in the *Magazine* is historically trustworthy.

Given the nature and parameters of this study, it is interesting to see how wide a cross section of early Methodism is represented in QS4 and the computer analysis. The male dominance of

society during this period and the tendency of Methodism to focus on the heroes of the movement are reflected in the fact that men outnumber the women by nearly two to one.[5] These early Methodists come from almost every county in England and the majority of counties in Ireland, Scotland, and Wales.[6]

The quantitative study gives some interesting information about the family background of people who became Methodists. The oldest Methodist in QS4 was born in 1677 and the youngest in 1776, with 108 of the 555 birthdates missing. From the year of John Wesley's birth in 1703 until the final date of 1776, only two years lack a representative.[7] Even more surprising is the distribution over the 75-year period. Every year is marked with more than one birth except 1773 and 1776; and, no year has more than 17 or 4% of the total.[8]

One finds that 90% (441) were born into non-Methodist homes and only 7% (33) were clearly second-generation Methodists. These figures are based on 491 known cases. Another fourteen persons (2.9%) were born into households which cannot be shown to be either Methodist or non-Methodist and two (0.2%) were from homes where the parents were hearers but not members.

In 320 of the total 555 cases, one finds a clear indication of the religious tradition of the childhood home. Of these 320, ten (3.1%) were clearly not religious (see table 2). The established church provided the early environment for the majority (203 or 63.4%) of those who later would become Methodists, while the Quakers (5 or 1.6%), Roman Catholics (9 or 2.8%) and known Non-Conformists (32 or 10.0%) combined to make a total of forty-six or 15.4% of the remainder.

The attempt to measure the level of religious observance within the childhood home is necessarily subjective. In order to provide some degree of objectivity, terms for measuring this factor were defined in the following manner:

● actively irreligious—active opposition to God and religion;

● inactive—no known attention to religion or religious duties;

● moderately active—head(s) of household and/or family attended religious services occasionally;

● active—head(s) of household and/or family attended regularly;

● very active—head(s) of household and/or family attend regularly with some form of family prayer, worship, or instruction in the home;

● evangelically active—encompasses all

contained within the definition of "very active" with the added dimension of intentional effort to reach others outside the community of committed Christians.

Table 3 presents the picture contained within the sources for the 290 individuals whose biographies, letters, and diaries contain sufficient information to measure. These results must be interpreted with caution, particularly in the silence of the 265 individuals who did not supply sufficient data for a reasonable evaluation to be made. Nevertheless, the picture one finds shows a minority (18 or 6.2%) of these early Methodist people come from irreligious or apathetic homes.[9]

In this discussion one must always bear in mind that the quantitative analysis is comprised of 555 individual accounts, of which the John Barritt account is only one. We must also be aware that this study is naturally biased toward the literate; it can tell us nothing of the thousands of experiences that were never recorded. In addition it is limited to those sources that have survived. One can only speculate on the historical value of the Wesley manuscript documents burned by John Pawson, the well-meaning Methodist preacher, soon after John Wesley died.

Before turning to a more thorough discussion of early Methodist spiritual experience and John Barritt's account, a brief statement concerning style and content would be appropriate. The interest in spiritual autobiographies and accounts of religious experience appears from the very beginning of John's and Charles' own religious experiences. Each of them had a documented account of "Old Jeffrey," the Epworth rectory ghost. Both kept diaries similar to those of the 17th century Puritans. Early in the revival they asked people to record their personal spiritual experiences and forward them in the form of a letter. When John Wesley returned from his visit to Herrnhut in August of 1738 he brought back written accounts of the spiritual experiences of Christian David, Michael Linner, David Nitschmann, Albinus Theodorus Feder, Wenzel Neisser, and others.[10] In December of 1738 John Wesley was reading letters of personal spiritual experiences to his societies.[11] Grace Murray, in her *Memoirs* for 1739, records the fact that "Mr. Charles Wesley desired as many as could to write out their experience, I wrote mine, and sent it in. He requested that I would come and speak to him the next morning, which I did; but shall never forget his piercing look. He examined me closely; I answered him with simplicity, so far as I knew."[12]

Minutes of the first Conferences include specific "letter days" each month.[13] Evidence from the early Methodist preachers indicates that every traveling preacher carried a packet of spiritual letters describing religious experiences which were read to the society on letter days.[14] As one would expect, the content of these letters of spiritual autobiography tends to become stylized as time goes on; however, the diversity of both expression and experience forces the historian to be cautious about discounting the value of any particular account.

Observations on Experience

Having provided the reader with this summary of the sources, sample, and method, let us return to our original queston: "How well does the manuscript account of John Barritt's experience represent this aspect of early Methodist spirituality?"

The fact that John Barritt was born into a home where his parents were members of the Church of England is certainly typical. As we have shown, this was true for 63% of the persons in QS4. His awakening to the need for salvation through the preaching of an itinerant Methodist is also typical, though his age (17 years) is not. Most of the people in QS4 were closer to 20 years old when they became convinced of the need for and possibility of an inward relationship with God. Table 4 provided a complete statistical analysis of the 332 valid cases where sufficient information exists.

It is interesting to note the absence of any personal contact or reference to John Wesley, Charles Wesley, or George Whitefield in the manuscript account of John Barritt. It appears that at the three critical points of spiritual transition (conviction, new birth, and sanctification) that one encounters repeatedly in early Methodist documents, lay persons have by far the greatest identifiable role. When one looks for an explicit reference to a human catalyst at each of these key transition points, lay persons are mentioned three times more frequently than clergy in relation to awakening or conviction, twice as often in relation to the new birth, and four times more often in relation to sanctification. The following chart will demonstrate this clearly.

Some of the implications of this information are obvious and others far-reaching. First, these facts suggest that the primary force in the Evangelical Revival was laity rather than clergy. The Wesleys encouraged and mobilized gifted lay persons to help spread the gospel as itinerant preachers (included as laity above). While this does not diminish the role of clergy leaders in

Experience:	Awakened	New Birth	Sanctification
Valid Cases	287	181	73
Laypersons (sex unclear or both)	11 or 3.8%	11 or 6.1%	7 or 9.6%
Layman	161 or 56.1%	84 or 46.4%	40 or 58.4%
Laywoman	21 or 7.3%	23 or 7.2%	10 or 13.7%
Subtotal	191 or 67.2%	108 or 59.7%	57 or 78.1%
John Wesley	35 or 12.2%	26 or 14.4%	6 or 8.2%
Charles Wesley	6 or 2.1%	29 or 16.0%	7 or 9.6%
Geo. Whitefield	20 or 7.0%	2 or 1.1%	--0--
Subtotal	61 or 21.3%	57 or 31.5%	13 or 17.8%

directing and shepherding the movement, it appears that the impact of a given clergyperson decreased as an individual progressed in the spiritual life. The breadth and depth of the revival had something to do with the ability of the laity to understand and experience God for themselves and then to enable others to enter into a personal relationship with God as well.

One should observe that in many accounts there is no immediate human catalyst identified with a particular spiritual experience. Often this was due to the number of different persons that had been involved over the course of time; thus no particular person or group was mentioned at the moment of the experience.

We should note the fact that John Barritt joined the Methodist society prior to his experience of the new birth. He makes it clear that "the first time I met in class my knowledge of the plan of salvation through Jesus Christ was much increased." The quantitative study indicates that in 209 of the 370 cases (56.5%) where information exists, people joined the society prior to their experience of the new birth. Table 7B provides a detailed analysis of the level of Christian experience at the time persons joined the society. Table 7A describes the chronological age at the time an early Methodist joined the society. While the age range is between seven and sixty-nine years, the mode and the median are both twenty-one years of age. This information suggests that the local community of believers had a significant role in pre-evangelism as well as post-evangelism and discipleship.

Barritt's account implies that less than a year passed between the time he was awakened to his need for a personal relationship with Christ and his experience of the new birth. Table 5A indicates that in the 402 valid cases the median is 0.808 and the mean is 2.381 years. This fact means that more than half the individuals found an evangelical experience within the first year. However, for one individual it took 48 years and the overall time lapse (mean or arithmetic average) is 2 years and 4 months between conviction and conversion. The average age for early Methodists to experience the new birth is 24.035 years while the mode is 20 and the median is 21.604.

The social environment of the new birth is significantly different from that of the awakening and may challenge some of the common stereotypes of evangelical experience. The most frequent social context for early Methodist conversion was while the individual was alone (131 cases or 42.8%; see Table 8), and more than two-thirds of the identifiable cases involved no more than a small group (sub-total 206 or 67.3%). The second most frequent context remained the large religious group (91 cases or 29.7%).

The events related to the moment of conversion are even more diverse than those of awakening. Eleven people are known to have been converted on their deathbeds (3.3%); eight were converted reading or singing a hymn (2.4%); eighty-three were in prayer of one form or another (25.8%); ninety-two were at a preaching service of one variety or another (27.7%); twenty-seven were reading the Bible or some other religious literature (8.1%); twenty-four were involved in spiritual conversation (7.2%); and fifteen were either preparing for or actually receiving the eucharist at the moment of their conversion (4.5%).

The most frequent location for the new birth experience to occur was in the person's own home or room (104 cases or 36.9%; see Table 9). This fact suggests that evangelical conversion for early Methodism was a slow process involving significant thought and reflection. The second most frequent location was in a religious meeting open to the public (58 times or 20.6%); and the Methodist band/class/society meeting (26 or 9.2%) had a significantly smaller impact than one might expect.

Sanctification is perhaps the least understood experience within early Methodist spirituality. Barritt's account is significant, for it sheds light on the role of the written and the spoken word. It is particularly interesting to see how scripture, poetry, and prose all contribute to the process whereby his expectancy and his experience are changed. While John Barritt seems to have experienced sanctification in a little more than a year after his new birth, the quantitative study would indicate that the norm was usually much longer. Based on 193 valid cases, the mean is 5.78 years and the median is 2.48 years. The range moves from 0.0 to 54.0. Tables 6A and 6B will provide a complete statistical summary of the time lapse between new birth and sanctification as well as the age when sanctified.

Most readers will be aware of the importance that John Wesley attached to the doctrine of entire sanctification or scriptural holiness. What can be known of this experience and its significance for the early Methodist people themselves? The quantitative study yields some interesting insights here, even though the number of cases where sufficient historical evidence exists is limited. Analysis of the 131 valid cases for the social environment of the sanctification experience implies that it was the most personal of all the spiritual experiences. One of every two persons sanctified appears to have experienced this transformation alone (45.6%) and nearly 80% of the known cases happened in a small group at the very most (combined total is 102 cases or 77.9%). However, the Spirit of God was active in the large group as well for almost 20% of the early Methodists found sanctification there (23 or 17.6%).

The events related to the moment of entire sanctification are less diverse than at the other two stages of Methodist spirituality, perhaps

because of the smaller number of cases (245), or perhaps because of the nature of the experience itself. The deathbed was the single most frequent event (32 or 22.1%) while various types of prayer combine to make the largest general category (51 or 33.2%), followed by attendance at preaching (16 or 11.1%), spiritual conversation (13 or 9.1%), and the normal routine of life (8 or 5.5%).

The physical location at the moment one was perfected in love reflects this same tendency for the experience to be personal and more likely to be private. The majority of cases occurred within the personal home or room of the individual (69 or 56.6%; see Table 10). The parish church or Methodist chapel were just as likely places for someone to be sanctified as the more private meetings of the society, class, or band (each of these general headings had 15 cases or 12.3% respectively).

Conclusion

From the historical accounts that have survived it appears that early Methodist spirituality could be characterized as a positive process in which lay leadership and direction played a key role along with that of the local community rather than sudden experiences related to a fear of death and hell. In addition, the empirical evidence implies that the pattern represented in John Barritt's diary is more the norm than the exception.

NOTES

1. John Barritt (1756-1841) was an early Methodist farmer who was later called by John Wesley to become an itinerate lay preacher. The Barritt manuscript is housed in a diary box at the Methodist Archives in the John Rylands Library, University of Manchester, Manchester, England.
2. I am indebted to the University of Cambridge Computing Services for their help with SPSS and Phoenix.
3. "QS4" is my abbreviation for "Quantitative Study 4." The numeral "4" represents the most current and correct version of the data base.
4. One of the best examples of Wesley's editorial work on documents published in the *Arminian Magazine* is the spiritual autobiography of Thomas Hanby (1733-96), now housed in the Woodruff Library Special Collections of Emory University. This manuscript has all of John Wesley's editorial marks and comments. It was written Nov. 12, 1779, published in the *Arminian Magazine* in the 1780 (pp. 508-551), reprinted by Jackson in *The Lives of the Early Methodist Preachers* (2:131-157) and by Telford in *Wesley's Veterans* (2:51-77).
5. There are 192 females and 362 males in QS4 with one person whose sex was impossible to determine, resulting in a relative frequency of 34.6%, 65.2% and 0.2%, respectively. In this study, any percentage figures are to be understood as adjusted frequencies unless expressly stated otherwise.
6. Only one county of the 45 possible in England was not represented, Monmouth. Early Irish Methodists were from 18 different counties while Scotland and Wales each had 5 counties represented.

7. No one included in QS4 was known to have been born in 1719 or 1775.
8. The mode is 1761 when there were 17 births or 3.8% of the adjusted frequency.
9. This observation is supported by an unpublished study by Susan Durden based on obituaries published in Methodist periodicals of both Calvinistic and Arminian persuasion.
10. These men were significant leaders in the Moravian Church; see John Wesley's *Journal*, 2:28-49.
11. See Curnock's note in John Wesley's *Journal*, 2:113.
12. *Memoirs of Grace Murray* (np., nd.), p. 8.
13. Bennet's *Minutes* for June 29, 1744, p. 17, sets July 23; Aug. 20; Sept. 17; Oct. 22; see also p. 51, June 18, 1747 where the letter days are monthly—July through December.
14. See the *Arminian Magazine* for 1786, p. 114; for 1791, p. 422; for 1795, p. 321.

TABLE 1

MAJOR DATA SOURCE FOR ENTRY IN QS4[1]

CATEGORY LABEL	ABSOLUTE FREQ	RELATIVE[2] FREQ (PCT)	ADJUSTED[3] FREQ (PCT)	CUM FREQ (PCT)
A Combination	3	0.5	0.5	0.5
Manuscript	78	14.1	14.1	14.1
Jackson's EMP[4]	38	6.8	6.9	21.5
AM/WMM[5]	285	51.4	51.4	72.9
CW JOURNAL[6]	4	0.7	0.7	73.9
JW JOURNAL[7]	6	1.1	1.1	4.7
Minor Account[8]	31	5.6	5.6	80.3
Other Printed Source[9]	109	19.6	19.7	100.0
Missing	1	0.2	MISSING	100.00
TOTAL	555	100.0	100.0	

VALID CASES   554   MISSING CASES   1

[1] See note 3 above.

[2] Relative frequency is derived by dividing the absolute frequency by the total number of cases with no adjustment made for "missing values."

[3] The adjusted frequency is derived by dividing the absolute frequency by the number of valid cases where adequate information exists.

[4] Thomas Jackson, ed. *Lives of the Early Methodist Preachers* (Wesleyan Conference Office, 1871), 6 vols. Abbreviated here as EMP. Jackson collected and edited these lives which were originally published in the *Arminian Magazine* or its successors.

[5] John Wesley, ed. The *Arminian Magazine* (1778-97), continued as the *Methodist Magazine* (1798-1821), and the *Wesleyan Methodist Magazine* (1822-1913).

[6] Thomas Jackson, ed. *The Journal of the Rev. Charles Wesley*, 2 vols. (John Mason, 1849).

[7] Nehemiah Curnock, ed. *The Journal of the Rev. John Wesley . . . enlarged from original MSS*, Standard Ed., 8 vols. (Charles H. Kelly, 1909-16).

[8] A "minor account" would denote an experience described within another story. These minor acccounts were found in one or more of the above sources but differ because experiences shared within this category were not the main thrust of the source document.

[9] "Other printed source" would identify persons whose stories were published in separate volumes such as a memoir, biography, or autobiography. It might also include various types of history books.

TABLE 2

RELIGIOUS TRADITION OF PARENTS

CATEGORY LABEL	ABSOLUTE FREQ	RELATIVE FREQ (PCT)	ADJUSTED FREQ (PCT)	CUM FREQ (PCT)
Known Unchurched	10	1.8	3.1	3.1
Church of England	203	36.6	63.6	66.6
Non-Conformist (??)	4	0.7	1.2	67.8
Sure Non-Conformist	32	5.8	10.0	.8
Methodist	45	8.1	14.1	91.9
Quaker	5	0.9	1.6	93.4
Roman Catholic	9	1.6	2.8	6.2
Other	12	2.2	3.7	1.0
Missing	235	42.3	MISSING	100.0
TOTAL	555	100.0	100.0	

Valid Cases   320   Missing Cases   235

TABLE 3

RELIGIOUS OBSERVANCE IN CHILDHOOD HOME

CATEGORY LABEL	ABSOLUTE FREQ	RELATIVE FREQ (PCT)	ADJUSTED FREQ (PCT)	CUM FREQ (PCT)
Active Irreligious	1	0.2	0.3	0.3
Unconcerned or Inactive	17	3.1	5.9	6.2
Moderately Active	36	6.5	12.4	18.6
Active	85	15.3	29.3	47.9
Very Active	108	19.5	37.2	85.2
Evangelically Active	39	7.0	13.4	98.6
One Parent Active	4	0.7	1.4	100.0
Missing	265	4.47	MISSING	100.0
TOTAL	555	100.0	100.0	
Valid Cases 290	Missing Cases 265			

TABLE 4

AGE AWAKENED OR CONVINCED

Mean[1]	21.467	Std Err	0.508	Median[2]	19.735
Mode[3]	20.000	Std Dev[4]	9.253	Variance	85.615
Kurtosis	6.408	Skewness	1.921	Range[7]	64.000
Minimum[5]	5.000	Maximum[6]	69.000		
Valid Cases	332	Missing Cases	223		

[1] The "mean" is the arithmetic mean more commonly known as "average." This number is calculated by adding all the numbers in a list and dividing by the total number of cases.

[2] The "median" is a measure of the central tendency. It is the value of a variable which splits an ordered list of cases into two halves, so that there are as many cases with values below the median value as there are with values larger.

[3] The "mode" is the value that occurs most often.

[4] "Std Dev" represents the standard deviation. It describes the amount of dispersion or diversity of data around the mean. It is calculated by taking the square root of the arithmetic average of the squares of the deviations from the mean.

[5] The "minimum" is the smallest value of any case represented.

[6] The "maximum" is the largest value represented in any given list of numbers.

[7] The "range" is the diversity represented by subtracting the minimum value from the maximum value in a given list of numbers.

TABLE 5A

TIME LAPSE BETWEEN CONVICTION AND NEW BIRTH

Mean	2.381	Std Err	0.261	Median	0.808
Mode	0.0	Std Dev	5.241	Variance	27.463
Kurtosis	31.988	Skewness	4.841	Range	48.000
Minimum	0.0	Maximum	48.000		
Valid Cases	402	Missing Cases	153		

TABLE 5B

AGE AT NEW BIRTH

Mean	24.035	Std Err	0.455	Median	21.604
Mode	20.000	Std Dev	9.142	Variance	85.581
Kurtosis	5.371	Skewness	1.881	Range	64.000
Minimum	7.000	Maximum	71.000		
Valid Cases	403	Missing Cases	152		

TABLE 6A

TIME LAPSE BETWEEN CONVICTION AND NEW BIRTH

Mean	5.782	Std Err	0.616	Median	2.481
Mode	0.0	Std Dev	8.562	Variance	73.306
Kurtosis	8.630	Skewness	2.687	Range	54.000
Minimum	0.0	Maximum	54.000		
Valid Cases	193	Missing Cases	362		

TABLE 6B

AGE AT NEW BIRTH

Mean	31.287	Std Err	1.072	Median	27.500
Mode	24.000	Std Dev	13.125	Variance	172.272
Kurtosis	2.270	Skewness	1.483	Range	73.000
Minimum	11.000	Maximum	84.000		
Valid Cases	150	Missing Cases	405		

TABLE 7A

AGE AT ENTRY TO SOCIETY

Mean	23.827	Std Err	0.460		Median	21.409
Mode	21.000	Std Dev	9.115		Variance	83.075
Kurtosis	3.737	Skewness	1.661		Range	62.000
Minimum	7.000	Maximum	69.000			
Valid Cases	392	Missing Cases	163			

TABLE 7B

CHRISTIAN EXPERIENCE WHEN JOINED THE SOCIETY

CATEGORY LABEL	ABSOLUTE FREQ	RELATIVE FREQ (PCT)	ADJUSTED FREQ (PCT)	CUM FREQ (PCT)
Known None	4	0.7	1.1	1.1
Awakened/Convinced	209	37.7	56.5	57.6
Born Again	152	27.4	41.1	98.6
Sanctified	5	0.9	1.4	100.0
Missing	185	33.3	MISSING	100.0
TOTAL	555	100.0	100.0	

Valid Cases   370   Missing Cases   185

TABLE 8

SOCIAL ENVIRONMENT OF NEW BIRTH

CATEGORY LABEL	ABSOLUTE FREQ	RELATIVE FREQ (PCT)	ADJUSTED FREQ (PCT)	CUM FREQ (PCT)
Alone	131	23.6	42.8	42.8
One Other	17	3.1	5.6	48.4
Friend or Family	20	3.6	6.5	54.9
Small Rel. Group[1]	35	6.3	11.4	66.3
Small Non-Rel. Group[2]	3	0.5	1.0	67.3
Lg. Rel. Group[3]	91	16.4	29.7	97.1
Lg. Non-Rel. Group[4]	1	0.2	0.3	97.4
Mass or Crowd[5]	6	1.1	2.0	99.3
Not Applicable	2	0.4	0.7	100.0
Missing	249	44.9	MISSING	100.0
TOTAL	555	100.0	100.0	

Valid Cases   306   Missing Cases   249

[1] This group could be a class, band, or prayer meeting.

[2] This group could be a small group at a tavern, a group traveling together in a coach, etc.

[3] This group could be an open air service, a religious society similar to those within the Church of England, the Moravians, etc.

[4] This group would include any large secular group such as a concert, etc.

[5] This group would indicate a large disorderly group like a mob gathered to persecute the Methodists or witness a public execution.

TABLE 9

LOCATION OF NEW BIRTH

CATEGORY LABEL	ABSOLUTE FREQ	RELATIVE FREQ (PCT)	ADJUSTED FREQ (PCT)	CUM FREQ (PCT)
Own Room/Home	104	18.7	36.9	36.9
House/Home of Other	13	2.3	4.6	41.5
Open Air or Field[1]	46	8.3	16.3	57.8
Church/Meeting Place[2]	21	3.8	7.4	65.2
Open to the Public[3]	58	10.5	20.6	85.8
Band/Class/Society	26	4.7	9.2	95.0
Love Feast/Watch-Night	5	0.9	1.8	96.8
Other/Not Applicable	9	1.6	3.2	100.0
Missing	273	49.2	MISSING	100.0
TOTAL	555	100.0	100.0	

Valid Cases   282   Missing Cases   273

[1] This location indicates an outdoor setting only. It could be a person walking alone on the road or an open air service on the green or in the market square.

[2] This location could be an Anglican church building, Methodist chapel, or non-conformist meeting house.

[3] This location would be a Methodist service which was open to the public such as the public preaching time prior to the society meeting.

TABLE 10

LOCATION WHEN SANCTIFIED

CATEGORY LABEL	ABSOLUTE FREQ	RELATIVE FREQ (PCT)	ADJUSTED FREQ (PCT)	CUM FREQ (PCT)
Own Room/Home	69	12.4	56.6	56.6
House/Home of Other	9	1.6	7.4	63.9
Open Air or Field	4	0.7	3.3	67.2
Church/Meeting Place	4	0.7	3.3	70.5
Open to the Public	15	2.7	12.3	82.8
Band/Class/Society	15	2.7	12.3	95.1
Other/Not Applicable	6	1.1	4.9	100.0
Missing	433	78.0	MISSING	100.0
TOTAL	555	100.0	100.0	

Valid Cases   122   Missing Cases   433

2. WESLEYAN SPIRITUALITY: MEETING CONTEMPORARY MOVEMENTS

Mary Elizabeth Moore

Spirituality is a wonderfully elusive reality, which is able to embrace many dimensions, but never to fit neatly into defining categories. Studying John Wesley's spirituality, then, may be a little like gathering water from a river in your hands. You can only gather a small amount from the river as it flows by, and even that runs through your fingers and back into the river. However difficult the task may be, we can presume that the portion of water we do lift from the river will tell us a great deal about the larger body of flowing waters to which it belongs.

The problem of studying John Wesley's spirituality is complicated further by the fact that Wesley himself did not use this word to describe his life and work. This problem was exemplified in the 1982 Oxford Institute of Studies in Methodist Theology in the working group dealing with Wesley's spirituality. Some persons had prepared for the working group by probing Wesley's sermons and theological treatises and the minutes of early Methodist conferences. They sought particularly to grasp Wesley's beliefs and practices in relation to justification, sanctification, and holiness. Some participants had studied Wesley's personal life, particularly his critical turning points and his relationships with significant others, such as his mother, Susanna. Still others had explored Wesley's own prayer practices and his advice to others regarding prayer and other disciplines of self-examination, study, and devotion. In all cases, principles of selection were functioning based on what persons understood spirituality to be. Each person was dipping into the river and removing a different handful of water, but the water in each hand was somehow related to the others because, after all, they were drawn from the same river.

Whereas the elusiveness of the concept of spirituality is part of its charm, that also creates a problem. People read various content into it so that discussions of spirituality are often vague and unfocused. This becomes especially problematic when we speak of the spirituality of a historical figure such as John Wesley. We are tempted to look back and revere Wesley's spirituality, wishing to revive it in our day. Unfortunately, this is difficult to do if we do not have any common understanding of that spirituality which we reverence. We can do no more than put Wesley's spirituality on a pedestal and admire it unless we are willing to describe, define, and critique it.

This problem is nowhere more evident than in the questing for the relationship between spirituality and social action. This quest is an interesting one when we look at Wesley because he clearly valued both. If we do not know the nature of his spirituality, however, his understanding of the relationship between personal and social transformation is difficult to grasp and critique and reclaim.

The purpose of this paper is to take heed of contemporary movements in spirituality, to look back to John Wesley for guidance, and to look forward to the possibility in the future for a new spirituality. We are paddling downstream from John Wesley, surrounded by a different environment, but we move in the streams which have flowed from the Wesleyan tradition. This is especially true if we belong to one of the seventy-three communions which have emerged from the work of John and Charles Wesley. In some ways, the spirituality of many non-Methodist communions has also been shaped by John Wesley's spirituality, for that early Methodist stream of spirituality has flowed out in different directions and has merged with other streams along the way.

Currents in Contemporary Spirituality

Shifts in the understanding of spirituality have taken place throughout history, and at this time we may be on the edge of a major shift.[1] At least five currents are particularly evident in the spirituality literature. As these currents feed into the Wesleyan stream, our boats may be tossed around a bit, or we may get pushed back into the Wesleyan currents, flowing with clearer direction than ever.

Spirituality as a Response to Life

One shift is toward the idea that spirituality is a response to life, to its beauty *and* its injustice. This may not sound like a shift, for the word "life" seems broad and noncontroversial. What is bold in this shift, however, is the refusal to separate physical life from the life of spirit. The tendency in the church's spiritual teachings (especially since the Enlightenment) has been to dichotomize these two and to elevate the value of the spirit, or mind, over the physical life, or body. This splitting is much documented and much bemoaned, but the bold reformulation of spirituality without this dichotomy is only beginning to emerge.

This new understanding of spirituality is particularly reflected in Matthew Fox, who speaks of sensual spirituality. He believes this to be compatible with the early Hebrew understandings of the spiritual life.[2] For Fox, sensual spirituality is clearly responsive both to the beauty and to the injustices of life. *On Becoming a Musical, Mystical Bear* poses prayer as the radical response to life which takes place in both the enjoyment of beauty (mysticism) and the response to injustices (prophecy).[3] Prayer, then, is not a withdrawal from the world, but a pulling into the world with all of its beauty and its ugliness.

In a similar vain, J. B. Libânio speaks of spirituality as seeking the will of God in everything. This impulse toward seeking God in all of life stirs the Christian community into apostolic activity.[4] Libânio describes this seeking of the will of God as spiritual discernment, and he sees it as "a way of incorporating love, concrete charity, into our lives."[5] But Libânio keeps spiraling in more deeply, refusing to leave love as a general or sentimental category. He describes social justice as one of the more important works of charity, and politics as "the privileged field for the realization of justice."[6] His understanding of prayer, like Matthew Fox's, is to pull people into the world so that they might discern more fully what is God's will in the midst of everything.[7]

To understand spirituality as a response to life is to look at *all* of life for the imprint of God. Such aliveness to life requires that we give attention to our senses and to our personal and communal intuitions, for God is as fully manifested in the physical world as in the revelation that seemingly breaks in from beyond the world.

Life as Interconnected

A second current in contemporary spirituality is an increasing recognition of the interconnectedness of life. Until very recent times, disconnectedness has been the dominant assumption, and the Christian church has tended to separate the individual from the society, the human from the non-human, the Northern Hemisphere from the Southern, the Eastern world from the Western, and so forth. The relations among these separate entities have been seen as exter

nal; therefore, we encourage individuals to be interested in the society and the society to be interested in individuals without any awareness that they are already connected at a very deep level.

This disconnected universe is being questioned on many fronts, and spirituality is being reformulated as a result. Libânio is particularly concerned with the church's tendency to dichotomize the individual consciousness and social reality, and he is also distressed with the accompanying tendency to value the former over the latter. He insists that we need to recognize the dialectic between individual consciousness and social reality and the impact that each has on the other.[8] This means that we could not make a simple choice between individual spirituality and the social order because each affects the other. We need a spirituality, therefore, which lives in the dialectic.

Furthermore, the different parts of the social reality are interrelated, affecting one another. A spirituality which ignores this is actually dangerous, for it fosters self-serving actions in one society which are detrimental to another society. Frances Meehan has particularly highlighted this in describing the interconnectedness of the first, second, and third worlds. Ignoring these connections can contribute to a lack of awareness and responsiveness, as happened when Christians in the first world were unresponsive to the plight of the people in Chile and unaware of their own silent complicity.[9]

So far, we have focused on the human interconnections, but human life is also related with all other life and with the earth itself. Whatever happens in the human community affects the ecological balance and vice versa.

In short, the interconnectedness of life is cause for both celebration of, and care for, the totality of life.[10] It calls us to embrace all of creation as our family. Our spirituality is inadequate if it is related to only one dimension of life, or if it denies any part of life in favor of some other part.

Spirituality as Social

All of the above leads quite naturally into a third current which recognizes spirituality to be a social phenomenon. Not only are the individual and social related, but both are important to our relationship with God. Thus, Meehan speaks of a "social spirituality," and Libânio paints a picture of spirituality which exists in the dialectic between the individual and the social. These words suggest that our relationship with God is inseparable from our relationship with society. Whatever happens between God and the individual will be affected by the social milieu, and will in turn affect the social milieu. Furthermore, God relates not simply with separate individuals, but with communities and with the whole of creation. This is particularly witnessed to in the Old Testament narratives of God's relation to the Hebrew people, and it is nowhere more clearly spoken than in the deliverance of the Hebrews from bondage in Egypt.

Frances Meehan speaks of the intrinsic relationship between the vertical and horizontal dimensions of spirituality.[11] This relationship means that one pulls us into the other. When we turn outward toward others, we are not distracted from God, but rather this turning outward can actually lead to new understanding of God.[12] The reverse is also true. If spirituality is social and God addresses whole communities, we can speak of the spirituality of a particular congregation or denomination. God reaches out to these communities, and they seek to discern the will of God.

If an individual's spirituality is connected with her or his social relationships, then we cannot consider that person's relationship with God in isolation from those social ties. When Christians from two different cultures meet and share their faith, their understandings of God are almost certain to be affected. When someone becomes deeply involved in the life of another person, this will affect both persons' relationship with God. In fact, just living in a society with its cultural values and practices and its dominant ideologies will influence our understanding of God and our spirituality.

This all suggests that the relations we have with the world connect us with God, and that our relations with God send us more deeply into our relations with others. It also suggests that the analysis, even suspicion, of our own social position is an important aspect of spiritual discernment. This is the way we discover our built-in biases, and this is the way we come to reinterpret reality and revelation.[13]

Spirituality as Response to the Poor

The recognition of the intertwining of spirituality and social relationships has led to another current in spirituality, that is, the conviction that spirituality is response to the poor. The bias of Jesus to the poor is often noted, especially among Latin American liberation theologians. If the spiritual life is to be authentic to the gospel, then it must be responsive and responsible to the poor.

J. B. Libânio has emphasized the idea that the church is "a community where the poor have a double precedence: both as recipients and as proclaimers of the gospel."[14] This suggests that the poor are not simply recipients of charity, but they have a significant voice in announcing and interpreting the gospel.

In her address to the Sixth Assembly of the World Council of Churches, Dorothy Sölle especially emphasized this point. She said that if we do not listen to the poor, we do not listen to God. She probed into this, radicalizing at each step. She noted that the effort to meditate without touching one's economic position is to foster a spirituality which is empty and disconnected from reality. She radicalized still further by suggesting that what is needed is for persons to actually become poor, seeking less after security (with the violence that ensues from that search) and seeking more after fullness of life (which has to do with sharing and relating with others).[15]

Spirituality, which is a response to the poor, is based on listening to the poor and responding to their needs. The response needed is not simply to their immediate and obvious needs, but also to their far-reaching needs for justice. Without such a response, spirituality is thwarted.

Prayer and Contemplation as Related to Action

The final current in the spirituality literature is the relating of prayer and contemplation to action. This has been a growing accent and is being expressed with increasing clarity.

J. B. Libânio, who has been cited frequently here, is clear that the purpose of spiritual discernment in the first place is to lead to concrete action. He is especially concerned with the selection of political programs.[16] For him, then, prayer is instrumental in searching for the concrete mediations which move toward the kingdom of God.[17] He does not view prayer, however, as related to the Kingdom in a simple cause-and-effect way. The concrete mediations which move us toward the Kingdom are always in dialectical relationship with the eschatological ends, and they should not be equated or confused.[18] What prayer does is to aid us in our search for concrete mediations by serving to clarify faith, stimulate hope, and purify charity.[19] In so doing, prayer awakens in us the motivation and insight to discern and to act.

Thomas Merton approaches prayer and contemplation in a somewhat different way, but with a similar stress on the relation to action. Merton is dismayed that prayer so often takes the form of petition or intercession with the emphasis on immediate efficacy. He thinks the immanentist approach to prayer is more appropriate in that its aim is the realization of union with God.[20] Interestingly, Merton believes that this union with God itself arouses sensitivity to the critical needs which need to be addressed. Prayer serves to heighten freedom, illumination, and love so that we might act in ways which are renewing and oriented toward the unknown future.[21] In this way, prayer is not understood as a tool to get things done, but as a way to relate with God. The action, then, flows from that relationship.

All of this points to the idea that action is somehow rooted in the traditional spiritual disciplines. These disciplines exist, not for their own sake, but to inspire and guide faithful action. To speak of spirituality without reference to action is inadequate. In fact, the old debating and tugging between spirituality and social action must become mute if we fully realize how intertwined these two dimensions of discipleship are.

We are indeed on the edge of a major shift in our understanding of spirituality, and the waters are churning. The five currents described above flow into the stream, as do others. Such a situation might tempt us to steer clear of the incoming waters in hopes that our boats will navigate the rough waters and come out relatively unaffected. On the other hand, the boats might be swirled around in the waters and could even crash into the bank. Perhaps the most creative approach is to paddle downstream in an alert, deliberate manner with an attempt to read the currents and a willingness to be swept by them in some new directions. New pathways might be carved which would be worthy of our travel.

John Wesley's Spirituality

If we stop to examine the river farther upstream, our understanding of these flowing waters may be more adequate. We may be able to navigate the river with greater wisdom, rather than be tossed from one surging current into another. Here we will look at the dominant emphases in John Wesley's spirituality as background for exploring the adequacy of his spirituality in relation to these new currents described above.

At the outset, we can say that Wesley's writing about spirituality was shaped by his contexts, just as that of the moderns reviewed above. Most of this writing was in the form of sermons, public tracts, letters, and conference minutes. He was often addressing a very particular issue in the writing, and, therefore, the accents vary from piece to piece. This in itself is significant because it suggests that Wesley related spirituality to the concrete events of life and the critical issues of his day. In so doing, he developed a clear and powerful statement on spirituality, which itself has currents running through it.

Faith as a Gift of God

Whatever else can be said, Wesley's most ardent claim was that faith is a gift deriving from God. God's love initiates the spiritual life. This is the first current that we feel sweeping through early Methodism. It is the current which reminds us that God is the source of the river.

Faith as the Path to Justification and Righteousness

God's gift of faith is the way by which we are justified and made righteous. This is the second sweeping current. This fact removes all cause for human pride because we are justified by God and not by ourselves.[22] Wesley spoke of faith in various ways, but one dominant theme is that faith is "a spiritual sight of God and the things of God."[23] He was associating faith with insight, or understanding, from which action flows. Faith is not at all static, for it yields fruits, namely, "peace, joy, love, power over all outward sin and power to keep down all inward sin."[24] The human response to faith does make a difference, but not as a way of earning faith. Good works are both the fruit of faith and the way by which faith grows. When good works are absent or when persons willfully sin, the gift of faith is diminished.[25]

We can see a progression for Wesley in that he saw the consciousness of sin as the prerequisite of faith, and faith as the prerequisite of love for God and neighbor.[26] Even the consciousness of sin is made possible, however, by God's grace which is acting within a person before the person knows it.

Salvation as a Lifelong Pilgrimage

We can already detect the third current in all of this talk about faith and sin. That is the recognition that salvation is a lifelong pilgrimage. Colin Williams has gathered the elements of Wesley's order of salvation and has presented the overall picture of the transitions from the natural human state to the state "under the law" to the state "under grace."[27] In so doing, he has noted the points of confusion in Wesley's own work over a period of several years. Whatever the ambiguities, however, one can sense the power of a spirituality understood as a lifelong pilgrimage.

Prevenient grace is God's working in persons to awaken conscience. Here the law becomes very important as the way to arouse an awareness of sin, turn persons to Christ, and guide persons in growth in grace.[28] God continues to work in persons to justify, and then to sanctify them. Justification is "what God *does for* us" through

Jesus Christ, and sanctification is what God "*works in* us" by the Spirit.[29] Wesley insisted on the unity of justification and sanctification. He refused to ignore one or subsume one under the other (as he thought Luther and the Romists did).[30] Even the frescoes in Wesley's City Road Chapel in London testify to this unity, for the dove with the olive branch (signifying deliverance, or justification) is inside a circle (signifying healing, or sanctification). Finally, the sanctifying work of God can lead to perfection—a state of complete sanctification, or perfect love.

In all of this, Wesley was *not* assuming that the path would be smooth and would lead always onward and upward. In fact, he spoke quite frankly of the dangers of lapsing, or falling into "the wilderness state."[31] He also spoke of the danger of pride in one's own experience of God's salvation.[32] At the same time, Wesley put forth the possibility of perfection in human life and some ways by which sanctification might be enhanced.

Wesley's doctrine of perfection is probably the doctrine most puzzling to the modern mind. He explained perfection as "loving God with all our heart, mind, soul, and strength." For him, this meant "that no wrong temper, none contrary to love, remains in the soul; and that all the thoughts, words, and actions, are governed by pure love."[33] The debate, of course, has raged as to whether Wesley understood perfection as a sinless state. He himself was ambiguous on this point. Certainly, he allowed for the possibility that mistakes could still be made.[34] What may be more important here, however, is the vision he put forth of Christian perfection as an ideal. Even as an ideal, perfection was not understood as static, but as a continued growing in perfect love.

In short, Wesley understood the entire path of salvation as one that could be described in terms of an unlimited number of degrees.[35] Because salvation was seen as a pilgrimage, guidance was critical along the way. Especially important were preaching the gospel and perfect love, self-examination, and meeting in small communities for accountability and discipline.[36] Gordon Wakefield also reminds us of the centrality of communion for Wesley. As the symbol of God's grace, it became the centering point for Wesley's spirituality.[37]

Spirituality as a Universal Gift

A final current in Wesleyan spirituality is the catholic spirit. This is particularly stressed by Wakefield, who sees this expressed both in Wesley's openness to loving all human beings and his willingness to recognize God's gospel from different sources.[38] This same catholic spirit is described by Lindstrom in terms of concentric circles of love. In the inner circle is the congregation; in the middle circle, the fellow Christians; and in the outer circle, the whole of humanity.[39] This image suggests a spirituality that is based in a visible community and that reaches outward.

At this point, the language of contemporary spirituality and the language of John Wesley seem worlds apart, and they are. The hope for mutual enrichment, however, is sufficient to motivate the last phase of this journey.

Amid the Swirling Waters

Into the waters swirling with the new currents, we come on the steady, flowing waters of the Wesleyan tradition. We come into this new place with a powerful conviction that God has gifted us with faith and that this faith is life-changing. In fact, this faith will never cease to yield fruit in our lives if we will only respond to the pushes and pulls of God. God's justifying act in Jesus Christ is *for us*, and we can do nothing to deserve it. God continues to work *in us* though, and as we respond, we can multiply our love for God and our neighbors. On this journey, there seems to be no end to the possibilities for loving, nor any limits to the neighbors whom we can love.

This seems quite sufficient until we consider seriously the incoming currents. If modern spirituality in the first current is understood as a response to life, Wesley's contribution is significant. His understanding of prevenient grace would suggest that God is already present in the midst of all of life (at least, human life); therefore, responding to life is a response to the indwelling God. The phrase "seeking God in everything" would be particularly appropriate in a Wesleyan spirituality.

We reach the limits of Wesley's contribution, however, when we recall his strong view of original sin which led him to the idea of a totally depraved human and physical world. He saw the natural self as set over against God so that coming to God requires the rejection of self:

> He that cometh unto God by this faith must fix his eye singly on his own wickedness, on his guilt and helplessness, without having the least regard to any supposed good in himself, to any virtue or righteousness whatsoever. He must come as a *mere sinner*, inwardly and outwardly, self-destroyed and self-condemned, bringing nothing to God but ungodliness only, pleading nothing of his own but sin and misery.[40]

This total rejection of the natural state suggests that spirituality responsive to all of life would be impossible. Robert Tuttle poses an argument that Wesley was influenced both by the Aristotelian emphasis on reason and by the Platonic emphasis on sense experience.[41] Wesley, however, seems to have maintained a dualism between reason and experience. Certainly he elevated the mental/spiritual world above the physical world. This problem is particularly evident in Wesley's inward asceticism which led him to reject the beauty and joy of the world.[42]

Perhaps a new spirituality could be based on a strong sense of God's participation in the natural world as well as a recognition of the inherent evil in the world. This could lead to a spirituality in tune with all of life, but alert to the evil which poses itself.

As to the second contemporary current flowing into the river, Wesley had no way of knowing the degree to which life is interconnected. This idea has only begun to appear in the knowledge explosion of the late twentieth century. Wesley did, however, have a strong sense of the individual's connection with the society. His own individualistic thinking was based on an assumption that changing individuals would change the social order. For example, he believed that convincing individuals of the evils of smuggling would lead to change in those harmful social practices.[43] Wesley's fervor for addressing social issues through individual persons must be heard and renewed. We must, however, not limit the connections to that idea, for the changes in society also affect individuals. Spirituality which is only concerned with the transformation of individuals is no longer adequate. Spirituality must be concerned, also, with the analysis and transformation of society's patterns and structures.

A Wesleyan spirituality would be more adequate if a strong sense of social spirituality were engendered. The means for doing this were present in early Methodism in the large preaching services and in the societies, classes, and bands. Wesley even recognized the essentially social nature of religion.[44] Furthermore, perfection was understood as a turning outward into love of God and neighbor. What was missing, however, was a sense of social sin and of communal experience of faith.

Wesley dealt both with sin and with faith experience in highly individualistic terms. The Methodist groups served to support, guide, and test the individual's experience, as well as to motivate service in the larger community. What was lacking was an awareness that however free a person may become from conscious, deliberate

sin, the person is always participating in social sins (often unconscious), such as abusing the environment, participating in oppressive political and economic systems, and so forth. The awareness of social sin calls us to new dimensions of repentance and to new avenues of service. Similarly, an awareness of communal faith experience calls us to new depths of community life. Communities may not exist solely to support individuals, but to support the communities themselves and the larger Christian community and the larger community of all peoples and all life.

As to the fourth contemporary current, John Wesley was more bold in his actions toward the poor and oppressed than are many who put this on their spoken agenda today. He ministered in the prisons, among the poor and the sick, and among the struggling miners and laborers of his day. Furthermore, he was bold in speaking out against slavery and other social ills that particularly afflicted the poor. His challenge is inescapable to the proponents of a spirituality which is responsive to the poor. It is simply this: *Be responsive to the poor.*

Finally, Wesley's message to those who wish prayer and contemplation to be related to action is equally clear. In fact, he modeled in his own life an ongoing process of action-reflection. He continually reflected on his own experience in order to make new decisions for action. All aspects of this were supported and guided by prayer. In fact, Wesley believed that everything one does is a prayer if it is done out of a desire to please God.[45] The early Methodists also modeled prayerful action-reflection in the life of the classes and bands. In these groups, persons prayed and studied together as they reflected on their own actions in the presence of one another.

Wesley was clear in his belief that loving God would lead to concrete acts of love.[46] Wesley saw prayer as a way of living for God, so naturally, prayer could not be divorced from ordinary life and action. He was clear, for example, in advising persons to pray without ceasing, and he often advised this in particular situations, as he did when he addressed the drunkard.[47] The power in Wesley's understanding was that it was an active understanding and one which contributes to the whole of Christian spirituality.

The power of Wesley's spirituality is great, but it cannot be felt if the river is diverted into Methodist channels. The meeting with currents from other traditions and other parts of the world is essential if Wesleyan spirituality is to make its impact and itself be reformed. Only then can we participate in a new, richer spirituality which has potential to transform our lives and the life of our globe.

NOTES

1. This shift is noted by Francis Meehan, who sees the shift as continuous with the recent past, but moving in some new directions. The shift which he describes is away from the Platonic and individualistic world views. See particularly Francis X. Meehan, *A Contemporary Social Spirituality* (Maryknoll: Orbis Books, 1982), pp. 1-6.
2. Matthew Fox, O.P., *Whee, We, Wee, All the Way Home: A Guide to the New Sensual Spirituality* (New York: Consortium, 1976), pp. 147 ff. See also John Macquarrie's description of spirituality in Celtic Christianity. It was characterized by an ardent sense of God's presence in creation, and that sense has been picked up by a few moderns. See Macquarrie, *Paths in Spirituality* (London: SCM Press, 1972), pp. 122-126.
3. Matthew Fox, O.P., *On Becoming a Musical Mystical Bear: Spirituality American Style* (New York: Paulist Press 1976), pp. 93-102; cf:49-76.
4. J. B. Libânio, *Spiritual Discernment and Politics: Guidelines for Religious Communities*, trans. Theodore Morrow (Maryknoll: Orbis Books, 1982, 1977), p. 33.
5. Ibid., p. 2.
6. Ibid.
7. Ibid., pp. 26-30. Libânio speaks of the importance of prayer in clarifying faith, stimulating hope, and purifying charity (or awakening the conscience). It is not at all an abstract activity, but is, rather, a searching for concrete mediations of the kingdom of God (p. 26).
8. Ibid., pp. 8-11. This awareness is also echoed by Francis Meehan, who notes that individuals impact, and are impacted by, the social structures (*Social Spirituality*, pp. 8-9).
9. Meehan, *Social Spirituality*, pp. 17-20.
10. This is what Matthew Fox sees as the origins of compassion. The interconnectedness stirs in us joy and concern for creation. See particularly *A Spirituality Named Compassion and the Healing of the Global Village, Humpty Dumpty and Us* (Minneapolis: Winston Press, 1979).
11. Meehan, *Social Spirituality*, p. 6.
12. Ibid., pp. 14-16.
13. Libânio sees the questioning of one's social position as an initial stage in interpreting revelation. This suspicion, or self-questioning, does not guarantee change in one's interpretation, but it opens the way. This is particularly true if the person or group has an attitude of openness (see pp. 15-18). Libânio also sees analysis of the social and personal situation as critical for the discernment of concrete mediations of God's kingdom (see *Spiritual Discernment*, pp. 46-65).
14. Ibid., p. 22; cf: 22-25, 37.
15. Dorothy Sölle, Address presented to the Sixth Assembly of the World Council of Churches, Vancouver, British Columbia, July 27, 1983.
16. Libânio, *Spiritual Discernment*, p. 3.
17. Ibid., p. 26.
18. Ibid., pp. 42-43, 44.
19. Ibid., pp. 26-30.
20. Thomas Merton, *Contemplation in a World of Action* (Garden City, N.Y.: Image Books, 1973), pp. 173-76.
21. Ibid., pp. 177-79. Merton thinks that this understanding of the role of prayer is particularly important during this time when persons have more power to control and less sense of "the inner ground of meaning and of love." He says: "We are living through the greatest crisis in the history of man; and this crisis is centered precisely in the country that has made a fetish out of action and has lost (or perhaps never had) the sense of contemplation" (p. 179).
22. John Wesley, "Justification by Faith," in Albert C. Outler, ed., *John Wesley* (New York: Oxford University Press, 1964), pp. 206-08.
23. John Wesley, "The First Annual Conference," ibid., p. 137; (cf. "Justification by Faith," p. 205).
24. Wesley, "The First Annual Conference," ibid., p. 138; (cf. "Christian Perfection," in ibid., pp. 259ff.).
25. These are recurring themes in Wesley, probably repeated often due to the frequency of questioning about it. Wesley refused to fall on the side of seeing good works as the way to earn faith, and he likewise refused to deny the value of good works. See "The Doctrine of Salvation, Faith and Good Works, Extracted from the Homilies of the Church of England," in Outler, *Wesley*, pp. 128-29; "The First Annual Conference," p. 138; "Sermon XLVI: The Wilderness State," *The Works of John Wesley*, vol. 6 (Grand Rapids: Zondervan Publishing House, 1872), pp. 78-85.
26. Harald Lindström, *Wesley and Sanctification* (London: Epworth Press, 1946), p. 33. Wesley asserted that faith "was originally designed of God to re-establish the law of love" ("The Law Established by Faith: Discourse II", in Outler, *Wesley*, p. 228).
27. Colin W. Williams, *John Wesley's Theology Today* (Nashville: Abingdon Press, 1960), pp. 57-73. This *ordo salutis* is also presented by Wesley in "The Scripture Way of Salvation," in Outler, *Wesley*, pp. 273-75.
28. Lindstrom, *Wesley and Sanctification*, pp. 81-82, cf.: p. 135. The law and gospel are actually seen as two dimensions of the same thing. See, e.g. "The Law Established by Faith: Discourse II," in Outler, *Wesley*, pp. 222-23.
29. Wesley, "Justification by Faith," in Outler, *Wesley*, p. 201.
30. "On God's Vineyard," in Outler, *Wesley*, pp. 107-9; "Justification by Faith," pp. 200-201.
31. See esp. Wesley, "Sermon XLVI: The Wilderness State," pp. 77-91.
32. One example of this warning is a letter to his sister in 1766. See Wesley, *Works*, vol. 12, pp. 265-66.
33. Wesley, "A Plain Account of Christian Perfection," *Works*, vol. 11, p. 394. See also "Brief Thoughts on Christian Perfection," ibid., p. 446; 1763 Letter to Mrs. Maitland, ibid., vol. 12, p. 257.
34. Wesley, "A Plain Account of Christian Perfection," *Works*, pp. 394-97, (cf: pp. 366-446). Wesley's ambiguity on this subject is evidenced in his various writings on the subject. See particularly the 1763 letter to Mrs. Maitland, pp. 257-58; and "Brief Thoughts on Christian Perfection," p. 446. Newton Flew acknowledges, as did Wilfrid J. Moulton before him, that Wesley spoke of sin in two different ways. Wesley thought we could be sinless in terms of "voluntary transgression of a known law of God which it was within our power to obey," but not in terms of "any falling short of the divine ideal for humanity." See R. Newton Flew, *The Idea of Perfection in Christian Theology* (London: Oxford University Press, 1934), p. 326.
35. Lindstrom, *Wesley and Sanctification*, pp. 120-21.
36. These are mentioned in many places, but are particularly highlighted in Flew, *Idea of Perfection*, p. 313; Wesley, "Sermon XLVI: The Wilderness State," pp. 85-91; "On God's Vineyard," in Outler, *Wesley*, pp. 109-16; and "The Rules of the United Societies," ibid., pp. 177-81.
37. Gordon Wakefield, *Fire of Love: The Spirituality of John Wesley* (London: Darton, Longman & Todd, 1976), p. 23.
38. Ibid., pp. 14-15, 20.
39. Lindstrom, pp. 191-93.
40. Wesley, "Justification by Faith," *Wesley and Sanctification*, p. 208; cf: in Outler, *Wesley*, "A Plain Account of Christian Perfection," ibid., pp. 366, 439; Wesley, "Advice to an Englishman," *Works*, vol. 11, pp. 185-186.
41. Robert G. Tuttle, Jr., *John Wesley: His Life and Theology* (Grand Rapids: Zondervan Publishing House, 1978), pp. 70-73.
42. Flew, *Idea of Perfection*, pp. 338-341.
43. Wesley, "A Word to a Smuggler," in *Works*, vol. 11, pp. 174-78.

44. Wakefield sees the theme of social holiness in Wesley's spirituality (*Fire of Love*, p. 22), and he quotes Wesley as asserting the social nature of Christianity (p. 67; cf. Wesley, *Works*, vol. 5, p. 296). See also *John & Charles Wesley: Selected Writings & Hymns*, ed. Frank Whaling (New York: Paulist Press, 1981), p. 13.

45. Wesley, "A Plain Account of Christian Perfection," p. 438.

46. Ibid., pp. 372-73.

47. See, for example, ibid., pp. 437ff. Wesley, "A Word to a Drunkard," *Works*, vol. 11, p. 171.

3. SOME BIBLICAL FOUNDATIONS AND METAPHORS OF VOCATIONAL IDEALS IN THE WESLEYAN TRADITION

Donald M. Joy

I have begun, but not completed, the journey through the more than six thousand poems and hymns of John and Charles Wesley. Since I am limiting my work to the primary sources, I am not always sure which of the Wesleys is responsible for a given work. Sample any of the thirteen volumes, however, and biblical images abound. What is more, the early Methodist poetical expressions strongly tended toward the ballad—the story of a pilgrimage from sin toward salvation. One specimen of that genre is titled simply, "Genesis III. 15." The subtitle verse is quoted: "I will put enmity between thee and the woman, and between thy seed and her seed." (*The Poetical Works of John and Charles Wesley.* London: Wesleyan-Methodist Conference Office, 1868, vol II, p. 66.)

Albert Outler got my full attention when, in the midst of one of his addresses at the Summer Theological Institute at Asbury Theological Seminary, in 1982, he quipped as an apparent aside: "How do you explain the fact that it seems never to have crossed John Wesley's mind to construct and publish a systematic theology, large or small, and that every attempt to transform Wesley's ways of teaching doctrine into some system of doctrine has lost something vital in the process?"[1] Dr. Outler was painting a portrait of Wesley as one who constantly took Scripture to experience and then back to Scripture, all the while working both through reason and tradition. Given such a multifaceted task, Wesley was never able to escape the immediate needs of the thousands of members of his class meetings to lock himself away for the luxury of writing a primarily cognitive "theology."

Although Outler did not reflect on it then, it began to occur to me that it may have been the poems and hymns of Charles Wesley which continuously were transforming John's preaching into the distinctly affective domain. And it is self-evident that the theology we sing gets more immediately into our life-styles than does the theology which we hold in literary or spoken theological creeds or formulations.

Elsewhere I have introduced the exploration of left- versus right-brained philosophy and theology, with likely prices paid for closing down either hemisphere.[2] I want now to hypothesize that John and Charles Wesley, perhaps unwittingly, formed the most viable holistic theology since the close of the apostolic age. To provide a background for that hypothesis, I am taking the position that "systematic theology" is as old as the fall, and that its central tendency is "scholastic," anti-experiential, and is uniquely rooted in those left-hemisphere-dominated cultures which have been spawned and have dominated the world to the west of Babel. It is unlikely, therefore, that our perspective will survive to leaven a technological, Cain-based world unless we take pains to differentiate our perspective from those which have given us the various distortions which characterize virtually all of classical "theology" today.

Albert Outler's concern, expressed in the address cited above, that United Methodist theologians tend not to have been trained in Wesleyan theology and hence United Methodist seminaries are not teaching Wesleyan theology is not particularly an indictment of one denomination. It is, instead, a "state of the art" observation. What does one study and where does one go to study systematic theology? To the extent that we put ourselves in the systematic theology trajectory, we will become preoccupied with merely codifying Wesley. Should we succeed in making a systematic theology of Wesley, our brittle dogmas will then be of little more use to us or to our world than if we had bought into the schemas of others. In an important sense, Wesley's way is not that of a verbal "confessional" theology, but of a dynamic holistic "way of grace."

What we need is a different way of doing theology. I am appealing here for a holistic theology, a theology that is "systemic." By systemic, I mean a theology which fully synchronizes all of reality and shows up everywhere from the root system to the finally ripened fruit—just as a systemic gardener avoids systematic spraying of vegetables and fruit in favor of a way of gardening which fosters health and resistance to disease and predators by getting the proper nutrients and inhibitors into the *system* of the plant. Given the indisputable evidence of the locus of written and spoken expression in the brain in contrast to the expressions of poetry and song, a systemic theology could only emerge where a happy synchronization of both "reason" and "image/heart" were present. Looking backward, it is easy to identify John and Charles Wesley; the future requires a similar corporate contribution.

Jacques Ellul makes the point that Cain is the first human to substitute "human achievement" for the creation. He suggests that it was the curse on Cain that engendered fear and that Cain's urge to build the "city" was a means of contriving "security" and safety from that curse.[3] But in Cain we also see the contrast to Abel, who "by faith . . . offered God a better sacrifice than Cain did. By faith he was commended as a righteous man, when God spoke well of his offerings. And by faith he still speaks, even though he is dead."[4] Thus Abel is allied with God, "the judge of all men, to the spirits of righteous men made perfect, to Jesus the mediator of a new covenant, and to the sprinkled blood that speaks a better word than the blood of Abel."[5]

The impulse of Cain is to "do it my way," to marshall all human ingenuity to exalt the self, leading ultimately to the city, of which the tower of Babel is but one tower—all poised to defy the creation and the Creator and to exalt human mastery. And it is at Babel that God came down to confuse human language. Evolutionist Carl Sagan projects backward through imagination and sees early humans having redundant brain hemispheres of a left-handed, right-hemisphere sort.[6] My recent colleague, Dr. John Oswalt, distinguished Old Testament linguist, himself left-handed, notes that clay tablets chronicle the shift when Akkadian ceased to be written vertically with the left hand and became a horizontal, left-to-right, right-handed language. The widely diverse cultures of East and West are now seen by some linguists and neurosurgeons as likely differentiations rooted in the highly imaging languages housed in the right hemisphere (East) in contrast to linear/abstract languages housed in the left (West).[7]

Behind Babel and Cain, however, lie the primal thumbprints of the serpent: "Did God really say, 'You must not eat from any tree in the garden'?"[8] Seduction was couched in an appeal to "systematize" the God-human relationship. This strategy of dividing "relationship" from

"cognition" by exalting cognition leads to the original sin. It is original sin because it incites the humans to pride and rebellion which fracture the God relationship. But it is also original sin because it established a fault line between "affect" and "cognition." This split between cognition and affect predicted the cognitive power plays by which relationships continue to be devalued and destroyed. Yet to be fully human is to be in full synchrony with cognition and affect fully integrated and fully functioning. It is to be in the line of Adam, Abel, Seth, Jesus, the apostles, Bernard of Clairvaux, Count Zinzendorf, and the Wesleys. To exalt cognition at the expense of affect and relationships is to be in line of descent from Cain, Nimrod, the Gnostics, Augustine, Descartes, Calvin, and Darwin.[9] Paul Bassett ably traces the line of his present life from the Wesleys back to the New Testament, documenting its near eclipse following what he calls the "Augustinian bypass" which relegated these to the future life alone.[10]

Ironically, the detour to the left-brain—the cognitive power play which devalues affect—left the laity without literacy, without cognitive balance, and the "dark ages" of magic, fear, and childlike license and games in the name of Christianity formed the alternative bypass to the right. Today's charismatic movement, tending largely to the affective imbalance, is a reminder of the tragic deformity when the affective right hemisphere is deprived of the balance of reason and the cognitive in theology.

Both detours emphasize the urgency of each generation to forge ahead to hold left and right in dynamic and synchronic union. Who are the prophets and saints of ages past whose life and vision encompassed the whole of our humanity? Who, to make a simple test, are those enshrined in the names of orphanages and hospitals—two expressions focused on the whole person? Are there ministries bearing the names of Augustine, Cain, Calvin, Knox, Darwin, or Paine? How do you account for that?

My appeal, then, in this introduction, is for a radicalization of theology that is truly in the Wesleyan spirit. This is clearly a call for a new style of theology—a systemic theology, not simply another systematic theology with a variation in content. Delbert Rose once called for a "theology of Christian experience."[11] Albert Outler long ago called John Wesley a folk theologian.[12] Neither captures the expansive and encompassing balance necessary when truly cognitive and truly affective dimensions are kept in dynamic synchrony in our theology.

I move, now, to examine some of the biblical

foundations and metaphors of vocational ideals in the Wesley tradition. In doing so, I will be deliberately tilting toward that right-hemisphered set of images which both articulate and shape the more left-hemisphered ideas which are intrinsic to Wesley's theology. I wish to identify four of the major features which characterize Wesley's system, all of which I find to be conspicuously absent in other theological systems: (1) Life is pilgrimage; we go on from grace to grace. (2) Righteousness is both real and relative, immediate and progressive. (3) All of life is transformed; suffering, pain, and repentance are the catalysts. (4) Salvation is the recovery of innocence.

Life as Pilgrimage: Going On from Grace to Grace

Elsewhere I have described life as "pilgrimage" and have described that pilgrimage as dynamic, relational, aspirational, epochal, and cumulative.[13] When I wrote that chapter, it had not occurred to me to check the Wesley hymnody. Other theologies tend to be concerned to note the effects of grace by focusing on the change in status as the believer becomes a child of God. Some theologies attend almost not at all to integrating past, present, and future, but focus entirely on the status/standing issues. Imagine my sense of discovery, then, in preparing for this conference, as I walked through set after set of Wesley poetry cast in this ballad, sometimes epic, poetic style. Look, for example, at the four poems which open part 2 of volume 2 of the complete poetical works. Here, in sequence, are "Christ the Friend of Sinners," "On the Conversion of a Common Harlot," "Romans IV. 5," and "Acts I.4." As you read them, note the over-all pilgrimage flow. The next three hymns recapitulate salvation in a Trinitarian sequence, with the heightening of the salvific grace visible from hymn to hymn. These are "Hymn of Thanksgiving to the Father," "Hymn to the Son," and "Hymn to the Holy Ghost."

The image of inner cleansing by the Holy Ghost was placed on the pilgrimage timeline as the "rest" that awaited at the climax of the long and toil-filled pilgrimage. If we examine the text built around "Hebrews IV. 9," including the editor's note regarding the later excision of stanzas four and five, we glimpse the amazing Wesley paradox: "rest" is attainable in this present life (in contrast to Augustine's notion, for whom purgatory became the sanctifying furnace), yet the struggle against sin, sinning, and ordinary trouble goes on. One of my students began a presentation by suggesting that

John Wesley's vision of salvation was such that he should, instead, have taken up dog racing. When I asked whatever for, he said, "Remember that the rabbits which racing dogs chase are mechanical, and they are always kept out of reach of the dogs to spur them on." Perhaps. But life's pilgrimage is not made up of artificial rabbits; the struggles are real. And John Wesley's own reluctance to claim, personally, the attainment of the "rest" in his imagery, suggests that the "motor" of discipleship in the Wesleyan spirit may well be the paradox which always separates full embracing of the vocational aspiration from the Jack Horner collapse of claiming arrival.

Righteousness as Real and Relational, Epochal and Continuous

Whereas Reformed theology consistently regards righteousness as positional and imputed, John Wesley holds plainly for righteousness which is real and which shares the divine nature, imparting it to us.

> And at the same time that we are justified, yea, in that very moment, sanctification begins. In that instant we are born again, born from above, born of the Spirit: There is a *real* as well as a *relative* change. . . . From the time of our being born again, the gradual work of sanctification takes place. We are enabled "by the Spirit" to "mortify the deeds of the body," of our evil nature; and as we are more and more dead to sin, we are more and more alive to God. We go on from grace to grace. . . . It is thus that we wait for entire sanctification; for a full salvation from all our sins, —from pride, self-will, anger, unbelief; or, as the Apostle expresses it, "go on unto perfection."[14]

These lines from the sermon "The Scripture Way of Salvation" strike at the heart of mere positional righteousness and of delayed righteousness through purgation after this present life, but they do so unself-consciously. By "*relative* change," Wesley explains elsewhere, "in all relationships," hence righteousness is visible in interpersonal exchanges, in one's stewardship of the earth, and, of course, in relationship to the righteous God.

If we were to lift one metaphor from Wesley sources which most fully illustrates the idea of pilgrimage as real and relational, epochal and continuous, it would have to be the central character of Genesis 25–37, Jacob. A fourteen-stanza hymn, traditionally called "Wrestling Jacob" focuses exclusively on Genesis 32. The Jacob material is plainly metaphoric to the theological reality Charles Wesley wishes to express. Nevertheless, Jacob's life story in more than ten chapters of Genesis overlays Wesley's

"Way of Salvation" or Outler's *ordo salutis* in a magnificent way.[15] Steve Harper's new book *John Wesley's Message for Today* details and documents the sequence of grace stages from an examination of a wide range of Wesley material.[16] I have offered here my own effort to plot the successive phases of grace in the life pilgrimage alongside other structural perceptions of human development.

Grace as Transformational: Suffering, Pain, and Repentance as Catalysts

James Loder has developed in theory what the Wesleys were developing in practice, when he published *The Transforming Moment: Understanding Convictional Experiences*.[17] Loder notes that at the purely human level, when (A) the *lived world* is experienced by (B) the *self*, ordinary growth occurs, moving a person toward increasingly complex ways of coping with reality. But we begin to accumulate unanswered questions, even pain, which Loder calls (C) the *void*. Without supernatural help, the void turns inevitably to despair and cynicism—the lot of "natural man" as Wesley pictures him. But when God breaks through with (D) the *Holy*, he transforms the very pain, catastrophe, or ambiguity that constituted the void: tragedy is turned into divine comedy. Loder explicates the Emmaus event to illustrate how with a "double negation," the Emmaus couple receive the "broken body" (bread) from the "risen Lord," and he disappears from their sight, denoting the transformation of blinding grief into the blinding light of grace-bestowed reconstruction and discovery.

John Wesley, in his first sermon in the series on the Beatitudes, notes, but scarcely develops, the developmental structure of those eight rungs of "blessedness." Wesley notes potentially conflicting views of the Beatitudes: (1) that they constitute "the steps which a Christian successively takes in his journey to the promised land,"

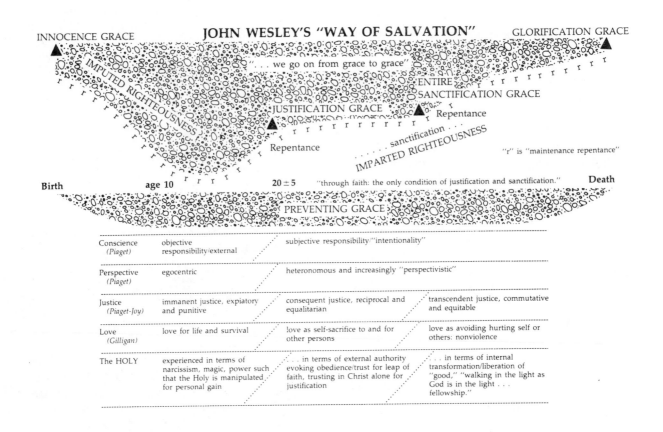

JOHN WESLEY'S "WAY OF SALVATION"

INNOCENCE GRACE   GLORIFICATION GRACE

". . . we go on from grace to grace"

IMPUTED RIGHTEOUSNESS

JUSTIFICATION GRACE   ENTIRE SANCTIFICATION GRACE

Repentance   Repentance

sanctification

IMPARTED RIGHTEOUSNESS

"r" is "maintenance repentance"

Birth   age 10   20 ± 5   "through faith: the only condition of justification and sanctification."   **Death**

PREVENTING GRACE

Conscience (Piaget)	objective responsibility/external	subjective responsibility/"intentionality"	
Perspective (Piaget)	egocentric	heteronomous and increasingly "perspectivistic"	
Justice (Piaget-Joy)	immanent justice, expiatory and punitive	consequent justice, reciprocal and equalitarian	transcendent justice, commutative and equitable
Love (Gilligan)	love for life and survival	love as self-sacrifice to and for other persons	love as avoiding hurting self or others: nonviolence
The HOLY	experienced in terms of narcissism, magic, power such that the Holy is manipulated for personal gain	. . . in terms of external authority evoking obedience/trust for leap of faith, trusting in Christ alone for justification	. . . in terms of internal transformation/liberation of "good," "walking in the light as God is in the light . . . fellowship."

and (2) that they list "all the particulars which . . . belong at all times to every Christian." He then appeals that both may well be true, ending with this: "Real Christianity always begins in poverty of spirit, and goes on in the order here set down, till the 'man of God is made perfect.' "[18] Had Charles imaged the Beatitudes in a hymn or a series of poems, we can be sure that this structure would have been visible in another grand epic ballad. John Wesley, however, spiritualized the first three of the Beatitudes, likely missing a cardinal plank in Wesleyan theology: the role of prevenient/innocence grace which undergirds the poor (helpless, infants, defectives, insane—all the morally incapacitated), the persons blinded by grief, and those whose resources of character are being trampled in the winepress of suffering—the meek, the "poor in spirit," in Luke's version is simply, "you poor." Poverty, grief, and humiliation may be literal and inescapable. Sometimes they are pathological inward attitudes of negative self-worth. When they are transformed by God's grace, they may finally become inner marks of a transparent spirit; the grace-transformed person has allowed the *void* to be transformed by the *Holy.*

The Wesleys' conception of God's salvation was as if it is a grace-lubricated conveyor belt by which we are enabled to move from one transformation to another. In early or otherwise innocent experience, the grace is "prevenient." In later or otherwise self-reflective, choosing experience, the grace is "converting" and "justifying," "sanctifying," even "entirely sanctifying" in its effects. So the Beatitudes of Jesus, prototypic of all other transformational models throws light on Erikson's epigenetic stages or "life crises," and on Levinson's "seasons of a man's life," or even Maslow's "hierarchy of human needs." In all of these structural trajectories a "prepotency" may obtain: each advance is dependent upon the completion of the previous task or obligation. And like Piaget's structural stages, they are hierarchically integrated—all previous masteries remain accessible and undergird the highest functioning stage.[19]

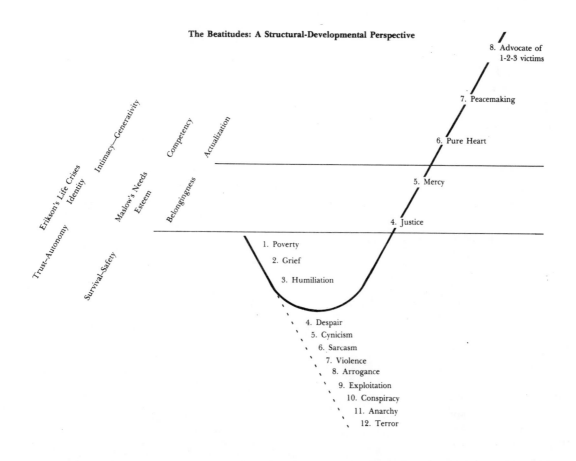

The Beatitudes: A Structural-Developmental Perspective

The helplessness and pain and tragedy denoted by "poor, mourning, and humiliated" persons living out the first three of the Beatitudes' conditions are not meritorious or grace filled in any deterministic sense.

There is no guarantee that poverty, grief, and humiliation will establish a person in the pursuit of righteousness, mercy, or the pure heart—only that during that phase of the life pilgrimage, God takes the sole initiative. Only with the first three of the Beatitudes is there the unconditional assurance of the reward of grace; thereafter, each blessing has its price clearly stated. And a person might more easily slip out of God's prevenient/innocence grace into a negative trajectory. Without the transformation of the void by the Holy, poverty, grief, and humiliation more likely predicts despair, cynicism, sarcasm, violence, arrogance, exploitation, conspiracy, anarchy, and terror. One's first estate in both original sin and original innocence may give way, not to converting, justifying, and sanctifying grace, but to culpable sin and ultimately to unpardonable sin.

Wesley's poetry regards the years in Egypt and the journey through the wilderness as the pain-filled, tragic early phase of the pilgrimage. The promised land, Beulah, becomes analogical to the New Testament "promise" and "rest" which define the urgency of faithfulness and moving ahead in the present struggle. "Milk and honey" are markers in the poetry texts pointing to the long-awaited rewards at the summit of life's vocation.

Salvation: The Recovery of Innocence

Wesleyan theology is populated with images and concepts which announce that the estate of creation is being recaptured by re-creation through Jesus Christ. While all systematic theologies in the Christian tradition would acknowledge these boundary markers, most are impoverished by the lack of their attention to the doctrine of creation.

Perfect innocence and perfect love are anchored in Genesis 1 and 2. So also is the loss of the first Adam defined only in terms of what he has lost and how far he has fallen. But given these defining images and concepts, the Wesleys show how grace will restore the lost image, how Abel can live again, and how the second Adam will bring all things back into focus with perfect love and perfect innocence. "None is like Jeshurun's God" is typical of these poetic image packages. (*Poetical Works,* vol. II, p. 305.)

Now, the recovery of innocence as a target of the life vocation would be absurd if righteousness were not both "real and relative." And repentance as life orientation is necessary if innocence is to be maintained across a lifetime of increased sensitivity to sin and heightened perception of failure. C. S. Lewis has likened the life pilgrimage to the increasing sense of responsibility a person would have in coming off a drunken spree. At first, denial of drunkenness. Later, embarrassment and apology. But only clear perception of the debauchery when stone sober.

We must ask at this consultation: What does the future require of us? Each phase of our section's consideration must answer, of course. But we may wish now to pause to ask these kinds of questions:

1. What are the images which have nourished or impoverished our individual and our collective theological concepts in the late twentieth century?

2. Are our spiritual leaders deliberately cultivating both right- and left-brain images and concepts on crucial aspects of theological perception?

3. What are the questions worth addressing if we would better understand the link between the arts in worship (hymn, poem, drama) and didactic in preaching? Between ecstasy and reason? Between story and interpretation?

4. Are all of us capable of theological ambidexterity? Or, as in marriage, are "image" and "concept" the opposing, but magnetic, halves of one whole? If so, how might we avoid the power plays which devalue the other's gifts?

NOTES

1. Albert C. Outler, "Repentance and Justification" (Wilmore, Ky: Asbury Theological Seminary Tape Library, No. 82BB3, July 13, 1982).
2. This entire introduction is adapted from the section, "A Call for Truly Wesleyan Theology," in the chapter "The Contemporary Church as 'Holy Community,'" in Melvin Dieter and Daniel Berg, eds. *The Contemporary Church and Ministry,* part of the series "Wesleyan Perspectives on the Church," in press, 1983. My right/left brain discussion may be traced back to chapters 2 and 12 of *Moral Development Foundations: Judeo-Christian Alternatives to Piaget/Kohlberg* (Nashville: Abingdon Press, 1983).
3. Jacques Ellul, *The Meaning of the City* (Grand Rapids: Wm. Eerdmans, 1970), pp. 1-9.
4. Heb. 11:4 NIV.
5. Heb. 12:23-24 NIV.
6. Carl Sagan, *The Dragons of Eden: Speculations on the Evolution of Human Intelligence* (New York: Random House, 1977), pp. 173-174.
7. Atuhiro Sibatani, "The Japanese Brain: The Difference Between East and West May Be the Difference Between Left and Right." *Science/80,* December, 1980, pp. 22 ff.
8. Gen. 3:1 NIV.
9. Charles Hampden-Turner, *Maps of the Mind* (London: Mitchell Beazley Publishers, 1981), pp. 30-37.
10. Paul M. Bassett, *The Historical Path of the Doctrine of Entire Sanctification.*

11. Delbert R. Rose, "The Theology of Joseph H. Smith." Doctoral dissertation, University of Iowa, 1952.
12. Albert C. Outler, *John Wesley* (New York: Oxford University Press, 1964).
13. Donald M. Joy, "Life as Pilgrimage" in *Moral Development Foundations*.
14. John Wesley, *Sermons on Several Occasions*, vol. 1 (New York: Waugh and Mason, 1836), pp. 45-46.
15. Donald Joy, "Life as Pilgrimage: Jacob and Us." Sermon at Warm Beach Camp, Wilmore Kentucky: Donald Joy tape library.
16. Steve Harper, *John Wesley's Message for Today* (Grand Rapids: Zondervan, 1983).
17. James E. Loder, *The Transforming Moment: Understanding Convictional Experiences* (New York: Harper & Row, 1981).
18. John Wesley, *The Works of John Wesley*, vol. 5 (Grand Rapids: Zondervan [1892]), p. 252.
19. See my extended discussion of this in "Pain: Catalyst for Christian Holiness," *Preacher's Magazine*, vol. 58. no. 4, June/July/August, 1983, pp. 26 ff. See also the section, "Wesley's Way of Salvation," in "Toward Christian Holiness: John Wesley's Faith Pilgrimage," in *Moral Development Foundations*, pp. 223 ff.

X. Ecumenism and Methodism: Issues in Ministry, Sacraments, and Order

1. WESLEY'S THEOLOGY
AND THE FUTURE OF THE CHURCH

Norman Young

As it enters its third century, how can United Methodism continue (as Wesley intended) as leaven in a more catholic expression of the church? What is implied for its present life in preparing for such a future? What is the "vision"? Those questions, posed to give direction to the discussion in one working group at the Emory Consultation, should at some stage lead us beyond issues in ministry, sacraments, and order if these are interpreted in too narrow a sense. The more I have become involved in bilateral and multilateral conversations with other churches the more I have become convinced that when Wesley's theology is taken seriously it does more than give Methodists a common accent in which to carry on dialogue with others. It can, to use the metaphor of the consultation program, help to build bridges over ecclesiological chasms that are far older and deeper than those resulting from Methodism's shift from movement to church.

So, how can Methodism continue as a leaven in a more catholic expression of the church? One most important contribution, I believe, is to offer theological insights that can help to overcome some of the most deep-seated divisions in Christendom. What is implied, therefore, for its present life? To take the theology of the Wesleys far more seriously than we have been inclined to do, not only as a corrective to Methodism's often-cited preference for evangelism and social action over theological reflection[1] (as though they were mutually exclusive if not downright destructive of each other!), but also as a move toward wider unity. "Back to Wesley" is often heard as the rallying cry of Methodist triumphalists, and it can be that, however unfaithful to the spirit of Wesley himself. My experience, however, of living within Methodism and now in a united church, and of teaching Wesley's theology in both contexts and in a wider one still,[2] leads me to a different vision—of a revitalized study of Wesley's theology that within Methodism will give depth to evangelism and direction to social action, and beyond Methodism will suggest new approaches to old and intractable problems.

But is that vision any more than an idle dream? I believe that it is, and offer as evidence some reflections on the theme of conscience and authority which the World Methodist/Roman Catholic commission discussed during its last round of conversations.

We began by recognizing that on this theme Protestants (not just Methodists) and Catholics have long been understood to divide. How do I know what I ought to do? Protestants are supposed to reply, "Follow your conscience"; Catholics, "heed the voice of authority." So widespread and ingrained has this type-casting been that the commission rightly concluded that "the nexus between conscience and authority has often been seen less as a relationship than as a Protestant/Catholic antithesis."[3] But it does not take an appeal to the theology of Wesley to see that this is a false antithesis. Imagine a Catholic nurtured in the faith by committed parents, prepared for confirmation by catechesis, enjoined to make a good confession and to live in the world as a good Catholic not being aware of the duty to obey conscience! That is about as likely as a Protestant brought up in a God-fearing, Bible-reading, church-going family, listening to the preacher week by week and regularly attending prayer meeting, not being aware of standing under authority. Thus a down-to-earth look at the way things are clears up the false antithesis. Where does reflection on Wesley's theology come in?

It comes in when, having agreed that both conscience and authority are involved in moral decision-making, we go on to ask how they are related. How is conscience informed? What does authority prescribe?

Wesley, of course, would never have defined his position over against Rome by opting for individual conscience rather than for more objective forms of authority as the final guide to Christian obedience. He defined conscience as "that faculty whereby we are at once conscious of our own thoughts, words, and actions; and of their merit and demerit, of their being both good and bad, and, consequently, deserving either praise or censure."[4]

Thus conscience does not give detailed instructions about what course of action to follow in every given circumstance. It does, however, provide the capacity to know that there is a difference between good and evil, and, in general terms, to grasp broad moral principles; for instance, that it is good to honor parents and to do right to others as we would have them do to us. Rather than shedding light on everything we should do, conscience makes sure that we know when we have turned away from the light we do have. Using another metaphor, this time from the law courts, he says that conscience has a three-fold office: as a witness, "testifying to what we have done in thought or word or action"; as a judge, "passing sentence on what we have done, that it is good or evil"; "it also in some sense executes the sentence by occasioning a degree of complacency in him that does well and uneasiness in him that does evil."[5]

In his sermon "*On Conscience*" Wesley strikes three additional notes that are important for us to hear. First is his insistence that while this faculty is universal it is not strictly speaking "natural," at least not in the sense of belonging to ordinary human endowments. It is a supernatural gift of God. "Not nature but the Son of God which enlighteneth every man that cometh into the world."[6] Second is his view of conscience in Christian perspective. Those without faith are, as we have seen, aware of the faculty of conscience, but the Christian discerns it as a means by which the Spirit of God reveals "the real quality of our thoughts, words, and actions," enabling us to know the extent to which these are in conformity with the will of God. Third is his concern to keep the conscience sensitive to the Word of God—not that conscience communicates a private word that bypasses the means of grace but that it enables us to feel the force, to get the point of the written Word. By the assistance of the grace of God, conscience brings us under the rule which is to direct us in every particular, "none other than the written Word of God."[7] That conscience does not stand alone to provide privileged and untestable knowledge of God's will is clear even in a passage in which Wesley calls most vigorously for obedience to conscience:

> If you desire to have your conscience always quick to discern, and faithful to accuse or excuse you, be sure to obey it at all events; continually listen to its admonitions and steadily follow them. Whatever it forbids, *if the prohibition be according to the Word of God*, do; however grievous to flesh and blood. Whatever it forbids, *if the prohibition be grounded on the word of God*, see that you do it not; however pleasing it may be to flesh and blood.[8]

My own limited reading of classical and contemporary Catholic writing on conscience suggested that there were significant points of agreement here, and subsequent discussion provided confirmation.[9] Thus Wesley had in fact provided Catholics and Methodists with considerable common ground in an area we had explored separately often enough but hardly ever together. But what of the claim that Wesley's theology has ecumenical significance on a much broader front?

This possibility begins to emerge as parallels between Thomas Aquinas and Wesley are recognized. Although Thomas did not hold, as Wesley did, that conscience was a separate faculty, contending instead that it is a reasoning act in which knowledge is applied to conduct, the *form* that such application takes finds an echo in Wesley, namely, to testify as to what has been done, to incite us toward the good and to accuse us when we have done wrong.[10] And both men were convinced that this capacity is directly the gift of God. For Thomas, "The light of natural reason whereby we distinguish good and evil, which is the function of natural law, is nothing else but the impress upon us of the divine light itself."[11] Commenting on that, a contemporary Catholic theologian concludes that "conscience is simply the extension or application of this natural law to a particular act."[12]

Surely here we have reached an impasse far more fundamental than the superficial "Protestants follow conscience, Catholics the authority of the church." Would not Wesley stand with the Reformers and dismiss natural law as the basis for moral obligation? For he, no less than they, denied that the rational creature participates in the eternal law, sharing in a finite way God's judgment of good and evil. That, they declared, is impossible, because although humans were created in the image of God this was destroyed, or so distorted in the fall that no natural capacity now remains to discern the will of God in and for his creation. And even those Methodists for whom Wesley's theology has remained an antiquarian, if not a closed, book may have reached the same conclusion, influenced by the Barthian denial of any analogy of being between Creator and creature. A theology based on God's unprecedented initiative in Jesus Christ, which remains a scandal to reason and can be apprehended only in faith, demands that Christian ethics too must have its grounding in the same revelation. God's self-disclosure in Jesus Christ, not the natural law, must therefore be the starting point for moral theology.

This fundamental disagreement about natural law and revelation has long resisted attempts to overcome it, yet despite its persistence as a barrier and its neo-orthodox reinforcement in our own time, I believe Wesley's theology offers a way through. Although as far as I know this has not been considered in ecumenical discussion,[13] it could have far-reaching implications, and this becomes more apparent as we recognize that Wesley faced the issue from ground he fully shared with the Reformers—a thorough-going conviction about the extent and effects of original sin.[14] According to Wesley, original sin is the state of rebellion of all creatures against the Creator, a state into which all have fallen, leading to pride and idolatry:

> Man was created looking directly to God, as his last end; but having fallen into sin, he fell off from God, and turned into himself. Now, this infers a total apostasy and universal corruption in man; for where the last end is changed, there can be no real goodness. And this is the case of all men in their natural state: they seek not God, but themselves. . . . Here is a three-fold cord not easily broken—a blind mind, a perverse will, distorted affections.[15]

So far, then, Wesley stands squarely in the tradition of Luther and Calvin, and of Augustine before them all. His distinctive contribution, however, stemmed from his practice of never speaking of human depravity brought about by evil without at the same time affirming the grace of God that overcomes evil and restores wholeness. It was Wesley's understanding of this prevenient grace that enabled him to refute the logic of predestination that argued that since no one is free to respond in faith, and not all are saved, it follows that God saves whom he will by selectively apportioning saving grace. True, said Wesley, in the state of nature none of us is free to opt for faith, *but none of us is now in a mere state of nature.* Because of God's act in Jesus Christ grace is given that restores lost freedom, and that prevenient grace gives the capacity to accept or reject the redeeming grace that leads us along the path of salvation. Why then are not all saved? Not because of any decree of God that they should die, but because they will not be saved.[16]

Beginning then from a stance that belongs to the Reformation, Wesley advocated a view of prevenient grace that is by no means alien to Catholic theology. It finds recent and influential expression in Karl Rahner's writing where the phrase "supernatural existential" is used to refer to this universal offer of grace to all people. "Existential" because it is a real possibility given to the existence of everyone, "supernatural" because, although never lacking in the existential situation, it does not belong as natural but comes as God's gift:

> Even prior to justification by sanctifying grace, whether this is conferred sacramentally or outside the sacraments, man already stands under the universal, infralapsarian salvific will of God which comprises within its scope original sin and personal sin. Man is redeemed, and is permanently the object of God's saving care and offer of grace. . . . This situation, "objective justification" in contradistinction to its subjective application by sanctification, is all-inclusive and inescapably prior to man's free action. . . . As an objective consequence of God's universal salvific will, it of course supervenes through grace upon man's essence as "nature," but in the real order is never lacking to it. . . . That man is really affected by the permanent offer of grace is not something which happens only now and again. It is a permanent and inescapable human situation. This state of affairs can be briefly labelled "supernatural existential," to prevent its being overlooked. It means that man as he really exists is always and ineluctably more than mere "nature" in the theological sense.[17]

It has been said often enough that Wesley combines a Protestant view of sin with a Catholic view of grace, and that this view of grace enables those who hold it to stand in the tradition of the Reformers without being obliged to endorse their predestinarian view of salvation.[18] What has not been seen so clearly is that this same recognition—that no one is now in a mere state of nature—also overcomes the major Protestant objection to natural law theory, which, as we have seen, is that the fall has so hardened our hearts and blinded our eyes that we cannot know when we have contravened the orderly purpose the Creator has built into the creation. Not so, says Wesley:

> Allowing that all the souls of men are dead in sin *by nature* this excuses none, seeing that there is no man, unless he has quenched the Spirit, that is wholly void of the grace of God. No man is entirely destitute of what is vulgarly called *natural conscience.* But this is not natural: it is more properly termed, *preventing grace.* . . . Every one, unless he be one of the small number whose conscience is seared with a hot iron, feels more or less uneasy when he acts contrary to the light of his own conscience.[19]

This is not to say that Wesley, by substituting conscience for natural reason, was maintaining that the natural law of God is fully accessible to everyone. That view of the natural, law which affirms such a congruence between human beings and God's purpose embodied in the natural world that full knowledge of this will is open to all, Wesley does not support. To know what is the will of God rather than just sensing unease when we have contravened it comes only when, in faith, we accept the saving grace of God.

Then the image is restored. Our reason is healed and our moral nature renewed. Through the intercession of his Son, God gives us the Holy Spirit "to renew us both 'in knowledge,' in his natural image . . . and also in his moral image, viz. 'righteousness and true holiness.' "[20]

For my part I agree that no one is so in tune with the ordered creation that the natural law is fully accessible to reason unaided by faith. I'm not sure that it is fully accessible even then, but the purpose of God for his creation does come into sharper focus from the standpoint of the incarnation. Nevertheless, that there is such a purpose built into the ordered creation and that our lives are diminished or enhanced as we contravene or fulfill that purpose I firmly believe, and see that as the soundest basis for Christian ethics. That aspect of natural law at least seems to me to be essential unless we are to live under an arbitrary God whose moral demands are unrelated to the fulfillment of human nature within the context of a creation that is good, that is, as God intended, having its own being and integrity. My conclusions here depend upon my understanding of what it is to believe, from the standpoint of Christian faith, in God as creator, and I have been struck with the parallel conclusions of contemporary Catholic author Gerard Hughes, and by what I hear as clear echoes of Wesley:

> If we can see no connection between our human fulfilment and the obligation under which God places us, then we would have no ground for believing that our God was a moral God at all. . . . Even if one were to accept that the effect of original sin was totally to blind our minds to our true nature and destiny we would have to remember that precisely because Christ dies for all men we are *not* left simply with our unaided sinful minds when we consider morality. The grace of Christ is offered to us. . . . Revelation commends itself to us partly because it does harmonize with our moral aspirations present antecendently. I conclude, then, that the Christian theologian must not hold that man has the ability to understand morality independently of God's grace, but of his coming to believe in Christ on the basis of God's revelation.[21]

It therefore seems to me that natural law theory need constitute no great divide between Catholics and Protestants if, as Wesley has suggested and contemporary Catholics reiterate, we recognize on the one hand that natural law morality is not "ungraced" at all but is a morality in which God's grace is already involved, and on the other, that the "ethics of revelation" do not negate but are consistent with the created order within which God brings our human nature to its fulfillment.

If there is any force in that conclusion at all then it does demonstrate that there are resources in Wesley's theology which can contribute significantly to ecumenical debate and, through that, to overcoming long-standing barriers to common worship, witness, and service in the world. If the next century of Methodism in the United States were therefore to begin with a commitment to revitalized study of Wesley's theology, this would be more than a Methodist-centered enterprise, for studied in ecumenical context Wesley emerges as more than the reluctant founder of a denomination. He gives theological impetus and shape to the hopeful vision of the church of God on earth no longer divided against itself, anticipating the fulfillment of the Creator's purpose for the whole of his creation.

NOTES

1. Would *Life* Magazine's comment, "Methodism is long on organization and short on theology," have been so long-remembered without Colin William's citing of it in the introduction to his still influential *John Wesley's Theology Today*? (Nashville: Abingdon Press, 1959).
2. As a minister in the Methodist Church of Australasia, which, together with the Congregational and Presbyterian churches in that country, became the Uniting Church in Australia in 1977. The United Faculty of Theology in Melbourne in which I now teach comprises the theological colleges of the Uniting Church, the Anglican Church, and the Jesuits.
3. "The Holy Spirit, Christian Experience and Authority." Report of the Joint Commission between the Roman Catholic Church and the World Methodist Council, Nov. 1979, 25.
4. John Wesley, "On Conscience," *Works* (London: John Mason, 1856), vol. 7, p. 178.
5. Ibid.
6. Ibid., p. 179.
7. Ibid., p. 181.
8. Ibid., (italics mine).
9. With Jesuit colleagues in Melbourne, and at WMC/RC commission meeting in Rome. A more detailed comparison of Wesley with the Fathers is given in my article "Conscience and Authority" (in the Toombs Festschrift, by University Press of America).
10. Eric D'Arcy, *Conscience and its Right to Freedom* (London: Sheed & Ward, 1961), p. 48.
11. *Summa Theologia*, I.I, q.91, a.2. Cited by J. V. Dolan, *Conscience: Its Freedom and Limitations*, ed. W.C. Bier (N.Y.: Fordham Press, 1971), p. 1.
12. Dolan, *Conscience*.
13. Excerpt in the WMC/RC commission in response to a paper I read on the subject.
14. This, he insisted, was one of the essential doctrines. "A denial of original sin contradicts the main design of the Gospel, which is to humble vain man and to ascribe to God's free grace, not to man's free will, the whole of his salvation." Wesley, *Works*, vol. 9, p. 409.
15. Ibid., pp. 435-36.
16. Ibid., vol. 7, p. 364.
17. Karl Rahner, in *Encyclopedia of Theology*, ed. Karl Rahner (London: Burns & Oates, 1975), pp. 494-95.
18. Note Colin Williams' thorough discussion in *John Wesley's Theology Today*.
19. Wesley, *Works*, vol. 6, p. 485.
20. Ibid., p. 209.
21. G. J. Hughes, *Authority in Morals* (London: Heythrop, 1978) pp. 5,6.

2. EUCHARIST, ECUMENISM, METHODISM

J. Robert Nelson

I. Remembrance: A Re-Presentation of Methodist Origins

We who are pleased to be known as Methodists, until the time of a more inclusive church unity arrives, are in deep debt to various writers of history and theology who have taught us who we are. Explorations of the thought of John and Charles Wesley and sympathetic recital of events which constitute the first hundred and fifty years of American Methodism have been combined with the discoveries and rediscoveries of the authentic nature of the church of Jesus Christ as these have taken place in the arena of modern ecumenical theologizing. As with our history and our general theological heritage, our liturgical and sacramental doctrines and styles have come under critical study and have been compared to similar investigations in other churches. For these studies we are indebted especially to J.E. Rattenbury,[1] Albert C. Outler,[2] John C. Bowmer,[3] and Ole E. Borgen,[4] among others. The books of Rattenbury and Bowmer were published more than thirty years ago; but only recently have they exercised a significant influence upon the pastors and theologians of Methodist churches. The revived appreciation of the Wesley brothers as sacramental theologians is rapidly reshaping the theology and practice of worship in Methodist churches.

Those books, like St. Paul, were "born out of time": that is, not too late but too early. What their time lacked was the intensity of liturgical concern which has lately become manifest. That concern and desire for renewal have arisen and spread in Methodism, not because of merely historical and archaeological interest in eighteenth-century Methodism, but because of the extending and ripening of our ecumenical experience. Both within the sphere of Protestantism and in relations with Roman Catholics and Orthodox, we have been witnessing some astonishing developments in respect to liturgy and sacraments. It is no mere coincidence that the new flowering of liturgical practices in The United Methodist Church has been prompted largely by the writings of our own experts who have become fully involved in the ecumenical liturgical movement. Notable for their effectual efforts are James F. White, Hoyt L. Hickman, Don E. Saliers, Richard L. Eslinger. Where most other persons have failed to stimulate a theological renewal in The United Methodist Church, these men have succeeded: namely, in the publishing and disseminating of denominational materials which penetrate not only the protective membrane of local churches but also those of ecclesiastical agencies.

As never before in this century, soon to end, the person of John Wesley has again become an authoritative criterion for the faith and practice of many Methodists. Of course, in diverse ways we have done violence to Wesley, using his words selectively to validate our own various positions. For example, we have turned him into a theological relativist by constantly quoting, "Is thine heart right as my heart is right with thy heart?" The assumption here is that the cardiac congeniality of two persons is sufficient to overcome—or else to conceal—any differences of faith, doctrine, and theology. Two hearts, strangely warmed, equal one warm handshake, and—*voila!*—the problem of church divisions is resolved.

In similar ways Wesley has been cast into differing roles by various directors of the theological stage. Was he actually a Calvinist with just a "hair's breadth" difference? Read George Croft Cell.[5] Was he an anti-Calvinist? Read William R. Cannon.[6] Was he a high church Anglican? Read Bowmer.[7] Was he a broad church Anglican? Read Albert Outler.[8] Did Wesley prefigure the theology of Karl Barth? Read Colin Williams[9] and John Deschner.[10] Was he primarily a soul-winning evangelist to lost sinners, declaring, "Church or no church, there are souls to be saved"? Read some of the evangelism literature. Wesley claimed to be *homo unius libri*, "a man of one book." But just as he read and published many books, so he was a man of several faces, who in his eighty-eight years experienced some changes of conviction and emphasis.

Some changes meant that he left behind a contrary view. So far as justification and salvation are concerned, the Wesley who sailed to the colony of Georgia was not the same as at Aldersgate on May 24, 1738. With regard to his understanding of bishops in apostolic succession, he changed his mind upon reading the books of two young, rather radical Anglicans, Edward Stillingfleet[11] and Lord Peter King.[12] On the basis for these studies, he justified years later his acts of ordination as a presbyter who is as much a bishop as any man! It is possible, however, to experience significant changes of mind without forfeiting other convictions. Contrary to one popular and distorted notion, John Wesley did not begin his ministry as an Anglo-Catholic, non-juror ritualist and then, following the Aldersgate experience, emerge as just an itinerant revivalist. *That* he was a high churchman at Oxford and in Georgia none could dispute. *That* he gave up his church concept of Anglicanism, with its focus upon the centrality of the Holy Communion, is simply not supported by historical evidence. Bowmer adduces many data to refute such an unbalanced picture of John and, *fortiter*, of Charles. Ole Borgen is often critical of Bowmer's penchant for stressing the Wesley brothers' pure Anglicanism; but he agrees completely with Bowmer on *this* point, as he writes: "The distinction between evangelicalism and 'sacramentalism' must never be applied to Wesley. For him these two aspects were one; and later Methodism has paid dearly for tearing apart what God has united."[13]

A favorite and quite dependable proof of Wesley's lifelong consistency with respect to the Lord's Supper is his oft-cited sermon, "The Duty of Constant Communion." The words of this title are definitive and categorical: "duty" and "constant." Not the "the rich personal values" or the "spiritual blessings" of the Eucharist, but "duty!" Not even a rather frequent reception, but "constant!" What is to be stressed here is not the persuasive argument as such, but the dates of the publication of this sermon. It was one of the first pieces he published in 1733 for the benefit mainly of his Oxford students. Just fifty-five years later, John republished the sermon, 1788, with the important comment: "I thank God, I have not yet seen cause to alter my sentiments in any point which is therein delivered."[14]

And as for his abiding by his own admonition, his lifetime average of communicating could be judged by any standard short of the Catholic priest's daily Mass to be called virtually "constant."

Wesley's regularity as either celebrant or recipient at the altar was not considered solely for his personal edification as a Christian. The frequent Communions which he urged upon all Methodists had a distinctly missionary purpose. When he spoke the familiar invitation, "Ye who do truly and earnestly repent you of your sins and are in love and charity with your neighbor, and intend to lead a new life . . . draw near with faith, and take this holy Sacrament to your comfort," Wesley meant this not only for persons secure in their faith, but also for uncertain, unconverted seekers after salvation. A remarkable example of how he and Charles combined evangelistic with sacramental purposes is their Hymn No. 39:

> (1) Sinner with awe draw near,
>   And find thy Saviour here,
> In His ordinances still,
>   Touch His sacramental clothes;
> Present in His power to heal,
>   Virtue from His body flows.
>   Touch His sacramental clothes;
>
> (3) Pardon, and power and peace,
>   And perfect righteousness
> From that sacred Fountain springs;
>   Wash'd in His all-cleansing blood
> Rise, ye worms, to priests and kings,
>   Rise in Christ, and reign with God.[15]

The address is what any old-time gospel preacher would use: "Sinner, with awe draw near." Near to what? To the proclaimed Word, to the Bible. To Jesus. To God in his mercy and forgiveness. As thousands of Christians and "almost Christians" have drawn near in response to preaching and invitation, they have had the experience of knowing deep within the heart that they want to be followers of Jesus Christ. So they take the step; make the good confession; are baptized (if not already so) and become members—or now *converted* members—of a denominational church. This is the standard pattern of evangelistic mission. And eventually, in most but not all churches, such persons come to the Table of the Lord's Supper to have their new-found faith confirmed and nourished. But the Wesleys' invitation in this hymn is an immediate one: "Touch His sacramental clothes!"

The Sacrament is not Jesus Christ himself but his garment, which to touch is to receive the Lord's "virtue" or power of healing. As Harald Lindstrom has demonstrated, Wesley often called salvation "healing." [16] This New Testament idea is not entirely unique. In the *Acts of the Apostles* 19:11, handkerchiefs blessed by the apostle Paul had therapeutic powers—a report which has been exploited by faith-healers today. In India, this is called *darshan*, when only the shadow of a holy person falling upon you brings blessing and healing. So clearly it is as "means of grace" that this hymn refers to the "sacramental clothes."

The third stanza speaks of the familiar fountain of Jesus' blood, the offering of atonement and the sealing of the covenant in Hebrew biblical terms. While other evangelistic invitations have summoned sinners to be "washed in the blood" in a forensic or rhetorical way, *here* it is obviously the eucharistic blood which is meant. "He who eats my flesh and drinks my blood has eternal life," said Jesus to the doubting and offended Capernaiticans (*John* 6:54). "Who are these clothed in white robes? They have washed their robes, and made them white, in the blood of the Lamb" (*Rev.* 7:14). Thus the Wesleys made concrete what the ex-slave-trading Methodist, John Newton, extolled more nebulously as "amazing grace." Here they take from Newton's colleague, William Cowper of Olney, "the fountain fill'd with blood" and give it a eucharistic setting.

So the challenge is sung to Methodists then and now: "Rise, ye worms, to priests and kings!" For Wesley, as for Calvin, men and women abiding in their sins are "worms." "But I am a worm, and no man," moaned the psalmist (*Ps.* 22:6). Human depravity for both Calvin and Wesley is not relative, but total. In a rhetorical triumph of inversion, Wesley preached of the wicked people before the deluge and before his pulpit, "They never deviated into good."[17] But so great is the redemptive power of God in Jesus Christ that even these vermiform sinners can be raised to "priests and kings—a royal priesthood." Like Jesus Christ himself, and like the paradigmatic figure of Melchizedec, King of Salem, the general priesthood awaits the sinful worms of fallen humanity who are transformed into justified believers, as by grace they move on to sanctification and perfect love.

Both Colin Williams and Ole Borgen have emphasized the thesis that Wesley's theology is defined by the *ordo salutis*, the order or economy of salvation. More than other writers, they perceive the central place of the Holy Communion in the saving work of God for each person. The sacrament is not incidental, tangential, or merely ancillary to salvation. It is the indispensable means by which Christ is known as Savior, that is, known in the breaking of bread.

Unless we have read of the lamentable state of public worship in the Church of England of the eighteenth century, we cannot appreciate how extraordinary Wesley's strong-minded views must have seemed. It is easy, whenever we picture him as an Anglican priest, to have a benign and optimistic image of typical parish worship. We see the pious parishioners coming to the square-towered Norman church, with possibly a reduced version of the King's College choir singing Purcell, and the cultivated rector celebrating the Eucharist every Lord's Day and feast day, using the dressed altar and Cranmerian ritual to high effect, as communicants kneel on the cushions of needlepoint, for the making of which the Holy Spirit has given a special charisma to Anglican ladies. Nothing of the sort! A noted historian, the late Norman Sykes, found evidence of a much degraded sacramental practice in Wesley's century and church. The drab atmosphere of seventeenth-century Puritanism lingered on in chancel, choir, and nave. Celebrations were infrequent and communicants few. In the Archdiocese of York there were 836 churches: 72 had monthly celebrations, 363 had them quarterly, 193 varied between four and six times a year, and 208 celebrated less than four times annually.

What were the reasons for this dreadful condition of the Church of England? Bowmer offers several plausible causes: the lingering, suppressing mood of the Cromwell Protectorate; the fear of "popery" or charges of it; the lack of sufficient clergy; "the indolent clergy and the brutal populace" (see William Hogarth's pictures and Henry Fielding's novels of English life); the inroads into both established and Non-conformist churches of rationalism, deism, and Arianism (by which was meant Unitarianism).[18]

No wonder that Wesley's insistence upon both "constant Communion" and a highly sacramental theology, as well as the enthusiastic vigor of Methodist preaching, caused angry resistance from the very churchmen whom they could most help.

Wesley could link Eucharist and evangelism together because of a firm conviction. It was his famous assertion that the Lord's Supper is a "converting ordinance." Not least of the reasons for his belief was the personal example of his mother, Susanna. She marked her true conversion as an experience at the communion rail. So did others whom John knew or knew about. He could not refute the evidence. He knew well enough how churches from time to time in history had imposed strict discipline upon communicants. And, rather paradoxically, he supported the practice in Methodist societies of issuing "tokens" or "notes" as tickets of admission to the sacrament. Nevertheless, astute Bible reader that he was, Wesley observed that the apostles had neither been baptized nor received the Spirit when they took part in the Supper with Jesus.

Despite his strictness, on the one hand, Wesley gladly opened the way to the communion rail for those who sincerely sought assurance of their salvation in Christ. Here could be appropriated the saving grace in its fullness: prevenient (preventing), justifying, and sanctifying grace—all together.[19]

Did Wesley's openness on the matter of admitting any sincere person mean that he rejected the traditional doctrine and practice of requiring that communicants had to have been baptized? Many American Methodists assume that such was Wesley's intention; and they appeal to this reading of the founder's mind as the warrant today for admitting "whosoever will come." If "God is no respecter of persons, and if the Eucharist is a possible, or probable, means of conversion, why not encourage everyone who might "love the Lord" to come? This practice implies either a total trust in the grace of God beyond all defining doctrines of the church; or else it implies a virtual indifference to Baptism.

But *were* those British communicants unbaptized? Laurence H. Stookey provides a most plausible explanation of Wesley's seeming indifference to Baptism. It was simply his assumption that *all* persons in Great Britain were baptized as a matter of custom. The comprehensiveness of the established church left very few babies unbaptized.[20] It is, to say the least, a very unsubstantial claim that Wesley's openness and encouragement for people to come to the "converting ordinance" set a legitimate pattern for casual invitations today. Geoffrey Wainwright and James F. White are clearly of this mind, too.[21]

Just as Wesley's alternating policies of strict discipline toward the ungodly and leniency toward the sincere may seem to have been contradictory, so there was a lack of outward consistency between his attitude toward ritual and his eucharistic theology. Anglo-Catholics since Edward B. Pusey, John Keble, and John Henry Newman of the early nineteenth century have been happy to claim the Wesley brothers as their own in terms of sacramental theology. With respect to high church ritual, or ritualism, however, John could not have been comfortable with their Roman-like preoccupation with the details of manual and bodily motions, liturgical colors, vestments, and incense. With regard to diverse forms of worship he was tolerant of wide scope. He even seems to have been more sympathetic toward Quaker simplicity than Catholic ritualism, for which he expressed distaste.[22] Perhaps it was because he was so concerned with the attraction and conversion of ordinary people to Christ's gospel that he knew which style of the "converting ordinance" would draw them. Such, at least, is a guess.

There is no need to guess about his sacramental theology, however. He and Charles made it clear where they stood, how firmly they stood, and what they stood for. They stood with the seventeenth-century non-juring Anglicans: that small group of clergy and laity who remained faithful to King James II, for they considered the monarch's Roman Catholicism to be more acceptable than the alternative favored by the Dutch-born Calvinist King of England, William. One of the non-jurors whose writing influenced the young Wesley was Robert Nelson, an aristocratic layman, whose books on liturgical piety were subsequently read by six generations of Anglicans. Wesley took with him to Georgia a copy of *The Great Duty of Frequenting the Christian Sacrifice*.

Another molder of Wesley's mind was the sometime dean of Lincoln Cathedral, Daniel Brevint. Although not considered important enough today to be mentioned in *The Oxford Book of Church History*, Brevint's significance for Methodists has been well demonstrated. Rattenbury, following both the great scholars L. Tyerman and J. S. Simon, writes of Brevint's *Tract on the Christian Sacrament and Sacrifice* (Oxford, 1679): This "must be accepted as the sacramental doctrine of the Wesley's."[23] When John and Charles published the one hundred sixty-six *Hymns on the Lord's Supper*, 1745, they republished Brevint's tract as the explanatory theological preface. Then the structure and headings of Brevint's essay, with a slight modification, were chosen as the framework of the Wesleys' collection. Thus:

1. The *Memorial* of the Sufferings and Death of Christ
2. The *sign* and *means* of grace (combining two of Brevint's)
3. The Sacrament as *Pledge* of Heaven
4. The Holy Eucharist as it implies a *Sacrifice*
5. The *Sacrifice* of our persons
6. After the Sacrament, our appropriation of benefits[24]

Note how the Wesleys used interchangeably the words "sacrament" and "ordinance"; also, "Lord's Supper," "Holy Communion," and "Holy Eucharist." In modern Protestantism, unnecessary distinctions have been placed on the meanings, and especially the connotations, of these words, provoking and perpetuating prejudices which only now are being dissolved.

One who has become informed about the contemporary ecumenical discussion of eucharistic theology, noting the remarkable converging toward consensus, cannot read about the Wesleys' understanding and faith without noting how up-to-date they seem. This observation has been one of the most unexpected and illuminating that we Methodists have been privileged to have. It means that, having been challenged and stimulated by ecumenical encounters, we have been driven back to our sources, and there have found exactly what our contemporaries are urging us to consider.

This foregoing recollection of the beliefs and teachings of the Wesleys is, therefore, a timely introduction to our present rediscovery of the genuinely catholic and evangelical dimensions of the Lord's Supper.

II. Is It Really the Sacrament of Unity?

Again and again we hear the rhetoric of Christian unity: One Lord, one loaf, one cup, one church. The Holy Communion is the "sacrament of unity!" In the nice phrase of Lionel S. Thornton, "the common life in the Body of Christ" is nourished and strengthened and integrated by sharing (koinonia) in the bread and wine. To employ a pietistic phrase, "the fellowship of kindred hearts is like to that above"—especially when gathered together to ask the Lord's blessing in the foretaste, antepast, or aperitif of the promised messianic feast. It is easy to fill in the blanks to express in exuberant prose and hymnody this unifying virtue of the one Eucharist.

And we can mean it. We really do! But the veracity of these expressions and sincerity of our intentions are called into question by some cruel facts. One is that even in relatively small congregations there seems to be minimal evidence that this sacrament, above all else, is the binding glue of koinonia. When membership of the whole denomination is considered, the evidence is even less. Where two denominations have entered a formal agreement on shared Communion, the appropriating of spiritual benefits is infrequent and usually limited to official leadership. This has been true, for example, of the mutual relation of the Episcopal Church and the Polish National Church in America and the Old Catholic Church in Europe. It is to be tested now by the new agreement between the Episcopalians and Lutherans.

Where two or more denominations have a de facto relationship of intercommunion, due to the absence of any doctrinal or canonical inhibitions, that fact hardly persuades them to embrace each other in eucharistic shalom. This describes the rather indifferent attitudes of Methodists to Presbyterians, Baptists, Disciples of Christ and, for that matter, Episcopalians (with whom there is no formal understanding).

Is, then, the very concept of the "sacrament of unity" as devoid of reality as the rhetoric? No! It is not the defect of divine grace which accounts for persistence in either mutual indifference or separation. It is lack of our wills to accept the divinely offered grace of unity. As heirs to Arminianism, we can argue that grace is not irresistible. But it is freely offered: a gift to be received, a power of love to be appropriated.

Methodists share with many other Christians a casual unconcern about the ruptures of communion, which are the outward and visible sign of an inward and long-tolerated disunity. They recognize no compelling interest in the theology of the sacrament and its significance for the body of Christ. Their indifference might be due to the unmitigated belief that their church and its sacramental life are so completely catholic, or whole, that communion with other churches is just unthinkable. Certainly this is the prevailing conviction of many Orthodox, Catholics, Episcopalians, and Lutherans. For them, there is no such thing as inter-communion because there can be either communion or none. But this is rarely the attitude of Methodists.

Far more prevalent is the unconcern about intercommunion for the plain reason that the Holy Communion itself is not important, much less central, in their own worship. It is scarcely mentioned when one describes the normative elements of the church's life. This is a condition which must not be forgotten when, in ecumenical conversations, we wax optimistic about our converging theologies.

So there is a coincidence of opposites: a meeting of extremes on the common position of indifference. "You cannot be in communion with us!" "But we don't mind, because the Lord's Supper is no big deal anyway!" This deep cleavage is described in the final report of the United Methodist–Roman Catholic conversation, 1982, as follows:

Infrequency of celebrating the eucharist—quarterly or even less among some United Methodists—indicates the idea that eucharist is an occasional act of worship which the church does; whereas frequency of celebration—as practiced by Roman Catholics—indicates that the eucharist constitutes the church, determining what the church is.[25]

Between such extremes are churches in which the Holy Communion has a regular, consistent, indispensable, and central place, but balanced by the vigorous preaching of the Word and emphasizing the mission of the whole body. It is here in the middle, fortunately, where some Methodist congregations are to be found today.

How are Methodists doing in the ecumenical parliament on sacraments and worship? In fact, very well! To be sure, Methodists are not quite abreast of some other churches in their commitment to dialogue, nor have achievements of theological agreement been so dramatic as those involving Episcopalians, Lutherans, and Roman Catholics. The intensity of common study and dialogue on the part of those communions is manifestly due to two factors. One is the primary importance of eucharistic liturgy in their regular life. The other is that these, unlike Methodists, have experienced painful polemics and ruptures in past centuries, which they are now the more eager to overcome through reconciliation.

Where are American Methodists actively involved in critical and constructive ecumenical exchange? In *five* places of major importance, apart from all the individual scholarship and participation in theological seminaries and societies.

1. The Consultation on Church Union. Chapter VI of *In Quest of a Church of Christ Uniting* (Rev. 1980) represents a final digest of the common consideration of sacramental worship as agreed by delegated representatives of ten (now nine) denominations.[26] Agreements on the Eucharist in various church union plans were studied in the preparation for this report.

2. Conversations with Roman Catholics, on world and national levels. The World Methodist Council and the Vatican's Secretariat for Promoting Christian Unity held common talks which eventuated in two notable reports, styled Denver (1971) and Dublin (1976). The American conversations, as noted, reported favorably in 1982. (There was almost no operational relation between these national and global ventures except for taking the former's provisional reports into consideration.)[27]

3. The World Council of Churches Commission on Faith and Order: its historic trio of common statements, *Baptism, Eucharist, and Ministry* (1982).[28] Several Methodists played key roles in the long history of this ecumenical achievement—over fifty years!—but the fact that their contributions in the reports are anonymous is indication of the genuinely ecumenical character of them. By the last day of 1984, the Methodist churches are expected to have made official responses.

4. United Methodist—Lutheran agreement on Baptism.[29] This good document is indirectly pertinent to eucharistic thinking,

being in theological congruence with the ecumenical convergence.

5. Local voluntary ecumenism, where the sometimes detached and academic deliberations of the theological commissions are transcended by practices in the parishes and communities. The COCU program called Interim Eucharist Fellowships has demonstrated how local churches of differing denominations and sociological nature can, if they will, find experiences of that unitive *koinonia*. Likewise in united parishes, in university and seminary chapels, and in institutional and military chapels. Here must be mentioned the immense influence of available literature, the fruit of international studies on common texts and English translations of rituals. The increasing use of common lectionaries is contributing immensely to Methodist worship, as also to the sense of the reality of Christian unity in worship.

In all these movements, ventures, and projects it has become clear that the ecumenical exchanges are authentically reciprocal. Contrary to some kinds of criticism, Methodists are not becoming more Anglican or more Roman, and thus ignoring the accumulated values of two centuries of Methodism. How the Roman Catholic Church has benefitted since Vatican II by communication with non-Catholics is a familiar story. Each church is both donor and recipient in this process. But the receiving requires well-considered response; and this has been provided by Methodists in a manner generally described as follows.

III. How Methodists Might Respond Theologically to the Ecumenical Convergence[30]

God, creation, grace, salvation

The Eucharist is the gift of God to his people. It is not a religious ritual invented and devised by people for their delectation. The God who gives such a "means of grace" is the one who created all things and called them "good." In the Eucharist, God reaffirms the reality and integrity of created things as instrumental values for his human creatures. His purpose is that people be saved *in* the world, not *from* the world; saved *for* fulfilled life, not *from* sin. The eternal Word or Son of God is thus truly incarnate, made flesh, assuming our fallen humanity within temporal history. God's immanent action upon human lives is the work of the Holy Spirit. What we are able to know of God's purpose for humanity, and for each person, is perceived in the biblical witness to Jesus Christ and illumined by the Holy Spirit. Despite aberration and distortion by many Methodists, we hold in the *Response* that the theology of Eucharist is based upon the revelation of God who is tri-une, sovereign, loving, and immanently active. His acts are pure grace: divine love and power directed actively toward us. God's grace mysteriously leads us as individuals: it is prevenient. His grace forgives us: it is justifying. His grace sustains and blesses us: it is sanctifying. His grace finds a particular and concrete means of communication in the Word, the words, the faith, the bread and the wine of the Holy Communion.

Objectivity: the Atonement (opus) *having been done* (operatum) *by God in Jesus Christ.*

A. "Sacrifice" is a concept which comprehends the wholeness of Jesus Christ. It is not limited to the cross. It includes his incarnation and birth as truly human, his obedience before the will of the Father, his ministry of teaching and healing, his sorrowful passion and humiliating death, as well as the wondrous miracle of rising from death. The hymn of *kenosis* in Philippians 2 raises difficult theological questions, but in so doing answers still more important questions about Jesus Christ. John and Charles Wesley, as we noted, tended to give inordinate emphasis to the passion and death of Jesus at the expense of his kenotic life and his resurrection. In the theology espoused by increasing numbers of United Methodists, the synoptic understanding of sacrifice is professed.

The objectivity of Jesus Christ is thus asserted in its fullness against any kind of Gnostic or Docetic thought, against any "merely human" Jesus, and even against any fixation upon one element of what is called rather abstractly the Christ-event.

B. The church is objectively given under two aspects: the communion (*koinonia*) of the Holy Spirit, and the body of Christ. The Eucharist is an act, an indispensable action, of the church. It is not a church-sponsored occasion for the edification of the Christian child, woman, or man who participates in it. Wesley identified his view with those of all churches of the Reformation by holding that the church is seen in a body of faithful people, a congregation, where the word is preached and the sacraments administered. The church is indeed more than this, but it is not less than this.

The strong Methodist testimony to the reality of the Holy Spirit goes well beyond a formal confession in the creed. The church is a *koinonia* of the Spirit as well as in the Spirit. The Spirit is the divine power which awakens faith in God, enables the gospel to be personally appropriated, and gathers people into community. So the people of faith have common sharing (*koinonia*) among themselves. But what they share is also the Spirit as such, the Spirit's present power and gifts (*charismata*).

This gathered community is not independent. In Wesley's diction, it is "connexional." But its connection is not limited to a denominational cluster, Methodist, Lutheran, or Catholic. If "the world is my parish" for John Wesley, the world-church (ecumenical and universal) is the wider connexion for Methodists. And this can be so only because there is one Lord, one body: one earthly, historical, visible body of Christ which contains many members and offers membership to all.

The body of Christ as Christian community in the world, the body of Jesus nailed to the cross, the Body broken and shared in the breaking of bread—clear distinctions cannot be made. For there is one Lord, one body.

This objectively given church is also known as a covenant people. The typology of a limited covenant between Yahweh and Abraham and Moses has been widened to include potentially all persons besides those of Israel. The ancient covenants with Israel are neither abrogated nor annulled by the New Covenant in the blood of Jesus. The new recapitulates, renews, and universalizes the old. This was done by the whole sacrifice of Jesus Christ, but announced at the Last Supper and consummated on the cross. Thus, each Eucharist is convenantal in the sense that it takes place within the divine-human covenant already effected by Christ. Each person as both individual and member of the body needs to renew and reaffirm the terms of that covenant. This is because persons are fallible, forgetful, and irresponsible. John Wesley adopted and commended the special covenant service of Holy Communion deliberately to hold before each person this obligation and opportunity.

C. The presence of Jesus Christ, insofar as we can conceptualize this, is objectively given. His presence is either "real" or it is not at all. But speculations and polemics have unhappily served to divide the belief in presence into two alternatives. Either Christ is "really" present on the altar, in the priest's hand, in-with-and-under the bread and wine, it is claimed; *or*, Christ is "truly" present in "the hearts and minds" of the gathered believers, say others. Wesley's Anglican sense of comprehension is shared by contemporary Methodists. They cannot affirm the Catholic doctrine of transubstantiation nor the Orthodox mystery of *metabole*. They are even hesitant about the old Lutheran idea of consubstantiation. To account for the change of substance, whether by Scholastic formula or by mystery, is not a compelling kind of theology. But neither is it enough, for many Methodists, to "spiritualize" and subjectivize and localize the presence of Christ with no reference to the sacramental action and elements.

If the whole Christ (*totus Christus*) is the risen Christ plus his church, and if the whole sacrifice is what we have described, then the whole presence of Christ should be expected in the whole eucharistic action: persons, words, actions, elements.

D. The Word and sacrament together are primary constituents of the church, according to formal Methodist teaching. They are given by God objectively, visibly, audibly, legibly, tangibly, even edibly. Further, as noted above, Wesley held them to be on parity and inseparable. Many, not all, Methodists agree with him today. Those who disagree are content to read and hear the Word, or to say that the Eucharist and Baptism are just the enacted Word. Those who agree with Wesley can "taste and see that the [Word] is good."

E. Implicit in the Eucharist is God's justification of sinful persons. For God in his mercy and grace to "make us right" in his sight by forgiveness is nothing of our own doing. Wesley was as stoutly positive in his affirmation of justification by grace and faith alone as Luther or Calvin had been. And this, too, is *opus operatum*, done by God in Christ. The liturgical over-run of Cranmer's Book of Common Prayer on abject confession and plea for forgiveness should have been corrected by Wesley with his own powerful doctrine of sanctification. In the eucharistic action he should have seen how Good Friday is transcended, not only by Easter, but by Pentecost. Had he felt free to amend the liturgy, he might have given expression to this. Conscientious and obedient Anglican that he was, he found no special warrant for amending the liturgy as he later reinterpreted the legitimacy of ordaining.

An Alternate Text, 1972 is the result of a disregard for such inhibition, and fortunately so. Confession and absolution are certainly there at the beginning; but then the text moves on briskly to thank God and extol his name for the justifying and saving work he has done in Christ. Atonement, reconciliation, renewal, self-giving, joy, and mission are declared in the prayers and responses. Having once swallowed this breach of canon law in prayer book revision, Wesley could have been in theological agreement with his descendants.

Subjectivity: the Atonement applied and appropriated

In one most important respect Methodists through the past two centuries have remained in accord with John Wesley: that is the personal inwardness of faith's objects and benefits. The triune God and the gospel of redemption are *pro me* and *pro nobis*. Two favorite words in Wesley's lexicon were "experimental" and "applied." By the former he meant "experiential," the realization in personal consciousness and affection of the love of God which by the Holy Spirit has been shed abroad in our hearts (Rom. 5:5). The same Spirit bears witness with our spirits that we are children of God (Rom. 8:16).

A. The Holy Spirit provides the enabling power for the objective gift and reality of the presence of Christ in the Eucharist to become the subjective experience of the believers who participate. Methodists may be faulted at times for a lack of doctrine concerning the objectivity of the sacrament; but they can never be in the attitude of spectators beholding an action at the altar which does not personally involve them. If it is not subjective, it is nothing to them. And this personal appropriation they attribute to the Spirit, who takes "the things of Christ" and makes them their own (John 16:15). Neither Wesley nor many Methodists have spoken of the *epiclesis* as an integral part of the liturgy. This has awaited the instruction from the side of Eastern Orthodoxy in the ecumenical exchange. But it seems evident that there has been an implicit, unexpressed *epiclesis* in Methodist usage all along. The Spirit is "called down" in the 1972 text, first, "on us gathered here out of love for you," and then "on these gifts."

B. Another currently employed Greek word, *anamnesis*, is no stranger to early Wesleyan or later Methodist vocabulary. To be sure, there have been, and are, many Methodists who have regarded "remembrance" as "recalling," in the sense of looking back in reverence to the time and person of Jesus. What is usually called Zwinglianism may not be entirely fair to Huldrych Zwingli himself; but insofar as it means "memorialism" it is aptly applied to many Methodists. Not so with Wesley. Not so with our present Methodist interpreters. J. Ernest Rattenbury some years ago was observing that Wesley's understanding of the prayer book words, "in remembrance of his death and passion," was exactly what Odo Casel meant by

Vergegenwärtigung and Gregory Dix by "re-presentation." The 1972 text rightly broadens the *anamnesis* to include "what your Son has done for us in his life and death, in his resurrection and ascension," or, as we have been indicating, the wholeness of Christ and his work. Borgen's approving expression of Wesley's approval of Dean Brevint finds approval today, as follows:

> The Lord's Supper does not only function as a memorial which *shows* Christ's death and suffering; in it, by the power of the Holy Spirit and through the enabling means of faith, time and space are transcended. Christ does not only invite men *to* his sacrifice; he actually offers to make this sacrifice theirs; as he offers himself to God, so he offers himself to man.[31]

What has not yet been sufficiently explored is the meaning of *anamnesis* for hope: in fact, remembering the future. If time and space are transcended, then the eschatological *now* becomes an experienced reality for us in the present eucharistic moment. The God who in Jesus Christ "was, and is and is to come" (Rev. 1:8) makes the Kingdom present now. The object of hope can be seen only dimly and darkly in the mirror of faith, but somehow the Eucharist reinforces our confidence in God's future. Another one of Wesley's favorite phrases of the New Testament applies here: "the substance of things hoped for, the evidence of things not seen" (Heb. 11:1). That is faith in the inward meaning.

C. Sacrifice as offering has effect in two directions, so to speak, between the risen Christ and ourselves. If "every good and perfect gift" comes from God (James 1:17) to us as faithful though unworthy recipients, our response in making an offering can only be, "We give thee but thine own." Thanks are given; *eucharistia* is thus essentially an offering in response to the far greater gift of salvation and new life and hope in Christ. Despite the rich phrases in the Book of Common Prayer expressing our offering of souls and bodies as well as our "sacrifice of praise and thanksgiving," Methodist practice has detracted from the power of these thoughts by its routine triviality. A few coins tossed into a passing plate, morsels of chopped Sunbeam batter-whipped bread, and a tray of tiny glasses of Welch's juice (called shot glasses by some irreverent Lutherans) hardly symbolize the full discipleship which we offer to God in response to his "inexpressible gift" of Jesus Christ. The relevant words of the 1972 text are less fulsome than those of 1964 or earlier; but the rubric directing the procession of the money offering and the communion elements (gifts) connotes a theological understanding superior to what was formerly implicit. At the risk of seeming to adopt current jargon, it may be asserted that the whole person is what we have to offer, not as debt but as love.

D. The applying of "the benefits" of Christ means salvation, according to Wesley. The full appropriation means sanctification. Wesley dared to go beyond the Reformers and speak positively of the possibility of sanctification, exceeding even the teaching of the Council of Trent on the matter. So greatly did he believe and trust both the New Testament and the Holy Spirit. He held up the primitive Christian community as the model of what Wesleyan Christians of his own time could hope for:

> They were "sanctified throughout" . . . they "loved the Lord their God with all their heart, and mind, and soul and strength"; . . . they continually "presented" their souls and bodies "a living sacrifice, holy, acceptable to God"; in consequence of which, "they rejoiced evermore, prayed without ceasing, and in everything gave thanks." And this, and no other, is what we believe to be true, scriptural sanctification."[32]

If Calvin could be a pessimist without despair, could Wesley and his train be optimists without illusions?

The Eucharist as sacramental rite was thought by St. Ignatius to be "the medicine of immortality.' Such a pharmacological notion is not seriously advanced by many Methodists today. But can all that we have said Eucharist implies and conveys be regarded as a means of sanctification? The same people who gave the Methodists *epiclesis* have offered *theosis*, which defies adequate or exact English translation. It has been partly expressed, as we saw above, in the ritual use of being "partakers of the divine nature." And the dangerous ambiguity of this concept was indicated: namely, the illusion of a monistic identification with God, or even a becoming divine. However, recent ecumenical exchanges have shown that the *theosis* of St. John of Damascus is not unlike the sanctification of John of Epworth. To be "made perfect in love" is, after all, the farther stage on the Christian way.

NOTES

1. J. E. Rattenbury, *The Eucharistic Hymns of John and Charles Wesley* (London: Epworth Press, 1948).
2. Albert C. Outler, *John Wesley* (New York: Oxford University Press, 1964).
3. John C. Bowmer, *The Sacrament of the Lord's Supper in Early Methodism* (London: Dacre Press, 1951).
4. Ole E. Borgen, *John Wesley on the Sacraments* (Nashville: Abingdon Press, 1972).

5. George Croft Cell, *The Rediscovery of John Wesley* (New York: Holt Rinehart, 1935).
6. William R. Cannon, *The Theology of John Wesley* (New York: Abingdon Press, 1946).
7. Bowmer, *The Sacrament*.
8. Outler, *Wesley*.
9. Colin W. Williams, *John Wesley's Theology Today* (New York: Abingdon Press, 1960).
10. John Deschner, *Wesley's Christology* (Dallas: Southern Methodist University Press, 1960).
11. Edward Stillingfleet, *Irenicum. A Weapon-Salve for the Churches Wounds* (London, 1661). Erroneously called *Irenikon* by Borgen.
12. Lord Peter King, *An Enquiry into the Constitution, Discipline, Unity and Worship of the Primitive Church* (London, 1691)
13. Borgen, *On the Sacraments*, p. 282.
14. John Wesley, *Works*, vol. 7, p. 147.
15. Rattenbury, *Eucharistic Hymns*, p. 207.
16. Harald Lindstrom, *Wesley on Sanctification* (London: Epworth Press, 1946), p. 41.
17. Wesley, *Works*, vol. 6, p. 57.
18. Bowmer, *The Sacrament*, pp. 3-5.
19. John Wesley, *Journal*, June 28, 1740, vol. 3, p. 361. Cf. *Works*, vol. 5, p. 187.
20. Laurence H. Stookey, *Baptism, Christ's Act in the Church* (Nashville: Abingdon Press, 1982).
21. Geoffrey Wainwright, *Eucharist and Eschatology* (London: Epworth Press, 1971), p. 131; James F. White, *Sacraments as God's Self Giving* (Nashville: Abingdon Press, 1983), p. 129.
22. Wesley, *Works*, vol. 5, p. 497.
23. Rattenbury, *Eucharistic Hymns*, p. 15.
24. Ibid., p. 17.
25. *Origins* 11:4 (March 25, 1982), p. 656.
26. *In Quest of a Church of Christ Uniting* (Princeton: Consultation on Church Union, rev., 1980), Ch. VI. In June 1983, the two Presbyterian churches in COCU became one.
27. "Report of the Joint Commission between the Roman Catholic Church and the World Methodist Council, 1967–1970," *Information Service* [The Secretariat for Promoting Christian Unity, Vatican City, No. 21 (May 1973/III)], pp. 22-24; "Growth in Understanding," Report of the Joint Commission (London: The Methodist Ecumenical Committee, 19 Thayer St., 1976).
28. World Council of Churches, Commission on Faith and Order, *Baptism, Eucharist, and Ministry* (Geneva: WCC, 1982). A United Methodist Response to the provisional draft was published by the General Commission on Christian Unity, 1977.
29. For the United Methodist-Lutheran agreement on Baptism, see *Quarterly Review*, vol. 1, no. 1 (1981) with text and comment.
30. The following section is adapted from my article, "What Methodists Think of Eucharistic Theology," *Worship* (Sept. 1978): 409-23. See also my article, "Methodist Eucharistic Usage," *Journal of Ecumenical Studies*, 13 (1976): 88-93.
31. Borgen, *On the Sacraments*, p. 183.
32. Wesley, *Works*, vol. 6, p. 526.

3. BAPTISM—THE ECUMENICAL SACRAMENT AND THE WESLEYAN TRADITION

James C. Logan

Introduction

Faith and Order's publication of *Baptism, Eucharist and Ministry* (*BEM*)[1] comes at an opportune time as American Methodism observes its bicentennial. The following paper is an attempt to initiate dialogue with both the Wesleyan tradition and the *BEM* statement regarding Baptism. Historical and theological background have been reduced for sake of brevity in order to focus upon the critical issues for discussion. In cases of summary, additional background is referenced in the notes at the end of the paper.

Since the Reformation, Baptism has increasingly become the ecumenical sacrament with mutual recognition on the rise among the various Christian churches and traditions. Obviously, this is not without significance for ecclesiology in general and has, I believe, a direct bearing upon the Ecumenical status of Eucharist. These issues will be discussed in the closing section.

The current liturgical revival, with the various Methodist traditions participating fully, and sometimes at the forefront, has centered more on the eucharistic theology and practice than on Baptism. Various reasons account for this. One reason certainly no less important than others is that Eucharist is our ecumenical problematic—the scandal of separated tables of the Lord. Baptism has not, however, been ignored. As evidence simply examine the ecumenical documents such as "A Lutheran–United Methodist Statement on Baptism," "The Report of the Consultation with Baptists" (sent to the Faith and Order Commission of the World Council of Churches, March 28–April 1, 1979), and Thornwald Lorenzen, "Baptists and Ecumenicity with Special Reference to Baptism," *Review and Expositor*, (78:42). Certainly the liturgical literature grows annually.

The purpose of this paper is to raise in the light of the recent Faith and Order statement, *Baptism, Eucharist, and Ministry*, some of the dilemmas and challenges confronting Methodism (particularly United Methodism) as it continues to participate in the ongoing ecumenical dialogue regarding Baptism. For Methodists in general the issue of Baptism is a confused and confusing one. From the British Methodist scene, J. E. Rattenbury in 1928 remarked: "The Methodist beliefs about baptism have always been varied. They certainly are today." He illustrates this: "I once heard baptism discussed at a gathering of eight or nine Wesleyan ministers, and there were eight or nine different doctrines pronounced at that meeting!"[2] Yet Methodists have not been alone. As early as 1957, D. M. Baillie wrote: "There is no doubt that from very diverse quarters, from high Anglicanism to continental Protestantism, there has in recent years been a new consciousness of the problem surrounding this sacrament [of baptism]."[3]

As American Methodists our nineteenth-century history has not left us with an unambiguous tradition regarding the theology and practice of Baptism. Shaped as the various Methodist bodies were by the revivalism of the nineteenth century, revivals which in many instances proclaimed the gospel to unbaptized persons unlike Wesley's day, a form of "believer's baptism" became a fairly normal occurrence among the people called Methodists and related churches. If the sketchy statistical records indicate anything to us, they show that it was not until the twentieth century that infant Baptism became the more normative practice among Methodists, United Brethren in Christ, and the Evangelical Church.

Russell E. Richey in an article published in *Quarterly Review*[4] has mapped out what he calls the "ecclesial sensibilities" and "a sense of the catholicity of the church" manifested in two treatises authored by Nathan Bangs and Abel Stevens[5] in nineteenth-century American Methodism. A careful reading of Bangs and Stevens reveals that their prime concern was to defend the Methodist system of polity. The treatises, however, do reveal that early American Methodism was not without ecclesiological concerns and sensitivities. Only in Bangs, however, is Baptism treated at all, and this only obliquely so. He was concerned primarily to refute the Episcopalian practice of separating Baptism and confirmation by the episcopal imposition of hands—the two distanced by an interval of time. In a note on Cyprian's claim that by Baptism one is cleansed and purged from sin, Bangs adds a footnote:

> I do not vouch for the correctness of these sentiments of Cyprian respecting the efficacy of

baptism. It certainly should not be considered anything more than a divinely appointed means of grace, which, when rightly administered, is accompanied, as all duties are, with God's blessing. It is "not the putting away the filth of the flesh"—it is not to be considered in the light of a common washing, resorted to for the cleansing of the body, "but the answer of a good conscience"—it has a *moral* or spiritual influence upon the mind when done in obedience to God's command, in the *spirit* of the requirement.

. . . Though we ought not to doubt that, when rightly administered it is always accompanied with God's blessing, yet it should be considered only as a means, in the use of which we are to look for the "inward and spiritual grace," prefigured by this outward rite, which is wrought in the soul by the Spirit of God.

While Bangs still espoused the practice of infant Baptism, the text reveals an ambivalence regarding the regenerative power of Baptism even when accompanied immediately by the laying on of hands. "We have reason to believe that most of those who receive the ordinance are strangers to the regenerating influences of the Holy Spirit."[6] As will be revealed later, a tension in Wesley's doctrine of Baptism becomes in nineteenth-century America an equivocation which continues in United Methodism to the present day. It is particularly appropriate to note that the *Book of Worship* of the former Evangelical United Brethren Church includes an order for the dedication of infants. This all too brief historical excursus does reveal that there lurks implicitly within the consciousness of many United Methodists a doctrine of "believer's baptism" while they may still practice infant Baptism but rationalize it as a dedication service.

The patterns of practice of Baptism among Methodists and related churches in the nineteenth century are not unrelated to a theological transition which can be mapped more clearly than practice in the writings of the Methodist theologians in this period. Wesley's doctrine of prevenient grace did make it across the Atlantic. There is still debate regarding the precise theological meaning of the doctrine in Wesley, some holding that Wesley meant by this the divinely given power of decision, and others, including myself, who find Wesley claiming prevenient grace to the point of a legal repentance before the law but not the evangelical repentance which he definitely saw as subsequent to justification. What cannot be denied is that by mid–nineteenth century the Methodist theologians in polemical controversy with the Calvinists were increasingly resorting to such terms as "gracious ability" as substitute for "prevenient grace." By the advent of the twentieth century, Methodist theologians under the influence of increasing rationalism and experientialism were quite plainly speaking the language of "freedom of the will." The christologically grounded doctrine of prevenient grace in Wesley had been transposed beyond recognition into an unabashed avowal of the freedom of the will grounded in human nature through means of a general metaphysical world view of divine immanence.[7]

Some broad parallels can be seen when this transition is compared with the various revisions in the rituals of Baptism of the books of worship of the Methodist Episcopal and Methodist Episcopal, South, churches. The original Methodist service, borrowed from the Anglicans, read in the ritual for Baptism of infants: "Forasmuch as all men are conceived and born in sin . . . ."

By 1910 The Methodist Episcopal Church, South, reformulated the statement to read: "Forasmuch as all men, though fallen in Adam, are born into this world in Christ the Redeemer, heirs of eternal life and subjects of the saving grace of the Holy Spirit . . . ."

The 1916 service of the Methodist Episcopal Church read: "Forasmuch as God in his great mercy hath entered into covenant relation with man . . . ."

By 1932 the same body had transformed and reduced the opening of the service (depending upon whether the longer or shorter version was employed) to: "Forasmuch as all children are members of the kingdom of God and therefore graciously entitled to Baptism . . . ," or, "Forasmuch as this child is now presented by you for Christian Baptism . . . ."

My colleague, Laurence Stookey, has argued in his recent book on Baptism that in these various revisions we witness a transition from "an original guilt theology, to a covenant theology with an implied universalism, to a rather explicit universalism, to an almost blatant humanism."[8] I would argue that the theological transition in the earlier century from prevenient grace to gracious ability to freedom of the will provided the theological background for the theological/liturgical transitions of the early twentieth century. Is there any wonder that by 1953 a Methodist could write on baptism the following words:

So that today in a great democratic country like America there are those who cling to the Catholic inheritance of original sin and baptismal regeneration; but as democracy increases, in both state and church, the worth of the individual advances, and the "whosoever will" teaching of Jesus is on the march![9]

Does this quandary about Baptism antedate the appropriation of the Wesleyan tradition in nineteenth- and twentieth-century America? It is at the point of Baptism in Wesley's "folk theology" that he has been more variously interpreted and criticized than at any other point. At least five interpretations of Wesley can be delineated in twentieth-century appropriation of his thought regarding Baptism. They range the gamut.

(1) Wesley maintained consistently his Anglican inherited view of baptismal regeneration (Ole Borgen, John R. Parris, and Frederick Hockin).[10]

(2) Wesley's Aldersgate experience swung his view more and more toward that of the Dissenters or what some Americans call the evangelical view (William R. Cannon, Lycurgus M. Starkey, Jr., Irwin Reist).[11]

(3) Wesley softened the edges but retained the core, or appropriated the Anglican view with some minor revisions (Franz Hildebrandt).[12]

(4) There were elements in Wesley's view of Baptism which he simply never reconciled (Paul S. Sanders).[13]

(5) While not a theory, nevertheless, the pointed judgment has been made that Wesley simply used language carelessly when contrasting Baptism and the new birth (John R. Parris).[14]

Not only the curious historian, but the contemporary Methodist who senses some linkage with the Wesley of yesteryear, cries out, "Will the real Wesley stand up?"

Obviously within the limits of this paper it is not possible to answer the question about the "real Wesley" on Baptism. One can only point to certain key issues in Wesley's thought and indicate some of the problems in subsequent interpretation. The primary and perennial "bone of contention" has been: Did Wesley consistently throughout his ministry hold to baptismal regeneration? No doubt exists concerning his earlier years. Joined with his brother Charles at Oxford, he fully embraced the Anglo-Catholic doctrine of baptismal regeneration. His *Journal* records his reflection that until he was ten years old he had not sinned away the "washing of the Holy Ghost" given in Baptism. This can in no wise be a definitive statement written as it was on the eve of his departure from the ill-fated Georgia experiment. At least in Wesley's case, with the vacillations in spirit and mood, the autobiography of the *Journal* will hardly suffice for theological underpinnings! Wesley's foundation stones for the doctrine of Baptism (consistently or inconsistently held)

must be found in his edition of his father's treatise on the subject and in Wesley's own sermons.

In 1756, Wesley edited a portion of a tract of his father's called *The Pious Communicant Rightly Prepared; or, a Discourse Concerning the Blessed Sacrament . . . To which is added, a Short Discourse of* [sic] *Baptism.* Wesley excised the "Short Discourse" and edited it.[15] For those who make so much of the Aldersgate experience as providing the pivotal point of reference for Wesley's theological development and particularly for the great stress which he placed on the experience of the new birth, it should be pointed out that Wesley published this treatise on Baptism approximately eighteen years after Aldersgate, and he published it precisely for the people called Methodists. He intended that it be taken seriously as Methodist doctrine with his own endorsement.

Concerning the origin of Baptism, the treatise rested the case upon two important premises: (1) The Baptism of John the Baptist and Jesus' submission to that Baptism. This secures the case that Baptism is accepted and ordained by Christ. (2) The origin of Baptism is to be found in the Old Testament practice of circumcision. A parallel therefore exists between admission to the old covenant through circumcision and admission to the new covenant through Baptism. "When the old seal of circumcision was taken off, this of baptism was added in its room."[16] The latter argument is of particular import for Wesley's defense of infant Baptism.

The treatise held forth five benefits of Baptism: (1) "The washing away the guilt of original sin, by the application of the merits of Christ's death."[17] (2) Entrance into covenant with God.[18] (3) Entrance into the church, "we being consequently made members of Christ, its Head."[19] (4) "By nature children of wrath," we are now made children of God.[20] (5) Since Baptism admits us "into the Church here, so into glory hereafter", hence, we are made heirs of the Kingdom.[21] In particular Wesley omitted two words from his father's treatise. In writing of the guilt of original sin, Wesley omitted the word "damning"—no doubt under the influence of his doctrine of prevenient grace and his fear that the Calvinist doctrine of reprobation rendered the atonement unnecessary or ineffective. Where Samuel described the third benefit, union with Christ in the church, as sacramental, Wesley omitted the word "sacramental." The omission in this case could have been made to avoid loading Baptism with more freight than Wesley thought it could carry. Would the word "sacramental" carry the connotation for the early Methodists of *ex opere operato*? Certainly this was not Samuel's intention. These are his own words, "We say *not* that regeneration is always *completed* in this Sacrament, but that it is begun in it." While Wesley did not repeat his father at this point, he did say that "a principal of grace is infused in the sacrament." The judgment of Ole Borgen and others regarding Wesley's edition of his father's treatise is to the point. By avoiding the language of damnation he escapes the Calvinist dilemma of seriously questioning the efficacy of the atonement. By deleting the word "sacramental" he avoided the conclusion of automatic salvation to all who were baptized.[22] It is interesting to note also that while prevenient grace is not mentioned in the discussion of Baptism, it seems to be presupposed through the discussion. So, one could also conclude that Wesley sought thereby to avoid the dangers of Pelagianism.

To place such a doctrine of Baptism within the Wesleyan *ordo salutis* requires a christological focusing. Christ is the agent of justification, and he is the mediator of all the benefits of Baptism. Through justification as communicated through Baptism the formal relationship with God has been changed—from "wrath" to "grace," or in Wesley's personal terms, from "servant" to "son." Baptism does not end with justification, however, but embraces regeneration and the growth in baptismal grace which is sanctification. In short, Baptism is Christ's act "washing," covenanting, incorporating, making new, and promising. At least to this writer, Wesley seems to have intended this to be the grand background for his subsequent treatment of new birth.

This so-called objective side of Wesley's doctrine of baptism is crucial for United Methodists, whether they be of evangelical or liberal theological persuasion. Perhaps the reason why conservatives and liberals fight so well with each other is that they unknowlingly accept similar premises. The evangelical insistence upon repentance and faith as prior to Baptism, and the liberal insistence that nothing can possess any efficacy unless it registers in one's experience, both need a corrective which Wesley's doctrine offers at this point. Both positions, evangelical and liberal, tend to justify a doctrine of Baptism where the primary emphasis falls upon human agency, and in the end both really affirm Baptism as dedication. Particularly in a time when Baptists are coming increasingly to agree to the reality of divine agency in Baptism, United Methodists need to recover the Wesleyan insistence upon the initiatory character of God's grace in Baptism.

Fine so far. But there came the day when Wesley preached his much-discussed sermon on "The New Birth." Here the debate regarding Wesley's real view of Baptism becomes heated. Hear Wesley's own words.

> Baptism is not the new birth: they are not one and the same thing. . . .But indeed the reason of the thing is so clear and evident, as not to need any other authority. For what can be more plain, than that the one is an external, the other an internal work; that the one is a visible, the other an invisible thing, and therefore different from each other?— the one being an act of man, purifying the body; the other a change wrought by God in the soul: so that the former is just as distinguishable from the latter, as the soul from the body, or water from the Holy Ghost.[23]

The key word in this passage is "distinguishable." Wesley was not attempting to separate the two—Baptism and the new birth. Quite to the contrary, on other occasions when speaking of the Baptism of adults he quite explicitly stated that ordinarily the two occurred simultaneously or were "ordinarily annexed" one to the other.[24] In reality what Wesley was attempting was a personal, relational understanding of Baptism in contrast to grace as some metaphysical substance implanted at Baptism. Hence, he could say, "Lean no more on the staff of that broken reed, that ye *were* born again in baptism."[25] One could document with further citations from Wesley's sermons indicating the same line of argument— an argument that remains in basic agreement with the edited treatise on Baptism. Ole Borgen has documented this fully, and a careful reading of Borgen offers a definite corrective for much of the history of Wesleyan interpretation on this subject.[26]

It appears to me that in actuality in the midst of the revival Wesley was attempting to do justice both to the objective (divine initiative) in Baptism and the experiential, or subjective, side of the same reality in terms of human participation in divine grace. It should, however, be noted that while "conversion" (a term Wesley used sparingly) could be translated as "human response," the term "new birth" refers rather to the divine work in human experience. One does not have to resort to such artificial constructs as two Baptisms (infant and adult) or two regenerations to make sense of Wesley at this point. For Wesley Baptism was at once the divine-human encounter in grace and the beginning of the process of sanctification. Baptism was for him regenerational and encompassed the full scope of the *ordo salutis* from justification through regeneration to sanctification.

This is not to say there are no theological problems with Wesley's treatment. While avoiding the language of damnation regarding the guilt of original sin, he nevertheless insisted that

Baptism "washed" that guilt away. How, then, is his understanding of Baptism to be related to the doctrine of prevenient grace? Earlier in this paper mention was made of the fact that throughout much of the edited treatise on Baptism he seems to presuppose prevenient grace, yet to my knowledge nowhere in Wesley's writings does he bring Baptism and prevenient grace into conjunction with each other. Recently the United Methodist theologian and liturgical scholar Laurence Stookey has treated prevenient grace along with incorporation into the body of Christ as the two foundational stones of infant Baptism. This interpretation seems to be consistent with the basic shape and direction of Wesleyan thought, though Wesley himself never makes this explicit.[27]

Wesley, for some reason—churchman that he was—did not make as much of the incorporation aspect of Baptism as an adequate doctrine requires. Maybe it was because he presupposed the Anglican Church and did not want to encourage his followers into thinking he was creating another church. This remains, however, for conjecture. Baptism, for the most part, still lingers in Wesley in an individualistic hiatus. At the same time he was the man who insisted that he knew of no religion other than a social one (and this was for Wesley an ecclesiological statement). If he could have possessed the prophetic vision to see later into the nineteenth and twentieth centuries, envisioning some of the problems his inheritors would have with ecclesiology, he might have prepared his children better.

Further, Colin Williams has pointed out one of the most significant differences between Wesley and Luther. It was Luther who could cry in assurance, "I have been baptized." Wesley could relate assurance only to the present internal witness of the Spirit.[28] Wesley was fearful that persons would place their faith in the means rather than grace itself. The danger is no doubt there. At the same time, however, he was attempting to do justice to both the subjective and the objective aspects of the sacrament. Here, however, the accent fell decidedly on the subjective side.

Before turning finally to the *BEM* statement, one further step needs to be taken. I turn to the official doctrinal statements of The United Methodist Church as they pertain to the issue at hand. A most careful delineation of these statements has been set forth in an unpublished paper by Dr. Thor Hall written in 1968.[29] In this paper Hall reveals "an equivocation" in the Articles of Religion. The first such statement in

sequence is Article XVI:

> Sacraments ordained of Christ are not only badges or tokens of Christian men's profession, but rather they are certain signs of grace, and God's good will toward us, by which he doth work invisibly in us, and doth not only quicken, but also strengthen and confirm, our faith in him.

This is the formal definition of a sacrament. Article XVII of the Articles of Religion addresses this issue in specific reference to Baptism: "Baptism is not only a sign of profession and mark of difference whereby Christians are distinguished from others that are not baptized; but it is also a sign of regeneration or the new birth. The baptism of young children is to be retained in the church."

Place along side this statement the relevant sections of Article VI of the Confession of Faith of the Evangelical United Brethren Church:

> We believe Baptism signifies entrance into the household of faith, and is a symbol of repentance and inner cleansing from sin, a representation of the new birth in Christ Jesus and a mark of Christian discipleship.
>
> We believe children are under the atonement of Christ and as heirs of the Kingdom of God are acceptable subjects for Christian baptism. Children of believing parents through baptism become the special responsibility of the Church. They should be nurtured and led to personal acceptance of Christ, and by profession of faith confirm their baptism.

When comparing these statements it is significant to note the usage of the terms "badges or tokens," "sign," and "signifies," and how these are placed in the syntax of the sentence. In the first instance (Article XVI), the intention of Wesley is preserved, that is, the conjoining of the sign and that signified, Baptism and regeneration. The second statement (Article XVII) enters a bit of the Wesleyan dilemma, or what some have even called equivocation, in that "sign" covers both human "profession" and divine "regeneration." Note that Article XVI states "not only . . . but rather"; whereas Article XVI states "not only . . . but *also* . . . " I fear that there is more than a nuance of difference here. The statement from the Confession of Faith is in closer agreement with Article XVI and clearly places both "sign" and that which is "signified" in dialectical relationship. In fact, Article XVI (Articles of Religion) and Article VI (Confession of Faith) clearly state the objective character of the action of grace while giving due importance to the experiential or existential side as well. In other words, Baptism is not *ex post facto* of the action of grace, but it is the means of grace in the here and now. The element of uncertainty or "equivocation" in United Methodism's official understanding of Baptism as sacrament (and this is reflected in actual theological rationale as well as practice) lies in Article XVII (Articles of Religion). Stated in another way, followers of the Wesleyan tradition on the American scene have manifested a certain lack of clarity regarding the relationship between Baptism and faith. The problem arises in Wesley's revival, and while he did not definitively answer it, he nevertheless never departed from a basic regenerational view of the sacrament. Much of American theological reflection and practice has been to make a virtue out of one side of the Wesleyan dilemma, and, in effect, dilute the objective means of the grace character of the sacrament.

Turning now to the *BEM* document and confining ourselves exclusively to the statement on Baptism, we can first note the areas of similarity and agreement between this document and elements of our tradition.

The opening definitional statement is at one with the various elements of our tradition in affirming that Baptism "is incorporation into Christ, who is the crucified and risen Lord; it is entry into the New Covenant between God and God's people. Baptism is a gift of God."[30] Likewise, that Baptism is "the sign of new life through Jesus Christ" (regeneration) is certainly in line with Article XVI (Articles) and Article VI (Confession).

The *BEM* document, however, manifests some of our Wesleyan equivocation or uncertainty when it states that "baptism . . . implies confession of sin and conversion of heart." Does "implies" mean "conveys," or does it mean "presupposes" or even "anticipates"? One looks to the treatment of "Baptism and Faith"[31] for a possible answer. "Baptism is both God's gift and our human response to that gift."[32] The following sentence could almost be a direct quote from Wesley himself, "It looks towards a growth into the measure of the stature of the fullness of Christ (Eph. 4:13)."[33] The sentence which follows simply raises the question again, "The necessity of faith for the reception of the salvation embodied and set forth in baptism is acknowledged by all churches."[34] Yes. But does Baptism impart this faith, presuppose this faith, or anticipate this faith? The statement offers a descriptive account: "When one who can answer for himself or herself is baptized, a personal confession of faith will be an integral part of the baptismal service. When an infant is baptized, the personal response will be offered at a later moment in life."[35] Either the statement is purely descriptive, or there are implicitly in it some theological assumptions which need considerable examination.

Where United Methodists can be most fruitfully theologically engaged with the *BEM* statement is at the above-mentioned point of the relation between Baptism and faith. This is our inherited and current problematic, and apparently the *BEM* statement shows that it is also an ecumenical problematic. Where United Methodists will be most challenged by the *BEM* statement will be with its forthright endorsement of Baptism as incorporation into Jesus Christ, that is, into the body of Christ. United Methodists seem to operate ecclesiologically on two tracks simultaneously. One is *movement*, and the other is *institution*. We began in Wesley as a *movement* and subsequently became an *institution*. Nowhere is this more obviously evident than in our practice of infant baptism. We baptize infants and place them immediately on "preparatory membership rolls."[36] In what sense have baptized infants then really been incorporated into the body of Christ? Is such practice in conflict with our theological affirmation of the meaning of the sacrament? Because of our history, *movement* became *institution*, and this is sociologically and theologically necessary—who today would argue for a docetic ecclesiology? At the same time we have come dangerously close to being an ecclesiocracy without an ecclesiology. Such issues as Baptism and church membership (one could also mention a somewhat parallel issue of ordination and conference membership) serve as constant reminders, in the light of as ecumenically significant a document as *BEM*, that ours is still very much an unfinished task.

Where the *BEM* document engages and challenges all Christians and all churches is at the point of the conjunction of Baptism and Eucharist. If increasingly churches of varying confessions can participate in a fellowship of the one Baptism, does this not lead to conclusions for eucharistic fellowship? The theological stresses, strains, and differences even within a particular tradition, such as the Wesleyan tradition, do not prevent mutual recognition and participation in one Baptism. I submit that the theological stresses, strains, and differences in eucharistic theology are no greater than those in Baptism. If Baptism be incorporation into the body of Christ, then by what logic do we deny full participation in the body around the Table of the Lord?

NOTES

1. *Baptism, Eucharist, and Ministry*, Faith and Order Paper No. 11 (Geneva: World Council of Churches, 1982). Hereafter, referred to as *BEM*.
2. J. E. Rattenbury, *Wesley's Legacy to the World* (Nashville: Cokesbury Press, 1928), p. 193.
3. Donald M. Baillie, *The Theology of the Sacraments* (New York: Charles Scribner's Sons, 1957), p. 72.
4. Russell E. Richey, "Ecclesial Sensibilities in Nineteenth Century American Methodism," *Quarterly Review*, vol. 4, no. 1 (spring 1984), pp. 31-42.
5. Nathan Bangs, *An Original Church of Christ* (New York: T. Mason and G. Lane, rev. ed., 1837); Abel Stevens, "An Essay on Church Polity" (New York: Carlton and Phillips, 1835).
6. Bangs, *An Original Church*, p. 328.
7. Robert E. Chiles, *Theological Transition in American Methodism 1790–1935* (Nashville: Abingdon Press, 1965).
8. Laurence H. Stookey, *Baptism: Christ's Act in the Church* (Nashville: Abingdon Press, 1982).
9. Robert W. Goodloe, *The Sacraments in Methodism* (Nashville: The Methodist Publishing House, 1953).
10. See Frederick Hockin, *John Wesley and Modern Methodism* (London: Rivingtons, 1887); John R. Parris, *John Wesley's Doctrine of the Sacraments* (London: Epworth Press, 1963); Ole Borgen, *John Wesley on the Sacraments* (Nashville: Abingdon Press, 1972).
11. See William R. Cannon, *The Theology of John Wesley, with Special Reference to the Doctrine of Justification* (New York: Abingdon Press, 1946); Lycurgus M. Starkey, Jr., *The Work of the Holy Spirit: A Study in Wesleyan Theology* (Nashville: Abingdon Press, 1962); Irwin Reist, "John Wesley's View of the Sacraments: A Study in the Historical Development of a Doctrine," *Wesleyan Theological Journal*, (1971): 41-54.
12. Franz Hildebrandt, *From Luther to Wesley* (London: Lutterworth Press, 1951).
13. Paul S. Sanders, "John Wesley and Baptismal Regeneration." *Religion in Life*, 23 (1953/54): 591–603.
14. Parris, *John Wesley's Doctrine.*
15. John Wesley, *Works*, vol. 10, pp. 188-200.
16. Wesley, *Works*, vol. 10, pp. 194-95; cf. Wesley, *Notes on the New Testament*, Matt. 26:26.
17. Ibid., vol. 10, 191-92.
18. Ibid., 191.
19. Ibid.
20. Ibid., 191-92.
21. Ibid., 192.
22. Borgen, *On the Sacraments*, pp. 124-25.
23. Wesley, *Sermons*, vol. 2, pp. 237-38.
24. Ibid., vol. 1, p. 283.
25. Ibid., 296.
26. For example, instructive is Borgen's careful delineation of the differences between the new birth, which is the act of God, and conversion, which is the human response empowered by convincing grace. See *On the Sacraments*, pp. 153-55.
27. Stookey, *Baptism*, p. 46.
28. Colin Williams, *John Wesley's Theology Today* (Nashville: Abingdon Press, 1972), p. 120.
29. See Thor Hall, "The Meaning of Church Membership," unpublished paper, 1968.
30. *BEM*, p. 2.
31. *BEM*, p. 3.
32. *BEM*, p. 3.
33. *BEM*, p. 3.
34. *BEM*, p. 3.
35. *BEM*, p. 4.
36. See Hall's, "Church Membership."

4. THE DEVELOPMENT OF THE 1972 UNITED METHODIST EUCHARISTIC RITE

James F. White

Few subjects are as central in ecumenical discussion these days as the Eucharist. Virtually all such discussions are grounded in eucharistic practice such as that discussed here. The present paper is a portion of a presentation to the 1983 annual meeting of the North American Academy of Liturgy on "Making Changes in United Methodist Euchology," a paper reprinted in full in the July, 1983 issue of *Worship*. The occasion gave me an opportunity to speak in a personal way about the genesis of the 1972 eucharistic rite.

Authorized by the 1970 General Conference, the new rite received its first national use at the 1972 General Conference. In slightly revised form, it was officially commended to United Methodist congregations for trial use by the 1980 General Conference. For a decade and more it has been in widespread use among American Methodists.

I

In the whole process of liturgical revision, one question keeps coming back to haunt me: "What right do we have to change the way people pray?" It is the only liturgical question that ever keeps me awake at night. Basically it is an ethical question although I doubt many ethicists lose much sleep over changing other people's forms of behavior, and educators positively seem to relish promoting new ways of learning. But there is something intimate about prayer, more intimate even than action or education. Do we really serve people by changing the way they pray either in public or in private?

Since prayer is such an intimate act, does another person have a right to interfere in such a personal relationship to God? Familiar ways of praying are unthreatening. Change can make them startlingly frightening. I remember once during the early years of liturgical revision at a celebration of the old—basically 1662—United Methodist rite thinking how much I loved that service myself, and yet I was working on replacing it. And I wonder, wondered whether what I was doing was beneficial or harmful to others. It seems so presumptuous for anyone to assert that there is a "better" way of praying, to infer that we know a "better" way to address God. Do we know or are we just meddlesome

busybodies? These are not questions easily dismissed, and yet anyone who refuses to wrestle with them has no right to tinker with the way other people pray.

At last, I can give more certain answers to those questions about serving people through making changes in the way they pray. But this came only after hearing people tell me how the 1972 Methodist Eucharist has shaped their piety and hence their very being. When a few minor changes in the service were suggested in 1980, people began telling us they loved the 1972 rite too much to want it changed. And to be loved is what a liturgy needs to function well, although creating it may not make the revisers particularly lovable. Indeed, the more cantankerous the revisers are, the better the liturgy produced may become.

I think one can say "yes, we *can* serve people well by changing the way they pray," but this is only possible after having thought through the reasons for making changes in prayer. I suggest four reasons which, for me, justify interference in the way people have been accustomed to address God. The first is to make liturgical or personal prayer reflect more accurately the true nature of God and God's relation to humans. For example, prayer addressed to God as the purveyor of success needs change. Second, prayer must be made to reflect and teach justice, though it ought not preach. Prayers in former wedding services, which prayed that the woman alone "fortify herself against her weakness," certainly needed replacing. In the third place, the language must be made accessible to all, not just to those who understand what it is to be "sore let and hindered." "Plight thee my troth" always made me think of how we feed hogs, hardly what Cranmer intended! And fourth, the way we pray has to be shaped to relate to the prayer of all Christians. Christian prayer demands the company of many voices, present or unseen. We proclaim the same story and implore God's continuance of the same work.

Apparently we succeeded in accomplishing some of these goals in the 1972 service. So naive were we, that we hoped that, with luck, fifty or sixty thousand copies would be sold to a small number of progressive congregations. Currently, over two and a quarter million copies have been sold, and about twenty-eight thousand more sell each month, to say nothing of the millions of times it has been photocopied or mimeographed. When one considers what a drastic break the service meant with the Anglican-Methodist pattern of euchology, this is remarkable. It also shows how much we may underestimate our peoples' eagerness to grow. Even more surprising is that its use seems as common in conservative congregations as in progressive ones, in country churches as in city congregations. Astonishingly, a major change has occurred in the way many of our people pray the Eucharist. It is a change many have welcomed, perhaps for the reasons I have just enumerated, perhaps for others.

II

Some words about the process of preparing the 1972 United Methodist rite will help explain how the theology developed. I was a young assistant professor when the previous rite, that of 1964, was being prepared, and no one wanted my advice. I remember being told at that time, when I pled for the inclusion of the fraction, that "even the Anglicans have given up that Dix stuff!" My very first association with the Commission on Worship of the Methodist Church was at a service dedicating the 1964 *Book of Worship*, in Champaign-Urbana in 1965. Somehow, just five years later, at a meeting in Dayton, a few of us were able to persuade weary members of the commission that it was already time to start over again.

Out of that discussion came a new project, shepherded by the Committee on Alternate Rituals, and ably chaired by Professor Grady Hardin. And this time around, I was chosen to be the writer for the Communion service with a committee of ten to supervise my efforts. The choice of members of such a committee, of course, determines in great measure the final outcome. Fortunately, that committee included Hoyt Hickman whom I looked on as conspirator at every stage and who always lent knowledgeable support. Most of the others were chosen as representatives of various constituencies within the church rather than as liturgical experts. One member even claimed that we were not out "to impress Massey Shepherd." Yet, I maintained that scholarship was vital, for what would please Massey Shepherd would also serve the church best. The committee chosen was in marked contrast to the Roman Catholic *coetus* of the liturgy concilium which initially included only one woman and scores of men, all liturgy experts

and almost all clergy. We have gone to the other extreme with democracy replacing expertise, representation overcoming specialization. Theology is done by nontheologians, liturgy by nonliturgists. At present there is not a single liturgical scholar on the Section on Worship although there is a most competent staff. Minorities are represented, but it is highly questionable whether they are served well by nonexperts. In other words, the patients now vote on how surgery is to be done.

Late in 1970, I began work on the new rite. My second text was mailed out for the Committee on Alternate Rituals to discuss at its first meetings in Chicago, March 14-15, 1971. I well remember how despondent the committee was when it saw the text, partly because some of them had never encountered the Eucharist in contemporary English. They missed the Cranmerian cadences, if not the vocabulary. I had to leave before the meeting was over, and, I understand, there was much hand wringing about the flatness and unpoetic nature of my prose. Indeed, Albert Outler later told me that, in writing it, I had loved the Lord Jesus but not the English language.

Be that as it may, I am strongly convinced that it is necessary to get one's theology straight before one can proclaim it with flair. The current Presbyterian attempts at new eucharistic prayers more than confirm that belief. In my lifetime, I have only written two such prayers, the 1972 one and one another, written in 1978 and included in *At the Lord's Table*. The latter is obviously better language but was impossible without the theological clarity of the 1972 effort. Actually, I am not sure whether the language of 1972 got better or we just got more accustomed to it, but I think it has worn rather well.

Far more important for me than language at that first meeting was that the structure I had proposed was accepted with only minor changes. Those changes were: the *Kyrie* was dropped, the *Gloria in excelsis* was not to be printed in full, the offertory prayer was dropped, and an invitation as a spoken rubric was added. But most of the structure I had proposed survived the committee's scrutiny even though some ingredients were unfamiliar. Encouraged by Hugh Old's book, I had deliberately borrowed the use of a prayer for illumination from the Reformed tradition. I had included three lessons and psalmody, recovered the ancient kiss of peace, and highlighted the four-fold eucharistic actions. All these ancient patterns, then just reemerging in the rites of other churches, were accepted much to my gratification. My recommendation to follow the International Consultation on English Texts

(ICET) texts was also agreeable to the members of the committee except to a New Testament scholar who was not content with the ICET version of the Lord's Prayer.

Equally important, the theology which I had tried to incorporate was accepted, almost without question. As a consultant, David Buttrick was helpful in making us realize what we were doing with language. Larry Stookey, also a consultant, who was soon to play a similar role as writer in reforming our initiation rites, affirmed our theology.

A third draft followed that spring, and a fourth was prepared for the committee's meeting in St. Louis in late May. At that meeting, I lost one major battle when the United Church of Canada Creed was substituted for the Apostles' or Nicene. But by that time I was learning to be obnoxious for the Lord! I could concede the creed if I could hold the line on the eucharistic prayer. I was learning that a person who comes to a committee meeting with mind made up or agenda prepared has a good chance of prevailing. Planning is power. I won on substituting the *Benedictus qui venit* because I could quote Psalm 118; I lost on the introduction to the Lord's Prayer since I had no ammunition ready. But out of the heated give and take, personal crochets and pet phrases were eliminated, greatly improving the results. At this time, it was decided to invite Fred Gealy to rewrite entirely the confessional acts and to retool the prayer for illumination and for Grady Hardin to write completely new intercessions. Both improved the synaxis considerably.

Through some procedural unclarity, due to minutes of the meeting not being available immediately, I produced a fifth text in June, unaware that others were also at work on another fifth version. I first saw their version at the third meeting, held in July in Arlington, Vermont. I was stunned by the theological alterations. Some of these, but not all, were compromised before the sixth text was printed for the First World Methodist Consultation on Worship in Denver the next month. By this time the post-communion prayer had been changed from unison to responsive. I think it has become the most popular part of the entire service, even though a novel form for this prayer. At Denver, the theology of the eucharistic prayer was threatened inadvertently by the comment of a well-known Methodist ecumenist that the phrase in the *epiclesis* "that they may be for us the presence of the crucified and risen Lord" was certainly a strong statement of real presence. Some of the weaker brethren quailed at that

thought, and I was forced to withdraw the phrase.

A new, the seventh version, was circulated by mail that fall to the members of the committee. On the basis of their written comments, a final text, the eighth, was prepared and sent to the printers, incorporating the refinements of Grady Hardin and me. Both of us read proof on it, and the service was used officially for the first time by the General Conference in Atlanta, April, 1972. I might add as a footnote that two years later I taught summer school at St. John's University in Minnesota and asked a number of prominent Roman Catholic liturgical scholars present then to comment on it. Interestingly, their comments were almost all literary rather than theological. I was able to propose some improvements, mostly in better transitions in the eucharistic prayer and in removing some of the sexist language which, inexcusably, had crept back in when we were concerned about other problems. I was forced to probe deeper into the area of discriminatory language and actions and the resulting sacramental injustice. I am considered as indulging in mere trifles by those whom I regard as insensitive, and damned as reactionary by those whom I regard as irresponsible. This latter conflict arises when I refuse to surrender the name "Father" at certain key points in the Eucharist. But maybe I have succeeded in making a few people angry enough to think about our liturgical sanctions of injustice.

A happy sequel to the 1974 refinements is that I was able to incorporate them in a 1980 revision which appeared in *We Gather Together*. This time, I was also able to design the graphics as well as to edit the booklet. I believe that the way a page appears is almost as important as what is printed on it. We were finally able to eliminate the Canadian creed and to move the acts of confession to a less prominent position. In this case, a new committee was open to persuasion on these matters, as well as minor retuning on the initiation, marriage, and burial rites. In 1981, Hoyt Hickman's *At the Lord's Table* gave us a collection of twenty-two eucharistic prayers, a book which, I think, stands unequalled among the other churches and which, along with Don Salier's book on Lent and Easter, *From Ashes to Fire*, give me considerable pride in United Methodist liturgy, a new experience for me. I also take much delight, but no credit, for the work of Larry Stookey and his committee on the reform of initiation. I hope the rest of the thirteen volumes now available in the *Supplemental Worship Resources* series will serve the church as well as these have.

III

When the Methodist-Catholic statement, "The Eucharist and the Churches" was released February 12, 1982 (cf. *Origins*, XI, March 25, 1982, pp. 651-59), it commented on the "surprising convergence" evident in the "remarkable unity and agreement on the structure of the eucharistic celebration and on the central eucharistic prayer." I was hardly surprised but certainly was gratified to have my intentions thus recognized in such a document.

At this point, I want to spell out those things that I was trying to do theologically in the 1972 service, and for which I was obstinate, if not obnoxious. I shall not try to defend my convictions but simply articulate them so I can be understood rather than excused. I am sure it never occurred to anyone else, but I felt at times that I had been entrusted with the most important theological task The United Methodist Church could delegate, changing Methodist euchology by altering the language and structure of the Eucharist. I believe I have a responsibility to make explicit what I was trying to do as writer for the 1972 rite. This should be helpful for others who will push us beyond it and, I hope, of interest to you who listen.

I had been prepared for liturgical revision by spending the year 1967–68 in Rome, looking over the shoulders of the Concilium for the Implementation of the Constitution on the Sacred Liturgy, reading all of its publications, and keeping up with every issue of *Notitiae* and the *BCI Newsletter* since. I had likewise made, and still make, it my business to read everything published by the Standing Liturgical Commission of the Episcopal Church, the Inter-Lutheran Commission on Worship, the Presbyterian Joint Committee on Worship, and all publications on worship of the United Church of Christ and Disciples of Christ. Ecumenism, then, was a basic given of all I tried to do. This was reflected in the nine basic rites I had ever before me: the most recent revisions of Methodists, Roman Catholics, Episcopalians, Presbyterians, Lutherans, the Consultation on Church Union, the United Church of Christ, the Church of England, and the Church of South India. I also made frequent use of the Byzantine rite.

But certain basic decisions had to be made which not all of these reflected. I was convinced that the eucharistic prayer is the church's central doctrinal statement and key to understanding ordained ministry. The eucharistic prayer proclaims the church's faith in the form of prayer by reciting and giving thanks for those acts of God that make the community one. But any look at the previous eucharistic prayers in any of these traditions (save the Orthodox) shows how completely this function had been lost. The redundancy of the inclusion of a creed demonstrates how oblivious we all were to this loss.

I had become convinced that, as a first step of recovery, a basically Antiochene structure, what Robert Taft calls "the ever-so-neat Antiochene pattern," for the prayer would function best. This would incorporate the full breadth of commemoration beginning with creation and ending in the final consummation in Christ's victory. This is quite an expansion from the passion narrative to which we had hitherto limited ourselves. The Antiochene pattern would allow inclusion (for the first time in our tradition) of creation, fall, exodus, covenant, and prophets in the preface, all compressed into fifty words. At the same time, the *Sanctus* could be expanded into a much fuller proclamation of the works of the new covenant.

The defects of the 1662 prayer—penitential obsession, the absence of the old covenant, eschatology, and pneumatology, plus a decidedly negative approach to sacrifice—could be overcome in such a structure. I think now it may be time to try other patterns, but the Antiochene proved the best place to begin. At the same time, it was possible for us to avoid the preliminary epiclesis which seemed to me an unnecessary intrusion in the new Roman prayers and the recent Church of England efforts. The intercessions, I felt, belonged elsewhere and can easily be heard here as a bit of moralizing.

Having established these prejudices, I needed guidance as to content. Two sources seemed most appropriate, John Wesley and Hippolytus. The conjunction need not surprise you. Wesley was a patristic scholar who would have welcomed Hippolytus had he known the *Apostolic Tradition* as well as he knew and esteemed the *Apostolic Constitutions*. Hippolytus provided structure and specific phrases for us. Wesley's contribution was theological; in his 1784 edition of the 1662 eucharistic prayer he had altered only one word, a redundant "one." But the Wesley brothers had provided a marvelous collection of 166 eucharistic hymns (cf. J. E. Rattenbury, *Eucharistic Hymns of John and Charles Wesley*. [London: Epworth Press, 1948]). I felt that one has to affirm one's own tradition even while being ecumenical, maybe especially while being ecumenical, and that the Wesley's eucharistic hymns are Methodism's distinctive contribution. John Wesley's patristic interests loom large in these hymns and sing the theology which I tried to reflect. Thus I can argue that the 1972 eucharistic prayer is more Wesleyan than Wesley's own 1784 version. The chief exception I made to Wesley's theology was in expanding the breadth of his vision of commemoration beyond just the passion narrative.

Wesley's study of patristics had led him beyond the negativisms of the sixteenth-century Reformation on eucharistic sacrifice. Indeed, a major portion of the eucharistic hymns is entitled "The Holy Eucharist as It Implies a Sacrifice," and the imagery of the hymns is replete with Old Testament images of sacrifice. I think it was important that, by using Hebrews 9 and 13, Romans 12, and Augustine, I was allowed to make a strong positive statement of the Eucharist as sacrifice, perhaps for the first time in a Protestant liturgy. This I consider an important ecumenical step which Wesley encouraged.

Another important element in the Wesleyan eucharistic hymns is the frequent use of imagery about the work of the Holy Spirit. Contemporary works, especially John McKenna's brilliant book, *Eucharist and Holy Spirit*, show how essential it is that we recover an *epiclesis* invoking the work of the Spirit in consecrating the gifts and uniting the communicants. Another Wesleyan characteristic is the eschatological dimension, certainly present in the New Testament accounts but long lacking in Western worship until recently. Recovery of this has been strengthened by Geoffrey Wainwright's classic study, *Eucharist and Eschatology*. I think subsequent prayers will need to reflect eschatology even more strongly and to tie it to present efforts for justice.

I felt it important to turn from a rather penitential prayer tradition to a more joyful offering of thanks. If we believe that ultimately everything depends upon God, then less concentration ought to be focused on human efforts and failures. In the 1972 prayer, God's work is thankfully commemorated and presently invoked, and God is begged to keep up the good work by bringing it to completion. Human activity is mentioned only at the end of the *epiclesis* and in the post-communion prayer as response to God's self-giving.

The fellowship of the gathered community is stressed by the action of breaking bread. We may have erred in 1972 in tying the fraction too closely to the spoken words of I Corinthians 10:16-17. Indeed, the fraction may be more eloquent as action alone. And we may need to explore further the ethical dimension of I Corinthians 10:21, in which sharing at the table and in the cup excludes us from compromise with the demons of the world. The sense of community is also stressed in the benefits sought in communion: "Make us one with Christ/one with each other/and one in service to all the world."

On the statement of the presence of Christ, as mentioned already, we were forced to compromise, but finally managed a more dynamic approach: "Help us know/in the breaking of this bread/and the drinking of this wine/the presence of Christ." (Perhaps a more ontological text will again be possible in the future such as "be for us.") In the institution narrative Fred Gealy, a New Testament scholar, persuaded us to translate *anamesis* as "experience anew." To some, that sounds too subjective a sense of presence although "recall" and "remember" may be no less so.

My own approach to sacraments as God's self-giving comes out rather strongly in the post-communion prayer: "You have given yourself to us, Lord/Now we give ourselves for others." It was tempting to push that sense of self-giving further in the direction of justice, but I fear preaching in prayer. And, after all, the whole of the liturgy, sensitively celebrated, is a strong statement of the Christian contribution to justice just as, insensitively celebrated, it can be an act promoting injustice in the church and eventually the world.

Well, these were the chief theological principles that guided our efforts in making changes in United Methodist euchology. Much that was done in the 1970s I think is irrevocable. Things that will endure include reading from both testaments of the Bible, the use of contemporary language, the concentration on eucharist as action, and the understanding of the eucharistic prayer as thankful proclamation of the church's faith. In time, our words will be refined and be exchanged for other words that function more adequately.

It has been a pleasure and a privilege to share in this exciting age in the rethinking and reformulation of how Christians give thanks. This stage in my own life may now be past, but it is equally exciting to be moving on to teach those who will be able to improve on what I was called to do when Methodism finally burst out of the tight confines of the Anglican-Methodist liturgical tradition in the early 1970s. There are times when we have an opportunity for *making* history rather than *teaching* history. I am pleased that you have given me this chance to record my perceptions of one such occasion. I hope it will help you in your work of teaching and making history.

5. ORDINATION, RECONCILIATION, AND THE ECUMENICAL FUTURE: Reflections from and to the Wesleyan Family

Gerald F. Moede

After fifty years of work the Faith and Order Commission of the World Council of Churches has produced and accepted a draft formulation, bringing about agreement on the traditional church-dividing issues of Baptism, Eucharist, and ordained ministry. This agreement (*Baptism, Eucharist, and Ministry—BEM*) is now being submitted to the three hundred member churches of the World Council, beginning a "reception" process, a process with more potential for unity than any so far envisioned in the ecumenical movement. As a member of the WCC, The United Methodist Church will be asked to respond to this agreement by the end of 1984.

A second agreement, in development for twenty years, will soon be published by the Consultation on Church Union. This document, in its conception of ordained ministry, is basically similar in direction to the WCC document; it will be submitted to the COCU member churches for their reception by 1988.

Thus the stage is set for major and far-reaching ecumenical agreements on a question that has divided the churches for centuries. How will the various churches of the Wesleyan tradition respond to this challenge, so rich in terms of promise and potential? What contribution will Wesleyan, subsequent Methodist, thought have to make to a *rapprochement* in the area of ordained ministry? And in what areas will present-day Wesleyans need to incorporate elements of ecumenical agreement on ministry (based on very early tradition) which may at first seem strange or even alien? These are some of the questions I shall discuss in this paper.

In a perceptive essay on the reconciliation of ministries written in the early seventies, Albert Outler posed this crucial question: "Is there any way schism and separation can be overcome without forfeiting the values of continuity (apostolic succession) or denying the validity of schismatic orders?" A second statement underlay the first: "The ecumenical task is to find a formula that can allow for regularization without abjuration."[1]

In his usual succinct manner, Dr. Outler encapsulated in these sentences what had become the classic ecumenical dilemma. After all is said and done in terms of theological agreement, at some point the ministries of the churches will need to be reconciled one to another. This will be the case, regardless of the "model" or goal chosen: conciliar fellowship; a communion of communions; covenanted fellowship; church union. How can a Heads-I-Win-Tails-You-Lose posture be avoided? How will the truth preserved on each side be honored and integrated? How can any "sign" of reconciliation be adopted without one group denying its past?

I will argue in this paper that the section on ordained ministry of *BEM* offers both "catholic" and "protestant" churches a way beyond their traditional positions regarding ministry. (Since the basic approach of COCU's agreement on ministry is similar, I shall make the same claim for it. But I will cite the WCC text for the sake of convenience.)

Further, I shall attempt to illustrate that at important points, Wesley (and early Methodism) blazed a trail that anticipated the theological position of *BEM*, even if his thinking was not compatible to it at every point. I shall argue that John Wesley, child of the Reformation and Anglicanism that he was, with thorough insight into the Greek Fathers, in his writing and actions, anticipated the direction taken by this most promising ecumenical agreement on ministry the churches will see in this century.

I shall *also* attempt to identify aspects of the agreement which will probably seem strange to United Methodists, aspects which will demand our (and Wesley's, were he here) stretching beyond where we have been.

In the first section of the paper I shall examine the question of ordination. It is in this section that Methodism has still the most to learn and "gain." In a second section I shall look into the question of "sign," and succession, and "orders" of ministry, including a reconceptualized ministry of bishop. In both sections I shall quote relevant paragraphs of the *BEM* document.

I. ORDINATION
Laying on of Hands with Prayer for the Holy Spirit

The church ordains certain of its members for the ministry in the name of Christ by the invocation of the Spirit and the laying on of hands (I Tim. 4:14; II Tim. 1:6); in doing so it seeks to continue the mission of the apostles and to remain faithful to their teaching. . . . In ordaining, the church, under the inspiration of the Holy Spirit, provides for the faithful proclamation of the gospel and humble service in the name of Christ. The laying on of hands is the sign of the gift of the Spirit, rendering visible the fact that the ministry was instituted in the revelation accomplished in Christ, and reminding the church to look to him as the source of its commission (*BEM* No. 39, p. 30). "The act of ordination by the laying on of hands of those appointed to do so is at one and the same time invocation of the Holy Spirit (*epiklesis*); sacramental sign; acknowledgment of gifts and commitment (No. 41).

The place where the *BEM* text on ordination will impinge most directly on United Methodist history and practice is its firm insistence on the inclusion of the *epiklesis* in the ordination prayer—the prayer for the gift of the Holy Spirit in the life and ministry of the ordained.

Agreement in the text on the centrality of this prayer offers hope of resolving one of the longest standing bases for division in the church. For many centuries the Western church went the way of formalization and juridicizing, pretending that it could control God's actions by its words, actions, and formulations. Over the centuries the simplicity of early church ordination (prayer and the laying on of hands) had been forgotten and replaced by evermore elaborate and presumptuous liturgy.

A. Evaluation of *Epiklesis*

"Ordination was originally conferred in the Church by the Holy Spirit through the laying on of hands and prayer. As more and more candidates came to be ordained at one time, the recitation of a lengthy Ordination Prayer over each ordained became repetitious and time consuming. To solve this problem, hands were imposed on each candidate in *silence*, followed by a single recitation of the Ordination Prayer for all the candidates by the bishop with hands extended over them.

"During the Middle Ages, a short *imperative formula* was added to many ordination rites to be said over each ordinand at the actual laying on of hands, meeting an apparent need for interpretative action and completion which the silence could not supply. Because he presumably lacked liturgical evidence to the contrary, Cranmer retained the imperative formulas with the laying on of hands in the English Ordinal of 1550, from which they passed unquestioned into the ordination rites of American Methodism.

"As a result of these historical developments, the recent practice of the United Methodist Church—and of other Churches of the West—represents a departure from the original imposition of hands accompanied by the prayer of the Church."[2]

In his rite for the ordination of a priest, Cranmer copied Martin Bucer's text almost *verbatim*, except that Cranmer omitted entirely the central section of Bucer's prayer, which was a *petition* that the Holy Spirit might be poured out on the candidates (*Precamur ut spiritum sanctum tuum, in nomine filii tui, opulente in hos ipsos tuos ministros effundos. . .* in Martin Bucer, *De ordinatione legitima ministrorum ecclesiae revocanda*, printed in his *Scripta Anglicana* [Basel, 1577], pp. 239-59).

In his book *The Anglican Ordinal*, Paul Bradshaw traces the reasons for the appearance, and gradual disappearance, of these so-called imperative formulae (*Accipe Spiritum Sanctum*) and the corresponding slow ascent of prayer *in this century* for the outpouring of the Holy Spirit to take the place of the "man-conferred" power in the *Accipe* formula. It is the genius of the *BEM* document (probably under the influence of Eastern Orthodox thought) that it puts a *prayer* at the center of ordination.

B. Wesley and the Invocation of the Spirit

Although proposals for change to more of a prayer format in ordination had been published during the time that reconciliation was being sought between the bishops of the Church of England and the Puritans, the failure of the movement toward the comprehension of Dissenters in 1689 weakened the desire to find ways of reuniting episcopal and nonepiscopal ministries. Thus during the early years of the eighteenth century the Anglican position hardened, the concept of apostolic succession became narrower and more rigid, and the validity of nonepiscopal ministries came under greater siege in the Church of England. This mentality partly explains Wesley's early "high" statements (1774) regarding the necessity of a three-ordered ministry of deacon, priest, and bishop.

It also signifies why Wesley's century was not to see any significant breakthrough in moving away from the imperative formula in ordination rites. Thus, even in his 1788 *Sunday Service of the Methodists with other Occasional Services*, although he calls the bishop "superintendent" and the priest "elder," he repeats the traditional imperative of the 1662 Book of Common Prayer: "Receive the Holy Ghost for the Office and Work of an Elder in the Church of God, now committed unto thee by the imposition of our hands."

In his "Form of Ordaining a Superintendent" we read: "Receive the Holy Ghost.... And remember that thou stir up the grace of God which is given thee by this imposition of our hands, for God hath not given us the spirit of fear, but of power, and love, and soberness."

Although Wesley had retained this imperative formula, the Methodist revision of 1792, fearing the sacerdotal sound of the imperative, altered the text to read, "The Lord pour upon thee the Holy Ghost," in a kind of transitional half command, half request. At least this request used most of the words of Hippolytus' prayer: "Pour forth now that power which is from thee, princely Spirit, which thou gavest to thy beloved Son, Jesus Christ."[3] But these early third-century words were clearly within a *prayer*, whereas the Western version had evolved into a *declaration*.

The transition from Cranmer we have been tracing is completed in the 1980 Alternate Rite for Ordination. A commentary lays the foundation:

Ordination, like baptism, is the gift of the life-giving Spirit of God at work in the community of faith.... The biblical basis of ordination in the Pauline doctrine of the gifts of the Spirit (I Cor. 12) should not be confused with the corporate priesthood of the whole community (Ex. 19:5, 6; I Peter 2:5-9).... Although the ordained ministers of the community share in the priesthood of the community, their representative ministry is based on particular gifts of the Spirit.

Ordination is the gift of the Holy Spirit who acts in and through the action of the Spirit-filled Church. In free and gracious response to the Church's faithful invocation, the Spirit affirms, increases and strengthens the Spirit-given gifts and graces (charisms) which are the evidence of the divine call on which the ecclesiastical call to ordained ministry is based.[4]

The proposed rite includes both the traditional *Veni Creator Spiritus*, which all sing together, but then proceeds further to an intentional *epiklesis*:

We praise you, eternal God, our Creator and Preserver,
because you have called us in your infinite love
to be a priestly people,
Offering to you acceptable worship
through Jesus Christ our Lord,
whom you have given us
to be the Apostle and High Priest of our confession
and the Shepherd and Bishop of our souls.
We thank you
that, by dying, Christ has overcome death,
and, having ascended on high
has poured forth your gifts abundantly on your people,
making some apostles, some prophets,
some evangelists, some pastors and teachers,
for the perfecting of the saints for the work of ministry,
for the building up of Christ's Body, the Church,
and for the fulfilling of your gracious purpose in the world.
As once you looked upon your chosen people
and commanded Moses to choose elders
whom you filled with the same spirit you had given him,
now fill with your Holy Spirit,
through Jesus Christ our Lord,
for the ministry of an elder in your Church,
your servants ...[5]

How close this understanding is to the WCC thinking can be discerned by quoting the ministry document again:

Properly speaking then, ordination denotes an action by God and the community by which the ordained are strengthened by the Spirit for their task and are upheld by the acknowledgment and prayers of the congregation. (No. 40).

Ordination is an invocation to God that the new minister be given the power of the Holy Spirit in the new relation which is established between this minister and the local Christian community and, by intention, the Church universal. The otherness of God's initiative, of which the ordained ministry is a sign, is here acknowledged in the act of ordination itself. "The Spirit blows where it wills" (John 3:3); the invocation of the Spirit implies the absolute dependence on God for the outcome of the Church's prayer. This means that the Spirit may set new forces in motion and open new possibilities "far more abundantly than all that we ask or think" (Eph. 3:20; No. 42).

Ordination is a sign of the granting of this prayer by the Lord who gives the gift of the ordained ministry. Although the outcome of the Church's *epiklesis* depends on the freedom of God, the Church ordains in the confidence that God, being faithful to his promise in Christ, enters sacramentally into contingent, historical forms of human relationship and uses them for his purpose. Ordination is a sign performed in faith that the spiritual relationship signified is present in, with and through the words spoken, the gestures made, and the forms employed (No. 43).

We have tried to indicate how the ecumenical convergence is offering a more primitive, and more promising way of praying for the Spirit's gifts in ordination, than that which Methodism has traditionally used. As Bradshaw indicates, there is great hope in restoring a *prayer* for the Spirit's presence and blessing of a person's ministry. The "imperative formula" had no place in primitive rites, it detracts from the ordination prayers, and it suggests that grace can be bestowed by command rather than being sought in prayer.[6] Use of the ancient prayer including the *epiklesis*, will enrich the ordination prayer by which United Methodists ordain their representative ministers.

C. Other Aspects

Other elements of the agreement on ordination will impinge, in a derivative fashion, on United Methodists. The ecumenical agreement stresses that ordination best takes place in the context of the Eucharist, or Lord's Supper. Orthodox ecclesiology has been especially effective in bringing into this agreement the inescapable relation between the early presbyter/bishop and the gathered community around the Lord's Supper. From this derives the placing of ordination itself in the setting of Eucharist.

A long and early Christian tradition places ordination in the context of worship and especially of the eucharist. Such a place for the service of ordination preserves the understanding of ordination as an act of the whole community, and not of a certain order within it or of the individual ordained (No. 41).

This is the position accepted by the new alternative Ordinal of United Methodism:

The alternative Ordinal recommends that ordination normally take place within the service of Word and Table—its traditional context—and be concluded by the Lord's Supper, with Holy Communion served to the entire congregation. Not all apparent change demands a painful surrender of the past, nor is all reverence for the past the result of romantic illusion. Sometimes progress is made by the recovery of a valuable heritage. According to the tradition of the former Methodist Church, provision for the Lord's Supper at ordinations is not innovation, but restoration. Although the Lord's Supper was eliminated from the ordination of elders in 1792, it was retained at the ordination of deacons and at the consecration of bishops until 1858 in the Methodist Episcopal Church, South, at the ordination of deacons until 1886 and at the consecration of bishops until 1916 in the Methodist Episcopal Church.[7]

Thus accepting the *BEM* text would strengthen our resolve to return to the early church practice. It is a "restoration" for which many have yearned. For example, in commenting on the lack of the Lord's Supper in the 1964 Ordinal, Albert Outler hopes:

In some future revision one might hope that the ancient linkage between ordination and Eucharist will be restored, as we come to understand their quintessential connection of ministry and sacraments, both in the life of the church and her ministry in Christ's name.[8]

This is also a position in which Wesley had sound instincts, but varying practice. He struggled his entire life to hold eucharistic ministry to his ordained elders, and he constantly urged his societies to receive the Lord's Supper from them or from Church of England priests. But he could still ordain Coke, Whatcoat, and Vasey in a small room in the middle of the night, in the absence of the community and the Eucharist. (But Archbishop M. Parker had also been ordained at 6:00 a.m. in a very similar setting!) We do not know enough about Wesley's other ordinations to be able to say whether they were always in the context of the Lord's Supper. We do know however, that in the Service of 1788, he stipulated: "After delivering the Bible, the Superintendent shall go on in the Service of Communion, which all they that receive Orders shall take together."[9] So by that point in his thinking, Wesley agreed that the ordinands at least should receive the Lord's Supper. But American Methodism dropped this connection between ordination and the Lord's Supper in 1792. With the *BEM* agreement, however (which is reflected in the *Alternative Rite*), the ancient rite is restored in which the entire community joins in the Communion. What better place for the new presbyters to first administer the Lord's Supper than this?

1. *Gifts, graces, and fruit*

Wesley, in his "gifts, graces, and fruit" criteria for ministry, accurately anticipated modern stipulations. The "call" also appears prominently in the *BEM* text.

Ordination is an acknowledgment by the Church of the gifts of the Spirit in the one ordained, and a commitment by both the Church and the ordinand to the new relationship. By receiving the new minister in the act of ordination, the congregation acknowledges the minister's gifts and commits itself to be open towards these gifts. Likewise these ordained offer their gifts to the Church and commit themselves to the burden and opportunity of new authority and responsibility (No. 44).

People are called in differing ways to the ordained ministry. There is a personal awareness of a call from the Lord to dedicate oneself to the ordained ministry. This call may be discerned through personal prayer and reflection, as well as through suggestion, example, encouragement, guidance coming from family, friends, the congregation, teachers, and other church authorities. This call must be authenticated by the Church's recognition of the gifts and graces of the particular person, both natural and spiritually given, needed for the ministry to be performed. God can use people both celibate and married for the ordained ministry (No. 45).

2. Secular ministry

In his early use of "part-time" preachers, Wesley also anticipated later agreement, where it is assumed that *some* presbyters may serve in "tent-making" ministries. To be sure, Methodism very soon moved to a "full-time" presbyteral ministry, and the *BEM* document assumes that as the normal pattern as well. But paragraph 46 is clearly making way for a new and different type of deacon, one who will live a Christian presence in some professional "secular" occupation:

Ordained persons may be professional ministers in the sense that they receive their salaries from the church. The church may also ordain people who remain in other occupations or employment (No. 46).

Deacons represent to the Church its calling as servant in the world. By struggling in Christ's name with the myriad needs of societies and persons, deacons exemplify the interdependence of worship and service in the Church's life. They exercise responsibility in the worship of the congregation: for example by reading the scriptures, preaching and leading the people in prayer. They help in the teaching of the congregation. They exercise a ministry of love within the community. They fulfill certain administrative tasks and may be elected to responsibilities for governance (No. 31).

Thus the great importance in Methodism continuing its search for a new type of deacon, one not bound to apprenticeship and transition to the elder's ministry, but exercising a professional ministry in its own right.

3. Sequence, progression of orders

From his practice, more than his words, we can deduce that John Wesley did not really challenge the sequential ordination practice which had developed in the Western church (and was then current in the Church of England), which assumed "deacons' orders" were, to all intents and purposes, a first step to that of a presbyter. In the score or so people he ordained, "in most instances, probably in all, they were ordained deacons one day; and, on the day following, received the ordination of elders."[10] Having no integrity as a ministry itself, the diaconate could be superseded by elder's ordinations of which we have record. Wesley *did* challenge the developing petrification of the ministry of *bishop*, but apparently did not see that a challenge to an "ascent" from presbyter to bishop also called into question a "ladder progression" from deacon to elder. The final collect of the Cranmer rite for the diaconate, for example, expected the candidate to pass "from this inferior office" to "higher ministries."[11] And Wesley wrote, concerning his estimate of this office: "That the seven deacons were outwardly ordained, even to that low office, cannot be denied."[12] Only in 1916 was "inferior" dropped from that phrase "inferior office."[13] But the lowliness of the ministry of deacon has continued to the present disciplinary definition of diaconate as the preparation for a ministry one does not yet have.

It will therefore represent a change for United Methodism to accept the implications of a departure from this traditional ladder concept, even though Methodism developed only a two-step, rather than a three-step, ladder.

But the *BEM* document, avoiding the legalistic *ordo* language of the past, develops a three-fold ministry in which each office has its own biblical and early church integrity, and offers us all a more authentic understanding of ordination, set-apart ministry, and "orders" as such. We turn now, in the second part of this paper, to a consideration as to how ordained ministries might be reconciled.

II
RECONCILIATION OF MINISTRIES

Introduction

In the second part of this paper I shall attempt to do two things: After observing the *BEM* recommendations as to how reconciliation of ministries might be achieved (Para. 53a, b), I shall examine how Wesley's use of *sign* in ordination (laying on of hands) and his concern for orderly *succession* were vital parts of his own practice. They also underlie what *BEM* recommends in a reconciliation procedure. Key to the entire matter is an understanding of succession within the apostolicity of the church.

I shall also argue that the theological understanding of ministry in *BEM* (assuming a three-fold ordained ministry of service) would represent a justifiable strengthening of the present two-order position of United Methodism; concentration will focus on the ministry of bishop.

A. Apostolicity—Faith and Works

> Churches which have preserved the episcopal succession are asked to recognize both the apostolic content of the ordained ministry which exists in churches which have not maintained such succession and also the existence in these churches of a ministry of *episkope* in various forms (No. 53a.).

I believe accepting and receiving the ministry text of *BEM* will represent an authentication of Methodism's own past, reminding us of the vital places where we have maintained early church ministry, of where we have departed *from* it, and bringing some new impulses to our present understanding that we lack and need.

Wesley struggled for many years to maintain the unity of his movement with the Church of England by steadfastly refusing to ordain, even after he became convinced that in the early church presbyter/bishop were of the same order and that therefore he had a *theological* right to proceed. He could abide with this position as long as the mission of the church as he understood it was not being damaged. In England he could appoint preachers to preach a more authentic gospel (he scrutinized them very carefully), and his people could receive the sacraments in the Church of England. His was a movement of reform and "completeness."

But when there was no more established church in the United States from 1784 onward, his scruples were ended. Now the mission of the church *was* being adversely affected, and thus he not only *could* ordain, he *must*.

Almost forty years earlier he had articulated the insight upon which he now acted:

> Lord King's *Account of the Primitive Church* convinced me many years ago that bishops and presbyters are the same order, and consequently have the same right to ordain. For many years I have been importuned from time to time to exercise the right by ordaining part of our traveling preachers. But I have still refused, not only for peace's sake, but because I was determined as little as possible to violate the established order of the National Church to which I belonged.
>
> But the case is widely different between England and North America. Here there are bishops who have a legal jurisdiction: in America there are none, neither any parish ministers. So that for some hundred of miles together there is none either to baptize or to administer the Lord's Supper. Here, therefore, my scruples are at an end.[14]

To Wesley, faithful mission demanded wholeness *and* unity. Thus in England, Wesley believed it was his responsibility to fulfill that part of the mission of the church which had been neglected, to reconstitute the apostolic obedience of the church—thus he and his preachers rode the length and breadth of Britain preaching that the Holy Spirit might awaken faith in his hearers, that the church might hear a *whole* gospel. But in accordance with his concern for the *oneness* of the church, which was also constitutive in its mission, Wesley believed that he *dare* not allow unordained preachers to administer the sacraments in his societies—for (in accordance with his interpretation of the sacraments and ordination), the administration of the sacraments was being legitimately cared for by the ordained priests of the Church of England. As Colin Williams put it:

> Wesley struggled to an amazing degree to keep unity within the Church, because he believed that not only the true preaching of the Word, but also the unity and continuity of the Church were vital to her mission. . . . He struggled ceaselessly to keep the unity of the Church in terms of its continuity through the historic ministry, sacraments, and liturgy.[15]

The overall point I am driving at in this section is that Wesley's basic intention in organizing a movement and ordaining presbyters was that the *apostolic* gospel in the Church of England continue to be heard, believed, and acted upon. He saw himself as an extraordinary messenger ("sent out," *apostello*) to keep this apostolic gospel before the people in all its fullness and vigor.

This gospel included repentance, living faith in Jesus Christ (justification), and works of loving service and growth toward perfection (sanctification).

Wesley's holding together of these dimensions of apostolicity is also found in *BEM*:

> In the Creed, the Church confesses to be apostolic. The Church lives in continuity with the apostles and their proclamation. The same Lord who sent the apostles continues to be present in the Church.

The Spirit keeps the Church in the apostolic tradition until the fulfilment of history in the Kingdom of God; Apostolic tradition in the Church means continuity in the permanent characteristics of the Church of the apostles: witness to the apostolic faith, proclamation and fresh interpretation of the Gospel, celebration of baptism and the eucharist, the transmission of ministerial responsibilities, communion in prayer, love, joy, and suffering, service to the sick and the needy, unity among the local churches and sharing the gifts which the Lord has given to each (No. 34).

Thus Wesley, in his insistence on a ministry which combined preaching the apostolic faith with full involvement in works of mercy and love, anticipated the direction of modern ecumenical thinking on the meaning of apostolicity. This means that Methodism (which has maintained Wesley's bifocal concern) will have every reason to have its apostolicity recognized by the "catholic church" as they "receive" and act on the *BEM* agreement. This attempt to hold together the various elements of apostolicity *within the church* was truly one of Wesley's vital insights and contributions.

B. The "Sign" of Reconciliation

The second half of the "reconciliation paragraph" of the *BEM* document directs its recommendation to the churches which have not through the centuries put stock in, or attempted to maintain, a "historic succession" in the episcopacy.

> Churches without the episcopal succession, and living in faithful continuity with the apostolic faith and mission, have a ministry of Word and sacraments, as is evident from the belief, practice, and life of those churches. These churches are asked to realize that the continuity with the Church of the apostles finds profound expression in the successive laying on of hands by bishops and that, though they may not lack the continuity of the apostolic tradition, this sign will strengthen and deepen that continuity. They may need to recover the sign of the episcopal succession (No. 53a).

This somewhat convoluted paragraph states a position, and then recommends that the churches without "succession bishops" be willing to reconcile their ministries with the "catholic" churches by accepting some kind of laying on of hands within a larger reconciliation. Such a recommendation, in the context of the entire ministry document, clearly presupposes the acceptance of a three-fold ministry.

The chronology of the evolution of Wesley's thought on the subject of three-*ordered* ministry is well known. He had begun his ministry believing

in the necessity of episcopal ordination and the validity of apostolic succession.

> We believe it would not be right for us to administer either baptism or the Lord's Supper unless we had a commission to do so from the bishop whom we apprehend to be in succession from the Apostles. . . . We believe that the threefold order of ministers . . . is not only authorized by its apostolic institution, but also by the written word.[16]

In July 1756, he wrote to Charles:

> As to my own judgment, I still believe the Episcopal form of Church government to be both scriptural and apostolical: I mean, well agreeing with the practice and writings of the Apostles. But that it is prescribed in Scripture I do not believe.[17]

In 1784, explaining his ordinations of Coke, Whatcoat, and Vasey, he based his right, not on the theory that *anyone* could ordain, or that ordination was only a sociological phenomenon, but rather that he had ordained as a *presbyter*, and that ordination by presbyters had been done validly (more often than he knew) in church history. Samuel Drew, who was Coke's biographer and had known him personally, cites the history of the church at Alexandria, as having been in Wesley's mind when he ordained. In that church the presbyters, on the death of a bishop, ordained one of their own number as the new bishop, and this practice continued until the time of Dionysius. In a 1785 letter to Charles, John reiterated his position: "I firmly believe I am a scriptural *episkopos* as much as any man in England, or in Europe; for the uninterrupted succession I know to be a fable, which no man ever did or can prove."[18]

What is clear in this is that Wesley did not equate succession with a juridical chain of laying on of hands by persons called bishops. To him apostolicity was vital, and orderly transmission of a commission was valuable as well. But this is the very position on the basis of which paragraph 53b can suggest to the "catholic" churches that the others are apostolic!

Other factors can be mentioned to remind the reader of Wesley's great concern to maintain the sign and orderly succession in regard to ordination.

1. *Fluvanna schism*

There is, for example, the incident during the Revolutionary War (1779) when a group of Methodist preachers established a presbytery and ordained themselves presbyters (Fluvanna Schism). Asbury, in hiding at the time, was in touch with Wesley, and finally prevailed upon them to desist from exercising these ordinations in sacramental ministry until a constitutional ordination could be provided.[19] In Wesley's eyes, such "ordinations" were invalid.

2. *Application for ordination*

Wesley also applied to the bishop of London for ordination for some of his preachers, without success. His application to Dr. Louth shows how seriously he took orderly transmission and the "sign," even as late as 1783! There is also the intriguing story of his having applied for ordination to a wandering Orthodox bishop, (but this may well be in need of de-mythologizing).

3. *Terms employed*

There is, third, good evidence that even Wesley's "setting apart" of Coke as a superintendent was intended to be an ordination, not merely an installation. Although the ordination was certainly "irregular," in his diary he used the word *ordination* to describe his action. And even though he did *not* use the word "ordain" in public documents, Charles Wesley surely understood that John had indeed intended his laying on of hands to be ordination. The hymn Charles wrote immediately on hearing the news of Coke's ordination did not get into the hymnbook, but it illustrates his realization that John had indeed meant to ordain.

So easily are Bishops made
   By man's, or woman's whim?
W_____ his hands on C_____ hath laid,
   But who laid hands on Him?

Hands on himself he laid, and took
   An Apostolic Chair:
And then ordain's his Creature C_____
   His Heir and Successor.

Episcopalians, now no more
   With Presbyterians fight,
But give your needless Contest o'er,
   Whose Ordination's right?'

It matter not, if Both are One,
   Or different in degree,
For lo! ye see contain'd in John
   The whole Presbytery![20]

4. *The American church*

The services John provided for the American church clearly include ordination for deacon, elder, and superintendent. And the authority he conferred on his superintendents is the administrative and sacramental authority that has been traditionally associated with bishops.

But more important, the episcopacy of Methodism, even as it adapted to the democratic spirit of American life, did not relinquish or even share with others the traditional right to ordain. Thus, although eventually almost all administrative functions of a bishop could be delegated to the annual conference, ordination was reserved to the bishop alone.

Even more remarkable, in its rite for the ordination of deacons, Methodism retained the traditional practice in which *only* the bishop laid on hands!

These factors indicate that Wesley went to great lengths to fulfill the very elements mentioned in paragraph 53*b* of *BEM* regarding the *use* of the apostolic sign and the proper transmittal of the ministerial commission.

There is another demurrer in the *BEM* document which will help United Methodists accept the "sign." In paragraph 38 it is stated, that although churches "engaged in union negotiations are expressing willingness to accept episcopal succession as a sign of the apostolicity of the life of the whole Church, . . . they cannot accept any suggestion that the ministry exercised in their own tradition should be invalid until the moment that it enters into an existing line of episcopal succession. Their acceptance of the episcopal succession will best further the unity of the whole Church if it is part of a wider process by which the episcopal churches themselves also regain their lost unity."

That is to say, the *BEM* text makes a point of refuting any suggestion that "accepting the episcopal sign" is in any way an abjuration of existing ministry. This is all the more important to United Methodists, whose own "episcopal succession," as I tried to show in a book written twenty years ago, fulfills all the theological criteria of what succession is intended to accomplish.

C. The "Churchly" Context

In this paper, I have, at several points, mentioned how important Wesley felt it was to maintain communion with the Church of England—"If the Methodists leave the Church, God will leave them." Although his ordinations broke the law of his church, he stoutly held to a succession of transmission of authority from it, many times mentioning his own "episcopal" authority as an ordained priest in the Church of England; he even used a "presbytery" of three persons (Creighton, Coke, and himself) to ordain Whatcoat and Vasey.

Here was the dilemma: orderly transmission he saw as essential, as a theological and "right teaching" criterion, even if that transmission was a breaking of church law. But he also, in the teeth of accusations of inconsistency, held to membership in the church. He would not leave it voluntarily, and the bishops did not expel him. It is my contention that the reason for this apparent inconsistency is Wesley's realization that, as the *BEM* statement puts it, the "primary manifestion of apostolic succession is to be found in the apostolic tradition of the Church as a whole." He knew the uninterrupted succession of bishops "to be a fable," but he strove mightily to maintain it in an orderly fashion among his own followers, *always however, in relationship to the national church*, and the means of grace which he believed it communicated. Succession had its primary value as part of the apostolic tradition which that *whole* church embodied!

At this point it is valuable to quote paragraph 35 of *BEM*:

> The primary manifestation of apostolic succession is to be found in the apostolic tradition of the Church as a whole. The succession is an expression of the permanence and, therefore, of the continuity of Christ's own mission in which the Church participates. Within the Church the ordained ministry has a particular task of preserving and actualizing the apostolic faith. The orderly transmission of the ordained ministry is therefore a powerful expression of the continuity of the Church throughout history; it also underlines the calling of the ordained minister as guardian of the faith.

Although he would not have phrased it in just those words, Wesley's actions indicate that he saw that succession did not validate the apostolicity of the church, but rather that succession found its meaning and value as part of the larger apostolic *tradition* of the whole church.

The hinge on which paragraph 53 of *BEM* rests is clear: the paragraph carefully balances its suggestion that "non-episcopal" churches accept the sign of laying on of hands of a bishop with a proposal that the "episcopal" churches, on their part, recognize the apostolic content and the *episkope* of the "synodal" churches' ordained ministry.

What more could be required by Methodists, or admitted by others? The basic reason Wesley dared risk a rupture in the unity of the church was his concern for its *full* apostolicity. If that point is not conceded by the "catholic" churches, can we not, and *should* we not, accept the traditional sign on a wider basis, for the sake of the *catholicity* of the church? It is my contention that we should, that we can do just that in the context of this agreement produced over fifty years by representatives of most of the world's churches, and that Wesley's thinking and actions offer us a rationale as to why such an action will be appropriate at this point in history for christians who trace their family tree to this extraordinary minister.

Albert Outler wrote in 1964:

> [Methodism] has never developed—on its own and for itself—the full panoply of bell, book, and candle that goes with being a "proper" church properly self-understood. This makes us *Une église manqué*, theoretically and actually. . . . One of our difficulties, I suggest, is that Methodism's unique ecclesiological pattern was really designed to function best *within* an encompassing environment of *catholicity* (by which I mean what the word meant originally: the effectual and universal Christian *community*). . . . We need a catholic church within which to function as a proper evangelical order of witness and worship, discipline and nurture.[21]

Already fifty years ago J. E. Rattenbury perceived that Methodism was feeling after a kind of catholicity.[24] I am arguing that participation in a service of mutual "laying on of hands" in a national service of reconciliation of COCU, or in some larger endeavor of a similar nature as suggested in *BEM*, would indeed relate Methodism to the universal Christian community, and begin to provide that "encompassing environment of catholicity" still lacking. Indeed, the so-called catholic churches would become more truly catholic in such a reconciliation as well!

Whether or not Methodism might serve as an order within the *Una Sancta*, it certainly needs to be related to the whole in a more integral fashion, in order that its concern for holiness and evangelism might serve more as a "leaven" (the word is Wesley's) in the ecumenical movement. As Geoffrey Wainwright puts it:

> A more catholic environment will in turn restore to it [Methodism] the sacramental dimension which the Wesleys' teaching and practice never lacked. The visibility of the Church and its unity is at stake. The alternative to visible unity is not spiritual unity, but visible disunity; and that is a counter-testimony to the gospel.[23]

And last but certainly not least, United Methodism has a contribution to make to a process of reconciliation. Out of several elements that could be named, one must at least mention its growing, fruitful, and promising experience with the ordained ministry of women, including the episcopacy! Methodism's superintendency continues its "frontier" ministry, and others can gain "catholicity" from us! Reconciliation is a two-way street. Another would be this: "We have a vital linkage with every major bloc in Christendom, and yet our independent mission in the modern world continues to cast us in a role that needs to be maximized within a catholic whole: as catalysts, critics, and pragmatists."[24]

(After Vatican II there was a joke to the effect that, to Vatican III the bishops would be bringing their wives, and that to Vatican IV the bishops would be bringing their husbands!) United Methodists will be able to interpret their experience, if called upon, when the catholic churches catch up.

D. An Implication of Reconciliation—Threefold Ministry

To conclude this paper I shall explore in more depth, one dimension that would need to accompany such a reconciliation.

To truly reap the benefits from, and enter fully into, shared *episkope*, or united episcopal ministry with other churches, it would seem necessary for United Methodism eventually to conceive and exercise its episcopacy as a third ministry, and not just an extension of the ministry of elder. I am intentionally avoiding the term *order*, because I believe that we no longer need to accept uncritically all the historical accretions that make up the concept "order". Neither the WCC document nor the COCU agreement ever employs the term—that silence is not coincidental.

In our day scholars understand better the origin, cultural conditioning, and aberrations that order has undergone through history. There is great difference between the Greek *cheirotonein* of the New Testament (which could mean an act of extending or laying on of hands, or even of appointing), and the Latin translation *ordo* or *ordinare*. *Ordo* was inevitably associated with Roman law and quickly took on the notion of a special status and class which was foreign to the early church.

Some years ago I tried to demonstrate that Wesley was right when he affirmed that in the first Christian generation there was a parity in the ministry of presbyters and bishops, and that ordination by a presbyter would therefore be *valid*, even if irregular. That truth is now widely accepted by scholars; it substantiates Wesley's

claim that his ordinations were theologically justifiable by primitive church standards. He was struggling (rightfully) against a juridical notion of order which had separated the work of a presbyter and bishop in a mechanical and legalistic fashion.

It is my conviction that *BEM* and *Quest* now make it possible to speak of an ordained three-fold ministry of deacon, presbyter (elder), and bishop, without needing to subscribe to the juridical and fullness elements of *ordo* to which Wesley objected, and therefore, that we can and should accept a renewed episcopacy as an ordained ministry distinct from that of elder.

To be sure, both the documents of Vatican II on episcopacy and the new Episcopal Church prayerbook continue to use the three-*order* description. But in both churches, scholarly work is making more modest historical assertions about the first and second centuries. And interestingly, the Canterbury agreement on ministry between these two churches is more restrained on this score than the individual claims of either! In fact, the Canterbury Statement does not use the term "three orders" at all! The joint statement on ministry and ordination of these two churches more faithfully reflects the present position of the academic communities of both churches than either individual position.

1. United Methodist movement

When, in the mid-70s, the WCC published the interim results of its attempt to find agreement on the ordained ministry, precursor of *BEM*, The United Methodist Church was asked, and agreed to make an official response to this document. Representatives (including theologians, pastors, and lay persons) of our church were assembled by the Council of Bishops through the Division of Ecumenical and Interreligious Concerns. To illustrate United Methodist openness on the question of order, I shall quote one paragraph from this *Response*:

> We have emphasized that the episcopacy is not a third order, but presbyters are consecrated to that particular office. In the light of the COCU discussion, we realize with added force that our use of the name and office of bishop has not been totally in keeping with the usage in the wider tradition of Christianity and requires continued rethinking.[25]

Regarding the sacramentality of ordination, it should be noted that in the final report of the United Methodist–Roman Catholic bilateral conversation, *Holiness and Spirituality of the*

Ordained Ministry, it was agreed that "Ordination is a sacramental act by which the church recognizes and authenticates the Spirit's call of certain persons to fulfill the particular functions." It is clear that The United Methodist Church is moving toward agreement that ordination has a sacramental dimension.

2. Ordo or ordering?

Our conception of "orders" as such, has come to us through the Western part of the church, through Rome and Canterbury. Even in these churches the exact *meaning* of order has fluctuated throughout history. As eminent a theologian as Thomas Aquinas believed that the bishop shares the *basic* order of the priest, at least in its medival setting. Cranmer held this viewpoint as well.

But what about that setting? Perhaps the single most influential person in the development of the concept of "order" was Augustine, who in *De civitate Dei* developed a highly "ordered" explanation of the structure of the world. "From Augustine was drawn in large part the consequent patristic and medieval emphasis on order, rooted in Neo-platonic thought. . . . In this view everything has its proper place, . . . and the notion of the church as hierarchical is cast in the image of a multi-level society."[26] The concept was basic in Roman law.

Perhaps what needs most to be questioned today is how *order* was later made normative in the church. The emerging ecclesiastical structure was rationalized, and the result was "the elevation to the status of an intrinsically necessary and essential reality a structural evolution that was, at least to some extent, the result of human decision and specific social needs."[27]

But since the *juridical* notions of order are being called into question in today's ecumenical thinking, and emphasis is being placed more on a three-fold ministry of diverse gifts and service, I believe that The United Methodist Church can include *its* bishops within such a three-fold ministry, stripped of traditional legalistic and hierarchical baggage. We authorize and lay hands on bishops, but do we not also recognize God's call and gifting, and invoke God's presence and grace in the bishop's ministry? Do we not understand this ministry as identifiable and accountable? The calling, function, and gifts of United Methodist bishops *are* different from those of the elder. Is not this what *ordering* meant in the early church?

The description of ordination in paragraphs 429-32 of the *Discipline* are completely compatible with my proposal. Could not The United Methodist Church thus serve as a bridge between traditional Reformed and Roman Catholic conceptions of episcopacy?

Reinforcing the logic of this question is our present ambiguous use of *two* orders. We have gradually forgotten *why* the deacon should represent an order by itself; we behave as if the deacon is the introductory step to elder's ordination. Thus we need to take seriously the recommendations of the committee that has proposed a new kind of diaconate. There is now, de facto, greater difference between the ministry of a bishop and an elder than there is between that of the elder and the deacon. Yet we claim that the bishop and elder are part of the same order, while the deacon and the elder are of *different* orders! Clearly we have not been consistent.

Furthermore, scholars have noted that Asbury and Coke utilized the word "ordination" to describe the service which set *them* apart to the episcopacy.

If the logic of the previous paragraph is convincing, it would seem that The United Methodist Church can also employ the term "ordination" to describe the rite by which the bishop is commissioned to service. Its New Testament usage refers to an appointing; let us restore the original context. It should also be noted that our Methodist cousins in Great Britain felt able to utilize this term in the ordinal they prepared with the Church of England in the mid-sixties.

3. Possible implications for United Methodists

Several results can be expected if The United Methodist Church moves in the direction I am arguing. First, at some point in the future United Methodist ministries will probably be reconciled to those of other churches. If the theological basis worked out in the COCU is accepted, the common terminology will be of great assistance.

Second, I believe that a shift to traditional ordination terminology will allow us to reemphasize, in a healthy fashion, some of the early church responsibilities of the bishop. Professor Robert Nelson puts it forcefully:

The member of another episcopal-type church who reads *The Discipline* is no doubt disappointed in the total lack of any theological or historical warrant for episcopacy. . . . Nothing is said about the bishop's ministry as made familiar in recent ecumenical discussions of the office. Is the bishop *pastor pastorum*? Is he guardian of the faith "once delivered to the saints," and hence a teacher? Is the bishop a sacramental figure, a eucharistic leader? Does the bishop symbolize the unity of the whole church on earth?[281]

Many of these traditional roles of the bishop are indeed referred to in the alternate ordinal the 1980 General Conference approved. United Methodist bishops do, in fact, serve many of these ministries already. And there is general mention of them in such disciplinary paragraphs as 518-22.

In Methodist and Evangelical United Brethren history we maintained a *feeling* for the traditional roles of early bishops. For example, although the annual conference can replace the bishops on many occasions, we traditionally insisted that only bishops ordain. Why? Our bishops have been exemplary for their zeal in the early church episcopal responsibility of evangelism. In recent times they have led in the struggle for social justice. But would not our *intentions* be made more clear, if we spelled out more specifically areas of episcopal responsibility such as those one finds in the COCU text: liturgical leader, teacher of the apostolic faith, pastoral overseer, leader in mission, representative minister in the act of ordination, administrative leader, servant of unity.

A third result of a united, ordained episcopacy would probably be a questioning of Methodism's traditional *itinerant* episcopacy. Is our itinerant episcopacy something helpful for a past era which we can now leave behind, or is it something essential for which we must contend?

I would argue the former. It is clear that Wesley's practice of constant itineracy as the first Methodist superintendent was greatly influenced by the milieu. He felt the need to oversee (super-vise) the whole, and only he could do it adequately. Methodism was a movement *in* the Church of England, and thus he could not and would not be settled in a diocese as the bishops were. For a movement *within* a national church, this made good sense.

But does it still? We have made a principle of the itineracy of our bishops, until now many pastors remain in one congregation longer than our bishops may stay in an area! To be sure, bishops need to be bishops who can function anywhere they are called. And they need to personify and embody the national and world church where they serve.

But I would suggest that they also need a longer and visible connection to the *place* they serve. Would not the church be enriched if each bishop could develop and maintain more lasting relationships with pastors and congregations of their areas? Surely what New Testament evidence we have, scanty as it is, would call for a more personal relationship of the bishops to their elders, as well as to their flocks. By his person, the bishop has traditionally testified to the interrelationship of all congregations in the one body of Christ; for this symbol to be alive it is necessary that a bishop be able to visit the congregations with some frequency, be able to listen *to* them, and interpret universal concerns *for* them. The New Testament exhortations concerning the focus of episcopal responsibility are always quite local.

To be sure, such an episcopacy would require more bishops, each with fewer numbers of persons to oversee, with less staggering geographical responsibilities.

Such "localization" would also have the effect of giving more attention to the organized mission of the congregation and annual conference. Ecumenical study has called attention once again to the church's responsibility to serve and sanctify the community and society around it. To do this, the church and its bishop need to be living parts *of* that society. Historically there has been a close relationship between the *polis* (city) and the bishop. How can a bishop truly be an integral part of a city if he or she needs to move every eight or twelve years? We can surely find a better symbol of the universal role of the bishop than this constant movement. At any rate, our pilgrimage from *ecclesiola in ecclesia* (England), to *ecclesia*, to a more complete ecclesiological form of life in the future indicates our taking more seriously the smaller diocesan patterns of episcopacy of the early church.

But does this mean giving up our traditional episcopal concern for the *whole*? On the contrary, it means enlarging our *conception* of the whole. In the words of Professor John Deschner of Perkins School of Theology:

> The whole, for whose unity episcopacy is responsible, cannot be merely a denomination, but must be the whole community of God, both in its visible form as the one church of Jesus Christ, and in its latent form as "all persons of good will." . . . Hence ecumenical responsibility is the first responsibility of Christian bishops, and ecumenical recognizability is crucial to their efforts and authority.[29]

This enlargement of responsibility and recognizability is precisely what the ecumenical documents on ministry are intended to accomplish. For these and similar reasons it is my conviction that United Methodist bishops' authenticity and service will be enhanced in the future church by their being ordained into a three-fold ministry.

Even an English Methodist, Geoffrey Wainwright, who has not experienced episcopacy at first hand, can write:

> I join with the Lima text in holding that the ministry of bishop, presbyter and deacon may serve today as an expression of the unity we seek and also as a means of achieving it, always supposing that churches with and without this pattern should together seek "how its potential can be fully developed for the most effective witness of the Church in this world."[30]

Crucial, of course, will be end of the *BEM* sentence: the acceptance of the episcopal succession by those churches without it should be part of a wider process by which the episcopal churches themselves also regain their lost unity.

Albert Outler concluded an essay on ministry with these words:

> Given the undiminished imperatives to Christian unity under which all the churches stand (condemned, one thinks, for their apathy and indifference) and given our recent but enlarging experiences of mutual recognition and mutual cooperation in ministry, can we hope and pray for yet another ecumenical breakthrough—in which the gap between the "ordinary" and "extra-ordinary" ministries thrown up by the tragic vicissitudes of our separate histories might be bridged, by divine grace and human magnanimity?[31]

I have been arguing that the *BEM* text on ministry, with its suggested way of reconciling ministries, can indeed provide such an ecumenical breakthrough—one in which United Methodists will experience new richness and treasures, but also one in which they may feel very much "at home," given Methodism's origin, its history, and its goal.

In 1964 Outler wrote:

> Every denomination in a divided and broken Christendom is an *ecclesiola in via*, but Methodists have a peculiar heritage that might make the transitive character of our ecclesiastical existence not only tolerable but positively proleptic. On our pilgrimage toward the actualization of the unity in Christ that God has given us and still wills for us to have, we can take both courage and zest from the fact that what we really have to contribute to any emergent Christian community is not our apparatus but our mission.[32]

"The transitive character of our ecclesiastical existence"; those lines are a good description of traditional Wesleyan Methodism—transitive in the sense of active verbs, whose object is direct.

It is my conviction that United Methodism's *mission* (on which we have general agreement) will be enlarged and enhanced through an integration of our "apparatus" (ministry) into a more catholic understanding and exercise of ordained leadership as the *BEM* document requests.

Where such reconciliation might lead is not yet clear. Although denominations might continue for some time, certainly some sharing of identity is involved in being "one body" in the New Testament sense. According to Wesley's intention, Methodism was to serve as leaven in the loaf. Might the vision of its founder(s) be most fully carried out with this leaven freed of its denominational form, enabled to flavor a "conciliar fellowship" (using the WCC terminology)?

> Who should know better than we [Methodists] that denominations may be justified in their existence for this "time being" or that, but not forever? We were commissioned by the Spirit of God "for the time being" to carry out an extraordinary mission of witness and service, for just so long as our life apart is effective in the economy of God's providence. We are, or ought to be, prepared to risk our life as a separate church and to face death as a denomination in the sure and lively hope of our resurrection in the true community of the whole people of God. The price of true catholicity may very well be the death and resurrection of the churches that we know—in the faith that God has greater things in store for his people than we can remember or even imagine.[33]

In these eloquent words Professor Outler poses an ultimate question. Out of his concern for the existing catholicity of the Church of England, Wesley did not wish his movement to separate from it. At what point can we, with most integrity and hope of a future life of our witness, seek wider catholicity in a wider reconciliation?

I have suggested that Wesley's own thinking and practice offer justification, and even a mandate, for such a reconciliation of ministries. It is my hope that as Methodism enters its third century in the United States a needed discussion will take place that will eventuate in our reacting affirmatively to the agreement and *rapprochement* proposed in the *BEM* and COCU documents.

Although such reconciliation will be but one more step along a long ecumenical road, it will have been a decisive movement toward that time when

Love, like death, hath all destroyed,
Rendered all distinctions void.
Names and sects and parties fall:
Thou, O Christ, art all in all.

NOTES

General reference: Baptism, Eucharist, and Ministry (BEM) (Geneva: World Council of Churches, 1982), Faith and Order Paper no. 111.

1. Albert Outler, "A Methodist Reply," *The Plurality of Ministries, Concilium,* ed. Hans Küng and Walter Kasper (New York: Herder & Herder, 1972), pp. 83, 84, 88.
2. *An Ordinal, The United Methodist Church, for Alternative Use* (Nashville: The United Methodist Publishing House, 1979), pp. 13, 14. Cf. Paul F. Bradshaw, *The Anglican Ordinal,* Alcuin Club Collections No. 53. (London: SPCK, 1971), p. 3.
3. H. Boone Porter, *The Ordination Prayers of the Ancient Western Churches* (London: SPCK, 1967), p. 7.
4. *An Ordinal,* pp. 10, 11.
5. Ibid., 46, 47.
6. Bradshaw, *Anglican Ordinal,* p. 209.
7. *An Ordinal,* p. 18.
8. Albert Outler, "The Ordinal," *Companion to the Book of Worship,* ed. William Dunkle Jr., and Joseph Quillian Jr. (Nashville: Abingdon Press, 1970), p. 133.
9. John Wesley, ed. *Sunday Services of the Methodists with other Occasional Services,* (London, 1788), p. 300.
10. L. Tyerman, *The Life and Times of the Rev. John Wesley, M.A.,* vol. 3 (London: Hodder & Stoughton, 1876), p. 442.
11. Bradshaw, *Anglican Ordinal,* p. 39.
12. Wesley, *Letters,* vol. 3, p. 200. Quoted in William Cannon, "The Meaning of the Ministry in Methodism," ms. p. 12.
13. Outler, "The Ordinal," p. 115.
14. Ibid., vol. 7, pp. 238, 239.
15. Colin W. Williams, *John Wesley's Theology Today* (Nashville: Abingdon Press, 1960), p. 146.
16. Wesley, *Letters,* vol. 2, pp. 55, 56.
17. Ibid., vol. 3, p. 182.
18. *Methodist Magazine,* 1786, p. 50.
19. Francis Asbury, *Letters,* Sept. 20, 1783.
20. Frank Baker, *Representative Verse of Charles Wesley* (1962), p. 368.
21. Albert Outler, "Do Methodists Have a Doctrine of the Church?" in D. Kirkpatrick, ed., *The Doctrine of the Church* (Nashville: Abingdon Press, 1964), pp. 26, 27.
22. J. E. Rattenbury, *Wesley's Legacy to the World* (London: Epworth Press, 1938), p. 198.
23. Geoffrey Wainwright, *The Ecumenical Moment* (Grand Rapids: Wm. B. Eerdmans, 1983), p. 199.
24. Albert Outler, "Methodism's Theological Heritage: A Study in Perspective," in Paul M. Minus Jr., ed., *Methodism's Destiny in an Ecumenical Age* (Nashville: Abingdon, 1969), p. 69.
25. *Response of the United Methodist Church to BEM* (New York: Ecumenical and Inter-religious Concerns Division, United Methodist Church, 1977), pp. 32, 33.
26. Bernard Cooke, *Ministry to Word and Sacraments* (Philadelphia: Fortress Press, 1976), p. 77.
27. Ibid., p. 557.
28. J. Robert Nelson, "Methodism and the Papacy," *A Pope for all Christians?* ed., Peter McCord (New York: Paulist Press, 1976), p. 156.
29. John Deschner, "Structure," ms., pp. 9-10.
30. Wainwright, *Ecumenical Movement,* p. 13.
31. Outler, "A Methodist Reply," pp. 90, 91.
32. Outler, "Do Methodists?" p. 28.
33. Albert C. Outler, *That the World May Believe* (New York: Board of Missions of the Methodist Church, 1966), pp. 74, 75.

XI. Wesleyan Thought and Christian Social Ethics

1. THE METHODIST SOCIAL CREED AND ECUMENICAL ETHICS

Walter George Muelder

I. Contextual Introduction

The focus of the church's attention on the morality of society in the latter decades of the nineteenth century was on gambling, card-playing, stage plays, novels, dancing, the Christian sabbath, the sanctity of the marriage tie, prostitution, divorce, the "single standard," and such diversions as cannot be taken in the name of the Lord Jesus Christ. Methodism proscribed the use of intoxicating beverages and helped launch the great moral and political crusade that placed an amendment in the federal constitution and destroyed for more than a decade a whole industry.

These concerns were not the first efforts to spread scriptural holiness and to reform the nation. Slavery, peace, and education refer to issues of economic, political, and social policy which were not mentioned in the Social Creed of 1908, but which consumed Methodist social passion and continue in terms of racism, militarism, and pedagogical dialogue and reform.

Great leaders of that era were more than single-cause advocates. Frances Willard proposed to the Women's Christian Temperance Union, of which she was president, to include promotion of equal suffrage for women, government regulations of monopolies, direct voting for President, government issue of money, confiscation of land not used or occupied, and free and unlimited coinage of silver at the ratio of sixteen-to-one. Thus, one of the most astute Christian socialist reformers of her age grasped the correlation of social questions to include not only personal sobriety, but institutional organization as well: the need for political power to effect social and personal change, the role of government in the economic order, the universal rights of citizens to choose their chief executive, and the problems of land ownership attending private speculation after large tracts of it had been transferred from the public domain to private ownership for development.

For a period in her career Frances Willard ardently supported the work of Dwight L. Moody, the great revivalist in the era of individualistic soul-saving; but he was no reformer in the rising tradition of the social gospel. Everything hung on personal conversions; and he opposed the Prohibition movement, breaking with Miss Willard over signing a temperance pledge and remarking, "Only conversion could save a man from drink." Moody *versus* Willard represents a dramatic contrast in late nineteenth-century Protestantism, just prior to the first formulation of the Social Creed by the Methodist Federation for Social Service. Moody did not lack concern for the poor. Indeed, he hoped the Moody Bible Institute would "raise up men and women who will lay down their lives alongside the laboring class and the poor," but in response to the question of what should be done with and for the working man, he simply asserted, "Save their souls." By contrast Willard represented the new theology of comprehensive evangelism that united the inner and outer redemption. In this her colleagues were Washington Gladden, Richard T. Ely, Josiah Strong, and Walter Rauschenbusch. In these devotees of kingdom of God theology were to be numbered others like Anna Howard Shaw, the Methodist Protestant, who became famous in the woman suffrage movement.

Methodism as a whole was late in entering the social gospel era. Why? Largely because Methodism was overwhelmingly rural and its members had been recruited by narrowly conceived revivalism. Ignored were the persistence of racism, the rise of exploitative capitalism, the scandals of city politics, the "manifest destiny" of the Spanish American War, labor rebellion as in the Pullman Strike (1894), and the trust busting of Theodore Roosevelt. Rural populism was wedded to frontier individualism.

The social ethos of Methodism included a hunger for education, as witness the growth of the Sunday school movement, devotion to the public school with its ideology of democracy and Americanism, and the astoundingly rapid spread of Methodist academies and colleges, even of universities. Of special note are the black colleges as a missionary response to the post–Civil War situation among former slaves. Of great significance for our theme is the fact that education was perceived as the single most effective means for upward social and economic mobility. And it was linked thereby to the American dream of success. The educational system, far from being the seed of radical ideology, fed the hunger for equality of opportunity in the mainstream of free enterprise. Indeed, private educational institutions joined the public sector in correlating the prospects for economic advancement with years and levels of educational achievement. Hence, the educational system served as a conservative brake on an emerging social gospel and rather empowered middle-class values. Social liberalism in the colleges was to come much later. The social gospel took root in the theological seminaries first. As late as 1950 *Readers Digest* called it "the pink fringe."

Before turning to the actual evolution of the Social Creed, it is well to lift up some of the Wesleyan motifs in theology which have had persistent social consequences, though it is not the function of this paper to deal with theological ethics systematically. The Wesleyan doctrine of grace is activist, personalistic, social, and perfectionistic. The love of God calls forth human love for the neighbor in a universal context and manner. When one who is converted to Christ confronts another person, no matter how wretched, one deals with such a one in a three-fold way: (a) as a person created by God in the divine image and likeness; (b) as a creature for whom Jesus Christ gave himself in self-sacrificing love; and (c) as a human being endowed with an immortal destiny, thus as a fellow pilgrim to eternal life. God is thus covenantally engaged with humankind in redemptive history, and there is no upward bound limit to human fulfillment short of the manifestation of the perfected image and likeness which all persons share with each other. The love of God includes but transcends justice; love requires justice and justice is fulfilled in love. It is inherent in the Wesleyan understanding of the kingdom of God that this is the kind of world that can be made better than it empirically is; for as God is active in love, and all God's children are to love their neighbors, so they ought to participate with a sense of self-worth in reforming society, despite their sinfulness and shortcomings. God's grace is sufficient for all; and the divine grace makes of each forgiven sinner a "somebody" equally precious in relation to every other participant in the realm of redemption. Such participation in history has radical social implications and consequences.

II. Evolution of the Social Creed

From one perspective the Social Creed of 1903 reflected a recovery of the whole gospel, following the individualistic era of late nineteenth-century revivalism. From another perspective the creed was a specification in the response of one denomination to incoherent industrialism and abuses of the factory system. In this respect it was a breakthrough that trumpeted a prophetic response to the new American revolution characterized by triumphant capitalism, reckless development, the "Great Barbecue," the "Gilded Age," the "Robber Barons," the dynamism of inventions and manufacturing, and the creation of a national marketplace. The revolution was urban, suburban, and agricultural. But whereas in Europe the proletariat was pressed into the ranks of socialist and labor parties, in the United States free land and torrents of immigrants overcame socialist impulses and kept the political economy in the paths of middle-class aspirations and the excesses of the super-rich. Despite economic depressions and industrial unrest, despite great concentrations of wealth and industrial ownership, the masses of Americans clung either to the ideals of the family farm or to the narrow goals of bargaining unionism and craft guilds.

Capitalist concentration and abuses of power held center stage. This concentration has since the 1890s come in three great waves: first, with the closing of the frontier and the establishment of the transcontinental railroad and telegraph systems, thus creating a national market and outmoding state-bound corporation law; second, with the invention and popularization of an affordable automobile, which modified local markets and set in motion the drive for a hard-surface highway system; and third, the collapse of the European colonial empires after World War II, combined with a communications revolution that created an American dominated world market with the conglomerate and/or transnational super-corporation. During the first wave of the organizational revolution, the Spanish American War set the nation on its imperialistic course. During the second wave, World War I transformed the United States from a debtor to a creditor nation. During the third wave, initiated in World War II, the colonial empires were set on the course of extinction. Concurrently, America became a super-power confronting the U.S.S.R. In this era of the super-corporation, we have witnessed both the debacle of the Vietnam War and the compounding of militarism, science-technology, the neocolonialism of the multinational corporation, and the exhausting price of nuclear terror.

There have been important developments of the social creed corresponding to these waves of industrial and military concentration and power. Industrial relations tended at the outset to push social gospel attention away from even woman suffrage and temperance movements. They were treated as specialized or independent moral and political issues, though earlier, as we have noted, they were parts of the correlated social question. As for the peace movement, its promising beginning in the first decade of the century was dealt a devastating blow by World War I. The "war to end war" and "to make the world safe for democracy" had no place for conscientious objectors. This peace movement recovered briefly in the twenties when idealism fused with disillusionment regarding the causes, the prosecution, and the consequences of World War I; but it was shunted to one side by World War II. Only now, in the aftermath of the Indo-China War and the horrors of nuclear deterrence, has a massive peace movement coalesced.

A. First Phase: 1908 – 1929

The first social creed owes its origin to the initiative of clergy who organized The Methodist Federation of Social Service in 1907. In 1908, it was adopted by the General Conference of the Methodist Episcopal Church and by the Federal Council of Churches. A few years later it was adopted by the church, South, and in the thirties by the Methodist Protestant Church. This creed was primarily labor-industry oriented, dealing with specific problems and reforms, such as the national political parties featured in their platforms. Such were the right of labor to organize, abuses of child labor, working conditions of women, and the equitable distribution of the products of labor. In the twenties the social concerns of the church included also civil liberties, the Japanese Exclusion Act, company unionism, the Kellogg-Briand Peace Pact, the League of Nations, disarmament, lynching, enforcement of the Volstead Act, and the beginnings of attention to the birth control movement. The woman suffrage amendment was, of course, endorsed. Methodists played prominent parts in all of these segmented issues, and annual conferences varied in their attention to them, the Methodist Federation being the acknowledged unofficial leader. It is worth noting that Bishop Francis J. McConnell was its president and Harry F. Ward its executive secretary from 1912 to 1944. A special case was the role of Methodists in the Interchurch World Movement, which investigated the steel industry following the strike of 1919 and which led to the abolition of the twelve-hour day in the industry.

B. Second Phase: 1929 – 1952

The second phase runs from the Crash and the Great Depression to the establishment of the official agency in 1952, the Board of Economic and Social Concerns. The year 1932 was a watershed for both the Methodist Episcopal Church and the Federal Council of Churches because the new formulation of the creed radically moved from single-interest reforms to a more systematic examination of the social-economic system. The whole capitalistic profit system was addressed. In large numbers church persons and the General Conference asked whether there was not something basically amiss in the industrial and financial order. The Federal Council of Churches did likewise. In some respects it anticipated reforms of the New Deal; in others it had an affinity with the proposals of the Socialist Party platform. The essential elements of the creed were to be read to the congregation on the Sunday before Labor Day. Following the creed was a body of commentary and resolutions dealing with such subjects as human rights in education, in industry and economic relations, in agriculture, in race relations, and in international relations. A direct responsibility was laid on the local church to investigate local moral and economic conditions as well as to know world needs. The whole statement heralded the eventual development of systematic social principles, a process that is not yet completed.

One of the prophetic statements in the section on industrial relations resolved: "The right of labor to organize with representatives of their own choosing, and where able, to share in the management." The first clause became federal policy through the Wagner Act in 1935. Another statement reaffirmed and went farther than the 1908 creed: "The supremacy of the service, rather than the profit motive in the acquisition and use of property on the part of both labor and capital, and the most equitable division of the product of industry that can be devised."

Methodism's historic concern for peace was also accented. On this subject the words of the Social Creed adopted at the Uniting Conference of 1939 are noteworthy: "We insist that the agencies of the church shall not be used in the preparation for war, but in the promulgation of peace. We believe that war is utterly destructive and is our greatest collective social sin and a denial of the ideals of Christ. We stand upon this ground, that the Methodist Church as an institution cannot endorse war nor support participation in it."

Given this strong collective persuasion before World War II, The Methodist Church's participation in the Crusade for a New World Order during it was a constructive consequence. This crusade was organized as a complement of the

Federal Council of Church's work in the Commission to Study the Bases of a Just and Durable Peace. John Foster Dulles was chairman, and fourteen of its members were Methodists. The crusade, headed by Bishop G. Bromley Oxnam, was a major contributing factor in the adoption by the United States of the Charter of the United Nations.

In this era we should note the impact of the larger ecumenical movement on social Christianity and Methodism's participation at the Oxford Conference (1937) and the Amsterdam Assembly of the World Council of Churches (1948). Two slogans carried historic significance: "Let the Church be the Church!" and "the responsible society," of which we shall speak more later.

Cooperative ecumenism in America, as in Europe, proceeded from the oft-expressed presumption that doctrine divides and service unites. But as we now know, both theology and practice may be divisive. And even when there is consensus on doctrine and ethics, the introversion and institutionalism of denominations may still forestall visible, organic, and truly conciliar unity. The career of Life and Work greatly influenced Methodism's developing social thought, nevertheless.

In response to the devastation of World War 1, European Protestant representatives met in 1925 in Stockholm. As earlier in America, so at Stockholm, the unifying theological concept was the kingdom of God. This basic gospel idea reinforced the then-widespread contrast between churchianity and Christianity, thus weakening the link between the church and the world and between Christ and history. But at Oxford a dynamic development took place due in part to the following elements: (1) the excellent seminal preparatory studies on such issues as the kingdom of God and history; (2) the Christian understanding of the person; (3) the relation of church to community and state; (4) the Christian critique of both capitalism and communism in theological and ethical terms; (5) the recovery of the activist and theological idea of the church as in the dictum, "Let the Church be the Church!"; (6) the paradoxes of the church's relation to war in the light of the Christian faith; and (7) bridging the gap between the rising Neo-Augustinian view of the human person and the natural-law tradition, thus bringing into vigorous dialogue the Reformation and the Anglican perspectives. In all these issues Methodists were active participants and from Oxford carried forward the discussion in the American setting. The "message" and the study reports and volumes of Oxford became for many Methodists stimulating reference points for their own developing social doctrine. The Oxford volumes still have a classic quality.

With the establishment of the World Council of Churches in 1948, the ecumenical impulse gave new directions to Methodist reflection. With G. Bromley Oxnam as president of the WCC, the Council of Bishops made the preparatory volumes of the Amsterdam Assembly available to all pastors through the omnibus volume entitled *Man's Disorder and God's Design*, the four component books being "The Universal Church in God's Design," "The Church's Witness to God's Design," "The Church and the Disorder of Society," and "The Church and the International Disorder." Inasmuch as the Amsterdam Assembly brought together both the Life and Work and the Faith and Order movements and was also in association with the International Missionary Council, the principal motifs of ecumenism and of Methodist concerns were mutually stimulated and enriched. Since the postwar preparatory volumes were symposia of leading theologians and expert laypersons from many nations and traditions, Methodist clergy were enabled to update their interdenominational orientations and their perspectives from the earlier Oxford Conference.

When at the General Conference of 1948 Bishop Oxnam read the Episcopal Address, he lifted up a theme also accented at Amsterdam, namely religious liberty as a principle. "We are determined," he said, "that free preachers, occupying a free pulpit, preaching to free laymen in a free land shall proclaim the freeing truth of the religion of Jesus." In all the social legislation passed at that session the emphasis on freedom and responsibility was marked. The idea of the responsible society became the leitmotiv of both ecumenical and denominational social ethics for most of the next twenty years. It states:

Man is created and called to be a free being, responsible to God and his neighbor. Any tendencies in state and society depriving men of the possibility of acting responsibly are a denial of God's intention for man and His work of salvation. A responsible society is one where freedom is the freedom of men who acknowledge responsibility to justice and public order, and where those who hold political authority or economic power are responsible for its exercise to God and the people whose welfare is affected by it.

This "middle axiom" had the fruitful consequence in the churches' struggles to clarify East-West tensions and to speak to both established capitalist and communist powers.

But since it presupposed the world social order of 1948, it had soon to be supplemented with responses to the rise of postcolonial independent nations and states and their dynamics of development. Suddenly the concept of the "third world" challenged Christian social doctrine everywhere. The idea of the responsible society was not in error, but it did not sufficiently anticipate and incorporate development issues and the tensions of themes like self-reliance and dependency in North-South world relations. Today the slogan of a Just, Participatory, and Sustainable World Society is superseding, but not replacing, the earlier ecumenical "middle axiom." Self-reliance, as we shall note, development, and the tensions which liberation create require modifications in the theory and practice of social change.

C. Third Phase: 1952 – 1972

The third phase of the developing social creed of uniting Methodism begins in 1952, in the midst of the McCarthy Era, with the official establishment of the Board of Economic and Social Relations. The unofficial Methodist Federation for Social Action was under attack as being under Communist Party influence by some Methodist leaders who helped write the legislation for an official agency. Some, indeed, were active in *Circuit Riders*, an association dedicated to drive liberal ministers out of the church. Despite this conservative midwifery the board proceeded to lay out careful and solid foundations for work which was representative of The Methodist Church as a whole. Fortunately, the organized female side of the denomination was typically in advance of the majority of white males and provided an ambiance of urgency on social questions which was truly prophetic. In addition, in 1956 the General Conference granted full clergy rights to women.

A major product of the board was the landmark, four-volume study under the general title, *Methodism and Society*. It was a comprehensive historical, theological, and contemporary analysis and interpretation, plus guidelines for action. This study, undertaken cooperatively with Boston University School of Theology, provided a solid foundation in Scripture, tradition, experience, and reason for subsequent social thought and action. Its scientific questionnaire of the current mind of the church among all the jurisdictions, and of both laity and clergy, clarified many points of moral consensus and significant differentials on others, particularly on race. Local churches seemed to follow local patterns of attitude and practice. The General Conference of 1956 took a position on race,

however, similar to that of the 1954 Assembly of the World Council of Churches. Taken as a whole, the questionnaire demonstrated the representative quality of the social actions of the General Conference. The MESTA volumes, as they were called, also indicated how deeply social concerns had penetrated the various boards and agencies and also, institutionally speaking, the leadership power of the General Board secretaries.

In *Methodism and Society in the Twentieth Century* I summarized as follows:

Methodism in the Twentieth Century has developed an impressive social witness. It has made a significant transition from the individualistic evangelism of the Nineteenth Century to the inclusive personal and social evangelism of the present. The social concern which was manifested in the organization of the unofficial Methodist Federation of Social Service in 1907 and in the Social Creed adopted in 1908, in the temperance movement of that period, and in only a slight attention to questions of race and world peace, has become a major aspect of the life of The Methodist Church. Almost every phase of the closely knit organization of the church has some direct relationship to social education and action. In a broader and perhaps deeper sense than John Wesley knew, its message today through conferences, boards, agencies, and local churches reflects the historic mark of Methodist preaching: "The Gospel of Christ knows no religion but social, no holiness but social holiness." (P. 383)

The social character of the gospel was not only compassionately interpersonal and universal, but it also reached to questions of structures, institutions, processes, and power. Belatedly, a constitutional amendment and enabling legislation provided for the abolition of the Central Jurisdiction through a voluntary transfer procedure.

The two decades of the third phase of the Social Creed were marked by the Civil Rights revolution and the Indo-China War. Within the church the major development institutionally was union with the Evangelical United Brethren Church. Ecumenically speaking social doctrine was profoundly affected by the Second Vatican Council, by the entrance of the Russian Orthodox Church into membership in the WCC, by more participation of churches in the third world, and by the emergence within an ethic of development of the demands of "liberation" theology. Concurrently, the feminist movement increased its power and effectiveness at home.

Questions of practical racial inclusiveness; of full rights for women; of the justice of the war in Vietnam; of violence, nonviolence, and the struggle for justice; of Christian participation in revolution; of the ethics of development; and of the revolutionary impact of the technological breakthroughs in microbiology—became new themes for social doctrine. Methodist seminaries trained nonviolent black leaders for boycotts and marches, and white bishops marched arm in arm with black civil rights protesters in the South, in Washington, D. C., and in northern cities. The black church discovered a renewed identity, and black theology took its place along with liberation theology and feminist theology. Meanwhile, the struggle against authority and established institutions raged on college campuses, and trustees were bewildered, asking, "Who's in charge?" The Methodist Church, seeking to become The United Methodist Church shared the agonies of a deeply divided nation whose young men dropped napalm in Asia while its cities went up in the flames of riots. A black nationalist, a President, a senator, and a Nobel laureate for peace were victims of assassination. The Social Creed sought a fresh formulation. Congress wrote a strong voting rights act into law, and the new United Methodist Church wrote inclusiveness into its constitution and stated: "In The United Methodist Church no conference or other organizational unit of the Church shall be structured so as to exclude any member or any constituent body of the Church because of race, color, national origin, or economic condition" (*The Book of Discipline of The United Methodist Church*, 1968, para. 4). Again, at the federal level, the government inaugurated a "war on poverty" which limped into an ineffective demise because no adequate tax base was established for it, the resources of the nation having been wasted in war. The absurdity of a guns-and-butter policy bore the bitter fruit of a subsequent debilitating inflation and widespread unemployment for Vietnam War veterans when they returned from Southeast Asia. Methodism opted for "butter" over "guns."

D. Fourth Phase: 1972 – 1980

The *Discipline* of 1968 recorded the status quo of social principles at the time of uniting. They stand as significant social documents at that historic juncture. In 1972 a new statement of social principles was adopted. It was revised in 1980 and is here briefly analysed. The General Conference intended these principles to be "instructive and persuasive in the best of the prophetic spirit." Its seven sections cover (1) the natural world, or the ecological realm, a perspective important to the sixties and seventies; (2) the nurturing community, dealing with the family, sexuality, life, and death; (3) the social

community, including the wide scope of human rights and welfare; (4) the economic community dealing with issues of property, work, and differing economic systems; (5) the political community, therein affirming basic freedoms and responsibilities, issues on crime, and service to the state; (6) the world community with its basic unity, problems of war and peace, and justice in relation to law; and (7) a summary statement of the Social Creed for regular emphasis in every congregation. This formulation is holistic and comprehensive, illustrating Methodism's theological quadrilateral of appeal to Scripture, tradition, experience, and reason.

When we move from the Social Principles to the 1980 *Book of Resolutions*, we note at once a principal ingredient in the development of social doctrine and policy during a seventy-year period. There are eighty-five resolution headings, some with multiple recommendations. Of the eighty-five, fifty-four request reform and/or action by the federal government. Hence, more than half demand political action at the national level. Twenty call for or imply action at the level of state government. Seventeen refer to international or United Nations issues and policies explicitly. Therefore, whatever United Methodists may think of church-state relations in the abstract, when they are assembled in General Conference they readily appeal to national political action on a wide range of reform. Most of the major resolutions appeal to the official Social Principles for moral and spiritual authentication.

To a historian of Methodist social teachings, the development of position papers with theological and empirical social argumentation on many themes in *The Book of Resolutions* is noteworthy. This constitutes a quasi-official and systematic United Methodist position on many issues and invites close criticism, particularly when the position and policy statements are taken in conjunction with the Social Principles. As noted above the resolutions often lead off with an appeal either to Scripture or to the Social Principles. There are systematic position statements on penal justice; population; peace, war, and conscription; racial justice and equality; health and health care; gambling; interreligious relationships; housing; human rights; sexuality, church, and government; and sexuality in general. This is a truly impressive list, especially instructive when numerous particular issue statements are combined with general argumentation. Over time, The United Methodist Church may be developing a coherent body of social doctrine. In view of this prospect, close ethical and theological analyses are important parts of the church's local and conference dialogue. One way of conducting this criticism is to compare Methodism's social principles with the development of those in the ecumenical movement. Thus far our comparisons have been mostly on congruences. In the balance of this paper divergences will be stressed.

III. The Social Creed and the World Council of Churches

Social doctrine reflects its generating nexus of social conditions, denominational provenance, and contextual dialogue. By the nature of its membership, that is, denominations, not local congregations or annual conferences, and the prompting historically by the world missionary movement, the WCC has struggled to express social doctrine, service, and witness, and recently action in a world forum. The ignition point of ever new formulations has been the locus of conflictual traditions, increasingly diverse crises as in East Asia, southern Africa, Latin America, the U.S.S.R., and the North Atlantic basin. Wars and revolutions have engaged its commissions and world assemblies and demanded a normative response. In some areas during its brief history the status of Christianity has been radically altered and weakened; in others, because of the program to combat racism, Christianity is growing more rapidly while development and nation building shape new patterns of the relation of church and state. Conflictual creativity penetrates both the North-South arena as well as the older East-West forum. Indigenous churches have become impatient with perspectives that missionaries from older churches assumed to be normative. The first order of business in the WCC has always been to create a valid dialogue and to keep the conversation going.

As we have seen, Methodist Social Principles, while influenced by ecumenism, have had a different provenance. Of course, Methodism is a world denomination, and its far flung missionary effort receives stimuli from a global encounter. Yet, despite its official and practicing openness to ecumenical influences, the place of decision making is American, white, and middle class; and it is still male dominated. America is wealthy and highly developed; it is powerful and creates dependency patterns which other developing countries increasingly resent. America still functions out of a sense of manifest destiny. Secular America is militantly missionary, while the churches have reformed their theology of mission to be more cooperative with formerly receiving countries. For this reason, Christian America is increasingly at odds in all the world's hemispheres with the nation's overseas policies. The United Methodist Church is largely preoccupied with domestic issues, though it *has* an overseas environment. That environment still seems external to it. By contrast the WCC *is* its own total environment; nothing is external to it. Hence the selfhood and the self-consciousness of the Methodists and of the WCC are radically different. As the WCC has grown from a European dominated council to a truly global entity, its selfhood has changed with the scope and intensity of the dialogue.

We may characterize the inner movement of the ethical themes of the WCC along seven lines: (1) from individualized reforms to major institutional and structural change in society; (2) a persistent quest through biblical, theological, and scientific analyses of community, state, nation, property, human nature, war and peace, and the church's function in society and history; (3) a journey from conflict over the ultimate norms of Christian faith to the use of "middle axioms" like the "responsible society" and the current phrase, a "just, participatory, and sustainable world society"; (4) from Western and East-West, or capitalist-communist issue orientation to North-South and third world development awareness; (5) from development as "growth" to "liberation", seen from the "underside of history"; (6) from "Let the Church be the Church" to "the unity of the Church within the unity of humankind"; and (7) from white male domination in doctrine and organization to the struggle for true inclusiveness and shared power.

These issues and trends are, naturally, shared to some degree by all the member churches of the WCC, but they are more of the conflictual essence and dialogue in ecumenism than in the reforms envisaged in the domestic life of The United Methodist Church. The contrast here is not denigrative, but it is real and has had real consequences in the level of wrestling with many problems. Of necessity the World Council statements have provoked more theological, philosophical, and ideological debate. Its preparatory documents invariably evoke symposia whose contrasting traditions make challenging theses which are not finally resolved. Thus, ultimate theological debate sharpens moral questions respecting economic order, secular community, war and peace, human rights, and the nature and purpose of the church in history. United Methodist statements, coming out of a common tradition, tend to have a more implicit and less theologically sharp formulation. They focus more on the practical aspects of broadly stated social principles. Methodists do not challenge each other so radically at the theoretical level, but tend to strive for prophetic postures in a democratic political forum of debate.

Both the UMC and the WCC statements reflect the process that gives them birth. World Council assemblies and conferences have long preparatory study periods and preconference research. The documents are generally scholarly and academic, and their findings are reflected in the conference conclusions. The UMC generally does not produce comparable preparatory and study documents in anticipation of its annual conferences, or even the General Conference. Its materials are aimed at a less "expert" audience with arguments readily comprehensible by the conference membership. Methodist "specialists" seldom have a wide-ranging debate, for that is not the structure of the process. Resolutions are generated in the hurly-burly of relatively short periods of time with an eye to state and national legislation. This observation does not denigrate the increasingly good scholarship and diligence of the various boards and agencies.

The nature and substance of social statements differ also because of their level and accountability. The WCC assemblies and conferences speak for themselves to the member churches in various cultural settings and tend to address and challenge the denominational "top." A world meeting has a significant action-distance from the political arena of a local congregation. But a denominational pronouncement has its audience of accountability closer at hand. The danger of an ecumenical statement is Olympian universality; the danger of a denominational statement is adaptability to the point of accommodation. Here the difference of a General Conference utterance from one in the annual conference is often noteworthy. The more removed from immediate accountability, the more radical and the more a pointing to ideal ends.

From these considerations we may note further a contrast in the teaching function of the Social Principles. For example, issues like Marxism and socialism, so essential to ecumenical debate, are generally external to middle-class American Methodists. When the World Lutheran Federation, with ecumenical collaboration does an existential study like "The Encounter of the Church with Movements of Social Change in Various Cultural Contexts" (with special reference to Marxism), it is hardly noticed by American Methodists. Since the demise of the leadership of the Methodist Federation, socialism has not been considered as an option in American social doctrine, as tolerable when present among democratic allies in Europe, and as positively evil in communist countries, including those in which The United Methodist Church is an active minority. On the other hand, the WCC must carry on with its member churches who seek a viable life in various cultural settings, some prerevolutionary, some revolutionary, and some postrevolutionary; some in which Christianity is a dominant force; some in which it is a tiny minority, as in China; some in nations where the ruling ideology is positively hostile to the Christian faith. In an ecumenical perspective the teaching function of the church varies greatly in these contrasting cultural contexts.

Although world Methodism operates in some varying settings, such as Sweden, West Germany, East Germany, India, Zimbabwe, and Brazil, the dominant posture is reformist so far as social principles go. Instead of having an inclusive interdependent consciousness, the Social Creed seems to assume that the world of Marxism or socialism is part of its external environment. This situation shapes the teaching function of the Social Principles both at home and abroad. The possibility that some agencies of the WCC may be doing constructively a Christian mission by cooperating with socialistically oriented regimes in certain cultural settings is often not seriously entertained.

Meritorious as the Social Principles and many of the resolutions of The United Methodist Church are when taken in the domestic setting, there is a gap between their spirit and substance and that of churches of the disinherited. Missing is the theological and practical commitment of the idea of development as liberation and of the "church of the poor." In 1975, the Nairobi Assembly affirmed: "The development process should be understood as a liberating process aimed at justice, self-reliance, and economic growth. It is essentially a peoples' struggle in which the poor and oppressed are and should be active agents and immediate beneficiaries. The role of the churches is to support the struggle of the poor and oppressed towards justice and self-reliance." The relevant issue, argues Dickinson, is not whether churches should be in solidarity with the poor, but how. *The Book of Resolutions*, 1980, makes only a passing favorable reference to the principle of liberation (p. 41).

From a critical perspective ecumenical social action suffers from internal structural and theological dilemmas which can only be listed here: (a) professionalization, with a tendency to be dominated by experts; (b) specialization of concerns in isolation from overall debate; (c) institutionalization of the professionalism and specialization; (d) development of conflicting theologies of causes, each claiming normative insights as in black theology, feminist theology, consensus theology, and liberation theology; (3) gaps between these social action ideologies and those of non-church-and-society interests, such as faith and order theology, evangelism, refugee presumptions, and the leading theological concepts with respect to other faiths and ideologies. Ecumenism has less coherence and greater complexity than at the time of Oxford and Amsterdam. It needs a strong effort in consensual social ethics. Among the congeries of many bewildering dialogues in the Christian world community, there is need to discover and carry forward a comprehensive dialogue. Methodism has much to contribute in such a dialogue because of its long experience in stable dialogues; it has much to learn from the liberation and development needs of the nation's ethnic minorities.

IV. Questions for the Future

A. The social witness (and the formalized Social Creed) of the UMC have been aspects of the larger movement of ecumenical response to the modern world, but also distinctive expressions of reflection on (1) the nature of the church, (2) the demands of the gospel, and (3) the nature of Christian unity. Yet Methodism needs greater internal coherence with respect to its special doctrine and greater struggle for coherence and consensus in the whole body of Christ, including Eastern Orthodoxy and Roman Catholicism. On questions of the family, sexism, sexuality, and church and state, the UMC represents the defensible theological and ethical position.

B. Growing out of these comprehensive problems we may cite three issues: (1) does inclusiveness as a mark of the UMC require the rejection of racism and sexism as a criterion of its consensus with faith and order ecumenically? (2) What does it mean in relation to the third world churches to affirm as a demand of the gospel "solidarity with the poor?" (3) What combination of full conciliar participation and diversity of polity is consistent with global responsibility?

C. What theological foundation and ecclesiastical strategy will overcome the tensions between the introverted structures of the UMC and its social action and ecumenical agencies, on the one hand, and those groups of the oppressed who regard themselves as Christian but who regard mainline churches as defenders of oppressing social orders, on the other?

D. How can the UMC develop a self-criticism which recognizes its operating polity and empirical practices as a statement of its real social principles? In the interest of realism, however, we must neither overestimate the moral goodness of the actual church (viewing it grandiosely, too powerful, or as always prophetic), nor must we denigrate it as always in collusion with the status quo (always spiritualizing and lost in other-worldliness or triumphalism). Similarly we must avoid a "children of light" and a "children of darkness" dualism. The ongoing problem is to be ethically and liturgically coherent, so that we know who the Christ is that we meet in Baptism and Eucharist. We must strive more humbly to be covenantally responsible at the local and denominational level, being an effective sign of the Kingdom diaconally and in confrontation with the powers that be.

E. The combined witness of the UMC and the WCC already has disproved the standpoints of enlightened self-interest and of those in the spiritual intelligentsia who hold that problems like hunger, stagflation, unemployment, poverty, trade disorder, world population, militarism, environmental destruction can be solved with simply more personal morality and scientific facts and technology. The assault must be stepped up on institutional powers and structures and on unjust patterns of participation in social and economic political orders. For, if present trends continue, the balance in 1990 and 2000 A. D. will be a world much worse off than it is today: increased polarization of rich and poor, with racism, sexism, and militarism, and readiness for violent attacks on unjust and oppressive systems escalating despite defensive national and class measures by those in positions of present power and affluence. Highest priority should be given to the policy and practice of nuclear militarism; high priority should be given to land and water reform (the United Nations made a decision to call the 1980s the "water decade" since only 15 percent of the rural poor have an adequate water supply); and in the long view a strong priority for the United States to accept the distributive justice of the "Law of the Sea" and to submit to it democratically.

For the balance of the century, we are challenged by the actualities of the global village (inclusive interdependence), by the "global factory" (dominance of the transnational corporation), and by the "global arsenal" (militarism dominating in international politics and budget allocations and commanding the genius of scientists and engineers). Cutting across these are the tensions between interdependence and self-reliance, of obsessive technology and human autonomy, and of computer-collectivism and the dignity of privacy. Meanwhile the gap between rich and poor widens, the maldistribution of food intensifies, poverty and unemployment escalate, and people explode in violent desperation. Terror becomes endemic. Cultures and religions are torn between accommodation to outmoded establishments and hungers for holistic salvation. The ecumenical movement is attacked as being allied to subversion, and pressure mounts for mainline churches to take a priestly rather than a prophetic course of moral action. In these years there is likely to be increasing use by established major powers of military might against their own people, as in Poland, and for dissidents to be suppressed by any means necessary. In one form or another the neocolonial powers rely less on overt "gunboat diplomacy" involving their own nationals abroad and more on training and supplying arms and technology to the forces abroad whom they wish to control. In such an era The United Methodist Church must gird itself with a total gospel of righteousness and compassion and speak the whole truth to those who hold places of authority and power. This vocation was adumbrated at the birth of the first Social Creed; it now is required as a mature nonviolent dedication.

To fulfill this vocation in the era of the global village, the global factory, and the global arsenal a new self-awareness with respect to the sinfulness of American power, similar to what has been achieved in part in the church regarding the nature of racism, must be accomplished. Racism, it is now commonly recognized, is not just a feeling of color prejudice, but an awareness of structural discrimination and injustice with respect to ethnic minorities. Persons who have felt no personal prejudice have come to acknowledge the reality of structural racism in which they often unwillingly participate. The remedy must be structural. Similarly, what is now required of The United Methodist Church is to recognize that the American nation in the world is structurally arrogant in the world community, structurally an exploiter of the world's poor industrially and commercially, and structurally militaristic and not peace-loving. To recognize this evil is the first step to overcoming nuclear terror.

2. TOWARD A WESLEYAN SOCIAL ETHIC

James C. Logan

I. Introduction

On the American scene the people called Methodists in the nineteenth and twentieth centuries have manifested an active, energetic spirit in evangelism, missionary endeavor, and various kinds of social reform. Much of this activity has been carried out with only passing explicit reference to John Wesley. Usually a captive quotation or slogan has been considered sufficient. Methodist evangelistic and missionary activity has marched under the banner "The World Is My Parish." Methodists engaged in social reform have at times cited Wesley's statement: "The Gospel of Christ knows of no religion, but social; no holiness, but social holiness."[1] Why search any farther? Isn't this sufficient to show that we have not lost our ties with our ancestor in the faith? This energetic spirit of American Methodism was characteristically summarized in the Episcopal Address to the General Conference of The Methodist Church in 1944:

> The Methodist insistence has not been so much upon opinion as *upon life*. Its distinguishing mark is not so much what men believe, as *what they are, what they experience, how they act*. The unique traditions of Methodism are, therefore, to be sought in *patterns of action* rather than systems of doctrine.[2]

Wilhelm Pauck credits this subordination of doctrine to action to the historic Wesleyan antipathy for Calvinism and a perennial stress on the practical and experiential character of the life of faith. As an on-looker he finds Methodists

> are primarily concerned with developing among their members a personal commitment to the gospel and to the life of moral perfection which they see implied in it. They regard Christianity as a social movement which through its organization endeavors to bring about a Christian transformation of the whole of human life. They are not hostile to theology but they relegate theological responsibility to a minor place in the life of both the Church and the individual members.[3]

This observation can be balanced with the claim that the Wesleyan "spirit" has lived on through the transmission of the "Wesley story," though at times this has been considerably sentimentalized. The Wesleyan emphasis on the universality of divine grace, in contrast to the Calvinistic doctrines of election and limited atonement, has always been a common assumption of the people called Methodists.[4] The stories of Wesley's practical concerns for the poor, imprisoned, under-educated, and socially and economically abused children have provided inspiration and justification for continued social involvement.

Then, why raise the question of peculiarly Wesleyan theological foundations? After all, the various branches of Methodism compare favorably with most other Protestant denominations in their social record. If for no other reason, the demands of historical accuracy mandate the question. While Wesley's social statements and actions were occasioned by the conditions which he encountered during the Revival, his reasons were nevertheless theologically grounded. Historical curiosity is healthy and a legitimate enterprise. The question of Wesleyan theological foundations is, however, more important for another reason. Wesley did not in his time stake himself haphazardly on the social and political issues. Even though he wrote no systematic theology nor a systematic ethics, his positions were grounded in his theology, and those theological premises have projected trajectories into the present and, perhaps, from the present into the future.

In recent theological literature John Wesley's long neglected thought has received attention by past ethicists. James Gustafson has given an extended treatment to Wesley's sanctification ethics in *Christ and the Moral Life*.[5] Likewise, Stanley Hauerwas in his quest for the formation of ethical character has insightfully compared Wesley's sanctification ethic with the reformers, Luther and Calvin, and the progenitor of modern liberal theology Friedrich Schleiermacher.[6] These ethicists are not uncritical, but they do find Wesley's theology fruitful for ethical deliberation.

This has not always been the case. In the nineteenth century Wesley was very much the possession of the Wesleyans. This is understandable. Both British and American Methodists were busy institutionalizing themselves from a religious movement into a church. From Tyerman, if no others, they found their *raison d'etre*: "Methodism is the greatest fact in the history of the church."[7]

Beginning probably with George Croft Cell in 1935[8] Wesleyan theology sailed out of its protected harbor into the open seas of ecumenical dialogue. Cell was concerned to see that the Calvinist side of Wesley's thought got its fair treatment. William Cannon sought to bring Wesley into dialogue with both of the reformers Luther and Calvin.[9] Albert Outler secured him a place in *The Library of Protestant Thought*.[10] And Colin Williams summarized it all with his survey of Wesley's theology in constant dialogue with various ecumenical issues of the time.[11] Wesley was now not simply Methodism's cult hero, but he was out in the open marketplace of the free interchange of theological discourse.

Generally when the ethical stance of Wesley has been investigated, the result has been a catalogue of Wesley's various positions on issues and conditions of his day. Such cataloging seems to have been the chief approach to "getting at" Wesley's ethics in the late nineteenth and early twentieth centuries. D. D. Thompson wrote of Wesley as a social reformer.[12] J. A. Faulkner attempted to secure a place for him as a sociologist, theologian, and churchman.[13] On the German scene, J. W. Ernst Sommer catalogued Wesley's "social questions."[14] Probably Wellman Warner came closer than any other person to bringing Wesley's theology and ethics into an integrated picture.[15]

In Wesleyan and Methodist literature on social ethics, certainly the action of the 1956 General Conference provided a watershed mark. It inspired what became the four volume the MESTA project.[16] Here the richness of Wesleyan and subsequent Methodist historical scholarship was brought to bear upon the future direction of the church in its social engagement. Since that time a new Wesleyan literary genre has been born seeking to integrate the evangelical message of the Wesleyan revival with the social involvement of Wesley and the Methodists who followed him. Mere cataloging of Wesley's positions was not enough. What was needed was a holistic picture of Wesley's theological grounding for the socio-ethical trajectories launched from that grounding. Interestingly, much of this new Wesleyan research has been carried out in western Germany and Czechoslovakia.[17] On the American scene the research into Wesley's theological ethics has proceeded mostly in terms of doctoral research.[18] These beginnings offer hope that Wesley's thought may yet make its impact upon the discipline of Christian ethics as it has made its impact upon evangelism and the disciplines of the spiritual life.

Our purpose is not to offer a bibliographical essay but to indicate that the movement of Wesley studies is in ferment and probably nowhere more than precisely in the area of social ethics. From this point we shall proceed, both retrospectively and prospectively, or to employ two different metaphors, we shall examine "roots" and "anticipations" in Wesley's theological ethics.

II. An Exercise in Retrospection: Roots

Generally when Wesley's ethics have been treated in a theological context, the tendency has been to select certain key theological themes in Wesley and explore the ethical content and implications of these themes. For example, the Arminian doctrine of the universality of grace has been mined for the power which it conveyed in giving the dispossessed and disspirited persons at the bottom of the economic and social ladder a new and positive self-image, thereby empowering them for the reform of their personal lives and the corporate life of their communities. In particular, this is what Gordon Rupp had in mind when he coined the apt aphorism—"the pessimism of nature and the optimism of grace"—as a summary of the Wesleyan message.[19] Others have chosen the theme of sanctification and have utilized it almost to the exclusion of other themes as the leitmotiv from which all of his social and ethical motivation and action flowed. In particular, the isolating of the theme of sanctification is what flaws the interpretations of both James Gustafson and Stanley Hauerwas in their treatments of Wesley. Gustafson rightly scores the individualism which arises from such interpretation,[20] and Hauerwas seems destined to limit the scope of ethics to personal and familial concerns as the consequence of his constriction of Wesley's theological horizon.[21]

"Theological horizon" is an apt expression and a suitable beginning point from which to gain a "retrospective" view on the "roots," of Wesley's theological ethics. Historically, American interpretations of the theology of Wesley have limited themselves to an explication of the so-called *ordo salutis*.[22] The adequacy of this form of interpretation needs to be called into question. Accepting these limits, John Deschner claims that Wesley operated with a view of "salvation-history," and its locus was the interior soul of the believer. One is sometimes tempted to think that Americans view the theology of Wesley through the lenses of the Second Great Awakening. Is there not a larger theological horizon within which the Wesleyan *ordo salutis* is then to be placed? If there is not, then Wesley's theology may well be progenitor of the individualism and subjectivism which many have criticized.

My awakening to the possibility of a wider horizon of Wesley's theology came in a conversation with Gordon Rupp one fall afternoon in 1973. I had just finished reading Wesley's notes on the book of Revelation. The eschatology in these notes seemed to me to be a somewhat conventional form of premillennialism. I was troubled because at the same time I sensed an ethical theological thrust which ran through the sermons, or in Rupp's terms "an optimism of grace." Rupp suggested that I read the sermons on the Sermon on the Mount. "You may find another Wesley there and a more authentic Wesley, because the sermons are not as dependent on another source (Bengel's commentary) as the *Explanatory Notes upon the New Testament*. There I read these words:

For this also we pray in those words, "Thy kingdom come": we pray for the coming of His everlasting kingdom, the kingdom of glory in heaven, which is the continuation and perfection of the kingdom of grace on earth. Consequently this, as well as the preceding petition, is offered up for the whole intelligent creation, who are all interested in this grand event, the final renovation of all things, by God's putting an end to misery and sin, to infirmity and death, taking all things into His own hands, and setting up the kingdom which endureth throughout all ages.[23]

Then, in the commentary on Matthew 3:2:

The kingdom of heaven, and the kingdom of God, are but two phrases for the same thing. They mean, not merely a future happy state in heaven, but a state to be enjoyed on earth: the proper disposition for the glory of heaven, rather than the possession of it. . . . It properly signifies here, the gospel dispensation, in which subjects were to be gathered to God by his Son, and a society to be formed, which was to subsist first on earth, and afterward with God in glory. In some places of Scripture, the phrase more particularly denotes the state of it on earth: in others, it signifies only the state of glory: but it generally includes both.[24]

To be sure Wesley also emphasized that the kingdom of God is *within us*.[25] More important, however, is the manner in which he balanced the *inward* and the *outer*: "It is termed, 'the kingdom of God,' because it is the immediate fruit of God's reigning in the soul. . . . For whosoever they are that experience this, they can aver before angels and men,

Everlasting life is won,
Glory is on earth begun;"[26]

The earth "shall be full of the knowledge of the Lord, as the waters cover the sea," and nations shall "beat their swords into ploughshares, and their spears into pruning hooks." There will be "no oppression, . . . no extortion to 'grind the face of the poor.'"[27] These are selected quotes, but they can be paralleled with others indicating that, contrary to the accepted interpretation of his day, Wesley understood that the kingdom of God established by Jesus Christ, takes hold of the hearts of human beings, and has tangible social consequences on earth, in society. One is tempted to use a modern phrase from New Testament studies and say that Wesley's view is that of an "inaugurated eschatology."

And if inaugurated, then to be consummated as well. Such a consummation includes the summing up of all things in Christ. It is not disembodied souls which make up the consummation; rather, it is the whole cosmic order.

But will "the creature," will even the brute creation, always remain in this deplorable condition? God forbid that we should affirm this; yea, or even entertain such a thought! While "the whole creation groaneth together," (whether men attend or not,) their groans are not dispersed in idle air, but enter into the ears of Him that made them.[28]

And if consummation, then also creation. The two, consummation and creation, are inseparably joined. Therefore, Wesley is forced back to the original intention of God in creation. Certainly, creation logically precedes consummation, but I suspect that Wesley's order or method (*methos*, "to gain access") moves in a contrary direction. And for good reason, it moves from future to beginning. His objections to the Calvinists were rooted in the fact that he was convinced that they loaded the end in the beginning. Hence, no real flow and movement of history could take place; hence, no real teleological development of creation or of the human being was possible under such conditions. The kingdom which is the consummation of creation surpasses the creation itself, and within that kingdom are those whose citizenship is marked by justification, new birth, and growth in holiness. Such, I believe, is the wider horizon within which we can place the Wesleyan message of salvation. Upon these grounds rests the possibility for a Wesleyan social ethic that will do full justice to Wesley and at the same time project his followers today into new fields of social responsibility.

The neglected factor in treatments of Wesley's social ethics has been the doctrine of creation, or, more specifically natural law or what Wesley

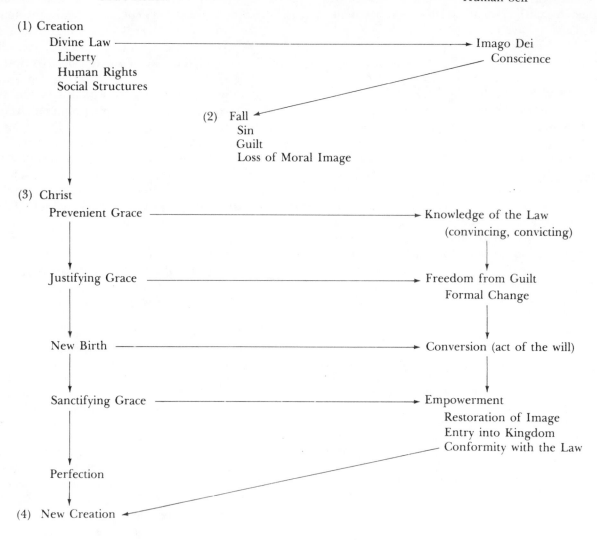

God's Action | Human Self

(1) Creation
    Divine Law ————————————————————→ Imago Dei
    Liberty   Conscience
    Human Rights
    Social Structures

                           (2) Fall
                                 Sin
                                 Guilt
                                 Loss of Moral Image

(3) Christ
    Prevenient Grace ——————————————————→ Knowledge of the Law
                                     (convincing, convicting)

    Justifying Grace ———————————————————→ Freedom from Guilt
                                     Formal Change

    New Birth ——————————————————————→ Conversion (act of the will)

    Sanctifying Grace ——————————————————→ Empowerment
                                     Restoration of Image
                                     Entry into Kingdom
                                     Conformity with the Law

    Perfection

(4) New Creation

more frequently and for good reasons chose to call "the law of God."[29] Wesley authored, or more accurately, edited an extended two-volume work entitled *A Survey of the Wisdom of God in the Creation*.[30] For the most part this work consists of observations and speculations about the natural order of creation. Virtually no consideration of the moral law is contained therein. For our purposes here what is relevant is the conclusion regarding the theistic rational character of the created natural order:

I have not looked upon thy works inconsiderately, and passed them over as ordinary things. But I have studiously and diligently searched into them, as things of great eminence and wonder; and have esteemed it part of the duty, which the wise God of nature requires of the children of men, who, for that very end, exposed these his words to the view of his intelligent creatures, and gave us not only eyes to behold, but reason, in some measure, to understand them.[31]

What is true for the natural order is equally true for the moral order. Yet there is a difference. The laws of nature are like nature created by God. He could, therefore, declare, "The world around us is the mighty volume wherein God hath declared himself."[32] As such, the laws of nature are contingent and depend upon their Creator. He would not permit any concept of the material world, or the laws thereof, to be absolute. What is eternal, and thus absolute, is God. In this manner he avoided the determinism of materialism and defended the freedom of God.

The moral law, however, is rooted in the very nature and being of God.

The whole difficulty arises from considering God's will as distinct from God: otherwise it vanishes away. For none can doubt but God is the cause of the law of God. But the will of God is God Himself. It is God considered as willing thus or thus. Consequently, to say that the will of God, or that

God Himself, is the cause of the law, is one and the same thing.[33]

For this reason he can, in what would otherwise appear to be exaggerated terms, speak of the law as "the face of God unveiled" and "a copy of the eternal mind, a transcript of the divine nature."[34] Because God is holy and just, the moral law is likewise holy and just.

At this point one may rightly ask: What makes Wesley so certain of the law of God and its morally holy and just nature? In one sense, Wesley's answer to this query is the human conscience. Because human beings were created in the image of God and therefore with moral conscience, the *imago Dei* and the moral conscience of which it is part are simply extensions of the natural law or law of God. Wesley defined conscience accordingly: "That faculty whereby we are at once conscious of our own thoughts, words and actions; and of their merit and demerit, of their being both good and bad, and, consequently, deserving either praise or censure."[35] Conscience was intended to provide the knowledge of good and evil and to grasp the ultimacy of the moral law.

But what of sin? Did not Wesley, like the reformers Luther and Calvin, and Augustine before them, subscribe to the doctrine of original sin? Did not Wesley on occasion even say that the doctrine of original sin is what distinguishes the Christian from the pagan (surely a polemical remark!).[36] Wesley, however, did not exaggerate the consequences of sin; the chief of which is that "the eyes of thine understanding are darkened, so that they cannot discern God, or the things of God."[37]

Wesley operated with a tripartite understanding of the *imago Dei*: the natural image ("a picture of His own immortality; a spiritual being endued with understanding, freedom of will, and various affections";) the political image ("the governor of this lower world, having 'dominion over the fishes of the sea, and over all the earth' "), and the moral image ("righteousness and true holiness").[38] The pervasiveness of sin means that all three facets of the image are affected, corrupted, and distorted. In particular, however, the moral image has been turned completely from relationship with God and the divine law to the human self and a law-unto-ourselves. Somewhere Albert Outler has observed that while Wesley believed in total depravity, he did not believe in tee-total depravity. The image was defaced and severely distorted, but it had not been totally destroyed. Yet, even granting this qualification, the sinner still cannot discern the law of God.

Precisely at this point the first and universally applicable consequence of the work of Christ applies, that is, prevenient grace. A "blind mind, a perverse will, distorted affections" cannot discern the divine law,[39] but no one, said Wesley, is in that completely forsaken state of nature. Prevenient grace, which is Christ's gift to everyone born into this world, provides the eyes by which one can discern the divine law, and thereby know oneself as disobedient unto that law. Prevenient grace re-sensitizes the deadened moral conscience. It is important to note here that Wesley never referred to natural conscience; conscience was always seen to be the divine gift whereby one is made aware of the demands of the law of God.

Why, then, the law? Harald Lindstrom explains how Wesley answered this question:

> It [the moral law] is regarded as an expression both of God's justice and of His grace. This is seen in Wesley's three uses of the law. The first use is to instill conviction of sin. . . . The second use is to lead man to Christ that he may live. . . . The third use of the law concerns its place in the Christian life. The law does not only lead man to Christ; it also strives to keep the justified and regenerated man alive and helps him to grow in grace.[40]

Wesley did not maintain that the natural law of God is fully accessible to everyone. Only through prevenient grace does one know anything of that law, and then no doubt not perfectly.

Precisely at this point Wesley's theology offers us one of the greatest of his contributions to ethical discourse and a continuing debate in contemporary Christian ethics. The Barthian or neo-orthodox rejection of any natural law theory because of the radical nature of sin is well known to all of us. Behind this rejection of natural law ethics is also the Barthian rejection of the so-called *analogia entis*. Wesley, without resorting to some Thomistic or idealistic analogy of being, is able, nevertheless, to maintain the importance of the natural law of God, and, without minimizing the sinful condition of humankind, can at the same time maintain the possibility of some knowledge of that law.

A genuine social ethic will either have to affirm forthrightly or boot-leg in by the back door something that resembles a natural law argument. Otherwise, on what ground do we rightly discourse about "right" and "wrong" and the various shades between? Likewise, on what other basis in a global community can ethical discourse proceed if there be no universal grounding of some kind? The genius of Wesley lies, not in his originality, but in the synthesis whereby he is able to hold to an "engraced" creation, an "engraced" reason or conscience, and the divine revelation of the holy and just law of God.

In terms of recent Protestant theological debate, Wesley is no less Christocentric in his theological epistemology than a Barth or a Brunner. The knowledge of the moral God of creation is gained through the benefits of the atoning death of Christ, that is, prevenient grace. In Wesley the doctrine of creation and the concomitant natural law rest no more upon a so-called natural theology than does it rest upon such in Barth or Brunner or, for that matter, in Júrgen Moltmann. In no wise, however, does this imply a rejection of the positive, constructive role which a rightly founded natural law can play in contemporary ethical deliberation.

This is not the place to enter into the "detective work" of deciphering the influences which played upon Wesley in the development of his understanding of the natural law. Of the Anglican-Arminian influence upon Wesley, two examples can, however, be cited. Hugo Grotius visited England in 1613 and gained the friendship of Bishop Andrewes. Wesley was acquainted with Bishop Andrewes' thought which is generally interpreted as leaning toward the general position of the Arminians. Another Anglican source was Dr. Isaac Barrows, who was an eminent divine as well as a mathematician. His works have an Arminian tone, and Wesley believed Dr. Barrows's views on Arminianism to be clear and excellent.[41]

As for the contents of the moral law as Wesley viewed it, he did not make extensive claims regarding his knowledge of such. "It is our duty to contemplate what he has wrought, and to understand as much of it as we are able."[42] Wesley was able to discern the following:

(1) *Liberty.* Human nature is neither totally matter nor wholly spirit. We are a composite of both. As body, we are under necessity; that is, under the laws of cause and effect. On the other hand, human beings are endowed with the *imago Dei.* Philosophically, this was the faculty of reason and conscience. Psychologically, this was the love of liberty.

All men in the world desire liberty; whoever breathes, breathes after this, and that by a kind of natural instinct antecedent to art or education. Yet at the same time all men of understanding acknowledge it as a rational instinct. For we feel this desire, not in opposition to, but in consequence of, our reason.[43]

It would be a naturalistic reductionism to reduce a spirit to matter or freedom to necessity. Theologically, Wesley rooted his belief in human

freedom in God. Because God's basic nature includes free-agency, it was God's crowning work of creation when the human creature was endowed with a similar liberty.

On this premise Wesley defended religious liberty or freedom. He refused to deny that Quakers were Christians simply because they had not submitted to the sacrament of Baptism and defended their right to practice Christianity according to their own dictates of conscience.[44] Even when it came to non-Christians, Wesley reserved judgment as to their eventual salvation:

. . . because I have no authority from the word of God "to judge those that are without"; nor do I conceive that any man living has a right to sentence all the heathen and Mahometan world to damnation. It is far better to leave them to Him that made them, and who is "the Father of the spirits of all flesh"; who is the God of the Heathens as well as the Christians, and who hateth nothing that he hath made.[45]

This did not spell an indifference regarding the evangelical zeal. That is another issue!

Another illustration of Wesley's ethical concern for what John Macquarrie has called the "freedom to be" is illustrated from his ministry. When one of his women followers was criticized for exercising a pastoral ministry among the people, Wesley answered:

But may not *women* as well as men bear a part of this honourable service? Undoubtedly they may; nay, they ought—it is meet, right and their bounden duty. Herein there is no difference: "there is neither male nor female in Christ Jesus." Indeed it has long passed for a maxim with many that "women are only to be seen; not heard." Accordingly many of them are brought up in such a manner as if they were only designed for agreeable playthings! But is this doing honour to the sex? Or is it real kindness to them? No; it is the deepest unkindness; it is horrid cruelty; it is mere Turkish barbarity. And I know not how any women of sense and spirit can submit to it. Let all you that have it in your power assert the right which *the God of nature has given you.* Yield not to that vile bondage any longer. You, as well as men, are rational creatures. You, like them, *were made in the image of God:* you are equally candidates for immortality.[46]

Though this is hardly the charter for women's rights as understood today, it is nevertheless slightly less than heretical for Wesley's day! And the foundation for the position? The God of nature! The image of God!

No doubt the most revealing and probably the most extensive treatment of liberty on a specific subject was Wesley's treatise on *Thoughts upon Slavery.*[47] Thomas Madron[48] has analyzed the treatise and claims that Wesley's case against slavery rests upon three basic premises: theological, ethical, and anthropological. We are concerned here with the theological-ethical. Many Wesley readers are familiar with the oft quoted, "The blood of thy brother 'crieth against thee from the earth, from the ship, and from the waters.' "[49] But Wesley in the treatise goes farther to give one of the clearest statements on civil liberty:

> Give liberty to whom liberty is due, that is, to every child of man, to every partaker of human nature. Let none serve you but by his own act and deed, by his own voluntary choice. Away with all whips, all chains, all compulsions. Be gentle toward all men; and see that you invariably do unto every one as you would he should do unto you.[50]

Here coupled with the compelling divine law ("to every child of man") Wesley emphasizes equally the Christian ethic of "faith active in love."

(2) *Political and Economic Power.* Wesley treated the doctrine of God under two basic rubrics— Sovereign (or Creator) and Governor. As Sovereign, God is loving, gracious power. As Governor, God acts in providential self-restrictions. God as Sovereign grants political power and authority to corporate representatives on earth.[51] It is at this point that Wesley joined the social issues of freedom (treated above) and human responsibility. In prevenient grace human beings have the possibility of responsible cooperation (synergism) with God and God's human creatures. At the same time prevenient grace does not save humans from the plight of sin. Out of sin the various forms of corporate evil (war is one example) arise. For this reason God as Sovereign delegates political responsibility to certain corporate representatives as the "check" on evil. While Wesley undoubtedly changed from the ardent Tory which he was in early years, he nevertheless did not change the basic formal position that political power was delegated by God. It did not arise from the people as in Locke.[52]

> Now, I cannot but acknowledge, I believe an old book, commonly called the Bible, to be true. Therefore I believe, "there is no power but from God: The powers that be are ordained of God.'"
>
> . . .
>
> The supposition, then, that the people are the origin of power, is every way indefensible.[53]

Regarding economic and property rights Wesley has often been hailed as the champion of the "Protestant work ethic." That later Methodists give witness to such is a matter of historical record. Wesley, however, deserves a more careful reading, for, indeed, Wesley discovered the poor![54] As in political theory, regarding the rights of property Wesley differed profoundly with Locke. Once again, God as Sovereign is pivotal in understanding Wesley's position. All property rightly belongs to God as Sovereign. Wesley's stress was not upon property rights or the equal distribution of property, but upon a stewardship of the economic materials which one possessed. In other words, the moral law grants stewardship rights but not property rights. The failure to exercise such stewardship is the root of poverty.

> Has poverty nothing worse in it than this, that it *makes men liable to be laughed at?* . . . You that live at ease in the earth, that want nothing but eyes to see, ears to hear, and hearts to understand how well God hath dealt with you, is it not worse to seek bread day by day, and find none? Perhaps to find the comfort also of five or six children crying for what he has not to give. . . . O want of bread! want of bread! Who can tell what this means, unless he hath felt it himself? I am astonished it occasions no more than heaviness even in them that believe.[55]

If the propertied failed to manifest their God-given stewardship, then they had no right to that property. It is a well-known historical fact that Wesley in the early days of the Methodist movement actually experimented with a communal holding in common of all property, convinced that this was the practice of primitive Christianity. What was grounded in the law of God was not the right of property but the responsibility of stewardship. This principle of the law of God, when coupled with the Christian motivation of faith active in love, became the fundament of much of the Wesleyan social and economic ministries to the poor.

Closely allied with Wesley's insistence that the law of God was stewardship, not property rights, was his abhorrence of "inheritance." "Have pity," Wesley counseled, "upon them and remove out of their way what you may easily foresee would increase their sins, and consequently plunge them deeper into everlasting perdition!"[56] In the light of these brief observations, one is forced then to question the thesis that Wesley himself was an advocate of the "Protestant ethic." To the contrary, as long as property rights are divine and stewardship is the divinely established law governing all, the ethical conclusions to be reached are quite different.

If prevenient grace opens sinful eyes to the divine law and convicts them thereby, sanctifying grace offers the empowerment for the fulfillment of that law. Once again, I wish to refer the reader to what I have called the larger horizon of Wesley's theology, namely, creation as it moves through Christ to new creation. Many of the interpretations of Wesley's view of sanctification have missed this context, and this has been the chief reason why sanctification has so frequently ended up in an ethical individualism. Sanctification and Wesley's view of the kingdom of God go hand in hand.

It is true that Wesley on occasion spoke of the kingdom as inward, but as has earlier been pointed out, there was equally an outward dimension to the kingdom. Speaking of "evangelical repentance" in contrast to "legal repentance," Wesley remarked:

> But, notwithstanding this, there is also a repentance and a faith (taking the words in another sense, a sense not quite the same, nor yet entirely different) which are requisite after we have "believed the gospel"; yea, and in every subsequent stage of our Christian course, or we cannot "run the race which is set before us." And this repentance and faith are full as necessary in order to our *continuance* and *growth* in grace, as the former faith and repentance were, in order to our *entering* into the kingdom of God.[57]

The italicized terms of "continuance," "growth," and "entering" are Wesley's, not mine! On another occasion he preached:

> For this also we pray in those words, "Thy Kingdom come": we pray for the coming of His everlasting kingdom, the kingdom of glory in heaven, which is the continuation and perfection of the kingdom of grace on earth. Consequently this, as well as the preceding petition, is offered up for the whole intelligent creation, who are all interested in this grand event, the final renovation of all things.[58]

In this context sanctification is seen as the entry by faith (justification) into a new life in the kingdom (sanctification). Sanctification, therefore, has two sides or two dimensions, "inward and outward holiness." Beginning with regeneration, sanctification is processive or theological in that the diseased and distorted image of God is now through the Spirit being restored. Sanctification is therefore not the collection of individual virtues, as though the sanctified life is itself a human project. Such a view is rightly subject to the criticisms of "self-righteousness," "self-justification," and "moralism." Rather, sanctification is the restoration of human life under the divine law of God or life lived under the reign of God (kingdom). Wesley, therefore, could preach regarding the Kingdom and life in the Kingdom:

> The meaning is, that all the inhabitants of the earth,

even the whole race of mankind, may do the will of their Father which is in heaven, as *willingly* as the holy angels; that these may do it *continually*, . . . yes, and that they may do it *perfectly*—that "the God of peace through the blood of the everlasting covenant, may make them perfect in every good work to do his will and work in them" all "which is well-pleasing in his sight." In other words, we pray that we and all mankind may do the whole will of God in all things.[59]

The crucial importance of this passage is that within the framework of a doctrine of the Kingdom Wesley states the theological goal itself—"may do it perfectly"—or *perfection*. In contrast to Calvinism, where perfection is deferred to life after death, Wesley held to the possibility of doing the perfect will of God within the scope of time and history. When this teleological goal is set beyond history, an ethical nerve is severed. When this same teleological goal is set within history, an ethical dynamic is unleashed which in the truest sense is both inwardly and outwardly, in Niebuhr's term, "transformationist." In modern ethical terms, Wesley's ethic is a dialectic between the teleological, on the one hand, and the deontological, on the other. The dominating theme in Wesley seems to be the grand work of God by which one's life is transformed at its core so as to produce the fruits of obedience.

It is also appropriate to observe at this point another related difference between Calvinism and Wesley. For Calvin, the structures of human society (such as government) appear to have a purely negative function. They are established because of the evil in the world and as a dam for the flood wave of sin. For Calvin, the human community with its various social structures will never conform to the standards of the Kingdom. The kingdom of God will come and extinguish the present life, and then the civil government will be entirely superfluous. Despite the so-called Calvinistic attempt at a "theocracy," there is nevertheless a negative assumption and finally a negative conclusion to the matter. Wesley, too, held that such social structures as government are "checks," but he grounds these ontologically in the law of God. There is, however, a different assessment of these social structures for Wesley in that the Christian has ethical responsibility to see that the divinely instituted structures perform the divine will. To be sure, Wesley did not speculate in terms of political power and social influence. The reformation of society would spring from the reformation of human beings. Nevertheless, the mandate "to spread Scriptural holiness throughout the land" carries with it the assumption that social structures as well as individuals can be transformed and brought more and more into conformity with the divine law. This is not to argue that Wesley espoused some facile idea of "building the kingdom of God." The Kingdom was still God's doing. Nevertheless, the Kingdom through the new birth had been implanted and of necessity it must reveal visible consequences; hence, his sense of Christian social responsibility, his courageous moral pronouncements, his practical humanitarian initiatives, and his strong personal example.

Here is not the appropriate place to enter into a discussion of Wesley's eschatology. All that I have attempted to do is to indicate that there is a larger horizon in Wesley's theology—a horizon which extends from creation to new creation. Without a recognition of this larger horizon the Wesleyan *ordo salutis* is left without a theological context and tends toward an ethical individualism which later Methodists have exemplified. Likewise, without this larger horizon we are hard pressed to explain the undeniable teleological thrust of Wesley's ethical thought and action. Also the Wesleyan emphasis upon the new birth, sanctification, and perfection as these relate to a new creation provide the retrospective vantage point to see the utter necessity for Wesley's emphasis on the doctrines of creation and of universal sin. Though Wesley was no systematic theologian nor systematic ethicist and though his theology is not particularly original, it manifests a remarkable consistency, an inescapable evangelical social ethic, and an ingenious synthesis that is truly catholic, reformed, and evangelical.

III. An Exercise in Anticipation: Development

It now remains for us to indicate in brief form where possible engagement of Wesley's social thought can best take place in the midst of contemporary ethical discussion. If the theology of Wesley has emerged from its institutional ghetto and has for several decades now been a part of the ecumenical conversation, it should now be ready for a new venture which is basically anticipatory in nature. There is no need for a Wesleyan scholasticism. While it is important to know Wesley for what he actually said and did, it is no longer sufficient simply to replicate Wesley. We need to find new ways in which the past can be projected into a more usable and viable future. As with the earlier metaphor, "roots" are important, but they can never be "branches." Yet without the "roots" there can never be "branches." Having set forth in outline something of the Wesleyan roots, it remains for us to anticipate future growth and development.

(1) *Natural Law Ethics*. The natural law tradition has been a venerable one, though in recent decades it has been under serious attack from quarters such as situational/contextual ethics and relational ethics. In many instances, this attack has presupposed an outmoded metaphysics of a traditional Thomistic variety. On this ground the attack has been a misplaced one! Few ethicists operate today from a traditional Thomistic stance. Neo-orthodoxy has waged an assault which is basically related to theological epistemology. As has already been indicated, Wesley's approach to the "law of God" is hardly subject to this criticism, since the knowledge of the law is predicated on the ground of prevenient grace. The neo-orthodox attack is wide of the target in the case with Wesleyan theology.

Even with these attacks the natural law tradition has continued to survive, and even in some quarters thrive. It lives today in new and philosophically defensible forms. To name only a few ethicists who appeal to natural law, three Protestant figures in particular stand out, both for the vigorous character of their thought and the fact that they have common roots in the personalistic tradition, which has made a major contribution to the development of American Methodist theological thought. The ethicists I have in mind are Walter G. Muelder, L. Harold DeWolf, and J. Philip Wogaman. The personalist tradition from its inception has operated with a dynamic metaphysic which is not subject to the criticisms of static abstraction directed toward traditional Thomistic philosophy. In the cases of Muelder and DeWolf,[60] they have attempted to update and enlarge upon the earlier formulations of natural law of the personalist tradition. They classify four complementary expressions of the natural law: the purely formal (ideals necessary for rational action of the will), axiological (principles to which the values willed by a moral agent ought to conform), personalistic (consideration of the effect of conduct upon individuals), and communitarian (consideration of the social context in which choice is made). In the case of Wogaman, the argument centers upon what he terms "moral presumptions."[61] Such a "presumption" indicates that certain actions are mandated unless a distinct case can be made for a different judgment. The task of the Christian ethicist is to ask what presumptions are most compatible with Christian faith. The Roman Catholic ethicists have, likewise, continued to develop and not been content to be fixated with an out-moded metaphysical underpinning of the moral law. Simply take note of Bernard Häring and Charles Curran as illustrations.[62]

Certainly in Wesley's understanding of divine

law there is a considerable amount of static fixity. Even dividing the doctrine of the nature of God into two divisions: Sovereign and Governor, would be difficult for many of us to defend today. Nevertheless, by grounding natural law in the very nature of God, and not external to God, provides an opportunity for a more dynamic interpretation of natural law, particularly if one simultaneously seeks for a biblically more dynamic understanding of the nature of God. The point, however, is that Wesley was able to maintain the essentials of the Reformed tradition without jettisoning the doctrine of creation; he was faithful to much of his own Anglo-Catholic tradition in his doctrine of sanctification, and he remained faithful to the evangelical commitments in his Christocentric approach. Wesleyan social ethics, particularly in regard to the doctrine of divine law, stands in a unique position today. It offers possibilities for a trilateral discourse not yet explored.

(2) *An Ethics of Formation.* Stanley Hauerwas has pointed to the fact that much of recent Protestant theological ethics has placed a prominent emphasis on the "command/obedience" metaphor.[63] Joseph Fletcher, Paul Lehman, and Joseph Sittler are illustrations of such. The result is an "occasionalistic" or "episodic ethic" with little clarification of the phenomenological self which does the deciding. Such an ethic is primarily rooted in the doctrine of justification. Hauerwas calls for a renewal of an ethics which places major emphasis on the metaphor of "growth/character." This allows for discourse, not only on "the way of acting" as a Christian, but also on "the way of being" Christian. Obviously such an emphasis will center upon sanctification. Hauerwas's claim is that Wesley fits this metaphor of ethics. I would not claim that Wesley fits this category as exclusively as does Hauerwas. It is interesting to note that nowhere does Hauerwas take into account the theology of law in Wesley's ethics. On the other hand, Wesley offers considerable possibilities both constructive and corrective for an ethics of "character formation."

Wesley's doctrine of sanctification and its concomitant ethics have been criticized for encouraging "moralism," "legalism," and "perfectionism." These criticisms generally arise when Wesley's views of sanctification have been removed from an over-all theological structure or context. Mildred Bangs Wynkoop has recently argued correctly:

As is true with the other key theological terms which characterize Wesleyan theology (or any other, for that matter), perfection considered alone fails to do justice to its evangelical meaning. It is not an abstract term which has an independent theological status. It is one facet of the larger truth which Christian theology seeks to rationalize systematically and must be considered in connection with the whole.[64]

One must confess that there are areas in Wesley's treatment of sanctification which do indulge in moralism. Part of the problem lies in that in his sermons he more frequently preaches about "sins" than "sin." When sin is so individualized as isolated violations, the resultant effect is that sanctification takes the character of a collection of virtues. The general argument of this paper has been that this need not be the case in appropriating Wesley for the future. When sanctification is placed within a theology of the kingdom of God, the issue becomes one, not of collecting virtues, but of faithful obedience in discipleship. At this point there is certainly an unfinished task in Wesleyan ethics. What would a doctrine of sanctification look like if it focused upon the formation of "discipleship character"? Such an effort would of necessity bring Wesley's thought into dialogue with developments today in theories of moral and faith developments.[65] This would not mean an uncritical acceptance of moral development theory to which, unfortunately, some Christian educators have succumbed. Such a dialogue would provide for an unusual interdisciplinary effort involving systematic theology, social ethics, psychology of religion, and Christian education.

The "anticipations" toward which this paper points are not for a replication of Wesley's thought, nor, for that matter, even a Wesleyan ethic so-called. The anticipations point through Wesley toward possibilities for a future Christian ethic where the polarities of teleological/deontological, justification/sanctification, and "command/growth" are transcended in a new synthesis. The genius of Wesley, again, was not his originality but precisely his ability to synthesize. To continue in that spirit would truly be the Wesleyan contribution to a future Christian ethic.

This would not imply that we ignore the content of Wesley's own thought. Perhaps a story expresses it best. The most poignant scene in the television series *Roots* (though not found in Haley's book) depicts Cissy attempting to explain to her son George why at the last moment she had canceled her impending wedding to Howard. Cissy's words to George speak relevantly to us. "George," she said with tears in her eyes, "Howard wasn't like us. Nobody ever told him where he come from, and, so, he didn't have a dream of where he ought to be goin'."

1. John Wesley, *Works*, vol. 14, "List of Poetical Works," pp. 321-22.
2. *Conference Journal, 1944*, p. 44. Italics mine.
3. Wilhelm Pauck, "Theology in the Life of Contemporary American Protestantism," *Religion and Culture: Essays in Honor of Paul Tillich*, ed. Walter Leibrecht (New York: Harper & Bros. 1959), pp. 273-74.
4. Bernard Semmel, *The Methodist Revolution* (New York: Basic Books, 1973).
5. James Gustafson, *Christ and the Moral Life* (New York: Harper & Row, 1971). See chap. 3, "Christ the Sanctifier."
6. Stanley Hauerwas, *Character and the Christian Life: A Study in Theological Ethics* (San Antonio: Trinity University Press, 1975).
7. Luke Tyerman, *The Life and Times of the Reverend John Wesley M.A.*, 3 vols. (New York: Harper & Bros., 1872), vol. 1, page 1.
8. George Croft Cell, *The Rediscovery of Wesley* (New York: Henry Holt, 1935).
9. William R. Cannon, *The Theology of John Wesley* (Nashville: Abingdon Press, 1946).
10. Albert C. Outler, ed., *John Wesley*. (New York: Oxford University Press, 1964).
11. Colin Williams, *John Wesley's Theology Today* (Nashville: Abingdon Press, 1960).
12. D. D. Thompson, *John Wesley as a Social Reformer* (New York: Methodist Book Concern, 1898).
13. J. A. Faulkner, *Wesley as Sociologist, Theologian, and Churchman* (New York: Abingdon Press, 1918).
14. J.W. Ernst Sommer, *John Wesley und die soziale Frage* (Bremen: Verlagshaus des Methodistenkirche, 1950).
15. Wellman J. Warner, *The Wesleyan Movement in the Industrial Revolution* (London: Longmans, Greene, 1930).
16. The four volumes were:
   S. Paul Schilling, *Methodism and Society in Theological Perspective* (Nashville: Abingdon Press, 1960).
   Richard Cameron, *Methodism and Society in Historical Perspective* (Nashville: Abingdon Press, 1961).
   Walter G. Muelder, *Methodism and Society in the Twentieth Century* (Nashville: Abingdon Press, 1961).
   Paul Deats, Jr., and Herbert E. Stotts, *Methodism and Society: Guidelines for Strategy* (Nashville: Abingdon Press, 1962).
17. J. Weizbach, *Der neue Mensch im theologischen Denken John Wesleys*, Beiheft 2 (Stuttgart: Beitrage zur Geschichte des Methodismus, 1970); Vilem Schneeberger, *Theologische Wurzeln des sozialen Akzents bei John Wesley* (Zurich: Gotthelf Verlag, 1974); Manfred Marquardt, *Praxis und Prinzipien der Socialethik John Wesleys* (Göttingen: Vandenhoeck & Ruprecht, 1977).
18. Egon Walter Gerdes, "John Wesley's Attitude Toward War," Ph.D. dissertation, Emory University, 1960; Allen Lamarr Cooper, "John Wesley: A Study in Theology and Social Ethics," Ph.D. dissertation, Columbia University, 1962; Leon O. Hynson, "Church and State in the Thought and Life of John Wesley," Ph.D. dissertation, University of Iowa, 1971; Thomas Madron and Leon Hynson have made a number of contributions to journals on Wesley's theological ethics. Hynson particularly has consistently emphasized a major point of this paper, namely, the crucial importance of the doctrine of creation for Wesley's ethics.
19. Gordon Rupp, *Principalities and Powers* (London: Epworth Press, 1963), pp. 64-78.
20. See note 5 above.
21. Stanley Hauerwas, *A Community of Character: Toward a Constructive Christian Social Ethic* (Notre Dame: University of Notre Dame Press, 1981), where the ethical considerations hardly extend beyond the family and sexual ethics.
22. See the treatments by Cannon, *Theology of John Wesley*, John Deschner, *Wesley's Christology* (Dallas: Southern Methodist University Press, 1960); Lycurgus Starkey, *The Work of the Spirit: A Study in Wesleyan Theology* (Nashville: Abingdon Press, 1962); Williams, *Wesley's Theology*.
23. Wesley, "Upon Our Lord's Sermon on the Mount: VI," *Works*, vol. 5, p. 336.
24. Wesley, *Notes*, "Matt. 3:2," p. 22.
25. Wesley, "The Way to the Kingdom," *Works*, vol. 5, pp. 76-86.
26. Ibid., vol. 5, p. 81.
27. Wesley, "Scriptural Christianity," *Works*, vol. 5, p. 45.
28. Wesley, "The General Deliverance," *Works*, vol. 6, p. 248.
29. See, for example, Wesley's sermon on "The Original Nature, Property, and Use of the Law," *Works*, vol. 5, pp. 433-446.
30. Wesley, *A Survey of the Wisdom of God in the Creation*, 2 vols., 4 parts.
31. Ibid., p. 463.
32. Wesley, *Compendium*, vol. 1, p. 313.
33. Wesley, "The Original, Nature, Property, and Use of the Law," *Works*, vol. 5, pp. 440-41.
34. Ibid., p. 439.
35. Wesley, "On Conscience," *Works*, vol. 7, p. 157.
36. Wesley, "Original Sin," *Works*, vol. 6, p. 55.
37. Wesley, "The Way to the Kingdom," *Works*, vol. 5, p. 82.
38. Wesley, "The New Birth," *Works*, vol. 6, p. 66.
39. Wesley, "The Doctrine of Original Sin," *Works*, vol. 9, pp. 435-36.
40. Harald Lindstrom, *Wesley and Sanctification* (London: Epworth Press, 1950), p. 57.
41. In an unpublished paper I have attempted to trace the background and influences upon Wesley at this point.
42. Wesley, *Wisdom of God in Creation*, vol. 2, p. 440.
43. Wesley, "Thoughts upon Liberty," *Works*, vol. 11, p. 34.
44. Wesley, *Letters*, vol. 3, p. 36.
45. Wesley, "On Living Without God," *Works*, vol. 7, pp. 353-54.
46. Wesley, "On Visiting the Sick," *Works*, vol. 7, pp. 125-26.
47. Wesley, "Thoughts upon Slavery," *Works*, vol. 11, 59-79.
48. Thomas Madron, "John Wesley on Race: A Christian View of Equality," *Methodist History* 2 (1964): 24-34.
49. Wesley, "Thoughts upon Slavery," *Works*, vol. 11, p. 78.
50. Wesley, ibid., p. 79.
51. Wesley, "Thoughts Concerning the Origin of Power," *Works*, vol. 6, pp. 47-48.
52. See Leon Hynson's dissertation, "Church and State in the Thought and Life of John Wesley," referred to in note 18 above, for the clearest and most accurate mapping of their development in Wesley.
53. Wesley, "Thoughts Concerning the Origin of Power," vol. 11, pp. 47-48.
54. Maldwyn Edwards, *John Wesley and the Eighteenth Century*, 3rd ed. (London: Epworth Press, 1956), p. 148.
55. Wesley, "Heaviness Through Manifold Temptations," *Works*, vol. 6, p. 96.
56. Wesley, "The Use of Money," *Works*, vol. 6, p. 132.
57. Wesley, "The Repentance of Believers," *Works*, vol. 6, p. 57.
58. Wesley, "Upon Our Lord's Sermon on the Mount, VI," *Works*, vol. 5, p. 336.
59. Wesley, ibid., p. 337.
60. Walter G. Muelder, *Moral Law in Christian Ethics* (Richmond: John Knox Press, 1966); L. Harold DeWolf, *Responsible Freedom: Guidelines to Christian Action* (New York: Harper & Row, 1971).
61. J. Philip Wogaman, *A Christian Method of Moral Judgment* (Philadelphia: Westminster Press, 1976).
62. Bernard Häring, *Free and Faithful in Christ: General Moral Theology for Clergy and Laity* (New York: Seabury Press, 1978).
   Charles Curran, *Transition and Tradition in Moral Theology* (Notre Dame: University of Notre Dame Press, 1979). See also Curran's *Christian Morality Today: The Renewal of Moral Theology* (Notre Dame: Fides, 1966).
63. Stanley Hauerwas, *Character and the Christian Life*.

64. Mildred Bangs Wynkoop, *A Theology of Love: The Dynamic of Wesleyanism* (Kansas City, Mo.: Beacon Hill Press, 1972), p. 274.

65. James W. Fowler, *Stages of Faith* (San Francisco: Harper & Row, 1981).

66. awrence Kohlberg, *Philosophy of Moral Development* (San rancisco: Harper & Row, 1981).

67. ohn Westerhoff, *Will Our Children Have Faith?* (New ork: Seabury Press, 1976).

3. IMPLICATIONS OF WESLEY'S ETHICAL METHOD AND POLITICAL THOUGHT

Leon O. Hynson

Purpose, Procedures, and Limits

In developing this essay, I make no claim to comprehensiveness in surveying Wesley's political thought or ethical method. No topic is exhausted, but the attempt is made to give suggestive lines of development which assist us in following Wesley's thinking. That Wesley's ethics have received minimal consideration in the discipline of Christian ethics is unhappily apparent to this company. While that gives us latitude in our survey it also burdens us with the responsibility of innovation and structure. It will be easy to slip into questionable extrapolations, analogies, or inferences. Our efforts in this seminar will assist in the clarification of Wesley's ethics and his contribution to the future of the Wesleyan heritage and to the collective life of the human race.

The essay assumes the principled nature of Wesley's ethics, that is, that Wesley developed a moral theology of enduring merit built upon the solid footing of faith. It should show how forcefully, helpfully, and hopefully Wesley spoke to the serious moral, social, economic, and political issues of his century. If we share with him a vision of social holiness, holiness fleshed out and vitalized in a fragmented and despairing society; if we accept his example in offering a relevant holiness which functions as light and leaven in the world, we shall become initiators of a revolution in the human spirit which may shake the foundation of society, even as early Christianity shaped the structure of the world in which it was born. There are times when Wesley's optimism was that sweeping and dramatic. On other occasions he was more realistic and pessimistic about a "Christian world." We will do well to challenge his "realism" by his spirit of faith which works through love.

From the simple assertion that Wesley offered moral principles for social and religious reconstruction, we will move toward analysis of political positions which Wesley developed. Sometimes concurrent with those themes, but more deliberately as a separate discussion, the investigation of his ethical methodology will proceed. Finally, on the basis of the ethical principles perceived, movement toward future application will occur. Here will be addressed some of the serious social and political problems of our own era, problems which decisively, and often fearfully, impact the future, the life of our children and grandchildren, or more ominously, as Jonathan Schell portrays, the awesome uncertainty that our grandchildren will ever come to life.[1] As an exercise in futurism, in which I have such narrow experience, the essay will extrapolate Wesleyan ethical norms, applying them to the four or five questions which vex our minds and souls in 1983 and beyond. The prognosis which Wesley would offer, in my estimation, would be a calm hopefulness in the face of peril; a hope which avails the gloomy totalitarianism of Orwell's *1984* or Zamiatin's *We*. Wesley would not buy into the apocalyptic pessimism of certain Christian millenarians, nor would he glibly declare that everything will be all right. He would portray outcomes in terms of divine sovereignty.

The issues which may be addressed here represent the staggering problems of nuclear holocaust and other modes of warfare; ecological entropy; world population problems with all of the parallel horrors attending overstocked, undernourished societies, for example, famine, disease, demoralization, to suggest a few possibilities; the problem of a world order which overcomes the rights of man, or vice versa, leading either to totalitarianism or to world anarchy; violence; and the lure of unchastened revolutionism. This discussion will be largely propositional rather than an extended essay.

The Politics of Order and Liberty

In summarizing Wesley's political opinions, some accounting needs to be made of his early immersion in the conservative Tory ideology of order. Decisively educated in the politics of divine right, passive obedience, and nonresistance, Wesley followed the pattern of Tory politics with its focus on the divine origins of political authority. Although the Tory position was sharply modified by the events of the Glorious Revolution, it remained a constant ideal for many persons. For the non-jurors, it sustained a particularized interpretation, that is, specific monarchs like James II had received by divine authority the right to hold their offices. Citizens had no right to change that divine grant.

Others modified that position, holding somewhat uncomfortably to the pragmatic conception of authority held by the force of revolution, but not revolution by the masses. Rather, it was a quiet, ordered procedure carried out by a responsible body, that is, Parliament, to deal with an emergency created by the flight of the monarch and the vacant throne.

As H. T. Dickinson has shown in his brilliant analysis *Liberty and Property*, the bulk of Tory opinion after the revolution moved to an uneasy acceptance of the new state of the affairs. They were mollified in part by the argument that James II had vacated the throne. Even more satisfying for many was the assertion that William and Mary became monarchs as the result of divine providence. Even so absolutist a figure as Francis Atterbury, a high Tory, came to accept the argument.[2]

Dickinson demonstrates further that the Whig appeal to government by consent, while indebted to Locke's appeal to the original contract and the right of revolution, reflected a conservative modification of Locke. The Whigs were as anxious about a radical application of the logic of revolution as many Tories. Whigs were more likely to appeal to the concept of an ancient constitution which regulated and continued to shape the political life of the English people.

Dickinson, finally, demonstrates that the Whigs balanced out a firm commitment to protect the interests of property holders alongside the advance of liberty for all. They were "careful to distinguish between liberty under the law and the excess of freedom which resulted in anarchy and licentiousness."[3]

As the eighteenth century moved into the last three decades, the more radical emphasis of Locke, and others, such as Joseph Priestley, Richard Price, and Thomas Paine, began to gain strength. Popular sovereignty, holding for moderates the specter of mob rule or anarchy, received strenuous explication. The radicals held the optimistic belief that social institutions could be continuously improved, shaped by the power of enlightened reason. Corollary to this was the necessary freedom of every man to exercise his reason in producing social and political change.[4] For the conservatives of the time, including John Wesley, these arguments were designed to undermine stable government and to unleash a wave of confusion and anarchy which could bury the nation. Furthermore, Wesley argued *reductio ad absurdum* that the radicals were not pursuing democratic government since they were not committed to the participation of women and minors in government.

Wesley's Synthesis

When we consider the dominant political trend of the eighteenth century, we will locate Wesley in several political centers (homes?). The politics of order was a constant factor for him, but there is a shift in the instrumental channels for maintaining order. From the belief in a divine right monarchy to whom one offers the quiescence of passive obedience and nonresistance, Wesley moved to a firm affirmation of limited monarchy. Employing a Lockean form of the doctrine of an original compact, Wesley extrapolated a conservative, stabilized political order. Since government had been achieved by contract in England (in some misty past which Wesley does not define, except to locate it at the time of the ancient flood), it is now necessary for citizens to live by the terms previously achieved. However, Wesley seems to allow that revolution creates a political *tabula rasa* (not his term) in which persons, like the revolutionaries in America, enter into a new compact. Undergirding Wesley's concern, first through the Hanoverian limited monarchy's fight against revolution, and then, when the American revolt has succeeded, in the new providential situation in America,[5] is his profound commitment to human rights—life, liberty, and property, and happiness which is synonymous with holiness.

Human Rights

The simple thesis which underlies all of my research on Wesley's political thought is: Wesley's mature political arguments, from his support for the Glorious Revolution, his treatment of political authority, his attack against slavery, to his resistance toward, and subsequent acquiescence in, the results of the American Revolution, rest upon the bedrock of commitment to human rights. There are many historical, theological, and personal reasons for this, but they all converge to this end.[6] To provide one example, Wesley's mature affirmation of limited monarchy builds upon his position that English liberties began with the revolution (1688), which is the beginning of modern constitutional government in England. Further, his appeal to that form of government is made on functional or instrumental grounds, that is, the monarchy is the most sure bulwark against tyranny and guarantor of human liberties. There is no reason to believe that Wesley, in his mature years, could have supported a system which weakened or diminished the rights of humanity.

Consider, then, the key political values to which Wesley dedicated much of his thinking from 1765–83, in a series of fifteen political and social tracts. His underlying agenda throughout these tracts—whether he speaks of liberty, slavery, authority, revolution, monarchy or democracy, hunger, population, or other socio-political issues—is the foundation, attainment, and preservation of life, liberty, property, and happiness. The form of government is never seen as an end in itself. His political teleology is the alter ego of his theological view of man. Created *imago Dei*, every person has the right to those benefits which are constituent to human life. In illustration, Wesley argues in his "Thoughts upon Slavery" that the denial of freedom involves the specter of dehumanization. A slave is deprived of the power to be fully human, that is, the power of contrary choice.[7] In "Thoughts on the Present Scarcity of Provisions," Wesley laments the misplaced values which for the rich produced sleek, grain-fed horses, while the dehumanized poor went to dung heaps looking for a few bits of grain to satisfy their hunger.[8] An ethical perversion!

As stated earlier, the tracts reflect a concern for life, liberty, property, and happiness. For Wesley these concerns are set within the framework of a theonomous ground of value. Appealing to natural law, which Wesley incorporates into a theology of creation, he insists upon the divinely given source of law which regulates or orders the benefits of life, liberty, and property. Whatever contradicts natural law, including positive (legislated) laws, cannot stand.

Life. Wesley's concern for the values of life are expressed in concert with many other voices in his era, latitudinarian and evangelical, revolutionary or conservative. Wesley differed from many spokesmen on the basis by which life could bear its distinctive worth. On God's creation of Man *imago Dei* rests Wesley's persuasion of the meaningfulness of life. Life possesses meaning because Man is free, rational, and self-conscious. Like God in the power of self-analysis, able cognitively and spiritually to step out and apart from one's self, Man may understand the meaning of life as God sees it. Life has "meaning" within the human context alone. All of creation contributes to that evaluation which humanity places on life, but only the human species perceives the worth of the whole.

Life has meaning for Wesley both on the quantitative and qualitative levels. Separate the two dimensions and life is no longer meaningfully human. It is possible to be physically alive and spiritually dead; physically alive but enslaved to another, hence not in full possession of the divinely given humanity; physically alive, but so deprived of the essentials of life that subsistence is impossible. Each of these—spiritual life,

freedom, and meaningful existence—are contained in Wesley's approach to life.

The folly of wasting human life in war—war between Christians, particularly, and wars fought between two heads of state who have no moral principles to guide their conflict, only self-aggrandizement, evoked a biting sarcasm from Wesley. He could not imagine reasonable men resorting to such a meaningless destruction of life. He wrote: "And surely all our declamations on the strength of human reason, and the eminence of our virtues, are no more than the cant and jargon of pride and ignorance, so long as there is such a thing as war in the world."[9] Here is a reference to reason which is characteristic of the eighteenth century's enlightenment spirit. Wesley obviously considers war to be a tragic rebuttal to the optimism of his age.

Liberty. The theme of liberty should be recognized as the centerpiece of his political thought. Thomas G. Hoffman has analyzed Wesley's moral philosophy and has concluded that freedom is the philosophical principle which sustains and gives coherence to Wesley's interpretation of human existence. He claims "that freedom is the ground on which true existence can become a reality for each man. Wesley's moral dynamic supplies the basis for authentic self-hood; it is the condition by which one can become a real person."[10] From another perspective, Bernard Semmel, analyzing Wesley's Arminianism, has shown the importance of Wesley's stress upon freedom in the development of the Methodist "revolution" in England. According to Semmel the Arminian influence seems to have helped shape a Whiggish tendency in Wesley's thought which led in the direction of constitutional government.[11] Whigs, too, gave dominant focus to liberty, as accented earlier.

A third variation on this theme proposes that in church-state questions, which Wesley encountered and addressed, his politics and ecclesiology are shaped by a central commitment to liberty, civil and religious.[12] Whether speaking of political or ecclesiastical order or human rights, liberty is the interpretative key to understanding his commitments.

But what is his definition of liberty? Like many others in his day, it included civil and religious liberty. By civil liberty he meant the freedom to exercise responsibly the rights which belong to every citizen. It is "a liberty to enjoy our lives and fortunes in our own way; to use our property, whatever is legally our own, according to our own choice."[13] Or, again, it is "a liberty to dispose of our lives, persons, and fortunes, according to our own choice, and the laws of our country.[14] While Wesley's definition of civil liberty seems to be grounded in political reality, that is, the guarantees of the state, his position on religious liberty is conceived more broadly. It links *both* political guarantees *and* the pledge of natural law and the Creator's endowment. Religious liberty is

> a liberty to choose our own religion; to worship God according to our own conscience. Every man living, as a man, has a right to this, as he is a rational creature. The Creator gave him this right when he endowed him with understanding; and every man must judge for himself, because every man must give an account of himself to God. Consequently, this is an unalienable right; it is inseparable from humanity; and God did never give authority to any man, or number of men, to deprive any child of man thereof."[15]

Wesley's definition is thorough, covering a series of issues which are important to him. He accentuates liberty of conscience, the power to choose one's own religion. He appeals for liberty to choose God, but he allows that other religious choices may be made.[16] Next, Wesley notes that liberty is a corollary of human rationality. Rational creatures require liberty in order to pursue the full reaches of human possibility, or, to be fully human. Rationality is combined with understanding and private judgment. If the actions of persons involve responsibility toward God, then we must possess the freedom to judge for ourselves. Another person, who cannot be our responsible substitute before God, cannot make our decisions, no matter how wise a counselor, or, by coercion, force us to an act which places our soul in peril before God. Wesley espouses an ethics of freedom in which human decision stands in bold relief. God does not impose an irresistible will upon humanity, but persuades, warns, and pronounces judgment on the disobedient. From the existentialist perspective, this power of choice includes both great benefits and terrible *anfechtungen* and anxiety. Wesley saw it as the happy opposite of every deterministic approach, whether psychological (as with David Hartley), philosophical (as with Henry Home, Lord Kames), or theological (Jonathan Edwards, Calvinism).[17] It is the mark of authentic humanity to freely exercise the power of judgment, to make decisions which we understand, for which we will be responsible.

Hoffman, commenting on Wesley's position that every judgment we make must be our own or we are not held accountable, states that, "conscience is the faculty which must be postulated as the means for man to be conscious of the value of these judgings."[18]

Finally, Wesley argues that the divine gift cannot be subverted or diminished by either church or state, under the pretext that God has granted church or state a variance or exemption to his order for humanity.

The privilege of religious freedom in the political state is a problem of recurring magnitude. While it will be analyzed further in a later section of this paper, it is fair to say that Wesley's position represents an appeal for responsible judgment on the part of the religious person and considerable restraint by the political powers. Serious dialogue between church and state concerning the limits of authority and the needs and rights of each order of creation, must be constantly carried on. This is true even where the state has assumed omnicompetency, where the church is outlawed or forced underground. Wesleyan ethics offers strong affirmation to the recognition of religious liberty, whatever the nature of the political state.

Property. Wesley's position on the right of property represents the least explicit part of his human rights ethics. By the right of property he does not mean that everyone has the right to the kind of property which will ensure the right of franchise. He himself lacked that privilege and seemed not to be perplexed by its absence. On the other hand, he deplored the prostitution of the franchise through bribery, and the like.

Nevertheless, Wesley does take a position on property which coheres with his position that certain essentials must be available, or owned, which make life good and decent. In *Thoughts on the Present Scarcity of Provisions*, he appeals for some government regulation of the use of grain for distilling alcohol or the development of fine horses and other patterns of luxury. He insists that people suffer for lack of work; that the distilling of immense amounts of corn or wheat consumes needed food; that taxes are so unevenly distributed that the burden falls on the "middle class" employers, and hence upon their employees who cannot be continued in their employ.

Wesley believes, further, that the monopolizing of farms, the so-called enclosure system, has placed farmland in the hands of a few, depriving small farmers and their tenants of the opportunities for sustenance. The little farms offered the setting for small entrepreneurs to raise their chickens, hogs, or vegetables and to make a living. Since that has been sharply curtailed by the increasing monopoly of land, many people lack both work and food, and the flow of food to the markets has sharply declined. Prices have increased leading to increased suffering on the part of those who only recently were faring reasonably well. The contrast between the luxurious life-style of the gentlemen or the "persons of quality" and the deepening poverty of the poor is so sharp that thousands are perishing for want of food.

In order to meet the needs of these poor, Wesley proposes the prohibition of distilling which he thinks would reduce the price of grain by a third. The number of horses should be reduced by a tax on exportation and on the carriage horses of gentlemen. Sheep and cattle should be increased in order to provide more food. Then Wesley argues that luxury should be repressed, "whether by laws, by example, or by both. I had almost said, by the grace of God; but to mention this has been long out of fashion."[19]

Finally, he proposes that the national debt should be reduced and that "useless pensions" shall be abolished. By useless pensions, Wesley refers to the money paid out for a century to governors of castles whose forts have done nothing but shelter crows.

What is the essence of Wesley's argument? It would be easy to lampoon some of his ideas as unrealistic. He himself admitted that the nation would not accept his appeals, because it was a nation in which the contempt of religion opened the way for social and economic demoralization.

In effect, however, Wesley was calling for several radical steps. One was the redistribution of the tax burden, easing the load on the common man and woman, resisting the trend toward land monopoly, and adding to the tax burdens of those who were able to enjoy the luxuries of life. Another step, even more unrealistic, was the use of grain for feeding the hungry and not for distilling. Unrealistic because it would cut the jugular of a national pastime. But alcoholism as Wesley (and Hogarth and others) knew was a serious threat to society. A third step or implication is the appeal for control by government. Wesley was not speaking here of moral suasion, but of regulation by the governmental powers. It is this appeal that leads to Philip Watson's thesis that Wesley would support the modern welfare state.[20]

Wesley has a consistent philosophy with respect to the Christian's use of possessions. He appeals for simplicity. His "Gain all you can, save all you can, give all you can,"[21] is not a philosophy by which zealous entrepreneurs become rich. It is from his sermon "The Use of Money." Money earned and saved is for the purpose of satisfying "whatever nature moderately requires for preserving the body in health and strength," for meeting household needs, and then for doing

good unto all. If the Protestant ethic flows in any sense from Wesley's sermon, as Max Weber believes,[22] it represents a misuse of his intention. For there is no question in my mind that he was affirming Christian stewardship in all of our activities. The sermon is on *use*, taken from our Lord's parable of the poor steward who became a reverse example of taking care of the future. Stewardship is the issue!

What may we then say concerning Wesley's teaching on the right of property? He is preeminently concerned that everyone shall have enough for subsistence. To achieve that he appeals to moral, religious, and political considerations. To achieve the larger goals of tax adjustment and national economic improvement, he will seek government action.[23] He is not simplistic in assuming that persons of goodwill will choose to give up their privileges. Beyond this is his articulated appeal to Christians, especially his societies, to practice a genuine spirit of *caritas*. Here he builds an ethics of love which expects the Christian to care for the persons who cannot work. Absent in Wesley's economic reflection is any suggestion that their distresses are due to the laziness of the poor. They would work if work were to be found. Bound up in all of this analysis is the gradual shift from an agrarian to an industrialized society. Wesley perceived the process from the side of agrarian dislocation. While some economists have downplayed the enclosure movement with its consequent disruption of the lives of many simple people, and have lauded the larger process which lead to economic growth, Wesley assumed a posture of commitment to the poor. That economic growth would be secured, even at the expense of the disadvantaged, did not appeal to him. His biting attack on slavery contains his sharp assertion that the colonies of England had rather be buried in the sea than developed at the expense of slaves. Whether wrestling with physical or economic slavery, Wesley's conscience and charity would not permit him to remain passive or to allow others the ease of an unenlightened morality. I believe that his concern for human liberty—the substance not the shadow—and for satisfying human needs is part of a coherent Christian ethics based upon the worthfulness of man, male and female. Hence political, social, and economic strategies are morally correct and necessary. Correct because for Wesley they are grounded on the divine evaluation of humanity. Necessary because ethical advance is not a matter of wishful thinking. Always these strategies must be held within the constraints of holiness, love, and justice.

happiness. The motif of happiness was a

constant theme in the discourse of eighteenth-century England and America. Written into the American Declaration of Independence, explicated by Thomas Paine and Jeremy Bentham, it participated in the era's optimistic belief that perfection was to be anticipated. In arts and reflection, in religious and civil expression, one could see or hope for a "future of unlimited progress."[24] Bentham was committed to the utilitarian ethic of the greatest happiness of the greatest number.

Wesley echoed the language of happiness with such frequency that one might suspect him of becoming a bedfellow with Paine, Bentham, or Jefferson. Wesley was dedicated to the happiness of humanity, but his interpretation of happiness must be seen primarily from a soteriological, not a political or social, perspective. Happiness and holiness are inseparable. Happiness is the end of life; the love of God is the source and center of life.[25] In God is found that perfect love which casting out fear creates happiness;[26] the contemplation of God's perfection is a "continual addition to the happiness of a Christian."[27]

The ethical implications which flow from Wesley's view of happiness are drawn out in Hoffman's important thesis. "The criterion," he writes, "for evaluating an act as morally sound according to Wesley is to be discovered in its effectiveness to make man happy. . . . Happiness serves as a measurement of God's successful work in His creature."[28]

If humanity cannot be happy without being holy, or if the norm by which happiness is measured is holiness, the universal human experience may be characterized as at best a marginal happiness. Wesley's stance virtually echoes Augustine's confessional dictum: "Our hearts are restless until they find rest in Thee." The "optimism of grace" which Wesley ceaselessly proclaimed is surely the counterforce to the negations of human alienation and restlessness.[29]

Summary

In this review of Wesley's political opinions, I have not exhausted the topics or offered comprehensive analysis of the issues addressed. Certainly there is only the most narrow focus on the sources or criteria for ethical analysis, a task which is before us. To this point the essay has sought to indicate that Wesley demonstrated great concern for the preservation of human rights within an established or dependable political order. At times, as in certain appeals for economic change or in his attack against slavery, Wesley appears in the liberal tradition, well ahead of many, if not most, persons in his age.

While echoing the familiar anthem of the liberal tradition—the right of all persons to life, liberty, property, happiness—he insists on the theonomous undergirding for these rights. The rights of Man are not interpreted through soteriology. That would be an elitism resting upon a personal, spiritual relationship to God in Christ. Rather, the rights are based upon the appeal to creation and natural law; therefore, everyone in all the whole round world is included in the Creator's pledge and gift. But this is an aspect of the next section on ethical methodology. To that we must turn.

Wesley's Ethical Method and Style

If Wesley is categorized in terms of theological ethics, it would be fair to say that his is a Trinitarian approach. He is surely theocentric in his ethics of creation; Christocentric in his analysis of *imitatio* and reconciliation; and, pneumatological in his discussion of the Christian dynamic for ethical transformation. Any attempt to assess the relative weight which he places upon one category or another, for example, theocentric or pneumatological ethics, will probably involve us in the familiar Trinitarian debates over what is the proper and adequate role of Father, Son, and Holy Spirit in the salvific process. That we are in constant danger of a unitarianism in theological analysis and religious life is well understood by all of us. The same risk is seen in Christian ethics. The criticism leveled at Barth's use of the christological analogy to define and interpret political ethics is an illustration of the problem.[30] Barth's evident reluctance to give any credence to the *analogia entis* seems to lead him to a Christomonism in theology. That is a debatable point. What is more important here is what this illustrates: the problem of a practical negation of the Trinity of God in ethical discourse.

Wesley does not appear to err in that regard, but a more definitive evaluation awaits the structuring of a pneumatological ethics in the discipline of Christian ethics.[31]

Ethics of Creation

An ethics of the "first person,"[32] or the Father, is called an ethics of creation, building upon the conception of God as source. In Wesley's thought several methodological keys introduce us to the purpose of the Creator and his provision for human life and society. In these may be recognized certain criteria of evaluation; criteria which are neither relativistic[33] nor heteronomous[34] as Wesley concluded regarding Francis Hutcheson's *Essay on the Passions*. While I believe Wesley misread Hutcheson, his concern remains valid. How does one develop an adequate "moral sense"[55] apart from the divine ground? Nor are Wesley's criteria *simply* utilitarian (in the Benthamite definition).

Wesley proceeds first to develop the ethic of creation on the ground of divine existence and reality. God exists as the One, Holy, Sovereign God of all creation. God has established a moral universe wherein his holiness is regulative of every relationship. Man is the centerpiece of that universe. Wesley does speculate about the great chain of being,[36] but his interests are far more in the sphere of human conduct under the divine superintendence and providence.

Two concepts leap to mind in any consideration of Wesley's "ethics of creation." First is the idea of man as the creation *imago Dei* and what that represents in ethical valuation. Second is concern for natural law and the way in which natural law shapes and modifies positive law. Concerning the first, it is argued that this theological assessment continues to shape Wesley's ethics throughout all of his reflection regarding Man. Never, even in his most negative assessment of Man, does Wesley forget the gift of God in creation. The fall, equally cataclysmic in Wesley's mind as in Calvin's, does not detract from human worth, and cannot be employed by despisers of the race to strip persons of their created value. Thomas Hobbes could construe the struggle of one person against another in such gloomy terms as to justify totalitarianism.[37] Wesley never saw the problem in such pessimistic terms, although he remained aware of the dangers of that possibility in his resistance to an unprincipled revolutionism which may become anarchism. Certainly totalitarianism was unacceptable to him.

In Wesley's interpretation of natural law he appeals to a constant and consistent reality which stands amidst the caprice of human society. Conscience is considered under the natural law rubric, even though it may be legitimate to trace conscience to grace.[38] Indeed, natural law itself may be legitimately expressive of God's graced outreach toward his creation. It is best, I claim, to analyze natural law in creational or ontological terms instead of under soteriological categories. My stance here is affirmative toward natural law ethics, although one must carefully avoid the casuistry which accompanies it historically, especially the way in which human reason may be manipulated toward desired ends. Caution must necessarily be exercised in assessing the power of reason. Since the natural law argument rests so solidly upon the right exercise of reason, we may be counseled not to lean too heavily. Nevertheless, for Wesley, the checks and balances of his authority quadrilateral—Scripture, reason, experience, tradition—surround the use of reason with corrective restrictions.

Image of God. In Wesley's theology of Man created *imago Dei* may be recognized the ineradicable depth of value which God has placed on his creature. The affirmation of all creation is contained in the words, "And God saw that it was good" (Gen. 1:10,12,18,25). After the creation was completed, "God saw all that he had made, and it was very good" (Gen. 1:31 NIV). Wesley perceives the drive of the divine creation toward the creation of Man. The creation is "very good." For now *Man* is made, who is the chief of the ways of God, the visible image of the Creator's glory." Wesley accentuates the perfection or completion of creation, the complementary significance of every part.[39]

If the descriptive intent of Wesley's analysis is evident, even more so is the normative. Man was made to be both happy and holy.[40]

The *imago Dei* represents humanity's constituent reality. Man is not merely a mirror image of God, but is godlike in nature and essence. The "moral image" of God is represented in the holiness of God's creation. Humanity was formed by God to bear the very nature of God. Righteous in all of the relationships which characterize the *imago Dei*—toward God, others, self, the world—humanity possessed all of the possibility of total holiness *and* happiness in the paradise God had given.

Moreover, the human race was granted the awesome gifts of freedom, rationality, will, and spirituality. Wesley describes this as the "natural image." Freedom, without which humanity would be "as incapable of either vice or virtue, as any part of the inanimate creation.[41] Rationality or understanding which involves power of discrimination and judging what is the truth. A will which before the fall was able to exert itself without a wrong bias. Spirituality, which, participating in the very nature of God who is Spirit, makes humanity capable of knowing and loving God. All of these benefits were given to the human family in order that it might possess the power to be fully human, standing in total dependence upon God which is the quintessence of human liberty. The paradox of human existence is found in Man's perfect freedom under the perfect sovereignty of the Creator.

A third aspect of the *imago Dei* is the "political image," expressing Wesley's interpretation of the governmental role assigned to this lower world.[42] "As he has the government of the inferior creatures, he is as it were God's representative on earth. Yet his government of himself by the freedom of his will, has in it more of God's image, than his government of the creatures."[43] The distinctiveness of humanity is contained in the divine assignment to Man to be "God's vice-regent upon earth, the prince and governor of this lower world."[44]

The ethical significance of the concept of *imago Dei* is apparent. First to be noted is the holiness motif which dominates the discussion. It is this which so clearly marks humankind as the creature and God as Creator in a relationship of complementarity, wholeness, and worth. That God is holy means that unequivocal worth inheres in the divine nature. If it is not possible to detract from divine perfection by any ascription of evil, then God may be known as worthful in a total sense. Humanity in a constituent sense bears that worthfulness. Nothing about humanity could detract from the quality of character which God gave in creation.[45] That humanity is finite cannot serve as the ground for self-denigration or devaluation of others.

If, adhering to Wesley's interpretation of holiness as love of God and neighbor, we affirm that God is love, we then link holiness and love in a more attractive picture of God than a simple focus on holiness permits. As Rudolf Otto affirms, the experience of the holy evokes tremor and fear, mystery and fascination.[46] To say that "God is love," a theme so vitally attuned to Wesley's proclamation of the gospel, is to attenuate the fearfulness of holiness with the tenderness of a caring which inheres in the subject whether or not the object is worthy. The doctrine of creation, however, affirms human worth.

The natural image concept with its focus on freedom, will, and understanding offers us a highly tuned ethical construct. Understanding is applied to decision making (or choice), and choice applied to ability (i.e., liberty, or the power to give expression to the choice). In the original state of humanity, Wesley claims, understanding was capable of clear apprehension and true judgment; the will was not biased. "His [Adam's] liberty was wholly guided by his understanding: He chose, or refused according to its direction."[47]

By the "political image" Wesley has indicated that humanity has the power of self-government, a power or authority given by the Creator. Human government is not given by God in anticipation of the fall, but as an expression of the special dignity of his creature, Man. Wesley seems to suggest a primeval autonomy, that is, self-government in the context of paradise. If that is so, it all changes in the sequence of rebellion where human government is required because of the antipathies which are created

between human beings, tragically pictured in the death of Abel at the hand of Cain.

We may summarize the importance of the *imago Dei* concept by asserting the responsibility which accrues to humanity as the result of choices freely made.[48] Alone among the creatures, Man is addressed by God, and answers God.[49] After the fall Man answers God in petulance and blame, but still there is response. In the response is the admission of sin, that is, of a choice self-serving and rebellious. Humanity is responsible!

The Fall. For heuristic purposes, we have been addressing Man in terms of that which constitutes humanity, that is, humanity in terms of creation, not the Fall. Now it is necessary to ask what sort of disvaluation occurs in the alienation of humanity from God. Wesley stresses that the fall brought about the loss of the moral image, the forfeiture of righteousness and true holiness.[50] Describing the consequences of the fall, he uses such theological concepts as "foundations out of course," "utterly perverse and distorted," "prone to evil," "alienated," "out of frame," "undue in their degree, or placed on undue objects," "inbred corruption," and more.[51] These convey the impression of both moral lapse, seen in such terms as corruption or perversion, and of relational conflict, in terms like "distorted," "out of course," "alienated," "prone." Indisputably, Wesley stands in the Augustinian-Reformation understanding of human departure from the will of God, hence depravity and alienation are stressed.

With respect to the natural image or the political image, he is able to affirm a quite different sequel. While the fall has weakened humanity's exercise of the will,[52] spirituality, and understanding, to the extent that no salvific possibility accrues to or inheres in Man, yet these powers remain in significant degree so that humanity is still characterized by a unique dignity and worth.

The question of worth or value returns to this discussion. Asserting that holiness is a "category of value," inhering in the divine nature and in the *imago Dei*, has the fall, with the loss of righteousness, stripped humanity of its worth? Does human rebellion and self-asserted autonomy result in a less worthy or even worthless creature? Basing the worth of humanity on the criterion of holiness, does the defacing of the image of God mean diminished value?

The answer which Wesley's thought offers us is contained in his doctrine of prevenient grace (while the focus on grace is reserved to a later section of this essay, some preliminary assertions may be made). Wesley is soundly orthodox in his definition of sinful humanity. However, as Umphrey Lee pointed out in 1936, for Wesley the natural man is "a logical abstraction."[53] He could articulate this apparently surprising and controversial thesis on the basis of Wesley's belief in the universality of precedent grace.

The ethical significance of the concept of prevenient grace suggests the affirmation of the goodness of creation. Grace affirms fallen humanity; grace affirms the value of deprived and depraved human life. Grace promises that whatever humanity has been, it may be again. Holiness is forfeited; grace promises restoration. Human abilities are impaired; grace renews and sanctifies. Even the earth, groaning under its inexplicable subjection to suffering, because of humanity's self-slavery, will again know the liberty of the children of God. Grace proposes all of the potential for value which sinfulness diminished and threatened but could not destroy—*could not destroy* because grace is stronger than sin.

Natural Law. H. T. Dickinson has demonstrated that the Whig party in England, following Locke, had appealed to the law of nature to counter the divine right theory. Locke had argued that reason was the best resource for interpreting the law of nature and that the law of nature was the unwritten law of God. "The law of nature was sovereign over all human actions and set the bounds to man's freedom."[54] By the law of nature all are made free and equal. Locke derived the rights of Man—life, liberty, property—from the law of nature.

The implication of this position is a high assessment of human reason. Certainly this opinion was congenial to the eighteenth century, even if certain events like the tragic Lisbon earthquake, or certain empiricists like Hume, who stressed the evidence of human experience (and the difficulty of theodicy), shaped a more negative opinion regarding the "reasonable man."

Wesley strongly affirmed the linkage between reason and religion, insisting that "knowledge and vital piety" belonged together. Nevertheless, he tempered the high place given to reason, by appealing to the experience of history. His criticism of warfare, which followed the more gloomy critiques of Jonathan Swift, shows that Wesley did not buy into the idealism of many of his contemporaries. All of this simply means that he sustained an awareness of the powers and perversions which are possible for human understanding.

In addressing the use of natural law in Wesley[55] we are attracted to his analysis of liberty of conscience, civil rights, and human liberty (the freedom to determine one's situation, i.e., the right to be a free person, not a slave).

Regarding both civil and religious liberty, Wesley insisted on "English liberty," "the liberty of Christians," "yea, of every rational creature, who as such has a right to worship God according to his own conscience."[56] In "Thoughts upon Liberty" he wrote:

All men in the world desire liberty; whoever breathes, breathes after this, and that by a kind of *natural instinct* antecedent to art or education. Yet at the same time all men of understanding acknowledge it as a rational instinct. For we feel this desire . . . in consequence of our reason.[57]

In his most explicit appeal to the law of nature Wesley argues the case for the supremacy of natural law over positive law in the case of human slavery. In natural law theory two major questions are asked: What is justice? and, How do we discover what justice demands?[58] Wesley's answer to these questions would seem to be: Justice is conformity to the nature of things, established by a just God, and discovered by reason. Liberty is perceived as consistent with nature; Wesley would call it a "natural instinct," a concomitant of life, like breathing. If positive (enacted) laws deprive anyone of the freedom of choice, which is a constituent aspect of human personhood, the positive laws must be changed.

"The grand plea is, "They [slaves and slaveholding] are authorized by law." But can law, human [positive] law change the *nature of things*? Can it turn darkness into light, or evil into good? By no means. Notwithstanding ten thousand [positive] laws, right is right and wrong is wrong still.[59]

The validity of appeals to natural law has long been tested. To those who have been nurtured on Barthian thought, natural law is evaluated in negative terms as potentially devastating to human society. Thielicke argues that to base human rights on natural law will surely be regarded skeptically by "Reformation theologians." Nevertheless, he affirms the insight, "however dubious the wrapper in which it is contained."[60]

Contrariwise, Wesleyan theology has incorporated natural law theory into its ethics. It is congenial to the Wesleyan quadrilateral which appeals to reason. Permitted to stand apart from Scripture, and from tradition and experience, natural law arguments may tend toward such a base human experience as the totalitarianism of National Socialism.

I believe we should cautiously affirm natural

law emphases, first, in the hope that we may discover, as James Luther Adams asserts, "something that abides in the midst of change and serves to measure it," or as he defines the task: Natural law is "the problem of establishing and justifying ethical standards in the relation to the essential nature of man and of things."[61] Second, we may surely hope that some degree of rationality and order survives in our world. And, it does!

Conscience

Earlier in this essay the concept of conscience was considered briefly and placed under an ethics of creation for structural purposes. The ability to recognize right from wrong seems implicit in the divine command to avoid the tree of the knowledge of good and evil. This suggests that God impressed upon Adam and Eve the consciousness of a correct path to traverse and a way which was wrong. The tempter initiated a dialogue which was designed to obscure that sense by an invitation to self-deification. When the allurement seemed reasonable and in their self-interest, they accepted the appeal. Immediately their consciousness of the difference between right and wrong, obedience and disobedience, is transmuted into a sense of shame and guilt.

Wesley asserts that immediately upon the act of transgression, their eyes were opened, that is "the eyes of their consciences." They "felt a disorder in their own spirits which they had never before been *conscious* of."[62] Conscience is certainly a gift of God in creation, "above all his [humanity's] natural endowments."[63]

In his political tracts, Wesley asserts that conscience must be free. This right is firmly based on the gift of God in creation. "The Creator gave him this right when he endowed him with understanding."[64] On this basis Wesley affirms the faculty of conscience as a benefit of God in creation. Conscience is a constituent part of our created humanity.

Nevertheless, Wesley is concerned to avoid naturalistic interpretations of conscience. Therefore, sinful humanity stands consciously responsible before God by that conscience which is now sustained for human benefit by the grace of God. Commenting on Francis Hutcheson's *Essay on the Passions*, Wesley declaims against the Scottish philosopher's claim that the "moral sense" is natural to humankind:

But it is not true, that either the *public* or the *moral sense* (both of which are included in the term conscience) is now natural to man. Whatever may have been the case at first, while man was in a state

of innocence, both the one and the other is now a branch of that supernatural gift of God which we usually style, preventing grace.[65]

Hutcheson, who taught Adam Smith at Glasgow, is known as the philosopher of the "moral sense."[66] The moral sense is the human avenue of perceiving virtue or vice. Virtue is found in that which evokes pleasure or agreeableness; vice is displeasure. Is it possible for the moral sense to approve the vicious and disapprove the virtuous? Hutcheson allowed the possibility but argued that instances of such "disorder" would be hard to find.

An action could be virtuous even when it was performed without any conscious prior intention or purpose to please God. It was this stance, not intended by Hutcheson to undermine the theistic ground of virtue, which Wesley took to be subversive of Christian ethics. In fact, Hutcheson insisted that acts performed to please the creature rather than the Creator, when the choice was present, indicated great perversity of human affection.[67]

A sharp contrast exists between Hutcheson's optimism and Wesley's pessimism regarding human conduct in response to the consciousness or understanding given through the moral sense. Hutcheson assumed a rather consistent goodness in human conduct, while Wesley was sure that humanity consistently acted against the invitation to right living. Nevertheless, for Wesley prevenient grace offers, not only the gift of perceiving right or wrong, but the enablement, through penitence, and faith, to do the right. This Hutcheson could not offer. Therefore his conception founders on the familiar ethical dilemma taught by Butler: "I see the right and I approve it, too. Condemn the wrong, and yet the wrong pursue." Hutcheson's ethics remains naturalistic at the level of performance.

Wesley's discussion of conscience, set largely against Hutcheson's analysis, stresses the affirmative response of conscience to right acts or thoughts and negative responses to wrong. Conscience possesses a cognitive function; it is "that faculty whereby we are at once conscious of our own thoughts, words, and actions; and of their merit or demerit, of their being good or bad."[68]

What are the implications which flow from Wesley's understanding of conscience? From the perspective of personal ethics, human beings are conscious of the quality of their thoughts and deeds, and are morally responsible for that which is known. At the level of theological ethics, Wesley would insist on the recurrent failure of humanity to adhere to the right way, even when that is clearly known. In the undergirding of pervenient grace lies a possibility for pursuing the goals of goodness provided by the insights of conscience. In the sphere of political ethics, the claim is made that individual conscience perceives its inherent dignity and priority over the will of the state, or the church, or other extraneous powers, significant though they may be. Above all of these the conscience answers to God. That stance is an assertion of the exalted possibilities in humanity and of the denigrations which occur to persons and powers, which in concert or separately deprive others of their worth by removing the very essence of humanity from them, that is, whether it is the right of worship, of persons, or of subsistence. Whenever these areas of our lives are structured by external coercion, not inner decision, to some degree we have suffered harm or loss of humanity.

Appeal to History. When Wesley's conception of conscience with its freedom or responsibility is fully analyzed, it will be seen that his valuation of liberty of conscience is largely drawn from his historical sense. Out of the Protestant Reformation he has drawn a conception of the right of private judgment. This right is pressed well beyond Luther's individualism. In Wesley it becomes a dynamic doctrine with the potential for misuse and fanaticism, but once again his quadrilateral, and his conception of the church as community, holds the individual in a structure of checks and balances.

From the Puritans, including his grandparents, and from others, he received a strong affirmation of religious liberty. The intolerance of English monarchs before the Glorious Revolution assisted him in the recognition that force, whether psychological, physical, or religious, is not the way of faith or reason.

Expressed in other terms, Wesley's ethical perspectives were shaped by historical illustrations which often formed, and surely reinforced, his preeminently biblical judgments.

Christological Ethics

If the ethics of creation has been adequately asserted, it must be confessed that the discussion has trespassed on the considerations of a second article of ethics. That Wesley developed an ethical structure on the significance or meaning of Christ for human life is now affirmed. Because the task of developing a Trinitarian ethics looms so large, we shall seek some shortcuts to interpretation. It is hoped that the fuller explication of Wesley's creation ethics will show some of the potential lines for our use in dealing with contemporary issues.

In christological ethics, Wesley is primarily concerned with grace, salvation, and imitation.

Grace. The ethical possibilities for humanity after the fall were and are sharply changed. Conscience, understanding, will, liberty, were all rendered impotent. The human race *coram Deo* was unable to carry on the reflective processes by which conscience is able to determine good or evil. However, as Wesley's theology recurrently teaches, humanity is not left in a natural state, untouched by the divine mind and will. Standing under the grace of God, which as it were fills up the vacuum created by our estrangement, we are assisted by grace in the areas of conscience, choice, contrition, and faith. Christian ethics for Wesley, then, is certainly a reaffirmation of creation ethics. Christian ethics is grounded in the grace of God, revealed through Jesus Christ through whom grace and truth came (John 1:17). While creation began with the divine initiative and the raw material of the universe came by his command, the soteriological process begins with a different product. Now defaced and defiled, rebellious and discordant, humanity requires another act of God. The saving acts of God are consummated in Jesus Christ; in Christ the totality of human experiences are recapitulated. But whether with creation or salvation, the initiative belongs to God, whose will is made known to us to the end that we may assume our moral burden. We are responsible! Another way to express this insight is to affirm the continuing obligation to God which grace undergirds. Persons are no less morally responsible because of the fall. Although Adam sought to shift the blame from himself to Eve, and to God, God confirmed his own guilt, hence his ethical astuteness or sensitivity. Prevenient grace means that humankind is still very human, that is, still an ethical being.[69]

Salvation. The major ethical lines of Wesley's doctrine of salvation may be summed up in terms of restoration, reconciliation, and sanctification. Somewhat arbitrarily the analysis of sanctification is deferred to pneumatological ethics.

The work of Jesus Christ is portrayed in Pauline theology as a reconciling work. Reconciliation is amplified in patristic theology by Irenaeus and infused into the stream of Christian soteriology. It seems evident that Wesley was impressed by the style of Irenaeus in developing his view of reconciliation.[70]

Wesley's discussion of the meaning of the death of Christ appears mainly to follow the lines of Anselm and of the major Reformers. Atonement conveys the sense of propitiation, the objective satisfaction for the sins of the race.[71]

The inclination of Irenaeus toward reconciliation seems less accented, presumably because it implies a subjective participation, perhaps even a synergism. In any event, the concept as it was developed by Wesley reflects Irenaeus' concept of *anacephalaiosis*. "When he [Christ] was incarnate and became man, he recapitulated in himself all generations of mankind, making himself the center of our salvation, that what we lost in Adam, . . . we might receive in Jesus Christ."[72] The purpose of incarnation is to bring humanity into union with the divine, "that man might become a son of God once more." Perhaps recapitulation suggests restoration more than reconciliation, but the latter is surely implied and understood.[73]

The theology of reconciliation links together and balances the doctrines of incarnation and atonement.[74] It concerns itself with humanity (human-ness?) as well as with the divine initiative toward humankind. The forensic theology of justification lacks (often lacks) this balance because the tendency is toward the objective decision of God toward us.

I believe the ethical significance of the concept of restoration and reconciliation are evident, containing the undergirding of the participation of Jesus Christ in our humanity. We are enabled then to affirm a depth of moral obligation which objective theories of the atonement often miss or are unable to bear.

Reconciliation according to Pauline theology conveys the "in Christ" prospect of a restoration of the original relationship between God and Man, man and woman, and Man and the earth. "In Christ," writes St. Paul, "there is neither Jew nor Greek, slave nor free, male nor female, for you are all one in Christ Jesus" (Gal. 3:28). "In Christ" the walls are taken down and the hostility is overcome by the reconciling work of Christ (Eph. 2:11-18). "In Christ" the whole universe drives toward the consummation, the overcoming of all of the anguish and discord which the long history of the world has recorded (Rom. 8:18-27).

Imitation. In the perspective of the reconciling work of Christ—atoning, making one, restoring—one is able to see the relevance of an ethics of imitation, the *imitatio Christi*. In particular dependence upon Thomas á Kempis, Wesley developed the concept of *Christ the Pattern*, his title for the edited *Imitation of Christ*. Included in the Christian Library, the work of Kempis provided a major source in the stream of Wesleyan ethics.

Wesley did not believe that one could make a simple human choice to imitate Jesus' life or adhere to his teachings. Grace is the factor, from outside or beyond us, which assists us in following Christ. With the grace factor in place, however, Wesley would strongly affirm the exemplary significance of the life and teachings of Christ.[75] This is evidenced in his sermons on the Sermon on the Mount, thirteen in all, but particularly in sermon nine. Wesley speaks of "imitating or resembling" God in the spirit of our minds for here "the true Christian imitation begins."[76]

From the standpoint of his early legalism, that is, his effort at self-perfection, Wesley perceived Kempis as too strict, and expressed anger, and presumably frustration, at the regimen he proposed. Subsequently the liberating word of the gospel, mediated through Luther and the Moravians, opened up the possibilities of a vigorous discipline within the power of faith. When faith works through love, a new kind of energy is operative in the life of the seeker.

While the *imitatio Christi* emphasis in Wesley does not receive as detailed an interpretation as one might expect, the disciplinary implications, that is, the life of discipleship and holy living, are very thoroughly crafted. That is evident in his lifelong dedication to the teaching of Christian perfection defined as the love of God and the neighbor. All of the duties that flow from that outreaching spirit are aspects of following Christ.

What it means to follow Christ's example would require an extended ethical discourse. Certainly it must involve the recognition of his spirit and mind. St. Paul's "Let this mind be in you which was also in Christ Jesus" (Phil. 2:5), with the hymn of kenosis and exaltation which follows, is an important clue for the servanthood which is to characterize Christian men and women. It surely requires deep concern for the neighbor's needs, whether the neighbor is "one of us" or not, as in the parable of the good Samaritan. It means "social holiness" lived out in the world where all of the prejudices of life, irritations, or abrasions are so sharply "up front." The Wesleyan model of servanthood in the imitation of Christ can never be the cloister, as appealing as that may be (even to academics in tower or dungeon).[77]

Fides Caritate Formata. A theme of primary significance in Wesleyan theological ethics is that of the faith which works through love. Representing the important Pauline relationship between faith and ethics (Gal. 5:6, "In Christ Jesus . . . ," gives this concept its christological reference), the insight is employed by Wesley to show both the priority of evangelical faith and the certainty that faith nurtures, and is nurtured in, love. A spiritual energy flows outward from faith toward love, that is, personal and social ethics. Love in turn is the context for maturing faith.

For Christians in the tradition of the Reformation, *fides caritate formata* echoes a Catholic theology which leads to the submersion of faith by love, or the departure from the certainties of objective justification to the subjectivity of sanctification. There is little doubt that the central peril of Wesleyan theology becomes a tendency toward moralism, that is, sanctification which does not continually rest on the footing of justification. Reformed theology faces the inverse problem of a justification that does not adequately protect against spiritual inertia.

For Wesley, once the priority of faith is fixed in his experience, the relationship of faith and love may be developed creatively. As long as he lived, faith remained the ground on which he stood. On and from this ground he moved to the *telos* of Christian life, that is, love. Love is never separated from faith. If and when this happens (and it has repeatedly in the heritage), love (or works of love) preempts faith and the Christian life is once more the familiar regimen of salvation by good works.

When *faith works through love*, the possibility for moral renewal and spiritual transformation, for both individuals and institutions, is in place. The energy is present (through faith) to prevent the reformer from becoming worn out and cynical. The motivation (through love) is healthy (holy) so that the agent of transformation does not repetitively draw the program of reform around self in another variation of *incurvatum in se*. When love balances faith in the ethical equation, it is possible to avoid the antinomian aberration of faith without love.

Ethics of the Spirit

In this third stage in the development of Trinitarian ethics, pneumatological or spiritual ethics are considered. Earlier it was noted that the ethics of sanctification would be deferred to this section. While sanctification may technically be considered under theology, soteriology, and pneumatology, the decision to incorporate it here is based on the pattern of traditional dogmatics. Two issues represent the Wesleyan "ethics of the Spirit." The first concerns sanctification as the purity of intention. The second considers the dynamic of spiritual life, the empowerment of the Holy Spirit for life.

Purity of Intention. From his early contacts with the proponents of earnest Christianity—Jeremy Taylor, William Law, and Kempis—Wesley learned the importance of the simplicity and purity of intention and the purity of affection. Concerning his experience in 1725 he wrote: "I saw that 'simplicity of intention and purity of affection, one design in all we speak or do and one desire, ruling all our tempers, are, indeed the wings of the soul,' without which she can never ascend to the mount of God." In the next sixty-six years Wesley developed the implications of this purity and simplicity in his doctrine of holiness as love for God and neighbor. In christological terms sanctification means purity through the reconciling death of Jesus at Calvary. The "blood and righteousness of Christ" or, "all that Christ hath done and suffered for us," brings "full salvation," "perfect love," which means "love excluding sin, love filling the heart, taking up the whole capacity of the soul."[79]

Purity and simplicity are the benchmarks of Wesley's doctrine of perfection. Applied to the sphere of moral influence in the world, or to ethical motivation, the doctrine offers the prospect of a cadre of Christian servants who may approach human need with an uncommon quality of concern. Admitting the ease with which humans overlook their faults and sins, falling repetitively into the Adamic sin of passing the blame, the Wesleyan teaching holds forth the possibility of persons no longer conformed to the present age. The pure in heart belong to God and to his world.

If it is possible to fashion persons after this model of Christian simplicity, the mixed motivations which subvert so much good in the world may be transmitted into a singular power. The flaw of reformers is frequently discovered in their distraction toward those spoils which belong to the victor. The most exalted programs are undermined by the will to power, self-assertion, or other variations on flawed commitment.

The Spiritual Dynamic. The practice of the Christian ethic is the goal of Wesleyan ethics. The value, adaptability, and application of his view of the Christian life lived in church and society, both of them communities of Man, finally turns on the issue of power, the power to carry out what is known and believed to be just, true, holy, or even prudent. Ethics always finds its nemesis in the power to achieve. Christian ethics declares that in the power of the Holy Spirit, the church is able to overcome its centrifugal tendencies and become the agency of moral renewal. The church *may* be selfish, oriented toward the arrogance of power, and materialistic. It *may* be as moribund as any other human agency. In the Spirit, however, resides a dynamic for achieving the Lord's purposes. Were the church to seriously open itself to the simplicity and purity of intention, dedicate itself to a transcendent *telos*, and become consistently the channel of the Spirit, then moral dynamic would pervade God's world. Idealistic? Of course, but a Christian idealism.

Charles Wesley wrote a hymn regarding "Primitive Christianity."

> Ye different sects, who all declare
> "Lo, here is Christ!" or "Christ is there!"
> Your stronger proof divinely give,
> And show me where the Christians live.
>
> Your claim, alas! Ye cannot prove,
> Ye want [lack] the genuine mark of
>   love.[80]

Come, let us show where the Christians live! *Veni Creator Spiritus!*

Trajectories from Wesleyan Ethics

The time has finally come to venture on the limb of futurism (having carefully laid aside all saws, axes, or other sharp instruments lest I land below(?) in a heap). If Wesley were addressing the problems and promise of the future, what would be his extrapolations? In particular, how would he speak to our most pressing, most overwhelming issues?

1. He would address them realistically, but hopefully, ever aware of the grace of divine sovereignty.

2. He would consider the Christian church, under the Spirit, replicating primitive Christianity, to be the potent force by which social transformation will take place.

3. Wesley affirmed human life as the great gift of the Creator. He would insist that we seek solutions to the abortion issue, not on pragmatic, naturalistic, or political bases, but on the ground of divine gift and grace. He would argue that reason, to say nothing of religion, would prevail in our pursuit of answers to nuclear confrontation. He would plead for Christian grace and sense in meeting the needs of the disadvantaged, hungry, or unlearned. He would press us to affirm the humanity of persons, and thus their need to develop their potential through education, Christian faith, and all that is meant by being human. He would call for both private and public sector programs and legislation which would ensure that some floor to provide for human subsistence would be established. He would press for elimination of those slaveries which keep persons on a subhuman level, but he would insist that we recognize the recurrent pride which drains off the moral force of our integrity, creating new kinds of slavery. Wesley would powerfully check our abuses of creation by appealing for simpler lifestyles, emphasizing the stewardship of the benefits we enjoy.

4. Affirming liberty under God, Wesley would call for universal acknowledgment of human freedom. His concern would be less for the form of government than for that system which preserves liberty. Religious oppression would be vigorously resisted wherever it is found.

5. Politically Wesley would stand firmly on the side of an ordered system which guarantees human rights. The uncertain course of revolution would call forth a stringent caution, lest present liberties and rights be exchanged for less, not more, opportunities for human life.

6. He would write carefully crafted letters to Prime Minister Thatcher, Queen Elizabeth II, and perhaps even the Council of Bishops in the United States, calling for an end to nuclear proliferation and conversations toward an eventual Geneva Convention–type control of weapons that threaten to annihilate Man. He would never consider human self-destruction to be the way the sovereign God brings about the *telos* of history.

7. He would caution church and state against alliances which negate the constructive function of each sphere. Wesley would be unable to identify or understand our wall of separation, but he would warn us against a post-Constantinian church which bears too many of the marks of temporizing and expediency.

8. Finally, he would counsel us to sustain a Trinitarian perspective in our ethics which holds creation, reconciliation, and sanctification in a dynamic unity, until the whole creation comes into the liberty of the children of God.

NOTES

1. See Gordon Kaufmann. "Nuclear Eschatology," *Journal of the American Academy of Religion* (March 1983): 1-14.
2. See H. T. Dickinson, *Liberty and Property* (London: Werden Feld and Nicolson, 1977), pp. 33-36.
3. Ibid., pp. 70-72, 8-89.
4. Ibid., pp. 197-206.
5. See Wesley's letter to "Our Brethren in America," 10 September 1784, in *Letters*, vol. 7, pp. 238-39: "By a very uncommon train of providences many of the Provinces of North America are totally disjoined from their Mother Country and erected into independent states." Dickinson's discussion of the appeal to providence in the Glorious Revolution should be noted as we look at Wesley's parallel emphasis on providence in the American Revolution. See Dickinson, *Liberty*, pp. 35-36.
6. Locke had stressed that every person possesses natural and unalienable rights to life, liberty, and property. The rights of life and liberty are civil liberties, not the right to exercise political power. Freedom of conscience, the right to a livelihood and of personal freedom under due process of law. See Dickinson, *Liberty*, p. 68. Wesley's position in the 1760s and following is a mirror of this, but

he is more cautious about the principle of consent or contract.

My thesis is consistent with the judgment expressed by J. Munsey Turner. Speaking of Dr. R. F. Wearmouth, who wrote on the influence of Methodism among the working class, Turner asserts: "Dr. Wearmouth clearly accepted the . . . familiar view that in Wesleyanism a 'dominant Toryism' made way for an 'underlying Liberalism.' " See Turner's "Robert Featherstone Wearmouth (1882–1963): Methodist Historian," *Proceedings of the Wesley Historical Society*, 43:5 (September 1982): 111-12.

7. See Wesley's "Thoughts upon Slavery," *Works*, vol. 11, pp. 74-75. He specifically describes the slave holders as "inhuman masters."

8. Wesley's "Thoughts on the Present Scarcity of Provisions," (1773), ibid., pp. 53-54.

9. See Wesley's "The Doctrine of Original Sin," *Works*, vol. 10, pp. 196-464, esp. 221-25. Wesley sums up his concern: "Now, who can reconcile war, I will not say to religion, but to any degree of reason or common sense?" Wesley's extended comment is from Jonathan Swift's *Gullivers Travels*. Compare the comments of Swift (New York: Rand McNally and Co., 1940), pp. 279-88.

10. Thomas G. Hoffman, "The Moral Philosophy of John Wesley: The Development of His Moral Dynamic," Ph.D. dissertation, Temple University, 1968.

11. Bernard Semmel, *The Methodist Revolution* (New York: Basic Books, 1973), p. 60.

12. See my "Church and State in the Thought and Life of John Wesley," Ph.D. dissertation, University of Iowa, 1971, p. 9.

13. See Wesley's "Thoughts upon Liberty" (24 February 1772), *Works*, vol. 11, p. 41.

14. See Wesley's "Observations on Liberty," (1776), ibid., p. 92.

15. Ibid. In "Thoughts upon Liberty," p. 37, Wesley interprets worship according to our own conscience to be "according to the best light we have." He further calls it an "indefeasible right, . . . inseparable from humanity."

16. See Wesley's emphasis in "A Farther Appeal to Men of Reason and Religion," *Works*, vol. 8, p. 125.

17. See "Church and State in the Thought and Life of John Wesley," p. 230, for a brief comment. See *John Wesley*, Albert C. Outler, ed., A Library of Protestant Thought (New York: Oxford University Press, 1964), pp. 473-74.

18. Hoffman, *Moral Philosophy*, p. 196.

19. Wesley, "Thoughts on the Present Scarcity of Provisions," *Works*, vol. 11 , p. 58.

20. Philip Watson, ed., *The Message of the Wesleys* (New York: Macmillan Company, 1964), p. 67, n.75.

21. Wesley, "The Use of Money" (1744), in *Sermons*, vol. 2, pp. 309-27. See esp. Sugden's introduction which describes the ways in which the "misuse" took place in the Methodist societies.

22. See Kemper Fullerton, "Calvinism and Capitalism: An Explanation of the Weber Thesis," in *Protestantism and Capitalism: The Weber Thesis and Its Critics*, ed. Robert W. Green (Boston: D. C. Heath, 1959), pp. 6-20, esp. 19-20, which despite its title incorporates some analysis of Wesley. Fullerton's concluding words are parallel to Wesley's lament over the increasing riches of Methodism. Fullerton states that Wesley had appealed to people to save in order not to rob God. "Capitalism saw the business significance of calling, removed the transcendental, other-worldly motive, and transformed 'calling' into a job."

23. In describing the attitude toward the common people in the early eighteenth century, Dickinson says, "Even these men with a social conscience would have been horrified at any suggestion that political action should be taken to ensure a fairer distribution of the material good of this world." By the time Wesley was writing his "Thoughts on the Present Scarcity" (1773), the horror was mitigated, but even such a fervent reformer as Joseph Priestley, whose republican views on liberty evoked Wesley's tracts on liberty, was cautioning against undue concern for the subsistence of the poor. He like others believed that many poor would not work if the state were too ready to help them. Dickinson, *Liberty*, pp. 87,230, 255-56. Some of the radicals in the 1790s echoed Wesley's concern. Even they could not consent to any forcible redistribution. Therefore, Wesley's stance in the 70s assumes remarkable proportions by his suggestion that goods, and therefore labor, might be regulated toward meeting subsistence levels.

24. See Dickinson, *Liberty*, pp. 242-43.

25. See Wesley's "Letter to Dr. Burton" 10 October 1735, *Letters*, vol. 1, p. 189, where he traces happiness to "faith and love and joy in the Holy Ghost."

26. Wesley, "Character of a Methodist," *Works*, vol. 8, p. 342. "Every believer may be happy as well as holy." Ibid., vol. 3, 271.

27. Wesley, "Letter to the Rev. Dr. Middleton," *Letters*, vol. 2, pp. 378-80. Note Albert C. Outler's pertinent comment that the "Holy Club" was not a "Happy Club." Only after Aldersgate does Wesley link holiness and happiness in a creative union.

28. Hoffman, *Moral Philosophy*, p. 158.

29. See E. Gordon Rupp, *Principalities and Powers* (London: Epworth Press, 1963), pp. 64-78, for his contrast of the "pessimism of nature" and the "optimism of grace."

30. See George W. Forell "The Ethics of Dietrich Bonhoeffer," in Martin E. Marty, ed., *The Place of Bonhoeffer* (New York: Association Press, 1962), pp. 204-7.

31. See my " Church and Social Transformation: An Ethics of the Spirit," *Wesleyan Theological Journal* (Spring, 1976): 49-61, as an attempt at structure.

32. "First person" refers to God the Father, confessed in the Apostles' Creed; "Second" refers to the Son; and "Third" to the Spirit.

33. As Wesley concluded in his critique of Bernard Mandeville's *Fable of the Bees*. Wesley said of Mandeville that he "loves and cordially recommends vice of every kind; not only as useful now and then, but as absolutely necessary at all times for communities!" *Journal*, (April 14, 1756), *Works*, vol. 2, p. 361.

A similar relativism in moral values expressed by Thomas Hobbes created a moral vacuum because it removed the possibility of any distinction between good and bad. Wesley referred to Hobbes's excessive valuation of reason, but not to his moral judgments. See *Works*, vol. 6, pp. 356-57.

34. "Derived from sources outside the divine will and revelation." H. Richard Niebuhr would call these "henotheistic." He writes that "it seems true to say that monotheism *as value dependence* [my emphasis] and as loyalty to One beyond all the many is in constant conflict with . . . a pluralism that has many objects of devotion." *Radical Monotheism and Western Culture* (New York: Harper & Bros., 1960), pp. 24-25.

35. See my "Church and State in the Thought and Life of John Wesley," pp. 204-6. Wesley believed Hutcheson removed the divine ground. Hutcheson argued that beneficent action, even if performed without specific reference to God, is virtuous.

36. See *A Survey of the Wisdom of God in the Creation*, or *a Compendium of Natural Philosophy*, 2 vols., second American edition, revised and enlarged; with notes by B. Mays (Philadelphia: Jonathan Pounder, 1816), II, pp. 179-80.

37. See the article "Thomas Hobbes" in *Oxford Dictionary of the Christian Church*, ed, F. L. Cross (London: Oxford University Press, 1958), pp. 642-43; and Clyde L. Manschreck, *A History of Christianity in the World: From Persecution to Uncertainty* (Englewood Cliffs: Prentice-Hall, 1974), p. 354.

38. See my "Creation and Grace in Wesley's Ethics," *Drew Gateway* 46:1,2,3 (1975–76): 50-51.

39. See John Wesley, *Explanatory Notes upon the Old Testament* 3 vols. (Bristol: William Pine, 1765), [reprinted Salem, Ohio: Schmul Publishers, 1975], vol. 1, p. 9. Wesley emphasizes the special attention God gave to the forming of Man (Gen. 2:7), "Man is a little world, consisting of heaven and earth, soul and body."

40. Ibid., p. 11 (Gen. 2:8-15). See the happiness motif, which Wesley relates particularly to the world of the sense. See also *Works*, vol. 6, p. 243, for the relation of holiness and happiness.

41. Wesley, "The General Deliverance," *Works*, vol. 6, pp. 242-44.

42. See Wesley, "The New Birth," ibid., pp. 66.

43. Wesley, *Explanatory Notes on the Old Testament* (Gen. 1:26-28), p. 7.

44. Wesley, "The General Deliverance," *Works*, vol. 6, pp. 243-44.

45. Is holiness a category of value? Does the holiness of God, which Wesley and Calvin emphasize as the constituent dimension or essence of the moral image of God, possess value or worth? Is holiness a moral category?

46. Rudolf Otto, while emphasizing the ethical significance of the Holy less than the nonrational, i.e., the numinous, declares that the Holy possesses "supreme worth or *value.*" In worship the confession of the holiness of God "recognizes and extols a value, precious beyond all conceiving." See *The Idea of the Holy*, 2nd ed. (New York: Oxford University Press, 1958), "The Holy as a Category of Value," pp. 50-58, esp., 51-52. See also John P. Reeder, Jr., "The Relation of the Moral and the Numinous in Otto's Notion of the Holy," in *Religion and Morality*, eds. Gene Outka and John P. Reeder, Jr., (New York: Anchor Books, 1973), pp. 255-92. Richard A. McCormick, S.J., defines value as "an intrinsic good to man, not something that is good simply because it is evaluated as such by human beings." *Notes on Moral Theology: 1965 through 1980* (Washington, D.C.: University Press of America, 1981), p. 645. The expectation of God in the Old Testament that only unblemished sacrifice could be offered conveys the principle of value associated with the Holy. Only the Holy possesses value when one comes before the Holy.

47. Wesley, "The General Deliverance," *Works*, vol. 6, pp. 242-43.

48. Wesley is not describing physical liberty or suggesting that there are no human limits. Rather he speaks of "moral liberty," the ability to choose and follow after either right or wrong.

49. H. Emil Brunner identifies this as "answerability" or responsibility. Man is made in God's image and knows it, is aware of it. See his *Man in Revolt*, discussed in J. S. Whale *Christian Doctrine* (London: Cambridge University Press, 1966), pp. 44-45.

50. See Wesley, "The Way to the Kingdom," *Works*, vol. 5, pp. 82-83.

51. Ibid.

52. Wesley's sermon "The Way to the Kingdom" describes the will as "utterly perverse and distorted, averse from all good." However, Wesley does not teach that the will has no power to function on the diminished level of existence in which humanity finds itself. The sermon, "What Is Man?" *Works*, vol. 8, pp. 228-29 states: "And although I have not an absolute power over my own mind, because of the corruption of my own *nature*; yet, *through the grace of God assisting me*, I have a power to choose whom I will serve." (my emphases). The major factor here is prevenient or assisting grace which brings a new dimension into fallen humanity's existence. Because of prevenient grace, it is not legitimate, *coram Deo*, to consider humankind as simply natural. Humanity, in other words, lives in a graced relationship, despite its alienation.

53. Umphrey Lee, *John Wesley and Modern Religion* (New York: Abingdon-Cokesbury, 1936), p. 124, cited in Wm. R. Cannon, *The Theology of John Wesley* (New York: Abingdon Press, 1946), p. 108.

54. Dickinson, *Liberty*, p. 65.

55. Professor Logan's paper deals with this issue in detail. I will restrict the development of the concept here.

56. Wesley, "To William Wilberforce" (July 1790), *Letters*, vol. 8, p. 231.

57. Wesley, "Thoughts Upon Liberty," *Works*, vol. 11, p. 34 (my emphasis). At the outset he cites Matthew Prior: "I scorn to have my free-born toe Dragoon'd into a wooden shoe."

58. See Richard Wallheim, "Natural Law" *Encyclopedia of Philosophy*, Paul Edwards, ed. (New York: Macmillan Company, 1967), pp. 451ff.

59. Wesley, "Thoughts upon Slavery," *Works*, vol. 11, pp. 70ff. (my emphasis). Following Judge William Blackstone, Wesley insists that warfare gives no right to victors to make slaves of prisoners. Locke had argued for this right. But Wesley agreed with Locke that no person may forfeit the power over his own life. See "The Origin of Power," *Works*, vol. 11, p. 52. Criminal activity is an exception to this theory of rights. (See ibid., p. 97.)

60. Helmut Thielicke, *Theological Ethics: Politics*, Vol. 2 (Philadelphia: Fortress Press, 1969), p. 67.

61. See David Little, "Natural Law Revisited: James Luther Adams and Beyond," *Union Seminary Quarterly Review* 37:3 (1982): 217ff. Little sees that Christians have an enormous stake in natural law thinking.

62. *Explanatory Notes on the Old Testament* (Gen. 3:6-8), pp. 15-16. (my emphasis).

63. Wesley, "On Conscience" *Works*, vol. 7, pp. 187-88.

64. "Observations on Liberty," *Works*, vol. 11, pp. 92-93.

65. "On Conscience," p. 189. Wesley does state that "natural conscience" is "an expression frequently found in some of our best authors," including presumably Joseph Butler.

66. In his later years Hutcheson used "moral sense" and "conscience" interchangeably, a possible sign of Butler's influence. See W. R. Scott, *Francis Hutcheson: His Life, Teaching, and Position in the History of Philosophy* (London: Cambridge University Press, 1900), pp. 198-99, 246.

67. See Francis Hutcheson, *An Essay on the Nature and Conduct of the Passions and Affections with Illustrations on the Moral Sense*, 3rd ed. (London: A. Ward, 1742), p. 333.

68. Wesley, "On Conscience," *Works*, vol. 7, p. 187.

69. Wesley, "The General Spread of the Gospel" *Works*, vol. 6, pp. 280-81 for an excellent resume of human ability through prevenient grace.

70. See Outler, ed., *John Wesley*, p. 195.

71. See Cannon, *Theology of John Wesley*, pp. 208-9.

72. Wesley, "The Holy Spirit" in *Works*, vol. 7, p. 513. Cannon has directed me to this source in his work, pp. 207-13.

73. See Wesley, "Justification By Faith," *Works*, vol. 5, p. 554, for discussion of satisfaction (sec.7) and reconciliation (sec. 8).

74. Irenaeus shared with the Eastern Church a particular concern for incarnation. See J. N. D. Kelly, *Early Christian Doctrines*, 2nd ed. (New York: Harper & Row, 1960), pp. 170-74.

75. But not the Abelardian doctrine of atonement as an exemplary work which evokes the response of contrition and love.

76. Wesley, "Upon our Lord's Sermon on the Mount:IX," *Works*, vol. 5, pp. 381-82.

77. The theme of imitation is developed in my forthcoming book *To Reform the Nation: Theological Foundations of Wesley's Ethics.*

78. Wesley, *Works*, vol. 11, pp. 366-67. See Outler, *John Wesley*, pp. 6-7.

79. Wesley, "The Scripture Way of Salvation," *Works*, vol. 6, p. 45, sec. 3, and pp. 46-47, sec. 9.

80. See Wesley, "Primitive Christianity," *Works*, vol. 8, pp. 43-44.

4. THE WESLEYAN TRADITION
AND THE
SOCIAL CHALLENGES OF THE NEXT CENTURY

J. Philip Wogaman

I. Methodological Problems

The papers by Professors Hynson, Logan, and Muelder[1] have highlighted important aspects of the Wesleyan tradition[2] in theological ethics and social thought, noting also a number of implications for the facing of current and future social problems. The task of the present essay is to address more directly the question of how the Wesleyan tradition may be used in facing the social challenges of the next century.

Two formidable methodological problems are immediately evident. First, there is the question of how we should define the tradition. The Hynson, Logan, and Muelder papers have already suggested the complexity of the "Wesleyan tradition." Clearly that tradition is not just what John Wesley thought about selected social questions he had to face in the eighteenth century—important as his observations on politics, slavery, family life, education, and economics were. The more fundamental question is What were the formative theological conceptions at work in Wesley's thought and how do such conceptions relate to moral issues? It is conceivable—and even probable—that the deeper currents of Wesley's thought may have been in conflict with his attitude on some specific problems (such as the American Revolution) which circumstances required him to address. The Wesleyan tradition includes both Wesley's specific response to particular social problems and his fundamental theological insights, but the latter are more important than the former.

But, as Muelder's essay reminds us, the tradition includes much more than the writings of John Wesley. It goes beyond Wesley to include the theological and social teachings of two centuries of Methodism in its flowering in all parts of the world—greatly influenced, but not precisely determined, by the work of the primary founder. Above all, our attitude toward Wesley and the early Wesleyan movement must not be nostalgic, idealizing the person and movement beyond human proportions and treating this as the *sine qua non* of contemporary Methodist identity. Muelder's essay is a useful reminder of the important developments since Wesley, including the development of a very substantial body of social teaching, particularly through the elaborations of the early twentieth-century Methodist Social Creed. Moreover, Muelder makes clear that Methodism has influenced and been influenced by the wider ecumenical movement. The Wesleyan tradition has affected that movement in important ways, but through ecumenical interaction Methodism has also been greatly influenced in turn. So it is no simple thing to speak of "the Wesleyan tradition"! Any attempt to do so is necessarily selective and interpretative, and in attempting to use that tradition we do well to focus upon major, recognizable themes that are more or less indisputably "Wesleyan."

The other methodological problem, then, is how to draw out the implications of those major themes so as to illuminate particular social problems facing us now and in future decades. This, too, is an extraordinarily complex undertaking, not least because the very definition of "problems" already assumes, to some extent, a frame of reference based upon values derived from that very tradition. None of us can claim omniscience in predicting the dominant problems several decades in advance. In attempting to predict the future, most of us tend to project current issues and problems far ahead, sometimes quite overlooking how transitory and faddist our assessments can be. The best we can do is to try to understand the likely shape of the future in light of present trends, designating as problems those points where empirical realities are or may become opposed to values that are central to our faith tradition.

II. The Theological Tradition

Commentators on the Wesleyan theological tradition typically note its soteriological emphasis. The focal theological problem to John and Charles Wesley was the drama of salvation, the broad outlines of which can be sketched fairly simply:[3] Human beings are, since the fall, lost in their willful, sinful alienation from God. Their foremost need is to repent and be restored to God. Through the work of Christ they are convicted of their sins, recognize their need for repentance, and are given the power to repent. Through the work of the Holy Spirit they are given the assurance of the complete forgiveness of their sins and the power to go on to a life of holiness in Christian perfection. Their ultimate destiny is eternal happiness in heaven. The internal evidence of salvation is personal assurance. The external evidence is supplied by good works.

Throughout the eighteenth and nineteenth centuries, this soteriological scheme was profoundly relevant to the success and development of the various branches of Wesleyanism in Great Britain, North America, and elsewhere; and it has not been altogether irrelevant to twentieth-century experience. But one might wonder whether its evident individualism and subjectivism are really helpful in the development of a serious response to the complex social problems of the present era. Certainly the drama of salvation, as it unfolds in Wesleyan theology, can be (and often has been) used to distract attention from questions of social justice. That is so wherever the social gospel is rejected in the name of a personal gospel, as if the two were really opposed to each other.

But, as the papers of Professors Hynson and Logan remind us, a purely individualistic, subjectivistic interpretation of Wesleyan theology is far off the mark. The profound concern for each individual already contains important social implications. Nobody can any longer be regarded and treated as inconsequential, and the effects of every social policy or institution upon actual human beings must be considered important. Active doctrines of stewardship and vocation further emphasize that Christians should assume responsibility for some part of the world before God. Stewardship implies that wealth and power are never to be treated simply as personal possessions for selfish enjoyment; rather, they are resources to be used to advance God's purposes. Vocation implies that our very being is from God and that our life purposes must be brought into utter conformity to God's. Stewardship and vocation mean that our life and our possessions become the instruments of love and service. The communitarian implications of this are not fully developed in early Wesleyanism, except through the backdoor of ecclesiology. But, as Muelder reminds us, ecclesiology itself is an expression of social doctrine. We form the church in accordance with what we believe God's purposes for society ultimately are. Wesleyan ecclesiology is thoroughly communitarian in that it treats human interactions as important along-side the divine-human interaction, although both originally and currently it reflects an uneasy mixture of democratic and hierarchical elements. Every person must (individually) repent. But the fruit of repentance is not further isolation; rather, it is salvation *from* isolation into relationship with God and the community of the redeemed.

Implied in this, and stated in Wesley's own theology, is a doctrine of creation. However imperfectly this may be stated by Wesley, it is this element in his theology that preserves it from any purely otherworldly interpretation, bridging the gaps between spirit and nature and between present and future forms of human existence. Professor Logan reminds us that Wesley's doctrine of creation, while consuming many pages of writing, is not very well-elaborated theologically. Nevertheless, it is very important in making the connection between a soteriological theology and a conception of the world as a sphere of value and responsibility in which stewardship and vocation make sense.[4]

The theological emphasis upon Christian perfection also has potential social ramifications, particularly when combined with Wesley's rejection of the full Calvinist scheme of election. All people, as candidates for salvation, are also candidates for perfection. One cannot therefore be completely cynical or pessimistic about human nature. The perfection of humanity—that is, every human being—is something to be *sought* and even to be expected. The Wesleyan tradition certainly recognized the power of sin. But its doctrine of perfection prevented it from conceding too much to the dark side of human nature. Even the most egregious sinner is to be approached, not as a fixed, immovable, evil force, but rather as a project for redemption and change.

III. A Tradition of Engagement and Reform

This brief summary is restricted to the broadly recognizable themes of Wesleyan theological tradition. While rooted in the thought of the founder, they are clearly discernible in the unfolding of subsequent Methodism. How have they actually affected the approach to social problems?

The historical record certainly would not support the charge that Methodism has been led by its Wesleyan tradition into quietism or the substitution of personal religious experience for the expression of social concern.[5] One might not always agree with Methodist positions or actions on social questions, but there is a long historical record of dealing with such questions beginning with John Wesley himself. One is struck, however, by the style of pragmatic reformism that has been typical of much of that history, again beginning with Wesley. Reformism tends to be reactive. It responds to particular problems or evils or injustices that appear to need correction, or to particular opportunities to do good. The Methodist style has not typically been to develop social doctrine systematically. It has tended to be more intuitive than ideological. There is consequently a risk, to which we shall return later, of some incompleteness or even inconsistency.

But this may not be all bad. At least the bearers of Wesleyan tradition have not typically allowed ideological commitment to substitute for active pursuit of concrete results. On the assumption that it is more important to affect reality than it is to hold correct abstract opinions, Methodist activism may be more strength than weakness. Similarly, the emphasis upon reform rather than revolutionary change may in most instances reflect theological wisdom. The Wesleyan tradition would not lead one to locate perfection in institutional structures. By absolutizing the drama of salvation, the tradition tends to relativize the material and structural conditions of human existence. Conditions are relatively very important. Particular evils, once identified, need to be attacked. Particular needs, once discovered, should be addressed. But one is not to be under the illusion that revolutionary changes of human society will eliminate evil per se.

So the Methodist style has been one of expressing concern for persons and for being engaged, where possible, in dealing with the forces that oppress persons. This has led Methodists into the struggle over slavery (unfortunately, on both sides), into the temperance movement, into the movement to reform labor practices and to organize labor for collective bargaining, into various peace movements and civil rights movements, and into a myriad local causes. This style has been effective and, in the main, faithful to the basic traditions from which it has sprung. In the main, one can argue that Methodism has been a great force for good in the countries where it has had a substantial presence and opportunity.

Having said this, however, it must be acknowledged that the activist, reformist style has limitations. There is also an important place for well thought out social doctrine, not as a substitute for active concern, but as its source of insight, clarification, and direction. Over-reliance upon intuition risks mistakes in a world where not everything is as it first appears. It also risks loss of a sense of proportion when one devotes all one's attention to an immediate problem or fad issue while neglecting problems of more fundamental and enduring importance.

Social doctrine may play an even more important role for Christians—that of preserving the integrity of faith and life. Most of us exist in a variety of social roles and simultaneously entertain attitudes on a variety of questions. The culture of which we are a part is almost infinitely complex, constantly influencing our values in many directions. In face of the complexity of life, nobody can live or think with perfect consistency. It is especially difficult to live and think in such a way that Christian faith is expressed at all levels of one's life and network of relationships. It is possible to hold the Christian faith on one level while, perhaps unconsciously, existing in a variety of concrete relationships that are in serious contradiction to the faith. Or one may venture, as a Christian action or teaching, something that could not be maintained consistently without doing violence to Christian faith. A purely intuitive approach to such complexities can make it more difficult to live as a faithful Christian.

Professor Muelder's paper points to Methodist participation in two twentieth-century endeavors to create a body of social doctrine: the development of the Methodist Social Creed, commencing in 1907–8, and the ecumenical articulation of social principles, particularly at the level of the World Council of Churches. The Social Creed now appears as the statement of Social Principles adopted by the 1972 General Conference six years after the merger of The Methodist Church with the Evangelical United Brethren Church. The World Council's social doctrine represents especially the work of the six assemblies of that body, commencing in 1948. Both of these emerging traditions are important and increasingly sophisticated, but both are also incomplete.

As it faces its third century, American Methodism is challenged to develop bodies of social doctrine that are commensurate with its traditions of concerned engagement. The task is vastly beyond the scope of a paper of this kind, but I wish to suggest several areas in which the development of more adequate social doctrine may prove especially important. In part, this means continued responsible participation in the thought processes of ecumenical bodies like the World Council. In part, it means ongoing refinement of the United Methodist statement on Social Principles. In part, it means greater care in articulating the basis of particular statements and actions at every level of the church's life.

IV. The Quest for Peace with Justice

Echoing John Wesley's own concern for peace, twentieth-century Methodism has devoted substantial energy to this commitment.[6] Highlights have included the Crusade for a New World Order of the World War II era, substantial participation in the Vietnam peace movement, and current participation in the nuclear disarmament drive. Recent church statements, particularly the Social Principles and subsequent resolutions, are careful to couple the commitment to peace with an affirmation of justice. The Social Principles reject "coercion, violence, and war . . . presently the ultimate sanctions in international relations . . . as incompatible with the gospel and spirit of Christ" (para. 74). At the same time a series of social and political rights are affirmed (paras. 72-74), and reference is made to "the duty of governments to establish police forces, courts, and facilities for rehabilitation of offenders." Support is given both to those who refuse to serve in armed forces and to those who conscientiously serve (para. 74).

At a certain intuitive, activist level such statements may constitute an adequate framework to sustain the church's witness. But they leave serious problems unanswered and important dilemmas unresolved. Violence, crime, international tension, political oppression, and war are likely to continue to be among the most serious problems faced by Christians in the decades to come. If so, what illuminating counsel does the church offer? The church is generally clearer in identifying the evils of war and injustice than it is in articulating a coherent policy to deal with those evils. A major unresolved tension in the church's social doctrine is over the extent to which coercion and violence may be necessary in order to maintain a structure of justice protecting human rights and how far the church should go in legitimizing such negative means.

Should the church adopt a thoroughly pacifist position, in keeping with the judgment of the Social Principles that "violence . . . is incompatible with the gospel and spirit of Christ"? If so, it needs to illuminate fully and consistently the implications of its position for the whole range of situations where use of violence appears necessary if justice is to be served. It could, for instance, take the view that antisocial people will respond positively if they are treated lovingly and not repressively, inviting people to join in actions consistent with that faith (the Tolstoyan and, to some extent, Gandhian view). Or it could adopt the stance of a John Howard Yoder in actively pursuing justice by noncoercive, non-violent means, knowing that many sinners will continue to behave like sinners but trusting God finally to make things come out right in the end. Or it could take the view that violence is morally permissible only if it is exercised responsibly by the state (i.e, as a police action), but that it must be rejected at the international level where there exists no responsible state. Or it could accept certain forms of violence, defined as conventional warfare, while rejecting others, such as nuclear bombs and nerve gas (these last two options would not, of course, be thoroughly pacifist approaches).

On the other hand, should the church adopt the view that it is the responsibility of the state to protect a defined range of human rights by necessary and proportionate means, including as a last resort violence and coercion? If so, then it must be prepared to illuminate the limits and constraints under which violence can morally be used, perhaps in the manner of the traditional "just war" formulations. Wesley himself does not appear to have rejected all use of force and violence, but he was well aware of the terrible evil that war lets loose upon humanity. In his spirit, it would appear that the church should at least acknowledge a serious responsibility to keep all violence in responsible check. In our own time—and looking toward the future—the church must above all acknowledge the awful dilemma posed by nuclear weaponry: Christians who argue that nuclear stalemate helps maintain the peace between the superpowers must force themselves to see clearly the moral effects of preparing for the actual use of such weapons of wholesale destructiveness; Christians who believe such weapons should be repudiated categorically must force themselves to grapple responsibly with the full political implications of their position.

The problem of violence is also posed for the church as it faces the moral dilemmas of revolution—another feature of contemporary world life that is likely to continue for some decades into the future. Professor Hynson notes Wesley's own reticence about supporting revolution. Wesley lived to see his more negative assessments of the American Revolution fail to materialize; he did not live long enough to see how fully the French Revolution would substantiate his fears about it, how it would "devour its own" and eventually pave the way for Napoleon. But in his appraisal of both revolutions he saw the dangers to society when an established order is broken, and he thought the quest for power by common people to be based on illusion. That judgment was not shared by many of the American Methodists, then or now, but Methodists still have not produced coherent doctrine on the subject of revolution. One result is that some Methodists sound rather like pacifists when criticizing the World Council of Churches for aiding "violent" liberation movements in Africa while also criticizing the antinuclear arms movement in the United States for weakening this country's military posture. Or then again some Methodists who sound a good deal like pacifists in their critiques of the U.S. defense budget are quite uncritical of the use of violence by third world revolutionaries. I venture no judgments here on the merits of particular cases. But the use of violence is terribly important and, in the case of nuclear warfare, awesomely important, and the dilemmas faced by Christian citizens and politicians are frightfully real. The church's stance on such a subject needs to be well thought through if it is to commend itself to people who want to be Christian in their actions but don't know quite how.

V. The Quest for Responsible Government

While John Wesley was doubtful about the case for democracy (and his English successor Jabez Bunting was apparently even more so), subsequent generations of Methodists have been much clearer in their support. Methodist commitment to democracy in America has in fact been well-nigh absolute for the past two centuries, to the point that the commitment could simply be assumed. The United Methodist Social Principles document has a good deal to say about various political and social rights and matters of church-state relationship, but reference to democratic participation in self-government is limited to a few scattered sentences. At the ecumenical level, the WCC's 1948 conception of a responsible society and the later emphasis upon the "participatory" society (to which the Mueder paper refers) are certainly forms of democratic political doctrine. But this cannot be said to exist at the denominational level.

This would not matter if the lack of carefully articulated statements of support and interpretation simply reflected general agreement, or if commitment to democracy by people throughout the world could be considered universal. In point of fact, however, there may be very serious disagreements emerging within the church, and there is no question that political democracy is flatly rejected in many parts of the world. I am among those who believe that the charges of groups like the Institute on Religion and Democracy that United Methodist agencies are not fully committed to democracy are usually overblown. Nevertheless, if commitment to democracy is important, the position of the church should be unambiguously clear. In particular, as the church finds it expedient to support or work alongside groups of doubtful democratic commitment, it should remove any public doubt about the church's own commitments.

The problem of responsible checks on political power is perennially important and may be particularly critical in the decades to come. A large number of countries are currently governed in a highly authoritarian way, with very limited opportunity for the general citizenry to participate in self-government, or even in open criticism of those who do govern. In countries influenced by Marxism, it is fashionable to argue that Western democracies are only a facade for the exercise of real power by economic elites. In those countries, the party generally claims moral authority to govern in behalf of the people, but that authority is rarely tested by open debate and secret ballot. Conservative authoritarian governments may be less pretentious in their moral claims, but they are no less oppressive in their unwillingness to brook opposition.[7]

The very large number of authoritarian governments in the world today poses a great responsibility upon the church to be as clear as it can be on the subject of political power. The traditional Wesleyan doctrine of perfection offers a conception of human nature that is commensurate with a positive view of the potentialities of government as servant of human good. There remains enough of a doctrine of sin in that same tradition to provide a basis for criticizing the pretensions of any elite thinking itself good enough or wise enough to rule without subjecting itself to the currents of open debate and the disciplines of an electoral process in which all are free to participate and in which an organized opposition is permitted.

VI. The Quest for World Order

Nothing in the Wesleyan theological tradition necessarily commits the church to the nation-state system as it has been inherited. Comparatively recent at the time of John Wesley, the system is still not very old in historical terms. The question is whether that system sufficiently serves human need, as seen in the gospel, or whether it is no longer adequate to human need.

One could argue that the inadequacy of this system is the great message of the twentieth century, and that the central political task of the twenty-first century will be to create new political and economic institutions of universal scope.[8] The world federalist dreams of some who invested much hope and enthusiasm first in the League of Nations and then in the United Nations have proved elusive, for the sources of conflict and group self-interest appear almost intractable. In some respects the United Nations seems less competent to resolve conflicts than it did in the immediate post–World War II situation. That is in part due to the fact that the world is much more complex now than it was then, partly because of the breakup of the old colonial empires in the third world and partly because of the scale of economic, environmental, and demographic problems the world now faces. Moreover, the Marxist and non-Marxist states have very different conceptions of what a new world order ought to be. The absence from Marxist doctrine of a recognition of the permanent necessity for democratic institutions for conflict resolution and the very different Western commitments respecting economic organization make it almost unthinkable that the world could quickly achieve universal government.

Still, humanity faces deepening problems that cannot be solved simply at the local or national level.[9] The problem of international institution building will engage us increasingly in the decades to come. The United Methodist Church has made substantial contributions already through its initial and enduring support of the United Nations, its support for the Law of the Sea treaty, its support for such international ventures as the World Health Organization's Code of Marketing of Breast-milk Substitutes, and its center at the United Nations headquarters. Such activities can be woven together in a context of meaning derived from theological recognition that the whole world is, in God, a single community, and from practical recognition of the interlocking, systemic character of many of the problems the world faces. In formulating its own conception of a new world order, the church needs to wrestle with the problem of how humanity can begin to transcend the major East/West tensions and the North/South imbalances, and with the problem of how to preserve the values of local and national community in some kind of federal design. Such things are not the work of a moment, but the underlying problem of achieving world order will be present with increasing urgency in the decades to come.

VII. The Quest for a Responsible Economic Order

From the beginning, the Methodist movement expressed concern for the meeting of human material needs. John Wesley himself showed great compassion for poor people, utterly rejecting the canard that poverty is merely the result of the laziness or wastefulness of poor people.[10] He also gave some rudimentary attention to the systemic problems of economic distribution, recognizing a relationship between the profligate consumption of the privileged classes and the destitution of the poor. He was—and most subsequent Methodists have been—thoroughly capitalist in his ideological assumptions. (Wesley, interestingly enough, provides substantial illustrative material for the "Protestant ethic" in Max Weber's celebrated work.[11]) But the beneficiaries of capitalism have, as a stewardship responsibility, the obligation to share their good fortune with poor people.

The Social Creed (now Social Principles) has affirmed throughout most of the twentieth century the conviction of Methodists that vulnerable people need to be protected in the economic process, thus placing some limits upon the workings of the capitalist market system. This Methodist conviction has included an enduring support for the right of collective bargaining and for most of the reforms embodied in the half-century of the New Deal era. It has also included strong support for international economic assistance programs and other programs to combat the somewhat loosely designated "hunger." The current Social Principles deal with a variety of economic questions but without attempting to articulate a coherent economic philosophy. The latter is an especially difficult task today because of the inherent ambiguity of many economic questions and the wide diversity of ideological orientation among Christians. I suspect that debate in coming years will center on five formative issues.

First, how can the formidable development problems of the impoverished areas of the world be solved and the vast chasm separating the rich and poor nations be diminished? The ideological diagnoses of this issue range from the Marxist or semi-Marxist view that the underdevelopment of poor countries is a function of the imperialism of the rich ones, to the capitalist conception of poverty as resulting from the inhospitable climate of poor countries to private investment from abroad. Other diagnoses, less committed to an inclusive ideological framework of left or right, emphasize the importance of such particular factors as population growth rates, unfavorable trade relationships, cultural factors, resource shortages, mismanagement, inadequacy of international assistance programs, and/or natural catastrophes and climatic variations. The inherent difficulty in amassing dependable information may tempt Western Christians to adopt faddist interpretations or extreme ideological views of left or right too easily. But the church certainly needs to work its way toward economic doctrine in which it can have confidence and on the basis of which it can coordinate its advocacy and ameliorative actions. No doubt the various hunger campaigns of the past few years accomplished much good, but one could scarcely accuse them of having been well thought out in relation to a defensible conception of the economic world.

Second, can we relate effectively to the new reality of transnational corporations? Occasionally church rhetoric implies that this phenomenon is fundamentally evil and can simply be made to go away, but the value judgment is overdrawn, and the view that the system can be abolished soon is more than doubtful. The relevant question is whether such enterprises can be made accountable, not only to their stockholders, but to the world public affected by their operations. In part this comes down to business ethics, the question of how corporate leaders can be challenged to a high sense of corporate responsibility. Given the fact that many corporate leaders are also church members, the vocational and stewardship implications of their positions of leadership should be apparent. But competitive economics places limits upon what any corporation can do by itself. Nor can business ethics codes of conduct be developed on a purely national basis in a world where some corporations are more powerful than many countries. The challenge is to find ways of institutionalizing "rules of the game" that affect corporations of entire industries throughout the world.

Third, what is the proper role of government in economic life? The United States and Great Britain have recently taken a surprising turn toward laissez faire economic policy commitments after half a century of New Deal or welfare state policies. Resulting high levels of unemployment and increases in the numbers of people below the "poverty line" should not be surprising to students of economic history, and it seems doubtful that the actual course of economic events will permit this to continue for long. Nevertheless, the question will remain to vex us: What exactly is the right mix of public and private sectors in economic life?[12] Worldwide the debate will continue between various forms of socialist doctrine and the advocates of free enterprise, and we may expect a variety of experiments to be tried in different countries. Methodists may not be prepared to commit themselves to the theological or ethical preferability of either capitalism or socialism. But they

should in any case be asking the deeper questions of the proponents of both socialism and capitalism: Will socialists commit themselves to political democracy and really institutionalize it? Will capitalists accept the necessary role of government in redistribution of welfare benefits to those who need them? Will socialists preserve opportunities for economic creativity and find ways of keeping public bureaucracies accountable and creative? Will capitalists encourage public regulation and overall planning in economic life?[13]

Fourth, how can labor, worldwide, be accorded sufficient job opportunity, job security, and compensation to sustain human fulfillment in a world where high technology increasingly displaces workers and where workers in more advanced economies must increasingly compete with workers in subsistence or near-subsistence economies? There are exquisite dilemmas written into this question, for who could question the advancement of technology insofar as it replaces purely mechanical labor performance and is environmentally sustainable, and who could object to increasing the job opportunitites and economic well-being of people in subsistence economies? But underneath are the broader questions of how technology can be made to serve all people, not merely those who own or control it, and how economic development can proceed in the third world without destabilizing the lives of workers in the developed countries. Sole reliance upon market forces to resolve these dilemmas is likely to be no more satisfactory now than it was during the early decades of the Industrial Revolution. Labor needs to be protected, both by collective bargaining and by appropriate legislation. The problem will be how to protect labor in countries like the United States without resort to purely protectionist measures and how to spread the benefits of increasing technological productivity. Over the long run, this is likely to involve serious expansion of work opportunity in service and cultural areas, for increased productivity does mean that fewer people are needed to produce more goods. Relevant applications of the doctrine of vocation enable us to understand that all people need secure opportunities to serve humanity and that such opportunities can go far beyond the production of physical necessities— indeed, that such opportunities need not be restricted to work as defined in market economic terms.

Fifth, can we articulate defensible theories of just wage and just price, commensurate with the sensibilities and needs of a new era? An important lesson of an era of combined inflation and recession has been the fact that prices and wages do not simply reflect market forces; they also are greatly influenced by cultural assumptions about what is "fair."[14] Culture probably plays a much more important role in economic life than economists generally assume. It greatly influences what people are willing to work for, what they are willing to pay, the restraints they are willing to accept. The hard medicine of a major economic recession worked to alleviate inflation in the United States, not just because of economic laws, but because in the climate of anxiety thus engendered, many people were willing to abate their expectations. Other influences leading to restraint might have had the same effects without necessarily causing the hardships of recession and unemployment. Most economists and governmental policy-makers are reluctant to accept wage and price controls, but some form of controls will, in my judgment, be necessary over the long-term future. But they will be accepted only to the extent they are perceived as "fair." Serious reflection on what fairness means in wages and prices is an important task the church has scarcely begun to address, but this is preeminently a task for normative, not technical, judgment. It will entail reassessment of social priorities in light of what are ultimately theological norms, along with serious attention to how relative social rewards affect the quality of social interactions within the community.

VIII. Pluralism and Integration

It is interesting to speculate why the Wesleyan tradition has spawned such social diversity within the churches based upon it. This may partly be the result of the comparatively loose doctrinal structure, opening the way to tolerance on a wide range of points. It may partly reflect the early appeal of Methodism to common people and the commitment to the value of every person regardless of accidents of birth. And it may be, in part, mere historical happenstance. In any case, the sociological diversity of this family of churches is quite remarkable. In The United Methodist Church, the ethnic mix comes fairly close to replicating that of the society as a whole. (This is no longer true in economic class terms, however, for United Methodism does not represent very many really poor people.)

In the specific case of black/white relationships, Methodism enacted within itself the whole history of American struggle: the slavery controversy, segregation, desegregation, and (lately) affirmative action. While unguarded rhetoric sometimes appears to make a supreme value of pluralism per se, and while official declarations are sometimes ambiguous at key points, the underlying doctrinal model of the church is integrative in character. Those who seriously believe in a completely separate existence for different ethnic or cultural groups would hardly be attracted by membership in a denomination of such diverse elements. Still less would they struggle for the achievement of such integrative policies as "open itineracy" for clergy. At the same time, the relevant problem posed by a doctrine of integration is how to preserve cultural values derived from each and all of the subgroups making up the whole without perpetuating social alienation. An accompanying pastoral problem is how to make it possible for persons of different backgrounds to feel equally comfortable in the liturgical expression and cultural patterns of group life without, again, contributing to estrangement from persons of differing backgrounds.

Resolving such problems within the church may be a necessary, but not sufficient, condition of resolving them in society as a whole. While the trend lines are largely positive over a period of forty years or so, there is still a good deal of racism and intergroup conflict in America and in parts of the rest of the world. Much of it is based upon the continued vitality of bad cultural stereotypes and ancient animosities; much of it is perpetuated by continuing legacies of economic and educational deprivation. United Methodism's loss of contact with broad masses of urban poor people permits the church to ignore the worst aspects of the continued legacy of racism in America, but here the example of Wesley and the early Wesleyans might well put the present church to shame. The early Wesleyans may not have been very sophisticated in their analysis of social systems, but they persistently sought out direct contact with the underclass of their era.

IX. Other Issues

Of course, this does not exhaust the list of even the predictable social challenges we are likely to face in the coming decades. For example, a whole host of issues relate to changing patterns of sexuality. Some of these are likely to prove ephemeral. (I suspect that may be so of the homosexuality issues so greatly exercising the church today, and I suspect the nuclear family and the marriage institution itself will prove to be quite durable despite the anxieties engendered by divorce statistics and life-style experimentation). In the main, I would agree with Professor Muelder that the existing body of church teaching on marriage and family constitutes theologically defensible social doctrine. The feminist movement has opened up what may prove to be the really revolutionary changes. United Methodist emphasis upon the full equality of women and men, articulated in the Social Principles and implemented ecclesiastically through ordination of women and affirmative action policies, constitute theologically defensible ground. But the subordinate status of women is so deeply embedded in the cultural history of most human societies that we may expect to have to address that legacy for years to come. United Methodism has already begun to give serious attention to the problem of liturgical and theological language conveying symbolically the identification of the divine life with masculinity, and the controversy engendered by that issue points to its depth. The task of clarifying the theological truth that God is not a sexual being, while preserving the truth that God is personal being is, not easy, for here we are indeed dealing with the liturgies and hymnodies that form our corporate ways of thinking and praying and singing together. But that task must be completed.

A whole range of issues in what is loosely termed bioethics will probably become more important in the years to come. The increasing success of medical technology in saving the lives of severely handicapped persons creates problems of adjustment in social policy. The abortion issue continues to vex us, although I suspect there will be no turning back from the present American legal stance of permitting this procedure to occur at the discretion of women and their physicians. Major breakthroughs in genetic science and engineering may pose important dilemmas in the future, tempting the church to a reflexively negative posture toward "playing God," which forgets that the doctrines of stewardship and vocation always entail acting for God in response to God's acting for us. Or such major advances may lull Christians into uncritical acceptance of changes that are contrary to God's purposes for human good, as best we can understand them.

The Wesleyan tradition contains all the elements necessary for concerned engagement with this society's myriad of problems with crime and punishment. The tradition is sufficiently realistic about sin not to yield to sentimentalism, yet sufficiently hopeful about redemption to support creative efforts at rehabilitation. But it must be admitted that Methodists have been very negligent about the vast human waste and misery represented by the American penal system. They are challenged to do better in the years to come.

X. Controversy Within the Church

We have seen some of the major social issue

that the inheritors of the Wesleyan tradition will have to wrestle with in the years ahead. Even so cursory a summary suggests the importance of deepening the body of social doctrine by which the church understands and interprets problems in the light of faith. Another reason why such a body of doctrine is important is to provide a clear frame of reference for more responsible conduct of controversy within the church. The variety, complexity, and depth of the issues the church faces will preclude total agreement within the church on very many subjects. But open expression of disagreement can contribute to the church's strength insofar as the grounds of disagreement are sufficiently clear and it is evident that all parties are seeking to base their views on Christian faith.

It is even more important that the church communicate the grounds for its views on particular questions clearly to the world beyond the church. The capacity of the church to relate the faith coherently to the great problems of the age is always on trial, and the church's success makes it easier to draw people into commitment to faith and fellowship and common service. Well-grounded, coherent social doctrine is very important to the evangelistic task of the church. When the church is unclear and inconsistent in the positions it takes, this contributes to the loss of respect and influence. Muelder notes that The United Methodist Church is more prone to take positions on an ad hoc basis than is the ecumenical movement at the international level. One can indeed expect a denomination that is primarily based in one country to have less perspective than what can be summoned by the ecumenical movement as a whole, and a denomination may have to face issues of greater immediacy requiring quick response. Nevertheless, The United Methodist Church has immense resources at its disposal in terms of theological, ethical, and technical expertise appropriate to all of the issues discussed in this paper. There is no reason why the church's positions on great social problems should not be carefully thought out and reflect high standards of competence. The world will pay closer heed to what we say, whether or not it agrees.

We may note in conclusion that controversy within the church should always be conducted in such a way that the traditional Wesleyan respect for persons is maintained. The opponent is still a child of God, not an enemy to be viewed with contempt or destroyed. It is well to remember that error on social questions (or what we think to be error) is as often the result of insufficient exposure to life's hard situations as it is simple perversity of the will. Controversy within the church does not have to degenerate into mutual mistrust and moral condemnation, even though we are indeed called to correct one another in love.

NOTES

1. See the three previous chapters in this book: "The Methodist Social Creed and Ecumenical Ethics," by Walter Muelder; "Toward a Wesleyan Social Ethic," by James C. Logan; and "Implications of Wesley's Ethical Method and Political Thought," by Leon O. Hynson.

2. The terms "Wesleyan," "Methodist," and "United Methodist" as used in this paper are not simply interchangeable. "Wesleyan" refers to an intellectual and spiritual heritage derived from the work of John and Charles Wesley and elaborated and refined by many other thinkers and leaders over the past two centuries. "Methodist" refers to churches having their origin in the Methodist movement, of which John Wesley was principal leader in eighteenth century England. The term is broad enough to encompass denominations other than The United Methodist Church as well as the predecessor denominations to that church (it being understood that the Evangelical United Brethren Church, which united with The Methodist Church in 1968 to form The United Methodist Church, was itself a union of predecessor denominations which did not have their origin in Wesley's Methodist movement). "United Methodist" refers specifically to the denomination brought into existence by merger in 1968, which is in direct linear descent from the Methodist Episcopal Church, generally thought to have come into existence as a church in 1784. The paper is specifically addressed to United Methodists, although it is written in understanding of the close relationships existing between United Methodism and others who share the Wesleyan and Methodist heritages.

3. This paper is indebted to helpful theological summaries by the Hynson and Logan papers. See also S. Paul Schilling, *Methodism and Society in Theological Perspective* (Nashville: Abingdon Press, 1960), pp. 44-64; and Albert C. Outler, "John Wesley as Theologian—Then and Now" and "John Wesley's Vision of the Christian Life" in *Willson Lectures 1973* (Washington, D. C.: Wesley Theological Seminary, 1973) for useful summaries of essential points in Wesley's theology.

4. Karl Barth's extensively developed doctrine of creation helps to illuminate this relationship, not through neglect of Trinitarian theology, but by refusing to disconnect the work of God the Father from the work of God revealed in Christ. The divine-human covenant, christologically interpreted, conveys the ultimate meaning of creation; creation provides the conditions or "basis" of covenant. See esp. *Church Dogmatics*, III/1.

5. See Richard M. Cameron, *Methodism and Society in Historical Perspective* (Nashville: Abingdon Press, 1961); Walter G. Muelder, *Methodism and Society in the Twentieth Century* (Nashville: Abingdon Press, 1961); and A. Dudley Ward, *The Social Creed of The Methodist Church* (Nashville: Abingdon Press, 1961).

6. Muelder, *Methodism and Society in the Twentieth Century*, details the development of the Social Creed from 1907-8 to 1961. Since 1972 this document has appeared officially as a declaration of Social Principles, to which is appended a much briefer Social Creed designed for liturgical purposes. The Social Principles and Social Creed appear in the 1984 *Book of Discipline of The United Methodist Church* as paras. 70 through 76.

7. These are, of course, very broad generalizations encompassing dozens of left- and right-wing governments, each with a unique history and each with unique governmental structures and governing personalities. Occasionally efforts are made to classify oppressive governments as to the degree of oppressiveness, and the former American Ambassador to the United Nations, Jean J. Kirkpartrick, and others have sought to distinguish between "authoritarian" and "totalitarian" regimes, with the former representing mainly right-wing governments and the latter communist states—and with the latter considered far more dangerous and oppressive. It is well to recognize that oppressiveness comes in relative degrees, but Kirkpatrick's distinction may be too biased ideologically to be helpful.

8. A flurry of useful literature on this subject has accumulated in recent years. See, for example, Gerald and Patricia Mische, *Toward a Human World Order* (New York: Paulist Press, 1977); and Lester R. Brown, *World Without Borders* (New York: Random House, 1972). While such writings, and other contributions of United World Federalists, World Peace Through World Law, and similar groups are sometimes characterized as overly utopian, it is well to remember that one of the architects of postwar political realism, Hans J. Morgenthau, remarked in the preface to the 3rd ed. of his classic *Politics Among Nations* (New York: Alfred A. Knopf, 1960), "I am still being told that I believe in the prominence of the international system based upon the nation-state, although the obsolesence of the nation-state and the need to merge it into the supranational organizations of a functional nature was already one of the main points of the First Edition of 1948."

9. Pope John XXIII emphasized this point in his great encyclical, *Pacem in Terris*, where he remarks that "at the present day no political community is able to pursue its own interests and develop itself in isolation" (para. 131) and "at this historical moment the present system of organization and the way its principle of authority operates on a world basis no longer correspond to the objective requirements of the universal common good."

10. Having visited a number of poor people in 1753, Wesley recorded that he had "found not one of them unemployed who was able to crawl about the room. So wickedly, devilishly false is that common objection, 'They are poor only because they are idle.' " (*Journal*, vol. 4, p. 52); quoted by Cameron, *Methodism and Society in Historical Perspective*, p. 58.

11. Max Weber, *The Protestant Ethic and the Spirit of Capitalism* (New York: Charles Scribner's Sons, 1958 [1904-5]), esp. pp. 175-77.

12. We may therefore agree with the judgment of Robert Heilbroner and Lester C. Thurow that "all market economies must have public sectors. It is impossible to have an economic system in which government would play no role whatever in the allocation of resources, where the dollar would decide everything and the voting rights of individuals would decide nothing. What is at stake is where to draw the line, not whether to draw the line. Here there is ample room for debate, but there is no room at all for contending that the political voting process is somehow an illegitimate intrusion on the marketplace. On the contrary, it is essential for its survival." *Five Economic Challenges* (Englewood Cliffs, N.J.: Prentice-Hall, 1981), p. 77.

13. The recent attempt by the Institute on Religion and Democracy to suggest that capitalism is a necessary (though not sufficient) condition for political democracy needs to be resisted vigorously. The theological case for political democracy is much clearer than the case for economic capitalism, and very different issues are posed by the two realms which ought not to be mixed. Reinhold Niebuhr makes this point quite clearly in his *Children of Light and Children of Darkness* (New York: Charles Scribner's Sons, 1944) where, anticipating wide spread of bourgeois culture and individualism, he pleads that democracy not also be discarded as integral to that

culture. Bourgeois society is, he argues, a transitory phenomenon; the case for democracy is universal and enduring. The institute's attempt to link democracy and capitalism appears in its publication, *Christianity and Democracy* (Washington, D. C.: Institute on Religion and Democracy, 1981), pp. 6-7.

14. Especially illuminating on the importance of expectations in generating inflation and/or recession is John Hicks's small book, *The Crisis in Keynesian Economics* (Oxford: Basil Blackwell, 1974).

XII. Religious Affections and the Knowledge of God

1. JOHN WESLEY'S *SUNDAY SERVICE* AND METHODIST SPIRITUALITY

James F. White

Wesley's service book is a prime source for liturgical theology, that is, theology based on the liturgical witness to faith. The distinctive elements of the whole Wesleyan movement are shown in the way Wesley orders worship. The *Sunday Service* thus provides important data for theological reflection today. The liturgical circle begins by observing that which is said and done in worship as a reflection of belief, then examines systematically such evidence of faith, and finally reforms worship itself so as to express that faith more adequately. We can only briefly sketch here the evidence to faith found in the *Sunday Service* and shall not discuss its contribution to liturgical reform at all. (The "Articles of Religion," as revised by Wesley, are an entirely different kind of evidence of belief, one which we shall not consider here.) Wesley's liturgical documentation of faith stands as a challenge in our day, both to theological reflection and to the reform of worship.

Hymnody was a most important concern for Wesley. Bound with most copies of the *Sunday Service* was *A Collection of Psalms and Hymns for the Lord's Day*. This 104-page document insured that the Methodists would make hymnody a prominent part of every service. It was, as Wesley had said of an earlier collection, "a little body of experimental and practical divinity." Wesley's deletion of service music and anthems must be balanced by his abundant provision for congregational song in the form of hymnody. It is not our present purpose to examine this hymnal, but it, too, is an important source of Wesley's liturgical theology just as are Wesley's 166 eucharistic hymns which appear elsewhere.

The basic pattern, of course, remains that of Anglican practice and faith. Wesley, in his preface, testifies to belief that the prayer book was not exceeded in terms of "solid, scriptural, rational Piety" by any other liturgy whether ancient or modern. Yet his emendations of the BCP are systematic and consistent. The faith that Wesley witnesses to in these pages is obviously uncomfortable with some aspects of prevailing piety and thoroughly at home with others. Rather than analyze Anglican piety in general, we must be content to look more closely at those elements in which Wesley differed from the BCP and made his differences evident by revision. We shall try to deduce his liturgical theology on the basis of what he retains, revises, and omits.

First of all, Wesley's vision for the Christian life is firmly built upon the God-given means of grace, particularly sacrament, Scripture, and prayer. (Fasting is mentioned once, for "all Fridays in the Year, except Christmas-day.") Wesley's pattern for the Christian life is based on a community gathering each Sunday for morning and evening prayer, and celebrating the Lord's Supper "on every Lord's day." At a time when most Anglican parishes were content with three Eucharists per year, Wesley's advice and his own practice were indeed revolutionary. He himself was not content with only a weekly Eucharist but communed, more often than not, twice a week.[1]

Scripture there was in abundance in Wesley's services: a lesson from the Old Testament was provided for each Sunday, both for morning and evening prayer in his table of proper lessons, abundant psalmody was arranged over a thirty-day period, and the liturgical epistles and gospels were retained as provided in the BCP. A note suggests that a gospel chapter be read at morning prayer and an epistle chapter at evening prayer. By far the largest portions of the book are devoted to selections from Scripture.

Prayer, too, abounds, not only in the Lord's Day services, but in the litany for use on Wednesdays and Fridays, and in the call for extempore prayer on all other days. The *Sunday Service* calls for a highly disciplined life, structured on the appointed means of grace and lived in Christian community.

The whole focus of the book is strongly christological. Gone is the entire sanctoral (saints' days) cycle. Wesley felt that "most of the holy-days (so-called)" were "at present answering no valuable end." Even the abbreviation "St." disappears with few exceptions (pp. 133, 298). The focus, instead, is on Sunday as the day of resurrection, or "Lord's Day" as the Puritans demanded and Wesley often calls it. Even some of the christological festivals such as Epiphany, Maundy Thursday, and All Saints' Day disappear, together with the Epiphany, pre-Lenten, and Lent seasons. The year focuses on Christ's

birth and cycles with Sundays numbered after Christmas and Easter as well as after Trinity Sunday. The only exceptions to this exclusively Sunday scheme (all of them christological) are Christmas Day, Good Friday, and Ascension Day.

For the Lord's Day, the traditional Anglican lections and collects are retained with only minor adjustment to accommodate Wesley's method of numbering Sundays after Christmas until "The Sunday next before Easter." It is significant that the Sunday lectionaries for morning and evening prayer and the Eucharist are left intact. Christ's work is presented in orderly and systematic recital as the basis for reading and preaching.

Wesley did, however, take to pruning the Psalter rather severely. Of the 150 "Select Psalms," he excises 34 psalms (or more than a fifth) entirely. Verses disappear from another 58, to make a shrinkage from 2502 verses in the BCP to 1625 in the *Sunday Service*. This means a move from about 42 verses per service in the BCP to just under 28. William N. Wade has analyzed the deletions as falling into five general categories[2]: curses, wrath, killing, and war; descriptions of the wicked, lack of faith, or special personal circumstances; at odds with salvation by faith; concerns exclusively historical or geographical, especially pertaining to Jerusalem; and references to the use of instruments or dance in worship. Wesley defended his excisions, stating that there were "many Psalms left out, and many parts of the others, as being highly improper for the mouths of a Christian Congregation." He also occasionally made changes in the translation, using the King James Version for a verse when it made better sense.

Wesley is certainly not the first (nor the last) to be troubled by untoward portions of the Psalter.[3] His preference for literal interpretation makes allegory unpalatable, and so he prunes away what seems inappropriate for common worship. The high value Wesley placed on the "Select Psalms" should not be overlooked for they are by far the largest single item in the *Sunday Service*. Wesley had recited the psalms daily throughout his life. They were a major ingredient in his personal formation, and he intended to transmit such a tradition, reformed to make it even better.

Ever since 1603 the Puritans had urged that "canonical Scriptures only be read in the Church." Wesley consistently avoids readings from the Apocrypha with one exception: Tobit 4:8-9 is retained as an offertory sentence at the Eucharist although the previous verse is eliminated. No mention of the Apocrypha appears in the "Articles of Religion."

Wesley's perception of the nature of ministry is apparent throughout the book. He prefers the term "minister" in morning and evening prayer, the litany, and the occasional services. Only in the Eucharist and at a few points in the ordinal is "elder" specified. The "superintendant" [sic] has a special ministry as indicated throughout the ordinal, and a "deacon" is designated to read the gospel at his ordination. There are significant shifts away from signs of priestly power. The words "priest" or "curate" disappear completely, as the Puritans had argued in 1661 they should. "Bishop" also has been eliminated completely. No references to clerical garb or ornaments appear.

The term "absolution" has gone entirely. Wesley declared in *Popery Calmly Considered*: "For judicially to pardon sin and absolve the sinner, is a power God has reserved to himself." At morning and evening prayer, the collect from the 24th Sunday after Trinity is substituted for the absolution; at the Eucharist the absolution is made into a prayer by changing the pronouns to "thy" and "thee," while the elder identifies with the people by use of "us" instead of "you."

More freedom is allowed the minister in some instances. The elder "if he see it expedient, may put up an Extempore Prayer" at the Eucharist (although unmentioned elsewhere in the services). The Puritans had pled in vain for such freedom. Likewise, a sermon is to be preached at the Eucharist. Wesley eliminates any mention of using one of the printed homilies from the sixteenth century which BCP suggested. The rather tedious exhortations are scrapped at Eucharist and Baptism. Sixteenth-century didacticism has been put to rest in these instances, although similar elements, such as the Decalogue at the Eucharist or charges at matrimony and at ordination, are retained.

A significant shift occurs in the way the process of becoming a Christian is signified. The concept of baptismal regeneration, although biblical (John 3:5; Titus 3:5) is problematic for Wesley because of his emphasis on the personal experience of conversion. Wesley keeps the declaration in the "Articles of Religion" that Baptism "is a sign of regeneration, or the new birth." But he does make more moderate the references to baptismal regeneration in the rites of infant and adult Baptism themselves without eliminating such references altogether. The opening statement in the infant Baptism rite and the prayer after the gospel both refer to regeneration as taking place in Baptism. But after the act of Baptism, in the statement after the signation "that *this Child is* regenerate and grafted" the

words "regenerate and" disappear. In the prayer after the Lord's Prayer, "that it hath pleased thee to regenerate *this Infant* with thy Holy Spirit," Wesley removes the words "to regenerate . . . with thy Holy Spirit." Presumption that regeneration is inevitable seems offensive to Wesley, and so any suggestion of such is abolished. Similar disappearances occur in the adult rite: "that *these Persons* are regenerate" lose "regenerate and" while the "now" in "that being now born again" vanishes. In short, Wesley does not eliminate the concept of baptismal regeneration but seems to remove any presumption of it. The 1786 edition makes further changes. Criticism of the doctrine of baptismal regeneration was common in liberal theological circles in Wesley's time and broke out in the Gorham dispute within the Church of England in the 1840s'.

Wesley's omissions are often important statements themselves. The most baffling of these is his omission of a rite of confirmation. Eighty years later, the Methodist Episcopal Church found it advisable to add a service for the "Reception of Members," and a century after that this was renamed "Confirmation." The value of a separate rite of confirmation has long been problematic. The Puritans had asked in the Millenary Petition of 1603 that "confirmation, as superfluous, may be taken away." Apparently it had been little administered prior to the reign of James I. Wesley may have felt as the Puritans did, or was sensitive to the difficulties of travel for his superintendents in America, or felt that a conversion experience was a more personal and lasting experience. Perhaps Wesley anticipated the misgivings of modern theologians about confirmation and felt it better to exclude it rather than to perpetuate the mistakes of the Middle Ages and Reformation. At any rate, exclude it he did, but with no mention of his reasons for so doing.

Wesley's other omissions are significant but less puzzling. The legal documents often bound in eighteenth-century BCPs, the table of contents, the various Acts of Uniformity, "the Preface," "Concerning the Service of the Church," "Of Ceremonies," and the instructions on reading the Psalter and scripture lessons, Wesley recognized as irrelevant to the American situation. The daily calendar and tables and rules for the feasts and fasts were not necessary for a Sunday service book. Like many of his contemporaries, Wesley was happy to be rid of the so-called Athanasian Creed.

Private Baptism he omitted without indicating just why. Probably Wesley had a sound liturgical instinct that Baptism ought to be public. The catechism requisite to confirmation also disappears. Similarly absent is visitation of the sick, although Wesley keeps Communion of the sick. "The Thanksgiving of Women after Childbirth" disappears. Wesley eliminated Ash Wednesday so there is no need for "A Commination, of Denouncing God's Anger and Judgments against Sinners," appointed for that day. "Forms of Prayer to be used at Sea" is also removed.

It should be no surprise that the vehemently nationalistic state services, included by royal edict in eighteenth-century BCPs, should be removed. Gunpowder treason, the execution of one English monarch, the restoration of another, and the accession of a third (and the hated George III, at that) would hardly appeal to Americans. Episcopalians toyed with services for July 4 and Thanksgiving Day but only the latter made it into their 1789 book. Wesley did not try to anticipate American festivals but otherwise accommodated to a new country and its distinctive situation.

NOTES

1. John Bowmer, *The Sacrament of the Lord's Supper in Early Methodism* (London: Dacre Press, 1951), p. 55.
2. Cf. his important dissertation: "A History of Public Worship in the Methodist Episcopal Church and Methodist Episcopal Church, South, from 1784-1905." (South Bend: University of Notre Dame, 1981), pp. 52-76.
3. A topic on the agenda of the first synod of Roman Catholic bishops in 1967.

2. "WITH THE EYES OF FAITH":
Spiritual Experience and the knowledge of God in the Theology of John Wesley

Rex D. Matthews

Introduction

Three distinct types of language about faith can be distinguished in the writings of John Wesley. In the first of these types of language, faith means essentially *fides*, assent to propositional truth. In the second, faith means *fiducia*, trusting confidence. In the third, faith means direct spiritual experience of God and the divine realm. This paper intends briefly to examine these three types of language about faith, to explore the relationships among them, and to argue that the third type of language about faith comes to be foundational for the first two in Wesley's mature theology and to play a key role in his religious epistemology.

I. Faith as *Fides*

Wesley defines faith as *fides* in one of his earliest surviving letters, to his mother, dated 29 July 1725:

Faith is a species of belief, and belief is defined, an assent to a proposition upon rational grounds. Without rational grounds there is therefore no belief, and consequently no faith. . . . I call faith an assent upon rational grounds because I hold divine testimony to be the most reasonable of all evidence whatever. Faith must necessarily at length be resolved into reason.[1]

That Susanna was not quite happy with this exposition of the nature of faith is clear from her reply to John on 18 August 1725:

You are somewhat mistaken in your notion of faith. All faith is assent, but not all assent is faith. Some truths are self-evident, and we assent to them because they are so. Others, after a regular and formal process of reason, by way of deduction from some self-evident principle, gain our assent; and this is not properly faith but science. Some again we assent to, not because they are self-evident, or because we have attained the knowledge of them in a regular method, by a chain of arguments, but because they have been revealed to us, either by God or man, and these are the proper objects of faith.

The true measure of faith is the authority of the revealer, the weight of which holds proportion with

our conviction of his ability and integrity. Divine faith is an assent to whatever God hath revealed to us, because he hath revealed it.[2]

She made essentially the same point in a letter of 10 November 1725, apparently in response to a lost letter of John's in which he continued to insist that "faith must necessarily at length be resolved into reason":

Though the same thing may be an object of faith as revealed, and an object of reason as deducible from rational principles, yet I insist upon it that the virtue of faith, by which through the merits of our Redeemer we are saved, is an assent to the truth of whatever God hath been pleased to reveal, because he hath revealed it, and not because we understand it.[3]

Wesley was finally convinced of the inadequacy of his original formulation, which had been drawn from Richard Fiddes' *Body of Divinity* (1718), writing to Susanna on 22 November 1725 that

Fiddes' definition of faith I perceived on reflection to trespass against the first law of defining, as not being adequate to the thing defined. . . . An assent grounded both on testimony and reason takes in science as well as faith, which is on all hands allowed to be distinct from it. I am therefore at length come over to your opinion, that saving faith (including practice) is an assent to whatever God has revealed because he has revealed it, and not because the truth of it is evinced by reason.[4]

George Cell, in *The Rediscovery of John Wesley*, described this development in Wesley's understanding of faith as a transition from a *via rationis* to a *via auctoritatis*.[5] Wesley's initial formulation, borrowed from Fiddes, reminds one very much of a "religion within the limits of reason alone." This position is not essentially dissimilar to that articulated by such Deist authors as John Toland, who argued in his *Christianity Not Mysterious* (1696) that "faith is so far from being an implicit assent to anything above reason that this notion directly contradicts the ends of religion, the nature of man, and the wisdom and goodness of God," and replied to those who might argue that such a view had the effect of transforming faith into reason or knowledge that "if by knowledge be meant understanding what is believed, then I stand for it, that faith is knowledge."[6] This *via rationis*, to use Cell's term, insists that to any proposition which reason cannot comprehend, that species of assent which is called faith cannot be accorded.

The *via auctoritatis* upon which Susanna insisted, and to which John had "entirely come over" only a few weeks later, seems closely similar to that of John Locke's *An Essay Concerning Human Understanding* (1696). This was, of course, the position against which Toland was reacting directly, with its celebrated distinction of things "according to," "contrary to," and "above" reason, and its definition of faith as "assent to any proposition, not . . . made out by the deductions of reason, but on the credit of the proposer."[7] According to this position, reason is to inspect any offered proposition. If the proposition contradicts the principles of reason or conflicts with what is already known by reason, it is rejected as false. But if reason is unable to determine the truth of the proposition on its own terms, the question becomes that of the weight behind the proposition—"the credit of the proposer." This is still faith understood as a form of rational assent; in the case of divinely revealed truths, the assent of faith is required precisely because it is God who is the "proposer." Locke added explicitly what is implicit in the words of both Susanna and John: that without doubt what God has revealed is true, but it is still the task of reason to judge whether any particular proposition is, in fact, a divine revelation. Given Wesley's view of the divine inspiration of Scripture (which is infallible, though its human interpreters are not), the assent of faith is required to the revelation from God which it contains.

Along with many others, Cell claims that Wesley was to abandon this *via auctoritatis* understanding of the nature of faith, in the wake of his experience at Aldersgate, "to substitute experiential thinking for the purely logical use of the intellect," and to develop a theology of "transcendental empiricism."[8] This claim is attractive and contains some truth, but it requires careful examination, as it rests on a false antinomy. Wesley's mature doctrine of faith is much richer and more complex than Cell's analysis will allow.

II. Faith as *Fiducia*

The *locus classicus* for Wesley's understanding of faith as *fiducia*, trusting confidence, is of course his account of his experience on that May night in 1738:

> In the evening I went very unwillingly to a society in Aldersgate Street, where one was reading Luther's preface to the Epistle to the Romans. About a quarter before nine, while he was describing the change which God works in the heart through faith in Christ, I felt my heart strangely warmed. I felt I did trust in Christ, Christ alone for my salvation; and an assurance was given me that He had taken away *my* sins, even *mine*, and saved *me* from the law of sin and death.[9]

In that important passage of his "Preface to Romans," Luther argues that faith "is not something dreamed, a human illusion"; it is not the same as "belief." Instead, says Luther, faith "is something that God effects in us":

> Faith is a living and unshakable confidence, a belief in the grace of God so assured that a man would die a thousand deaths for its sake. This kind of confidence in God's grace, this sort of knowledge of it, makes us joyful, high-spirited, and eager in our relations with God and with all mankind. That is what the Holy Spirit effects through faith. . . . Offer up your prayers to God, and ask him to create faith in you; otherwise, you will always lack faith, no matter how you try to deceive yourself, or what your efforts and ability.[10]

Given the abject personal and ministerial failures of his Georgia experience, and his condition of profound emotional and spiritual depression upon his return to England in early 1738, one can understand how Luther's description of the nature of faith as *fiducia*, trusting confidence, could strike Wesley so powerfully. Despite all of his strenuous "spiritual athletics," Wesley had not been able to arrive at that "living and unshakable confidence" or the kind of "joyful, high-spirited" relationship to God of which Luther spoke. It was in fact his own experience of his lack of that "belief in the grace of God so strong that a man would die a thousand deaths for its sake," contrasted with the calm assurance of faith exhibited in the face of the raging storms of the North Atlantic by the Moravians, which first led Wesley to his association with them. And it was the Moravian, Peter Böhler, who gradually convinced Wesley, over the course of several months of disputation, that the concept of faith as primarily *fides*, rational assent, with which he had been working up to this point, was seriously deficient.

It was on Sunday, 5 March 1738, Wesley tells us, that he was "clearly convinced" by Böhler of his "unbelief, of the want of that faith whereby alone we are saved."[11] This marks, I think it is safe to say, Wesley's *intellectual conversion* to the understanding of faith as *fiducia*, trusting confidence, which Böhler had been urging on him. That Wesley so regarded it is clear from his following statement: "Immediately it struck my mind, 'Leave off preaching. How can you preach to others, who have not faith yourself?' "[12] The implication seems clear: Wesley now acknowledges the *theory*, but has not the *reality*, of saving faith understood as "a sure trust and confidence of salvation"; he is both intellectually *convinced* that Böhler is right about the nature of saving faith and spiritually *convicted* of his own personal lack of it. But Böhler would not let him off the hook quite so easily, and responded with an admirable bit of pastoral counseling: "Preach faith *till* you have it; and then, *because* you have it, you *will* preach faith."[13] And this Wesley did, "though my soul started back from the work."[14]

What Wesley's Aldersgate experience was all about, on this interpretation, was his coming to possess the reality of faith as *fiducia*, trusting confidence in God's grace and mercy. As A. S. Wood once remarked, "Already it was an intellectual apprehension; he must go on proclaiming it to others until it became a spiritual possession for him."[15] Colin Williams has made essentially the same point, writing that "the crisis in Wesley's life arose precisely from the fact that the doctrine which he accepted pointed to an experience which he did not have."[16] What Aldersgate did was to release Wesley from an excessive preoccupation with his spiritual condition, from what Stanley Ayling has aptly described as a kind of "religious hypochondria" which had led to "a constant fussing over his spiritual temperature."[17] Once freed from this, first by the new understanding of faith as *fiducia* to which Böhler led him, then by the assurance of his possession of that faith which was given to him at Aldersgate, Wesley's confidence in his spiritual state and condition never seriously faltered, even though he did have his moments of doubt and fear (he was, after all, human). And his new-found understanding and possession of faith as "a sure trust and confidence" of salvation also freed Wesley from a form of spirituality which had in reality been utterly self-oriented—through its focus on self-examination, self-discipline, self-denial, and self-doubt—to become truly "a man for others."

III. Faith as Spiritual Experience

Wesley's third type of language about faith is based on Hebrews 11:1, translated in his own *Explanatory Notes upon the New Testament* as "Now faith is the substance of things hoped for, the evidence of things unseen."[18] It was apparently in Georgia that Wesley first had faith defined for him in precisely these terms. In his *Journal* for July 1737, he records the substance of a conversation with the leaders of the Moravian community there. To Wesley's question, "What is faith?" the Moravian response was to quote Hebrews 11:1.[19] Wesley would certainly have been familiar with the discussion of faith in Hebrews 11 already, and the definition of faith as "the evidence of things unseen" had been used in discussions of the nature of faith by John Toland and Peter Browne, among others. But so far as I have been able to determine, this is the first time this type of language about faith appears in any of Wesley's writings, and this in a context which would connect the assurance of salvation which these Moravians seemed to have and the "witness of the Spirit" about which Spangenberg had closely pressed him with the understanding of faith as "the evidence of things unseen."

Wesley's understanding of faith as "spiritual experience" finds its first complete expression in *An Earnest Appeal to Men of Reason and Religion* (1743). There faith is described as

> . . . the demonstrative evidence of things unseen, the supernatural evidence of things invisible, not perceivable by eyes of flesh, or by any of our natural senses or faculties. Faith is that divine evidence whereby the spiritual man discerneth God and the things of God. It is with regard to the spiritual world what sense is with regard to the natural. It is the spiritual sensation of every soul that is born of God.[20]

The same understanding of faith as "spiritual experience" recurs in Wesley's extended debate with "John Smith" about the nature of faith and his perceptibility of divine inspiration or the "witness of the Spirit." In the original letter, "Smith" (who may or may not have been in reality Archbishop Thomas Secker) defined faith in terms typical of eighteenth-century Anglican theology: "It is the nature of faith to be a full and practical assent to truth. But such assent arises not momentaneously, but by the slow steps of ratiocination; by attending to the evidence, weighing the objections, and solving the difficulties."[21] Wesley's response is brief, succinct, and directly to the point:

> "It is the nature of faith to be a full and practical assent to truth." Surely no. This definition does in no wise express the nature of Christian faith. Christian, saving faith, is a divine conviction of

ing its denomination from that principle object, is ordinarily termed *faith in Jesus Christ*.[27]

This kind of language about faith comes to be increasingly important and prominent in Wesley's writings from about the time of his abridgment of Scougal's treatise in 1742. And though he will occasionally use the analogy of hearing (more rarely those of taste or touch, and almost never that of smell), it is the analogy between the physical sense of sight and the spiritual sense of faith which is predominant. This passage from his sermon "The Scripture Way of Salvation" (1765) may be taken as typical:

> Faith, in general, is . . . *an evidence*, a divine *evidence and conviction* (the word means both) *of things not seen*; not visible, not perceivable either by sight, or by any other of the external senses. It implies both a supernatural *evidence* of God, and of the things of God; a kind of spiritual *light* exhibited to the soul, and a supernatural *sight* or perception thereof. . . . By this two-fold operation of the Holy Spirit, having the eyes of our soul both *opened* and *enlightened*, we see things which the natural "eye hath not seen, neither the ear heard." . . . Taking the word in a more particular sense, faith is a divine *evidence* and *conviction* not only that "God was in Christ, reconciling the world unto Himself," but also that Christ loved *me*, and gave Himself for *me*. It is by this faith (whether we term it the *essence* of it, or rather a *property* thereof) that we *receive* Christ .[28]

IV. Wesley's Three Languages About Faith

On this analysis, then, three distinct types of language about faith can be discerned in Wesley's writings. But the balance among these three types of language is not constant. In the period prior to Aldersgate, Wesley uses primarily, if not exclusively, the language about faith as *fides*, rational assent to propositional truth, as we saw in his correspondence with his mother. In the period immediately following Aldersgate, the language of faith as *fiducia*, "a sure trust and confidence of salvation," becomes much more prominent. It is surely significant, as Albert Outler and others have pointed out, that by November of 1738 Wesley "began more narrowly to inquire what the doctrine of the Church of England is concerning the much controverted point of justification by faith."[29] One of the immediate results of this inquiry was the publication of his abridgment of the Cranmerian *Homilies*. The more important long-term result was his appropriation of Cranmer's language about the "sure trust and confidence" of faith as truly his *own* language.

However, contrary to George Cell's assertion, Wesley never completely abandoned the language about faith as rational assent. Instead, in the early post-Aldersgate writings, a "not only . . . but also" formula appears, as for example, in the sermon "Salvation by Faith," preached at St. Mary's, Oxford, less than three weeks after Aldersgate: "[Saving faith] is not barely a speculative, rational thing, a cold, lifeless assent, a train of ideas in the head; but also a disposition of the heart. . . . Christian faith is, then, not only an assent to the whole gospel of Christ, but also a full reliance on the blood of Christ. . . . It is a sure trust and confidence."[30] The same formulation appears in a letter of 1739, to Henry Stebbing, one of the earliest Anglican critics of the emergent Methodist movement: "that term 'believing' [implies], not only an assent to the Articles of our Creed, but also, 'a true trust and confidence of the mercy of God through our Lord Jesus Christ.' "[31] And in response to the assertion of "John Smith" in 1745 that faith is (simply) "a rational assent and a moral virtue," Wesley replies that he does believe that "a rational assent to the truth of the Bible is one ingredient of Christian faith," while insisting that such rational assent is not in itself the fullness of faith.[32] Faith *is* rational assent. But it is not *only* rational assent.

But by the time of his *Appeal* and his exchange with "John Smith," in the mid-1740s, the language about faith as spiritual experience becomes more prominent, and his emphasis on faith as rational assent becomes more muted, as Wesley evolves his complex mature doctrine of faith. Of course, he could, on occasion, be admirably succinct, as when he wrote to John Bennett in 1744 that "faith is seeing God; love is feeling God."[33] More typical is this formulation, in a letter of 1760 to the editor of *Lloyd's Evening Post*:

> *Faith* is an evidence or conviction of things not seen, of God, and the things of God. This is faith in general. More particularly it is a divine evidence or conviction that Christ loved *me* and gave Himself for *me*. This directly leads us to *work out our salvation with fear and trembling*; not with slavish, painful fear, but with the utmost diligence, which is the proper import of the expression. When this evidence is heightened to exclude all doubt, it is the *plerophry* or *full assurance of faith*. But any degree of true faith prompts the believer to be zealous of good works.[34]

And the concept of faith as spiritual experience becomes predominant in the writings of the elderly Wesley. Three of his last sermons, "The Difference Between Walking by Sight, and Walking by Faith" (1788), "On the Discoveries of Faith" (1788), and "On Faith" (1791), are all concerned primarily with the theme of the invisible things, a supernatural conviction of the things of God, with a filial confidence in his love. Now a man may have a full assent to the truth of the Bible (probably attained by the slow steps you mention), yes, an assent which has some influence on his practice, and yet have not one grain of this faith.[22]

There is of course a venerable history and a voluminous literature concerning the "spiritual senses" in Christian theology, which we have no time to review here. To cite only one example, Hans Urs von Balthasar, in the first volume of *The Glory of the Lord: A Theological Aesthetics*, identifies three *loci classici* of this history as being Origen, who "invented" the doctrine of the "five spiritual senses"; Bonaventure, who gave the definitive medieval explication of the "spiritual senses" as the expression of the mystical and intuitive experience of God; and Ignatius Loyola, whose *Exercises* call for the "application of the senses" of the exercitant to the mystery of faith under consideration each day.[23] And there are, of course, many others to whom von Balthasar could have pointed.

Given the extent of Wesley's reading and the range of his intellectual interests, he may well have been familiar with all of these figures. And in addition, the writings of John Norris, Nicholas Malebranche, John Locke, and Peter Browne, among others, certainly contributed to Wesley's understanding of sensory perception in general and of the "spiritual sensation" of faith in particular. The enterprise of tracing the sources or definitive influences on any particular point in Wesley's thought is of course exceedingly difficult, if not impossible. Still, I think it likely that a more important influence on Wesley's understanding of faith as "spiritual experience" was the tradition of English Puritanism.

Such Puritan authors as Baxter, Perkins, Sibbes, and Owen, all of whom appear in Wesley's *Christian Library*, frequently employed the analogy of the immediacy of sensory perception when describing the experience of grace, and the classical discussion about theoretical knowledge versus personal experience of "the taste of the honey" was well known to both John and Charles Wesley. The concept of "spiritual experience" plays a critically important role in Charles's sermon "Awake, Thou That Sleepest," preached at St. Mary's, Oxford, in 1742, and printed in John's collected *Sermons*. And it is there expressed in language powerfully reminiscent of those Puritan divines:

And most certain is it, that one dead in sin has not "senses exercised to discern spiritual good and evil." "Having eyes, he sees not; he hath ears, and

hears not." He doth not "taste and see that the Lord is gracious." He "hath not seen God at any time," not "heard His voice," not "handled the word of life." In vain is the name of Jesus "like ointment poured forth, and all his garments smell of myrrh, aloes, and cassia." The soul that sleepeth in death hath no perception of any objects of this kind. His heart is "past feeling," and understandeth none of these things.

And hence, having no spiritual sense, no inlets of spiritual knowledge, the natural man receiveth not the things of the Spirit of God; nay, he is so far from receiving them, that whatsoever is spiritually discerned is mere foolishness to him. He is not content with being utterly ignorant of spiritual things, but denies the very existence of them.[24]

But it is in John's writings, beginning with the passage from his *Appeal* quoted above, that the concept of "spiritual experience" is explicitly wedded to the notion of faith as "a divine evidence or conviction of things not seen." And it may well be the case that the most important influence upon this identification of faith with "spiritual sensation" was the little devotional book of Henry Scougal, *The Life of God in the Soul of Man* (1677). The importance of this work to Susanna Wesley, who first introduced her sons to it, has long been known. And as Winthrop S. Hudson points out in the introduction to his edition of it, the book has with some justice been described as the "text-book" of the "Holy Club" at Oxford; it was highly regarded by both John and Charles Wesley, and Charles's borrowed copy was the immediate agency of George Whitefield's conversion.[25] And Wesley's abridgment of the work went through seven separate printings between 1742 and 1808, in addition to being included in his *Christian Library*.

Scougal's concern is to present religion as a matter, not of external practices, but of internal experience: "True religion is an union of the soul with God, a real participation in the divine nature, the very image of Christ drawn upon the soul, or, in the Apostle's phrase, *it is Christ formed within us*. . . . I know not how the nature of religion can be more fully expressed than by calling it *a divine life*."[26] The root of this divine life, says Scougal, is faith; its chief branches are "love to God, charity to man, purity, and humility." And faith is described by Scougal in these terms:

Faith hath the same place in the divine life which *sense* hath in the natural, being indeed nothing else but a kind of sense or feeling persuasion of spiritual things. It extends itself unto all divine truths; but, in our lapsed state, it hath a peculiar relation to the declarations of God's mercy and reconcilableness to sinners through a Mediator, and therefore, receiv-

"spiritual senses" of faith as a remedy supplied by God to correct the deficiencies of our natural senses, which are utterly incapable of perceiving God and the things of God. But even in these late sermons, language about faith as rational assent and as "sure trust and confidence" is not totally lacking. For not only is there a significant shift in the *balance* among the three types of language about faith through Wesley's lifetime, there is also, more importantly, a shift in the *function* of these types of language.

Increasingly, the understanding of faith as "an evidence or conviction of things unseen" becomes Wesley's *general* definition of faith (the "genus"; or in Wesley's more characteristic language "the faith of a servant"), which is basic to the more *particular* understanding of faith as the perception of God's grace and mercy extended to the individual Christian (the "species"; or "the faith of a son"). This is particularly clear, for example, in the 1760 letter to *Lloyd's Evening Post* cited above: "*Faith* is an evidence or conviction of things not seen, of God and the things of God. This is faith in general. More particularly it is a divine evidence or conviction that Christ loved *me* and gave Himself for *me*."[35] Exactly the same distinction between the general and the particular understandings of faith as spiritual experience is found in the sermon, "The Scripture Way of Salvation" (1765):

Faith, in general, is . . . *a divine evidence and conviction* (the word means both) *of things not seen.* . . . Taking the word in a more particular sense, faith is a divine *evidence* and *conviction* not only that "God was in Christ, reconciling the world unto Himself," but also that Christ loved *me*, and gave Himself for *me*.[36]

It seems clear, then, that the *particular* understanding of faith as one's personal spiritual experience of God's grace and mercy becomes the *foundation* for faith as *fiducia*, one's "sure trust and confidence" of salvation, and for faith as *fides*, one's rational assent to the truth of divine revelation. In short, it becomes the basis for all knowledge of God.

V. The Knowledge of God

How does one come to the knowledge of God, in general, and to the particular knowledge of Jesus Christ as personal Savior? "Only through the eyes of faith," replies Wesley, meaning thereby "only through personal spiritual experience." Though his position is adumbrated elsewhere, Wesley's clearest epistemological discussions come in *An Earnest Appeal* (1743) and its sequels,[37] and in the sermon, "The Case of

Reason Impartially Considered" (1750?).[38] Put "in form," as Wesley might say, the general argument runs like this:

(1) Knowledge, whether of the spiritual or the material world, depends upon the working of human reason.
(2) Reason is "a faculty of the human soul" which has three functions: "simple apprehension," "judgment," and "discourse."
   (a) Simple apprehension is "barely conceiving a thing in the mind."
   (b) Judgment is "determining that the things before conceived [or apprehended] either agree or disagree with each other."
   (c) Discourse, or "reasoning" more particularly, is "the progress of the mind from one judgment to another."
(3) Reasoning (or discourse) on any subject presupposes true judgments already formed.
(4) The forming of true judgments depends on the apprehension of clear, fixed, distinct, and determinate ideas.
(5) There are no innate ideas; all ideas must originally come from sensory experience.
Therefore:
(6) If there is no sensory experience, there can be no apprehension, and so no judgment, and no discourse or "reasoning," and, consequently, no knowledge.

It has long been supposed that Locke is the immediate source for this epistemological stance. To cite only one example, Gerald Cragg, in his edition of the *Appeals*, asserts flatly that "Wesley's interpretation of the senses is a part of the epistemology he derived from John Locke."[39] More recent scholarship has tended to suggest a wider range of influences on Wesley's epistemological outlook. In his important doctoral dissertation "Epistemology in the Thought of John Wesley," Mitsuo Shimizu makes a good case for the importance of John Norris and Nicholas Malebranche.[40] And Frederick Dreyer, in his recent article "Faith and Experience in the Thought of John Wesley," one of the best and most balanced discussions of this topic to date, argues that although Wesley's empiricism "derived ultimately from Locke," it was in reality Peter Browne who was "the more direct and immediate influence on Wesley's mind."[41]

Regardless of its sources or the influences upon its development, it seems clear that Wesley's epistemology is thoroughly empiricistic. Wesley is at one with early Enlightenment thinkers in England, France, and Germany in his rejection of Cartesian innate ideas. On this point, at least, there is no essential difference between

Wesley and Locke (or Browne or Hume, or even Voltaire). And yet, like Locke, Wesley leaves unchallenged the assumption of the innate operating principles of the mind. Even though he is working with a very different understanding of the nature and function of reason (which, as I have argued elsewhere, is heavily dependent on the eighteenth-century Oxford Aristotelian logical tradition), Wesley, like Locke, is content merely to enumerate and describe the various "functions" of the "faculty" of reason, and to assert them as fundamental powers of the mind, or reason (the two terms are synonymous for him), without pressing questions concerning the details of their operation, their unity, or their source.[42]

However, it would seem that Wesley has a serious problem here which does not beset such figures as Locke. For, with his strong insistence on the radical debilitation of human nature by original sin, brought about by the fall from grace by the first parents of our race, comes his assertion that we have lost the image of God in all of its dimensions: natural, political, and moral. Is the functioning of the "faculty" of reason, along with its corresponding sensory apparatus, to be considered a part of the "natural" dimension of the image of God? If so, what is the extent of its disability in the condition of original sin? Although Wesley never discusses this issue in any detail, he does assert, in a footnote to his extract of Browne's *Procedure, Extent and Limits of Human Understanding* in his own *Compendium of Natural Philosophy* that "I believe all 'the light of nature,' so called, to flow from prevenient grace."[43] Apparently it is Wesley's position that our knowledge of the natural or material, physical world, obtained through sensory experience and the epistemological mechanics he has outlined, is in reality not "natural" but dependent on God's grace.

It is when Wesley turns to questions of specifically religious epistemology that his understanding of faith as "spiritual sensation" becomes critically important. Just as we have no innate ideas about the physical world, argues Wesley, so we have no innate ideas about the spiritual world. And the analogy which Wesley draws between the physical senses and our experience of the physical world through them, and the "spiritual senses" of faith and our experience of the spiritual world through them, is precise and exact. Lacking the requisite "spiritual senses" and consequently lacking any experience of the "things of God," it is impossible for "men of reason" (alone) to employ their reason in the religious realm: no senses, no sensory experience, no apprehension, no judg-ment, no discourse, and consequently no knowledge of God. What is required, says Wesley, is that they have "a new class of senses" opened up in their souls, through the gift, from outside them, by God's grace, of faith.

What is required, in other words, is that they be "born again." For that is what saving faith entails for Wesley: justification and regeneration, forgiveness for past sins and renewal of inward nature. The "new birth" is "that great change which God works in the soul, when he brings it to life; when he raises it from the death of sin to the life of righteousness . . . the change wrought in the soul by the Almighty Spirit of God when it is 'created anew in Christ Jesus,' when it is 'renewed after the image of God.' "[44] As Wesley repeatedly insists, the "new birth" is not only a *relative* but a *real* change. It is not only something that God does *for* us, but something that God works *in* us; it is a real transformation wrought in the soul. And one of the results of that transformation is the "opening up" of the new "spiritual senses" of faith. It is in this sense that Wesley speaks of the Spirit as "opening and enlightening the eyes of our understanding" or reason. And it is only *after* this transformation that it is possible, according to Wesley, for one to have any direct experience of spiritual reality, and consequently, to arrive at any knowledge of God:

> The Son of God begins his work in man by enabling us to believe in him. He both opens and enlightens the eyes of our understanding. Out of darkness he commands light to shine, and takes away the veil which the "god of this world" has spread over our hearts. And we see then not by a chain of *reasoning*, but by a kind of *intuition*, by a *direct* view, that "God was in Christ reconciling the world to himself, not imputing to them their former trespasses"; not imputing them to *me*.[45]

That such a transformation as the "new birth" must occur in order to the opening up of the "spiritual senses" of faith in the soul Wesley repeatedly insists. He is considerably less clear about precisely *how* he understands such a transformation to occur, or in precisely *what* it consists. Part of Wesley's lack of clarity on these points is, I think, the result of his reluctance to "meddle with the deep things of God." But a part of it is due to the fact that he certainly had not the leisure, and probably had not the ability, to press theological and philosophical questions or issues to these depths. Despite his broad general familiarity with the concerns of eighteenth-century philosophy—he had read works by such diverse figures as Locke, Berkeley, Hume, Browne, Norris, Malebranche, Butler, Hutcheson, and Edwards, to mention only a few—Wesley's mind was of a less systematic and penetrating, inquiring turn. He certainly was capable of being a fierce disputant, and had formidable skills in logic and debate which he used in controversy with such figures as Thomas Church, Conyers Middleton, George Lavington, and "John Smith." But, in general, he was much more concerned to defend his general theological, and epistemological, position against such critics than to trace out the conclusions and implications of his analogical and metaphorical language concerning such matters as the "spiritual senses" of faith and the "direct experience" of the divine realm which he claimed to be possible through them.

Still, Wesley does insist clearly that it is possible to know *when* such a transformation has taken place in the soul. This is his much-maligned doctrine of assurance or "the witness of the Spirit," which he describes as "an inward impression on the soul, whereby the Spirit of God directly witnesses to my spirit, that I am a child of God; that Jesus Christ hath loved me, and given Himself for me."[46] This doctrine of "the witness of the Spirit" was second only to his insistence on the possibility of entire sanctification or "Christian perfection" in the amount of difficulties which it caused Wesley, despite his attempts to use cautious language in its expression, and it laid him open to repeated charges of "enthusiasm," perhaps the most damning accusation which could be leveled in the Age of Reason.

To the question of how one could distinguish the real "witness of the Spirit" from presumption or "enthusiasm," Wesley gives this response:

How, I pray, do you distinguish day from night? How do you distinguish light from darkness; or the light of a star, or a glimmering taper, from the light of the noonday sun? Is there not an inherent, obvious, essential difference between the one and the other? And do not you immediately and directly perceive that difference, provided your senses are rightly disposed? In like manner, there is an inherent, essential difference between spiritual light and spiritual darkness; and between the light wherewith the Sun of Righteousness shines upon our heart, and that glimmering light which arises only from "sparks of our own kindling": and this difference is also immediately and directly perceived, if our spiritual senses are rightly disposed.[47]

Precisely *how* this comes to pass is a matter Wesley prefers not to attempt to explain: "To require a more minute and philosophical account of the manner whereby we distinguish these [i.e., spiritual light and darkness], and of

the *criteria*, or intrinsic marks, whereby we know the voice of God, is to make a demand which can never be answered; no, not by one who has the deepest knowledge of God."[48] Or as he put it elsewhere,

The manner how the *divine* testimony is manifested to the heart, I do not take upon me to explain. Such knowledge is too wonderful and excellent for me: I cannot attain unto it. The wind bloweth, and I hear the sound thereof; but I cannot tell how it cometh, or whither it goeth. As no one knoweth the things of a man, save the spirit of a man is in him; so the *manner* of the things of God no one knoweth, save the Spirit of God. But the *fact* we know; namely, that the Spirit of God does give a believer such a testimony of his adoption, that while it is present in the soul, he can no more doubt the reality of his sonship, than he can doubt of the shining of the sun, while he stands in the full blaze of his beams.[49]

So, while maintaining a healthy respect for the mysteries of the precise *manner* of God's activities, Wesley yields no quarter in his insistence that the *fact* of the "witness of the Spirit" can be directly and immediately perceived through the "spiritual senses" of faith, if they are "rightly disposed." But how can one be sure that one's spiritual senses are in fact "rightly disposed"? Wesley's answer is, "by the testimony of your own spirit":

by "the answer of a good conscience toward God." By the fruits which He hath wrought in your spirit, you shall know the testimony of the Spirit of God. Hereby you shall know that you are in no delusion, that you have not deceived your own soul. The immediate fruits of the Spirit, ruling the heart, are "love, peace, bowels of mercies, humbleness of mind, meekness, gentleness, long-suffering." And the outward fruits are, the doing good to all men; the doing no evil to any; and the walking in the light—a zealous, uniform obedience to all the commandments of God.[50]

So, to review: once the "spiritual senses" of faith have been opened up in our souls, we are as immediately able to perceive and distinguish God and the things of God through their agency as we are able to distinguish light and darkness through the agency of our natural senses; we are assured that this has taken place through the direct "witness of the Spirit" to our souls; and we are confirmed in our perception of this direct "witness of the Spirit" through the (indirect) "witness of our own spirit," by our possession of both inward and outward fruits of the Spirit. And though Wesley always claimed that, normally at least, the outward and the inward "fruits of the Spirit" occurred together, the more important for him were the inward, immediate fruits: love, peace, and joy "ruling in the heart." And we *know* these to exist because we *feel* them.

Inward *feelings* were an acid test for Wesley. In those dispairing *Journal* entries of early 1738, he uses the language of feeling extensively. "By the most infallible of proofs, inward feeling," wrote Wesley in January 1738, "I am convinced: 1. Of unbelief; having no such faith in Christ as will prevent my heart from being troubled; which it could not be, if I believed in God, and rightly believed also in Him."[51] At Aldersgate he "felt" his heart to be strangely warmed, and "felt" that he did trust in Christ alone for salvation.[52] In a time of struggle in January 1739, he used the same language: "I *feel* this moment I do not love God; which therefore I *know* because I *feel* it. There is no word more proper, more clear, or more strong."[53] Precisely the same claim appears in a different context in Wesley's "Thoughts upon Necessity":

> But it is certain I can trust none of my senses, if I am a mere machine. For I have the testimony of all my outward and all my inward senses, that I am a free agent. If therefore I cannot trust them in this, I can trust them in nothing. Do not tell me there are sun, moon, and stars, or that there are men, beasts, or birds, in the world. I cannot believe one tittle of it, if I cannot believe what I feel in myself, namely, that it depends on me, and no other being, whether I shall now open or shut my eyes, move my head hither and thither, or stretch my hand or my foot. If I am necessitated to do all this, contrary to the whole of my inward and outward senses, I can believe nothing, but must necessarily sink into universal scepticism.[54]

"John Smith" was correct in his assertion that Wesley held a doctrine of "palpable inspiration," as Wesley himself finally admitted (though with reservations). But, as Wesley replied, what is perceptible is not the *work* of divine inspiration but its *fruits*, not the *manner* of the Spirit's working but the *results* of that work. And the most important of these results or fruits is inward feelings or dispositions. These, as Wesley argued in his controversy with Thomas Church, *are* immediately perceptible or sensible:

> Do you then exclude all sensible impulses? Do you reject inward feelings *toto genere*? Then you reject both the love of God and of our neighbor. For, if these cannot be inwardly felt, nothing can. You reject all joy in the Holy Ghost; for if we cannot be sensible of this, it is no joy at all. You reject the peace of God, which, if it cannot be felt in the inmost soul, is a dream, a notion, an empty name.

> You therefore reject the whole inward kingdom of God; that is, in effect, the whole Gospel of Jesus Christ.[55]

At bottom, then, Wesley seems to come to a position strikingly similar to that of Jonathan Edwards, though from a different starting point and through a different route. Wesley's "spiritual senses" of faith seem to correspond to Edwards's "sense of the heart," and Wesley's "inward fruits of faith" to Edwards's "religious affections." Religious experience does not consist of dreams or visions, but of feeling in one's inmost self the love of God and of neighbor. And the knowledge of God to which one comes through this religious experience, through "seeing with the eyes of faith" does not consist of new data about God's being or inner essence, but of an awareness of what God has done for *me*. It is an intensely *personal* form of knowledge of God as Creator and Christ as Redeemer.

But such a position does not imply a retreat on Wesley's part from reason to a kind of incoherent and subjective emotivism, any more than on Edwards's. "Knowing God" properly begins with "feeling God," but does not end there. Reason has a critically important role to play. As Albert Outler once appositely remarked, in Wesley's view "reason generates neither its data nor its presuppositions; faith does not provide its own self-evident conclusions."[56] That Wesley yielded to none in his respect for the role of reason in the religious life, is made abundantly clear by his sermon, "The Case of Reason Impartially Examined"; he insists there that, though reason can never *produce* faith, yet faith is always *consistent with* reason.[56] The knowledge of God to which we come through religious experience, by "seeing with the eyes of faith," is not one whit less "reasonable," according to Wesley, than the knowledge of the natural world around us to which we come through physical sensory experience. In either case knowledge is what results from the application of reason, in its three-fold functioning, to the data of sensory experience.

Modern epistemological theory and contemporary discussions of the phenomenology of human emotions have long since outdistanced Wesley's eighteenth-century philosophical vocabulary. Yet Wesley may still have something important to say to us, with his insistence that the knowledge of God involves at once more than mere cognition and more than mere feeling. And a part of his continuing relevance may well prove to lie in his complex concept of faith as *fides*, *fiducia*, and *feeling*.

NOTES

The volumes from Wesley, *Works* (Oxford), will be abbreviated as follows: Vol. 11: *The Appeals to Men of Reason and Religion and Certain Related Open Letters*, ed. Gerald R. Cragg (1975) [=*Appeals*]; Vol. 25: *Letters I, 1725-1740*, ed. Frank Baker (1980) [=*Letters I*]; Vol. 26: *Letters II, 1740-1755*, ed. Frank Baker (1982) [=*Letters II*]

1. *Works* (Oxford), 25: *Letters I*, pp. 175-76.
2. Ibid., p. 179.
3. Ibid., p. 183.
4. Ibid., p. 188.
5. George Cell, *The Rediscovery of John Wesley* (New York: Holt, Rinehart, 1935), 168 ff.
6. John Toland, *Christianity Not Mysterious* (facsimile reprint of original 1696 ed., Stuttgart: Friedrich Frommann Verlag, 1964), p. 145. Spelling and punctuation silently modernized.
7. John Locke, *An Essay Concerning Human Understanding*, ed. P.H. Nidditch (Oxford: Clarendon Press, 1975), pp. 687-89 (IV.xvi.23, IV.xvii.2).
8. Cell, *Rediscovery*, pp. 84-86.
9. *Journal*, vol. 1, pp. 475-76.
10. Martin Luther, "Preface to Romans," in *Martin Luther: Selections From His Writings*, ed. John Dillenberger (Chicago: Quadrangle Books, 1961), p. 24.
11. *Journal*, I, p. 442.
12. Ibid.
13. Ibid.
14. Ibid.
15. A. S. Wood, *The Burning Heart: John Wesley, Evangelist* (Minneapolis: Bethany Press, 1978), p. 63.
16. Colin W. Williams, *John Wesley's Theology Today* (Nashville: Abingdon Press, 1960), p. 104.
17. Stanley Ayling, *John Wesley* (Nashville: Abingdon Press, 1980), p. 320.
18. *Notes*, p. 841 (Heb. 11:1).
19. *Journal*, vol. 1, p. 372.
20. *Works* (Oxford), *Appeals*, p. 46.
21. *Works* (Oxford), *Letters II*, p. 141.
22. Ibid., p. 159.
23. Hans Urs von Balthasar, *The Glory of the Lord: A Theological Aesthetics*, vol. 1: *Seeing the Form*, trans. Erasmo Leiva-Merikakis, ed. Joseph Fessio S.J. and John Riches (San Francisco: Ignatius Press and New York: Crossroad Publications, 1982), pp. 365-80.
24. *Sermons*, vol. 1, p. 74 ("Awake, Thou That Sleepest").
25. Henry Scougal, *The Life of God in the Soul of Man*, ed. Winthrop S. Hudson (Philadelphia: Westminster Press, 1948), "Introduction," pp. 12-13.
26. Ibid., p. 30.
27. Ibid., p. 38.
28. *Sermons*, vol. 2, p. 448-49 ("The Scripture Way of Salvation").
29. *Journal*, vol. 2, p. 101.
30. *Sermons*, vol. 1, pp. 40-41 ("Salvation by Faith").
31. *Works* (Oxford), *Letters* I, p. 671.
32. Ibid., *Letters* II, p. 157.
33. Ibid., p. 108.
34. *Letters*, vol. 4, p. 116.
35. Ibid.
36. *Sermons*, vol. 2, pp. 448-49 ("The Scripture Way of Salvation").
37. *Works* (Oxford), *Appeals*.
38. *Works*, vol. 7, pp. 350-60.
39. *Works* (Oxford), *Appeals*, p. 57.
40. Mitsuo Shimizu, "Epistemology in the Thought of John Wesley," Ph.D. Dissertation, Drew University, 1980.
41. Frederick Dreyer, "Faith and Experience in the Thought of John Wesley," *American Historical Review* 88 (Fall 1983): 12-30. The important new work of Richard E. Brantley, *Locke, Wesley and the Method of English Romanticism* (Gainesville: University of Florida Press, 1984), which argues many of the same points as Dreyer, appeared too late to be considered in this paper.
42. This argument is advanced in my unpublished paper "Reason, Faith, and Experience in the Thought of John Wesley," presented to the seventh Oxford Institute of Methodist Theological Studies (Keble College, Oxford, July 26–August 5, 1982). Further detail will be given in my Th.D. dissertation "Reason and Religion: A Study in the Theology of John Wesley" (Harvard Divinity School; in preparation).
43. *Compendium*, vol. 5, p. 211.
44. *Sermons*, vol. 2, p. 234 ("The New Birth").
45. *Works*, vol. 6, pp. 274-75 ("The End of Christ's Coming").
46. *Sermons*, vol. 1, p. 208 ("The Witness of the Spirit").
47. Ibid., p. 216 ("The Witness of the Spirit").
48. Ibid.
49. Ibid., p. 210 ("The Witness of the Spirit").
50. Ibid., p. 217 ("The Witness of the Spirit").
51. *Journal*, vol. 1, p. 415.
52. Ibid., p. 476.
53. Ibid., vol. 2, pp. 125-26.
54. *Works*, vol. 10, pp. 471-72.
55. Ibid., p. 8, p. 408.
56. Albert Outler, ed., *John Wesley* (New York: Oxford University Press, 1964), p. 28.
57. *Works*, vol. 6, p. 355.

3. "TRUE RELIGION" AND THE AFFECTIONS:
A Study of John Wesley's
Abridgement of Jonathan Edwards's
Treatise on Religious Affections

Gregory S. Clapper

The phrase "religious affections" has a quaint sound today. On the odd occasion that it is encountered, it more than likely conjures images of an over-dressed, nineteenth-century dandy, reading floridly romantic theosophy in an effort to cultivate new pinnacles of exquisite interiority. This was not always the case.

For Jonathan Edwards and John Wesley, the "religious", or "holy", or "gracious" affections were the essence of what Christianity was about, and neither man was a religious dilettante of the drawing room. At the very beginning of his *Treatise on Religious Affections*, Jonathan Edwards states that "True religion, in great part, consists in Holy Affections."[1] In his later abridgement of this work, Wesley puts his name to the same opinion.[2]

In this paper, I will attempt to make clear what Wesley did, and did not, mean by this. To do this, I will first make a few remarks about Edwards's thought and Wesley's relation to it. Next, I will briefly exposit Wesley's abridgement of Edwards's *Treatise* and compare the themes found there with the theology that Wesley's original works betray. Finally, I will draw a few inferences from all of this for the doing of theology in the Wesleyan tradition.

Edwards and Religious Affections

Jonathan Edwards was born in East Windsor, Connecticut, in the year of John Wesley's birth, 1703 (d. 1758). Educated at Yale, he had a lifelong fascination with both philosophy and natural science as well as theology. Locke and Newton were his intellectual companions every bit as much as Calvin was. Such interests were reflected in his writings as well as his readings, as seen in his papers titled "Of Insects," "The Mind," and even "Of Being."[3] While his *Freedom of the Will* is usually taken to be his major contribution to theology,[4] Edwards is more widely known for his sermon "Sinners in the Hands of an Angry God," which is most notable for its vivid depiction of the end that awaits the reprobate. Unfortunately, neither *Freedom of the Will* nor his famous sermon gives a true picture of the broad scope and creative nature of his work. Edwards was much more concerned with beauty and love than he was with either humanity's bondage to sin or the nature of hell.[5] It is these wider interests that are most relevant for our concerns.

Roland Delattre in his *Beauty and Sensibility in the Thought of Jonathan Edwards* claims that Edwards understood Divine Being to be most immediately and powerfully present to humanity as beauty.[6] This beauty is known through our sensibility; that is, it is *felt*, and not merely intellectually inferred by the understanding. Saving knowledge of God, then, is available only in and through the enjoyment of God. The fullness of God is encountered as a living reality "only according to the degree to which men find in [God] their entire joy and happiness, the fulfillment of their aesthetic-affectional being."[7]

This emphasis on the sensible apprehension of God, when linked with Edwards's appreciation for the philosophy of John Locke, has been taken by some of Edwards's interpreters as showing that Edwards's epistemology was nothing more than philosophical empiricism.[8] But Terrence Erdt has recently shown that a "sense of the heart" or a "sweetness" (*suavitas*) can be found in Calvin's thought, so that Edwards's emphasis on feeling and the "heart" has a rootage in the theological tradition which is deeper than is often suspected.[9] But regardless of its historical roots, Edwards's affectional "sense of the heart" was at the center of his psychology, epistemology, ethics, and, indeed, his whole theology.

Wesley and Edwards

It was Edwards's theoretical concern with the nature of religious experience and, more importantly, his burning practical desire to have such experience widely propagated, that put Edwards and Wesley on common ground. Wesley's first contact with Edwards's writings came in 1738. Wesley was traveling from London to Oxford when he "read the truly surprising narrative of the conversions lately wrought in and about the town of Northampton, in New

England. Surely 'this is the Lord's doing and it is marvelous in our eyes.' "[10]

What he read was Edwards's *Faithful Narrative of the Surprising Work of God . . .*[11] which was to be the first of five works of Edwards's that Wesley would abridge and publish.[12] The other four works which Wesley published also had direct bearing on the subjects of Christian experience and evangelism. These were *The Distinguishing Marks of a Work of the Spirit of God* (written in 1741, Wesley's abridgement published in 1744); *Some Thoughts Concerning the Present Revival of Religion in New England* (1742, 1745); *The Life of David Brainerd*, who was Edwards's son-in-law and a missionary to the Indians (1749, 1768); and, of course, the *Treatise on Religious Affections* (1746, 1773).

These five works by Edwards represent the largest number of separate works by one author that Wesley was to abridge and publish under his own name. The influence of Edwards on Wesley was so strong that Albert C. Outler has said that Edwards was a "major source" of Wesley's theology, and that, indeed, Wesley's encounter with Edwards's early writings was one of four basic factors that set the frame for Wesley's thought.[13]

This is not to say, though, that there were no important differences between the two, for there were. Wesley was familiar with Edwards's *Freedom of the Will*, but he published no abridgement of it and, instead, attacked the views contained in it in his "Thoughts upon Necessity."[14] Wesley thought that Edwards's denial of human freedom made nonsense of the moral life. In general, anything that smacked of Calvinistic "irresistible grace" or "unconditional election" was anathema to Wesley.

Edwards also had his disagreements with Wesley. In fact, the only record of Edwards's referring to Wesley was a disparaging remark which he made about Wesley's views on perfection.[15] If one were to give an irenic reading of their differences, one might say that Wesley and Edwards agreed about the sovereignty of God, but that while Edwards expressed this sovereignty through his Calvinist doctrines of predestination and the bondage of the will, Wesley expressed the same thing by emphasizing prevenient grace and the perfecting possibilities of the Spirit. Both the continuities and the differences between these two men can be seen in microcosm in Wesley's abridgement of Edwards's most widely read book, his *Treatise on Religious Affections.*[16]

Wesley's Abridgement of Edwards's *Treatise*

The task of discerning a man's views by looking at how he abridged another man's work must be approached with caution. Frank Baker in his article "A Study of John Wesley's Readings" states that one of the ways that Wesley dealt with a "dangerous" book was by publishing an expurgated version of it.[17] This might lead one to believe that Wesley's version of the *Treatise on Religious Affections* was merely the lesser of two evils; since the book was already in print, Wesley may have thought that it would be better if his followers read his version rather than Edwards's, if they had to read it at all. If this were the case, the abridgement would be less an endorsement of Edwards's views than a reluctant toleration of them.

Such doubts about attributing the abridgement's views to the abridger arise when it is noted that books did in fact appear in the first edition of Wesley's *Christian Library*[18] which contained views contradicting Wesley's own.[19] But this is less of a problem than it first appears to be, for the publication of the offending passages was the result of hasty abridging on Wesley's part. The second edition of the *Christian Library* was corrected with great care by Wesley to remove the contradictions. It is this second, corrected edition which contains Edwards's *Treatise*.

Most importantly, though, we can take Wesley's abridgement of the *Treatise* as representing Wesley's views because Wesley specifically endorsed the book. Wesley did not always write a preface for the books that he published, but in the case of the *Treatise* he did. In this preface, he both distances himself from some parts of the original *Treatise* and recommends the portion he retained. The end of this preface reads, "Out of this dangerous heap, wherein much wholesome food is mixed with much deadly poison, I have selected many remarks and admonitions which may be of great use to the children of God. May God write them in the hearts of all that desire to walk as Christ also walked!"[20] Our purpose now is to spell out what Wesley considered poison and what he considered food.

1) What Wesley Deleted

Determining what Wesley left out of the *Treatise* is more difficult than one might first suspect, since it appears that Wesley did not work from the original edition. John E. Smith has determined that Wesley worked from an abridgement made by William Gordon, published in London in 1762.[21] Gordon, who is listed as an "independent minister" in the *Dictionary of National Biography*,[22] reduced the text by more than one-third, omitted many notes and rewrote the text in hundreds of places. This means that in order to be sure that any omission was truly

Wesley's omission, all three texts must be compared.

But determining exactly what Wesley left out would be crucially important only if our purpose were to chronicle the differences between Edwards and Wesley on the topic of religious affections. The central intent of this paper, however, is to see what Wesley *liked* about the *Treatise*, not what he disliked. So, instead of a lengthy three-way textual comparison, I will just make a few general remarks about Gordon's abridgement and Wesley's deletions.

First of all, while he did remove much of the original text, Gordon's appreciation of Edwards was much less critical than Wesley's. The original *Treatise* consisted of a preface and three major parts: part 1 concerning the nature of the affections, part 2 containing twelve signs that *cannot* be used to judge whether or not particular affections are gracious, and part 3 containing twelve distinguishing signs of "Truly Gracious and Holy Affections." Gordon retains all four basic parts of the work, and in parts 2 and 3 both sets of twelve signs are fully represented. His excisions and revisions, which apparently occurred most often when he determined that Edwards was "too refined for common capacities"[23], do not, in my judgment, pervert the essential thrust of Edwards's work.

Wesley was a much more ruthless editor. Whereas Gordon's abridgement was about two-thirds of the original, Wesley's was one-sixth. He cut not only Edwards's preface, but the second, third, and fourth of the twelve signs of part 3 in their entirety, as well as considerably reduced the explanations of the remaining signs. One sign (the seventh) was so reduced that Wesley did not even bother to number it and, instead, merely included a brief summary of it in the preceding section. (This omission of the number, though, might be the fault of Wesley's notoriously bad printers. Later in the text, the numbering jumps from 4 to 6 with 5 never appearing.)

The omissions that Wesley made usually fall into one of two categories, both of which are alluded to in Wesley's preface. These two categories of edited material might be defined as (1) Calvinistic and (2) overly "subtle."

As he made clear in his preface, Wesley thought that Edwards's purpose in writing the *Treatise* was to show that backsliders were never true believers in the first place. In other words, Wesley saw the *Treatise* as a Calvinistic tract on the perseverence of the saints. Wesley claimed that Edwards's attempt to defend such an indefensible doctrine led him to heap together "so many curious, subtle, metaphysical distinctions, as are sufficient to puzzle the brain, and

confound the intellects, of all the plain men and women of the universe; and to make them doubt of, if not wholly deny, all the work which God had wrought in their souls."[24] After this broadside, Wesley goes on to admit, as quoted above, that there is much wholesome food mixed in with the "deadly poison."

As others have pointed out, it seems clear that Wesley misunderstood Edwards's purpose in writing the *Treatise*.[25] Edwards was trying to show valid signs for distinguishing true from false piety or "religion," not explain away the fact of backsliding. Wesley might justifiably be accused of being somewhat defensive here—seeing Edwards's Calvinism operating where it really was not. True, Edwards does mention the "elect" in a few places, and other Calvinistic tendencies which Wesley altered can surely be seen in the original, but Wesley's preface mischaracterizes the tenor of the *Treatise* as polemical when it is in fact constructive. Since Wesley was caught up in heated debate with the Calvinists at the time of the abridgement, his defensiveness can at least be understood, if not justified.[26]

The most substantive passages that Wesley omitted from the *Treatise*, however, are not the overtly Calvinistic ones, but the overly "subtle" ones which "puzzle" and "confound" plain-thinking humanity. Wesley shared Edwards's interest in science and philosophy, but edification was his ultimate criteria when evaluating the written word. Edwards was a brilliant speculative thinker who incorporated many of his philosophical theories into his theological works. Because of this, Wesley encountered much that could be dispensed with. This can be seen especially in two of the three signs that Wesley omitted.

The second of Edwards's twelve signs states that the "first objective ground of gracious affections is the transcendently excellent and amiable nature of divine things";[27] the third sign says that holy affections are founded on the "loveliness of the moral excellency of divine things."[28] In these two signs, we can see the metaphysics of "beauty" and "excellence" which Delattre has declared to be the linchpin of Edwards's speculations.[29] Wesley was probably content with Edwards's point (made in many other places) that divine things are the object of gracious affections, and that extended discussions of the "loveliness" or "moral excellency" of these divine things were therefore dispensable.

Conjecture about why Wesley deleted the fourth sign is more difficult, for it asserts something which Wesley would not want to deny—the intellectual component in the affections ("Gracious affections do arise from the

418

mind's being enlightened, rightly and spiritually to understand or apprehend divine things."[30]) Certainly Wesley was never tempted, as Luther was, to "tear out the eyes of reason" in order to promote faith. One can only guess that Wesley considered this sign to go too far in the other direction, that is, that it could be taken as a kind of rationalism.

2) What Wesley Retained

At the beginning of part 1, Edwards quotes the text of I Peter 1:8: "Whom having not seen ye love: In whom, though now you see him not, yet believing, ye rejoice with joy unspeakable and full of glory." In this text, Edwards sees the two archetypal exercises of true religion: love to Christ and joy in Christ. Based on this, he then formulates the proposition that he will defend throughout the entire book, that "True Religion, in great part, consists in Holy Affections."[31] His first step in this process is to define what affections are.

According to Edwards, the "affections of the mind" are "the more vigorous and sensible exercises of the will."[32] In drawing this out, Edwards goes on to say that God has imbued the soul with two faculties: the understanding which is capable of perception and speculation, and the inclination or will which either is pleased or displeased, approving or rejecting the things perceived. The mind with regard to the exercises of the will is called the heart. The crucial point here is that the affections are not exercised apart from the understanding.

Edwards makes his anthropology even more explicit when he says that it is the mind and not the body that is the proper seat of the affections. Herein lies the difference between affections and passions as well. Passions are more sudden, have a more violent effect on the "animal spirits," and in them "the mind is less in its own command."[33]

The next section of part 1 consists of several points which attempt to show that a great part of true religion lies in the affections. These range from the more speculative arguments ("the religion of heaven consists much in affection"[34]) to arguments based on observations of human behavior ("affections are the springs of men's actions,"[35] which, of course, are necessary for religion) to arguments based strictly on Scripture ("Holy Scripture places religion in the affections"[36]; "the Scriptures place the sin of the heart much in hardness of heart"[37]). From these and other arguments, Edwards draws these inferences:

1) That we cannot discard all religious affections.[38]

2) That "such means are to be desired, as have a tendency to move the affections."[39]

3) That "if true religion lies much in the affections, what cause have we to be ashamed, that we are no more affected with the great things of religion!"[40] In other words, we are to be held accountable for having certain affectional capacities.

Having established the connections between true religion and the affections in part 1, Edwards now moves on to the theme that occupies the largest part of the book: distinguishing the holy and gracious affections from those that are not. Part 2 consists of twelve points which deal with twelve different ways of analyzing affections. Edwards asserts that these twelve "signs" cannot give certain knowledge as to whether or not religious affections are "truly gracious."

One can imagine the sobering effect that these negative points must have had on many of the "spirit-filled Christians" of his day. Among the most interesting are points number 1: that religious affections are raised very high[41]; 2: that they have great effects on the body[42]; 4: that the persons did not make the affections themselves[43]; and 5: that they come with texts of Scripture.[44] Point number 3 can serve as a warning to all garrulous theologians of any age: that it is no sign to be fluent, fervent, and abundant in talking of the things of religion[45].

The final four signs, when seen together, show that, for Edwards, we can never know how another person's soul is seen by the eyes of God by observing his or her outward behavior. People can: spend much time in religion and worship[46]; praise God with their mouths[47]; be confident that their experience is divine[48]; or convince other people of their godliness[49] without being assured that their affections are gracious. This makes an important point about the entire book. It is to be an aid for one's own spiritual quest, not a guidebook for the judgment of others.

Part 3 of the *Treatise* is perhaps the most important section, for this is where Edwards explains what *are* valid signs of gracious and holy affections. The first sign is that gracious affections arise from "spiritual, divine and supernatural" influences on the heart.[50] In a sense, this begs the question and is of no practical help, but it does make clear that his epistemology is a kind of spiritual empiricism. The Spirit of God gives the believer a new "spiritual sense"[51] through which one has access to the divine things.

The second sign in Wesley's abridgement (Edwards's fifth sign) states that gracious affections are accompanied by a conviction of the reality and certainty of divine things. This conviction is not some sort of vague mysticism or a certainty about the existence of "divine things" in general, *a la* Schleiermacher. It is a "conviction of the truth of the great things of the Gospel."[52] The title of the *Treatise* may sound as if the book is about generic religious experience, but, in reality, the positivity of the Christian religion is constantly and unashamedly asserted.

The sixth sign states that gracious affections are attended with "evangelical humiliation", that is, a conviction of one's own "utter insufficiency, despicableness and odiousness, with an answerable frame of heart, arising from a discovery of God's holiness."[53] On this point, it is flatly put that "They that are destitute of this, have not true religion, whatever profession they may make."[54] For Edwards (and Wesley), humility is pervasive, it is a quality of all the other affections, and therein lies an important safeguard against "enthusiasm."

The material contained in the seventh sign in the original is treated in just a few unnumbered paragraphs by Wesley. This is perhaps because this sign simply states that gracious affections are attended with a change in the nature of the affected person, which is really already implied in several of the other signs (e.g., nos. 6, 8, 9, 11, 12 in the original).

The eighth and ninth signs show that while false affections have a tendency to harden the heart, truly gracious affections promote the spirit that appeared in Christ (no. 8), a tenderness of spirit (no. 9). In these sections, Edwards lays special emphasis on love, meekness, quietness, forgiveness, and mercy. From the very beginning, of course, Edwards has said that love is the first and chief of the affections—the "fountain" of all gracious affections[55]—but it is not until this eighth sign that we are given an overall view of what specific additional affections are, in fact, "religious."

The tenth sign is that gracious affections have beautiful symmetry and proportion. While there are echoes here of Edwards's philosophical contention that we know God through beauty, there is also something more important being stressed. In saying, for example, that love of God must be yoked with love of man, or that having hope does not mean jettisoning holy fear, Edwards is laying out a theological roadmap (or we might say a "grammar") of the affections. This grammar of the affections can be seen as the emotional manifestation of Christian doctrines. In one sense, the laying bare of this grammar is the main theological task of the entire *Treatise*.

The eleventh sign states that gracious affections increase the longing for spiritual attain-

ments, while the false affections tend to make one rest satisfied. This can be seen as a corrective against those who might think that Edwards is about a kind of mysticism which cultivates "religious experiences" for their own sake. This theme reaches its culmination in the twelfth and final sign where the emphasis is shifted completely away from inner experience to the necessary fruits of the affections: works of love.

This last sign, the explanation of which is by far the longest of the twelve in both the original and in Wesley's abridgement, contains many arguments for Christian practice as the chief of all the evidences of a "saving sincerity" in religion. So much is practice emphasized here that Edwards feels compelled to answer two objections that might arise regarding the importance of the works: the objection that Christian experience is to be the central sign of grace, and that emphasizing works could lead to a works-righteousness. Edwards smoothly answers these objections by showing that "experience" and "practice" cannot be separated, and that making a "righteousness" of experience is just as heretical as a works-righteousness.[56]

The Themes of the *Treatise* in Wesley's Original Works

We can see from the above exposition of Wesley's abridgement of Edwards's *Treatise* that Wesley endorsed the view that true religion consists, in great part, of gracious affections. These gracious affections find their apex in love and joy, but also consist of meekness and forgiveness, among others, all of which are marked by humility. The outward expression of these affections in dramatic bodily demonstrations is not a sign of their holiness, but they *must* issue in fruits—works—in order to be considered gracious.

It is not hard to find equivalent statements in Wesley's own writings. In commenting on Romans 14:17 ("For the kingdom of God is not meat and drink; but righteousness, and peace, and joy in the Holy Ghost.") Wesley says: *"For the kingdom of God*—That is, true religion, does not consist in external observances. *But* in *righteousness*—the image of God stamped on the heart; the love of God and man, accompanied with the *peace* that passeth all understanding, *and joy in the Holy Ghost."*[57]

On Galatians 5:22 ("But the fruit of the Spirit is love, joy, peace.") he says that "love is the root of the rest"[58] (cf. Edwards's statement that love is the "fountain" of the other affections). In the following verse, commenting on meekness, there is an unmistakable parallel with the "symmetry and proportion" of Edwards's tenth sign. Here

Wesley says that meekness means "holding all the affections and passions in even balance."[59]

Similarly, commenting on I John 4:19 ("We love him, because he first loved us."), Wesley says: "This is the sum of all religion, the genuine model of Christianity. None can say more: why should anyone say less, or less intelligibly?"[60]

In his sermons, the emphasis on the affective life is no less evident. For example, in "Salvation by Faith," saving faith is distinguished from the faith of a devil "by this: it is not a speculative, rational thing, a cold, lifeless assent, a train of ideas in the head; but also a disposition of the heart."[61] In "The Circumcision of the Heart" he begins the final section by saying, "Here, then, is the sum of the perfect law; this is the true circumcision of the heart. Let the spirit return to God that gave it, with the whole train of its affections."[62] Again, the sixth sermon in the "Sermon on the Mount" series contains the following:

> In praying that God, or His name, may be hallowed or glorified, we pray that He may be known, such as He is, by all that are capable thereof, by all intelligent beings, and with affections suitable to that knowledge; that He may be duly honored, and feared, and loved, by all in heaven above and in the earth beneath; by all angels and men, whom for that end He has made capable of knowing and loving Him to eternity.[63]

In his sermon "The Witness of the Spirit," Wesley tries to show how the testimony of God's Spirit may be distinguished from the "presumption of a natural mind." Wesley, again, sounds like Edwards here by (1) relying on Scripture as a guide; (2) emphasizing joy, but a joy that is humble; and (3) maintaining the importance of works as a sign of the presence of grace, especially the "keeping of the Commandments."[64]

All of the works of Wesley quoted above were written *before* he published his abridgement of Edwards's *Treatise*, so we cannot say that this particular work was germinal for Wesley's own thought on this topic. But I think it *is* fair to say that in the *Treatise*, Wesley saw a useful summary of insights into the nature of Christian experience which clearly reflected his own views on the matter. He could, in clear conscience, recommend this work as if it were his own to "all that desire to walk as Christ also walked."

True Religion and the Affections

Wesley recognized that by emphasizing the importance of the affections for "true religion" he would be parodied and ridiculed. Alluding to his sermon text of Acts 26:24 ("And Festus said with a loud voice, 'Paul, thou art beside thyself'"), Wesley says in "The Nature of Enthusiasm":

> And so say all the world, the men who know not God, of all that are of Paul's religion: of every one who is so a follower of him, as he was of Christ. It is true, there is a sort of religion, nay, and it is called Christianity too, which may be practised without any such imputation, which is generally allowed to be consistent with common sense—that is, a religion of form, a round of outward duties, performed in a decent, regular manner. You may add orthodoxy thereto, a system of right opinions, yea, and some quantity of heathen morality; and yet not many will pronounce, that "much religion hath made you mad." But if you aim at the religion of the heart, if you talk of "righteousness, and peace, and joy in the Holy Ghost," then it will not be long before your sentence is passed, "Thou art beside thyself."[65]

But in his abridgement of the *Treatise*, as well as in his original work, Wesley showed that one can talk about the inner life without losing one's reason, for his discourse is always rational in form, even when its subject matter is affectional. Similarly, he showed that focusing on the affections does not entail making them the primary source of revelation, as witnessed to by his constant use of the external checks of the Bible and tradition. The other great danger of linking true religion with the affections—an obsession with one's own inner experience—is also clearly excluded from Wesley's conception by his constant emphasis on the affections issuing in external behavioral "fruits," that is, making Christian love and joy manifest in the world through one's actions.

Clearly, the religious affections, as Wesley presented them, are relevant for many doctrinal issues. Obvious linkages could be made between the affections and the doctrines of assurance, sanctification, and perfection, to mention just a few. But the enduring importance of Wesley's conception of the religious affections can be summed-up without making reference to any of these specific doctrines.

If Wesley has a contribution to make to the contemporary theological concern with the norms and criteria which should govern our language about God, it is his contention that we only truly know God if we truly love him, and take joy in him. That inescapable inner reality which we describe by the metaphor "heart" stands at the center of what Christianity is about for Wesley, and a theology which ignores it is not a "Wesleyan" theology.

Certainly, true religion for Wesley does not start with the heart, its beginning is the gospel.

Neither is the end of true religion in the heart, for its *telos* in the human life is in the works of love, the "fruit" of the heart. But until the heart is addressed, the gospel will fall on deaf ears and the works will be empty moralism.

If theology is to be done in the Wesleyan spirit, the affections must be seen to be more than merely a source of error and confusion which confound our "higher" faculties. They are not dispensable luxuries which may or may not be indulged in (according to one's temperament) after all of the hard thinking is done. As both secular and pastoral counselors have long known, the affective dimension of life tells us who we are in our concrete existence. If it is this concrete existence which the church is to address, then the church must not hesitate to speak in a normative way about affective realities.

Wesley's message, like Edwards's, was simply that if you are not humbly filled with love and joy about what God has done for you, then you have not really heard the gospel and are not really a Christian. He saw that the rough contours of felt experience are where the gospel either grows or dies. If it is true that the gospel is "we love him because he first loved us," then theology, *qua* medium for the knowledge of God, must recognize that "True religion, in great part, consists in Holy Affections."

NOTES

1. Jonathan Edwards, *Treatise on Religious Affections*, in *Works*, vol. 2 (New Haven: Yale University Press, 1959), p. 95, hereafter *RA*. First published in Boston in 1746, all quotes will be from vol. 2 of this edition, John E. Smith, ed., Perry Miller, gen. ed.
2. John Wesley, *Christian Library*, vol. 30, p. 310, hereafter *RA* (W). Wesley's abridgement first appeared in his collected *Works* (vol. 23: pp. 177-279) 1773, reprint 1801, and later appeared in the 2nd ed. of *Christian Library* (vol. 30: pp. 307-76) 1827. See Frank Baker, ed., *A Union Catalog of the Publications of John and Charles Wesley* (Durham: Duke University, 1966) entry no. 294 for the complete publication history. All references in this paper are to the *Christian Library* edition.
3. Cf. J. Edwards, *Scientific and Philosophical Writings*, in *Works*, vol. 6.
4. Ibid., vol. 1 (1957).
5. Actually, there are less than a dozen imprecatory sermons written by Edwards among the more than a thousand which survive in manuscript form. See Sydney E. Ahlstrom, *A Religious History of the American People* (Garden City, N.Y.: Image Books, 1975), p. 370.
6. Roland Delattre, *Beauty and Sensibility in the Thought of Jonathan Edwards* (New Haven: Yale University Press, 1968), p. 50. Delattre's analysis is based on all of Edwards's works, but he draws most heavily on the *RA*, *The Nature of True Virtue* (Ann Arbor: University of Michigan Press, 1960), and the *Miscellanies* (forthcoming in the Yale *Works* series.)
7. Ibid., p. 49.
8. The most influential exponent of this view was Perry Miller, especially in his *Jonathan Edwards* (New York: Wm. Sloane Associates, 1949).
9. See Terence Erdt, *Jonathan Edwards: Art and the Sense of Heart* (Amherst: University of Massachusetts Press, 1980), esp. chap. 1, "The Calvinist Psychology of the Heart."
10. Wesley, *Journal,*, vol. 2, pp. 83-84.
11. The full title continues *in the Conversion of Many Hundred Souls in Northampton and the Neighboring Towns and Villages of New Hampshire in New England,* first written in 1736, Wesley's abridgement published in 1744.
12. For more detailed commentary on the abridgements, as well as an enlightening comparison of Wesley and Edwards, see Charles Rogers' "John Wesley and Jonathan Edwards" in *The Duke Divinity School Review*, 31 (Winter, 1966), 20-38.
13. Albert C. Outler, *John Wesley*, in Library of Protestant Thought (New York: Oxford University Press, 1964), p. 16. The other three factors, according to Outler, were his Aldersgate conversion, his disenchantment with Moravianism and his vital reappropriation of his Anglican heritage.
14. John Wesley, *Works*, Thomas Jackson, ed. (Grand Rapids: Baker Book House, reprinted, 1979) vol. 10, pp. 457-74.
15. Jonathan Edwards, *The Works of President Edwards*, vol. 4, p. 118, quoted in Rogers, "John Wesley and Jonathan Edwards," p. 36.
16. *RA*, Smith's intro., p. 78.
17. Frank Baker, "A Study of John Wesley's Readings," *London Quarterly and Holborn Review*, 1943, p. 240.
18. See Baker, *Union Catalog*, for the publication history of the *Christian Library* (entry no. 131).
19. See T. W. Herbert, *John Wesley as Editor and Author* (Princeton: Princeton University Press, 1940), pp. 26-27.
20. *RA* (W), p. 308.
21. *RA*, p. 79. Smith says that the chances of Wesley and Gordon independently making so many of the same omissions and substitutions is very small. Frank Baker's opinion, stated to me in a personal correspondence, concurs with Smith's.
22. *Dictionary of National Biography*, ed. Leslie Stephen and Sidney Lee (New York: Macmillan Company, 1890), vol. 22, p. 235.
23. William Gordon, ed. and abridg., *Treatise on Religious Affections*, p. 78.
24. *RA* (W), p. 308.
25. See Smith's introduction in *RA*, p. 80, and Rogers's "John Wesley and Jonathan Edwards," p. 30.
26. See John Allan Knight, "Aspects of Wesley's Theology After 1770" in *Methodist History*, 6, 3 (April 1968): 33-42.
27. *RA*, p. 240.
28. *RA*, p. 253.
29. See Delattre, *Beauty and Sensibility*, for in-depth discussions of primary and secondary beauty, the equivalence of beauty and excellence, and beauty as the "cordial consent of being to being-in-general."
30. *RA*, p. 266.
31. *RA* (W), p. 310.
32. Ibid., p. 311.
33. Ibid., p. 312.
34. Ibid., p. 316.
35. Ibid., p. 313.
36. Ibid.
37. Ibid., p. 316.
38. Ibid., p. 317.
39. Ibid., p. 318.
40. Ibid.
41. Ibid., p. 320.
42. Ibid., p. 321.
43. Ibid., pp. 324-25.
44. Ibid., p. 327.
45. Ibid., p. 324.
46. Ibid., p. 333.
47. Ibid., p. 334.
48. Ibid., p. 335.
49. Ibid., p. 342.
50. Ibid., p. 343.
51. Ibid., p. 346.

52. Ibid.
53. Ibid., p. 349. To avoid confusion, I will refer to the signs by Edwards's enumeration.
54. Ibid., p. 349.
55. Ibid., p. 316, e.g.
56. Ibid., pp. 372-76.
57. *Notes*, p. 575.
58. Ibid., p. 697.
59. Ibid.
60. Ibid., p. 915.
61. Wesley, *Sermons*, vol. 1, p. 40.
62. Ibid., p. 279.
63. Ibid., p. 436.
64. Wesley's sermon "The Witness of the Spirit," second part, ibid., pp. 211-18. Wesley was, like Edwards, always quick to emphasize the *gracious* nature of these affections. He thought any emphasis on the affections which was purely naturalistic to be heretical. For example, regarding Hutcheson's feeling-based ethics, he said that Hutcheson was a "beautiful writer; but his scheme cannot stand, unless the Bible falls" (*Journal*, Curnock, ed., vol. 5, p. 492).
65. Wesley, *Sermons*, vol. 2, pp. 86-87.

CONTRIBUTORS

J. William Abraham is Professor of Philosophy and Religion, Seattle Pacific University, Seattle, Washington.

Thomas R. Albin is Associate Minister of First United Methodist Church, Tulsa, Oklahoma.

Mortimer Arias is Professor of Hispanic Studies and Evangelization, School of Theology at Claremont, Claremont, California.

Carl Bangs is Professor of Historical Theology, St. Paul School of Theology, Kansas City, Missouri.

Bruce C. Birch is Professor of Old Testament, Wesley Theological Seminary, Washington, D.C.

Earl Kent Brown is Professor of Church History, Boston University School of Theology, Boston, Massachusetts.

Joanne Carlson Brown is Assistant Professor of Religion, Pacific Lutheran University, Tacoma, Washington.

Ignacio Castuera is District Superintendent, The United Methodist Church, Los Angeles.

Paul Wesley Chilcote is a doctoral candidate at Duke University, Durham, North Carolina.

Gregory S. Clapper is a doctoral candidate at Emory University, Atlanta, Georgia.

Sheila Greeve Davaney is Assistant Professor of Theology, Iliff School of Theology, Denver, Colorado.

H. Ray Dunning is Professor, Trevecca Nazarene College, Nashville, Tennessee.

Durwood Foster is Professor of Christian Theology, Pacific School of Religion, Berkeley, California.

Stanley Hauerwas is Professor of Theological Ethics, Divinity School, Duke University.

Leon O. Hynson is Professor of Church History and Historical Theology, Asbury Theological Seminary, Wilmore, Kentucky.

Robert Jewett is Professor of New Testament, Garrett-Evangelical Theological Seminary, Evanston, Illinois.

Donald M. Joy is Professor of Human Development, Asbury Theological Seminary.

Rosemary Skinner Keller is Associate Professor of American Church History, Garrett-Evangelical Theological Seminary.

Jean C. Lambert is Associate Professor of Theology, Saint Paul School of Theology.

Thomas A. Langford is Professor of Systematic Theology, Divinity School, Duke University.

C. Eric Lincoln is Professor of Religion and Culture, Duke University.

James C. Logan is Professor of Systematic Theology, Wesley Theological Seminary.

Robin W. Lovin is Associate Professor of Ethics and Society, Divinity School, University of Chicago, Chicago, Illinois.

Rex D. Matthews is Instructor in Historical Theology, Candler School of Theology, Emory University.

William B. McClain is Associate Professor of Preaching and Worship, Wesley Theological Seminary.

M. Douglas Meeks is Professor of Systematic Theology and Philosophy, Eden Theological Seminary, St. Louis, Missouri.

Paul A. Mickey is Associate Professor of Pastoral Theology, Divinity School, Duke University.

Mozella G. Mitchell is Assistant Professor of Religion, University of South Florida at Tampa; Pastor, Mount Sinai AME Church, Tampa, Florida.

Gerald F. Moede is General Secretary, Consultation on Church Union (COCU), Princeton, New Jersey.

Mary Elizabeth Moore is Assistant Professor of Christian Education and Theology, School of Theology at Claremont.

Walter G. Muelder is Dean Emeritus, Boston University School of Theology.

J. Robert Nelson is Professor of Systematic Theology, Boston University School of Theology.

Schubert M. Ogden is Professor of Theology, Perkins School of Theology, Southern Methodist University, Dallas, Texas.

Theodore Runyon is Professor of Systematic Theology, Candler School of Theology, Emory University.

Jean Miller Schmidt is Associate Professor of Modern Church History, Iliff School of Theology.

Roy I. Sano is Bishop of the Denver Area, The United Methodist Church.

James S. Thomas is Bishop of the East Ohio Area, The United Methodist Church.

Emilie M. Townes is Pastor, United Faith Affinitas Church of Chicago.

David Lowes Watson is on the staff of the Evangelism Section, General Board of Discipleship, The United Methodist Church, Nashville, Tennessee.

James F. White is Professor of Liturgy, University of Notre Dame, South Bend, Indiana.

J. Philip Wogaman is Professor of Christian Ethics, Wesley Theological Seminary.

Charles Wood is Associate Professor of Theology, Perkins School of Theology, Southern Methodist University.

Norman Young is Professor of Theology and Principal, Theological Hall, Ormond College, Parkville, Victoria, Australia.